W9-BXN-070

Lee's Miserables

Civil War America *Gary W. Gallagher, editor*

LEE'S MISERABLES.—"I want a copy of that book about Gen. Lee's poor miserable soldiers faintin'," said an old lady in West & Johnston's bookstore, the other day. The clerk was dumb-founded. One of the proprietors was sent for, made the old lady repeat her request, turned pale, rolled his eyes wildly, scratched his head and at last exclaimed, "Oh! ah! yes! I know what it is now you mean Les Miserables. Fantine by Victor Hugo." "No, I don't," replied the old lady. "I know nothing and care nothing about" Lays Meeserarbuls. "I want Lee's Miserables faintin'." As nothing else would satisfy her, she was allowed to depart without the book she so eagerly sought.
—*Richmond Whig*, 12 June 1863

They called themselves "Lee's Miserables." That was a grim piece of humor, was it not, reader? And the name had a somewhat curious origin. Victor Hugo's work, *Les Miserables*, had been translated and published by a house in Richmond; the soldiers, in the great dearth of reading matter, had seized upon it; and thus, by a strange chance the tragic story of the great French writer, had become known to the soldiers in the trenches. . . . Thus, that history of "The Wretched," was the pabulum of the South in 1864; and as the French title had been retained on the backs of the pamphlets, the soldiers, little familiar with the Gallic pronunciation, called the book "Lees Miserables!" Then another step was taken. It was no longer the book, but themselves whom they referred to by that name. The old veterans of the army thenceforth laughed at their miseries, and dubbed themselves grimly *"Lee's* Miserables!" The sobriquet was gloomy, and there was something tragic in the employment of it; but it was applicable. Like most popular terms, it expressed the exact thought in the mind of every one—coined the situation into a phrase.
—John Esten Cooke, *Mohun; or, The Last Days of Lee and His Paladins*
  (1869)

Life in the Army of Northern
Virginia from the Wilderness
to Appomattox

Lee's

The University of North Carolina Press

Chapel Hill and London

J. Tracy Power

Miserables

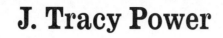

Set in Bell and Clarendon types
by Keystone Typesetting

Publication of this work was aided by a grant included in the
Mrs. Simon Baruch University Award of the United Daughters
of the Confederacy.

The paper in this book meets the guidelines for permanence and
durability of the Committee on Production Guidelines for Book
Longevity of the Council on Library Resources.

Library of Congress Cataloging-in-Publication Data
Power, J. Tracy.
Lee's miserables : life in the Army of Northern Virginia from the
Wilderness to Appomattox / by J. Tracy Power.
    p. cm. — (Civil War America)
Includes bibliographical references (p.   ) and index.
ISBN 0-8078-2392-9 (cloth: alk. paper)
1. Confederate States of America. Army of Northern Virginia—
Military life. 2. Soldiers—Confederate States of America—
History. 3. Lee, Robert E. (Robert Edward), 1807–1870. 4. United
States—History—Civil War, 1861–1865—Regimental histories.
I. Title. II. Series.
E470.2.P69 1998
973.7'455—dc21   97-17724
                          CIP

02   01   00   99   98   5   4   3   2

For my parents,

James Charley Power Jr.

and

Claudett Fagan Power

Contents

Maps and Illustrations

Maps

Illustrations

Preface

In May 1864, while the vicious battles at Spotsylvania still raged and not long before the bloody fighting at Cold Harbor, the *Richmond Whig* published an editorial on the Army of Northern Virginia. The *Whig*'s editors claimed, "It would take a historian years to tell the bare story of their deeds, and when that was done, complimentary comment would be almost ridiculous."[1] In the more than 130 years since, many historians and other writers have tried not only to "tell the bare story" of the Confederacy's most famous army but also to provide "complimentary [or other] comment" on its campaigns and personalities. The cumulative weight of such attempts has been aptly described by Richard M. Mc-Murry, who notes that the Army of Northern Virginia's "battles and leaders have become fixtures of United States history, and it would be difficult to find an educated American who has never heard of Robert E. Lee, Thomas J. 'Stonewall' Jackson, Pickett's charge, and Appomattox."[2] The influence of Douglas Southall Freeman, to name only the best-known historian of the army, still looms over all students who study it.[3] Books and articles on the army's major and minor campaigns and officers appear at the rate of several dozen a year, as the troops often referred to simply as "Lee's army" have never lacked attention from students of the Civil War.

The literature published to date on the Army of Northern Virginia, however, is only a fraction of the more than 50,000 books written about the war—at a rate of almost a book published a day for every day since the war ended. David Donald, writing almost forty years ago, observed, "There must be more historians of the Civil War than there were generals fighting in it." About the same time Clifford Dowdey commented that "An impression seems to exist that Civil War history, in contrast to all others, consists of a body of immutable facts, and all left to do is to present this material in a different way—or, as some say, 'rehash.' "[4] That impression, which not only persists but has even gained momentum in the years since 1960, is no more valid now than it was then.

Most military history is written about battles and leaders, and Civil War history is certainly no exception. But comparatively little substantive research has centered on the experiences of specific armies or their component units, on field, staff, or company officers, or on noncommissioned officers and the rank and file. The pioneering—and still unsurpassed—general studies in the field of Civil War soldier life are Bell Irvin Wiley's *The Life of Johnny Reb* and *The Life of Billy Yank*, published in 1943 and

1952, respectively.[5] Though a few articles and books appeared in the next thirty years, there seemed to be little sustained scholarly interest in Civil War soldiers before the 1980s.[6]

Since 1985, however, several new books have added significantly to our knowledge and understanding of the war's participants.[7] Their interpretations are most often based on evidence in soldiers' letters and diaries, postwar reminiscences, memoirs, and unit histories. Most of them take a general view of Civil War soldiers, whereas a few focus on specific armies or units. Among the best of these recent studies are Joseph T. Glatthaar's *The March to the Sea and Beyond* and *Forged in Battle*, Reid Mitchell's *Civil War Soldiers* and *The Vacant Chair*, Randall C. Jimerson's *The Private Civil War*, Larry J. Daniel's *Soldiering in the Army of Tennessee*, and James M. McPherson's *What They Fought For, 1861–1865* and *For Cause and Comrades*. Just as Wiley's earlier works were characterized by a generous sampling of soldiers' letters and diaries, these recent books are notable for their reliance on—and effective use of—unpublished manuscript material surviving in countless public and private collections.

The potential for creative research in and interpretation of Civil War manuscripts is virtually unlimited. In no American war before or since did so large a proportion of the population leave home for an extended period and produce such a detailed record of its experiences in the form of correspondence, diaries, journals, and other wartime papers. Earl J. Hess has reminded us: "Whether it is a narrative of a battle or an analysis of the mind of the soldier, personal accounts are the essential foundations of good studies of the war. . . . The historian's work is ephemeral, it will necessarily be superseded by another scholar's book. But the words of one who personally experienced the war has a special, unique value that transcends whatever interpretation is currently in vogue."[8]

Many manuscripts, furthermore, are readily accessible, having been collected and cataloged in repositories and other institutions throughout the United States. These institutions have enjoyed a remarkable increase in both the number of their holdings and the number of scholars visiting them in the past fifty years, and their Civil War manuscript collections, in particular, have grown due to the enduring public interest in the war. Such papers will amply reward the effort required to examine them. "In using manuscripts," Bell Wiley once advised historians, "the important thing is to know how to read the signs—to know what roads to go down—and to know the meaning of the sources, to know what they add up to." Using an example from the sources he knew better than almost anyone else, he continued:

If one reads only the printed accounts he gets a distorted view of the battle performance of Civil War soldiers, because most of the statements that tell of defection, cowardice, and panic in combat were usually omitted, or at best inaccurately recounted, in unit histories, personal narratives, and official reports. If one wants to get a realistic account of how soldiers behaved in battle he must go to the manuscripts. Then too, the use of manuscripts is eminently satisfactory to the historian. The reading of personal letters, for example, gives him a sense of closeness to his subject. If he is writing about a soldier he gets acquainted with his hopes and fears, his strengths and weaknesses, and his thought patterns. To him the soldier reveals his innermost and most intimate self.[9]

Despite the quantity, quality, and availability of such rich sources, however, relatively few Civil War historians have taken full advantage of the opportunities they present. As Gary W. Gallagher has recently noted, referring specifically to the Army of Northern Virginia, "These manuscripts contain abundant testimony about the meaning of the war, the problem of race, the state of politics, the nature of the enemy, and many other topics."[10] Though many scholars from Wiley to McPherson have, of course, used ample evidence from the Army of Northern Virginia to support their analyses of the Confederate soldier, no study published to date has focused solely on that army and comprehensively investigated its extant manuscript material. Gallagher's historiographical essay "Home Front and Battlefield" calls for "an analytical portrait of the army through the prism of the officers and men in the ranks," commenting that although several recent studies "have deepened understanding of the common soldier in the war," no historian has yet "trained a close lens on Lee's army in particular."[11]

This book not only trains "a close lens" on the Army of Northern Virginia but also further intensifies that lens by examining a finite period: the final year of its existence. The army's campaigns in 1864 and 1865, arguably the most significant and compelling of its entire history, have usually been neglected in favor of its great campaigns of 1862 and 1863. Lee's army was not only, as Gallagher points out, "the greatest obstacle to northern victory during the last year of the war," but it had also become, in many ways, the very embodiment of the Confederacy.[12] A study of the army's crucial last year may therefore contribute to our understanding of the possible causes of Confederate defeat.[13]

The present study was first conceived as an experiment, as an attempt to view the Army of Northern Virginia less from the vantage point of a professional historian writing in the last quarter of the twentieth century and as much as possible "through the prism of the officers and men in the ranks." Over twenty years' experience studying Civil War soldiers in general, Confederate soldiers in particular, and this army most of all has only strengthened a conviction that was shaped by the influence of Bell Wiley, first through his writings and later by his advice and encouragement. I am convinced that the best way, though certainly not the only way, to understand Civil War soldiers is to read the signs they have left us in their letters and diaries, to go down the roads their papers open up for us, and to discover "what they add up to." Though Walt Whitman's cynical observation that "the real war will never get in the books" has often been quoted to demonstrate that writers of fiction and nonfiction alike have failed to capture the essence and the meaning of the Civil War, the soldiers themselves are still the best authorities on the war they fought.[14]

This book is based on research in thousands of officers' and soldiers' letters, diaries, and other papers from 1864 and 1865, most of them manuscripts held by thirty major and minor repositories throughout the former Confederate states and the District of Columbia. The papers examined represent every grade from the commanding general to the lowliest private, every level of education and every class of society, every state that contributed troops to the army, all three major branches of the service, and almost every infantry and cavalry brigade or artillery battalion assigned to Lee in 1864–65.[15] Other significant sources include published letters, diaries, and other wartime papers; the massive documentary collection *The War of the Rebellion: A Compilation of the Official Records of the Union and Confederate Armies* (most often referred to as the *Official Records*); Confederate imprints; and major Confederate newspapers, all dating from the last year of the war.

To further enhance the immediacy and accuracy of these sources, I quote them frequently and often at some length. There is no better testimony on the Army of Northern Virginia than the accounts written by the officers and men who belonged to it. The best of their letters and diaries are often eloquent, and even the least expressive of them usually contain valuable insights. I have intruded as little as possible on each man's personal writing style, grammar, spelling, and punctuation, with rare editorial modifications in brackets when necessary.

Another major factor has helped define this study. The vast majority of sources examined and cited—with the notable exceptions of this preface and Chapter 10—date from the war years. This book is intended to convey that sense of contingency so evident in letters and diaries in which soldiers chronicled the daily, weekly, monthly, or yearly progression of events without knowing in advance how things were going to end. After the army's surrender at Appomattox, the passage of time softened veterans' memories of such events as hand-to-hand combat at the Bloody Angle or the sheer boredom of day-to-day life in the trenches at Petersburg. "Glamour was beginning to envelop the memory of the Confederates," Douglas Southall Freeman once observed, cautioning that memoirs often make "charming and therefore dangerous reading."[16] For the sake of a more accurate interpretation of the army's experience, postwar veterans' accounts have been excluded from consideration here.

A word on the relevant secondary literature on the Army of Northern Virginia, the campaigns of 1864 and 1865, and such related subjects as Civil War soldier life, the Southern home front, and causes of Confederate defeat is in order. Although my knowledge of the army has been influenced and immeasurably improved by the studies of many able historians over the years, I did not directly address their works in the original version of this study, which was completed in 1993 as a doctoral dissertation at the University of South Carolina. My intent was to avoid relying, even subconsciously, on the interpretations of others to form my own conclusions about the army's last year. In the end, however, this study is still a work of imagination, of choices made at every turn concerning sources, presentation, narrative, and analysis. It is not simply the inevitable product of an immersion in the sources as the "raw stuff" of history, which then reveal themselves to the diligent (and, hopefully, perceptive) historian.[17] This book, unlike the earlier study, cites the relevant secondary literature; it also features a concluding chapter that views the army's last year in retrospect and places this study in the context of other Civil War scholarship.

This study is a hybrid of social and military history. It is not, however, a social history that features extensive statistical evidence and quantification or a military history that highlights detailed battle narratives and analyses. It emphasizes, instead, the narrative form and is intended to be what David Hackett Fischer has called a "braided narrative," an interweaving of narrative and analysis.[18] Viewed from one perspective, this book is a broad history of life in the Army of Northern Virginia from May 1864 to April 1865. But viewed from another, equally valid perspective, it is a multifaceted presentation of many simultaneous narrative themes and interpretations, some of them with considerable interest as separate and specialized topics. The prologue and first nine chapters favor an implicit and understated style of analysis instead of the more explicit and forceful analysis often employed by historians, a style that may sometimes obscure rather than illuminate our understanding of the past. Though the last chapter is more direct in its analysis and in engaging the work of other historians, it, too, tends toward understatement rather than away from it. This book also differs from most studies of Civil War soldiers published to date by being restricted to their wartime writings rather than a blend of wartime and postwar writings, and by being organized in a chronological framework rather than a topical arrangement.

Officers and men cited in the documentation have been identified by name, grade, and unit in the notes and bibliography, placing each correspondent or diarist in his proper context within the Army of Northern Virginia. Unit identifications are in the following format: company or battery/regiment or battalion/brigade/division/corps/army or other administrative unit as appropriate.[19] The first note citing an officer or enlisted man identifies the soldier, his grade, and his unit—usually his company and regiment. Subsequent citations will identify the author simply by name unless his grade and/or unit had changed since the last citation given.[20]

I have no pretensions that this is *the* history of the Army of Northern Virginia during the last year of the Civil War but consider it a social history of Lee's soldiers in 1864 and 1865. Many of those who served under "Marse Robert," we may be sure, were not unmindful of their place in history even then. Lt. Col. William Ransom Johnson Pegram, a twenty-three-year-old Virginian whose Third Corps artillery battalion was one of the best in the Confederacy, was a perceptive young officer who often included assessments of the army's previous performance and its future prospects in his letters home. As the army continued to hold its lines between Richmond and Petersburg in the fall of 1864, he wrote his sister Mary: "Our troops are in remarkably fine spirits. The only drawback is that we have not enough of them. It would be impossible for the best writer in the world to do justice to this noble army."[21] Pegram was mortally wounded the next spring, only eight days before Appomattox. In July 1865, a few months after the war ended, Lee wrote his former generals and staff officers asking them to help him collect source material for a history of the army. "I am desirous that the bravery and devotion of the Army of Northern Virginia shall be correctly transmitted to posterity," he began his letter. "This is the only tribute that can now be paid to the worth of its noble officers and soldiers."[22] Writing more recently, and from the perspective of a scholar rather than a participant, Albert Castel has commented: "Perhaps setting (or keeping) the record straight is as much as the Civil War historian—or any historian—can hope to accomplish as a rule. If true, so be it. This is a worthy task, worthy of praise. And if more than that is done, then still more praise is deserved."[23] Though not presuming to meet Pegram's lofty standards, I hope that I have accomplished something toward Lee's and Castel's goals, and that I have done justice to the officers and men of the Army of Northern Virginia.

Acknowledgments

Few presents have ever meant as much to any fifteen-year-old as the copy of Bell Irvin Wiley's *The Life of Johnny Reb: The Common Soldier of the Confederacy* that I opened on Christmas morning 1973, and few parents have ever gone to so much trouble as my mother did, searching for weeks to find the lone copy for sale anywhere within a thirty-mile radius of Atlanta. Reading that remarkable book inspired me to begin work on a "book" of my own, one I then optimistically titled "The Morale of the Confederate Common Soldier, 1864–65" and the idea for which provided the spark for this study thirteen years later. All scholars who write about Civil War soldiers and their experiences owe a debt to Wiley, who led the way in an age when manuscript research was the exception rather than the rule. I am personally indebted to him as well. He took the time to promote my interest in the common soldier of the Confederacy while I was still in high school, and once I became an undergraduate at Emory University, where he continued teaching as a professor emeritus until his death in 1980, his frequent encouragement reinforced my desire to become a scholar and teacher. William C. Davis has stated in a book review that it would be "next to impossible for any graduate student of Wiley to leave Emory University without taking along some of the great teacher's passion for the common folk and common soldiers of the war." My experience as an undergraduate student there, I am happy to say, was no different.

If Bell Wiley's influence on this book is readily apparent, the influence of several other extraordinary teachers must also be acknowledged. Two of them had a lasting impact on my life far greater than could be measured by counting the number of their classes I took or the number of hours they spent with me either in or out of the classroom. Sally Parish, my English teacher at Berkmar High School in Lilburn, Georgia, taught me not only how to write but also how to take advantage of the rewards and endless possibilities of writing as expression and as communication. James Z. Rabun, my undergraduate adviser at Emory University, taught me much about Southern history but even more about research, the critical examination of sources, and the synthesis of historical evidence. The lessons I learned from both of them still help guide me years later.

From the moment I outlined the conception for this study to Clyde Wilson and asked him to serve as my major professor at the University of South Carolina, he urged me to approach it as a book manuscript that would happen to meet the requirements for a degree rather than a doctoral dissertation tailored to satisfy his views or those of a committee. He read every paragraph and every note with care and always combined praise and constructive criticism with questions or issues I had not yet considered. His influence and steady support were never more valuable than during the long months I wrestled with the critical final chapter, one that I wrote long after he had already fulfilled any obligations as an adviser. From major themes to minor details, this book would be vastly different without his guidance from beginning to end. I am also indebted to him for his continued support of every aspect of my career as a historian.

The University of South Carolina awarded me the Smith Richardson Fellowship for 1989, which helped fund a portion of the manuscript research. I am also grateful to the United Daughters of the Confederacy for granting the manuscript its 1994 Mrs. Simon Baruch University Award, and particularly to Mrs. June Smith Wells of Charleston, S.C., chair of the award committee.

Gary W. Gallagher first suggested the University of North Carolina Press as a possible publisher, provided valuable advice, and served as a reader for the Press. He and Richard M. McMurry recommended its publication but did so with the proviso that I should make an effort to place its subject, and indeed the book itself, in the context of other Civil War scholarship. Chapter 10 would exist in a drastically different form—if at all—without the benefit of their thoughtful comments. At the University of North Carolina Press, director Kate Douglas Torrey, editor-in-chief David Perry, and managing editor Ron Maner have all been remarkably supportive while leading an anxious first-time author through the acquisition and publication process. I especially appreciate Stevie Champion's fine copyediting, which combined equal measures of skill and sensitivity.

The South Carolina Department of Archives and History granted me occasional leave to complete the research, to write the original version of this study, and to revise the manuscript for publication. Several former and present colleagues there read portions of the book and provided general support; I am especially grateful to Paul Begley, the late Patricia Cridlebaugh, Charlie Hall, Alexia J. Helsley, Ian Hill, Charles H. Lesser, the late Nancy C. Meriwether, Lee Tippett, and George L. Vogt for their interest, friendship, and encouragement. Andy Chandler, who is at once a colleague, a "cousin-in-law," and my closest friend, has been a constant presence throughout, often lending a sympathetic ear to my musings about Marse Robert's army and just as often changing the subject when we both needed it most.

Friends and fellow historians Steve Davis, Rich DiNardo, Jim Legg, Chris Meyers, Henry Mintz, Karen Nickless, and Carol Reardon have carefully read the entire manuscript in draft, in its final form, or both, and have given me many valuable suggestions for improving it. Though I have not always followed their advice, I have always appreciated their opinions. Henry Mintz alerted me to manuscript and published sources I might have otherwise missed, obtained photographs of Lee's officers and men, and shared his vast knowledge of the North Carolinians who belonged to the Army of Northern Virginia. Other friends and colleagues have been particularly helpful in discussing major and minor themes of the book and offering additional support at various stages along the way, most notably Michael Bell, Robert E. L. Krick, Alex Moore, Bill Piston, Bob Valentine, and Steve Wise.

The staffs of all of the institutions listed in the notes and bibliography provided valuable assistance during my research. I am particularly grateful to William R. Erwin Jr. at Duke University; Virginia Cain, Linda Matthews, and Kathy Shoemaker at Emory University; Donald Pfanz at Fredericksburg-Spotsylvania National Military Park; Gail Miller De-Loach and Charlotte Ray at the Georgia Department of Archives and History; Corrine P. Hudgins and Guy R. Swanson at the Museum of the Confederacy; William H. Brown and Fran Tracy-Walls at the North Carolina Division of Archives and History, Department of Cultural Resources; Chris M. Calkins at Petersburg National Battlefield; Stephen Hoffius at the South Carolina Historical Society; Beth Bilderback, Henry Fulmer, and Allen H. Stokes at the South Caroliniana Library, University of South Carolina; Richard A. Shrader and John White at the Southern Historical Collection, University of North Carolina; Wilbur E. Meneray at Tulane University; Frances Pollard and Joseph Robertson at the Virginia Historical Society; Chris Kolbe at the Library of Virginia; Laura Endicott at the University of Virginia; and Michael P. Musick and Michael Meier at the National Archives.

In obtaining access to or copies of manuscripts in private collections, I appreciate the help of Elizabeth Jones and Sebron Hood of Myrtle Beach, South Carolina; Barnwell R. Linley and Sarah Linley Clingman of Columbia, South Carolina; Walker Gilmer Petroff and Julie Petroff of Beaufort, South Carolina; and Tommy Sims of Salem, Oregon. Charles E. Lee of Columbia alerted me to a scarce volume of published letters that proved to be extremely useful.

Several individuals have generously granted permission to publish photographs in their private collections; I am especially grateful to Ruth

Bedingfield, Robert J. Driver Jr., Ernest B. Furgurson, Charles W. Proffit, Joseph C. Shaner Jr., George M. Smith, and John A. Woodard for their assistance. I am also grateful to Special Collections, Robert W. Woodruff Library, Emory University; the Georgia Department of Archives and History; and the South Caroliniana Library, University of South Carolina, for their permission to publish photographs in their collections.

I have been richly blessed with a family that has always been there when I needed it. My parents, James C. Power Jr. and Claudett Fagan Power, of Lawrenceville, Georgia, to whom this book is dedicated, have been an unfailing source of support and have always believed in this book. My mother-in-law, Carolyn Smith Thompson of Olanta, South Carolina, has given me as much steady support and encouragement as if I were her own son. My grandparents, Harold C. and Willie Herndon Fagan of Law-renceville, and Charley and Katherine Rickman Power of Toccoa, Geor-gia, have shared that same faith in me and pride in my work, assuring me that I would succeed at whatever I wanted to do. They have my heartfelt thanks, as do the other members of my family who have asked so many times over the years, "how's the book coming?" only to hear, "it won't be long now."

I would be remiss if I did not mention three dear friends who have contributed nothing of substance to this book but have been faithful com-panions as well as frequently welcome distractions. Charlie—who will always be missed—Beauregard, and Maggie (Boston terrier, basset hound, and Boston terrier, respectively) spent countless hours by my side over the years while I wrote this study, the vast majority of them dreaming the grand dreams of dogdom.

It would be impossible to exaggerate the debt I owe to my wife Carol, who has spent far too much time waiting for me to finish something—a sentence, a note, a paragraph, a page, a chapter, this book—before I would leave the company of "Lee's Miserables" for a while and return to the twentieth century. She has cheerfully read or listened to far more about the last year of this army than anyone could ever wish for. But Carol's most important role has been—and is—to remind me that I have a full, rewarding life apart from the pursuit of history. She knows, in spite of her frequent tongue-in-cheek advice to "get a life," that she is the best part of the life I have.

Lee's Miserables

We are looking for marching orders every day

now and expecting for the Big Fight to open soon.

—*5th Sgt. Marion Hill Fitzpatrick*

45th Georgia, to his wife, 29 April 1864

. . . .

Prologue: Spring 1864

As the winter of 1863 gave way to the spring of 1864, and as the Civil War entered its third year with no clear resolution in sight, there was a sense of anticipation and renewed optimism within the Army of Northern Virginia. The previous year had been one of sharp contrasts for the Confederacy's most successful and most famous army, in which an exhilarating victory at Chancellorsville was followed by a disheartening defeat at Gettysburg. Since late July 1863 the army commanded by Gen. Robert E. Lee had been locked in a stalemate with its old foe, the Army of the Potomac. Though fighting had been infrequent and relatively small in scale, maneuvering had not, but neither the Confederates nor the Federals gained a lasting advantage before both armies went into winter quarters. A new year, a new season, and a new campaign, however, promised dramatic opportunities.

The prevailing opinion, particularly in the Confederacy, was that 1864 would be the last year of the war. Many soldiers in the Army of Northern

Virginia not only believed it but also believed that they would win a victory—or victories—as impressive as those of 1862 and 1863. "Every soldier feels as confident of success as if we had already achieved it," Lt. Robert Tutwiler of the 15th Virginia Cavalry wrote his aunt in April. "Genl. Lee's *old* army . . . is now generally considered to be in better spirits & health, also better armed equipped &c, than at any previous time during the war."[1] The relative quiet after Gettysburg had given the army some desperately needed rest, resupply, and recruits, and had also strengthened its resolve. "Our thinned ranks speak more eloquently than words of what we have suffered and endured," a North Carolina colonel proudly asserted in a short history of his regiment. "But the same Spirit that controled our actions in the beginning of this Struggle *still animates us.*"[2] The mood in the army this spring, unlike the three previous years, was more a spirit of calm determination than one of restless confidence.

Even so, overall morale was high among Lee's troops as they prepared for yet another campaign between Richmond and Washington. Many officers and men simply assumed that a Confederate victory was both forthcoming and inevitable. Some of them were quite ready, even eager, for the resumption of active operations. "There is hard Fighting to do," predicted Sgt. Thomas J. Gardner, "and our Army is in fine spirits and anxious for a Fight—the fighting has to be done and they Say they dont care how quick it commences."[3] Col. Gilbert Jefferson Wright, commanding Cobb's Legion Cavalry, wrote his wife, "I think we are ready for *Mr. Yank* now when ever he may think proper to come."[4] Similar expressions were common in letters written home from the winter camps of the Army of Northern Virginia.[5] In some instances soldiers seemed to relish the thought of fighting—and defeating—the Federal invaders. Others simply preferred the activity of campaigning to the tedium of camp life. Yet others, however, who believed that Lee would defeat the enemy, still acknowledged that bloody battles and heavy casualties lay ahead of them. A sergeant in the 12th Virginia commented of his comrades, "I cannot say with truth that they desire a fight but all express a determination to do their utmost when it does come and have confidence in the protection of Providence, their Leader, and themselves."[6] Andrew Boyd, a South Carolinian whose brother would soon join him in the ranks, wrote wistfully to his father, admitting, "I would like to bea at home to healp you. I think how loansum you must bea no one to healp you plow or feed the Stock in mornings . . . but our Cuntry call us for healp and we have to obey."[7] Many soldiers, who had no great desire for combat, still felt a grave responsibility to their comrades and to their families and friends at home. They viewed their military service as less something to be endured than a privilege to be appreciated.[8] All in all, predictions for the coming campaign differed more in their degrees of enthusiasm than in questions of whether the Army of Northern Virginia would succeed.

One readily apparent sign of the army's mood this spring was the voluntary—and involuntary—reenlistment of its officers and men. Confederate authorities, anxious to oppose the Federals with as many troops as possible, had worked throughout the winter to fill the ranks of all their armies. Congress debated, revised, and finally passed a law that extended soldiers' enlistments for the duration of the war and drafted all white men between the ages of seventeen and forty-five. The conscription act of 1864, enacted on 17 February, also eliminated the practice of hiring substitutes and abolished most exemptions from military service. It retained many veterans who had joined the rush of volunteers throughout the South in the spring of 1861 and who had fulfilled their original three-year enlistment.[9]

Before the new law and accompanying army regulations were widely circulated, numerous individuals and units in the Confederate armies voluntarily reenlisted "for the war." Many of them did so out of patriotism or a sense of duty, but some renewed their terms to avoid criticism from their comrades or the folks at home. Capt. Asbury Hull Jackson, a staff officer in Brig. Gen. George P. Doles's Georgia brigade, believed that such re-enlistments demonstrated "not only to our people at home, especially the whipped, but to the enemy, that we who have suffered most by facing them and fighting, bleeding & dying on the battle fields, who have suffered and withstood cheerfully the privations of hard marches in all sorts of weather, of cold & short rations & of being kept so long away from home & friends, are not ready nor willing to give up, in short, not whipped."[10] Sgt. Jacob Patton of the 14th North Carolina was less idealistic than Jackson. "About half the old members of our company has reenlisted," he informed his father. "I am one of that number, we have carid [carried] on the war this far, I thought I would see them out we have this war to fight out."[11] Lee, in general orders, praised those units in the Army of Northern Virginia that reenlisted, urging the rest of his soldiers to "imitate this noble example and evince to the world that you never can be conquered."[12] Some soldiers, who had originally joined for a three-year period in the summer of 1862, also voluntarily reenlisted for the rest of the war rather than waiting for the new law.

Even those soldiers who reenlisted before 17 February, however, were not always selfless patriots. Some regiments were strongly encouraged, even forced, to "voluntarily" renew their enlistments. A disaffected North Carolinian wrote home that one regiment's soldiers "swore to the very last that they would not" reenlist, but that handpicked officers spoke for their companies so that "it was carried that all the men were in favor of reenlisting." Christopher Hackett assured his parents, "I dont consider myself any deeper inn or any nearer out for the war cant last long no way in my estimation."[13] Hackett was representative of a slowly but steadily growing number of soldiers whose fondest hope was to end the war—or at least their own part in it—as soon as possible.

In the spring of 1864 Lee's army was not only retaining its veterans but was also gaining numerous new recruits and returning absentees. Many of the recent conscripts had been furnished by enlisted men who won themselves a thirty-day furlough for bringing them in.[14] Others, who had previously furnished substitutes to stay out of the army, helped to fill vacancies in depleted companies. "Bringing in these [men who had paid for] substitutes gives great satisfaction to the men [already in the army]," one staff officer commented.[15] Absentees, most of them either assigned to details or in hospitals with minor wounds or illnesses, also returned under the provisions of the conscription act of 1864 and the strict enforcement of existing regulations. Lee, who was anxious to increase his numbers by any means available, kept up a spirited correspondence with President Jefferson Davis, Secretary of War James A. Seddon, and other Confederate authorities. From army headquarters, such admonitions as "it is a matter of great moment that the recruits for this army should reach it in full time for the coming campaign" or "it is a matter of extreme importance to get every able-bodied man back to the field as soon as we can" were common.[16]

Such purely military improvements were not the only renewals occurring in the Army of Northern Virginia. Religious revivals in the army were sometimes extensive, other times more modest, but always charged with emotion and evangelical fervor. They took place almost daily in camp throughout the winter of 1863–64 and into the next spring and included sermons, prayer meetings, scripture lessons, and hymn singings. These activities attracted many different soldiers, from the deeply religious, to the curious, to those who simply wanted a diversion from the boredom of camp life. Such revivals were also recommended in the Articles of War and were warmly supported by Lee, who issued orders urging "a proper observance of the Sabbath . . . not only as a moral and religious duty, but as contributing to the personal health and well-being of the troops," and limiting military duties on Sundays to those "essential to the safety, health, or comfort of the army."[17]

Numerous Christians, both in and out of the army, believed that the Confederacy's military defeats, economic woes, political disputes, and social upheavals were all caused by the people's inability—or refusal—to obey God. Some of Lee's soldiers emphatically condemned the South's collective sins and warned of a prolonged war, possible defeat at the hands of a hated enemy, and the specter of eternal damnation. "Satan is reaping a great harvest now," wrote a Georgia captain in the Second Corps. "If the hearts of our People will get right God will give us Peace and not before."[18] Daniel Abernathy of the 16th North Carolina expressed both hope and pessimism when he reported to his parents, "we have regular preaching here in camp and some converts though their is so much wickedness going on it appears that the men dont care what they due."[19] Jefferson Davis, in a presidential proclamation, set aside 8 April as a day of humiliation, fasting, and prayer throughout the Confederacy. He urged soldiers and civilians alike to express "fresh gratitude to the Supreme Ruler of nations" while at the same time confessing "that our sins as a people have justly exposed us to his chastisement."[20] Lee endorsed Davis's proclamation and encouraged the Army of Northern Virginia to join the Confederate people in observing the day.[21]

Other officers and men had a more optimistic view of religious activity in the army. Lt. Harry Lewis returned from a furlough in Mississippi to find that "where formerly scarcely none attended preaching now crowds flock."[22] Many veterans, confronting the uncertainties and dangers of another year of combat and becoming even more aware of their mortality, embraced the Christian life. They hastened to repent for their sins and to win the promise of eternal salvation represented by Jesus Christ. "Life is so un certann and deth is shure," cautioned one private in Brig. Gen. John Rogers Cooke's North Carolina brigade. "We know not when it will come some die sudenly in camp some on the battle field. . . . We hav prayer meeting in the brigade evry day preaching evry night and preaching of Sundays it is agreate privilege . . . one hundred or more hav been changed from natures night in to the Marvelous light of the people of god at this camp."[23]

Chaplains and ministers often drew parallels between one's religious and patriotic responsibilities. They emphasized that God was on the Confederacy's side, but that only Christian soldiers could hope to triumph over both their earthly and spiritual enemies. Capt. W. R. Redding of the 13th

Georgia heard a typical sermon in April, one that admonished soldiers to obey the civil and military authorities because "we were due that to them and if we failed to discharge our duty in this respect we were dishonest before God." Redding wrote his wife that the chaplain "wound up by Exhorting us to love mercy give to the Poor clothe the naked and feed the hungry. I wish every Person in the Confederacy could have heard him."[24] The emotional and spiritual support of such a faith, and of a community of believers, gave many soldiers strength to face the grim days ahead.

Several army units made public pronouncements of optimism, determination, and patriotism that spring. The action of the 12th Mississippi, in the Third Corps, was typical. The Mississippians, wishing to thank Richmond residents for the hospitality shown to them earlier in the war, offered to donate one day's ration each week to destitute and hungry civilians in the Confederate capital. The gesture was greatly appreciated by the Virginians, who nevertheless refused to take the soldiers' rations.[25] A newspaper editorial later commented that the regiment's generosity surrounded it "with a halo of almost supernatural light."[26] The same sort of spirit led the Georgians of Brig. Gen. John B. Gordon's Brigade, of the Second Corps, to express their support for the Davis administration and their contempt for its critics. In several resolutions passed on 30 March the members of the brigade praised Davis and Lee while rebuking Gov. Joseph E. Brown and other Georgians who opposed the Confederate government's policies. They pledged, "while the privations and dangers of the army have no charms for us, we will cheerfully submit to them, even unto death, for the sake of our nationality and independence."[27] A few days later the *Richmond Dispatch* paid tribute to the 12th Mississippi, to Gordon's Brigade, and to the Confederate army as a whole: "the public virtue, the manhood, and all those qualities peculiar to the South, lie mainly in the army." The editorial exhorted: "the army is the country. Let those who stay at home labor to feed and clothe it, to invigorate and encourage it, to imitate it in endurance and self-sacrifice, and to be thankful that they live in the same land and generation with it."[28]

In spite of such inspiring words from both soldiers and civilians, all was not well with the Army of Northern Virginia in early 1864. Desertion, often resorted to by soldiers weary of the war and simply wishing to return home, was occurring at a disturbing rate; increasingly, those who deserted went over to the enemy. Veterans, who had fulfilled their initial three-year enlistment and participated in their share of battles, were sometimes encouraged by family or friends to leave the ranks and let others continue the fight. But conscripts, who had little if any desire to be in the army, frequently bolted at the first opportunity. The increase in desertions during the winter, which accelerated as the spring campaign approached, was a significant factor in Lee's—and the government's—efforts to replace them by bringing in absentees, recruiting new troops, and limiting exemptions from service.

Perhaps the most common reason given for desertions, particularly those to the enemy, was that of reduced rations. It was so difficult to obtain provisions for the army that the normal daily ration in early 1864 was three-quarters of a pound of meat—usually salt pork or bacon—and a quarter pound of salt, along with half rations of sugar and coffee.[29] This was about half the regular allowance, but soldiers often received quarter rations and sometimes even less. "Short rations are having a bad effect upon the men, both morally and physically," Lee complained to the War Department in January. "Desertions to the enemy are becoming more frequent. . . . Unless there is a change, I fear the army cannot be kept effective, and probably cannot be kept together."[30] Numerous pleas for additional subsistence usually accomplished little. A general order acknowledged the problem and assured the army that "no effort has been spared to provide for its wants." It ended with an appeal spurring the troops to emulate the sacrifices of their ancestors during the American Revolution: "You tread with no unequal step the road by which your fathers marched through suffering, privations and blood to independence. . . . be assured that the just God who crowned their efforts with success will, in His own good time, send down His blessing upon yours."[31] Many men who deserted to the Federals saw no parallels between their situation and that of the Continental Army. They were simply seeking something to eat.[32]

One of the hungry and discontented soldiers to whom Lee's order was addressed was Sgt. Christopher Hackett, of the 45th North Carolina, who had unwillingly reenlisted with the rest of his regiment. Hackett felt the pinch of short rations in late March and informed his parents that he received them "regular enough but getting enough is the thing." He sarcastically described his quarter rations of cornmeal and pork, supplemented by a little sugar, coffee, and rice, as "strong living" and announced that he and a few others were planning to desert. Hackett swore his family to secrecy, saying, "I intend to make the trip the first oppertunity that offers itself . . . for I intend to get out of this war in some way and there is but the one way that one can make a sure escape." He called his letter "among my last that I will write in the confederacy." Hackett evidently had a change of heart—or never found a suitable opportunity to escape. He stayed with his regiment until captured at Spotsylvania in May.[33]

Many Confederates, Lee's troops among them, were undoubtedly encouraged to desert by the obvious inconsistency in the trials and sentences administered by military courts. Soldiers who were tried for desertion were often convicted of being absent without leave instead. Even if offenders were found guilty of desertion, the Articles of War permitted a sentence of either death "or such other punishment" as a court-martial saw fit.[34] Deserters were frequently given that "other punishment," and even those sentenced to death frequently received more lenient sentences after review by the military or civil authorities. Punishments for desertion varied widely from court to court and from case to case. In March and April 1864, for example, deserters who avoided a death penalty were given sentences ranging from three months' to five years' hard labor, most often with a ball and chain, and usually forfeited their pay for the duration of their sentence.[35]

Lee generally recommended clemency toward soldiers who could claim extenuating circumstances, such as previous good conduct, extreme youth, or voluntarily returning to the army. By the spring of 1864, however, he had grave concerns about the increasing number of desertions and about the sentences given to convicted deserters. He wrote Davis at length on the subject, commenting in April that "the escape of one criminal [from punishment] encourages others to hope for like impunity . . . the effect of the example is the chief thing to be considered, and that it is injurious, I have no doubt."[36] Col. Bryan Grimes of the 4th North Carolina opposed the common practice of sentencing deserters to hard labor on the Richmond fortifications. He believed that men often deserted to avoid fighting, and that "labor and confinement is no punishment to a coward or to a man so devoid of principle as to desert. Any disgrace and punishment short of taking life is to him preferable to encountering the perils of battle."[37] Grimes observed that if the army would not execute deserters, it could at least punish them in camp and require them to fight.

The widespread tendency toward mercy notwithstanding, several deserters in the Army of Northern Virginia were indeed executed that spring. One North Carolina lieutenant declared that a deserter scheduled to be shot the next day "brought it on himself, therefore he does not get much simpathy."[38] An officer in Brig. Gen. John Marshall Jones's Virginia brigade, whose unit was ordered to witness an execution in mid-April, was more compassionate. Lt. Thomas Frederick Boatwright wrote his wife, "I had thought and hoped that I would not have to witness such a scene again but *alas* it will be so by Desertion or other disobedience."[39] It remained to be seen whether such infrequent strict punishments would deter future desertions.

By mid-April the unmistakable signs of an impending campaign were evident throughout Lee's army. General orders directed the troops to be ready to march at any time and required a ready supply of one week's rations for men and the same amount of forage for animals. Officers were ordered to stay with their commands, all soldiers not fit for field duty were transferred to hospitals, and all visitors to the front were sent beyond the lines. Detailed lists stipulated the number of wagons and animals allotted to each officer, staff, and unit.[40] "This looks like squally times are expected soon," noted a private in the 50th Virginia. "As soon as the weather will permit the ball will open."[41]

Other indicators that the Army of Northern Virginia was about to enter its third spring of fighting were increased activity among its sharp-shooters and a headquarters circular concerning soldiers' behavior if they were captured by the enemy. Regimental, division, and brigade sharp-shooters, most often used as skirmishers, worked almost daily on their drilling and target practice.[42] After watching his division's sharpshoot-ers a Second Corps courier commented, "they looked very warlike went through a sham battle charging and falling back, it was very interest-ing."[43] Lee's instructions for soldiers who found themselves in enemy hands cautioned them to give the Federals no information but their name, company, and regiment.[44] "There is something on foot different from what *has* been from a *circular* sent from General Lee to the army," remarked a lieutenant in the 44th Virginia. "This I say is a strange request comeing from General *Lee* it is the first of the kind during the war."[45]

As the army's officers and men prepared for the coming battles, they often expressed opinions of their own commanding general and of their enemy's newly appointed general in chief. Their evaluations of Lee, natu-rally enough, exhibited a simple yet profound faith in his ability to lead them to new victories. "All seems to be in tolerably good spirits and to repose the utmost confidence in Gen. Lee," noted Powell Reynolds, a Virginian in the Second Corps. "Although he has to contend against the ablest one of the Yankee Generals, all think he will be more than a match for him."[46] "The ablest one of the Yankee Generals" whom Reynolds referred to was Ulysses S. Grant, who had been promoted to lieutenant general and appointed to command the armies of the United States in March 1864. Though Maj. Gen. George G. Meade was still technically in command of the Army of the Potomac, Grant's headquarters would be with Meade in the field, and the promotion did not mean that he would now command from behind a desk in Washington. Most observers soon referred to the Army of the Potomac as if it were Grant's army. Sgt. W. H. Strayhorn of the 2d North Carolina Cavalry, on picket on the Rapidan River one day, struck up a conversation with his Union counterparts across the way. "They put all confidence in Gen Grant they say he is the man for Gen Lee," Strayhorn reported. "I toled them that Grant was a fine officer but that Lee would Soon nose him out as he had done all the balance."[47] Lt. Col. William Murdoch Parsley of the 3d North Carolina expressed similar opinions in a mid-April letter to his sister: "I feel certain that we will whip Mr. Grant well, and that he will be sorry enough to have been put in command where Genl. Lee can get hold of him."[48] Though Grant's victories at Vicksburg and Chattanooga the previous year had made him a Northern hero, and though Abraham Lincoln had given him full responsibility to prosecute the war for the Union, many men in the Army of Northern Virginia viewed him as just another general whom Lee—and they—would soon defeat and embarrass.[49]

Lee himself, meanwhile, was preoccupied with last-minute plans and preparations, all intended to use his force to its best advantage. Increasing the army's overall strength was a high priority. Several commands of various sizes had been detached since Gettysburg for various reasons, ranging from reinforcements for other Confederate commands to enforcement of the conscription law or the apprehension of deserters. The Army of Northern Virginia was about to enter the spring campaign opposing an enemy that significantly outnumbered it even under the best of circumstances.

The basic problem concerning the army's strength was more significant than counting numbers of soldiers. The question was how to increase the number of officers and men present and fit for duty. In mid-February, for example, though the Army of Northern Virginia numbered some 85,000 troops present and absent, only 38,000 were present for duty. A month later, the totals had increased to 98,500 present and absent, of which less than 44,000 were present for duty.[50] By mid-April Lee's strength was about 122,000, but only a little more than half of that number—some 64,500—represented soldiers present for duty.[51] Measures to acquire new recruits, regain absentees, and reduce the number of detailed men, such as offering furloughs to veteran soldiers who brought in recruits or sending nonessential detailed men back to their companies, had improved the situation somewhat but had not brought troops to the army in vast numbers.

The most important addition to the army that spring was the return of Lt. Gen. James Longstreet, with most of his First Corps, from Tennessee. Longstreet had taken two of his three infantry divisions, along with two battalions of artillery, to reinforce Gen. Braxton Bragg's Army of Tennessee in the fall of 1863. After playing a major role in the Confederate victory at Chickamauga in September, Longstreet was assigned to command the Department of East Tennessee, given more troops, and sent to oppose Federal forces in that vicinity. He suffered a bitter defeat at Knoxville in November and spent the winter of 1863–64 embroiled in various disputes with his subordinate generals, placing several of them under arrest. On 7 April Lee ordered Longstreet and his old corps—some 10,000 troops—back to Virginia.[52]

The veterans of the First Corps were overjoyed at the prospect of leaving Tennessee and rejoining their comrades in Virginia. One private in the 7th South Carolina described the scene when Longstreet's corps passed through Charlottesville on its way to rejoin the rest of the army. "We wer met by the ladys of the town to Cheer us and the yong girls from the Coledgs Came runing to meet us," Andrew Boyd wrote his father. "We are ruff weatherbeaten lookin fellowes dirty and raged but the womans and yong girles Seems to Say Stand of[f] you Cleen Shirts hospittle rats the town is filld with Such."[53] Another member of the brigade, which had long been commanded by Brig. Gen. Joseph B. Kershaw, appreciated "the luxury of sun shine and balmy winds of Va. from which we have been so long deprived while on in that detestable East Tenn."[54] Longstreet's officers and men, who had experienced the most active—and most frustrating—fall and winter of any troops in the army, could have been pardoned for being anxious to begin a new campaign.

Both to welcome Longstreet's veterans back to the army and to gauge their strength and effectiveness, Lee ordered a review of the First Corps for Friday, 29 April. After their hard expedition to Tennessee and back, they were indeed "ruff weatherbeaten lookin fellowes dirty and raged." Still, they did their best to be presentable for "Marse Robert," Longstreet, other officers, and a crowd of civilian spectators that included many young ladies. Officers and men sewed up holes in their jackets and pants, polished buttons and belt plates, and cleaned their uniforms, arms, and accoutrements as well as they could before marching out to the field where the review was held. A newspaper correspondent described the reception Lee received from Kershaw's South Carolinians: "a wild and prolonged cheer, fraught with a feeling that thrilled all hearts, ran along the lines and rose to the heavens. Hats were thrown high, and many persons became almost frantic with emotion."[55] David Hugh Crawford, a brigade courier, wrote his mother proudly:

> Everything passed off well. As the Gen. came on the field he was received by a salute of eight guns, and cheers from the troops. . . . In coming from the field Gens. Lee and Longstreet met the troops and were enthusiastically cheered by them as long as they were in sight. All the troops marched by Gen. Lee very well, but Jenkins' Brigade marched better than all others. My old company marched very well. Gen. Lee uncovered his head as the colors of each regiment were lowered as they passed by him.[56]

It was difficult for observers to tell whether the First Corps or Lee was more moved by this reunion. A sergeant in the 53d Georgia commented, "All were certainly glad to see General Lee. And I expect he was glad to have us again under his Banner."[57] This review was much more than a simple inspection by the commanding general. It was an exceptional occasion, almost a ritual, which carried with it all the participants' memories of past bravery, sacrifice, and victory, and all of their hopes for their future efforts.

With so many units from widely ranging localities, and so many officers and men from diverse backgrounds, it would have been difficult to single out a representative soldier in the Army of Northern Virginia at the end of April 1864. One candidate among many such men could have been 5th Sgt. Marion Hill Fitzpatrick of the "Ray Guards," Company K of the 45th Georgia. His regiment had an enviable record as part of Brig. Gen. Edward L. Thomas's Brigade, in the famous old "Light Division" of the Third Corps, and had seen all of the army's major campaigns and battles since June 1862. On the same day that Lee reviewed the First Corps near Gordonsville, Sgt. Fitzpatrick sat in camp near Orange Courthouse and wrote his wife the latest news. He described his two meals a day as "biscuits for breakfast every morning and cornbread for supper or dinner. . . . The meat we draw is very inferior and comes in small doses." Fitzpatrick was a member of his regiment's newly organized sharpshooters, whose target practice interrupted his letter home. After sharpshooting he attended a Masonic lodge meeting in camp that lasted until midnight. The meeting kept him from finishing the letter until the next day, after that morning's target practice. "The weather is fine and pleasant now, and buds are rapidly putting forth, which indicates the near approach of Spring in Old Va.," Marion told Amanda. "We are looking for marching orders every day now and expecting for the Big Fight to open soon. . . . I have but few notions about it. When the order comes to fall in, I will buckle on my armour, sieze my Enfield, and put forth with energy and devotion to my bleeding country."[58] The determination expressed by Fitzpatrick was typical throughout the Army of Northern Virginia as it marched from its camps toward another battle with the Army of the Potomac, toward the tangled growth known locally as "the Wilderness."

I am heartily sick of blood & the sound of artillery &
small arms & the ghastly, pale face of death and all the
horrible sights & sounds of war. I long more intensely
& earnestly for the sweet rest & quiet of home than ever
before.

—*Capt. Benjamin Wesley Justice*
  Commissary, Kirkland / Heth / III Corps,
  to his wife, 20 May 1864

1

The Wilderness and Spotsylvania, May 1864

In the days just before the spring campaign opened, a dramatic event occurred in the army that some soldiers might have interpreted as a sign. On the morning of 2 May, several units of the First Corps marched a few miles to new camps near Gordonsville. They had barely gotten settled when they were drenched and buffeted by "a heavy Storm from N.W. blowing down our tents, and the trees and creating a general stampede . . . the gale followed by a hard rain several narrow escapes from flying limbs by our boys," according to a member of the famed Texas Brigade.[1] Less than a week later the Texans and the rest of the army would find themselves in the midst of a quite different storm, with its own general stampedes and narrow escapes. At least one high-ranking observer thought that the thunderstorm might postpone fighting for a few more days. Brig. Gen. Porter Alexander, Longstreet's brilliant chief of artillery, wrote his wife, "We have just had a tremendous storm & the weather is very chilly &

damp (of course) but as it may give us a longer time to prepare for Grant I am very glad to see it."[2] By the next day, however, the weather had improved enough for drill and a sham battle in the Texas Brigade and for a preliminary movement by elements of Brig. Gen. Micah Jenkins's South Carolina brigade, also in the First Corps.[3] "This closing towards the front indicates something but what it is impossible to say," noted a colonel in Jenkins's Brigade. "It serves this purpose with soldiers (however unsatisfactory it may be in women and citizens), namely, it puts them in a condition to be surprised at nothing."[4]

With months of uncertain waiting behind them, and with certain battles immediately ahead of them, officers and men throughout the army wrote their families and friends in the first few days of May. Their letters, describing preparations for the coming fight and making their own predictions for the future, were often a blend of hope and fear, of confidence and apprehension. "Dear wife their is more talk a bout peace now then ever I herd of before," Sgt. Isaac Lefevers of the 46th North Carolina commented, "but I am afraid it is only Sine for a big fite Shortley." Lefevers, like many of his comrades, had alternating, if not contradictory, feelings about what lay ahead. "We all feel assured that if Grannt makes an attact hear that by the assistance of the almighty we will give him what he wont like," he reported, but then cautioned, "all tho I have no doubt a meney one of us will fall in the Strougle."[5] Lefevers's simple words were echoed by Maj. Gen. Wade Hampton's more polished but no more heartfelt observation: "I hope confidently for success, but at the same time I cannot feel but anxious. In any event, how many thousand of the brave hearts, now eager for the strife, will have ceased to beat when that great fight is over!"[6] One Virginian, a member of Brig. Gen. William Mahone's Brigade in the Third Corps, had given much thought to the army's past performance and its future prospects. "I find but few who agree with me," Robert Mabry wrote his wife. "I can see no more reason now for a defeat of the Yankee Army bringing them to terms than heretofore." After listing the Army of Northern Virginia's campaigns since Lee took command, and claiming that Gettysburg was the only defeat during that period, he asked rhetorically, "Where is the good resulting from all these victorys[?]" He thought Grant's defeat "almost certain" but saw "little reason for believing it will close the war," then ended his discussion with the optimistic but not entirely convincing words, "I humbly trust we may have an early peace."[7] Many of Lefevers's, Hampton's, and Mabry's fellow soldiers in the Army of Northern Virginia undoubtedly displayed similar conflicting emotions on the eve of the campaign.[8]

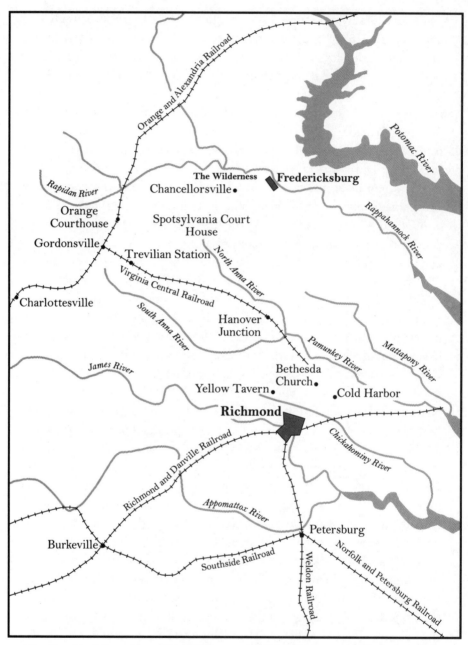

The Overland Campaign: The Wilderness to Cold Harbor, May–June 1864

The army's large-scale preparations and troop movements were launched in earnest on 4 May. Lee discovered that the Army of the Potomac was massed north of the Rapidan River and crossing it in force close to where the two armies had met a year before at Chancellorsville. The Federals had some 118,000 effective troops, whereas the Confederates had about 62,000 officers and men, or a little more than half of that number, present for duty. Lee immediately ordered Lt. Gen. Richard S. Ewell's Second Corps and Lt. Gen. A. P. Hill's Third Corps to check the Federal advance and Longstreet's First Corps to follow.[9] A sermon in the Third Corps was interrupted by orders "to strike tents, cut them up and distribute them among men, cook up rations and hold ourselves in readiness to march," an Alabama lieutenant wrote his wife that afternoon.[10] When Grant attacked Lee in the nearly impenetrable forest, thickets, and underbrush of the Wilderness early the next morning, he initiated a campaign—or series of campaigns—that would not end until the next April at Appomattox.[11]

Fighting on 5 May was heavy but resolved nothing. Lee, preferring not to fight a general engagement until his entire force arrived, kept the Second and Third Corps primarily on the defensive. The initial Federal assault, on the Confederate left, created considerable disorder in Ewell's corps and achieved some early success. When the Second Corps received reinforcements and counterattacked, however, the offensive stalled. Ewell spent the rest of the day and early evening turning back further Union attempts to break his line or turn his flank. Federal advances that afternoon, on the right against the Third Corps, were somewhat more effective. Though Hill held his position, his troops were greatly disorganized and weakened by the constant pressure, and though Lee's lines were intact at nightfall they would not remain so long. Poor communication between Ewell and Hill, combined with the usual confusion of battle and the natural obstacles of the Wilderness itself, allowed a gap between their corps. Grant would quickly exploit the opportunity presented by that costly error.

Early on the morning of 6 May, after repulsing an attack by Ewell, the Federals launched an offensive against Hill's weak position. The Third Corps fell back in disarray but was soon supported by elements of the Second Corps and of Longstreet's First Corps, just arriving on the field. By midday Longstreet found the Federal left flank exposed and committed a large portion of his force in an attempt to turn it. But the maneuver stalled when Longstreet was accidentally wounded by his own men. Fighting throughout the afternoon was characterized by Confederate frontal assaults that achieved little. Just before dark Ewell, on the other end of the line, discovered that Grant's right flank was unprotected. Though initially successful, the Second Corps's assault there was blunted by Confederate delays and Federal reinforcements, and darkness fell without either side gaining a tactical victory.[12] After two days of fierce combat, in which Grant lost nearly 18,000 casualties and Lee lost some 10,000 killed, wounded, and captured, the battle ended in a stalemate.

Combat in the Wilderness was defined by the forbidding region itself. The forest—primarily one of scrub pines and oaks—was overgrown with vines, briars, and other tangled vegetation, and it was divided by many small creeks and swampy areas. These features placed severe constraints on troop movements, on formations, on communication and coordination between units, and on visibility. Though officers in both armies attempted to create and exploit opportunities for flanking maneuvers, they were more often reduced to sending reinforcements into existing tactical situations. This was, above all, an infantry battle, in which elements of divisions, brigades, and regiments became hopelessly intermingled and in which individual soldiers often fought each other. When an officer in the 6th Louisiana wrote, "our Brigade got into the thickest of it," he referred to the terrain as much as to the combat.[13]

Confederate descriptions and assessments of the fighting shared several common characteristics. Accounts in letters and diaries, and to a lesser extent in official reports, often illustrated their authors' inability to write clear narratives describing their experiences. Such phrases as "a perfect wilderness," "a boundless forest," or "undergrowth almost impossible to penetrate," for example, were used to convey the difficulties encountered by the Army of Northern Virginia.[14] Some writers made explicit references not only to the Wilderness but also to the obstacles it created in the disposition of troops and in the use of arms other than infantry. Capt. James Hays, a staff officer in the Third Corps, wrote, "we have fought them in dense woods, only with musketry, & the Bayonet."[15] "I have never before seen woods so riddled with bullets," a South Carolinian in the same corps marveled after the battle. "At one place the battle raged among chinquapin bushes. All the bark was knocked off and the bushes are literally torn to pieces."[16] In their official reports of the Wilderness, officers described the challenges they faced in moving, positioning, and leading troops under such conditions. "The dense character of the woods in which the line was formed render[ed] it impossible for either men or officers to see the character or numbers of the enemy we were to attack," noted Brig. Gen. Goode Bryan, commanding a Georgia brigade.[17] The colonel of the 1st South Carolina reported that a regiment that should have been in line next to his was nowhere to be seen when an advance began. "In the density of the forest [I] concluded it had temporarily gotten lost," he wrote, "and I gave no more thought to it."[18]

This confusion helped create situations in which troops blindly fired at noises or at shadows, and in which they killed and wounded their comrades instead of the enemy. When William Mahone's Virginians of the Third Corps fired into a group of high-ranking officers on 6 May, it was only the most notable of several such occurrences in the Army of Northern Virginia. The volley from Mahone's Brigade injured James Longstreet, mortally wounded Micah Jenkins, and killed two members of Joseph Kershaw's staff. Most significantly, the mishap deprived the First Corps of its commander at a crucial juncture in the Confederate counterattack. Many observers in the army mentioned Longstreet's wounding, eerily close to the scene where Stonewall Jackson had been accidentally shot by his own troops almost a year to the day earlier. Some believed that the mishap kept Lee from winning a decisive victory in the Wilderness. Longstreet himself told one staff officer that he was wounded "in the very achievement of victory but his plans were frustrated when he fell," and another officer in the corps wrote a few days later, "Gen Longstreets wound I believe alone prevented us from routing Grants whole army on the 6th."[19] Similar accidents befell the 18th North Carolina, which "became somewhat confused, and commenced to fall back" when caught between Confederate and Federal fire, and the 12th Virginia, which was fired on by its own brigade, losing "some of [its] bravest and best men." Sgt. John F. Sale of the latter regiment observed that "the loss of these was more deeply regretted than of those who were shot by the enemy."[20]

Artillerymen and cavalrymen took relatively little part in the fighting but were keen observers of the battle. Some artillery batteries, placed on or near the few roads in the area or in the even fewer clearings, added firepower to Confederate defensive positions. The Second and Third Corps artillery, in limited action, "assisted materially in driving back the enemy" and participated "as far as the nature of the country permitted."[21] The First Corps artillery, however, remained in rear of the corps infantry and was not engaged. Its commander spent several hours "trying to find a place to get our arty to aid in the battle [but] could find none" and returned to corps headquarters.[22] Elements of Maj. Gen. J. E. B. Stuart's cavalry corps helped guide units through the woods, scouted to establish enemy troop positions, clashed with Federal pickets and skirmishers, and fought dismounted in support of infantry as needed. "Some Yankee prisoners remarked in my hearing today that 'that 4th Regt. fought like very Devils,'" a captain in the 4th Virginia Cavalry wrote proudly. "Our whole Division has been fighting just as Infantry most of the time in fact could only fight in that way in that Wilderness country."[23] It was, as a courier in the Third Corps observed, "almost entirely a musketry fight."[24]

One notable response to tactical obstacles was the extensive use of skirmishers or sharpshooters. Both armies, by this stage of the war, had gradually increased their employment of skirmish lines and had created special units, most often battalions, of sharpshooters. Such troops, with their tactical flexibility, seemed particularly suited to operations in the Wilderness. A North Carolina lieutenant described the experiences of his sharpshooters during the first day's fighting, which were typical. "We skurmished till late in the Eave at which time we advanced & run them back gaining some ground & held it," he wrote. "They kept up some fireing all night but we were relieved by a co of the 32d Regt so we got to rest & sleep all night."[25] On the same day Capt. George P. Ring of the 6th Louisiana was writing his wife when a Federal assault interrupted his letter in midsentence. "I am now out with my co. skirmishing and the bullets are whistling all around me," Ring observed when he resumed writing. "I have just had another man Killed but it is nothing when you get used to it."[26]

Soldiers threw up hasty field fortifications, improvising trenches and earth or log breastworks, almost as soon as the two armies made contact. This delineation of positions, and the resulting attacks and counterattacks against them, gave the fighting a sense of savage fluidity. A member of the 4th Georgia even received a letter from home while his regiment fought from behind breastworks on 6 May. "I was in line of battle when I received it," John LaRoque wrote his wife the next day, "not more than three hundred yards of the enemy who shot at evry head raised above the pile of logs we used as brest workes." LaRoque appreciated her letter all the more for arriving when it did and told her, "yours contained so much Christian advice & wrote in Such warm Spiritts &c, that I concluded the letter of yours the most appropriate letter for the ocasion I ever saw."[27] Earthworks, in most instances, created a tactical stalemate that was evident to the soldiers behind them. Samuel Finley Harper predicted that the Federals would "hardly attack us again & they are in an almost impregnable position . . . & it would be too great a sacrifice to charge it. . . . Altho we have gained another great victory I would like [it] if the yanks were in a position that we could attack & make it complete."[28] The ebb and flow of such a battle, in which both sides lost some positions they defended but captured some positions defended by the enemy, blurred distinctions between tactical success and failure.

Fighting in the Wilderness was almost relentless, a quality reflected in many soldiers' accounts of the combat. Most veterans in both armies were accustomed to the natural confusion of Civil War battles, and to relatively brief periods of close and violent contact with the enemy. Here, however, the forest magnified those characteristics, transforming confusion into chaos and close contact into a test of endurance. "Hear has bin the oflest site that I ever saw," George Pearsall of the 55th North Carolina reported to his wife a few days later. "I tell you I nevor was in as clost a place as I was the first day [5 May] I sot in one place and shot my riful 61 times and I was not more than 2 hundred yards from them." He was cut off from his regiment during the day but "got with the 11 Missippa [another regiment in his brigade] and went in a charge the 6 [6 May] in the morning and backed the yankees considerbal."[29] Pearsall's letter was more a statement of his actions than a description of his immediate surroundings. But Thomas L. McCarty of the 1st Texas told a graphic tale in his diary on the night of the sixth: "Many of our company killed and wounded among whomb my freind Frank Gearing shot in breast, [I] laid him down by a tree and passed on with boys. Had canteen and tin cup perforated by a ball, also one through breast of coat, and haversack strap cut—struck in face by a peice of tin, off a canister or some arrangement for holding balls by artillerymen. . . . Many wounded among whomb was Jno McCarty and myself in right breast glancy shot bled considerably but never left field."[30]

Such experiences, though these were described in somewhat more detail than in most Confederate letters and diaries, were so common as to be typical. Pearsall's and McCarty's dramatic narratives reinforce more understated accounts, such as that written by Capt. Andrew Jackson McBride of the 10th Georgia. McBride began his letter home, "Another day of blood and carnage, and after more than ordinary exposure, I am spared to write a few lines to my Darling." He informed his wife that he was "struck on the foot but not hurt. I dont think I would have objected to a very slight wound."[31] Louis G. Young, a staff officer in the Third Corps, complained, "Never have I fought on a more unsatisfactory battlefield," and described the Wilderness as "almost a battle in the dark."[32]

These scenes became truly horrific when portions of the forest, thickets, and underbrush caught fire while the fighting still raged on the second day. Many wounded soldiers burned to death before they could be rescued, and many other soldiers, already dead, were burned beyond recognition. One North Carolinian who encountered such gruesome sights wrote his wife: "I have neaver Saw Such a Site in no Battle as I have in this I have Saw lots of Dead bodes Burnt into a crips. . . . I Saw one man that was burnt that had the picture I suppose of his little Daughter in his pockett. . . . I neaver Saw enny thing that made me feel more Sorrow."[33] "Truly war is terrible in all its phases," a sergeant in the 12th Virginia commented after describing the inferno in his diary.[34]

The realization would soon spread throughout the Army of Northern Virginia, from the men in the ranks to the commanding general, that these two days of battle in the Wilderness signaled a new phase of the war in Virginia, one in which intense fighting would occur for days or weeks at a time—or even longer—rather than in one large-scale battle followed by a respite, as had so often occurred before. One soldier noted, "We hold all the battle ground now and I tell you hear is a offul site. . . . We have kiled a quanty of yankees and a good meney of our men too."[35] A captain on the staff of Brig. Gen. William W. Kirkland's Brigade captured the essence of the Wilderness in a letter written three days after the battle. Benjamin Wesley Justice observed on 9 May that "the fighting was in dense woods & pine thickets, & at very close range. . . . The discharge of small arms excelled anything I ever heard." His letter was full of phrases describing "many who groaned in agony or met terrible death all alone in the dense woods" or units that advanced "only to be slaughtered in heaps." Justice vividly recounted the battle's melancholy aftermath:

Night put an end to the bloody strife, & drew a sable curtain over the dead, the mangled, & the dying. Ambulances & litters brought the wounded to the rear, & the surgeons were soon busy cutting out balls, amputating limbs, & dressing ghastly wounds. The cries of the sufferers, the rumbling of wagons & artillery & ambulances, the hurrying to & fro of men & animals, the neighing of horses and mules, the glare of the ruddy campfires, all made a scene difficult to describe, but never to be forgotten.[36]

And the Wilderness was only the beginning. One Virginian characterized it as "a hard fought Battle & not over yet by a great deal."[37]

Many of Lee's veterans, turning from those "scene[s] difficult to describe," focused their attention on the results that they expected to follow. They claimed a victory, as defined by Grant's inability to break their lines and drive their army from its strong defensive position. Observations such as "the enemy are evidently much worsted & their plans frustrated," "we have got the best of the fight so far," "we have whipped them badly," "we have been driving them handsomely at every point," and the picturesque "our boys gave them 'hankins' today" were representative.[38] Notes of caution, such as a staff officer's opinion that "the grand results contemplated by the Country will not be realized," were much less frequent immediately after the battle.[39] There was some criticism of units that fought ineffectively or even badly, allowing the enemy temporary tactical advantages, such as one colonel's complaint that "some of our troops have not behaved as well as was expected."[40] But most cautions and criticisms were generally explained away, or forgotten, by Confederates anxious to proclaim a major victory.

Correspondents and diarists reported that they—and Lee—were ready for any attack or movement that the Federals wanted to make against them. The phrases "high spirits" or "fine spirits" were often employed to describe the army's mood immediately after the Wilderness.[41] "Our troops are in fine spirits, fine condition & no straggling," claimed one officer.[42] Maj. Gen. Cadmus M. Wilcox, commanding the old "Light Division" in the Third Corps, believed that "no battle of the war was fought with more valour on our part."[43] The troops' faith in Lee, though always unshakable, was even stronger after he attempted to lead a charge of the Texas Brigade on 6 May and had to be physically restrained by officers and men shouting "Lee to the rear!"[44] "Our army is in splendid condition & spirits, confident of success and victory, trusting in God & Gen. Lee," observed one staff officer; another reported, "General Lee was among the thick flying balls on the front lines, waving his hat and encouraging the men."[45] The Army of Northern Virginia's performance in the Wilderness helped reinforce a confidence that was, if not at the giddy heights of the year before, still a definite asset.

If Confederates' evaluations of their own deeds—and future prospects— were generally positive, their assessments of the Army of the Potomac, and of Grant, were correspondingly negative. Some believed that the Federals were demoralized by their failure to defeat the Army of Northern Virginia. "The enemy have been active but have accomplished nothing at all," observed Col. Bryan Grimes on 7 May. "They are regarded as badly whipped and greatly demoralized." The day before, Grimes had written his wife that the Federals "stampeded like sheep"; one enemy corps "broke and run before we could get a good chance to execute much punishment upon them."[46] Allusions to Grant's generalship often reflected the widespread belief that his previous successes, in the war's western theater, were against inferior Confederate generals, if not inferior armies themselves. "It is enough to say Grant is badly whiped so far," one Georgian believed; a North Carolinian claimed that "Grant [now] thinks this army composed of different material from our western army [the Army of Tennessee]."[47] There were several, perhaps reluctant, admissions that Grant's troops fought well, perhaps better than they ever had in the past. "We drove them like a storm," James Reynolds of the 16th Georgia wrote in his diary on 6 May; the Federals "fought us right tight but we drove them off leaving a great many dead boddies & wounded subjects."[48] Many soldiers would have agreed with the surgeon who wrote, "They seem very determined," but "I think we are certain to whip them. Our men fight desperately."[49]

On the whole, the officers and men of the army viewed the Wilderness as a resounding Confederate triumph. "Can such men as these under such a General ever be subjugated?" asked one Mississippi private.[50] The claims of a Virginia captain writing his mother on the night of 7 May were representative: "We have repulsed the Yankees in every instance, & have driven them several miles. We hold the field. . . . They say that no army in the world can stand our charges."[51] Lee's confident troops fully expected Grant, as so many Union commanders of the Army of the Potomac had done before him, to abandon his attempt to take Richmond and to turn his army back toward Washington. They believed that two days of combat, though fought under greater disadvantages and with heavier losses than in any battle since Gettysburg, had ended the campaign.

Their commander, however, recognized that his new opponent was made of sterner stuff than erstwhile foes George McClellan, John Pope, Ambrose Burnside, Joseph Hooker, or George Meade. Lee expected Grant to move around the Confederate right flank in an attempt to place his forces between the Army of Northern Virginia and Richmond and made provisions to block such a move. On 7 May he ordered the First Corps, now commanded by Maj. Gen. Richard H. Anderson in Longstreet's absence, to march to a strategically critical crossroads some ten miles southeast. Grant, that same day, had indeed ordered a corps in that direction. During the night lead elements of the Army of the Potomac and the Army of Northern Virginia, each corps commander unaware of the other, moved toward Spotsylvania Court House.[52]

On the morning of 8 May a corps of Federal infantry and a division of Confederate cavalry clashed just northwest of Spotsylvania, on the main road leading from the Wilderness. Stuart's cavalry, fighting behind improvised breastworks placed astride the road, held on until Anderson and his men, who had marched all night, could come up and even the odds. The Federals, intending to push on to the village itself, launched several attacks against Anderson throughout the day, as reinforcements arrived and were sent into the fight on both sides. Ewell arrived with the Second Corps late in the afternoon and repulsed a vigorous Union attack on the Confederate right. As night fell, Anderson and Ewell continued to hold the road and blocked Grant's way to Spotsylvania Court House. A meeting engagement between advance units had rapidly drawn in significant portions of both armies and made a major battle here inevitable.

The ninth of May was a relatively quiet day, though additional Union and Confederate troops made their way to the vicinity, were assigned their proper positions in their respective lines, and worked industriously to construct defensive works. Lee's final infantry corps, the Third, arrived under Maj. Gen. Jubal A. Early as Hill was too ill to command. Confederate engineers, expecting Grant to renew his push toward Spotsylvania, laid out a defensive line destined to play a pivotal role in determining the course of the battle. The defenses were roughly semicircular in shape, with a protruding salient that would soon become the focal point for both armies. There was occasional sharpshooting and picket firing throughout the day but little fighting of any significance. Large-scale maneuvering began in the afternoon and continued into the evening, most notably a Federal bid to turn Lee's left flank and a Confederate shift by elements of the Third Corps in response. Both commanders hoped that they could find, and exploit, an enemy weakness the next day.

Neither the Federals nor the Confederates accomplished much of consequence during the morning of 10 May. Grant withdrew his exposed force from Lee's left about the same time that Early advanced, and the resulting brief contact gave Confederate participants the impression that a pitched battle had taken place. Several Union assaults on the First Corps, poorly executed and without proper support, were launched during the day and repulsed with little difficulty.

By the afternoon, however, enterprising Federal officers had identified the salient near Lee's center—dubbed the "Mule Shoe"—as a point at which they might penetrate the Confederate defenses. The salient, occupied by Ewell's Second Corps, not only jutted out from the main line but was also masked by dense woods, through which an attacking force might approach unobserved. Infantry alone, without strong artillery support, could not hope to hold such an exposed position and even with guns in the works might not hold it long. Though a second and more secure line across the base of the salient was planned, it was still unfinished. Early in the evening of 10 May, a Federal column crashed into the salient, broke through it before the Confederates could mount an effective defense, and captured hundreds of prisoners. Ewell's counterattack, aided by reinforcements of infantry and artillery, drove the Federals back and restored the line. Grant's assault, which was well planned, failed only because it lacked both sufficient numbers and sufficient support.

The opposing forces spent 11 May building, or improving, earthworks and log breastworks and waited for full-scale attacks that never came, while the usual skirmishing and picket firing only served to heighten the troops' unease. In the afternoon Confederate cavalrymen, scouting the enemy's activities, interpreted signs of movement as indications that the Federals were about to retreat. Lee, acting on this assessment, ordered his army to prepare to follow the enemy withdrawal. The Second Corps artillery, massed in the salient, was withdrawn during the night in preparation for just such a move. Grant, meanwhile, recognized the great potential of a second, more substantial, attempt to break the Confederate center and ordered a corps into position. A cold rain continued falling throughout the night while soldiers on both sides waited for morning.

At about 4:30 A.M. on Thursday, 12 May, a massive Union column moved forward in fog, mist, and rain through dense woods, then into and through a clearing in front of the Confederate lines. The Federals, cheering, rushed over the point of the Mule Shoe salient and rapidly overwhelmed Ewell's stunned infantry, driving the Confederates a half mile and taking thousands of prisoners. An entire division of the Second Corps was shattered, and only a fierce counterattack by the other two divisions prevented a complete disaster. The Federals were pushed back to the outside of the salient, but no farther. While portions of the Third Corps, and still later of the First Corps, moved into positions supporting Ewell's hard-pressed corps, Grant pushed reinforcements of his own forward. The combat quickly degenerated into a savage fight for survival, a prolonged bloodletting that was shocking, even compared with the previous week's fierce battle in the Wilderness.

In the rain and mud, behind log breastworks and in slick trenches, Confederates and Federals fought with virtually no interruption for almost twenty-four hours, through the twelfth and into the early morning of the thirteenth. Combat here became a bloody embrace that neither army could break. One portion of the salient, where particularly brutal fighting raged, would earn the evocative—and accurate—name, the "Bloody Angle." The hail of musketry was almost continuous and at some points was so concentrated that it cut down trees as well as human beings. Soldiers fought literally hand-to-hand, pulling each other over the works, lunging with their bayonets, or clubbing heads with the butts of their

Pvts. William T. and Henry M. Bailey, Company C, 16th Georgia. Brothers William T. and Henry M. Bailey served as privates in the Hartwell Infantry; William was furloughed home in 1863, while Henry, who was captured at Cold Harbor, died a prisoner of war at Elmira, New York, in early 1865. (Vanishing Georgia Collection, Georgia Department of Archives and History)

muskets. Spotsylvania was truly, in the words of a contemporary historian writing a few months later, "a slaughter so sickening that the heart heaves at the details."[53] The Confederate units in the works held their positions throughout the day and well into the night, while comrades to their rear worked desperately to finish a second line of defenses across the base of the demolished salient. Finally, about 3:00 A.M. on 13 May the grim survivors in the Mule Shoe withdrew to their interior line and one of the worst days of the entire war was mercifully over.

Reeling from the fury of the twelfth, both armies were content to spend the next few days in relative inactivity, interrupted only by picket firing and by occasional withdrawals or rearrangements of troops. On the morning of 18 May the Federals advanced once more against the Bloody Angle, taking the unoccupied outer lines, but were repulsed with heavy casualties by a concentrated fire from the Second Corps artillery. When Ewell's corps attempted a reconnaissance in force on the Union right in the afternoon of the nineteenth, the action accomplished little other than inflicting additional casualties among the attackers and defenders. After eleven days of skirmishes, assaults, actions, engagements, and full-scale battles— with the heaviest combat occurring on 10, 12, and 19 May—the fighting around Spotsylvania finally ended.[54] The Army of the Potomac lost some 18,000 killed, wounded, and captured—about the same number as in the Wilderness—and the Army of Northern Virginia suffered about 12,000 casualties. Two weeks of fighting in the Wilderness and at Spotsylvania had cost the Federals a staggering 36,000 officers and men, and the Confederates' loss—22,000 casualties—was proportionately even greater.

Combat at Spotsylvania, both in its setting and its duration, was quite different from that in the Wilderness. Though the two armies still had to contend with stretches of dense forest, clearings and roads were more common, somewhat easing the soldiers' sensation of being trapped and allowing greater latitude in troop movements and dispositions. There was also more space in which to construct earthworks, log breastworks, and other obstructions such as abatis. Though Federal resources for such work, both in manpower and in entrenching tools, far outstripped those in the Army of Northern Virginia, the Confederates were still able to build extensive defenses. "Our position here is in an open field behind breastworks," a sergeant in the First Corps commented; on the next day he added in his diary, "in order to protect ourselves we have dug pits in the ground & are huddled up in them as closely as possible."[55] Lee's soldiers worked almost incessantly to improve their works, such as on the night of

10 May, after the complete surprise and partial success of the first Federal assault on the Mule Shoe salient. The commanding general himself wrote Ewell that evening, cautioning him: "It will be necessary for you to re-establish your whole line to-night. . . . I wish Gen'l Rhodes [Maj. Gen. Robert E. Rodes, commanding a division in the Second Corps] to rectify his line & improve its defenses especially that part which seemed so easily overcome this afternoon. . . . a ditch had better be dug on the outside & an abattis made in front."[56] Such field fortifications, whether planned or sim-ply improvised, played a major role in the fighting there.

Operations at Spotsylvania developed over almost two weeks, with alternating stretches of inactivity, increased activity, and almost over-whelming intensity, in contrast to only two days of continuous fighting in the Wilderness. If anything, however, combat at Spotsylvania was even more inconclusive than in the Wilderness. The skirmishes, assaults, ac-tions, engagements, and full-scale battles that occurred at Spotsylvania were more notable for their casualties than for their strategic, or even tactical, results. The day-to-day uncertainty, which produced anticipation in some and apprehension in others, was noticeably reflected in numerous diaries written in the Army of Northern Virginia. Sgt. Edward Richard-son Crockett of the 4th Texas commented, "We have to keep on the watch continuously, our fare is rough & our duty hard & we are getting very tired."[57] Though diaries had an immediacy that letters usually did not convey, Confederates writing home also alluded to the strain created by their ever-changing circumstances. Capt. Benjamin Wesley Justice de-scribed the mood around him—ironically enough, on the day *before* the vicious fighting at the Bloody Angle—in a letter to his wife. "The excite-ment & confusion are great; the suffering of the wounded, indescribable; the mental anxiety & solicitude, almost insupportable," Justice reported. "It *must* end before many days."[58] Late the same night a fellow North Carolinian optimistically wrote, "the report is old Grant is retreting and I think it is time for if he ant whiped now thair is no chans to whip him." But after participating in the fighting on 12 May, George Pearsall continued on the thirteenth, "that report is not so for the fight opend at day yestady morning and held all day." He concluded his letter on the fourteenth, "our scrumershs is firing and reglar buming going on . . . huney I will close for evry time I begin to write we have to leave."[59] A few days later Sgt. Marion Hill Fitzpatrick of the 45th Georgia scolded his wife, "you must write to me and not wait till the fight ends before you write, for there is no telling when it will end."[60] The cumulative effect of the first three weeks of May, greatly reinforced by events at Spotsylvania, would make many in the army question whether the war—or even their present situation—would ever end.

As for assessments of the battle itself, three major themes ran through Confederate letters and diaries, particularly those describing what occurred on 10 and 12 May. Soldiers often expressed astonishment at the ferocity, the extraordinary duration, and the physical and mental strain of the fighting. Yet just as often they simply alluded to such subjects without discussing them in any detail. It was as if correspondents and diarists could not find the words to express what they had done and seen.

An almost universal topic, mentioned by many officers and men who wrote soon after (or even during) the battle, was the incredible level of musketry fire during both the skirmishes and the larger fights. The firing on 12 May was variously described, for example, as "perfectly fearful," "an incessant roar," "an active fusillade—indeed, a terrific roar of musketry," and "a storm of balls which did not intermit one instant of time for eighteen hours."[61] One veteran noncommissioned officer called Spotsylvania "the hottest place I have been in since Manassas."[62] Walter Raleigh Battle, a private in the 4th North Carolina, shared his impressions of the musketry in a letter to his parents:

> There is not a man in this brigade who will ever forget the sad requiem, which those minie balls sung over the dead and dying for twenty-two long hours; they put one in mind of some musical instrument; some sounded like wounded men crying; some like humming of bees; some like cats in the depth of the night, while others cut through the air with only a 'Zip' like noise. I know it to be the hottest and the hardest fought battle that has ever been on this continent.[63]

Writing a few days later, Battle told his mother, "I shot away 120 rounds of cartridges myself, three cartridge boxes full."[64] Charles E. Whilden, a forty-year-old color bearer in the 1st South Carolina, observed, "the top of my Flag was shot away & a bullet tore open my clothes & gave a slight wound to my left shoulder, but I am allright."[65]

Perhaps the most graphic testimony to the sheer density of lead flying through the air was that an oak tree at the Bloody Angle, measuring some twenty inches in diameter, was cut down entirely by musket balls. The tree, which fell into the lines of Brig. Gen. Samuel McGowan's South Carolina brigade of the Third Corps, was visited by curious officers and men immediately after the battle and was the subject of considerable discussion throughout the Army of Northern Virginia for some time. In his diary entry for 12 May, a private in the 1st Texas, in the First Corps, mentioned "trees 1 foot to 18 in[ches] shot down by minnie balls." Lt. James E. Green, of the 53d North Carolina, walking over the battlefield a few days later, went to the Bloody Angle and "saw a White Oak tree cut down by [bullets] that would of maid 10 Rails to the cut, shot off & bent over to the ground."[66] McGowan alluded to the large oak in his official report, as did Brig. Gen. Nathaniel H. Harris, commanding a Mississippi brigade that fought beside McGowan's at the salient.[67]

If the destructive power of musketry often prompted statements of awe, the intensity of hand-to-hand combat was usually described with more restraint by correspondents and diarists. Lt. Charles E. Denoon of the 41st Virginia related his own experiences during the battle of 12 May. "We had a rough roll and tumble fight at one time," he wrote his parents. "I got hold of a Yankees musket while he was trying to shoot me and whacked him over the head with my sword until [he] cried out for quarters." Denoon failed to mention whether or not he captured his adversary.[68] One soldier in the 1st Texas, assigned to a burial detail on the night of the tenth, commented almost casually in his diary that he "helped to carry out the Federal soldier who bayonetted Jim Blalock, he was killed by Hickman of Co H, with a blow of Enfield rifle barrel on head." With considerable understatement, Thomas McCarty continued in the margin of his entry for that day, "The Federals and us were '*closer to each other* today than since the War commenced.'"[69] Even Denoon's and McCarty's simple accounts were atypical; most soldiers who mentioned the use of bayonets or rifle butts did so in general terms. "Never has such fighting been known before," one noncommissioned officer observed. "They have locked bayonets time and again and fought with the butts of their guns."[70] Further elaboration was seldom necessary.

Soldiers throughout the army wrote expressively, often eloquently, of the battle's appalling casualties. "I tel you their neaver has bin Such a Slaughter in men Sinse the war commensed," claimed a North Carolina sergeant; "we have lost a menny a good man But no comparing with the yankes."[71] Another veteran, in similar language, noted, "we have had one of the bloodyst campain so far that ever has bin since the war . . . we have lost A great many men out of our Army but they say nothing to what the yankees have lost."[72] Others wrote more vividly, whether with polished metaphors or with simple, even blunt words. A staff officer who had not witnessed the battle firsthand called it "one of the bloodiest that ever dyed God's footstool with human gore."[73] Samuel McGowan, who was wounded while commanding his South Carolina brigade, claimed in his official report that "The trenches on the right in the Bloody Angle ran with blood and had to be cleared of the dead bodies more than once."[74] A Charleston newspaper published the shocking description written by an unidentified soldier in the 1st South Carolina, in McGowan's Brigade: "I was splashed over with brains and blood. In stooping down or squatting to load, the mud, blood and brains mingled, would reach up to my waist, and my head and face were covered or spotted with the horrid paint."[75]

All too often "the dead bodies" went nameless in official reports, newspaper dispatches, and even in their comrades' letters and diaries. If they were mentioned by name at all, it was usually on a company or regimental casualty list, printed in a newspaper in their native state, under the heading "Killed." These men were, however, not simply statistics, but individual human beings, with friends in the army, with families at home hoping and praying for their safety, with their own motives for fighting the Yankees, and with their own personalities and their own life histories. The story of one Confederate soldier killed at Spotsylvania may help to underscore the human cost of such a war and of war in general. Five days after the fighting at the Bloody Angle a young soldier in the 1st South Carolina wrote his mother a graphic depiction of the hellish scenes he had witnessed there. Pvt. Francis Asbury Wayne's letter was not written for publication, but his account, unlike the letter printed in the *Charleston Courier*, identified at least one of the regiment's dead whose "blood and brains" had so horrified the anonymous correspondent:

> On the 12th we fought behind breastworks, & nearly every man that was killed or wounded on our side was shot through the head. Men were killed before behind & on either side of me. I met with several very narrow escapes a ball having struck the rim of my hat & one grazed my shoulder. I fought almost ankle deep in the blood & brains of our killed & wounded. . . . Sergt Force of our Co was killed just by me & his blood & Brains poured out on my right leg & Shoe. Such, is war *in reality*.[76]

The unfortunate Confederate killed next to Wayne was twenty-year-old 3d Sgt. Philip H. Force. In September 1861, at the age of seventeen, Force had enlisted as a private in the "Carolina Light Infantry" of Charleston, which became Company L of the 1st South Carolina. He was promoted to 5th sergeant, then 3d sergeant, and had been wounded at least three times—at Gaines's Mill in June 1862, Fredericksburg in December 1862, and Chancellorsville in May 1863—before his death.[77] Though a casualty list of his company in the Charleston newspapers simply listed him as one of the "Killed," an anonymous obituary published in the same papers a few days later gave readers a more detailed, if not intimate, portrait of "Serg't PHILIP H. FORCE." Titled "The Young and the Brave," the obituary called him "among the many whose epitaph, more lasting than brass and enduring than marble—[is] 'I died in the defence of my country'—and whose death will long be lamented by those who knew him best and loved him most."[78] Capt. William Aiken Kelly, who had himself been wounded at Spotsylvania, had not only reported his company's casualties to the papers but also wrote Force's father a letter of condolence. "No nobler sacrifice has been offered on the altar of our country than your son's," he eulogized, calling Force "a most gallant, brave and daring soldier" and "one of the most efficient non commissioned officers I had." Kelly also praised the sergeant for improving the company, stating that Force had been particularly helpful in training new recruits or draftees. He closed with a touching eulogy to "a good, brave and noble soldier . . . but also an esteemed and valued friend. . . . In life I honored and esteemed him, in death I revere his memory."[79] A few weeks later Kelly observed that writing such letters "was indeed a sad & mellancholly duty to perform but one which I felt it my duty to do."[80] Philip Force was only one of many men in both armies killed at Spotsylvania, but Frank Wayne's simple comment is a strikingly appropriate one on Force's death—and all the other deaths—there: "Such, is war *in reality*."[81] Such was Spotsylvania in reality.

Many Confederate participants, either in private letters and diaries or in official reports, referred to the extraordinary length of combat in and around the Mule Shoe salient. From early morning through the day, then from twilight through the night and into a second early morning, men fought not for victory but to survive. They loaded, fired, loaded, fired— again and again—and thrust bayonets or swung muskets over and over, until they ceased thinking about their actions and simply repeated them. Two North Carolina brigades of Robert Rodes's division in the Second Corps, for example, were instrumental in restoring the broken lines that morning and fought in the salient for more than twenty hours. Members of those brigades made pointed references to the duration of the fighting. The colonel of the 4th North Carolina, in Brig. Gen. Stephen Dodson Ramseur's Brigade, called it "a day of most trying hours that lingered oh how wearily."[82] A private in the 14th North Carolina described the brigade's evacuation of the works early the next day, commenting, "I don't suppose there is any man that can express the relief he felt after getting out of such a place."[83] Brig. Gen. Junius Daniel's Brigade fought beside Ramseur's in the salient, and Daniel was mortally wounded there. "This fight lasted from light till late in the night. . . . It was the hardest fight we have ever had & will be long remembered as the hard fight of the Twelf of May," declared Lt. James Green, commanding sharpshooters in the 53d North Carolina. Brigade courier Thomas Pollock Devereux undoubtedly expressed the feelings of many weary soldiers when he wrote home, "I am broken down—but I am all right."[84] Some members of the brigade, also "broken down," saw things quite differently. A soldier in the 45th North Carolina, who deserted to the Federals on the night of 16 May, told them that he thought "within [the last] few days the spirit of the men has somewhat failed."[85] One noncommissioned officer in the Third Corps summed up the situation perfectly. "There was quite a quiet resting over the whole army after the excessive fighting upon the preceding day," he observed in his diary on 13 May.[86] Such "excessive fighting" was beginning to wear down first the flesh and then the spirit of Lee's soldiers.

The physical and mental exhaustion of prolonged fighting was exacerbated by the dismal conditions under which the Army of Northern Virginia defended its position. A cold rain drenched troops to the skin, turned the ground into a treacherous quagmire, and fouled rifles. Fog further intensified the obscurity, and even at midday visibility was limited at best. Dead and wounded Confederates fell into the trenches and behind the log breastworks, amid discarded or ruined weapons and accoutrements that littered the ground. A Louisiana captain in the Second Corps wrote his wife, "We lay all day and night long in the Breastworks in mud five inches deep with every kind of shot & shell whistling over us, among us *in us* and about us, so that it was as much as your life was worth to raise your head above the works."[87] Pvt. Walter Raleigh Battle of Ramseur's Brigade observed, with a touch of humor, "There was no one too nice that day to drop himself behind the breastworks. Brigadiers and Colonels lay as low in the trench and water as the men."[88] Writing to his mother a few days later, he commented on the psychological strain: "add to all this the thought that the next minute may be your last, [and that] is another thing altogether. There is not a man in this brigade who will ever forget it."[89]

One member of the brigade who would certainly not forget it was with the 14th North Carolina. Pvt. David Fort of Company K, the "Raleigh Rifles," had been in the army only since September 1863—when he enlisted at the age of forty-three—and was near both physical and emotional collapse. On Sunday, 15 May, Fort's cousin Benjamin Wesley Justice, a captain on the staff of the Third Corps, visited the regiment and found him "looking thin & hollow eyed. He would have been pale but for the smoke & dirt on his face. He said he had been sick for several days." Justice wrote

Fort's wife Nancy for him, to let her know that he had made it through the battle, and enclosed a note in a letter to his own wife. When he asked his cousin if he would not rather be at home in North Carolina attending church with his wife, Fort "replied affirmatively, then hung down his head as if to hide his emotions from some soldiers near, & when he looked up again his eyes were filled with tears." The captain, though he held a relatively privileged position as a staff officer, felt great compassion for the men in the ranks. "O how much mute sorrow & suffering fill the hearts of the poor soldiers on the marches, by the camp fires, & in the trenches," Justice sympathized.[90]

Lee's soldiers, either because of or in spite of almost two weeks of such "sorrow & suffering" at Spotsylvania, expressed varying degrees of encouragement and discouragement after the fighting there. Some believed that the Federal offensives had been Grant's last desperate efforts to defeat Lee and that his failure to do so would hasten the end of the present campaign or perhaps even the end of the war. A member of the 1st Virginia Artillery, after describing the ease with which a Union assault was repulsed on 18 May, ventured the opinion, "It does not seem to me that Grant can do much more, & from accounts from Richmond every thing looks as bright as day."[91] Several North Carolinians in the Third Corps were confident enough to say that they " 'would give *$1.25 in gold* for *$1* in *Confederate money!* "[92] Many officers and men wanted to remain in their formidable entrenchments and act entirely on the defensive, simply waiting for the Federals to assault their positions again. A Virginian in the famous Rockbridge Artillery headed a letter to his parents "In position on the battlefield" and boasted, "we have got a splendid line of breastworks and we can whip any Army the Yankees can bring against us if the Lord is willing."[93] A South Carolina infantryman noted, "our men just lay in theare brest works and waits for them to charge."[94] These men, and many others like them, believed that the battle was an outright victory, won by a combination of Lee's generalship and their own hard fighting. Their letters and diaries expressed satisfaction with what they had accomplished at Spotsylvania and confidence that they would soon win the Confederacy's independence. "The victory so far is decidedly in our favor, though the enemy of course claim all advantages," asserted Capt. Watson Dugat Williams of the 5th Texas, in the First Corps. "A perfect enthusiasm prevails in the army and the men are so confident of a decisive victory that they exhibit a delight in fighting."[95] One young North Carolinian was even more emphatic than Williams. Writing just a day after helping to defend the Mule Shoe salient, he reported, "To day all is quiet and Grant is thought to be retreating. . . . We can whip the whole Yankee nation, and we will do it."[96]

Some civilian observers believed that the Confederates were just as optimistic as, and even more determined than, they had been before the Wilderness. According to one editor, who talked with some of the army's wounded recuperating in Richmond hospitals, " 'We just *mowed* them every time' . . . is the only account they give of the struggle."[97] Soldiers who had been wounded in some of the most brutal fighting of the war, and could still exhibit what the editor called "high spirits and unbounded confidence," were impressive spokesmen for a significant school of thought in the army.

Other Confederates who agreed that the Army of Northern Virginia had successfully defended its position also conceded that Grant was a formidable adversary and that the Army of the Potomac fought with more determination than it had displayed even in the Wilderness. "Grant is certainly a far more fearful adversary than any of his predecessors," admitted Robert Stiles, adjutant of a First Corps artillery battalion. "His pertinacity & courage are positively sublime." After Stiles had a conversation with "Marse Robert" himself about the Federal commander, he reported that Lee "frankly admits Grant's terrific power & successes, yet quietly knows his ability to meet him, & trusts the result to a Higher Power."[98] Frank Wayne expressed the same general sentiment in more simple words when he wrote his mother, "There never has been such fighting I recon in the history of wars. Old Grant is certainly a very stubborn fighter."[99] Grant's soldiers were given their due as well by men such as Lt. Charles Denoon, of Virginia, who stated, "The Yanks fought to the last," or by Pvt. William Slater, of South Carolina, who commented, "the yankees have ben more stauborn and Detirmin than they ever have bin with us."[100]

Such men recognized the likelihood of additional battles, and, as a result, their predictions for the immediate future—though hopeful—were somewhat more cautious than they might otherwise have been. Lt. Col. Charles S. Venable, aide-de-camp on the headquarters staff, reflected this mood in describing a pathetic scene that reinforced his own feelings about the campaign: "We hope to discomfit Grant entirely by the help of God. . . . I saw a poor little young soldier this afternoon sitting crying by his dead comrade. I was afraid it was his brother or father & could not ask him anything about it. May God send us peace & stop this fearful carnage."[101] A Georgia private expressed himself more colorfully than Venable a few days later when the sound of musketry interrupted his attempts to write a letter to his wife. "(Hush I hear small arms again and it scares me so bad I can hardly write) Ewells Bull dogs is barking pretty finely again, and old Grants Bulldogs is barking at Ewell, but Lee has dogs enough for all the dogs Grant can bring up," Pvt. James Wesley Williams commented.[102] Though these observers knew that more battles and more casualties lay ahead, they believed that those battles and casualties were an unfortunate necessity, part of a task to be completed rather than a great triumph to be enjoyed. Some soldiers, aware that they might not survive the next battle, wrote home outlining plans to be followed after their deaths. Charles Whilden instructed his brother William, "I have never made a will, but if it should be the decree of the Almighty that I should lose my life in this War, I wish you to take charge of & destroy such of my papers as you may think proper." He left William a pipe, specified that lots were to be drawn among several relatives for a watch and chain, and bequeathed the rest of his property to his two sisters, ending his letter with a simple "Farewell."[103]

Still other members of the army were convinced that they—and, indeed, the entire army—had barely escaped disaster, citing the surprise Federal assault on the Mule Shoe salient on 12 May. Officers and men in units that had endured the heaviest combat and had suffered the highest percentage of casualties were, understandably, among the most outspoken soldiers on this subject. They were often critical of the army's performance at Spotsylvania and disparaged its prospects for the future. Maj. Alfred D. Kelly of the 21st Virginia, in Maj. Gen. Edward Johnson's Division of the Second Corps, a division that had been overwhelmed at the Bloody Angle, wrote his brother bluntly, "Our old division has lost all of its past renown. My shattered nerves will not allow of my writing more."[104] Most of the division's officers and men, including its commander, were captured in the initial fighting. Capt. George P. Ring of the 6th Louisiana believed that many Confederates gave up too quickly and for selfish motives, commenting, "it is a well known fact that many an Officer and man allowed themselves to be taken prisoner as the safest way to escape the dangers of the rest of the campaign, as they thought the war would end this summer and if they were prisoners they would certainly come out all safe."[105]

A private in the 50th Virginia, meanwhile, reported: "Some forty or fifty of the regiment made their escape. Counting all the drummers, detailed men, nurses and sick, there is but eighty of the 50th left. It started into the fight with 490 men."[106] An artilleryman who had just joined the 1st Virginia Artillery saw his first battle on 10 May, when his battalion was overrun by the Federals. He served a gun in the salient all day and night of the twelfth and was badly shaken by the experience, calling it "the most terrible and awful one of my life." Pvt. Creed Thomas Davis of the famous Richmond Howitzers continued in his diary, "I pray God, that I may never experience another such an one." He admitted candidly, "I am already quite exhausted, and I must say also demoralized, others whom I might mention are in the same frame of mind." Davis reported to the hospital on the morning of 14 May, sick and "quite prostrated from working at the guns in the last fight," but the surgeon on duty suspected that some soldiers were only sick of fighting and tried to make them go back to their commands. Davis expressed the fears of many in the army when he wrote, "Oh God, will this war never end!"[107] These men, and others of like mind, had few, if any, illusions about easy Confederate victories over inept Federal opponents and wrote gloomily of stalemates and a war that seemed to have no end in sight. Benjamin Wesley Justice, who had not heard from his wife in North Carolina since before the Wilderness, wrote her plaintively, "I am heartily sick of blood & the sound of artillery & small arms & the ghastly, pale face of death and all the horrible sights and sounds of war."[108] A Georgian in the First Corps expressed the hope that "this may be the last battle we will fight in Virginia and I hope that what few of our Co. that is living will get home."[109]

Though postbattle opinions ranged from jubilation to dejection, after Spotsylvania correspondents and diarists throughout the army would have agreed on one major point. Lee could ill afford to continue losing his officers and men at such a rate. Col. Bryan Grimes, who was assigned to command Junius Daniel's North Carolina brigade after Daniel's death, commented, "although in all probability I gain a Brigade by his death I would for the sake of the Country have always remained in statu quo than the country should have lost his services." After mentioning that Col. Thomas M. Garrett of the 5th North Carolina had been killed, Grimes continued, "who else I cannot enumerate there were so very many—N.C. has suffered very much indeed, in killed and wounded."[110] On the same day that an Alabama surgeon observed, "a great many of our best men have already fallen," a South Carolina infantryman wrote his mother: "How many gallant officers & men we have lossed in this fight. Our regt has lossed three (3) hundred men in killed wounded and missing."[111] Joseph F. Shaner, referring to persistent rumors that the only way Grant could persuade his troops to charge the Confederate breastworks was to issue them whiskey, commented bitterly, "Oh how hard it is to think of having our best men butchered up by a set of drunkards as they are. . . . we have lost some good men in this fight."[112]

Many of those "best men" and "good men" were private soldiers, such as William D. Curry of Georgia. Curry had enlisted in the "Coffee County Guards," Company C of the 50th Georgia, but by 1864 was detailed to the headquarters of a Georgia brigade in Kershaw's Division of the First Corps. William Ross Stillwell, a courier at brigade headquarters, described the twenty-two-year-old Curry's death one night at Spotsylvania: "I have made many narrow escaps and pased through many dangers I had one of my frinds a Mr Curry killed by my side the other knight while aslepe he and I was Sleepeing together the ball struck him in the brest he awoke me struling but before I could get alight he was dead pore fellow he never knew what hit him oh God thy ways are past finding out and thy mercy endureth for ever blesed be the name of God."[113] Curry's family and friends could not even console themselves with the knowledge that he had lost his life in the forefront of battle, fighting for the Confederacy or for his comrades; instead, he died barely awake, shot by a stray bullet.

It was no wonder that Benjamin Wesley Justice exclaimed, "I am heartily sick of blood & the sound of artillery & small arms & the ghastly, pale face of death and all the horrible sights & sounds of war." Many of his fellow soldiers, heartsick at the loss of relatives and friends, perhaps suffering from their own wounds, and simply tired of fighting the enemy, would have agreed with Justice when he wrote, "I long more intensely & earnestly for the sweet rest & quiet of home than ever before."[114] Though the spring campaign was only a few weeks old, its impact on the army was already undeniable and lasting. Bitter fighting in the Wilderness and at Spotsylvania had taken the old Army of Northern Virginia—and, indeed, the war in the East as well—to a new dimension in American military history. It remained to be seen whether the officers and men who had joined the pre-Wilderness army could adapt to the demands now being placed on them by the post-Spotsylvania one.

*The yankes are trying to flank us again wee have
whiped the Yankes at every point but know wee will
take of[f] after them again and before we stop I expect
wee will be at Richmond.*

—Corp. Jonathan Fuller Coghill
  23d North Carolina, to his brother, 25 May 1864

Spotsylvania, the North Anna, and Cold Harbor, May–June 1864

In camp near Hanover Junction, the week after fighting ended at Spotsylvania, John H. Hartman began a letter to his wife at home in Salisbury, North Carolina. "I now seat myself to answer your cind letters that I received weak before last," he wrote. "I was truly glad to hear from you but I am sorry that I cold not rite eny sooner but you must excuse me for we have bin fighting now for the last 27 days we had fore men wonded but nary one cild." Hartman, a private in the 1st North Carolina Artillery, alternated between apologies for being an infrequent correspondent and colorful descriptions of the fighting he had just seen. "My dear I hant mutch time to rite I must just put up my letter as I can for I hant got time to rite mutch as we air on line of battle and fireing evry cople ours," he explained. "We have whipt the yankeys in evry fight yet we have had brest works to fight behind . . . our men wold just shoot them down like flys they lay three and fore men deep in front of our brest works they was enough yankeys cild to make fortifications all round Salisbury." Hartman lay his letter aside for a few days but finished it four days later, while his company was halted for a rest on its way to Richmond. "Rite soon and oftin I just haf to rite by chance," he closed.[1]

Though time was a luxury in short supply throughout Lee's army for most of May 1864, many men spent a significant amount of that time writing about their experiences in the Wilderness and at Spotsylvania. One of a Civil War soldier's greatest joys was receiving a letter from family or friends, but he often found it difficult to return the favor while in the midst of an active campaign. This situation was almost universal in the Army of Northern Virginia that spring. Correspondents usually began their letters with either an expression of gratitude for receiving mail or a grumble of complaint for not receiving it, followed by an apology for not writing earlier.[2] Soldiers who kept diaries—either instead of or, more often, in addition to writing letters—had no better success in keeping them up to date. They often settled for brief entries that provided only an outline of their experiences or wrote longer entries that recapitulated the events of a week or more in greater detail, but days after the fact.[3]

A lack of time to write, however, was not the only—or even the most significant—factor that shaped these accounts. Many letters and diary entries written during this period reflected their authors' struggle to describe and come to terms with the present campaign. In its previous three years of existence, in victories from First Manassas to Chancellorsville and in defeats from Malvern Hill to Gettysburg, the Army of Northern Virginia had helped to set new, if grim, standards for Civil War battles. But desperate combat in the Bloody Lane and on Cemetery Ridge was at least equaled, if not surpassed, by the ferocity of extended battle in close quarters in the Wilderness and at Spotsylvania. The war itself was evolving, and the language used by its participants to describe and assess it was evolving as well.

Descriptions of troop movements and their results, for example, were more often than not vague and imprecise. Most simply provided an outline of what happened rather than an explanation of how or why it happened. Capt. James Hays, on the staff of a Mississippi brigade in the Third Corps, wrote his mother from the Wilderness on 7 May, "heavy & continuous Battles have been fought on the 5th, 6th, and 7th insts. & thousands have been killed & wounded."[4] Another staff officer, writing on 19 May from Spotsylvania, briefly summarized two weeks of battle: "This is the eighth day of rain and the fifteenth in which our troops have been in the line of battle. The great days of fighting were the 5th, 6th, 8th, and 12th. Also yesterday morning. The intermediate days there has been no general heavy engagement, but skirmishing has been going on all the time, with occasional more severe attacks on some point of our line."[5] One Georgian gave his wife even less information, writing her, "This is the 9th day of the fight and no likelyhood of its Stoping yet. . . . The fighting was terrible on the 6th 10th & 12th not so sever on the other days."[6] Even those who described the fighting in somewhat greater detail, such as Corp. Jonathan Fuller Coghill, often left much to the imagination. "As for the fights that has ben fought in the Wilderness and at Spottsylvania C H," he wrote his brother, "I have not time to mention onely the yankes made a good meny assaults on our breastworks but war repulsed every time with the exception of once and that was on Thursday the 19th." Coghill then gave a brief account of the latter action, in which "the roar of cannon and musketry was terrific" but "the enemie did not gain eny advantages."[7] Many officers and men, taking advantage of the brief lull after Spotsylvania to write home, expressed themselves much as Coghill did. "Two weeks have passed since I wrote you," Brig. Gen. Alfred M. Scales began a letter to his wife, "two weeks of marching exposure & hard fighting. . . . Grant with a much larger army has been badly whipped in every fight & driven back we have suffered but one reverse & then as soon as our reserves came up they [the Federals] were driven back again."[8]

Many men wrote home that they could not possibly describe all they had done and seen, that their families and friends would get more accurate and more detailed information from newspapers. Some of them began letters with phrases such as "If I was with you I could tell you the newes . . . but I cant give you A full history of it in riting" or "I cannot enter in eny thing like a discription of the battle, you will get all the newes from the papers before you get this," then still made an attempt to recount their experiences.[9] Others, after writing relatively full reports, dismissed them with phrases such as "I will close about the war news as I cannot commence telling you enything about it" or "enough of these battles you will see better accounts of them in the papers."[10] Charles L. Burn of the 1st South Carolina ended a letter, "I suppose you will learn more of the fighting than I can communicate from the Papers."[11] One North Carolinian who began with the assertion that "Pen cannot describe or words relate the many adventures which we have passed through" proceeded to write a remarkably vivid depiction of combat at Spotsylvania and ended his letter by claiming, "I am too worn out to write anything of any interest."[12]

Some men tried to explain their inability to write detailed accounts of the fighting, commenting that participants in battles often made poor reporters of them. "I have never been in a fight that I knew as little about," an Alabama surgeon complained on 17 May.[13] Another surgeon, a South Carolinian, wrote home the same day, "I expect you know as much about the situation—or more—than I do, for, although we are right here, we know nothing unless we see the newspapers."[14] Capt. Benjamin Wesley Justice of the Third Corps, concerned that his wife might not have heard from him since the campaign began, wrote her this prologue to his description of fighting at Spotsylvania: "I will write & do my part, & leave the rest to Providence. We are completely cut off from communication with the rest of the world, & we are agitated by any number & quality of camp rumors. I have not seen a newspaper for more than a week. We do not even see or know Gen. Lee's dispatches from the battlefield to the War Dep'tm't; we do not even know, on the right, what occurs on the left, of our lines."[15] Still other members of the army, whether from lack of time, of desire, or of ability, did not even try to report the latest news. "I cannot attempt a description of the battle," Capt. Andrew Jackson McBride admitted on 20 May, adding, "(I have not time for the battle is not yet over, the enemy still confronts us, and a battle may commence at any time)."[16]

One common observation of Lee's soldiers was that Confederate casualties in the Wilderness and at Spotsylvania included an exceptionally high number of general officers. In only two battles Lee lost five generals killed or mortally wounded, another ten wounded seriously enough to turn their commands over to other officers, and two captured; casualties numbered an appalling seventeen generals, or nearly one-third of the total number assigned to the army.[17] Nearly every dispatch Lee wrote from the battlefields to the War Department mentioned one or more of his generals killed or wounded. "I grieve the loss of our gallant officers & men, & miss their aid & sympathy," he wrote in a private letter.[18] Others also commented in a similar vein. "Our loss in Gen. officers has been unprecedented," a North Carolinian observed, and a Georgian noted less formally but no less accurately, "Our loss in high officers is pretty heavy."[19] Surgeon Abner Embry McGarity of the 61st Alabama wrote that "Our loss in Generals has been very great. I am in hopes our future losses will not be so serious."[20] Even in this army, whose generals had repeatedly displayed a dangerous—and often fatal—preference for entering combat at the head of their troops rather than to the rear, the casualties among general officers in the Wilderness and at Spotsylvania were rivaled only by those in the Gettysburg campaign. Brigade, division, and corps commanders found themselves in battles with no identifiable rear and where demonstrating personal bravery in moments of crisis proved more valuable to their troops than any strategies or tactical maneuvers ever could.

Lee himself, on four separate occasions in the Wilderness and at Spotsylvania, seemed compelled to lead his men into combat in the literal as well as the figurative sense. A North Carolinian wrote admiringly to his father, "you would be astonished to see Moss-Bob all ways ride along the line in the thickest of the fight he should not expose him self so but it is his will to do so."[21] The first, and best known, of the four incidents occurred on 6 May in the Wilderness. A heavy Federal attack early in the morning forced troops of the Third Corps from their weak positions, and Lee arrived on the field in time to see most of a division streaming to the rear. Just then the Texas Brigade, near the head of the First Corps, came up, entering the battle in an attempt to hold the Confederate line. Lee rode forward, hat in hand, and tried to lead the charge himself. One of the earliest accounts of what happened next came from the pen of Pvt. Thomas L. McCarty, of the 1st Texas, who that night recorded in his diary, "Genl. R. E. Lee galloped into our ranks and wanted to lead Brigade,—Boys made him go back. Lt Randall—Capt Massie—Capt Kerr—& Others—Maj Venable & Genl Gregg on Horseback near Genl Lees horse at the time & forced him to go back."[22] Another member of the brigade, 3d Sgt. Edward Richardson Crockett of the 4th Texas, wrote a more dramatic narrative in his diary:

> The Texas brigade, Hoods old brigade, [was] in front, with Genl. Lee close in rear & cheering them on to deeds of desperate daring. He said that Texans had always driven the foe. Soon the command passes along the lines, forward guide center: (The harbinger of Death) one minute more. The Texas brigade is moving to the charge Genl. Lee following them slowly, soon the balls are whizzing by us and our rifles in fierce defiance are belching forth storms of leaden hail on the hated foe, now some one seizes Genl. Lee's bridle & says he must go no farther, he stops & to our great relief turns back.[23]

The Texans' fierce counterattack succeeded; one member of the Third Corps commented that "Soon the tide of battle turned and instead of their driving our men, our men drove them."[24]

The news of Lee's daring act quickly spread throughout the Army of Northern Virginia, and throughout the Confederacy as well, as officers and men repeated the details over and over in their letters and diaries. Sgt. John F. Sale of the 12th Virginia heard the story from an eyewitness and reported in his diary that "One of this Brigade [the Texas Brigade] speaking of the incident says he does not believe there was a man in it but would have died rather than have given back an inch."[25] A North Carolina colonel in the Third Corps described men "falling back in disorder until Gen'l Lee took Command in person and with raising hat in hand charged them [the Federals] driving them helter skelter"; a South Carolina private claimed, "we cannot afford to loose such as him, [the Texans] caught his horse by the bridle and restrained the old gentleman, it is said Gen. Lee cried on the occasion."[26]

Three other such incidents occurred at Spotsylvania, one of which took place near the Bloody Angle on 12 May. Just as he had done in the Wilderness, Lee reacted to a battlefield crisis by riding Traveller into the fight and trying to inspire his troops. "As he sat on his charger I never saw a man look so noble, or a spectacle so impressive," a correspondent for the *Richmond Sentinel* wrote a few days later. When Lee attempted to lead John Pegram's Virginia brigade and John B. Gordon's Georgia brigade forward, he was stopped by Gordon, who was temporarily commanding Jubal Early's Division. Gordon tried to convince Lee that he should go back, saying, "These men have never failed! They never will! Will you, boys?" The correspondent continued, "Loud cries of 'No!' 'no!' 'Gen. Lee to the rear.' 'Go back.' 'Go back.' 'General Lee to the rear!' burst from along the lines, and as one led the General's horse to the rear, Gen. Gordon gave the command, 'Forward, charge!' And with a shout and yell the brigade dashed on, through bog and swamp, and briers and undergrowth, to the breastworks."[27]

Though not as dramatic as these "Lee to the rear!" incidents, another narrow escape for the commanding general occurred at Spotsylvania when Lee visited the lines occupied by Lt. Col. William T. Poague's artillery battalion of the Third Corps. After Federal artillery opened on the position, a private in one of Poague's batteries, "becoming uneasy for the safety of the Gen., politely but earnestly invited him to take a seat in the gun pit. The Gen. in his polite and pleasant way declined." When a shell burst showered Lee with dirt, however, the soldier "seized him (Gen. Lee) by both hands . . . and did actually drag Gen. Lee to a place where he was less exposed." Poague, writing a few weeks later to his father, commented that "these little incidents will serve to show how Gen. Lee's boys value him and love him."[28]

Newspaper editorials observed that such behavior might be admirable in others but was reckless in an army commander, particularly one of Lee's stature. "It is abundantly established that General Lee has greatly exposed himself in the late battles," the editors of the *Richmond Whig* complained.

"Against this, we earnestly protest. . . . Too great a cause and too many hopes rest on General Lee's shoulders to admit the exposure of his life. Jackson and Stuart have fallen; Longstreet is disabled; Lee cannot be spared."[29] A correspondent for the *Richmond Dispatch* believed that "the whole country, with one voice, should protest against such rash exposure of [a] life in which we are all so deeply interested, and upon the preservation of which so much depends."[30] Even Jefferson Davis wrote Lee on the subject, calling him "my dear friend" and commenting, "I have been pained to hear of your exposure of your person in various conflicts. The country could not bear the loss of you."[31] If Lee could go so far as to place himself in immediate danger at the head of his troops—not once, but several times—his behavior dramatically underscored the Army of Northern Virginia's dependence on the experience and the example of its officers.

That dependence, which extended from its general officers down to its field and company officers, was severely tested by the heavy casualties of the first three weeks of May 1864. "The proportion of officers to privates killed and wounded is very much larger than in any previous fight," claimed a correspondent for the *Richmond Examiner* after the Wilderness.[32] Losses at Spotsylvania only reinforced that opinion. As a correspondent for the *Richmond Dispatch* explained: "Our loss in the rank and file is remarkably small, the men being well protected by the entrenchments. The casualties, however, [have] been unusually heavy among field officers, who were unprotected, and had to move frequently from one point to another, under the terrible infantry and artillery fire of the enemy, which swept every part of the field in rear of our entrenchments."[33] A North Carolina colonel commented, "The loss to N.C. in Soldiers has been very great indeed and many of her most gallant and valuable officers have fallen," and, according to a South Carolina colonel, "Our State has lost very heavily—more so than in any fight in the war. The loss is especially heavy among the officers."[34] Capt. George P. Ring of the 6th Louisiana estimated that the Confederate casualties of 12 May included "any quantity of minor Officers." He further noted that losses in the Wilderness and at Spotsylvania had reduced his regiment to only fifty-seven rank and file, and that Col. Louis Lay, Ring himself, and another captain were the only commissioned officers left in the unit.[35]

Confederates also wrote about casualties in varying degrees of detail. Some letters and diaries provided only estimates of losses; others, more precise numbers; and still others, names and fates of individual officers and men. "We had a pretty Sevier fight yesterday and had a good many wounded but fiew Killed that I could see," a South Carolina sergeant wrote the day after being slightly wounded in the Wilderness.[36] Others, though still writing in general terms, expressed themselves more color-fully, such as the North Carolinian who said that he was "well & hearty, but sick of blood & ghastly wounds & pale death and mangled limbs & gory faces," or the Texan who observed, "the day is ours though hundreds of our bravest & best are sleeping to wake no more on earth."[37] Some soldiers were slightly more specific when they summarized the army's, or their own unit's, losses. "My co wint in with 30 men," reported Pvt. George Pearsall of the 55th North Carolina, "and come out with 8 only and onley 2 taken prisner the rest all kiled and wonded . . . the strength of our regt was 350 and now 120."[38]

Brief casualty lists were often included in letters home. Capt. Andrew Jackson McBride, who commanded Company E of the 10th Georgia, in Kershaw's Division of the First Corps, wrote his wife, in a typical ex-ample, "The loss of Co 'E' in killed and wounded is 13—two killed 11 wounded most of them slightly Lt Thally and private Dickens killed—Jas Hudson [and] Will Waterson severely though not mortally wounded—D. I. Walden mortally."[39] Capt. Asbury Hull Jackson, a staff officer, wrote in somewhat greater detail about the losses in Company C of the 44th Georgia, in Rodes's Division of the Second Corps. Jackson, who began a letter to his mother, "I have deferred writing in order to be able to send you a list of casualties in my old company," provided more than a simple list: "Sergt. Wm. J. Whitehead wounded in both legs, one amputated. Pri. Wm. P. Bearden severely in shoulder & leg. J. J. Griffeth—right arm broken, N. Y. Hunt—ear slightly, L. C. Cooper—thigh flesh wound, Joe B. Langford—left arm, flesh wound. Gilmer Tiller—missing. . . . Sergt. S. T. Maxey & Pri. Henry Whitehead were killed, the latter shot through the head, the former bayonetted 3 or 4 times."[40] Even this specific list of soldiers' wounds was a dispassionate recital of particulars. The cumulative effect of these commentaries, estimates, and lists, repeated over and over throughout the army, was to reinforce the bloody reputation of the battles in the Wilderness and at Spotsylvania in an impersonal way.

A few members of the Army of Northern Virginia wrote more vividly and more intimately of those who had been killed or mortally wounded. Several officers and men not only provided concrete information on how friends or relatives died, but also paid tribute to the conduct of their lives and the manner of their deaths. Some officers were given posthumous recognition in their commanders' official reports. A division commander in the First Corps, for example, called Col. James D. Nance of the 3d South Carolina and Lt. Col. Franklin Gaillard of the 2d South Carolina "[two] of the most gallant and accomplished field officers of the command . . . both gentlemen of education, position, and usefulness in civil life and highly distinguished in the field."[41] William Ross Stillwell wrote this touching eulogy to a friend killed on the second day in the Wilderness: "pore John Steaphens was killed on the field while bering the flag and a braver and better Soilder never dide on that memorable feeld not only me but all who knew him mornn his deth."[42] John W. Stephens and his brother James had enlisted in the "Newton Anderson Guards," Company E of the 53d Georgia, in the spring of 1862. John, who enlisted as a private, had been promoted in 1863 and was first sergeant at the time of his death. "I hope our loss is his eternal gain," Stillwell commented in the letter to his wife. "I talked to him on the subget of religion but a few days before his deth I think he was a christian give my respect to his parents and frinds and tell them that I shear part of thare grief his b[r]other James is still with the Co and well."[43]

Soldiers were less precise when recounting their own battle experiences, particularly when writing home with the distressing news that they had been wounded. Virgil Lucas wrote a friend that "through the mercy of God I am still right side up though not handled with care. For 13 of the last 15 days I have been more or less under fire." After commenting on his regiment's and his company's losses, Lucas admitted, "I have been wounded twice—on the head by a piece of bomb & on the leg by a bullet—both slight."[44] One Virginian began a letter to his parents, "This will inform you that I am well with the exception of a wound in the arm. It is slight, and I am now writing without any inconvenience." Lt. Charles Denoon reassured his anxious family, "I am all right so far and you need not feel uneasy about the above mentioned, it being my rule to write all good and bad."[45] Many wounded men described their injuries, no matter how serious, as "slight" to prevent undue alarm among distant families and friends. One well-intentioned but not quite successful such attempt was the short postscript that Pvt. John A. Everett of the 11th Georgia added to a letter written a few days before the Wilderness: "Dear Ma as the fight has bin to day and is yet going on—I will write you afew more lines to informe you that I am not kild yet but the yanks come verry Near killing me I was wonded in the head again."[46]

Many Confederates referred to the almost constant activity around them, the knowledge that they could be called into battle at any moment, and the difficulty in finding time to eat, sleep, bathe, or change clothes, much less write long, informative letters. The chief of the First Corps artillery explained why he had sent only one letter home since the campaign began: "The continued marching fighting & lying in line of battle which has not yet ceased has kept me going always from daylight until dark & frequently during many hours of the night."[47] Some soldiers gave their families colorful descriptions of their own appearance after three weeks of active campaigning, such as the North Carolina colonel who told his wife, "you would blush to acknowledge your husband if you could only take a peep at him at present," for "only once since the 3d of May have I been able to change any apparel and if this continues much longer [I] expect to be covered with vermin as mingling with the men in such close proximity is apt to find such companions."[48] Others, such as Pvt. James Wesley Williams of the 16th Georgia, seemed much less disturbed by their inability to wash their clothes or even themselves. "Drucy you Just ought to have seen me yesterday and the day before (blame that louse) in to dough up to my elbows cooking for the company," Williams wrote, then mentioned two other soldiers who were with him in the rear, "keeping batchelors hall in the pine thicket about four mile from the Company, (I had almost forgot to tell you I have just pulled Williams inside of a boiled suit for the first time in nearly three weeks)."[49] A fellow Georgian, Sgt. Marion Hill Fitzpatrick, spoke for most members of the army when he admitted: "I am poor and thin and tired down. . . . We are looking for another fight at any time. I slept but little last night. It is useless to talk about how tired and sore I am. I have not changed clothes or shaved since the fighting commenced."[50]

After the fighting had been vaguely or graphically described, after the casualties had been enumerated or eulogized, after the reports of their safety or injury in battle had been dutifully made, and after venturing comments about how they felt and how they looked, officers and men often recorded their hopes and fears for the immediate future. Most—though certainly not all—letters and diary entries written in the days after Spotsylvania reflected the general optimism in the army. Capt. Thomas Claybrook Elder of the Third Corps staff exulted, "I dont suppose the world ever saw a more determined better contented people under similar circumstances than is presented by Genl Lee's army at this time," and Pvt. Joseph Shaner of the Rockbridge Artillery boasted, "we can whip any Army the Yankees can bring against us if the Lord is willing."[51] Others, though still confident of an ultimate Confederate victory, were more restrained in their claims and predictions. "Our business is to keep back Grant from Richmond & he is completely checked," noted Brig. Gen. Alfred M. Scales, commanding a North Carolina brigade in Wilcox's Division of the Third Corps.[52] A Virginia sergeant whose division had just rejoined the Army of

Northern Virginia after a lengthy period of detached service believed that the army was "in fine spirits trusting fully to Lee and seeming confident of defeating our enemies, and we will."[53] Still others, though hopeful, seemed more uncertain of success than they had before the Wilderness. A surgeon on the Second Corps staff commented that although the battles in the Wilderness and at Spotsylvania were fought "without arriving at any deffinite conclusion as to the result, both sides claiming to be the Victors, but there is one fact that is undeniable and that is our forces are more willing to renew the contest than the Yankees."[54] Capt. Council A. Bryan of the 5th Florida reported that his brigade, in Mahone's Division of the Third Corps, had left Spotsylvania for a new position on the North Anna River. "We have whipped Grant twice," Bryan observed, "but he has such a tremendous army that we *cannot rout* him—and consequently [our] victories dont amount to much."[55] One North Carolinian tried to convey a positive attitude in ending a letter to his father on 25 May: "the fight is not desided yet but I hope it will be soon and lasting . . . if I fall in the strougle I will trust in the lord and I hope you will too and not be troubled so adiew."[56] An artilleryman in the Richmond Howitzers, who had been with his company only a few weeks, undoubtedly expressed the feelings of many soldiers in both armies when he asserted, "Genl Grant shows no disposition to leave, and Genl Lee just as little, both are stubborn old soldiers."[57]

Yet another characteristic of post-Spotsylvania letters written by Lee's soldiers was their treatment of the fighting from 5 through 19 May as one long battle, or perhaps a series of battles, combats, engagements, skirmishes, and other military actions. Some writers made simple observations such as "There is no telling when the fight will end" or "the great battle is not yet over, there is only a lull."[58] Others wrote in somewhat greater detail, such as the South Carolina colonel who called the fighting "an unprecedented struggle; not so much one battle, but a series of battles," or the North Carolina private who began a letter home, "I am very much tierd down from the longe and sevear fighten that has bin progresing for the last 16 Days and Stil no Sine of Seasing."[59] William H. Slater wrote on 20 May that his South Carolina regiment had been "in line of battle for 15 Days night and day they have fighting every Day more or less untill To Day theare has ben no fireing up to this time—12 oclock but they may commence before night."[60]

There was, however, a more complex theme running through many soldiers' letters and diaries in the last two weeks of May. This theme, expressed in terms of intense physical exhaustion accompanied by an equally intense mental or emotional determination to persevere, characterizes the immediate post-Spotsylvania morale of the Army of Northern Virginia. Such observations as "we are all very much worn out but in good spirits & full of confidence" or "the troops are as badly worn out as I ever saw them but still in good spirits" were typical.[61] Even the Richmond newspapers took notice. On 19 May the correspondent of the *Examiner*, exaggerating only slightly, wrote: "It is, of course, true that the troops are tired and jaded, but there is no faint-heartedness, no demoralization. General Lee trusts his troops most implicitly, whilst they in turn confide in their chief with child like faith."[62] Maj. Alfred D. Kelly of the 21st Virginia opened a letter to his brother with the explanation, "After 21 days of the hardest campaigning and fighting I have ever gone through, for the first time I find myself in rear, not sick but completely worn down." Yet near the end of his letter Kelly wrote, "Our men are tired but in good fighting condition."[63] Similar opinions were voiced by Pvt. Samuel P. Lockhart of the 27th North Carolina, in Brig. Gen. John Rogers Cooke's Brigade of the Third Corps. Lockhart, though "very much fatigued and worn out, marching and throwing up fortifications," considered his fellow soldiers "in fine spirits and tolerable good health" with "less straggling than I ever saw; it appears like every body tries to keep at the front."[64]

Perhaps the most fully developed expressions of this theme were those of a staff officer whose letters to his wife often included thoughtful descriptions of the soldiers in the ranks. Capt. Benjamin Wesley Justice wrote, somewhat gloomily, that "Our men are confident & cheerful, but the extraordinary fatigues & exposures of 21 days & nights of marching, fighting, watching, & lying in the trenches begins to tell on them, in the loss of flesh, & sunken eyes, & falling asleep anywhere just as soon as they become still." Justice's next letter, written the following day, described the troops' plight with less emotion and emphasized the generally positive mood throughout the army. After visiting the brigade and talking with the men, he believed that they were "in excellent condition and fine spirits," though they were "much in need of a change of clothing, soap, tobacco, an increase of rations of meat, & postage stamps & paper"; moreover, "they are strongly intrenched & feel sure of repelling any assault the enemy may make on our lines."[65] Justice's letters, which alternate between pessimistic accounts of physical conditions and optimistic evaluations of the army's morale, are fitting commentaries on the state of Lee's troops near the end of May 1864.

Their commander, meanwhile, was trying to determine what Grant's plans might be and making arrangements to answer the Federals' next moves, whether against his army or against Richmond. On 20 May, the day after the last significant fighting at Spotsylvania, Lee reported that some Federal units were shifting toward his right flank but "whether [the movement was designed] for attack or defense is not apparent."[66] Grant, however, had no intention either of attacking from or defending his position. He was, instead, moving the Army of the Potomac southeast in an attempt to place his forces between Lee and Richmond. Lee responded by ordering his army southeast as well, toward the North Anna River and the nearby railroad intersection at Hanover Junction, some twenty-five miles north of the capital.[67] "Grant would not fight us again in our breastworks and moved down the river toward Richmond, so, of course, Lee had to move, too," a sergeant in the 45th Georgia wrote a few days later, explaining the situation to his wife. "I wish old Grant had fought us up there, but he knew we would whip him there and he wants to try another place."[68] Throughout the day and night of 21 May and into the morning of the twenty-second, the Army of Northern Virginia marched from Spotsylvania toward the North Anna.[69] A Florida captain in the Third Corps exclaimed the next day, "I dont think I ever suffered on a march so much as I did yesterday."[70]

As the first elements of Lee's army arrived at the river early on the twenty-second, they immediately began constructing earthworks to help them block Grant's path to Richmond. Sgt. Edward Crockett wrote in his diary that his regiment, the 4th Texas, "took position on bank of N. Anna & dug trenches with hatchets bayonets & boards & our hands."[71] Many Confederates believed that their formidable defensive line south of the river could withstand Federal attacks almost indefinitely. "I think if they leave our brigade whare we are now we need not be uneasy we hav agood posish [position]," one North Carolinian wrote his father on 25 May. "That and alittle time afew rails then our bayonets and hands we are r[ea]ddy for the blew Jacks."[72] On the same day Corp. Jonathan Fuller Coghill of the 23d North Carolina informed his brother, "wee are in a line of battle on the Northanna River and the yankes are trying to flank us again wee have whiped the yankes at every point but know wee will take of[f] after them again and before we stop I expect we will be at Richmond."[73]

The Army of Northern Virginia held its position along the river for five days, a period in which daily fighting, though small in scale and inconclusive in results, was at times quite sharp, with some 5,000 total Confederate and Federal casualties. "Our Regt fought the yankees for 11 hours on the 25 [of May] it was one continuous roar of musketry," Lt. Charles Denoon of the 41st Virginia wrote his parents a few days later,

"We used 5 boxes of cartridges and slayed many yankees."[74] But neither the Confederates nor the Federals were able to turn momentary tactical successes into strategic advantages.[75] On 26 May, Grant, unwilling to make a large-scale assault on Lee's impressive field fortifications, moved his army south—around the Confederate right flank and yet closer to Richmond. Lee, on discovering the next morning that the Federals had left his front, ordered his troops to follow.[76] "We advanced soon this morning but the yanks wer gon a cross the River," a North Carolina lieutenant recorded in his diary on the twenty-seventh. "So our hole Army moved to the right in the direction of Richmond as the yanks is gon in that direction."[77]

The Federals were indeed near the Confederate capital, and some members of Lee's army had already expressed their uneasiness at the prospect of retreating still closer to Richmond. "We may fall back to Richmond, but I do not like that idea and hope we will whip him here," one Georgian had written of Grant's move from Spotsylvania to the North Anna; a North Carolina artilleryman informed his wife, "we air exspecting abig fight before many days the fight will be close round richmond."[78] Others were more optimistic, such as the brigadier who commented, "it is true we are nearer to Richmond but have repulsed Grant in every instance so far. . . . There is then no grounds for uneasing, but everything to encourage us," or the private who remarked of Grant, "I think God has let him come nearer richmond to whip him the harder."[79]

Some believed that the move from the North Anna toward Richmond was more significant for what it revealed about Grant's generalship than for its strategic implications. A common observation was that he could have taken his army just as close to Richmond as it now was—without suffering appalling casualties in the Wilderness and at Spotsylvania—in the first week of May. "Grant, it is true, got nearer Richmond by making a detour," Charles Minor Blackford reasoned, "but when he got in his present position he was where he could have been at first without seeing a Confederate soldier or losing a man. As it is he has lost fifty thousand men and Lee and his army are before him, full of fight and unconquerable."[80] A courier in a Georgia brigade expressed the same opinion in less sophisticated language: "our army have only fell back to prevent Grant from flanking us wich he could have done by going along the banks of the river as wich he done [by fighting in the Wilderness and at Spotsylvania]."[81]

Still other observers in the Army of Northern Virginia expressed concern about the effect this latest move—which many admitted was a Confederate retreat—was having on the troops. One of these was Porter Alexander, who described the mood in the ranks as the army marched to the vicinity of Richmond and toward still more combat with the Army of the Potomac. Though Alexander was "hopeful of the result—if we can only catch [Grant] before he has time to fortify," he continued: "I noticed on the march to-day that the whole column of Infantry seemed to feel that a severe battle was immediately impending—They marched in such deep silence that a man with his eyes shut would only have known that any one was on the road by the occasional rattle of a canteen. It reminded me of Byron's description, 'Some thought about their children, wives, & friends. And others of themselves & latter ends.'" Alexander commented, "The prospect of battle every day has been hanging over us, & accompanied with such continued skirmishing that we are getting very much hardened to its anticipation."[82] Adjt. James M. McFall of the Palmetto Sharpshooters wrote his sister, "We are all about worn out. . . . Oh if we could get peace now without any more fighting but that is impossible we will have to whip peace out of them."[83]

When the "severe battle" expected by Alexander did occur, it would be fought by an Army of Northern Virginia with many officers, men, and units in new positions. The army was undoubtedly weakened by its heavy losses and by almost constant contact with the Federals, and Lee was forced to make critical decisions that would have a major impact on the effectiveness of his troops. Of Lee's three infantry corps commanders at the beginning of the 1864 campaign—Longstreet, Ewell, and Hill—the first was now absent wounded and the other two were often incapacitated by illness. Richard Anderson had been given temporary command of the First Corps, and Jubal Early alternated between temporary command of either the Second or the Third Corps. By the time the Army of Northern Virginia reached the outskirts of Richmond, Early had been assigned to temporary command—which would eventually become permanent command—of the Second Corps. The Third Corps, under the ailing Hill, was the only corps in the army still commanded by the general who had led it at the Wilderness.[84] Though only two divisions were under new officers—both of their original commanders having been given temporary corps command—sixteen brigades, some of them now consolidated, were under temporary commanders, many of them colonels.[85] Lee wrote to Richard Anderson about Joseph B. Kershaw's old South Carolina brigade, which he described as "much in need of a good brigade commander." He instructed Anderson to get Kershaw's recommendation for a new brigadier, commenting, "I am anxious that a brigade that has always done so well should

Sgt. William Henry Edwards, Company H, 4th North Carolina Cavalry. Edwards, who enlisted as a private in an independent cavalry company later assigned to the 4th North Carolina Cavalry, was appointed sergeant in 1863 and was killed 15 June 1864 in fighting near Petersburg. (John A. Woodard)

now be well commanded."[86] Losses in regimental and company officers were just as numerous, with the result that soldiers were often led by an entirely new slate of officers. After Spotsylvania, for example, Company B of the 13th South Carolina was commanded at the company, regimental, and brigade levels by a lieutenant, a major, and a colonel, respectively.[87]

Casualties in the rank and file—particularly in large numbers of prisoners taken—also necessitated the reorganization or consolidation of some units, the most significant of which involved the remnants of Edward Johnson's Division of the Second Corps. Johnson's four-brigade division, which had included the famed Stonewall Brigade and had consisted of twenty-six regiments, had been virtually destroyed at the Bloody Angle on 12 May. Most of its casualties were now Federal prisoners, and the division numbered only fifteen hundred men after Spotsylvania.[88] Powell Benton Reynolds of the 50th Virginia—one of the larger regiments in the pitiful division, boasting only eighty men—wrote on 19 May, "Our Division has been entirely broken up. . . . the remnant of the Division has been attached for the present to Early's Division. . . . The six Va. regiments in our Brigade and the five Va. regiments in the 'Stonewall' Brigade and the three Va. regiments in St[e]uart's Brigade have all been thrown together and make one Brigade."[89] Such consolidations and reorganizations would become commonplace in the coming months, as Lee and his subordinates struggled to increase, or simply maintain, both the strength and the fighting effectiveness of steadily weakening regiments, brigades, and divisions throughout the army.

One of the more dramatic changes in the army was taking place in the cavalry corps, which had always served Lee well in the past. The Confederate cavalry no longer enjoyed such a marked advantage over its enemy, however, since the Federal cavalry had made significant progress in its performance and in the quality of its generals over the last year. In addition, Stuart's cavalrymen now spent most of their time collecting information on reconnaissances rather than on exciting raids, and the relatively little combat they did see was most often as dismounted skirmishers. "Our operations have been confined to our branch of the service and the Infantry has been as separate and distinct from us as distance can make us," observed an officer in Cobb's Legion Cavalry. "We have no communication with the Infantry, and hence our inability to keep posted with their movements."[90]

The greatest obstacle to the cavalry's continued success was the death of Stuart and the absence of a dynamic leader to replace him. In the interval between the Wilderness and Spotsylvania, as the army's infantry and artillery prepared to defend their extensive lines, its cavalry rode to intercept a large-scale Federal cavalry raid intended to disrupt Lee's supply lines and to threaten Richmond. Though the Confederates forced the enemy away from the capital, the most significant result of the fight at Yellow Tavern was that Stuart was mortally wounded on 11 May and died the next day. With his death the cavalrymen of the Army of Northern Virginia lost their last claim to undisputed superiority over their Federal counterparts. "The Cavalry corps has lost its great leader the unequalled Stuart," William L. Wilson of the 12th Virginia Cavalry wrote his mother. "We miss him much. Hampton is a good officer but Stuart's equal does not exist."[91] Lee, unwilling to contribute to the rivalry that already existed between Hampton and Maj. Gen. Fitzhugh Lee—Lee's own nephew—promoted neither of them to corps command but ordered the three divisions to report to army headquarters until further notice.[92] "Among the gallant soldiers who have fallen in this war General Stuart was second to none in valor, in zeal, and in unfaltering devotion to his country," Lee declared in general orders announcing Stuart's death. "His achievements form a conspicuous part of the history of this army, with which his name and services will be forever associated."[93]

Reinforcements represented yet another—but welcome—change in the composition of the Army of Northern Virginia. Before the spring campaign began, Lee had sent pleas for help to President Davis and Secretary Seddon. "We are inferior in numbers . . . the absence of the troops belonging to this army weakens it more than by the mere number of men," he had written Jefferson Davis on 4 May—the day before fighting began in the Wilderness. After that battle and the appalling combat at Spotsylvania, Lee told Davis that if "fresh troops can be spared from Richmond it would be of great assistance. We are outnumbered and constant labor is impairing the efficiency of the men."[94] In the days immediately after Spotsylvania the army received substantial reinforcements from detached units returning to their permanent assignments as well as from units being assigned to it for the first time. Lee continued to ask for additional troops from the vicinity of Petersburg, units in the Department of North Carolina and Southern Virginia, commanded by Gen. P. G. T. Beauregard. Beauregard, who protested to Davis and Seddon that he could spare no men without placing Richmond and Petersburg in peril, proposed typically grandiose schemes instead and managed to keep his command intact for the time being.[95]

The largest body of troops belonging to the Army of Northern Virginia and now returning to it was Maj. Gen. George E. Pickett's Division of the First Corps, four Virginia brigades numbering some five thousand men.

Pickett's Division, after its moment of glory at Gettysburg, had been assigned to eastern North Carolina and southern Virginia from the fall of 1863 through the spring of 1864. Though Lee had requested its return shortly before entering the Wilderness, the division, as part of Beauregard's department, had fought at Swift Creek and Drewry's Bluff while its comrades were fighting in the Wilderness and at Spotsylvania. By the time the army had concentrated at Hanover Junction on 25 May, Pickett's veterans had rejoined their old command.[96] "We are with Lees army again fixing for another Big fight," Lt. Henry M. Talley of the 14th Virginia informed his mother. "I think the Big fight will come off in a Day or two I think this fight will Bring this war to a close. Nearly all the Boys think like myself Pervided Lee whips Grant, and that I think he will do and not half try."[97]

Other units, which had not previously belonged to the army, were ordered to join it in the days after Spotsylvania. Maj. Gen. John C. Breckinridge's two-brigade division, heading south from the Shenandoah Valley, was the largest new unit assigned to Lee and was about half the size of Pickett's Division.[98] A small brigade of three South Carolina cavalry regiments commanded by Brig. Gen. Matthew C. Butler also joined the army about this time and was assigned to Hampton's Division. Though two of these regiments had served on the South Carolina coast and were composed of veterans, one regiment had just recently been created and consisted of conscripts and recruits.[99] Sgt. E. O. Harkins of the new 4th South Carolina Cavalry wrote a brief note to a friend while his unit stopped in Richmond on the way to the Army of Northern Virginia. "I supose we will not stay hir long til we move to the sean of action," he commented, "thair it will be stand to it weather we like the tune or not."[100] Hugh Lide Law, a private in the 6th South Carolina Cavalry, told his father that "troops are coming in pretty fast now I expect Gen Lee will have a very large army soon."[101] Still more South Carolinians, some 1,200 of them, arrived in a single infantry regiment that reinforced Kershaw's old brigade of the First Corps and virtually doubled its strength. The 20th South Carolina, commanded by Col. Lawrence M. Keitt, had been organized in 1862 and had participated in the siege of Charleston. When Keitt and his men joined Kershaw's Brigade—without a permanent commander since Kershaw's promotion to major general—Keitt assumed command of the brigade as its new senior colonel.[102] "My regiment is a trifle larger than all of Kershaw's Brigade," he noted. "The regiments have been cut down very small."[103] Such reinforcements, and others, increased the army's effective strength to some 60,000 troops, just enough to offset, if only in numbers, losses incurred at Spotsylvania and the North Anna.

All of these factors—the army's proximity to Richmond and the necessity for it to defend the city at all hazards, the assignment of new or temporary officers, and the arrival of unfamiliar units—made Lee's already daunting task even more difficult. Such obstacles, further reinforced by the Federals' numeric and strategic strengths, helped create a situation in which the Army of Northern Virginia faced the very real possibility of disaster. Lee made troop dispositions as best he could, put his soldiers to work constructing defensive lines, and searched for an opportunity to go on the tactical offensive before Grant could take the initiative from him.

There was much work to be done throughout the army, and the troops, as usual, had a great deal to say about the tasks assigned to them. Some units, such as the Texas Brigade of the First Corps, were assigned new positions along the Confederate lines, and then returned to their original positions in an attempt to ensure that the works were adequately defended. In his diary Sgt. Edward Richardson Crockett of the 4th Texas described three consecutive days of such marching and countermarching, calling the second day's work "a tiresome feeling, ten-feet-at-a-time move" and noting that his brigade arrived back at camp about midnight on 30 May. "We were all well vexed by the time we got settled for the night," Crockett continued. The next day proved no better, as the Texans "got no sleep & were vexed beyond endurance accused all the generals of being drunk, & felt like tearing the world up generally, such is a soldier's life."[104] Other units spent their time building and improving earthworks. One member of the 27th North Carolina admitted, "Although it does not make much difference how tired I am, I am always ready to throw up breast works for they are a great protection in time of an engagement."[105] Lt. James E. Green's battalion of North Carolina sharpshooters began entrenching on the night of 29 May and completed the works just in time the next morning; in his diary Green reported, "Finished our works, for the sharpshooters is playing a right pretty fuss in front this morning."[106] The view from headquarters, as expressed by Lt. Col. Walter H. Taylor of Lee's staff on the same morning, was that the Army of Northern Virginia was "only waiting to have [Grant] located, to have his position &c well developed before [it] is let loose at its old opponent."[107]

Lee, meanwhile, seeking to preempt any Federal attempt to move between his forces and the Confederate capital, found a weak point in Grant's lines near Bethesda Church. He gave Jubal Early responsibility for planning and executing an assault there, and on the afternoon of 30 May Early sent a single brigade of his corps forward after little or no reconnaissance and almost no coordination with other units. Though the

Confederate attack gained some initial success, it was soon easily repulsed with moderately heavy casualties.[108]

Two of the Confederates killed or mortally wounded at Bethesda Church were promising young field officers destined for higher command whose deaths, like so many others, deprived the army of its experienced and able leaders. Both men—Col. James B. Terrill of the 13th Virginia and Col. Edward Willis of the 12th Georgia—were associated with John Pegram's old Virginia brigade of Early's Division, which had borne the brunt of the fight. Terrill had already been recommended for promotion to brigadier general. His nomination was being considered by the Confederate Senate when he was killed, and his commission was confirmed posthumously the next day. Willis, who was in temporary command of the brigade at Bethesda Church, had been recommended for promotion by Lee and earlier in the war by Stonewall Jackson. He was mortally wounded in the assault and died on 31 May.[109] A dispatch Lee sent to Davis the day after the engagement discussed numerous vacancies in the army's brigade and division commanders, beginning: "I regret that Col Terrill cannot be nominated to the command of Pegram's Brigade. In the attack last night, he was either killed or left wounded in the hands of the enemy. Col E Willis of Ga whom I had assigned yesterday to the command of the brigade, was mortally wounded, and I understand has since died. At present I can name no one to you to fill the vacancy in this brigade, but hope to do so tomorrow."[110] Terrill and Willis were only two casualties in only one afternoon of small-scale fighting, but they were representative of all the officers in the Army of Northern Virginia who were being killed, wounded, and captured daily. "Ther is skermish fiting and charging in hearing every day and I expect the worst aint come yet," wrote a member of the 57th North Carolina. "I dont look for this fite to stop til peace is made lee has fell back from Rapadan ten mile from or near Richmond this is the bludest time that ever was nown."[111]

Having failed in this bid to halt or delay Grant's advance to the outskirts of Richmond, Lee momentarily turned his attention from the offensive back to the defensive. The evening after Early's repulse at Bethesda Church, Lee warned Jefferson Davis that further failures to reinforce the army might have grave consequences. "General Beauregard says the Department must determine what troops to send for him," Lee wrote, his patience with the Confederate authorities and the recalcitrant Beauregard at its limits. "The result of this delay will be disaster. . . . Hoke's division, at least, should be with me by light to-morrow."[112] When Gen. Braxton Bragg, Davis's military adviser, gave Beauregard unequivocal orders to send Maj. Gen. Robert F. Hoke's small division to the Army of Northern Virginia later that night, Hoke was already on his way. Beauregard received the order from Bragg minutes after he had finally decided to reinforce Lee.[113]

As soon as Hoke arrived with his 7,000 troops on 31 May, he was rushed to the extreme Confederate right at Old Cold Harbor, a strategic junction of several roads less than five miles from Richmond that would be the focal point of both armies for the next few days. Cold Harbor, just north of the Chickahominy River, had been the scene of the June 1862 battle at Gaines's Mill—sometimes also called Cold Harbor—during the Seven Days' campaign. Not only was it the most likely place for a Federal crossing of the Chickahominy, but it also presented a relatively strong position for Confederates attempting to block Grant's path. Clashes between opposing cavalrymen on the thirty-first, which eventually included a portion of Hoke's infantry, ended when the Confederates withdrew and left the Federals in possession of the junction. This fighting was only the prelude to three days of skirmishes, maneuvering, and brief but exceptionally bloody combat at Cold Harbor.[114]

In the days and hours before yet another major battle with their Federal counterparts, Lee's officers and men voiced varying degrees of confidence and concern at what would happen next. After admitting to his wife, "I cant tell you what Grant is going to do—He seems, to have given up his plan of attack," a North Carolina general in the Second Corps claimed that "our glorious army is in splendid spirits. I hope & believe & pray that we will be able to overthrow Grant. If so the war will be brought to an end."[115] Whereas one artillery officer believed that "Our army is in very good spirits, but perhaps a little the worse for having fought recently principally behind breastworks," an infantry private expressed the hope that the Federals would advance against his position, writing, "if Mr. Grant dont mind, he wont go around this line like he did the others, and if he attacks us in our works, we will be apt to make a good many of them bite the dust."[116]

Such observations might have been of interest to the commanding general, who had no intention of remaining passively on the defensive but planned to take the crossroads from the Federals. Lee assigned this task to Anderson and the First Corps, with Hoke's Division in support. When Anderson and Hoke advanced toward Grant's dismounted cavalrymen in the morning of 1 June, their initial attack was repulsed quickly and handily. Their failure was due in part to the uncharacteristically poor performance of the troops, some of whom fled when pressed, and in part to a lack of cooperation between Anderson and Hoke. After the Confederates withdrew to their earthworks, Grant replaced his cavalry with an infantry corps and planned to launch a counterattack as soon as another corps could come up in support. Though the necessary dispositions took most of the day, a large-scale Federal force attacked Anderson and Hoke in the late afternoon, broke through a gap between two Confederate divisions, and captured not only numerous prisoners but also part of Lee's lines as well. When Anderson rushed fresh troops from his corps forward, they forced back the Federals and restored the broken defenses, ending the fighting for the day.

Both armies spent the rest of 2 June preparing to fight again. The Army of Northern Virginia worked diligently to complete its defenses, constructing new lines and strengthening existing ones to create a makeshift system of earthworks running northwest from Cold Harbor to the vicinity of Bethesda Church. In addition, Breckinridge's small division and most of the Third Corps, which together had been anchoring the Confederate left, were now shifted to the extreme right of the army to link with Hoke's Division and extend the defenses to the Chickahominy River. Meanwhile, the Federals postponed an attack originally planned for that morning. After skirmishes and brief clashes near each end of the lines, which were the only fighting of the day, apprehensive soldiers on both sides spent the night waiting for the Federal advance the next morning.

Before daybreak on the morning of 3 June, Grant, hoping to penetrate the Confederate lines, sent three corps forward against Lee's well-defended position. Some Federals, convinced that they were advancing to their certain deaths, had written their names, units, and hometowns on slips of paper and pinned them inside their jackets to aid the identification of their bodies after the battle. These soldiers' expectations of failure, sadly enough for them, were more realistic than their commander's hopes for success. As the Federals neared the earthworks, volley after volley of Lee's musketry, much of it catching the attackers in a deadly crossfire, first slowed, then staggered, and soon prevented their further progress. Confederate reinforcements quickly drove back the only portion of the assault that gained any foothold in their defenses. Within a matter of minutes— certainly within a half hour—the attackers had suffered some 7,000 casualties, and it was obvious to both sides that Grant's assault had been a colossal blunder. Under a withering fire, unable to advance or retreat, surviving Federals simply dug in where they were and waited for night so they could connect their new trenches to the existing ones behind them. It was all over by 5:00 A.M. At a cost of fewer than 1,500 casualties, most of them slight wounds, the Army of Northern Virginia had won one of the most complete tactical victories of the war to date.[117]

Five days of sporadic fighting, some near Bethesda Church but the vast majority in the vicinity of Cold Harbor, had cost Grant about 14,000 officers and men, more than half of them in the disastrous assault of 3 June. Most of Lee's losses over the same period—a comparatively few 5,000 soldiers—had occurred when the Federals managed to break through weak points in his lines. In just under a month of almost daily combat from the Wilderness to Cold Harbor, major and minor actions had now killed, wounded, or made prisoners of about 50,000 Federals and about 30,000 Confederates. If the bloodshed continued at this ghastly rate, the Army of the Potomac and the Army of Northern Virginia might destroy each other before the end of the year.

Lee's officers and men who wrote accounts of the fighting at Cold Harbor described conditions and circumstances unlike those encountered earlier in the spring campaign. The terrain, for example, played a slightly less significant role here than in the Wilderness and at Spotsylvania, as the two armies faced each other over stretches of open fields as well as through piney woods and the swampy bottoms of the Chickahominy. The Army of Northern Virginia held a naturally strong defensive position reinforced by Lee's reliance on an extensive—if hastily constructed—line of earthworks. Such defenses, which were beginning to be taken for granted, would have been shunned by many soldiers as less than courageous in 1862 or 1863.

By 1864, however, veterans on both sides had learned to dig rudimentary trenches and build simple breastworks as soon as they could when occupying a new position in close contact with the enemy. The Confederate works at Cold Harbor, to a somewhat greater extent than those in the Wilderness and at Spotsylvania, were the result of initiative displayed by the men in the ranks rather than of orders from their officers. "Since the fight began on the 5th May our Regt has throwed up 13 lines of works up to the 2 day June & charged on the yanks & drove them twice without works &c.," a lieutenant in the 53d North Carolina wrote in his diary a few days after Cold Harbor.[118] One Texan reported that his regiment, after a short march, arrived "just after dark, in an open field, & here with the sharpshooters bullets whistling around us all the time, we had to throw up breast works. We worked all night & by early dawn had our work completed."[119] Pvt. John G. Hall, whose North Carolina brigade had just joined the Army of Northern Virginia, described how his regiment "had nothing to work with but our ba[y]onets and hands we done the best we could until the evening," claiming, "we got us a right good breast work."[120] Federals, too, quickly threw up their own entrenchments, and the two armies remained extremely close to each other, usually within a few hundred yards and at some points as close as seventy-five or one hundred yards.

A more significant difference from the May campaigns was that most of the army's reinforcements since Spotsylvania had never served with Lee and were relatively unknown quantities when fighting began at Cold Harbor. Several of these units broke or faltered as soon as they were attacked or even fired upon, causing confusion in the Confederate ranks and occasionally stampeding veteran units along with them. One such incident occurred on the morning of 1 June when the First Corps attempted to drive the Federal cavalry from the crossroads. Kershaw's old South Carolina brigade, one of the units leading the assault, included the 20th South Carolina—Lawrence Keitt's regiment, which had only arrived from Charleston with him the day before. The regiment faltered, Keitt was mortally wounded trying to rally it, and most of the 20th South Carolina panicked and fled, sweeping Kershaw's veterans to the rear and precipitating a crisis in Anderson's corps. "Kershaw's brigade tried to flank the Yankees to day, but failed because the 20th broke, it was never in a fight before," wrote one of the brigade's couriers. "Col. Keitt was commanding the brigade, and was mortally wounded while attempting to rally his regiment."[121] A Georgian in Kershaw's Division commented, not entirely in jest: "Brother I dont want to say to much but if you have eny more troops on the Co[a]st like the 20th S.C. you may Jest keep them we dont want no such men in this army they run twice in one day they No was eleven hundred and (20) twenty nearly twice as larg as my brig. they want to know how long ear [ere] they will get back to Charlston ha ha its fun to an old Soildier in the first Army Corps."[122] One observer, after writing that the regiment's soldiers "behaved badly" on 1 June, reported that they "recovered their character . . . most handsomely" when engaged the next day.[123] Several other units new to the army, such as Brig. Gen. Thomas L. Clingman's North Carolina brigade of Hoke's Division, or the two Virginia brigades of Breckinridge's Division, had similar experiences when first engaged but managed to give a good account of themselves days or even a few hours later.[124]

Though these disappointing performances gave Grant a few fleeting successes, they made virtually no impact on the rest of Lee's army and none on the outcome of the battle. Officers and men throughout the Army of Northern Virginia, new arrivals and veterans alike, were awed by the relative ease of their victory on 3 June. The next day Sgt. Marion Hill Fitzpatrick of the 45th Georgia wrote, "Our boys had good works to fight behind, and I know they just poured it to them right."[125] Fitzpatrick's simple but particularly apt description illustrates a growing sophistication among Lee's soldiers. Though they recognized the almost certain futility of frontal assaults on earthworks, they still hoped that the Federals would continue to hammer against their lines. When Capt. Francis Marion Coker of the Third Corps artillery expressed his opinion that "if Grant will only keep *charging our works*, we can destroy his army with slight loss to our own," he was stating a view shared by many of his comrades.[126] The 1864 campaign was providing further confirmation of what had already been demonstrated on battlefields such as Malvern Hill, Fredericksburg, and Gettysburg, and though the grim lesson had been retaught by degrees in the Wilderness and at Spotsylvania, it was punctuated with a bloody exclamation point on the final morning at Cold Harbor. "We hav kild and Wounded five to one," claimed one South Carolinian whose estimate was a pardonable exaggeration. "If they continue to fight us behind our brest Works We Wil Whip them ever time."[127]

Several aspects of the fighting on 3 June left a lasting impression on many Confederate correspondents and diarists. One topic, a seemingly insignificant statistic, was the number of times the Army of the Potomac was supposed to have been repulsed. Confederate estimates ranged from five or six attempts to thirteen or fourteen. A surgeon in the 61st Alabama called Grant "a much more stubborn Gen. than we have ever fought before. It seems that he is determined to crush us or sacrifice his Army. He is doing the latter pretty rapidly."[128]

A more universal topic in Lee's army after Cold Harbor concerned the appalling numbers of enemy dead who lay on the field for days after the battle. "I have often heard about the yankees beeing piled up five deep around Richmond but I did not believe it until last week when I saw them with my own eyes," 2d Lt. Virgil Duc of the 25th South Carolina told his father. "I think that I saw about 600 dead and wounded yankees in front of our breastworks and our [brigade's] loss in that charge was 25 kill and about 150 wounded."[129] An Alabamian in the Third Corps described the field in front of his regiment's breastworks as "colored not only by its natural production but . . . varigated with blue, unburied, dead Yankees."[130] A shocked North Carolinian in the Second Corps wrote less grammatically but more graphically: "Father I have Ben over the Battle field and I have seed they yanks pile up where they had charge our men they never berried their dead I saw them where they was Rotten and they live things was just falling owtten them."[131]

Such horrors were compounded by Grant, who allowed two days to pass without attempting to care for his wounded or bury his dead lying between the lines. Unwilling to ask Lee for the customary flag of truce, as such a request would have been considered an admission of defeat, Grant waited until 5 June to begin negotiations with the Confederate commander.[132] "Grant is a barbarian: he cares neither for his living nor dead soldiers," commented Lt. Elias Davis of the 10th Alabama that day.[133] By the time the truce finally began, in the evening of the seventh, most of the Federal wounded had either died or been removed by comrades at night. "We had a good time for awhile as Gen. Lee gave Grant permishion for three hours to bury the dead," a private in the 2d Georgia Battalion reported to his brother. "We traded tobacco for coffee & knives. I got a little black handel, three bladed [knife] not mutch account. After the armistus was over we fired at each other & kept each other in the ditches very close."[134]

During the first week of June 1864, as the two armies "kept each other in the ditches very close," many officers and men in the Army of Northern Virginia took time to reflect on events of the past month and what might happen in the next month. Col. John Bratton apologized to his wife for not writing her an informative letter since before the Wilderness, "but we have been fighting, skirmishing, shifting position or marching all the time," he explained. "I have not pulled my boots off but two nights since the 4th of May. I have by dent of energy and strong resolve so to do succeeded in changing my clothes three times in the month." As for the future, Bratton wrote: "The probabilities are that we will have a long and tedious campaign. Grant hangs on like a bull dog and will, doubtless, be more shy about attacking our works hereafter and go Yankie like to ditching, but I will try to drop you a line every few days."[135] A North Carolina private in the Second Corps similarly wrote his parents, "Well the thing has been going on so long that I am just worn out but I guess we can stand it as well as the Yanks can, if not better."[136] Numerous soldiers, refraining from the temptation to predict a swift and overwhelming Confederate victory, contented themselves with observations such as "I hope this fight will soon close that we may get some rest, for I assure you we need it" or "O how dreadfull is war O that peace once more blessed our country how much O how much I should appreciate it."[137]

Others were confident, such as the Georgia sergeant who said that Lee's veterans wanted "no easier task than to whip the Yankees when they have works to fight behind" or the Florida captain who thought that "it will take but one more (if that?) battle to close the war."[138] Capt. N. A. Ramsey of the 61st North Carolina, encouraged by the victory at Cold Harbor, also believed that the Confederacy would soon win its independence. Noticing in the North Carolina newspapers that Gov. Zebulon B. Vance would appoint an agent to settle claims on behalf of deceased soldiers, Ramsey "most respectfully" asked Vance for the position. "I have faithfully served in the army for upwards of 3 years," he explained, "& if I thought the War would last for any considerable length of time, I would not accept the appointment. But the end of the strife is fast drawing to a close . . . & I wish to have an active employment when peace does dawn upon us."[139] One South Carolinian claimed, "I heard General Lee tell General Hoke that his campaign would be over this month. The war will be over this year. . . . I expect the great battle will come off before this letter reaches you."[140]

Still others in Lee's army, such as Lt. John B. Evans, were not as hopeful as they had been in May. Evans, under arrest for a minor infraction of army regulations—of which he was eventually acquitted—had not participated with the 53d Georgia in any of its engagements during the spring campaign. However, his brother James, a private in the 14th Georgia, had recently died of wounds received in the fighting along the North Anna River. Evans went to the hospital in Richmond to see his dying brother, but "When I got there they told me he was dead. I taken his things and brought them back to camps. . . . the doctor told me that James appeared to be willing to die, but spoke of his family that he would like to see them and perticular his farther." Evans's father, who had also arrived too late to see James, planned to start back home to Georgia the next day but wanted to stay until the battle was over. "This makes about thirty one or two days that the fight has ben going on," Evans commented. "It is the hardest and longest fight we have ever had I belive, but after all I belive we will rout the yanks and perhaps in three or four years we will have something like peace."[141] David Hugh Crawford, a brigade courier in the First Corps, wrote "with great sorrow" when he described the mortal wounds and intense suffering of a family friend, Capt. Ralph E. Elliott of the 2d South Carolina. "When will peace come to our land?" Crawford asked in a letter to his mother. "How many more good men must pour out their blood? I sometimes think it will be a *very* long time yet before this war ends."[142]

Crawford's opinion, though by no means the prevailing view throughout the army, contained more truth than the young South Carolinian could have known. The next few days, which some Confederates believed might be the last days of the war, would instead serve as the transition from a primarily active campaign to a primarily static one. Frequent marches and countermarches, complex strategic and tactical maneuvers, and large-scale combat would soon give way to primarily fixed positions, the virtual absence of maneuver, and daily sharpshooting and occasional skirmishing that did little to change the overall situation. Many of Lee's officers and men expected the next battle to be the one great Napoleonic clash that would decide the outcome of the war once and for all. They hoped for a battle that would end with the Army of the Potomac utterly defeated, in retreat, and perhaps even routed, and their own army victorious, in possession of the battlefield, and in a position to dictate terms. Several of them were more than ready for such a fight to occur. "The days are so very long and when there is no excitement the monotony is almost unbearable," an Alabama lieutenant complained from his trenches near the Chickahominy. "We have all long since ceased to see any pleasure in the excitement of a battle, but are always ready to meet the enemy as a stern duty. . . . I heartily wish this campaign was over and the war closed with it."[143] The next campaign would indeed close the war, but only after many more casualties and many more months, and with a far different ending from the one Lee, his army, and the Confederacy were hoping and praying for.

You hear that, boys? It's all right now in Petersburg.

General Lee's gone over there. I ain't goin' to make

myself miserable about the thing any more.

—*Unidentified Confederate*

> *on hearing of the arrival of the Army of Northern Virginia*
> *at Petersburg, 16 June 1864*

Cold Harbor to Petersburg, June 1864

When the sun rose over the battlefield of Cold Harbor on the morning of 4 June, the Army of Northern Virginia enjoyed its first respite since just before the Wilderness. Many Confederates took advantage of the opportunity to reflect on their experiences of the past month. William H. Brotherton, a private in the 23d North Carolina, headed his letter "In line of Battle Thirty Days" and reported to his parents, "I have come threw all they fights safe so far and I am in good heart yet." He continued: "It is true I have run some narrow chances I have ben shot threw my cloths in three difference places sceince this fight commence . . . Father I have Ben into four hard Battles . . . you kneed not to be oneasy About our side I think grant will get a complete whipin I think this fight will close the war."[1] A sergeant in the 53d Georgia ventured his opinion of Grant's campaign so far: "To day exactly one month ago he commenced his grand onward movement and now is in a position where I think he is somewhat puzzled to move. He will never take Richmond with his present force and if he continues to fight like he has been fighting, it will not take Gen. Lee's army thirty days longer to destroy his whole force."[2]

As officers and men throughout the army took stock of themselves and their adversaries in the trenches a few hundred yards away, Lee busily attended to the needs of his troops. On the previous day he had issued two circulars concerning preparations for additional enemy attacks and the necessity of putting as many men in the front lines as possible. The first circular ordered officers to inspect and modify their lines as necessary, to issue rations and ammunition to their troops, and to keep one-third of their force in the trenches all night, so they might be "on the alert against night or early morning attacks."[3] Lee's second circular addressed the return of extra-duty or detailed men to the ranks, stipulating that wounds, illness, or official business were the only acceptable reasons for soldiers to be in the rear. "It is a matter of great importance when the enemy is bringing against us all the men he can possibly get, that all our fighting material in the army should be armed and equipped, and on duty with their companies and regiments," the commanding general stated.[4] In a third circular, issued only two days after the second, headquarters criticized many officers' willingness to allow their able-bodied men to go to the rear for trivial reasons or no reasons at all. The practice, which was always common, seemed to be even more so during the present lull in the campaign. "This is all wrong," the circular admonished, "and the General Commdg. desires you to see that on your portion of the line no man is allowed to go to the rear or leave his position in the trenches without proper authority."[5]

Though the problem of sufficient manpower had long plagued his army—and all the Confederate armies—Lee now faced a more specific, and potentially much greater, problem than the familiar one of mere numbers. At every level, from corps command to company command, his army had lost a disproportionate number of officers in the Wilderness, at Spotsylvania, at Cold Harbor, and in the minor clashes and skirmishes overshadowed by those major battles. Some of the army's most prominent generals—Longstreet, Ewell, and Stuart, to cite the most obvious examples—and several of its lesser-known but promising division or brigade commanders had been killed, wounded, captured, or incapacitated by illness. Their successors, most of them placed in their positions in emergency situations, still awaited official appointments. A special order issued from army headquarters on 4 June not only named one major general and three brigadier generals, but, under the provisions of a new law, also appointed two lieutenant generals, two major generals, and four brigadier generals of temporary grade.[6] Vacancies at the regimental and company levels could not demand a fraction of the attention given to the appointment of corps, division, and brigade commanders and were simply filled by surviving officers. Such appointments, many of them made without permanent promotions, were all too often given to officers whose seniority was their only claim to their promotion and who had not demonstrated any particular aptitude for command. Even those fortunate appointments that involved officers whose past performance promised future success were frequently made out of sheer necessity.

In Brig. Gen. George P. Doles's Georgia brigade, in Rodes's Division of the Second Corps, the campaign from the Wilderness to Cold Harbor virtually wrecked the command structure. After Doles himself was killed on 2 June, a lieutenant in the 4th Georgia observed: "All unite in mourning his untimely end. He was universally honored by the officers & men of his command, for his daring & unsurpassed gallantry & loved for his gentlemanly & social qualities."[7] A sergeant in the 44th Georgia who called his dead commander "our brave & Gallant Brigadeer Genl George Doles" believed that "he was the greatest Genl we ever had with us."[8] Col. Philip Cook, of the 4th Georgia, who would soon be appointed brigadier general, succeeded to the command of the brigade after Doles's death and was in turn succeeded as commander of his regiment by Capt. Francis H. DeGraffenried. A few days after Cold Harbor, Company B of the 4th Georgia, the "LaGrange Light Guards," numbered only six privates and was commanded by 1st Lt. John T. Gay; 2d Lt. William S. Evans, the only other commissioned officer in Gay's company, was assigned to the command of another company in the regiment.[9] "Our Poore Boys are Seeing a very hard time," one member of the brigade wrote a friend. "Many of them Seene this morning's Sun will never see it any more."[10] Reporting Doles's death, Capt. Francis Marion Coker, adjutant of a Georgia artillery battalion in the Third Corps, commented, "the Georgians are falling thick and fast."[11] It must have seemed as if all too many of the Army of Northern Virginia's officers and men were "falling thick and fast" in all too many battles that spring. "Their has been meney a poor fellow fell in the last 40 days to rise no more," lamented a South Carolina infantryman. "Their is not a day no not a hour but their is som one falls."[12]

Lee's soldiers, quickly adapting to the new state of things, spent their time improving their entrenchments and waiting for something else to happen. Many veterans, after only a few days' exposure to the almost constant sharpshooting and little else occurring in the trenches, declared that they would much prefer an engagement, even a general battle, to the "continual pop, pop, from morn till night."[13] "We are rather at a loss to know what Grant means by lying so quiet," Edward Porter Alexander wrote his wife on 10 June, "& I wish he would do something for I am very tired of stooping & crawling thro the trenches every day in the hot sun, with minie balls shaving the parapet above, & soldiers crowding the ground beneath."[14] Lee's infantrymen were even more disillusioned with life in the trenches than Alexander was. "I long to see the day When the fight is over so We can get some rest," Sgt. Daniel Boyd of the 7th South Carolina wrote. "We haff to be up half the knight ever knight to Watch for the yankees I think that their Wil be afight som Wher on the lines in a day or too for We cant stay so close to geather With[out] fighting."[15] By "fighting," of course, Boyd meant a large-scale battle in which large numbers of troops were engaged. A sergeant in the 14th Virginia complained, "I can't see what they are waiting for both armies lying still within 3/4 of a mile of each other and has been so for the last 8 or 10 days," while a private in the 2d Georgia Battalion longed for the day "we get away from around Richmond, which I hope will not be long, as I am tired lying in line so long."[16] A correspondent of the *Richmond Examiner* wrote, "Now and then there is a discharge of artillery, and ever and anon the crack of the rifle tells that the sharpshooters are busy at their work of death, but with this saving, nothing of a warlike character is going on."[17] Alexander, Boyd, and their comrades had no idea that they would indeed move from these trenches in the next two weeks, only to occupy a new and more extensive line of works, one where they would spend most of their time for the next ten months.

For the moment, however, soldiers in the Army of Northern Virginia occupied themselves with various pursuits that had been long neglected. For example, while members of the 4th Texas washed clothes or bathed themselves, artillerymen in the Richmond Howitzers went fishing in the Chickahominy River. The officers and men of a Florida brigade laughed at their state's Confederate congressmen, who visited them in the trenches but dodged at every shot they heard nearby, while one soldier in the Stonewall Brigade picked flowers growing between the Confederate and Federal lines and sent them to his division commander's wife, who was boarding in Richmond.[18]

Many of Lee's veterans, who had paid relatively little attention to the quantity or quality of their rations during the last month of fighting, now devoted their energies to thinking about, writing about, acquiring, and enjoying the universal concern of the soldier. The common daily ration about the first of June had been one-half pound of meat, usually bacon; a pound of cornmeal or flour; and a little salt, or less than one-half of the ration allowed by regulations.[19] Opinions on the quality of this ration were divided; whereas one South Carolina private thought his daily allowance was "more than enough for me," a Texas captain alluded to his "accustomed breakfast of cornbread and rank bacon."[20] But in the lull after Cold Harbor the army's rations improved. The "1/2 lb. bacon & 1 lb. of coarse, raw, corn bread" eaten by Sgt. Edward Richardson Crockett of the 4th Texas on 4 June had been replaced by a supper of "peas and rice bacon boiled and fried, corn & flour bread, genuine coffee with sugar, and cherries and sugar" by 9 June.[21] "It is not comon for me to say any thing abowt what we draw," one North Carolina private wrote, "But I fell Bound to let you know how mutch we draw we are getting plenty of ever thing we draw half pound Bacon and plenty corn Bread and coffee sugar merlasses and vegtibel pees cabages and union I am just liveing as well as I want two."[22]

It was, of course, a welcome change. Sgt. William Horace Phillips of the 14th Virginia told his parents, "they are feeding us better now than they have in 18 month," and Lt. Elias Davis of the 10th Alabama boasted, "I am fattening, our rations are now splendid. . . . Some of us nearly starved at Spsylvania."[23] Some soldiers still complained, such as the South Carolinian who claimed, "we only get half rations and that is not cook," or the Floridian whose company was "so starved for a change of diet that we have eat all the poke—may flower tops—and other weeds that we could find—some of the boys says they will try '*rock* soup' next."[24] Most, however, were grateful for the increased quantity and variety of their rations. Lee wrote Secretary of War James A. Seddon, "I am glad to learn that you are exerting yourself to accumulate stores for the army. . . . If practicable, I hope that provision will be made to continue the supply of vegetables. It greatly promotes the health and comfort of the men."[25]

Some units, mindful of their good fortune, offered one day's rations out of every week's allowance to the poor in Richmond, sending their donations to the Army Committee of the Young Men's Christian Association there. "Well let me ask you all wheather this looks much like starvation," Pvt. Joseph F. Shaner of the Rockbridge Artillery wrote his parents, "when this whole Army is a getting a half a pound of bacon per day which is more than anyone man can eat and besides this we are a getting full rashons of good sugar and coffee and sich and sometimes onions and cabbage." Furthermore, "some of the Brigades and regments are a giving one days rashons out of six to the poor people of Richmond. my regment is a going to give them one days rashons this week."[26] Letters and editorials appearing in the *Richmond Dispatch* and the *Richmond Examiner* called such donations "a noble example" or an "extraordinary spectacle."[27] "We are gratified to know that our gallant soldiers are now receiving full rations, and we trust that their generous contribution will awaken throughout the country a hearty response," the *Examiner* observed. An editorial in the *Dispatch* asserted that "such deeds as these will be recorded on a page as bright as that on which are inscribed the battles in which they have shed their blood, that their country might live."[28] When Brig. Gen. Clement A. Evans's Georgia Brigade, in Gordon's Division of the Second Corps, donated one thousand pounds of bacon and two thousand pounds of flour, as well as coffee and sugar, Evans explained: "the troops have now more rations and in greater variety than they have had since the first year of the war; but we know that large numbers of families of women and children, whose homes have been plundered by the enemy, have gone into the city and may be suffering. We, therefore, desire to aid you in your efforts for their relief."[29] "A great deal is being done now in this way by the army," Gordon remarked after mentioning the contribution of his old brigade. Many other infantry and artillery units throughout the army participated enthusiastically in the association's relief effort.[30]

Though diversions such as fishing, sending bouquets to ladies, or donating food to the poor were a pleasant break from what one observer called "this terrible and seemingly interminable fight," just as many military matters still needed attention.[31] The proper placement and use of the army's artillery, for example, was one of Lee's pressing concerns. Some officers, such as First Corps chief of artillery Porter Alexander, resented the additional work and responsibility given to the artillery. "I have been so constantly occupied on our lines that I have had to leave camp very early every morning, & only returned after dark at night, too tired & sleepy to do anything but eat dinner & go to bed," Alexander claimed.[32] Other artillery officers, taking a more positive view, tried to devise innovative ways to fight the Federals. One of the most unusual proposals was suggested by Brig. Gen. William Nelson Pendleton, the army's chief of artillery, who argued for the introduction of gas warfare. Pendleton, writing on the reverse of the title page torn from an 1864 novel, said that the Confederates could design and manufacture artillery shells that would "combine destructive explosion and suffocating gases" and asked Alexander for his comments. With lukewarm encouragement from Alexander, who replied, "I am riding & can answer this but briefly," Pendleton then sent his idea to Lt. Col. Briscoe G. Baldwin, the army chief of ordnance. "It seems at least worth a trial," Pendleton commented after suggesting that mortars be employed to lob such shells into the Federal lines, or that special hand grenades might be used by the infantry in cases where the trenches were particularly close together.[33] Baldwin's response, and that of the War Department, was noncommittal at best. As far as can be determined, the Confederates conducted no experiments of the kind Pendleton proposed.[34]

Even without Pendleton's novel shells and grenades, the prevailing mood in the Army of Northern Virginia was much as it had been after the Wilderness and again after Spotsylvania. Most officers and men shared an optimism tempered by the trials of the past month and by the uncertainties of the immediate future. One sergeant in the Texas Brigade, capturing the spirit of Lee's troops perfectly, noted in his diary, "The suspense of the present days are great but we are confidant of victory."[35] The surgeon of the 61st Alabama observed, "I see that Gen. Lee and all the rest of the Gen's and all the lower officers and men seem perfectly cheerful and confident."[36] A good deal of that confidence, which might have been shaken by the hard fighting and high casualties of May, was undoubtedly restored by the relatively easy fighting and low casualties so far in June. "We have whip them at ever point we have met them," William Brotherton of the 23d North Carolina boasted, declaring, "Father their is no dowbt But what they have got the worst whippin they ever have got yet."[37] J. W. Tindall of the 20th South Carolina thought that the army was "anxious for the frey feeling certain that victory will be ours . . . we have beat the Yankees at evry point and if we can give them a good thrashing this time it will put an end to the Bloody Strife."[38] Many soldiers believed that Cold Harbor was a sign that the war was almost over, that Grant would soon make a last desperate attempt to take Richmond, and that his defeat in such a climactic and decisive battle would ensure Confederate independence.[39]

Lee himself, though he might well have been "perfectly cheerful and confident," recognized that the future success of the Army of Northern Virginia was not necessarily the certainty that some of his officers and men thought it was. "I have little fear of your ability to maintain your position if our men do as they generally do," he assured one of his corps commanders before cautioning him that changing circumstances required a corresponding change in their strategies and tactics. "The time has arrived, in my opinion, when something more is necessary than adhering to lines and defensive positions," Lee advised. Determined, if at all possible, to avoid placing his troops at such a disadvantage, he wished "the corps to be kept together and as strong and possible, and that our absentees will be brought forward and every attention given to refreshing and preparing the men for battle. Their arms and ammunition should be looked to and cooked provisions provided ahead."[40]

If Lee trusted his soldiers to do almost anything he asked of them, they, in turn, trusted him to know what was best for the army and the Confederate cause. "I tell you our Gen'ls are keen enough for them," one North Carolina private boasted to his parents.[41] A staff officer in the Second Corps maintained that though he had no idea of what Grant and the Army of the Potomac might do next, he was not worried. "Until I see anxiety and restlessness manifested in our great leader," Abner McGarity declared, "I shall be perfectly satisfied that all is going well. I have never seen Gen. Lee look more tranquil or cheerful than he does at present—quite different from his appearance at Gettysburg. I know that he knows what he is doing."[42] The already close bond between the commanding general and his men would only strengthen during the coming campaign, a campaign that would be less an example of brilliant generalship or even leadership than an exercise in shared endurance.

The high degree of confidence many members of the army expressed in Lee and in themselves after Cold Harbor was reinforced by a growing sense of superiority over, if not disdain for, their enemy. Grant's "on to Richmond," they were fond of pointing out, had cost him 50,000 casualties and gained him a position no better than George McClellan's at the beginning of the Seven Days' campaign in the summer of 1862. Though Confederate observers generally admitted that Grant and the Army of the Potomac fought stubbornly, they seldom—if ever—conceded that he displayed much imagination or his soldiers much enthusiasm. "I don't think that we need to fear Grant anymore," predicted one of the newly appointed brigadiers of the Third Corps. "His fury is expended, and his troops too."[43]

If a few Confederates thought that the Federal commander might soon abandon his campaign and retreat toward Washington, most believed that he was only waiting a few days before he began another move toward Richmond.[44] "Grant seems to have lost that vigor with which he commenced this campaign," a Georgia lieutenant observed. "Of late he has subsided into a stupid lethargy, so completely enchaining his faculties, mental & physical, that no challenge or demonstration on the part of Gen Lee can arouse him."[45] Correspondents and diarists throughout the Army of Northern Virginia expressed the common Confederate opinion that Grant did not know—or care—that he was beaten and that he was just another of Abraham Lincoln's failures. "I do want Grant to make his best efforts on Richmond and then if he fails I want him to retire and let our army have some rest," one weary sergeant wrote. "He would willingly sacrifice one half his army if by so doing he would be enabled to capture Richmond. I think that he will make a grander failure than McClellan."[46] Capt. Edward A. T. Nicholson, on Brig. Gen. James H. Lane's staff, claimed that Grant's initials stood for *"Unfortunate Strategist"* and that he was "the worse used up Yankee Commander that we have ever combated. He is the very man for us and will end the war in our favor, I trow—sooner than any other man in Yahooland."[47] Lee's veterans believed that Grant, whom they described as "determined to keep on as long as he can raise a man," "out generaled & badly defeated . . . [but] too ambitios & proud to acknowledge it," and "one of the most inhuman wretches now living," had so far displayed few, if any, traits that they associated with their own commander— or any successful general.[48]

As for Grant's soldiers, many of whom they had faced in battle since the beginning of the war, numerous observers in Lee's army considered them exhausted and demoralized after Cold Harbor. "Those captured now speak less hopefully of capturing Richmond than they did at the opening of the campaign," commented Col. David Lang of the 8th Florida, "and many declare that their men won't fight much longer."[49] Though most Federal captives were understandably discouraged at the prospect of spending time in a Confederate prison, some were said to be "highly pleased" and joked to their captors that "they were going to Richmond where they had started, and that they would get there along time before *Grant* did."[50] Other members of the army reported conversations with enemy soldiers who simply deserted to the Confederates instead of waiting to be captured. "Small parties come and give themselves up occasionally—say they are perfectly worn out and disgusted," a surgeon reported to his wife. "They tell some big stories about the demoralization of the Yankee Army."[51] The 25th South Carolina's 2d Lt. Virgil Duc, in charge of a picket detachment one night, was surprised early the next morning by a group of about fifty deserters who approached from the direction of the Federal lines. "50 Yankees came an surrender themselves to me," Duc wrote later that day. "Thay told General Lee that thay was not going to fight any longer thay said theire time was out. Thay also told General Lee tha[t] thousands more would come if thay could get an opportunity."[52]

Several members of Lee's army either cited current rumors or reported incidents that they had actually witnessed to the effect that numerous Federal prisoners and deserters were often drunk when they came into Confederate hands. Many maintained that morale in the Army of the Potomac had sunk to such depths that the soldiers were issued liquor to give them enough "artificial courage" to advance. "Grant brings his men up only by making them drunk," a South Carolina colonel claimed, passing on camp rumors. "Those we take are invariably drunk, and they tell us all are made so to get them to advance."[53] One private in a Georgia artillery battalion reported that his unit "took 49 prisoners in one squad who were made drunk in order to get them to charge us but they say all the spirits in Yankeedom cant make them charge the rebels. They say they like dixie *finely*."[54] To other Confederates, the Federals seemed to be drinking of their own free will, without any coercion or encouragement from their commanders. A captain in the 5th Florida, after describing Grant's disastrous frontal assault at Cold Harbor, commented, "This morning the Yankees had plenty whiskey aboard—some of them were *staggering* along and nearly fell over the breastworks."[55] Sgt. Edward Crockett of the 4th Texas, in the First Corps, recorded a remarkable episode in his diary entry for 3 June: "The prisoners taken by our division belong to the 18th Corps, Butler's command, late this evening a Lt. Col. came in to us, he said that his regiment was all killed & that he had been drunk all day & had just got sober & had as soon go to Richmond as not, he had lain in front of us all day, after the charge in the morning as a dead man, & late in the evening he hoisted a white flag & came in to us."[56] Though many Confederates undoubtedly believed—or wanted to believe—that Grant was not above sending inebriated soldiers to their deaths, the simplest and most plausible explanation for the Federals' behavior is that the sheer physical and psychological strain simply overwhelmed them.[57]

While most members of the Army of Northern Virginia spent their days and nights in the trenches, two divisions of the cavalry corps were sent to thwart a large-scale Federal cavalry raid. The raid, intended to disrupt Confederate supply lines and to reinforce a small Federal army that had been operating in the Shenandoah Valley since the spring, was already well under way when the Confederate horsemen—now commanded by Wade Hampton—left the rest of the army near Richmond. Hampton, after a forced march, caught up with the Federals at Trevilian Station, a crossroads near Charlottesville, on 11 June. In two days of both mounted and dismounted combat, first one force and then the other nearly overwhelmed its enemy, only to be driven back by fierce counterattacks and by the arrival of reinforcements. Some of the most intense cavalry fighting of the war ended with both commanders claiming a tactical victory—though a relatively insignificant one—and suffering a thousand casualties on each side.[58] "My men are jaded but in fine spirits," Hampton reported to Lee a few days later.[59] "The Cavalry have done & are doing very hard fighting," an infantry staff officer in the First Corps commented on hearing news of the battle. "It is no longer an easy place."[60]

This raid, along with numerous battles and skirmishes occurring in the Shenandoah Valley, convinced Lee and the authorities at Richmond that a major Confederate presence was needed there to rid that vital territory of Federal forces. Lee had already sent Breckinridge's small division back to the Shenandoah, but he now ordered Jubal Early and the Second Corps there as well. Before dawn on the morning of 13 June Early's corps, under strict secrecy, left the Army of Northern Virginia and marched toward Lynchburg. His force, reinforced by Breckinridge and by other scattered units from the Shenandoah Valley, numbered some 14,000 troops and was designated "the Valley Army."[61] Early and his army, which would operate from its base in the Shenandoah for the rest of 1864, inevitably invited comparisons with Stonewall Jackson and his earlier army of the same name from the spring of 1862. Jedediah Hotchkiss, who had been a member of Jackson's staff during the earlier campaign, called the move "some distant expedition," while Pvt. Virgil Lucas of the 26th Georgia, in Evans's Brigade of Gordon's Division, assured a friend back home, "Expect a glorious victory for us—the 'Old Guard.' God be with the right."[62] Only time would tell if Early and his small army would be as successful as their legendary predecessors.

When Lee's skirmishers moved forward later on the morning of Early's departure, "feeling" for Grant's position, they—and their commander— were astonished and chagrined to find the Federals gone from their front. During the night of 12 June Grant had somehow slipped almost 100,000 men out of his earthworks and moved south around Lee's flank, crossing the Chickahominy and proceeding toward the city of Petersburg. Lee, after his losses at Cold Harbor and after sending Early to the Shenandoah, now commanded only about 40,000 troops present for duty. He imme- diately moved them across the Chickahominy and hoped to strike Grant en route but was unable to find the main body of the Army of the Potomac before night on the fourteenth. By that time Grant had already begun crossing the James River; a day later the Federals were on the outskirts of Petersburg and threatening to overwhelm the skeleton Confederate force defending the city.[63]

Officers and men in the Army of Northern Virginia, trusting Lee to make the proper decisions and troop dispositions, either commented ap- provingly of their march south—considering Grant's move a retreat—or simply reported the fact that they were following the Federals. "We left

Capt. Ralph Emms Elliott, Company I, 2d South Carolina. Elliott, the brother of Gen. Stephen Elliott Jr., enlisted as a private in the Palmetto Guards and was promoted from lieutenant to captain in 1863; he was wounded at Fredericksburg in December 1862 and was mortally wounded at Cold Harbor in June 1864. (South Caroliniana Library, University of South Carolina)

our old camp about ten Oclock in the morning, we marched about 13 miles," a sergeant in the Texas Brigade noted on 13 June. "Both Yanks and Confederates, all hands are now striking for South side of James River."[64] A private in Brig. Gen. John Rogers Cooke's North Carolina brigade conveyed the Confederates' frustration in a letter to his father. "The nite of the 12th the enimy evacuated thare well fortified posish on Gains farm moved still more to our rite," wrote Jesse Frank of the 48th North Carolina. "We crost [the Chickahominy] . . . put up brest works stayed till morning of 14th when the yanks ware reported all gone we then started after them again did not go more than amile the yanks ware lost." By the morning of 15 June the Federals "ware reported advancing on us again . . . they ware dismounted cavalry . . . the prisners say they ware holdeing us back so they could finish crossing the James." In spite of Grant's stealing a march on them, Frank still believed that Lee had the advantage. "Lee did not retreat to richmond," he claimed, "but onley moved to the rite between richmond and U. S. [Grant] and is still between."[65]

Whether Lee was between Grant and Richmond, however, mattered little if Grant's immediate objective was Petersburg. When a Federal corps, numbering some 15,000 troops, reached the city on 15 June, the remaining 85,000 men of the Army of the Potomac were within a two-day march. Meanwhile, the defenders of Petersburg were a makeshift force of fewer than 2,500, including both regular Confederate troops and local militia, and represented about half of the troops in the immediate vicinity. P. G. T. Beauregard, who had already turned back an ineffective Federal raid against the city on 9 June, scrambled to prepare for a more substantive attempt at any moment. By the fifteenth he had ordered the other troops in his department—most notably, a division from the lines at Bermuda Hundred, less than ten miles northeast—to join him at Petersburg and was gathering together about 15,000 troops. Beauregard called desperately for additional troops from Lee and from Richmond, shifted the few troops he had from point to point along the Petersburg defenses, and prepared to hold off the Federals for as long as possible.[66] Though Beauregard sent his superiors typically dramatic warnings, such as "with my present force I cannot answer for consequences" or "my position [is] more critical than ever," his messages were more accurate—and the situation more critical—than Lee, Bragg, Seddon, or Davis believed.[67]

In early May, while Lee and Grant clashed in the Wilderness and at Spotsylvania, Beauregard's force, some 20,000 strong, had defended the area between Richmond and Petersburg against Maj. Gen. Benjamin F.

Butler's Army of the James, which numbered some 35,000 troops. A small but sharp engagement occurred at Port Walthall Junction on 6 and 7 May and was followed by a larger one at Swift Creek on 9 May. In the latter fight the Confederates, commanded by George Pickett, repulsed a Federal demonstration toward Petersburg. Seven days later, on 16 May, Beauregard attacked Butler at Drewry's Bluff—on the James River only five miles from Richmond—and forced the Federals back to the peninsula at Bermuda Hundred. The two armies, neither of them crippled by excessive casualties such as those being lost by Lee and Grant, spent the next month in a virtual stalemate until the Army of Northern Virginia and the Army of the Potomac marched in their direction in mid-June.[68]

Many soldiers under Beauregard's command, describing their fights at Port Walthall Junction, Swift Creek, and Drewry's Bluff, considered them hard-won victories. "I have been in three Battles and five Skirmishes since I left home," Lt. Virgil Duc of the 25th South Carolina wrote his sweetheart. "I was at the battle of Walthall Junction, also Swift Creek and Drewrys Bluff. . . . I saw about 1600 dead and wounded yankees on the battlefield at Drewrys Bluff we also captured about 2500 prisoners at that battle."[69] Duc, who was twenty-two years old, had enlisted at Charleston in February 1862. He joined Company B, the "Beauregard Light Infantry," as a second sergeant and was soon elected second lieutenant of his company. Duc was one of several members of Brig. Gen. Johnson Hagood's Brigade mentioned in official reports "for meritorious conduct" at Port Walthall Junction and was slightly wounded in the head while commanding his company at Drewry's Bluff. "I think of you Dear Antoinette every moment of the day," Duc assured his sweetheart. "I will also confess to you when I was wounded and fell upon the Battle field my thoughts was turned to thee. I think that I remained upon the battlefield for about five hours before I was able to rejoin my company."[70] Another Confederate— 2d Sgt. John Washington Calton of the 56th North Carolina—wrote his father, "You said you reckoned I had herd at mutch about the fite at Richmond I suppose I did for I was in it. I cant tell how many fites I hav bin in for it has bin anevery day bisness." He continued, "I tel you it is hard work the boys is all in good hart considering our hard duty I hope it will end som day."[71]

Some of Beauregard's soldiers, particularly those who had seen relatively little heavy fighting in previous service around Charleston, in eastern North Carolina, or in southeastern Virginia, seemed to be shocked at the scale and the intensity of combat here. "I tell you that this thing called fighting war is an awful affair," Pvt. William C. Leak of the 22d South Carolina wrote his wife and children. Leak, whose regiment had just recently arrived in Virginia, declared: "I never knew what war was until I got here. I can't tell you anything about [it] now, for I can't express my feelings. I think of all things in this world, I hate war and the army the worst, but I am here and here I will have to stay."[72] Leak's simple words were echoed by Sgt. Henry Greer, of the 25th South Carolina, who noted that the Confederate victory at Drewry's Bluff was won "at the expense of many valuable lives. . . . The suffering & trials said to be endured by troops here is not exaggerated."[73]

Most of Beauregard's soldiers were more optimistic than Leak and Greer, particularly after hearing the news from the Wilderness and Spotsylvania. "The great fight of the War will take place in a few days," 2d Lt. Luther Rice Mills of the 26th Virginia believed. "Waterloo will be a skirmish when compared with it. Lee's prospects will be good. He is stronger now when compared with Grant than at first. Besides the 'Esprit du Corps' of his army is good whilst Grant's is destroyed."[74] At the end of May Lt. Col. Theodore Gaillard Trimmier, of the 41st Alabama, a veteran of several campaigns in the war's western theater with the Army of Tennessee whose regiment was now in Beauregard's department, had observed, "The men generally are in fine health & spirits. We all hope the war is to close this year."[75]

By early June some of Beauregard's officers and men described living in the trenches and discussed the increasing Federal pressure on them. "One can easily imagine our condition," one South Carolinian observed in his diary, "rolling in ditches of red clay, with no protection from rain or sun, and a continued series of working details and pickets. . . . We have been in the trenches now twenty days without relief and there is no telling how much longer we will stay." Though Lt. Samuel Catawba Lowry of the 17th South Carolina observed that "Lee's success is so far uninterrupted," he made no prediction concerning the Army of Northern Virginia or the possibility that it might go to Bermuda Hundred or Petersburg.[76]

Others in Beauregard's department—from company officers, to general officers, to staff officers—spent more time than Lowry did writing or talking about Lee's, and Richmond's, failure to come to their aid. "Nearly all of Beauregard's Army has been sent to Gen. Lee," a lieutenant in the 26th Virginia claimed. "Hoke's entire Division and Matt Ransom's Brigade have gone lately. I think Lee must have gotten 25000 fresh troops since the fight at Spotsylvania C.H. I am expecting Lee to take the offensive."[77] One high-ranking officer who had a chance opportunity to discuss the situation with Beauregard himself was Stephen Elliott Jr., a newly promoted brigadier from South Carolina. The thirty-two-year-old Elliott had just arrived in Virginia after three years' service in his native state—including nine months as commander of Fort Sumter—and recently had been promoted to lead a brigade in Johnson's Division. On the day Elliott took command of his troops he went to see Johnson in the house where division headquarters had been established. Though Johnson was not there, Beauregard happened to arrive soon after Elliott did and the two "sat down in the piazza and had a long talk." Beauregard said, according to Elliott, that he had "tried his best to get some of Lee's troops after his big battles [at Swift Creek and Drewry's Bluff] for the purpose of thrashing Butler and capturing his army." He also claimed that his inability to get reinforcements, combined with his own officers' incompetence, prevented him from winning a more complete victory at Drewry's Bluff.[78] The week after Elliott's conversation a member of Beauregard's staff was even more critical of Lee and the Confederate authorities. On 10 June Maj. Henry Bryan, Beauregard's adjutant and inspector general, complained, "All is now quiet on our lines, but there is no telling when troops may be massed in our immediate front—Bragg or the President give us the minimum & Beauregard is expected to hold the back door for the benefit of Lee."[79] Such allegations, though obviously exaggerated, did have some basis in fact and were greatly influenced by messages Beauregard received from Richmond in the first two weeks of June that offered him little substantive assistance.[80]

Though some sought to cast blame on Lee and others, there were still officers and men in the Department of North Carolina and Southern Virginia who believed that the Federals would be defeated—if not by Beauregard alone, then by Beauregard with Lee's help. Some soldiers, such as James W. Albright, conveyed the anxiety and anticipation they felt while waiting for the great battle. "Gen. Beauregard made an inspection of the lines . . . & was lustily cheered by the troops on the line," Albright reported in his diary on 11 June. "His presence inspired all with confidence that all that could be done *would* be." Albright, ordnance sergeant of the 12th Battalion Virginia Light Artillery, wrote on the sixteenth, with still no sign of the Army of Northern Virginia, "All I fear is we may [be] deceived as to the real point of attack by Grant—if we knew it was either Richmond, from the South side, or Petersburg by this line—all would be right." He did, however, end with the observation, "I have so much faith

[in] Gen. Lee that I think he knows & will be with Grant—*whenever* & *wherever* he appears."[81]

Lee, meanwhile, neither knew Grant's precise whereabouts nor had significant portions of his army in contact with the Army of the Potomac. His anxiety for the safety of Richmond, coupled with uncertainty over the identity of the Federal troops massing around Petersburg, led him to act cautiously. He first intended to move his army "nearer the exterior lines of defences around Richmond" but could not get enough information to satisfy him as to Grant's intentions. "I shall remain where I am today," Lee wrote Bragg from near Richmond on 15 June, "as the enemy's plans do not seem to be settled."[82] By the next morning, with the First Corps on its way to Bermuda Hundred to take the place of Bushrod Johnson's Division, which Beauregard had ordered to Petersburg, Lee had reached Drewry's Bluff. On the sixteenth a flurry of telegrams passed between Lee and Beauregard, with Lee requesting, "Please inform me of condition of affairs," admitting, "I do not know the position of Grant's army," and asking, "Has Grant been seen crossing James River?"[83] Beauregard's messages to Lee were full of warnings such as "We may have force sufficient to hold Petersburg" or "We greatly need re-enforcements to resist such large odds against us. The enemy must be dislodged or the city will fall."[84]

Most officers and men in the Army of Northern Virginia, even those making their way toward Petersburg, had no idea that a crisis was at hand. When elements of Anderson's First Corps encountered Federals along the road between Drewry's Bluff and Petersburg on 16 June, they brushed them aside with little effort. Portions of Pickett's and Field's Divisions easily recaptured a section of Beauregard's former lines the next day and secured the works by nightfall on the seventeenth. "We made a charge upon them capturing them without any trouble & taking some prisoners," noted one sergeant in the Texas Brigade, and "we lost but little in this affair." Pvt. Thomas L. McCarty of the 1st Texas, in the same brigade, recorded in his diary, "at night we moved again by the right flank towards Petersburg, halted & stopped for night in a line of breastworks."[85] There seemed to be little, if any, sense of urgency among these soldiers or, for that matter, among the officers and men of the Third Corps, now at Chaffin's Bluff. Hill's troops, ordered to a point equidistant between Richmond and Petersburg so they might be able to defend either city as necessary, were of the opinion that Lee would have an answer ready for whatever Grant might do. "We are lying here resting from the fatigues of the ditches," one Georgia captain wrote his wife. "Grant's whereabouts [are] not exactly defined but the main portion of his army is already on the southside, and I think he intends to try to take Petersburg." The captain, a staff officer, further remarked that "Beauregard was fighting him near Petersburg yesterday, & repulsed several attacks . . . Longstreet's Corps is over, and we are yet on this side."[86] A brigadier general in Wilcox's Division described his troops as "all quiet behind our breastworks," predicting: "the next fight will, I expect, take place between Petersburg and Richmond. . . . 'tis all speculation, nobody knows anything. The Army has unbounded faith in Lee and is content with anything he does, knowing that he will do all that man can do."[87]

That officer's expression of contentment with Lee might have been true enough when speaking of the Army of Northern Virginia, but it was not always so in the case of Beauregard or his troops, who had spent the last three days fighting—against both Grant and immense odds—to save Petersburg. "I can inform you that we have awful times here now," one South Carolinian began a letter to his family, continuing: "We left our entrenchments last Thursday morning [16 June] and came to the city entrenchments. . . . There was fighting going on all along on the left next to the river. . . . It has been a continual ringing of musketry and roar of cannon ever since last Wednesday [15 June]."[88] Confusion reigned as regiments and brigades were moved into and out of the lines as the emergency dictated, often while other units were being forced from or withdrawn from the trenches. One Alabama regiment, for example, was held in reserve on the night of 17 June until a Virginia brigade "was driven from the entrenchments . . . falling to the rear in confusion." According to the commanding officer of the 43d Alabama, himself a temporary replacement for the colonel, the regiment "went in gallantly under a heavy fire and reached the Trenches just as the enemy were taking possession of them . . . with our charge the enemy were driven from the works in confusion and the 43d took possession of them and held them the whole night & until the lines were reestablished."[89]

On the morning of 18 June, as the first elements of Lee's army reached Petersburg after a few miles' march and a short railroad trip, they received an enthusiastic welcome from Beauregard's weary soldiers and from the city's residents. "We leave our position this morning about 8 Oclock & march for Petersburg which is now seriously threatened," a member of the 4th Texas recorded in his diary. "After marching a few miles we take the cars and reach Petersburg about a half hour afterwards. We immediately disembark & march out to the lines and take position."[90] Another member of the Texas Brigade reported that he and his fellow soldiers in the First Corps "found that the Feds had been quite close to the City, & had driven our cavalry and citizen soldiery before them into the City—people quite excited, and overjoyed to find Longstreet's Corps coming in to town."[91] A corporal in the 20th Georgia, describing his brigade's reception there, made sure to specify that "considerable excitement prevailed among the female population."[92]

A particularly poignant scene occurred in the streets of Petersburg when William Mahone's old Virginia brigade marched through the city "enveloped in a cloud of dust, to take their places in line of battle." According to one witness, a woman and her child stood "intently and anxiously surveying" the Confederates' faces as they watched the brigade march by. "Suddenly she sprang into the column and threw her arms around the neck of a soldier, so dusty and sunbrowned that you could scarcely tell whether he was white or black, or what his clothes were made of." As the two embraced, the soldier's emotions "seemed to be those of mingled astonishment and joy, as they both wept with delight. . . . He was crying, she was crying, the child was crying; and tears stood in many an eye that had never quailed before death or danger in the field of battle." The Virginian "could not, or would not quit his place in the ranks," and after the three embraced and kissed again "he took his place again in the ranks and continued his tramp to the front." His wife and child had not seen him for two years before that day.[93]

Beauregard's officers and men might not have been the most excited people in Petersburg that morning, but they were undoubtedly the most relieved. "Gen. Lee, reached the city at 10 o'clock, A.M. & the main body of his army during the day," one awestruck artillerist wrote. "I saw Gens. Anderson, D. H. Hill, A. P. Hill, Johnson, & Finnegan, & a host of lesser lights. It is a fine sight to see such an army of tried and true veterans. Little did I think two months ago that we would be in Gen. Lee's grand army."[94] Brig. Gen. Stephen Elliott informed his wife: "Kershaw's Division has arrived and A. P. Hill's is to be here to-day, is now perhaps, and Old Mars Robert Lee is either here or expected every minute. So we feel quite stiff."[95] These reinforcements were almost as welcome for their experience, their reputation, and the confidence they exhibited as for their physical presence in the earthworks.

Much of the confidence in the Army of Northern Virginia came from the soldiers' belief that Lee had the situation well in hand. "'Madam rumma' says Grant says that he came over here to fight Bory—but he met Lee," reported a hospital steward in the 37th North Carolina.[96] According to another North Carolinian, Federal prisoners claimed that "the yankees intend to take Richmond & Petersburg both by the 4th of July. I presume Gen. Lee will have a voice in that matter."[97] A day or two before the general himself arrived at Petersburg, Capt. Charles Minor Blackford of the First Corps staff met an ailing soldier in the Third Corps who had been in the trenches about thirty-five days. The man, "making his way slowly along in an effort to join his regiment," told Blackford that "he thought he would get well if a battle came on" and asked him about the latest news from Petersburg. Blackford replied that he knew little except that Beauregard was defending the city. "General Beauregard is a pretty good general," the sick man commented. After Blackford said that Lee was on his way to Petersburg, the soldier turned to a group of sick and wounded Confederates and exclaimed, "You hear that, boys? It's all right now in Petersburg. General Lee's gone over there. I ain't goin' to make myself miserable about the thing anymore."[98]

Lee's troops were almost as confident of their own abilities as they were of their commanding general's, assuring family and friends that "the great campaign of '64, about which so much has been said and possibly feared, has now pretty fairly developed itself, and with but little to cheer our enemies."[99] They described themselves in terms such as "a large and undaunted army," "in as good spirits as ever," "hopeful of an early peace," or a "wall of Southrons" confronting Grant and his army.[100] Many veterans thought that their battles of May and early June confirmed their innate superiority over their enemies. They also had, or at least expressed, few doubts about their ability to win the war with one last decisive battle at Petersburg. "Grant has thrown his army repeatedly against our earthworks suffering dreadful slaughter every time," one officer summed up the campaign from the Wilderness to Cold Harbor. "Now we are strong enough to whip every man he *ever* had & his best men who would *lead* assaults have all been killed."[101] Some soldiers in Lee's army seemed to be unconcerned at all, such as the members of the 20th Georgia described by Corp. Joseph Pryor Fuller on 20 June. Fuller wrote in his diary that his comrades were already at ease in their new earthworks and looking for ways to amuse themselves, only two days after reaching Petersburg. "At night—the boys shot up pieces of canon fuse—which resembled rockets," Fuller reported. "This was done for pass time."[102] Ira Traweek, an Alabama artilleryman in the Second Corps, believed that "our prospects for peace are brighter than they have been since the war commenced."[103]

Traweek's commanding general was not as sanguine as the young Alabamian. "I hope to go to church this blessed day & shall remember you all in my poor prayers," Lee wrote his wife the day after his arrival at Petersburg. "Never forget me or our suffering country."[104] His doubts about the Confederates' ability to withstand a prolonged siege, or their ability to prevent Federal disruptions of their communications and transportation routes, weighed heavily on him, and his correspondence with Davis, Bragg, and Seddon took on a more apprehensive tone. When he wrote "I do not see what can be done" or "if this cannot be done I see no way of averting the terrible disaster that will ensue," such phrases, coming from Lee, no doubt alarmed the authorities in Richmond.[105] There was no mistaking his confidential message to Jefferson Davis, written on 21 June: "The enemy has a strong position, & is able to deal us more injury than from any other point he has ever taken. Still we must try & defeat them."[106]

One way to defeat the Federals, Lee hoped, was by holding his position at Petersburg while Jubal Early and the old Second Corps secured the Shenandoah Valley, siphoning troops from Grant, protecting the area's vital subsistence, and perhaps threatening Baltimore and even Washington. "Grant is in front of Petersburg," he notified Early on 18 June. "Will be opposed there. Strike as quick as you can, and, if circumstances authorize, carry out the original plan, or move upon Petersburg without delay."[107] Reporting from New Market a few days later, Early briefly discussed plans for the immediate future, then reassured Lee, "If you can continue to threaten Grant I hope to be able to do something for your relief and the success of our cause shortly."[108] Though Lee and the country dared not hope that Early might prove himself another Stonewall Jackson, they could—and did—hope that the second Shenandoah Valley campaign might equal the first in its strategic results and in the dramatic impact it had on Confederate morale.

I think we are better off than if we had Been lying in

the Trenches round Petersburg & Richmond . . .

I had much rather stay up here than to go Back there.

—*Capt. Ruffin Barnes*

43d North Carolina, to his wife, 2 August 1864

4

The Shenandoah Valley, to Washington, and Back, June–August 1864

As they left the rest of the Army of Northern Virginia behind in mid-June, many soldiers in the Second Corps believed at first that they were moving to a more advantageous position along Lee's lines, or that they might be part of an attempt to flank Grant out of his trenches. "None of the numerous suppositions proved correct," an Alabama lieutenant admitted, and a North Carolina lieutenant observed, "We started at 2 A M & marched off towards Richmond, but unknown to us where we were going."[1] But after traveling northeast for a few miles, crossing the major railroads north of Richmond and proceeding in the direction of Louisa Court House, Early's veterans realized that they were going to the Shenandoah Valley. Some of them knew that a Federal force under Maj. Gen. David Hunter had already burned the Virginia Military Institute and much of the town of Lexington. Because Hunter was now threatening the strategic railroad junction at Lynchburg, they guessed that Lynchburg was their immediate destination. "We marched some 18 or 20 miles & then stoped about 3 P.M. to camp," a lieutenant in the 53d North Carolina wrote in his diary on 13 June. "We now think we [are] going to Lynchburg as the enemy Comd by Hunter is advancing on that place."[2] A few days later a Georgian with a sense of humor joked to a friend, "Perhaps this will be news to you as the move is veiled in secrecy as much as possible. Then shut the door & listen!" Virgil Lucas, writing from near Charlottesville, continued, "Ewell's Corps left R. Monday at 2 AM on a grand *Hunt(er)ing* expedition. . . . Expect to bag the game inside of 3 days."[3]

Early, whose first priority was to save Lynchburg and its railroad lines, was anxious to link his corps with Breckinridge's troops already in the town before Hunter arrived there. He pushed his soldiers through Louisa Court House and on to Charlottesville, hoping to reach Lynchburg by the seventeenth, then to defeat Hunter and force him from the Shenandoah Valley. Before leaving Charlottesville, Early's men enjoyed the hospitality of the citizens and the beauty of the town and neighboring countryside. One North Carolinian was given such luxuries as "ice cream, cherries, and ice water"; another described the town's young ladies as "so kind and patriotic" and wrote his parents, "[they] gave us soap tobacco &c—the latter article, you know I don't use."[4] Brig. Gen. Bryan Grimes, taking advantage of a relatively rare opportunity to see the sights, visited the University of Virginia and called it "even more beautiful than I had anticipated, for the buildings are Superb and everything unique."[5] The Confederates had little time to dwell on such pleasant thoughts, however, as two of Early's three divisions took the railroad to Lynchburg on 17 June and the third followed the next day. "Hold on and you will be amply supported," Early had telegraphed Breckinridge while waiting to board the trains at Charlottesville, and his prediction was confirmed when the first units of the Second Corps arrived in Lynchburg before the Federals did.[6]

For two days the newly constituted Army of the Valley worked on its defensive lines and waited for Hunter to advance in force against them. Brief clashes occurred on the seventeenth and eighteenth as the rest of Early's army came up, and the Confederates prepared for an attack on the morning of the nineteenth, but the Federals retreated toward the mountains of West Virginia during the night and deprived Early of his opportunity.[7] The Army of the Valley pursued Hunter for several days but was unable to overtake him; this prompted some officers and men to claim that the Federals were better suited for retreating than for fighting. "Yankee armies are seldom caught when they start on a retreat," one officer commented. "In that branch of tactics they generally excel."[8] A North Car-

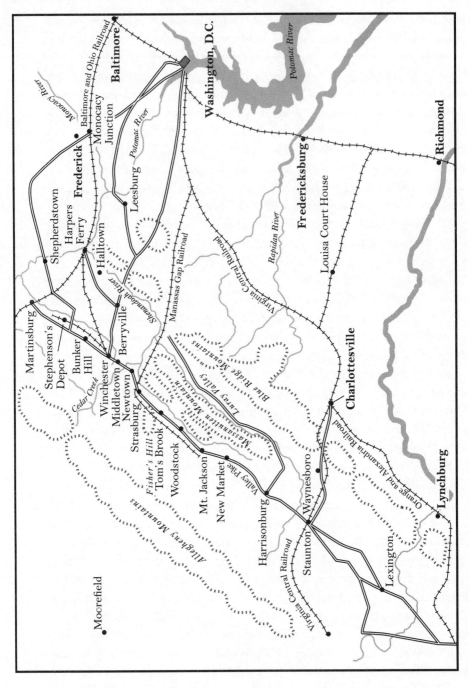

The Shenandoah Valley Campaign, 1864

olina private thought that Hunter "took the back track & run like a fox—so fast, that we couldn't catch much of him but stragglers."[9]

Other correspondents and diarists observed that extraordinarily hard marching since they left Cold Harbor was beginning to tell on the army, as officers and men alike fell from the ranks too sick or too exhausted to continue. Veterans who rarely mentioned marches except to note the number of miles they had traveled, or to refer to the weather, called their trip so far "very tiresome & dusty" or "a most fatiguing jaunt."[10] "I am awful tired marching though I am such a lightwood [k]not," Pvt. John S. Anglin of the 4th North Carolina reported to his parents. "I stand it nearly as well any one in the Reg't—a great many stouter men have fallen out & gone to Hospital, a much stronger than I am."[11] Others, such as Lt. James Green of the 53d North Carolina, were not so fortunate. Green admitted in his diary that "yesterday was the first time I have ever had to ride in the ambulance since I have been in service." A few days later, left behind when Early's troops departed Charlottesville for Lynchburg, he commented, "I am very unwell to day. I suppose it is fatigue, I have gon through with so much this spring."[12] Most of these soldiers had five more months of such marching—not to mention fighting—ahead of them in the Shenandoah Valley and beyond.

Their commander, meanwhile, had to decide what to do next. With Hunter out of the way, the Shenandoah Valley was free of Federal troops for the moment, and the first of Early's two major objectives had been achieved without fighting a general engagement. But much might still be accomplished by moving down the valley and into Maryland on a third Confederate invasion of the North. After giving most of his army a full day's rest for the first time since leaving Lee, Early marched toward the southern end of the Shenandoah Valley, passing through Lexington on 25 June and reaching Staunton on the twenty-seventh.[13]

The Confederates' brief trip through Lexington reinforced the determination of many soldiers in the old Second Corps when they saw two awe-inspiring, if depressing, sights. One was the ruins of the Virginia Military Institute, burned by Hunter; the other was the grave of their old commander, Stonewall Jackson. On orders from Early, his troops took a slight detour from the main road and through the town cemetery, where they marched by Jackson's grave as regimental bands played a dirge. Captain Cary Whitaker of the 43d North Carolina described the salute:

We marched through the Cemetery, by the grave of Jackson—men in two ranks at reverse arms in column the officers on foot and when they passed the tomb they uncovered [their heads]—the grave has no monument or stone of any kind over it, it could only be known by having the Confederate flag flying above it—It was beautifully decked with flowers the work no doubt of the ladies of Lexington who love his memory so well.[14]

Others in the army reflected on what that memory meant to them and to the Confederate people at large. "Though gone from among us, he still lives in the hearts of his countrymen," observed a soldier on signal duty at corps headquarters.[15] Brig. Gen. William Gaston Lewis, commanding a North Carolina brigade in Ramseur's Division, wrote his wife, "You have no idea what feelings passed over me as I went by his grave. There lay *the* great christian patriot & soldier, the unsurpassed warrior of his time." Lewis believed that "some of Jacksons spirit was instilled into the breasts of those hardy veterans who had followed him in so many hard marches, & fought with him on so many stubborn but victorious fields."[16] The sight of the Virginia Military Institute and of Jackson's grave seemed to arouse emotions of revenge and resolve in many officers and men in the new Army of the Valley.

Once in Staunton, Early paused to write Lee outlining his plans and to issue general orders intended to prepare his troops for their trip north.[17] His orders reorganized his force, assigning Gordon's Division to Breckinridge to form a two-division infantry corps and placing Maj. Gen. Robert Ransom in charge of the four cavalry brigades that had been under Breckinridge. The most detailed portion of the orders concerned a reduction in the allowances for transportation and for quartermaster supplies. It restricted regimental and company officers to what they could carry; they were to leave the rest of their belongings in the regimental wagons, which would be stored at some safe point until called for.[18] "The command is ordered to be ready for rapid marching," one company officer noted in his diary. "No officers baggage wagons are to be allowed on the expedition in contemplation, and all of us have left the greater portion of our clothing and all our company documents, papers, &c."[19] On 28 June, after a day's rest, the Army of the Valley left Staunton, marching through its namesake toward the Potomac River and enemy territory.[20]

Early's soldiers, naturally enough, spent a significant portion of their time speculating about the probable object of the campaign; many of them had already guessed that they were going to take the war into enemy country again. "I expect we will march down the valley towards Martinsburg Va.," one North Carolina private observed. "I tell you we can alarm Grant's Capital by moving on Washington City."[21] The commanding general himself seemed confident, assuring Lee on the morning of 30 June that his men were "in fine condition and spirits, their health greatly improved," and ending his brief message, "I shall lose no time."[22] The surgeon of the 61st Alabama was less optimistic, writing his wife: "Everything looks like we are going to Maryland again. I can't understand our movements—I suppose though our Generals do. I am in hopes all will go right. Our threatening the enemy's country may possibly draw him out of ours."[23] Lt. Robert Emory Park, a fellow Alabamian, spoke for many of his comrades when he commented, "We are all under the impression that we are going to invade Pennsylvania or Maryland. It will be a very daring movement, but all are ready and anxious for it."[24]

The "very daring movement" proceeded swiftly, as the Confederates marched about twenty miles a day. By 4 July the Army of the Valley was near the northern end of the Shenandoah, divided into two wings and encountering little resistance along the way. Early's troops began enjoying their expedition even more when one wing captured a huge cache of Federal stores at Martinsburg and the other confiscated the contents of abandoned enemy camps near Harpers Ferry.[25] "We Saw fine time 4th of July," wrote 3d Sgt. William Aycock of the 13th Georgia, describing the scene at Martinsburg. "The yankes dident know that we was eney whers a Bout," Aycock claimed in a letter to his captain, who was at home in Georgia on furlough. "They was fixing up for a grate Juberlee gonto give a Big Diner Barbacure [to celebrate Independence Day] they had eney thing that you Could mentionn. . . . We got plenty to eat and that ate was good."[26] Lt. Billy Beavans of the 43d North Carolina reported in his diary that his regiment "found a great deal of plunder" at Harpers Ferry, that he "Drank Ale, Porter, Lager beer & cider other things," and that "There was a great deal of Brandy, Whiskey, Wine, vegitables, crackers &c down at the Ferry." Beavans probably meant to include himself as one of the Confederate "casualties" when he commented wryly, "Some few men got wounded down there."[27]

Any officers or men who overindulged in food or drink, however, were given no sympathy and little time to recover. Two of Early's four infantry divisions crossed the Potomac into Maryland on 5 July, followed by the rest of the army the next day.[28] Concerned that the troops' willingness to plunder might ruin his army, Early lectured one of his generals on the necessity of maintaining discipline, then issued a stern general order reminding his troops that their march into Maryland was to be "no marauding expedition."[29] "The strictest discipline must be preserved, and all straggling, marauding, and appropriation of property by unauthorized parties must be prevented," the order warned, further directing officers to "take every precaution to prevent their men from obtaining ardent spirits."[30] Yet undoubtedly many Confederates had different ideas. The same day Capt. Asbury Hull Jackson, the commissary officer of a Georgia brigade in Rodes's Division, wrote his mother: "The boys have brought a great many things—clothing, eatables, tricks &c. . . . We [are] glad we are away from around Richmond. Hard marching & good Mtn. Water is more healthy than fighting & bad water."[31]

After crossing the river into Maryland Early concentrated his forces, marched north and east, then turned southeast, hindered briefly by skirmishes with scattered Federal and militia units but continuing in the general direction of Baltimore and Washington. Maj. Gen. Lew Wallace, the Federal commander in the area, assembled troops to oppose the Army of the Valley, hoping to delay it long enough for substantial reinforcements from Grant to reach Washington. Wallace managed to gather about 6,000 men—or fewer than half the number in Early's force—including militia, untried Federal units, and reinforcements from the Army of the Potomac. On the morning of 9 July, as the Confederates neared the Monocacy River south of Frederick, they found their way blocked by Wallace's makeshift force.

Skirmishing throughout the morning was inconclusive until elements of Early's cavalry forced their way across the river and found a route by which the Confederate infantry might flank Wallace's small force. About mid-afternoon Gordon's Division crossed the Monocacy and attacked the Federal flank, which was stubbornly defended by the veterans from the Army of the Potomac. Several Confederate assaults were blunted before one broke the Federal lines, and even then the attackers were eventually repulsed. An overwhelming assault by the rest of Gordon's Division finally forced Wallace from the field, at first in an orderly withdrawal and then, as pressure mounted, with some haste. "This battle," Gordon wrote a few days later in his official report, "was short but severe."[32] It ended when some of Early's troops briefly followed the retreating Federals but did not press their pursuit of them. Though Early rightfully claimed a tactical victory, having forced his way past the only substantial enemy force between his army and Washington, Wallace's holding action on the Monocacy might still prove to be a Federal strategic victory if reinforcements could reach the Northern capital in time. The casualties sustained were relatively light—though moderate to heavy for the troops engaged—

as Early lost some 800 killed and wounded, whereas Wallace lost some 1,900 killed, wounded, and captured.[33]

Most Confederate accounts of Monocacy were brief and matter-of-fact, emphasizing the end result of the fighting. Early devoted only a few lines to the battle in his official report of the Maryland expedition. "The enemy in a very short time was completely routed by Gordon," he observed, "and left the field in great disorder and retreated in haste on Baltimore."[34] Correspondents and diarists who did not participate in the battle wrote in much the same vein, characterizing the fight in such phrases as "we whipped the Yankees beautifully," "the rout was complete," or "Yanks routed & Gordon in hot pursuit."[35]

Members of Gordon's Division, however—particularly those in Gordon's old Georgia brigade commanded by Clement A. Evans, himself wounded at Monocacy—noted that their victory was hard won. A sergeant in the 13th Georgia reported, "The Brigade went in the fight with one Thoussand Guns lost 375 Kilded and wounded and the most of them was Kilded and Mortley wounded."[36] Gordon himself, in a letter written two days after the battle, lamented the death of his friend John Hill Lamar, colonel of the 61st Georgia. "It is one [of] the saddest events to me of this war," he wrote. "I feel as tho' I had lost a brother," Gordon continued, asking, "Oh Lord why am I spared & so many & so good men are taken around me[?]"[37] In his report of the battle Gordon called Lamar "a most promising young officer" who was "shot from his horse at the head of his regiment."[38] Despite such losses, the officers and men of the division were proud of their performance. "I did with my Div all the fighting nearly & won the victory—it was a decided success & the Enemy routed," Gordon summed up the battle in a letter to his wife.[39]

The next day the Army of the Valley pushed on toward Washington in what one company officer called "very hard marching indeed"; the journey was aggravated by the heat and dust as much as by the pace.[40] "The day was very hot and the roads exceedingly dusty," Early noted in his report, "but we marched thirty miles."[41] By nightfall on 10 June the Confederates were within another day's march of the city, and many of them believed that they had an excellent chance of capturing it. "Citizens report but a small force in the City," one private wrote hopefully.[42]

Marching orders for the next day called for an early start—at 3:30 A.M.—both to save time and to push the advance as far as possible before the oppressive heat slowed the column. Infantry and artillery were to alternate in the line of march.[43] Even so, Early later admitted, "the day was so excessively hot, even at a very early hour in the morning, and the dust

so dense, that many of the men fell by the wayside, and it became necessary to slacken our pace."[44] By the early afternoon of 11 June, the first of
his exhausted—but excited—Confederates reached the outskirts of Washington and halted just in sight of the works defending the Federal capital.
"All the citizens report but a small force in Washington," Pvt. B. L. Wynn
of the headquarters staff noted in his diary that afternoon. "Hopes are
entertained of the capture of the City."[45]

Early, with the force at hand too tired to fight immediately, sent skirmishers forward to test the city's defenses and to find out whether the
Army of the Valley faced home guards or regular troops. "We rested until
about three P.M. when our brigade was sent near the skirmish line,"
a North Carolina lieutenant reported. "Skirmishing and shelling going
on."[46] Later that afternoon, after the rest of his army arrived and he made
a closer inspection of the Federal fortifications, Early discovered that they
were both strong and extensive. A few days later he reported to Lee,
"They consist of a circle of inclosed forts connected by breast-works, with
ditches, palisades, and abatis in front, and every approach swept by a
cross-fire of artillery, including some heavy guns."[47] He also learned that
the works were manned by an entire corps from the Army of the Potomac
—a portion of which he had defeated at Monocacy—and that additional
reinforcements from Grant were probably on their way. John B. Gordon,
heading his letter "Near Washington," explained to his wife that afternoon, "We [are] at the Yankee fortifications around the City of Washington & in the District of Columbia & in sight of the Capitol." Gordon
ventured the opinion that "We could have gone in without great loss a few
hours ago for they were not prepared for us—Now we will hardly attempt
it—Works very strong."[48]

Early held a council of war on the night of 11 June, then surveyed the
fortifications and enemy troop dispositions once more on the morning of
the twelfth. He regretfully concluded that an assault on the defenses of
Washington, "even if successful, would be attended with such great sacrifice as would insure the destruction of my whole force . . . and, if unsuc-
cessful, would necessarily have resulted in the loss of the whole force."
Though he was disappointed to have come so far without trying to capture the city, Early was also a realist and knew that a Confederate defeat
there "would have had such a depressing effect upon the country, and
would so encourage the enemy as to amount to a very serious, if not fatal,
disaster to our cause."[49] He decided to retreat under cover of night and
spent the rest of the day skirmishing, demonstrating, and bluffing the
Federals, hoping that they would be content to stay in their works and not

force a general engagement with his small army. Several members of the Army of the Valley expressed their simultaneous disappointment and relief at not being ordered to charge the enemy's works. "It is generally believed now that no attack will be made on Washington," one private wrote while he was out "on the Skirmish Line noting movements of the enemy."[50] A North Carolina lieutenant who was ordered to advance a squad of skirmishers commented, "We are hanging around the city of Washington: The Yanks are shelling our sharp shooters from their forts, as they were yesterday."[51] In the evening a small Federal force came out of the works and advanced in Early's direction, but a brief clash did not develop into anything larger. The Confederates began their retreat toward Virginia late on the night of 12 July and recrossed the Potomac River, halting at Leesburg, on the fourteenth.[52]

Most of Early's soldiers, pausing to evaluate their grand trip to the Federal capital, considered it a success. "The object of the daring expedition was no doubt accomplished," one officer believed, "and Grant was forced to send large reinforcements to the threatened and demoralized Capital from his own army, and thus largely diminish his own force and lessen his ability to act upon the offensive."[53] One of Early's division commanders thought that "Natural obstacles alone prevented our taking Washington." Stephen Dodson Ramseur explained: "The heat & dust was so great that our men could not possibly march further—Time was thus given the enemy to get a sufficient force into his works to prevent our capturing them." Nevertheless, he thought that the Army of the Valley "accomplished a good deal—and I hope will still do good work for our cause."[54] William Gaston Lewis informed his wife of the army's adventures in a more humorous way. "I saw the dome of the Capitol," Lewis wrote, "but concluded that I would not visit such a detestable Black Republican place, so we turned round & came over to a more congenial clime."[55] A Georgia sergeant who had been wounded at Monocacy had little to say about the trip to Washington. "We staid there two day[s] & had a little skirmish," he wrote a friend, "[then] recrossed the Potomac on the 14th six miles above Leasburg."[56] Early's raid into Maryland and the District of Columbia had indeed accomplished a great deal, even if success was measured only in terms of Confederate expectations and corresponding Federal fears.

Once back in Virginia, the Army of the Valley was pursued by several Federal commands, including the two corps Grant had sent to Washington as well as elements of Hunter's small army, back in the Shenandoah. Sharp fighting resulted at Cool Springs and Stephenson's Depot on

18 and 20 July; in the first action Early easily repulsed a Federal attack, but in the second Hunter's cavalry routed Ramseur's Division and drove it from the field. The Federals, believing that Early was on his way back to Lee, ordered the units from the Army of the Potomac back to Washington and from there to Petersburg. A small Federal force was left behind in the Shenandoah Valley to make sure that the Confederates did no more mischief. Instead, that command was soundly defeated by Early near Winchester on 24 July in the second battle of Kernstown and soon left the area, once again clearing the valley of Federal troops. This turn of events convinced Grant to attempt to neutralize the threat represented by Early's small army. He not only sent his two corps back to the valley but also placed Maj. Gen. Philip H. Sheridan in command of the Federals there on 5 August. Sheridan's orders were to destroy both Early's force and the Shenandoah Valley's contribution of supplies to the Confederate war effort, and he would soon initiate a second and climactic phase of the 1864 campaign in the valley.[57]

Early's officers and men spent most of late July and August marching, countermarching, and otherwise maneuvering in the lower end of the Shenandoah.[58] "Well, My Love we are still wandering about up here, catching and frightening Yankees, gathering up wheat etc.," Surgeon Abner McGarity wrote his wife.[59] One Georgian, explaining, "I have to Close my leter in a few minuts to git Ready to march," broke off his narrative of the campaign with a list of casualties at Monocacy and did not even mention the trip to Washington and back. "I cant tell for my life which way we will go," he continued, admitting, "I have had a purty tuff time of it . . . though I have got A long very well so fare."[60] Almost two months of constant marching was beginning to wear the troops down, according to some observers. A North Carolina lieutenant who had been in the hospital and had not accompanied the army into Maryland rejoined his company and remarked, "found our boys very much worn out with their hard marching in Md. & back and only 18 Guns with the Co. to which belongs about 84 or 85 men &c. but all our officers present. the men looks very bad & poor."[61] Confirmation of these unofficial assessments was furnished by an inspection of Gordon's Division conducted in mid-August. The division inspector commented that since the division left the Army of Northern Virginia two months earlier, it had "performed 800 miles of route marching, independent of movements in the presence of the enemy . . . been engaged in seventeen battles and skirmishes . . . [and been] almost constantly in the presence of the enemy, either on the advance or in retreat."[62] The cumulative effect of such a strenuous campaign might seriously limit Early's future ability to achieve his objectives in the Shenandoah Valley.

The almost constant activity prevented all but the most industrious correspondents and diarists from providing thorough accounts of their exciting campaign. "Since leaving Richmond, on the 15th June last, we (I mean our little army of the Valley) have had an arduous, active, exhausting, and yet an interesting time," a staff officer wrote in August.[63] Letters were the best medium by which soldiers might recount details of where they had been and what they had done, but few men had—or took—the time to write much more than short notes letting family and friends know that they were safe. In addition, the procession of marches, fights, and sights from mid-July through the end of July was so rapid that letters were outdated almost as soon as they were written and certainly as soon as their recipients read them. Such excuses as "we've been so busy marching nobody has had time to write" or "I have given you a brief sketch of our trip I wished I had time to give you a full history" were common.[64] "I am fearful that my letter will prove uninterresting to you as I had to rite in Such a hurry," William Aycock of the 13th Georgia closed a typical letter. "I hope you will Excused Bad riting and Spelling and correct mistakes."[65] Capt. Edward A. T. Nicholson, a staff officer in Brig. Gen. Lunsford L. Lomax's cavalry brigade, interrupted a description of "marching & Countermarching" to comment, "I must stop writing about our expedition—for I have neither time nor paper nor patience to undertake anything like a detailed account of it and anything else I know must fail to interest."[66]

Diaries, though they were better suited than letters to communicate the day-to-day uncertainties, anticipation, and excitement of the campaign, were by nature more outlines than narratives and were often restricted to dutiful recordings of the numbers of miles marched or the names of towns passed through. Even those who regularly kept diaries—such as Lt. James Green, who wrote something in his virtually every day—described newsworthy events in a few lines and often resorted to comments such as "nothing going on at all," "no startling news to day yet," or "nothing of interest to day."[67] An entry such as "Gen. Early fell back from Martinburg to Bunker's Hill. Weather very warm" was as much as some soldiers had the time or inclination to write.[68]

Though few men wrote detailed narratives, many of them freely expressed their opinions on the success or failure of Early's campaign so far. "Our trip into M'd. was a success," Dodson Ramseur believed. Referring to newspaper editors in Richmond who criticized Early for not capturing

Washington, Ramseur pointed out, "If he had attempted it he would have been repulsed with great loss, and then these same wiseacres would have condemned him for recklessness."[69] At least one observer in the Army of the Valley thought that the expedition into Maryland might soon be followed by another march into the North. In late July Capt. George P. Ring of the 6th Louisiana remarked, "what the next move will be I can only surmise, but I would not be surprised to write you before a week elapses from somewhere in Western Pennsylvania."[70] Numerous soldiers interpreted the relative lack of combat since their return from the North as an indication that the Federals were now willing to acknowledge Confederate possession of and control over the Shenandoah Valley. One surgeon claimed to be "in better hopes than I have been since Grant fought us so stubbornly in May. . . . Unless they are heavily reinforced, we will not be apt to have much more fighting here, simply from the fact that they will not stand."[71] In early August Pvt. William Brotherton of the 23d North Carolina wrote his father: "I dont think their will Be mutch more hard fighting this campign I think that Early wants to show they yankees that he aint afraid of them I will inform you that Early has got ahigh name they soldiers [the Federals] had just as leave Risk him as general lee."[72]

Other Confederates, though generally optimistic, believed that the campaign in the Shenandoah Valley would not only continue but perhaps escalate as summer turned into fall. On hearing that troops from the First Corps were on their way to reinforce Early, a staff officer with a North Carolina brigade thought that "a big fight" was about to happen, "with a decided probability that the theatre of war is to be transferred [from Petersburg] to the Valley."[73] Lt. James Manning Goldsmith of the 60th Georgia reported to his father, "Of the military situation I can say but little, there is every prospect of a fight; as long as the winter will permit." Goldsmith observed gloomily, "This is the policy of the Confederacy, I think."[74]

As for the "military situation" elsewhere, many of Early's officers and men eagerly repeated rumors or news about Confederate success in Virginia and Georgia that summer. "Our rumours from Richmond are very pleasing," one general observed, without specifying what they were. "May our Heavenly Father turn back our enemies with a terrible defeat." A few days later, after passing on a rumor being printed and reprinted in many newspapers—that Grant had been killed at Petersburg by a shell—he exclaimed, "Oh! If we can be successful at Richmond & in Ga, I believe we can see the beginning of the end of this horrible war."[75] A private whose duty with the signal corps gave him an unusual opportunity to hear the latest war news recorded early reports of the battle of Atlanta in his diary.

"It is reported and believed that Gen. [John B.] Hood has beaten [Maj. Gen. William T.] Sherman's Army," he wrote on 24 July, adding three days later, "Off[icial] information of Hood's victory over Sherman just received at Head Quarters."[76] Unfortunately for both the general and the private, the specific reports they so hopefully referred to were manifestly untrue and similar disappointments would only multiply with time. The evolution in Abner McGarity's view of Confederate prospects at Petersburg and Atlanta from early to late August was a representative one. "I do hope this horrible war may close soon," McGarity wrote his wife on 8 August. "If Sherman's Army is routed, which I believe will be done, I think the war will end in less than six months. Almost all depends on the result at Atlanta—I mean that there is the point of doubt. There is none about the result at Richmond." Within three weeks, however, the Alabama surgeon's outlook was less optimistic. "The last news from Petersburg is not encouraging," he reported on 28 August, "but I hope the next will be. I am fearful the enemy will be hard to dislodge from the Weldon rail road, but it must be done, and Lee and Beauregard are the men to do it." As for operations in the Western theater, McGarity noted, "We have had no late news from Atlanta and Mobile, but hope all is going well. If Sherman is not routed pretty soon all that country will be ruined. . . . It is very hard but we must endure."[77]

Some of Early's weary soldiers, as well as some entire units, began displaying signs of dissatisfaction with their officers as the campaign progressed. Two of the three brigades in Gordon's Division, for example, had been created by merging two or more original brigades. Brig. Gen. Zebulon York's Louisianans and Brig. Gen. William R. Terry's Virginians had served in two and three separate brigades, respectively—including such famous units as the Louisiana Tigers and the Stonewall Brigade—but had been mauled so heavily at Spotsylvania that the surviving remnants of several regiments had to be consolidated. Maj. Edwin L. Moore, who inspected the division, commented: "Both officers and men bitterly object to their consolidation into one brigade. Strange officers command strange troops and the difficulties of fusing the incongruous mass are enhanced by constant marching and frequent engagements."[78] An endorsement on Moore's report elaborated, "The troops of the old organizations feel that they have lost their identity, and are without the chance of perpetuating the distinct & separate history of which they were once so proud."[79] Discipline in the division, particularly in these two new brigades, was described as "lax," though it was improving, and the division had fought so far in the campaign—especially at Monocacy—"with conspicuous gallantry and constant success."[80]

Combat reverses, such as the disaster at Stephenson's Depot, also contributed to low morale. Dodson Ramseur, as capable a division commander as there was in the entire Army of Northern Virginia, had been humiliated by his crushing defeat and wrote his wife that "for the first time in my life I am deeply mortified at the conduct of troops under my command." A few days later, describing his division running away "panic stricken" and "in wild disorder," Ramseur claimed, "I did all in my power to stop them—but 'twas impossible."[81] One of his noncommissioned officers, a member of the 23d North Carolina, had a somewhat different perspective on the engagement. Jonathan Fuller Coghill, in a letter to his brother, remarked: "I thank God that I came out safte, sound and unhurt although by bad management wee wase repulsed and I had to run about two miles to keep the yankes from getting me and that on level ground it was very hot and it was impossible to get eny watter on the way so I was completly exausted when I stoped." Coghill blamed the rout on another North Carolina brigade that "gave way and run that caused us to give back."[82]

Public criticism of Ramseur, both in the army and in the Confederate press, grew to such a level that his friend Robert Rodes was obliged to defend him. "I feel that it is due Ramseur as my friend, and as an admirable officer, that I should make some effort to relieve him at once of the embarrassing situation he finds himself in at Richmond," Rodes wrote to their old corps commander Richard S. Ewell, who had been assigned to command the Department of Richmond on the same day that the Second Corps had left for the Shenandoah Valley under Early.[83] Some of Ramseur's soldiers evidently believed that their commander was as much to blame as they were for what some in the army called "that nasty affair." Bryan Grimes, who had long led a regiment in Ramseur's old brigade but was now commanding another brigade in Rodes's Division, observed that "Ramseur is very unpopular with his command." When the troops marched by ambulances with Ramseur's name stenciled on them one day, one of them called out rhetorically, "who is Ramseur[?]" Another soldier replied "he is a Major General," but a third disagreed, saying, "No he is a dog," only to be corrected by a fourth man calling out, "No he aint a dog but we would like to swap him for a dog." Though Grimes asserted that the troops' disrespect for Ramseur "makes me like him more," such behavior could not have given him much confidence in the future.[84]

A more cheerful observation in the same letter concerned the army's adaptation to and appreciation of the Shenandoah itself, a highlight of the campaign that elicited many comments from Early's officers and men. "If we could remain quiet as at present," Grimes wrote his wife, "[we] would be pleased to stay until cold weather in this part of the State."[85] Other members of the army were more enthusiastic about the area, such as the corporal who remarked, "I am sitting on the margin of the Alagany [Allegheny] Mountains I wish I had the time to discribe its beautiful and magnificent seans."[86] A fellow North Carolinian called the valley "a vitall country," writing his parents, "I think if good spares me I will make my home here after the war is over."[87] Numerous Confederates would have agreed with the brigadier general who observed, "This Valley of Virginia is one of the most beautiful countries in the world."[88]

The Shenandoah Valley was also a region of great abundance in the early summer of 1864, and it contributed immense quantities of crops, livestock, and products to the Confederate war effort. Early's soldiers pursued food and drink more than any of the area's other attractions— with the possible exception of pretty young ladies. In a letter home, one private gleefully described himself as "fat and sawssy," remarking, "we are drawing some of they prettiest flour I ever saw and good Beef and we are getting some of they Best Apples you ever saw and some few peaches and milk. . . . I am in as good health as heart could wish for."[89] Another Confederate suggested that one reason Early's army had been formed and sent to the valley was to gather supplies for the Army of Northern Virginia at Petersburg. "It may be that we are after provisions," the Alabamian supposed in late June; by early August he was reporting: "Our Army is drawing sugar and syrup and plenty of flour and beef—all gotten from the enemy. We are a self sustaining army—besides we have sent a great deal to Gen. Lee."[90]

Troops serving in other theaters of the war, both Confederates and their enemies, would have been satisfied indeed to spend a few weeks in such a "Great milk, butter & Cherry country" as the Shenandoah. "I eat more cherries than ever before I think," a lieutenant in the 43d North Carolina admitted in his diary.[91] But some of Early's soldiers took unnecessary risks to obtain luxuries. One unfortunate corporal in the 12th Alabama, for example, scrambled into a tree near Harpers Ferry to pick some cherries on the Fourth of July and was wounded by Federal sharpshooters for his trouble.[92] John Anglin of the 4th North Carolina, who was assigned to guard duty near a private residence, had "ham, buiscuit, boiled mackerel, butter[,] stewed apples, coffee & milk" for breakfast one August morning.[93] Milk was certainly plentiful here and much sought after by thirsty soldiers traveling on hot and dusty roads. Anglin "saw one

Mrs Logan fill about twenty canteens with milk" for soldiers marching through the countryside near Lexington.[94] Water, particularly spring water, was also a valuable commodity on the march. "I am well & away up here in the mountains drinking cool limestone water," Anglin wrote his sisters in the same letter in which he described the pleasures of milk.[95]

Alcohol, in many forms, was just as abundant in the Shenandoah Valley as milk or water and probably more widely coveted. Cider was perhaps the most common of the spirits, as many farms with apple orchards produced "applejack" of varying strengths. Whiskey, many soldiers' liquor of choice, was almost as common as cider, and wine, though not as widely used, was occasionally made. While alcohol was plentiful in the valley, most men in the ranks—and most company and field officers as well—found it difficult to obtain. One day Capt. Cary Whitaker of the 43d North Carolina went to division headquarters to ask for leave to visit a lieutenant in his company on wounded furlough in Winchester. Though Maj. Gen. Robert Rodes turned down Whitaker's request, what most impressed the North Carolina captain was that "Gen R had his table under a nice shade with his friends around him and was just in the act of mixing and taking a drink, no doubt made of the best liquor, while the balance of us, that is we poor subordinates and soldiers, can hardly ever see a drop of mean whiskey even when wounds and sickness require such stimulants." Whitaker wrote in his diary, "I sat on my horse at a respectful distance and wished I had a good drink too, but the General didn't think proper to ask me to indulge so I had to forego that pleasure."[96] Accusations that some members of the Army of the Valley, including the commanding general himself, were all too willing to imbibe would trouble Early and his troops before the campaign ended.

Confederates who wrote glowingly of "the prettiest ladies you ever saw" populating the towns and the countryside doubtless considered them one of the valley's greatest charms.[97] Cary Whitaker's twenty-four-year-old cousin Billy Beavans, who kept a brief—but lively—diary during the campaign until he was mortally wounded, seldom missed an opportunity to comment on the girls and women he saw along the way. "Good looking ladies," "more pretty ladies," and "a good many pretty young ladies" often caught his eye.[98] William Gaston Lewis described roads lined with young ladies "who came from the surrounding country, to give a welcome & wave a nice white handerchief, & smile sweetly at the '*boys*' who had rid them of the Yankee plunderers & thieves." Lewis could not resist teasing his wife: "I paid considerable attention to some of the young ladies on the route. I believe I like ladies company now better than I did before I was married."[99]

Such enticements as cherries, cider, and charming young women helped offset, in some soldiers' minds, the heat, dust, and fatigue of a campaign in which a twenty-mile march was a typical day's work. A private in the 4th North Carolina, for example, began a letter to his sisters with the comment, "I am well & enjoying myself finely, though our hardships are awful."[100] Another member of the regiment, who had just returned to his command, noted at the end of August that "two or three days is a long time for us to remain in camp without some move." Walter Raleigh Battle of Company F, the "Wilson Light Infantry," had been slightly wounded during the last phase of fighting at Spotsylvania and had been sick for most of the period since. He had enlisted at New Bern, North Carolina, in June 1861, at the age of twenty-one. "The boys all seem to be in good spirits," Battle wrote his mother, "though they look quite thin from the hard marching they have had to do since they left Richmond."[101] Capt. Ruffin Barnes of the 43d North Carolina asked his wife, "Did you ever hear Tell of Troops marching Before as we have done this Spring & Summer since we first Started on this campaign?" His commentary on the Shenandoah Valley and on Early's campaign reflected the views of many Valley soldiers that summer: "But I think we are better off than if we had Been lying in the Trenches round Petersburg & Richmond, and we are more Healthy and are up here where we get the Best Kind of water to drink. I had much rather stay up here than to go Back there, though we get nothing up here to eat But Beef & Flour. A small piece of Bacon is a great thing. However, the Boys all Keep in fine Spirit."[102]

Meanwhile, from his headquarters near Petersburg Lee was keeping an anxious watch on Early, the Army of the Valley, the enemy, and the Shenandoah Valley itself. "I still think it is our policy to draw the attention of the enemy to his own territory," he had written Davis just prior to Early's raid into Maryland. "As before stated, my greatest present anxiety is to secure regular and constant supplies. At this time I am doing well, but I must look to the future."[103] A few weeks later, after Early's return to Virginia, Lee observed, "so far as the movement was intended to relieve our territory in that section of the enemy, it has up to the present been successful."[104] By the first week of August, however, he believed that the Federals intended to reinforce their forces in the Shenandoah in order to defeat Early and to regain control of the region. Lee's response was to order additional troops to northern Virginia to cooperate with, and, if necessary, reinforce, the Army of the Valley. A combined force under First Corps commander Richard H. Anderson, consisting of an infantry division, a cavalry division, and an artillery battalion, left Richmond for northern Virginia on 7 August and reached Early on the eighteenth.[105]

As they made their way north, members of Anderson's small force speculated on the reasons for their expedition. "I have no idea what the object of this move is unless Gen. Lee desires to transfer the field of operations from Petersburg to this beautiful Valley," a clerk with the 53d Georgia wrote.[106] Early's troops, for their part, were happy to have help. On 14 August a Georgia captain observed, "Longstreet is said to be on the move and within suporting distance of us I expect he will attack them in the rear if so they will have a good time going to the Potomac, Grants Army across the River."[107] After describing several maneuvers and skirmishes, Thomas Pollock Devereux, a courier in Grimes's Brigade of Rodes's Division, commented, "Where the enemy is—I can't say—but they can't do anything with Jubal Early."[108] Sgt. Daniel Boyd of the 7th South Carolina, in Kershaw's Division, believed that the reinforced Army of the Valley might be "on our way to penssylvania . . . if We go on We will force the yankees to leav petersburg. . . . We wil have a hard time of [it] but the Boys says that they Wil mak the yanks feel the War."[109]

While Early and the Army of the Valley had been marching and countermarching, Lee and the Army of Northern Virginia had been locked in a siege at Petersburg with Grant and the Army of the Potomac. Lt. Harvey Hightower, of the 20th Georgia, referring to the Federal mine that was dug and detonated under the Confederate lines, resulting in the cataclysmic battle of the Crater, wrote that his division had already left Petersburg "before the blow up." "I tell you I am not sorry we left either," he declared. "This way they have got blowing up people I dont believe in it."[110] Whether Hightower and his comrades believed in it or not made no difference. If Grant and his soldiers, who had already demonstrated their willingness to continue the campaign in spite of incredible casualties, were capable of such imaginative and frightening innovations, then Lee and his soldiers might not be able to withstand such pressure indefinitely. The siege of Petersburg might hold the key to Confederate victory or defeat in the East.

There is the chill of murder about the casualties of this month, and sad, sad is the regret when death thus strikes the brave.

—*Brig. Gen. John Bratton*

Bratton / Field / I Corps, report of operations for July 1864

5

The Siege of Petersburg and the Crater, June–July 1864

To most members of the First and Third Corps of the Army of Northern Virginia, sweltering in the summer heat in their trenches near Petersburg, the contrast between their position and that of their comrades in the Shenandoah Valley and beyond could hardly have been more pronounced. "While Grant has been besieging Petersburg & Richmond, Early has been thundering at the *very gates* of Washington & Baltimore," wrote one Georgia artillery captain.[1] The bulk of Lee's army settled into the earthworks alongside Beauregard's troops—who were now for all practical purposes part of Lee's army instead of Beauregard's—as soon as they arrived at Petersburg. They also settled into an everyday routine that they quickly took for granted, spending most of their time trying to improve their defensive positions and living conditions while trying not to be hit by a stray—or aimed—shot from the nearby Federal lines. One Texas private, in a typical diary entry, reported "considerable sharpshooting along the line and canonading, a man cant expose himself a second now without he hear the *Zip* of a minnie."[2] A few weeks later a South Carolina sergeant wrote his father, "every thing has bin quiet for several days With the exceptions of heavy Shelling and picket fighting Which has becom as coman as a mans voice."[3] The prevailing Confederate opinion, at least in late June and early July, seemed to be that such "Fighting, Working, day and night . . . sometimes aweek at the time" was the prelude to a new campaign rather than the campaign itself.[4] Sgt. Henry I. Greer of the 25th South Carolina, quoting an enemy officer captured by his regiment's pickets, reported that the Federal prisoner believed that "this campaign would not end the fighting" but added, "It is to be hoped that he will be mistaken."[5]

In their first few days at Petersburg, several officers and men thought that a single full-scale battle there might be decisive and might end in the Confederates' favor. They supposed, after inflicting frightful casualties on the Federals and frustrating Grant's offensives in the Wilderness, at Spotsylvania, and at Cold Harbor, that the Army of the Potomac, its commander, and the Northern people were almost ready to abandon the campaign. Some believed rumors that a massive Federal assault—one last great effort to occupy Petersburg and Richmond—would take place on Independence Day. "There are no means of determining whether there will be a great battle soon at this point," a North Carolina captain on the Third Corps staff wrote his wife.[6] "The noted day is close at hand & every one seems to be puzzled as to what Grant will do tomorrow," Corp. Joseph Pryor Fuller of the 20th Georgia recorded in his diary on 3 July. "Numerous reports are afloat as to when the enemy will commence the storm of artificial thunder." The next day, when the expected fight did not occur, it "remained quiet all day—at sun set the enemys' bands came near the line & played their national piece 'Yankee Doodle' a deafening cheer went up on their side."[7] Thomas McCarty, of the 1st Texas, who was evidently in no mood to fight, observed that the Federals "agreeably disappointed us all."[8]

Others thought, or hoped, that the prospect of additional heavy casualties would deter the Federals from attacking the city's defenses, and that they might try instead to flank the Confederates from their strong position. Additional fighting might even be unnecessary, they believed, if Grant would only acknowledge that he could not possibly take Petersburg and Richmond. "I think Grant is completely lost," Samuel P. Lockhart of the 27th North Carolina wrote his mother the day after arriving in the trenches. "He don't know where he is going when he starts to Richmond via Petersburg. I hope he will soon see the folly in trying to take Richmond and quit fighting and let us alone, so we can rest."[9] Several Confed-

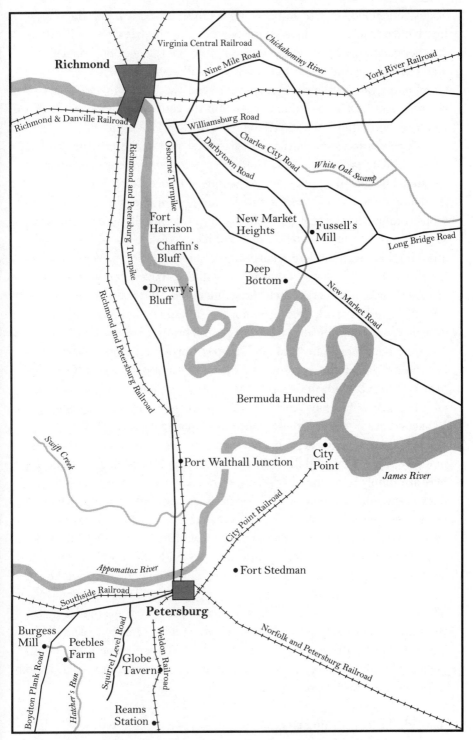

The Petersburg-Richmond Front, June 1864–April 1865

erates concluded, despite ample evidence to the contrary, that the opposing armies would soon leave their positions in the trenches and initiate another campaign rather than endure a prolonged siege. One Third Corps staff officer declared, "I do not think we shall stay long here."[10] A North Carolina private in the same corps observed, "we keepe them anoyed all the time and they us so I don't think that the too armies will stay in that condition long they have stayed longer now than I thought."[11]

As Lee's officers and men spent day after day in the trenches and as June and July wore on, most Confederate correspondents and diarists began acknowledging that they were indeed under siege. Some of them, no doubt reminded of Grant's successful siege of Vicksburg in the previous summer, feared that the Federals might eventually wear them down or starve them out of Petersburg. Few, if any, of Lee's soldiers thought anything like the humiliating surrender of July 1863 could ever happen in Virginia. "I dont know whether grant will ever take Petersburg or not," Henry Ferrell of the 31st North Carolina noted, "but I am of the opinion he will have hot work before he does it."[12] Other observers seemed to attach even less significance to the siege, accepting it as a matter of course. "Matters here remain in statu quo," a First Corps staff officer observed in late June.[13] Becoming resigned to the idea, surgeon Spencer Glasgow Welch of the 13th South Carolina thought in early July that "It now looks as if our army will have to lie in line of battle all summer to keep the Yankees back."[14] Later that month the quartermaster of Brig. Gen. Henry L. Benning's Georgia brigade sent his absent commander the latest news from the army and described conditions at Petersburg. "The duties here are simply to occupy the trenches from day to day being relieved for 2 days every 6 days that a brigade remains in," he told Benning, who had been wounded in the Wilderness.[15] Ord. Sgt. James W. Albright of the 12th Battalion Virginia Light Artillery vividly characterized life under siege in his diary: "The siege progresses slowly, & no new developments are transpiring. Dig, dig, dig! is the word; while boom, boom, boom! from the mortars, & the shrill whistle of the minnies, alone, break the monotony of the tiresome, demoralizing, debilitating siege."[16] Perhaps the most representative comments were those of Capt. Francis Marion Coker, of the Third Corps artillery, who wrote his wife, "The 'situation' here is unchanged in every respect. . . . It has become to be such a continual day and night business that it excites neither notice or remark."[17]

Though the lengthening siege's "continual day and night business" might not seem remarkable in terms of an army's—or a component unit's, or even an individual's—advantage over an enemy counterpart, it was certainly significant in terms of an individual soldier's life or death. As there were few places in the trenches where officers and men were truly protected, and few times of the day or night when they could rest easily, Lee's troops were often alternately apathetic or anxious about their safety. Pvt. Thomas Lafayette Alexander of the 37th North Carolina, one of the former, remarked, "we have becom use to it it is just like aman daly buisness."[18] An unidentified captain in the 12th Virginia was evidently a member of the anxious group. One night in July, as 1st Sgt. John F. Sale of Company H recorded it in his diary, the exhausted captain "fell to nodding" while commanding the picket line. "After a short while," however, "the Yanks opened a few shots which aroused him and the lightning bugs being plentiful he cried out Look at the guns boys! Pour it into them! They have a cross fire on us! Wax em! which brought forth shouts of laughter." Sale wrote that the abashed captain "no doubt felt, as the boys say, shamed."[19] Every exchange of musketry and artillery fire, which might be precipitated at almost any time by the chance discharge of a bored infantryman's rifle or the accidental detonation of an artillery shell, only further emphasized this campaign's fundamentally inconclusive character. "We wore through a weary month of guard duty, mortar shelling, and sharpshooting, watching and waiting for the affray," a South Carolina brigadier wrote in his official report covering events of July 1864, "but no assault was made."[20]

Numerous observers in the Army of Northern Virginia, particularly troubled by the indiscriminate manner in which their comrades were being killed and wounded every day and night, questioned the human cost of the siege. "Many is the luckless fellow, who, in an unguarded moment, shows his crown above the works & receives into it a ball that 'settles the hash' with him forever," one North Carolinian remarked. "Sometimes a man is struck down dead without himself or any one near hearing the report of the gun that sent the fatal bullet. Such is war as now conducted."[21] A staff officer in the First Corps described a freak incident in mid-July that underscored the essentially random nature of life in the Petersburg trenches in 1864. "The sharp shooting on both sides is murderously active and accurate," he wrote. "Yesterday, a Capt. Jones, 17th Georgia, and a private of 2nd Georgia were passing each other in the narrow covered way of the main trenches. Each raised his head a little too high, and a ball passed through the brain of each."[22]

A moment of inattention could easily be a soldier's last. "Most of our men have been killed & wounded by carelessness on their part," a Georgia staff officer stated.[23] Bushrod Johnson, one of Beauregard's division commanders, made daily reports that included the latest information on Confederate and Federal activity along the lines and listed casualties in his division in the last twenty-four hours. As the siege continued into July and his four brigades lost about five to thirty men killed and wounded every day, Johnson began noting when those casualties were soldiers killed or wounded by their own carelessness. Of the five members of Brig. Gen. Archibald Gracie's Alabama Brigade wounded on 15 July, for example, four were "shot by carelessly exposing their persons" above the parapet of the trenches.[24]

Many of Lee's officers and men believed that conditions at Petersburg helped create an usually high proportion of deaths to wounds, and that an equally high proportion of those killed and wounded were shot in the head. "The Yankees keep balls continuously flying over our heads, and no man can expose his head a minute above the breastworks without being struck, and most probably killed," one South Carolina lieutenant noted in his diary.[25] Brig. Gen. James P. Simms, commanding a Georgia brigade in the First Corps, corroborated this observation in his official report of operations in June and July. "The number of casualties occurring in the brigade at this place will give some idea of the difficulties which had to be contended against," Simms reported. "There were 15 killed and 31 wounded, most of which proved fatal."[26] One of the casualties in Simms's Brigade was Pvt. Alexander Parker, of the 53d Georgia, who died four days after being wounded in the head. "Sanda died last Sunday I was with him when he died," Lt. John B. Evans of Parker's company wrote his wife. "You can tell his wife if you see her soon that he was woun[d]ed on the 22 of June, he was shot in the back part of the head . . . Sanda was in his right mind untell about six or eight hours before he died."[27]

Most members of the army soon learned to respect, if not quite fear, what one officer called the "cowardly rascals," and many spent a great deal of their time, energy, and ammunition returning the Federals' fire.[28] An Alabama private told his family, "I cant write much about the war our men & the yanks are lying in thir ditches shooting at one another all the time." After admitting, "Thay kill & wound more or less of our men all the time," Timothy Morgan continued, "I mean we hurt som of them for our boys does thir best if a yank shows his head thay shoot at him."[29] Some soldiers in either army, using rifles with telescopic sights, could "pick off a man at the distance of nearly a mile," according to a North Carolina staff officer. "Their aim is most deadly."[30] But in some units, the relative scarcity of ammunition prevented many Confederates from engaging in duels with their enemy counterparts. "The losses and annoyance which the enemy occasion in my lines are simply due, in my opinion, to a want of proper ammunition," Bushrod Johnson stated in one of his daily reports. Johnson, proposing that the government should make extraordinary efforts to supply his division—and the rest of the army—with ammunition, warned, "Whilst we husband our ammunition and the enemy are thinning our ranks with comparative impunity—our men being compelled simply to suffer and endure—a moral effect is being produced which may prove very detrimental to our future success."[31] Spending day after day, week after week, and month after month in the trenches and under steady fire would indeed have a lasting negative impact on the Army of Northern Virginia.

Other Confederates found ways to test the enemy sharpshooters without firing at them. Capt. Benjamin Wesley Justice described how North Carolinians in Brig. Gen. William MacRae's Brigade occasionally amused themselves. "Some of our men place an old hat on a ramrod & elevate it just enough for the yankees to see it," he observed, "& then coolly count the shots that hit or miss it."[32] One private who watched others tempt fate this way but would not do it himself was William Thomas Casey of the 34th Virginia, in Brig. Gen. Henry A. Wise's Brigade. Casey, expressing what many others in the army must have thought that summer, wrote his brother, "The Yankee sharpshooters are so good on a man's head that I am afraid to raise my head above the ditches, &c."[33]

Though most casualties occurred in the earthworks, soldiers to the rear were often wounded, either by Federal design or by bullets or shells that missed their intended targets. "I am not loosing many men, but some are killed & wounded almost every day," Maj. William Sammons Grady of the 25th North Carolina informed his wife in early July. "George Wright was shot dead a day or two ago, he was in the rear of the intrenchments picking Blackberries and a stray ball [hit] him he was found dead." A few days later, interrupted in midsentence by the explosion of a nearby shell, Grady wrote, "Just this moment a Shell fell in the ditch about 20 yards to my feet & fortunately only wounded two men." He explained: "I allow one Company at a time to go out and bathe in the river during the day and it so happened that the shell fell where the Company was gone from so there was only a few men where it fell if the Company had all been in it would have hurt several of them."[34]

One result of all of these casualties—particularly the deaths, whether intentionally or unintentionally inflicted—was that many officers and men began to reflect on their own, and others', behavior when faced with the loss of their fellow soldiers. Some observers feared that Lee's troops were steadily becoming accustomed to this impersonal kind of death in the

Capt. Benjamin Wesley Justice, commissary, MacRae's Brigade. Justice served first as a lieutenant in the 47th North Carolina, then as regimental commissary, and finally as commissary of Kirkland's (later MacRae's) Brigade in the Third Corps; he surrendered at Appomattox. (Special Collections, Robert W. Woodruff Library, Emory University)

trenches and that they paid little attention when one more man was killed. "Even the death of [a] soldier is looked on as one of those inevitable results of War," Grady remarked, "and a man drops out of the ranks and is scarsly spoken of, after a few moments. I hear men talking laughing & singing when two were killed an hour ago and they appear as unconcerned as if nothing had happened." He and many of his fellow Confederates wondered if they saw "so much of Blood and death that our sensibilities become hardened that we can hardly be said to act & feel like Men."[35]

Others, perhaps the majority, believed that the army felt these deaths more keenly than those that occurred in full-scale battles or even skirmishes, where one at least died in combat. Brig. Gen. John Bratton, commanding a brigade in the First Corps, voiced that view in an official report that counted fifty-three men killed outright and seventy-two wounded, many of them mortally wounded. "Our daily loss was small," he commented, "but the sum total for the month, particularly when the nature of the wounds is considered (unusual proportion fatal), loomed up heavily, ay, and sadly." Bratton, in an eloquent tribute to his South Carolinians and to the rest of Lee's troops killed during the first few weeks of the siege of Petersburg, continued: "Many of my noblest veterans, whose kindling eyes had flashed out their staunch hearts' enthusiasm on so many glorious fields of battle, were stricken from our rolls, as it were, by the stealthy hand of the assassin. There is the chill of murder about the casualties of this month, and sad, sad is the regret when death thus strikes the brave."[36]

Several members of the army echoed Bratton's characterization of the Federals as "assassins." Some indignant Confederates complained that it was cowardly to wage war against anonymous soldiers; they were even more outraged when writing about the civilians killed, wounded, or driven out of their homes by the "vandels" or "vile Yankees" who periodically shelled the city with field artillery and mortars.[37] "Every day some shell are thrown into Petersburg by the relentless Yankees imperiling the lives of the women & children," a Texas sergeant noted. "Such is Yankee warfare."[38] A few men thought that the bombardment produced more noise than actual injury or damage, such as the South Carolina surgeon who claimed, probably with some exaggeration, "I would often see young ladies sitting on their porches reading quietly while shells were occasionally bursting near by."[39]

Frustrated at their inability to answer such sharpshooting and shelling in any meaningful way, Lee's officers and men were even more disappointed on the few occasions when significant numbers of them were ordered forward against the Federals. In late June and again in late July, what seemed to be excellent opportunities to break or at least temporarily disrupt the siege were thwarted by imprecise plans, by a lack of communication and coordination among officers, and by the performance of the troops. On 22 June, for example, Lee sent two divisions of the Third Corps and one division of Beauregard's force to exploit a gap left in Grant's lines by the movement of Federal infantry attempting to cut the Weldon Railroad. The assault was initially successful, surprising the Federals, driving them from their first line of earthworks, and capturing some 1,600 prisoners. When the enemy recaptured their lines the next day, however, the Confederates were forced to withdraw.[40] Though their offensive had forced Grant to temporarily suspend his operations against the railroad, Lee's men were well aware that they might have achieved much more than they did. Writing to his father in Alabama, a member of Mahone's Division accurately called the first day's fight "a very brilliant one" but admitted a few lines later, "our general situation remains unchanged from day to day."[41]

Another attempt at cooperation between a division of the First Corps and another division of Beauregard's, which took place on 24 June, was much less successful. The advance cost the attacking force moderate casualties, most of them prisoners, and was easily repulsed. Its chief result was a series of unpleasant recriminations in which officers and units blamed each other for the failure.[42] A Texas private whose division participated thought that the affair meant "lives sacrificed and nothing gained," and a South Carolina sergeant whose brigade suffered most of the casualties commented, "our men charged splendidly, & if the supports had come up, would have succeeded."[43] Some veterans, expecting better results from the army, hinted—or explicitly claimed—that some of Lee's generals had failed him, and that the quality of Beauregard's officers and men was particularly suspect. "The only cause I can assign is the incompetency of Generals," one staff officer remarked. "The truth is the 'Stonewalls' are nearly all dead, and a host of Generals now in this Army are wofully incompetent."[44] Lee, who had witnessed the fight, observed ruefully, "There seems to have been some misunderstanding as to the part each division was expected to have performed."[45]

An engagement on 27 and 28 July near Deep Bottom ended with results similar to those of the action on the Weldon Railroad in late June. This fight, in which a division of the First Corps, two divisions of the Third Corps, and elements of Ewell's Department of Richmond participated, was characterized by attacks and counterattacks of Federal cavalry and Lee's infantry. Though the Confederates blunted the enemy offensive and achieved some progress on the first day, they neglected to establish a unified command and were driven from the field in confusion on 28 July.[46] The field officers in one North Carolina brigade, for instance, explained their troops' conduct in their official reports with such comments as "my Regiment had to fall back under a most galling fire," "my lines were so short as to compel me to fall back," or "it became necessary to retreat in order to prevent their cutting us off & capturing us."[47] But the view from the ranks was quite different. "The[y] flank us an cross fired on us and runn us back threw the terable Swamp," Pvt. Augustin E. Shore of the 33d North Carolina wrote his brother and sister a few days later. "Colonel Cowens [Col. Robert V. Cowan, commanding Brig. Gen. James H. Lane's Brigade in Lane's absence] don sum of his big Swaring because the Regt was scattered so . . . we had our asses whip off us if the truth was knone."[48]

Lee attempted other maneuvers to gain some sort of advantage over the Army of the Potomac that summer. On the early evening of 8 July, for example, as a result of "Gen. Lee wishing to find out something," Charles Field's Division of the First Corps, with the assistance of the corps artillery, was ordered to make a large-scale demonstration along its lines in an effort to gauge the Federal strength in their immediate front. "At 5 o'clock there was considerable excitement on our line—heavy canonading musketry & cheers—the object of this we can't imagine," a corporal in the 20th Georgia noted in his diary.[49] Pvt. Thomas McCarty of the Texas Brigade described the scene in greater detail in his own diary. "Our men began cheering and yelling on our left which passed down the line, no one knew what the yelling was about, but everybody yelled like wild Indians. The Yankees answered by tremendous discharges of artillery, & musketry, which was returned by our batteries, and men, and *pandemonium reigned*, for sometime finally everything got quiet, & resumed its former way— 'What was it about?' "[50] The next day John Bratton wrote his wife that the demonstration "created quite a commotion in the Yankie line, and quite a cannonade which will doubtless be reported in the newspaper as a mysterious affair if reported at all."[51] The First Corps diary, kept as a brief record of the campaign, simply called it "something of a Chinese demonstration in the way of shooting and artillery firing to ascertain the enemys' strength."[52]

Most units in the Army of Northern Virginia, however, did not even have these opportunities to face the enemy outside the confines of the siege but remained in or near their trenches throughout June and July. A rotation system of sorts was devised, in which units spent a specified period on the lines—usually a few days—and then moved to the rear for a day or two before being rotated back into the works. Units in the trenches often kept part—usually one-third—of their strength awake and on guard at all times. Details to construct new earthworks, or to improve or repair existing ones, were also formed and maintained, often working through the day and well into the night. Soldiers built several types of improvements to their defensive works. These included traverses, or short trenches perpendicular to the main lines, intended to protect against enemy fire sweeping down the length of the trenches; bombproofs, generally made out of earth with log or plank roofs or doors, for protection against mortar shells; and covered ways or deep trenches designed to allow men to walk upright, sometimes with blankets stretched over them to provide relief from the sun. Infantry soldiers were also occasionally detailed to construct works for field artillery or mortar batteries to support their own works.[53] "We work day & night on our works making them better, safer, & stronger," reported a North Carolina major. "The work is done by details 35 or 40 working at a time, the ballance of the regt lay in trenches ready to meet the enemy if they should attack us."[54]

Because this labor was often done under enemy musketry and artillery fire, and always with less-than-adequate tools, it was little wonder that one noncommissioned officer noted, after his company worked through the night to build a covered way, that "there was considerable grumbling among the men."[55] Even so, most officers and men greatly appreciated the protection these lines afforded them. "The works are quite formidable on both sides and constantly improved—in so much so that both sides are afraid to attack," one Georgia staff officer wrote.[56] An officer in the Third Corps claimed that the men in his brigade were "willing to fight the yankees day after day, if the yankees will only come up & assault our breastworks."[57]

Lee encouraged his soldiers to improve their lines, not only for military purposes but also for their personal comfort, writing one of his corps commanders to that effect and reminding him that he wanted a report of progress "in constructing covered ways and other conveniences for the comfort and health of the men, &c."[58] A Texan in the First Corps referred to Lee's instructions in a letter to his uncle, describing conditions at Petersburg in words that would prove to be more accurate than he knew. "We are fixing up here though as if we intended to remain a life time," observed Sgt. Maj. J. Mark Smither of the 5th Texas. "Genl Lee has issued a circular to the Division Commanders ordering them to do everything here to their works and camps that will be conducive to the health and comfort of their commands, that we were liable to remain here a long time."[59] One officer explained to his wife that he and his men were "confined to the trenches in the broiling sun, which sounds terrible, doubtless, to you, but you would be amazed to see the little contrivances for comfort that we get up."[60]

One of the most common "little contrivances" was an improvised shelter, designed not so much for protection from the sharpshooters and shells as for protection from the sun. These shelters were sometimes made of earth and logs or planks but were more often much simpler. "By the ingenious disposition of blankets ramrods and muskets," Stephen Elliott wrote, describing the standard practice in his South Carolina brigade, and in many other brigades as well, "a tolerable amount of shade is obtained."[61] Though officers usually had advantages over their troops—Elliott himself admitted, "we are not much incommoded by the heat personally [but] the men have a harder time in the trenches"—any amount of shade at all was welcome. For most men in the ranks, who worked day and night extending and improving the lines, spent their time sharpshooting, or stood guard against enemy attacks, shelter from the heat was a necessity rather than a luxury. "The men suffer a great deal in the trenches," Lee told his wife in late June, "& this condition of things with the extreme heat of the sun nearly puts an end to military operations."[62]

When a sergeant in the 56th North Carolina complained, "it is so Dry & hot I cant hardly live," he was only confirming Lee's assessment in more simple terms.[63] Heat—dry, oppressive, stifling heat—was one of the defining elements of life in the trenches at Petersburg in the summer of 1864. Correspondents and diarists, even those who usually did not mention the weather, often referred to the high temperatures and the severe drought in the area. "The weather is exceedingly dry and hot, have not had a drop of rain for more than a month," 2d Lt. E. Harleston Barton of the 2d South Carolina Rifles wrote a friend in early July. "It seems to me that the soldiers can't stand it much longer."[64] One Texan reported that his regiment was "all in fine health tho the hot rays of a July sun pouring down on us in the fortifications has melted us down to not much more than greasy spot[s]."[65] Some members of the army, evidently repeating what local citizens had told them, wrote that June and July were the hottest and driest months in memory in that part of Virginia. They reported "*No rain yet* now in six weeks" or commented, "we have had no rain in two months, and the dust is stifling," or described crops in terms such as "every thing is parched up worse than thay are at home" and "corn looks like it will die as well as a great many other things."[66] Lt. John Hampden Chamberlayne of the 13th Battalion Virginia Artillery, in a short note to his sister, declared, "I would like to have some news—There is none here—Heat & drouth are all worth mentioning and that is no news."[67]

When badly needed rain finally fell on 19 July, many relieved Confederates reported the end of the drought. "Rained nearly all day which is badly needed," a member of the 1st Texas wrote in his diary, and Pvt. James Reynolds of the 16th Georgia exulted, "Thick clouds and a beautiful shower of rain falling upon this fertile vacinity how happy vegitation appears oh well soon have something good to eat I hope."[68] Lee's soldiers, of course, were equally pleased to have their own relief, even temporary relief, from the heat. Reynolds's fellow Georgian Benjamin Simms, whose brother commanded a brigade in the First Corps, spoke for many when he wrote cheerfully, "I feel very much refreshed today as it is the first rain we have had for two months and probably a longer period. The dust was excessively annoying."[69]

Soldiers being soldiers, however, it did not take long before some members of the army began to complain about living in water and mud instead of heat and dust. Within a few days, the same member of the Texas Brigade who had welcomed the "badly needed" rain said that he was "unable to sleep on account of the Slush & mud & soaked condition of ground in mud about trenches 'all suffered much.'"[70] "It has been raining now for two days and the trenches are nearly knee deep in mud," the adjutant of the 24th North Carolina wrote, reflecting that wet and miserable men, weary of the war, might well vote for the peace candidate in their upcoming election for governor.[71] By 25 July Capt. Frank Coker, adjutant of a Georgia artillery battalion, noted, "We had another rain last night, mixed with a storm, blowing and the rain dashing all night." Though Coker was "perfectly dry and comfortable" in his tent, he acknowledged that "many a poor fellow was drenched to the skin."[72]

One enterprising officer used the wet weather as an excuse to propose a fanciful scheme in which one thousand Confederates would cut down trees and lash them together to form a giant raft, which they would launch on the James River. If the freshets persisted and the river continued to rise, Bushrod Johnson argued, such a raft might "sweep the Yankee fleet out into the Atlantic Ocean, and leave Grant's army without pontoons, communications, or base of supplies . . . no Yankee power or ingenuity could withstand the crushing power of this raft, hurled down the stream by the accumulated torrents of the river." Beauregard, in spite of his own weakness for grandiose plans, did not dignify his division commander's ludicrous suggestion with a reply.[73]

Whether working on the trenches or manning them, whether in drought or downpour, officers and men alike throughout the army now seemed much more susceptible to exhaustion and disease at Petersburg than they had been in May and early June. A sergeant in the Palmetto Sharpshooters, returning to his regiment after spending several weeks in South Carolina on a wounded furlough, "found all the boys as well as could be expected considering the fategues and hardship thay have undergone yet thay are Looking Quiet thin and Much worn out from lying constantly in the ditches."[74] The sergeant's brigade commander asserted a few months later, in his official report of operations in July 1864, that "the fire upon us here was incessant night and day, and the labor of completing the works, added to the heavy guard-duty necessitated by the close proximity of the lines at this point, rendered this probably the severest tour of duty that my men have been subjected to during the war."[75] A Georgia lieutenant, giving his wife the latest news about his regiment in early July, noted, "our boys are very near run down at this time."[76]

As Lee's soldiers could hardly be expected to work or fight indefinitely under these conditions, they were periodically given a brief break from the trenches. Such breaks, even if only for a day or two, were often enough to revive the troops and make them more fit for duty. Numerous observers, such as Lt. Col. Theodore Gaillard Trimmier, thought that a lack of rest was the single major problem among officers and men. "I have come out to the wagons to wash up and get clean clothes today," he noted in early July. "I feel well, but somewhat fatigued and need rest."[77] Pvt. James Lee of the 43d Alabama—the regiment Trimmier was temporarily commanding— agreed with the lieutenant colonel. "We have been lying in the rifle pitts for ten or twelve days," Lee wrote his wife on 7 July. "We have been out here one day. we came out to wash. I judge we will go back to the ditches again in a day or so."[78] A South Carolina captain in the quartermaster's department noted that troops in his division received an opportunity "about two days in each week to refresh themselves a little with clean clothes, a stroll into the city &c."[79]

Other officers believed that there were close ties between the widespread fatigue and the illnesses prevalent in the Army of Northern Virginia that summer. Maj. Gen. Robert Hoke's Division, for example, was so weakened by hard duty and disease that he questioned its efficiency. Hoke's Georgians, North Carolinians, and South Carolinians had indeed been active since May, coming to Virginia from Charleston, fighting at Port Walthall and Drewry's Bluff under Beauregard, at Cold Harbor under Lee, and back under Beauregard at Petersburg. "My command is daily becoming much reduced from sickness which can be prevented by rest," Hoke wrote on 27 June, forwarding a report from one of his brigadiers and requesting permission to have one brigade in reserve at all times.[80] One of Hoke's noncommissioned officers, a sergeant in Johnson Hagood's South Carolina Brigade, substantiated his division commander's concerns when he described the pitiful condition of his company the next day. "I have only thirteen privates, & three non commissioned officers for duty to day," 1st

Sgt. Henry I'on Greer of the 25th South Carolina wrote his father. The twenty-three year-old Greer, who had been commended "for gallant conduct" at Drewry's Bluff and now commanded his company in the absence of any commissioned officers, continued: "Diarrhoea, & dysentery & hard work have used up the men terribly, & a sick man gets little or no attention here, & the food, dry corn Bread & Bacon does not help them. . . . one can hardly help wishing to get sick enough to go to the rear, so as to get a little rest."[81] A few days later, "sick enough" himself, Greer got his wish and spent a week in the brigade hospital. On returning to his company, he wrote home, "The rest I had while there was of great service to me & I hope that I will now be able to stand it without going to the rear again."[82]

Soldiers who were already "used up," as Greer put it, were unquestionably vulnerable to illness, and even more so when expected to live on the poor rations and even poorer water available to many of them at Petersburg. "I am afraid we are going to have a good deal of sickness this summer," Samuel Lockhart of the 27th North Carolina informed his sister. "The men are looking very badly and a good deal complaining. . . . We don't get anything to eat but bread and meat and coffee and peas; just one thing all the time. The Dr. says that is what makes the men sick so much."[83] A shortage of fresh fruits and vegetables produced numerous outbreaks of scurvy, while poorly maintained sinks and unsanitary wells contributed to widespread diarrhea and dysentery. One Georgia private wrote his mother, "We air not getting but verry Little to eate at this time it is all we can do to make out on Just Enough to keep sole and Boddy to gether."[84] In a letter to a friend, a North Carolinian remarked, "I can inform you that our fare is quite common. [W]e dont get but little, and that little is very common. . . . to tell the truth we are liveing hard."[85]

Other Confederates believed that most of Lee's troops were in good health and acknowledged that their rations were improving somewhat but still wanted greater quantities and more variety from their commissary officers. Those officers, attempting to feed an army spread out along the defenses around Petersburg, established cooking details that prepared rations behind the lines every day and carried them up to the men in the trenches.[86] Though this practice ensured an equitable share for each soldier, it hindered an individual's ability to enjoy foraging for whatever food he could find. "We can't get anything to eat only what we draw," Pvt. William Leak of the 22d South Carolina complained in mid-July. "We can't get vegetables of any description. Our rations are one pound of meal and one fourth pound of bacon a day." Leak, who reported, "I get about a tin cupful of peas cooked every other day," observed wistfully, "I just believe that I could eat as much more as I get and then not have enough."[87] Another member of Leak's brigade, a lieutenant in the 17th South Carolina, was "Living on corn bread and bacon, with cow peas occasionally" and thought that his regiment "Will not be apt to get anything better this summer."[88]

Numerous members of the army, whether anxious to ward off diseases or simply seeking to add some variety to their diets, bought food from enterprising civilians in the area. These vendors, most of them women and many of them slaves or free blacks, often came out to the lines carrying baskets of food—usually produce, some type of fruit or meat pies, or soups and stews—for which they charged exorbitant prices. Though the soldiers complained at both the cost and the poor quality, many bought what they could instead of settling for what the commissaries offered. A North Carolina private, reporting to his wife that he paid two dollars for a pint of potatoes, commented, "we get a plenty to eat such as it is but my dear you no that we get tired of bread and meat all the time."[89] Some men, such as Sgt. Daniel Boyd of the 7th South Carolina, refused to buy the civilians' wares. Boyd, whose regiment was paid in early July for the first time in more than two months, was happy enough to receive his pay and clothing allowance—nearly two hundred dollars—but was much less pleased at the prospect of spending it on food at such high prices. "Every thing is very high hear," Boyd noted, listing prices such as "flour 2 to 3 dollars a pound corn meal 2 dollars a quart Bacon 8 dollars per pound peas 2.50 a quart Beans 21 dollars a quart." Even pies sold for fifty cents each, and a drink of whiskey cost a thirsty soldier three dollars. Deciding that he would do without any luxuries, Boyd assured his father, "We are faring tolerble Well for Somthing to eat We get corn meal Bacon coffee Shugar peas rice som times."[90] Brig. Gen. John C. C. Sanders, commanding an Alabama brigade in William Mahone's Division of the Third Corps, bought some blackberry dumplings that were "better than we expected but not so good as they might be." Though the pies were "not of the best quality," Sanders remarked, "I see no prospect of starving as long as pies continue to be vended in the public streets."[91]

In spite of fatigue, illness, and poor, scanty, or expensive rations, most men in the Army of Northern Virginia did their best to adjust to life under siege. Many of them took advantage of their long stay near Petersburg and attended worship services at the city's various churches when possible or participated in services or prayer meetings in camp, often conducted by the town's ministers or by their own chaplains. Some Confederates went into town on Sunday mornings for a service and attended another in the evening in camp or in the trenches. Chaplain John Cowper Granbery, a Methodist minister who had served as chaplain of the 11th Virginia before becoming a missionary to the Third Corps, conducted three services in the corps one Sunday in late June. The first, in a North Carolina brigade, had no sooner begun with hymns and a prayer than the brigade was ordered to move. Unwilling to have his service canceled, Granbery marched a mile and a half with the brigade and resumed worship "so soon as the men were settled in their new position." He then went out to the trenches, where he preached to a Virginia brigade in one division later that morning and a North Carolina brigade in another division in the evening. Granbery's hard work was appreciated by a member of the latter brigade, who approached him after his sermon and gave him "a little bag of coffee, saying he had nothing else to offer and that he wished to give me some proof of his regard for my sermon."[92]

Several high-ranking officers, including the commanding general, also participated in religious services when possible. On 10 July, for example, Lee invited Rev. William H. Platt of St. Paul's Episcopal Church to hold an open-air service at his headquarters. Platt, whose church was one of several that had been forced to suspend services due to the frequent Federal bombardments of the city, preached what James Albright called a "very fine" sermon to an audience of officers, soldiers, and civilians. Albright, an ordnance sergeant in a Virginia artillery battalion, described the service in his diary, recording his impressions of Lee "humbly kneeling on the ground among the sunburnt soldiers of his army, & joining in the impressive ceremony of the day. . . . I shall never forget this sermon, nor the men who participated—so calmly, even within the range of the enemies guns."[93] On the same Sunday morning, unable to attend the service at Lee's headquarters or to go to a church in Petersburg, one Georgian wrote, "Tolerably pleasant Sabbath morning but alas far from home cannot visit any Sabbath School no Church as once was the case but only live as a soldier as has been the case for a long while past."[94]

Many correspondents and diarists, whether or not they attended worship services and prayer meetings, frequently mentioned their faith in God and His master plan for them, for the army, and for the Confederate people. "With brave hearts and trusting in God, we have only to persevere and the time is not far distant when days of fighting will be past and the much longed for peace will dawn upon our suffering land," a North Carolina private wrote in late June.[95] As the siege wore on day after day, and as events in other theaters also seemed to resolve nothing, some Confederates wondered just when that peace might come. Sgt. Calvin Conner, who had "thought Some time ago that the presant campaign would perhapse close the war," now believed that the Northern presidential election of 1864 would play a critical role in determining both the war's duration and its outcome. "If thay Succeed in electing a peace man I do not think the war will Last Long but Should thay elect a war candidate God alone knows when we will have peace," Conner observed, "but we must trust the issue to God alone and he will in his own good time bring it about when he thinks we are prepared for it."[96]

Some members of the army, anxious to do what they could to achieve peace on a day-to-day basis in their immediate vicinities, suspended hostilities with the Federals for brief periods, either by mutual consent or by informal truces. Pickets, skirmishers, and sharpshooters, whose duties placed them well in front of their own trenches and put them in frequent contact with their enemy counterparts performing the same duties, saw little reason for individual soldiers to shoot at each other day after day. Confederates and Federals often made agreements not to fire on each other unless an advance or general engagement was imminent and frequently met between the lines to trade newspapers, tobacco, coffee, or other items. An Alabama lieutenant, in a letter headed "Picket line near Petersburg," wrote his wife, "I am now in full view of Yankees. We are not shooting at each other. Papers are exchanged here daily."[97] On 10 July Sgt. Marion Hill Fitzpatrick of the 45th Georgia, whose detachment of skirmishers had been in advance of the Confederate lines for almost two weeks, noted: "The Yankee skirmish line is a short distance from us in full view. By mutual agreement, we do not fire at each other, there being no use of it unless an advance is made." Fitzpatrick then described the fraternization between his men and the Federals in some detail:

> They are quite friendly with us. We meet them everyday nearly and exchange papers. Only one or two go at a time, and they meet half way. We have traded with them some, too, but it is against orders, and it got to be so common that they have put very strict orders against it. . . . But occasionally some of the boys run the blockage and trade with them yet. Our boys give them tobacco and cornbread for crackers, knives, soap, pockette books, &c. I gave one of them the other day a plug of tobacco for a pockette knife and six crackers.

Evidently satisfied with his situation, Fitzpatrick commented, "They do not relieve us atall now, and we stay here all the time. I had much rather stay here than back at the Regt." A few days later he wrote his wife: "We are not so friendly with the Yanks now. All communications, trading, &c. is stopped except an occasional exchange of papers by the officers. There is still no firing between us, and I hope will not [be] till an advance is made."[98] Though Lee's officers were unable to keep their men from fraternizing with the enemy, they continued to oppose the practice, fearing with good reason that some soldiers might be tempted, or enticed, to desert. A member of the 8th Alabama, for example, approached the enemy's pickets one evening in July to exchange newspapers and trade with the Federals, fully intending to go back to the Confederate lines. Yet the Alabamian changed his mind and deserted after the Federals assured him that he would be treated kindly.[99]

Desertions, most often to the safety of the Federal lines, increased noticeably—even dramatically—during July, as weary veterans and recent conscripts alike saw little to inspire them and much to discourage them about their lives in the trenches. "There have been more desertions of late than ever before," Charles Minor Blackford remarked on 17 July. "The hard lives they lead and a certain degree of hopelessness which is stealing over the conviction of the best and bravest will have some effect in inducing demoralization hitherto unknown."[100] Though many deserters believed that the Confederacy could not win the war, just as many deserted because they were simply tired of the army, no matter which side finally won. Some were probably influenced by a Federal order assuring them that they would not be kept in prison or forced into U.S. service to fight against the Confederacy if they took the oath of allegiance.[101] Among the reasons deserters gave to Federal officers who interviewed them were that they were "tired of the war" or that "The men are getting weary of life in the trenches, and are complaining considerably of late."[102] Several of them talked freely about conditions in the Army of Northern Virginia, describing their units and the mood of the soldiers in them. Three men from the 48th Mississippi, for example, reported that their regiment had only 150 arms-bearing men and that their brigade was reduced to some 675 troops.[103] Numerous deserters had just been conscripted or had served with the army a short time and saw no reason to remain in the trenches any longer. For instance, ten soldiers from the 64th Georgia who deserted to the Federals over a three-day period told their interviewers that "their regiment was considerably demoralized" and that "Many of them would desert if they dared to. They are nearly all conscripts, and were forced into the army against their will."[104] Some North Carolinians claimed that they deserted because they were not allowed to vote. In a special election held in the army a few weeks before the general election, incumbent Gov. Zebulon B. Vance soundly defeated his opponent, newspaper editor and peace candidate William W. Holden, by a margin of about five to one. Veterans from North Carolina regiments in the Army of Northern Virginia and in Beauregard's command told Federals that Vance supporters in the army prevented them from casting their votes for Holden and that "in very few cases, and those depended on the character of officers, were any allowed to vote who did not vote for Vance."[105]

Many men who remained in the army that summer and did not take the drastic step of desertion found other ways to avoid doing their duty. Some of them hoped for, and some deliberately sought, slight wounds that would give them furloughs. Pvt. John A. Everett of the 11th Georgia, reporting that a member of his company "got shot through the hand the other knight," commented, "it is thought by the Company that he did it a-Purpose if he did it ought to of bin his head instid of his hand."[106] Others faked physical or mental illness to escape their responsibilities. A Third Corps chaplain described one soldier who "feigned madness" when interrogated by the provost marshal, answering most questions with the comment, "I don't know," but who remembered that he belonged to the 6th North Carolina "after a severe pumping" by the authorities.[107]

Poor discipline, which had always presented a problem in the Confederate army, was rapidly becoming a serious weakness in some units of the Army of Northern Virginia by the summer of 1864. Many regiments and companies, already understrength, had lost their officers to death, wounds, capture, illness, or retirement and were being commanded by officers or noncommissioned officers with little or no experience. "You'd scarcely know the old brigade and I fear the next fight will show that it is badly demoralized," Adjt. O. D. Cooke of the 24th North Carolina wrote his colonel, who was at home recovering from a wound received at Drewry's Bluff. "I wish I could get out of it."[108] Stephen Elliott's South Carolina brigade was in little better condition. "I think that the discipline of the Brigade has improved decidedly since I took it," he observed, "but it has to be drilled freely yet before the men will get into the way of listening to their officers voices as I wish them to and as they *must* do."[109]

Most of Lee's troops, with or without good officers, responded to the frustrations of the siege in less dramatic ways than desertion or faking injuries or illnesses. They often complained about, or just as frequently joked about, their own and their fellow soldiers' troubles. In spite of everything, however, numerous Confederates managed to retain their keen

Pvt. Joseph Fauber Shaner, Rockbridge Artillery. Shaner served as a private in
Virginia's famous Rockbridge Artillery from just after First Manassas until he
was wounded at Fredericksburg in December 1862 and again until he
surrendered at Appomattox. (Joseph C. Shaner)

sense of humor. In mid-July, for example, Lt. John Evans and several members of the "Jeff Davis Riflemen"—Company I of the 53d Georgia—sat in their camp "on Peckerwood Creek near Petersburg" and talked about the war. Evans asked his wife Mollie to tell Betty Thaxton that her husband Jim was well, but that Thaxton said that "he be blamed if he fights any more if they dont feed him better." Perhaps to reassure Mrs. Thaxton, Evans added, "but I can say for Jim he is as good a soldier as we have in our Regt." He also mentioned receiving a letter from Charles Foster, who had been absent from the company for some time and was sick in Richmond with the fever. "I was at the Regt when I recived the letter," Evans reported, "and some of the boys said that they bedamed if he dident have the fever as long as this war lasted."[110] According to Samuel Lockhart of the 27th North Carolina, if his sister "were to see our Company all together, you would say they were the toughest looking set you ever saw in your life: I think the girls would most disown their sweethearts if they could see them now." Dave Parks, the commissary sergeant of the regiment, while watching Lockhart write to his sister, asked him to "please tell her something for me" in his letter. Lockhart described a dream that Parks claimed to have had, in which he "got Mr. Grant around the neck . . . and all at once he got Grant on his horse and jumped up behind him and put spurs to the horse and brought him clear through our lines and never was halted at all, and he said he thought he was doing mightily to be a commissary Sgt. and capture old Grant in such a funny manner."[111]

Numerous members of the army, well aware that they sat in their trenches around Petersburg to prevent the Federals from capturing the city and forcing their way to Richmond, still believed that keeping Grant at bay was not the same thing as defeating him, and that they would much rather be fighting than waiting. But they also thought that the stalemate could not last forever and that something would soon force the Federal commander to make a move. James Farrow, a South Carolina civilian who visited friends in two brigades from his home state in late July, said that "the men of both were in fine spirits & confident of their ability to do whatever Gen. Lee would order to be done." Farrow's friends told him that they were "ready to pitch into 'Mr.' Grant whenever 'Marse Bob' gave the word."[112] "The Yankees have not gained an inch the advantage above Petersburg," a captain in the 5th Texas maintained, "and it is thought that Grant is only waiting a favorable opportunity to leave that vacinity honorably when he will withdraw to his own soil and give up the capture of Richmond as something impossible of accomplishment."[113] Lt. Col. William J. Pegram undoubtedly expressed the mood of many Confederates when he wrote his sister, "I would like to have this kind of warfare broken up, and get to field fighting once more. . . . I believe that such is the wish of every thinking man in the army."[114]

Excitement and speculation within the army grew considerably throughout July, though not nearly so much over its own operations as over those of Confederate armies in Maryland and Georgia. In the first half of the month Lee's troops filled their letters and diaries with rumors about the Army of the Valley's supposed exploits in Maryland, most of them involving the much-hoped-for capture of Washington. After Jubal Early's return to Virginia, however, most correspondents and diarists were more concerned with the Army of Tennessee's campaign in Georgia, particularly the removal of Gen. Joseph E. Johnston and his replacement by John B. Hood and the subsequent battles around Atlanta. To many soldiers in the Army of Northern Virginia, both campaigns seemed to be having a greater current impact on the war than the one in which they found themselves at Petersburg. Joseph Pryor Fuller conveyed the overwhelming sense of anticipation felt by so many of Lee's soldiers that month when he noted one afternoon, "Great expectations of a move, but we are puzzled to know in what direction." In the midst of the excitement Fuller dutifully reported, "Some rumors, say that we are going to Johnstons; others to Early," then added, somewhat regretfully, "but the last that came in, says, the enemys' works are to be carried in front of our divis."[115] As it turned out, Fuller's division was denied even that opportunity to contribute when the assault was called off at the last minute.

Expectations for Early's independent campaign, already high, increased dramatically once it was reported that the Army of the Valley had crossed the Potomac into Maryland. "The news from the North is very exciting," Sgt. Edward Crockett of the 4th Texas informed his wife. "Confederate cannon are knocking at the doors of Washington & all Lincolndom is in a great commotion."[116] That "great commotion," which soon spread throughout the Confederacy as well, subsided nearly as quickly when it became apparent that Early's small army could not possibly capture the Federal capital. Many observers, in spite of their disappointment that Baltimore and Washington were still in enemy hands—or still standing— believed that the move had drawn the enemy's attention away from Petersburg and Atlanta and demonstrated that the bold Confederate strategies of 1862 and 1863 were still possible. "Any way he has done much damage," Frank Coker remarked, "wofully scared the Yankees, & if he retires in safety with all his Captures he will have done well."[117] Others, opposed in principle to the idea of Confederate troops invading the North and preferring to wage a primarily defensive war, expressed their apprehensions at Early's operations. Brig. Gen. Stephen Elliott was "very much opposed to this movement into Maryland" and believed that "it will unite feeling at the North and scatters our army. . . . This campaign has been conducted in direct opposition to the principles laid down by military writers."[118] Most members of the Army of Northern Virginia, whatever they thought of Early or the probability that his campaign would improve Confederate fortunes, trusted in their commanding general and agreed with Henry Greer, of the 25th South Carolina, who wrote, "I suppose that Genl Lee knows what he is about."[119]

About the same time that Early was making his way back into Virginia, events in Georgia demonstrated not only the contrast between operations in the Shenandoah Valley and Maryland and operations near Atlanta, but also the more subtle contrast between expectations for the two campaigns. For the most part, Lee's officers and men based their assessments of the latter campaign on personalities. Some members of the Army of Northern Virginia believed that Johnston had skillfully maneuvered the Army of Tennessee from Dalton to the outskirts of Atlanta—fighting at Resaca, New Hope Church, and Kennesaw Mountain while they fought and marched from the Wilderness to Petersburg—and that he might be luring William T. Sherman into a siege similar to the one at Petersburg.[120] But according to many others—perhaps to Georgians more than to the rest—Johnston had given up so much territory and so much of the strategic initiative to the Federals that he could not hope to save Atlanta. "Johnston's army has been taught that falling back is the aim of a campaign and that fighting is an incident," Capt. Charles Minor Blackford observed. "Lee has taught us that an occasional retrograde movement is an incident and fighting is the aim."[121] Sgt. Marion Hill Fitzpatrick of the 45th Georgia wrote simply, "I do not know what to say about the war. . . . The news from Early is highly encouraging while that from Johnson is gloomy."[122] Jefferson Davis, contemplating a change of commanders in the Army of Tennessee, asked Lee for his advice and for his evaluation of Hood. "We may lose Atlanta and the army too," Lee wrote in a telegram. "Hood is a bold fighter. I am doubtful as to other qualities necessary."[123]

When Davis did remove Johnston from command on 18 July and replaced him with Hood, many observers in the Army of Northern Virginia believed that the change would benefit both the Army of Tennessee and the Confederate cause. They often referred to Hood's success as a brigadier and a division commander under Lee to support their views. "I am glad that Johnson has been removed," Stephen Elliott remarked. "He is a brave man personally but he never had done anything but get ready for a fight yet and then retreat. Hood is a fighter." Elliott also reported, none too seriously, "It is rumored here that Johnson was getting pontoons ready to cross over to Cuba and that a change was therefore necessary."[124] In the first few days after Hood succeeded Johnston, optimistic Confederates at Petersburg used such phrases as "Glorious news from Georgia today" or "we feel confident that Richmond is as safe as Washington if *Hood will hold Atlanta*."[125] On 25 July one Georgia artillery officer wrote, "We are in receipt of the news of Hoods beginning of his big fight, and so far it is very favourable—in fact excellent news. . . . I trust that the fight so well began may end in a complete victory for us, and that Sherman may be compelled to leave Confederate soil."[126]

As the month of July came to an end, Lee's soldiers had several different predictions for their own immediate future. Some of them saw no indications that significant fighting would occur along the lines at Petersburg, such as the South Carolina sergeant who noted, "I do not know whither we will have any fighting imediatly on this Line or not but it is the prevailing oppinion amongst the men that the enemy will not attact us here as our Lines are to Strong for them to do so with any hope of Success."[127] Others, such as the assistant adjutant general of a North Carolina brigade in the Third Corps, admitted that though they did not know what might happen, they did not trouble themselves about it. "Nothing seems to startle the imperturbable soldier," Capt. Louis G. Young commented to his mother on 29 July. "A great battle here to-morrow would not surprise me, while I would be signally unmoved by order to leave for Northern Va. & Maryland."[128]

Young's "great battle" did indeed take place the next day. It was initiated by one of the most extraordinary incidents of the entire war, in which the Federals made an ingenious attempt to force the Confederates from their strong defensive position. A detachment of Grant's soldiers had spent almost a month digging a long tunnel to a point underneath an enemy salient, where they planned to set off a mine and literally blast a hole in Lee's lines. An infantry division, specially trained for the task, would then assault what remained of the Confederates in the immediate vicinity and attempt to force its way through to the city itself.

Earlier, some observers in the Army of Northern Virginia, noticing an unusual amount of enemy activity at one particular point along their lines, had suspected that Grant might be digging a mine. Engineers were quickly authorized to dig countermines and listening galleries in an effort to prevent the Federals from completing their work. "We are tunnelling &

Grant is also," Virginia artilleryman James Albright reported in his diary on 20 July, "& some *mines* may be sprung any day, & many souls blown into eternity."[129] A few days later Albright commented, "we are not near enough in our mines to hear the enemies *picks*—still the *springing* of a mine, while it might startle us, would not surprise any one—at any moment."[130]

The Federals' mine, which did a great deal more than startle Lee's soldiers, was detonated at about 4:45 A.M. on 30 July. The fierce fight that followed, known forever after as "the Crater" from the massive hole carved out of the ground by the explosion of four tons of gunpowder, would in time become the best known of all the engagements around Petersburg. An infantry brigade and an artillery battery of Beauregard's command that occupied the salient were virtually destroyed, with most of the dead in those unfortunate units either killed by the blast or buried under a huge mass of earth. As soon as the smoke and dust had cleared somewhat, a Federal division advanced into the gap, which was later estimated to be about 125 feet long, about 50 feet wide, and about 25 feet deep. But the attackers milled around in the crater in confusion instead of bypassing it and were soon joined by reinforcements that repeated their mistake.

After the shocked defenders in the area regrouped and were reinforced by a division of the Third Corps, the Confederates secured their works, counterattacked with infantry and artillery that surrounded the crater, and inflicted appalling casualties on the Federals. Savage hand-to-hand fighting, reminiscent of the scene at Spotsylvania, took place not across log breastworks but in and around a chasm full of debris, of the dead and wounded and of soldiers struggling desperately with each other, in what one participant described as "the dreadfulest seen I ever wittnest."[131] Many of Lee's soldiers, infuriated by the sight of black Federals—the first they had met in combat—shot or bayoneted them as they tried to surrender or after they had already done so. Within a few hours, by early afternoon at the latest, the Confederates had recovered all of the ground lost to Grant's bold attack and forced those Federals who had not been killed or taken prisoner back to their own lines. Grant's casualties numbered some 3,800 killed, wounded, and captured out of an assaulting force of about 16,500 troops; Lee's defenders suffered about 1,500 casualties out of a defending force of about 9,500, with nearly half of that number being lost in the initial explosion by Stephen Elliott's South Carolina brigade and by Capt. Richard G. Pegram's company of Virginia artillery.[132] What had promised to be a significant, perhaps decisive, Federal victory had instead become another frustrating battlefield defeat. By the same token, what had threatened to be a Confederate disaster developed instead into yet another tactical success that had almost no lasting effect on the conduct of the war.

This spectacular battle was, of course, the topic of widespread discussion throughout the Army of Northern Virginia for some time to come. Though remarkably few Confederate units were engaged at the Crater—only one entire division and several brigades of two others, along with various artillery battalions and batteries—there were other factors that contributed to the almost universal interest shown by correspondents and diarists. Among these factors were the sheer novelty of the mine and the chaos created by its explosion; the relative ease with which the Confederate counterattack broke the Federal assault, capturing hundreds of prisoners and nearly a score of enemy flags; and the behavior of black Federals and their white officers, as well as the reaction of Lee's soldiers to such behavior. Most observers in the army would have agreed with the comment of the brigadier who wrote his father a few days later, "Since I last wrote, we have had some excitement and some very heavy fighting."[133]

Accounts of the Crater written by the few survivors in Elliott's Brigade and the other soldiers in Bushrod Johnson's Division, naturally enough, emphasized the surprise that accompanied the sudden explosion of the salient underneath them and the appearance of the Federals in their lines. "Just at sunrise as I had steped up on the step of the breastwork I herd a tremendous dull report and at the same time felt the earth shake beneath me," a sergeant in the 26th Virginia, in Wise's Brigade, observed. "I immediately looked down to our left & to my sorrow I saw an awful scene, which I never witnessed before."[134] Johnson's own official report, written a few weeks after the battle, described "The astonishing effect of the explosion, bursting like a volcano at the feet of the men, and the upheaving of an immense column of more than 100,000 cubic feet of earth to fall around in heavy masses, wounding, crushing, or burying everything within its reach." Johnson commended his troops for their conduct, claiming, "It is believed for each buried companion they have taken a twofold vengeance on the enemy, and have taught them a lesson that will be remembered as long as the history of our wrongs and this great revolution endures."[135] One of those "buried companions" was 2d Sgt. John W. Callahan of the 22d South Carolina. Callahan's friend Daniel Boyd, himself a sergeant in Joseph Kershaw's old brigade of the First Corps, wrote that "J W Calahan Was Kild by the blowing up of our breast Works he was buried wit[h] the dirt. When they found him he was Standing Strait up the ditch their was one hundred kild and buried with the explosion."[136] A captain in the 49th North Carolina, in Brig. Gen. Matt W. Ransom's Brigade, observed, "When the dust and smoke cleared away several of the enemy's flags were floating on our line. They re-enforced rapidly and overwhelmed our men in the trenches on either side of the chasm."[137] Though the blast and the Federal assault essentially wrecked Elliott's Brigade, the other brigades in Johnson's Division retained enough order to mount a stubborn defense until badly needed reinforcements arrived.

Those reinforcements, most notably three brigades of William Mahone's Division of the Third Corps, launched a vicious counterattack that was the focal point of the fighting at the Crater and that rightfully received the lion's share of attention after the battle. Numerous officers and men in these units, particularly Mahone's infantrymen, understandably believed that they had saved the Army of Northern Virginia on 30 July. "Alas many a noble Confederate sealed his devotion to his countries cause with his life in the struggle," commented Robert C. Mabry of the 6th Virginia. Two days later Mabry, who had been on picket duty at the time of the battle, wrote his wife, "it pains me to say that my company was almost entirely swept away; it carried in the Fight Twenty one muskets & three *commissd* officers, came out with two men & one officer. . . . I hear there are only Ten privates left in the entire Regt."[138] A contemporary history of the 48th Georgia called the battle "certainly one of the most sanguinary fights on record," claiming, "Nothing could withstand the desperate valor of our boys."[139]

Lt. Elias Davis of the 10th Alabama remarked to his wife: "Last Saturday (30th of July) is a day that will be long remembered by members of our brigade. . . . Our Brigade is said to have made the grandest charge of the war, capturing three stands of colors & five hundred Yankees & negroes."[140] Those captured Federal colors—nineteen flags or portions of flags in all, taken by David A. Weisiger's Virginia brigade, by John C. C. Sanders's Alabama brigade, and by A. R. Wright's Georgia brigade—were a particularly dramatic measure of the division's performance at the Crater. Secretary of War James Seddon endorsed a list of the flags and their captors with the comment, "let appropriate acknowledgement be made to the gallant general and his brave troops."[141] A Virginia artillery officer in the Third Corps believed that the battle demonstrated "the superiority of veterans to new troops—i.e. of Lee's to [General P. G. T.] Beauregard's troops. They had to take Mahone's Division from this portion of the line, to that point, near the centre, to retake & reestablish the line, because those troops failed."[142]

Many Confederate observers, both those who fought at the Crater and nonparticipants, made frequent references in their letters and diaries to the brutal combat there and to the appalling sight of dead and wounded soldiers in the crater itself. "We witnessed the charge of the negroes—we saw the desperate hand to hand fight—saw the bayonets lock—the thrusts given—the rifles clubbed," Capt. Henry A. Chambers, a North Carolinian in Johnson's Division, recorded in his diary on 30 July. "Maddened by the sight our men were nerved to fight in desperation."[143] The battle flag of the 48th Georgia was said to have been "pierced by one hundred and three bullets, and three times was the staff cut two in this engagement."[144] Shocked correspondents and diarists described the bodies of the Federal dead as they lay "in piles blacks whites and all together lying in piles three and four deep," "literally crammed in our trenches and bomb proofs," or "piled indiscriminately together, one hundred and thirty-three were buried in the bottom of the chasm."[145] One Georgia private thought that "the whole face of the Earth was utterly strewn with dead negroes Ys. [Yankees] and our men," and a fellow Georgian, a corporal in another brigade, claimed, "our men left them thicker than any place that ever yanks was killed on . . . in that hole there is three hundred yankees ded besids the wounded."[146] A Virginia artillery officer spoke for many witnesses when he told his sister, "I never saw such a sight as I saw on that portion of the line."[147]

Another indication of the battle's intensity was the relatively high proportion of dead and missing—much more than half—among Federal casualties. There was, furthermore, a logical, though hardly justifiable, explanation for this statistic. Though the number of troops engaged here was significantly less than in the previous battles of 1864, and still less when compared to the huge campaigns of 1862 and 1863, it was the composition of the Federal troops, not their number, that aroused the brutality displayed by many Confederate participants. Many of Lee's officers and men, already fighting desperately, were first surprised when enemy reinforcements proved to be an entire division of U.S. Colored Troops, then outraged when some blacks and their white officers shouted "No quarter!" as they entered the battle. "The reason of the casualties in the negro troops being so great was, that they jumped upon our works and cried, 'no quarters,'" a Georgia cavalryman explained. "Our boys replied, 'We ask none' and commenced a most desperate and determined conflict with their bayonets and the butts of their guns, and I did hear, that the officers had liked to have never stopped our boys from butchering them. Just what they deserved, every one of them."[148] Eyewitness and second- or third-hand accounts of the battle included such comments as "you may depend we did not show much quarters, but slayed them," "they came yelling 'no quarters!' and our boys took them at their word," and "the Negros charged up shouting no quarter our men trick them at their own proposition and gave them none."[149]

Numerous Confederates wrote with satisfaction, and some with pleasure, of the "great slaughter" of black Federals, who "had their eyes opened only to find out that they were to run for life or else be butchered like sheep."[150] Pvt. Dorsey Binion of the 48th Georgia wrote, almost apologetically, "some few negroes went to the rear as we could not kill them as fast as they past us."[151] Maj. Matthew Love of the 25th North Carolina described the reaction of his regiment: "such Slaughter I have not witnessed upon any battle field any where Their men were principally negroes and we shot them down untill we got near enough and then run them through with the Bayonet. . . . we was not very particular whether we captured or killed them the only thing we did not like to be pestered berrying the Heathens."[152] A Georgia sergeant in the First Corps repeated what he had heard about the Crater: "Negro troops were in the fray, they threw away their guns and attempted to surrender, but our men replied that they had arms and must fight, and continued to shoot them down."[153] One of the more powerful expressions of such attitudes came from the commander of an artillery battalion in the Third Corps. "It seems cruel to murder them in cold blood, but I think the men who did it had very good cause for doing so," he remarked on 1 August. "I have always said that I wished the enemy would bring some negroes against this army. I am convinced, since Saturday's fight, that it has a splendid effect on our men."[154]

Other members of Lee's army, disturbed by their fellow soldiers' bloodthirsty behavior, expressed misgivings or disgust in their accounts of the Crater. "Many negroes were killed after they surrendered," a staff officer in Mahone's Division admitted, and a lieutenant in Sanders's Brigade wrote his wife, "Troops that our Brigade fought were principally negroe and the slaughter was immense: *heart sickening*."[155] Pvt. Noble John Brooks of Cobb's Legion Cavalry observed in his diary that some Confederates "were persisting in the final destruction of the quarter undeserving captives, when Gen. Mahone with drawn sabre and awful threats caused them to desist from their barbarous work." Brooks exclaimed, "Oh! the horrors of war. Oh! the depravity of the human heart; that would cause men to cry out 'no quarters' in battle, or not to show any when asked for."[156]

The prevailing mood in the army immediately after the battle was one of increased confidence, due to the relative ease with which the enemy was repulsed, along with righteous indignation directed at Grant and the Federals for exploding a mine under the Confederate lines and then sending black troops to assault the position. Writing to his wife, Capt. Frank Coker of Cutts's artillery battalion summarized the battle, described the field, and evaluated the results of the whole affair: "Before night we had retaken every portion of our lines and captured over 1,000 prisoners, killed about 700 of them and wounded about 3,000 more. Here for the first time our army came in contact face to face with negro troops, but we slayed them. I have not seen the mine but Col. Cutts says it is 50 yards square, and 20 to 30 ft. deep. . . . It is said to present a shocking picture. But Grant failed totally in his trick and will now have to resort to something else."[157] A South Carolina sergeant believed that the Federals "got so badly Whipt at their oone trick I dont think they try it eney more," and a Georgia private, repeating rumors that Grant might try to explode other mines under Lee's troops, thought "if he can keep up at it we will try and stand it, but I think he will soon get tired of it, and try some other plan."[158] Most officers and men in the Army of Northern Virginia, adding the Crater to the list of their victories so far in 1864, had their faith in Lee and in themselves strengthened. They thought that they would frustrate whatever plans Grant might have in store for them in the future. "You can tell all of the folks that we are all rite and are not a fraid of being whiped," Corp. Thomas W. G. Inglet of the 28th Georgia closed a letter to his wife on 31 July.[159]

North of Petersburg, meanwhile, Jubal Early's small force was entering the second, and decisive, phase of its campaign in the Shenandoah Valley. Faced with a new adversary in Philip H. Sheridan, who commanded a significantly reinforced Federal army, Early would receive crucial reinforcements of his own from Lee in an attempt to maintain the balance of forces in the valley. After scouts reported considerable numbers of Federal units moving toward the Shenandoah—two cavalry brigades, for example, traveling in that direction the day after the battle of the Crater—Lee expressed his concern that Early's relatively small Army of the Valley might soon be overwhelmed. "I fear that this force is intended to operate against General Early," he wrote Jefferson Davis on 4 August, "and when added to that already opposed to him, may be more than he can manage. Their object may be to drive him out of the Valley and complete the devastation they commenced when they were ejected from it."[160]

As the excitement of the Crater subsided, and as the siege of Petersburg resumed its former character, the two armies in the Shenandoah Valley began the last few months of their 1864 campaign there. By the time that campaign ended, Early's and Sheridan's respective performances would, unfortunately for the Confederacy, confirm Lee's prediction of the result he feared from operations in the valley.

Wee cannot expect to gain every victory over the army that

is opposing us [in] large and superior numbers to ours.

—*Corp. Jonathan Fuller Coghill*

23d North Carolina, to his sister, 10 October 1864

The Shenandoah Valley,
Winchester, Fisher's Hill, and Cedar Creek,
August–December 1864

As Jubal Early's weary soldiers marched up and down the Valley Pike in search of, in pursuit of, or in retreat from the Federals throughout August and into September, several of them might have willingly traded places with their comrades back at Petersburg. Instead of returning at night to a camp they had just broken up days before, or marching yet another time through such towns as Strasburg, Winchester, or Bunker Hill, Early's troops would probably have been happy to sit quietly in the trenches and endure a little sharpshooting, shelling, and tedium. Writing from his camp near the last town one afternoon, an Alabama surgeon commented, "This is the fourth time we have camped here. We also have stopping places at Martinsburg and Strasburg. Our campaigning is like children playing baste—we give a dare and then the enemy gives one."[1]

Some members of the Army of the Valley saw little reason for their constant movements and wondered what their commanding general's intentions might be. "Gen. Early with infantry moved towards Berryville to cut the Yankee Calvary off—Found no calvary in that vicinity," one soldier reported in his diary on 2 September. "The move was to no purpose."[2] In a letter to his father, a South Carolina sergeant explained one possible reason for such activity: "We start out to meet the yankees every too or three days. . . . We do not Stay at one place more than three days at a time We half to run after the yankee cavelry to keep them of[f] our waggons."[3] Whereas some soldiers believed that they would fight if the two forces would only remain concentrated in one place long enough, others thought that neither Jubal Early nor Philip H. Sheridan wanted to bring on a major battle. Such observations as "there seems to be no chance to get anything like a respectable fight out of them," "I think neither side anxious for an engagement," and "we have a great deal of marching to do but little fighting" were frequent among the army's correspondents and diarists during this period.[4]

Shortly after the campaign ended, Col. David G. Cowand of the 32d North Carolina described this phase of operations in the Shenandoah in his official report. In August his regiment, in common with most other units in the Army of the Valley, "moved up and down the Valley for some days, one day running the enemy and the next falling back"; in early September it "moved down the Valley and back again several times.[5] Most of Early's soldiers would have heartily agreed with Lt. Robert Emory Park, of the 12th Alabama, who said that on a typical day his division left its camp, marched ten or twelve miles to disperse a small force of Federal cavalry, and then marched back to the same camp, noting: "These reconnaissances may be very important and very interesting to general and field officers, who ride, but those of the line, and the fighting privates, wish they were less frequent, or less tiresome [in] this sultry weather. We have walked this pike-road so often, that we know not only every house, fence, spring and shade tree, but very many of the citizens, their wives and children."[6]

Such movements confirmed a new Federal emphasis on operations in the Shenandoah Valley. This spirit was manifesting itself not only in raids, skirmishes, and running fights, but also in a deliberate and unprecedented campaign to destroy anything of value to the Confederate war effort. Sheridan, to an even greater degree than David Hunter before him, was waging war on the valley itself just as much as on the army defending it. Civilians often told harrowing tales of Federal cavalrymen who burned crops, outbuildings, and, less frequently, residences. This phase of Sheridan's campaign, which began about the same time that reinforcements from the Army of Northern Virginia reached Early, would last until the end of 1864 and would give birth to some of the most lasting bitterness produced by the war. References to the Federals as "vandals" or "miscreants" became more common in Confederate letters and diaries. "Such warfare is a disgrace to civilization," Lt. Park remarked, "but I suppose that Irish-Yankee Sheridan and that drunken butcher and tanner, Grant, have little comprehension of sentiments of humanity or Christianity."[7] A South Carolina sergeant, after noting that "the yanks is Burning all the Wheat as they go," warned, "We Wil pay them for it."[8]

Fighting during this period, though frequent, was usually of little consequence. Daily clashes quickly fell into a pattern, usually characterized by meeting engagements that began when cavalry attacked cavalry, often with some success, and ended when the attacking cavalry encountered elements of enemy infantry that easily drove it back. Combat between infantry units was less common, though some infantrymen clashed with cavalrymen on a regular basis, usually as the result of a reconnaissance in force rather than a desire to bring on a full-scale battle. Early, in particular, often deployed his infantry divisions in several different directions, hoping to anticipate or to counter the movements of Sheridan's cavalry; he used his small army more to harass the Federals than to drive them from the Shenandoah Valley.[9] "When we move up the enemy fall back, and when they come in force we edge off to toll them up the Valley," Bryan Grimes remarked on 10 September. "So far Gen'l Early has been very Successful indeed in all his Manoeuvres."[10]

Many of those maneuvers were conducted by Early's infantry for the simple reason that the Confederate commander had a long-standing—and largely justified—mistrust of the cavalrymen in the Army of the Valley. His horsemen, poorly equipped, poorly mounted, and just as poorly led by their officers, were proficient plunderers but unreliable fighters and were among the least-disciplined soldiers in the entire Confederate army. Though they had been embarrassed, and often put to flight, by Federal cavalry in the Shenandoah Valley, they seemed to believe that they could ride anywhere with impunity. Early had repeatedly proposed, in all seriousness, that if his cavalrymen could not be made to obey orders they might as well be transferred to the infantry, where the opportunities for misbehavior were not so great. The only problem with such a drastic step, he admitted, was that such newly created foot soldiers would probably desert immediately.

An extreme, though by no means unique, incident had recently demonstrated just how undisciplined these cavalrymen could be. On 30 July Brig. Gen. John McCausland, operating under orders from Early, demanded a ransom from the town of Chambersburg, Pennsylvania, in retaliation for Federal depredations in the Shenandoah Valley. McCausland allowed his cavalrymen to ransack buildings and steal whatever they could while he waited for an answer, then burned the town when the citizens refused to pay the ransom. Brig. Gen. Bradley T. Johnson, who commanded one of McCausland's brigades, included a graphic description of the Confederates' "outrageous conduct" in his official report. "Every crime in the catalogue of infamy has been committed, I believe, except murder and rape," Johnson declared. "After the order was given to burn the town of Chambersburg and before, drunken soldiers paraded the streets in every possible disguise and paraphernalia, pillaging and plundering and drunk."[11] Such behavior, on a much smaller scale, was common even in the midst of loyal Confederate citizens in Virginia and helped give the Valley cavalry its bad name. One soldier detailed to the signal corps, working to establish and maintain Confederate communications in the Shenandoah, described an apparently common complaint about Early's wayward horsemen in his diary. "Followed two men all the morning who had robbed a citizen of his horse," Pvt. B. L. Wynn reported, "[but] failed to come up with them."[12]

By August Early's superiors, all too aware of the serious deficiencies in his cavalry units, took steps to improve their discipline and efficiency. When Lee ordered additional troops to the valley he planned to send Wade Hampton's fine division, with Hampton in command, but was prevented by operations near Petersburg that required Hampton's attention. Lee's nephew Fitzhugh Lee, with his own cavalry division, went in Hampton's place, and Lunsford L. Lomax was promoted to major general and ordered to take command of the Valley cavalry. Lomax replaced Robert Ransom, who made a thoughtful report on the condition of the cavalry when he arrived in Richmond. Ransom's critical evaluation proposed a wholesale reorganization that consolidated some cavalry units and abolished others, replaced incompetent officers, and created two cavalry divisions of equal size, one commanded by Fitzhugh Lee and the other by Lomax.[13] His report was forwarded to Early with the observation that "too radical a change may produce dissatisfaction" but stressing that Confederate authorities believed that "some stringent measures are necessary to secure discipline and prevent disaster." Early, already inclined to dismiss his cavalry as worthless, did not reply.[14] The combination of the troops' deficiencies and their commanding general's contempt for them would prove to be a severe handicap before the end of the campaign.

The typical daily alarms, skirmishes, and affairs popularly referred to as "stampedes" undoubtedly contributed to a disturbing new tendency among many units during this period. Numerous soldiers, having become accustomed to raids and other movements that seemed to accomplish nothing and rumors of enemy attacks that never materialized, took the fluid situation for granted and assumed that significant operations in the Shenandoah were almost over for the year. Incidents in which pickets, skirmishers, or larger bodies of troops were surprised and significant numbers of them were captured occurred with increasing regularity in the Army of the Valley. On 7 August, for example, Johnson's and McCausland's cavalrymen, sleeping in their camps near Moorefield, West Virginia, were surprised by Federal cavalrymen who captured hundreds of them and scattered the rest, also taking hundreds of horses and four pieces of artillery. One civilian called it "a perfect rout, our men scattering in wild disorder and confusion, and running in different directions."[15] Johnson, for his part, believed that "had there been less plunder [earlier in the campaign] there would have been more fighting at Moorefield on Sunday, August 7."[16]

Jedediah Hotchkiss, Early's topographer, referred to this latest humiliation as "a disgraceful affair," and, a few days after the incident, William Brotherton of the 23d North Carolina advanced his own theory about why his regiment was suddenly marched to Winchester. "I herd the Reasin we came up hear," Brotherton wrote, "was they yankes takin our cavelary on serprise and capterd some of them and we was sent hear to hold this place."[17] Jubal Early's already strong prejudice against his cavalrymen, and his suspicion that they would not or could not fight, was clearly reinforced by the disaster at Moorefield. "Keep a strict lookout and keep your forces in constant readiness," he warned one of his infantry commanders a few days later; "do not let us have another surprise."[18]

Though Early's undisciplined cavalrymen were often the culprits when such a surprise occurred, his infantrymen occasionally became careless and suffered embarrassments as well. Most of these incidents were caused not only by the negligence of the Confederates but also by Sheridan's aggressive use of his own cavalry. One evening in late August, for example, a Federal captain noticed that nearby Confederate skirmishers were "sitting down roasting corn, and no person paying any attention, many of them having their backs to their line," as Early later reported it.[19] The Federal officer then received permission to advance a small force of cavalry and infantry against the oblivious picket line. The stunned skirmishers, members of a South Carolina brigade that had been part of the recent reinforcement from the First Corps, were overwhelmed. Many were captured or wounded and seventy-five to one hundred members of the 15th South Carolina, the majority of them with loaded muskets, were captured. Pvt. Charles Kerrison, an aide-de-camp at brigade headquarters, was caught in a crossfire and "scarcely expected getting out alive" but escaped injury when his horse "became so frightened by the confusion as to break off at full speed to the rear, throwing off my saddle bags with all my clothing, and causing me to loose my hat."[20] Sgt. Daniel Boyd, of the 7th South Carolina, whose regiment was on the picket line, described the affair to his father a few days later. "We had afight on the 26th we got the worst of it . . . the yankees saw our line Was Weak and they mased their force in a peace of woods and charg our lines With cavelry and infantry," Boyd explained. "The cavelry charged the 15th regment and broke their lines and captured about 75 of them We had to do some of our beast runing I tell you What it was a rite close place."[21]

Several skirmishes between elements of Confederate infantry and Federal cavalry near the northern end of the Shenandoah Valley during the same week increased Early's suspicions that Sheridan was timid and would not fight him. Sheridan, discovering that Early had received reinforcements from Lee, had already retreated from his position at Cedar Creek, about halfway down the valley, almost as far as Harpers Ferry and the Potomac River. Early, trying to arouse Sheridan into action, followed him and attacked with Rodes's and Ramseur's Divisions on 21 August and with Wharton's and Gordon's Divisions on the twenty-fifth. These sharp actions—the latter was described by one observer as "quite a lively skirmish"—inflicted moderate casualties on both sides.[22] They also initiated a series of advances and retreats by both commanders that ended in the first week of September with Sheridan's forces near Berryville and Early's army between Bunker Hill and Winchester.[23] "I believe now, we will have a few days quiet," courier Thomas Pollock Devereux wrote his sister a few days after the last significant skirmish; on 7 September Lt. Archibald Henderson remarked: "About the prospect of a fight I cannot speak with much certainty. It seems to be Gen'l Sheridan's policy to avoid [one] and Gen'l Early is equally as cautious in attack, he does not wish to lose men unnecessarily."[24]

Early was now so certain that Sheridan posed no great threat to him that he not only needlessly weakened his small army but also divided his forces. On 14 September he sent Kershaw's Division and Maj. Wilfred Cutshaw's artillery battalion, along with First Corps commander Richard Anderson, back to the Army of Northern Virginia, thinking that Lee needed them at Petersburg more than he did in the Shenandoah Valley. In the meantime, Lee, unaware that Anderson and the troops were already on their way to him, wrote to both Early and Anderson on the subject. Lee's proposal—that Anderson return and resume command of his corps but that Early retain Kershaw's Division if he needed it—was, unfortunately, too late. Early's hasty decision, which he would soon have good reason to regret, would cost him some 4,000 veteran troops.[25] "Andersons Division left here a day or two since for Richmond and only our original troops have been left here," a North Carolina brigadier noted.[26] Furthermore, on the seventeenth, Early himself accompanied an expedition toward Martinsburg while the rest of his army remained at Stephenson's Depot or near Winchester. "I will be gone until day after to-morrow," he notified Breckinridge, "and I wish you to keep a strict lookout, and keep all officers and men in camp so as to be ready at any moment to meet the enemy."[27]

Sheridan, meanwhile, had just assured Grant in a face-to-face conference that he could defeat Early's small army. Though intending to attack the Confederates south of Winchester, Sheridan quickly revised his plan to take advantage of Early's vulnerability. If all went well, he had an excellent opportunity to defeat each of the components of the Army of the Valley in turn. By 18 September those components, dangerously separated from each other, were spread up and down the Valley Pike for some twenty miles from Martinsburg south to Winchester. John B. Gordon, with his own division and a cavalry brigade, was at Martinsburg; Jubal Early, with Robert E. Rodes's Division and an artillery battalion, was at Bunker Hill; John C. Breckinridge, with Brig. Gen. Gabriel C. Wharton's Division and an artillery battalion, was at Stephenson's Depot, north of Winchester; and Stephen D. Ramseur, with his own division and Early's remaining artillery battalion, was near Winchester itself, guarding the road that ran east to Berryville. When Early learned during the day about the meeting between Grant and Sheridan, he feared the worst and quickly turned his expedition back south in a desperate effort to concentrate his forces. Rodes, by a forced march, reached Stephenson's Depot that evening, and Gordon marched as far as Bunker Hill, with orders to continue to Stephenson's Depot the next morning.[28] With tremendous odds against him—even if all of his units had been concentrated, the Army of the Valley would have numbered a little more than 12,000 soldiers—Early faced an energetic opponent commanding about 35,000 troops.

Sheridan opened the battle of Winchester early on the morning of 19 September, attacking from the east with his cavalry in the lead and his infantry close behind. After Federal cavalry quickly drove in a small line of Confederate cavalry and infantry skirmishers, the lead elements of Sheridan's infantry attacked Early's main line. Ramseur's Division and an artillery battalion, fighting stubbornly, were briefly overwhelmed but soon rallied, holding the Federals in check. Early then arrived in person and his other divisions marched toward the sound of the battle, reaching the field about midmorning. The rest of the Federal infantry wasted several hours struggling through a narrow gorge east of Winchester, and it was almost noon before Sheridan was able to mass his assaulting column. By that time Rodes's and Gordon's Divisions were supporting Ramseur's hard-pressed troops, and Breckinridge, who had been skirmishing with elements of Sheridan's cavalry during the morning, was ordered to move Wharton's Division to the Confederate left, north of the town. When three Federal infantry divisions finally charged Early's lines, Ramseur held his position while Rodes and Gordon delivered a vigorous counterattack that halted Sheridan's infantry and nearly drove it from the field. As the infantry battle slackened and both armies waited for its renewal, it seemed as if the crisis might be over for the Army of the Valley.

After a few hours of skirmishing, consisting primarily of cavalry fighting in which Early's dismounted horsemen were driven back, a Federal infantry division opened the second and decisive phase of the battle when it attacked the Confederate left flank about 3:00 P.M. Though Early's infantry and artillery fought fiercely for two hours, Sheridan threw fresh cavalry against them as well, and a mounted charge late in the afternoon finally broke through their lines. When Gordon's and Wharton's Divisions were forced to give way, they exposed Rodes's and Ramseur's flanks, and what began as a retreat soon degenerated into a rout and, among some Confederates, into a panic. Early's troops streamed south with Federal cavalry in close pursuit and barely paused until they reached the safety of Fisher's Hill, about twenty miles away near the town of Strasburg. For the first time during the war, the Second Corps of the Army of Northern Virginia—Stonewall Jackson's old corps, including many veterans who had won the first two battles of Winchester in May 1862 and June 1863— had been driven from a battlefield in confusion.[29]

Sheridan's casualties at Winchester were moderately heavy, numbering some 5,000 men killed, wounded, and captured. Confederate casualties, though fewer, were proportionately much greater than Sheridan's. Early lost more than 3,500 troops, or about one-quarter to one-third of his total force, killed, wounded, and captured, not including the hundreds of stragglers who were absent from their units for days after the battle. The loss of three pieces of artillery in an army that sorely needed them further underscored the magnitude of the defeat.

As Early tried to restore some semblance of order to his dazed army at Fisher's Hill on the night of 19 September and throughout the next few days, his soldiers took the opportunity to record their impressions of the fight in their letters and diaries. Some Confederates wrote detailed descriptions of the battle itself; others blamed particular officers or units for the disastrous defeat, and still others emphasized the confusion and shame of its aftermath. Many accounts reflected all three views. "Yesterday we had a most terrible fight at Winchester and were very roughly handled by the enemy," Bryan Grimes wrote his wife on the twentieth. "We lost a great many men and our troops did not behave with their usual valor. . . . Yesterday to me was the most trying day of the war."[30] A courier on Grimes's staff called Winchester "one of the hardest fights on record almost as heavy as the 12th of May," admitting, "We are right badly used up."[31]

The entire Army of the Valley was indeed "right badly used up," for the fighting at Winchester was some of the hardest combat Early's veterans had ever experienced. Soldiers in Ramseur's, Rodes's, and Gordon's Divisions, the units that bore the heaviest burden and suffered the most casualties, made frequent references to the severity of the battle. A North Carolina corporal in Ramseur's Division described it as "A op[e]ned handed fight in the clear open field . . . the most terriffic seen and carnage of this cruel warfare."[32] A fellow North Carolinian and sergeant major in Rodes's Division wrote, "I never saw minnie balls and grape shot rain so in all my life," and a Louisiana captain in Gordon's Division thought that his brigade's counterattack was "the prettiest stand up fair open fight that I have ever seen."[33]

In the aftermath of the battle, as Confederates evaluated their army's performance, several of them described the fighting of the morning and afternoon, before the wholesale rout. Numerous officers and men wrote accounts in which their division—or brigade—or regiment—fought bravely while units all around them were falling back. Some members of Ramseur's Division, including its commander, believed—with some justification—that their defensive stand had saved Early's army at Winchester. A few days later Ramseur asserted, "I *made* Earlys old Divn. do splendid fighting at Winchester."[34] A member of Brig. Gen. Robert D. Johnston's North Carolina brigade observed simply, "charge after charge was made on both sides and as the day closed the seen of action did also but finally wee was drove from the field."[35] Confederates in other divisions, naturally enough, made similar claims of their own. "Ramseur's division broke: all the Army ran—except our noble brigade," declared Thomas Pollock Devereux, a member of Grimes's Brigade of Rodes's Division. "Ramseur broke on our right [Brig. Gen. William Ruffin] Cox and [Brig. Gen. Cullen A.] Battle on our left. We went on through blood and fire a mile in advance of the army."[36] In his after-action report Col. David Cowand of the 32d North Carolina claimed that Grimes's Brigade "moved in fine order and without any hesitation for some distance through an open field beyond any other troops. If the balance of the troops had pushed forward like this brigade we would have driven the enemy from the field."[37] An officer in the 6th Louisiana, in Zebulon York's Brigade of Gordon's Division, reported that his brigade "drove them in our front about half a mile, and had the left of the line met with the same success, we would have made it a [Federal] rout." He explained that "from some unaccountable cause the 61st Ga. of Evans Brigade gave way and although they rallied and drove the enemy back afterwards, we had to fall back a short distance losing about half the ground we had gained."[38] Though these accounts, and others like them, all contained elements of truth, they were attempts to salvage some sort of pride from the disaster.

A common thread running through such chronicles was that once they assigned credit to various units for the Confederate successes of the day, they were virtually unanimous in assigning blame for the ultimate defeat to the cavalry. "Whose fault it was that this disaster occured is the subject of much discussion in the army," a captain in Gordon's Division wrote on 21 September. "All blame the cavalry and the general impression is that if the Yankee infantry fought half as well as their cavalry, we would not have any army here this morning."[39] Other narratives of the battle included comments such as "a heavy force of Yankee cavalry dashed up the Martinsburg pike, driving back our cavalry like sheep and penetrating to our rear" and "the Enemy's Cav'y in heavy force broke our Cav'y on the left & created a terrible disorder throughout our line."[40] At least one Confederate simply reported what happened without assigning blame. A North Carolina sergeant major wrote that his sharpshooters were rushed "at a double-quick to where our cavalry were fighting both Yankee infantry and cavalry. They [the Federals] came pouring down upon us like a thousand bricks which of course we could not stand."[41] Some soldiers, particularly officers, made more pointed criticisms of Early's cavalry. One staff officer thought, "If we had only had some good cavalry to resist that of the enemy, our infantry could have maintained its position, but our cavalry did not behave well, even if there were superior numbers against them."[42] Early himself stated in his report that he might have been able to prevent his defeat "if our cavalry would have stopped the enemy's; but so overwhelming was the battle, and so demoralized was a larger part of ours, that no assistance was received from it."[43] This report, it should be noted, was written a few weeks after Winchester and with the hindsight of further abysmal performances by his cavalry since then. One biting assessment of Early's horsemen at Winchester—but one that would have been seconded by soldiers throughout the army—came from a disgusted infantry officer who wrote, "After a feeble resistance, as usual, our worthless cavalry gave way exposing the infantry flanks and causing them to give way."[44]

The general theme of the Confederate accounts of Winchester, even more common than those of praise or blame for the army's performance, were accounts of the widespread confusion at the end of the battle and afterward. Capt. George P. Ring of the 6th Louisiana, a veteran of the first two battles of Winchester, included this vivid description of the panic in a letter to his wife a few days later:

> All over the plain men could be seen flying to the rear, Officers riding to and fro trying to rally and reform the men. It was a mortifying but very exciting scene. . . . our army or some portions of it had become so completely demoralized that they would not stop for anything or any body, but poured into and through Winchester out the Valley Pike and I dont think some of them stopped until they reached this point [Fisher's Hill] 22 miles from Winchester.[45]

A North Carolina staff officer believed that "It was equal to the 1st Manassa stampede. I never saw anything like it before," and an Alabama surgeon described a scene of "wild confusion": "It was utterly impossible to rally our men—Officers and men ran with all possible speed."[46] Capt. Robert Emory Park, of the 12th Alabama, who had only recently been promoted from first lieutenant of his company, was wounded in the leg just as Early's troops began to panic. He observed in his diary that the Confederates "became impressed with the horrible, unendurable idea that they were flanked, and began to retreat in confusion." After being taken to a makeshift hospital in Winchester with other wounded officers and enlisted men, Park watched the shaken Army of the Valley flee through the town. "It was a sad, humiliating sight," he admitted, "but such a handful of worn-out men could not successfully withstand such overwhelming odds. I never saw our troops in such confusion before."[47]

Early's veterans were all too aware that such conduct, on such a large scale, was unprecedented among the units belonging to the Army of Northern Virginia. Capt. James Mercer Garnett, the ordnance officer of Rodes's Division, was one of many officers who tried in vain to rally soldiers who were running to the rear. Two days later Garnett wrote that he was "fatigued in body and spirit, especially the latter. Cannot get over a feeling of sadness and humiliation at having been compelled to abandon Winchester in that style. . . . I haven't life enough left for anything."[48]

Other members of the army wrote with less emotion about the battle and their flight to the rear. Many not only frankly conceded their poor performance, but also expressed the natural tendency to be more concerned for their survival than for their reputation. Soldiers told their families "we have been badly whipped" or acknowledged, "I can say in plain langage that I never reallized such A whiping before in my life."[49] For all too many Confederates, the instinct for self-preservation proved to be stronger than the impulse toward patriotism at Winchester. Sgt. Maj. Samuel P. Collier of the 2d North Carolina provided a refreshingly unvarnished description of his—and many others'—flight to the rear:

The whole face of the earth was literally alive with rebels running for their lives. I would run a while and stop and laugh at others and think what fools we were making of ourselves, when some shell would come tearing among us and every thing would start off again, I would be among them. I never run as fast in all my life. To come out and tell the truth I ran from two miles the other side of Winchester to New Town a distance of ten (10) miles and I can assure you I had company from Brig Genl down to privates. But there is one thing that I did not do that was to throw away my gun and things. I always hold on to them let what may happen.[50]

One new and disturbing trend in Early's small army was that many soldiers easily accepted or even seemed to approve of the disgraceful behavior, which magnified the impact of their defeat at Winchester. That attitude, dramatically reinforced by subsequent events, would spread throughout the Army of the Valley in the next few weeks and would prove to be a major impediment to its success for the remainder of the campaign.

Another such obstacle, which was becoming a critical one, was the dwindling number of experienced officers still in command. Though the personal leadership displayed by Confederate officers had typically resulted in a proportionately high number of casualties among them, those casualties had greater consequences in 1864 than they had earlier in the war, particularly in an army as small as Early's. Several general officers were killed or wounded at Winchester while either directing their troops during the battle or attempting to rally them after the Federals broke their lines. The most notable of these casualties was Robert Rodes, one of the finest combat officers in the Army of Northern Virginia, who was killed during his division's fierce counterattack in the early afternoon. "Gen R. E. Rodes was killed instantly early in the day," a Louisiana captain wrote his wife; "his loss is one of the most regretted in the army since Jackson was killed."[51] An Alabama captain claimed that Rodes's troops "regarded him as second only to General Lee, excelled by none other"; moreover, a fellow Alabamian believed that Rodes's death "had a great deal to do with our stampede. He was the best Maj. Gen. in this Army, and probably in the C.S.A. and his death produced a tremendous impression on the minds of the men."[52] The army's cavalry lost its best officer when Fitzhugh Lee was severely wounded, and three of Early's infantry brigades were deprived of their commanders when Archibald C. Godwin and Col. George S. Patton were killed and Zebulon York was seriously wounded.[53]

Casualties among experienced officers at the regimental and company levels were even greater, such as those in Patton's small Virginia brigade of Wharton's Division. This brigade, consisting of one regiment and two battalions, boasted three field officers with military educations. Patton, colonel of the 22d Virginia who commanded the brigade at Winchester, and Lt. Col. G. M. Edgar of the 26th Virginia Battalion were graduates of the Virginia Military Institute; Lt. Col. Clarence Derrick of the 23d Virginia Battalion was a graduate of West Point. Patton was killed, and Derrick and Edgar were captured while trying to rally their men, "thus leaving the brigade without an officer above the rank of captain." An inspection report of the brigade written soon after the battle noted that "a large majority also of the company officers, the most gallant and efficient, either met their deaths on the battle-field or fell captive into the hands of the enemy."[54] Such casualties among the army's officers, from division to company levels, were losses Early and his soldiers could ill afford when they needed every possible advantage even to remain in the Shenandoah.[55]

These losses forced Early to make some changes in his officer corps, including the appointment of two new division commanders. Acting quickly, he announced his choices the day after the battle. Dodson Ramseur, who had been a superb brigadier under Robert Rodes and so far had performed well as a major general, was assigned to command Rodes's Division, and Brig. Gen. John Pegram succeeded to the command of Ramseur's Division. Early was losing a third division commander in John C. Breckinridge, who had recently been ordered to resume command of the Department of Southwestern Virginia and would soon be leaving the Army of the Valley, though the orders did not arrive until after the battle at Winchester.

At least for the moment, Early would be somewhat better off in numbers of troops than in experienced commanders, for Breckinridge's old division would remain with the army, commanded by Gabriel C. Wharton, who would report directly to headquarters. Lee, meanwhile, after hearing word of the disaster at Winchester, ordered Richard Anderson to be ready to send Kershaw's Division and Cutshaw's Battalion back to the Shenandoah Valley if Early needed them. The Army of the Valley might be gaining some important and badly needed reinforcements in the near future.[56]

In spite of its flight from the battlefield at Winchester, some Confederates thought that the Valley army was in good spirits and was ready to fight if Sheridan pressed it. On 20 September B. L. Wynn described Early's troops as "much jaded but not at all dispirited." The next day Capt. George P. Ring reported, "we have just received orders to man the breastworks and we are anxious for them to come at us here as we think we can get even with [them] for the repulse of Monday."[57] These breastworks, thrown up along the crest of Fisher's Hill and astride the Valley Pike, enhanced the natural strength of Early's defensive position, one that Pvt. Jonathan Fuller Coghill of the 23d North Carolina said was "considered the strongest persition in the Valley."[58] Coghill, his comrades, and his commander had good reason to feel confident about their position, for Sheridan had already declined to attack the Army of the Valley when it had occupied the same ground in August.

Even such a fine defensive position, however, could not fully compensate the Confederates for the advantages the Federals enjoyed in sheer numbers and in the confidence Sheridan's men felt after their victory at Winchester. Furthermore, Early's flawed disposition of the troops he did have at hand only magnified the obstacles facing him. Because he expected Sheridan to try to turn his right flank, near the Shenandoah River, Early anchored that end of his line with his artillery and posted his infantry along the ridge. On his left, near Little North Mountain, he unaccountably placed Lomax's dismounted cavalry—instead of a veteran division of infantry—on the most vulnerable portion of his line. "But strange to say," one officer later commented, "the weak, wavering fearful Cavalry were placed where the position was naturally weak & without fortification, while the infantry were posted in the strongest natural positions well fortified."[59] Early's decision was made, as he later reported, "with the hope of arresting Sheridan's progress" but would soon prove to be one of his worst mistakes of the campaign.[60]

The Federals to their immediate north, meanwhile, were not idle. Sheridan, anxious to press his advantage, had pursued Early all the way from Winchester and had arrived in the vicinity of Fisher's Hill by the night of 21 September. He never seriously considered a frontal assault against the entrenched Confederates but believed an attempt to turn their vulnerable left flank could succeed. Sheridan then detached most of his cavalry and sent it south, hoping that it would cut off any Confederate avenues of retreat and allow him to complete the destruction of Early's army. Signs of Federal activity during the morning and early afternoon of 22 September did not go unnoticed by Early, who recognized that his relatively small force could not hope to hold its position indefinitely and issued orders for the withdrawal of his army during the night. But while the Confederates waited for nightfall, and while two of Sheridan's corps skirmished and demonstrated in their front, a third Federal corps—screened from view by the woods on Little North Mountain—marched into position to threaten Early's thinly held left flank.

As soon as Sheridan's troops crashed down the mountain Lomax's stunned cavalrymen broke and fled in confusion, exposing the rest of the Valley soldiers to an overwhelming force on their flank and behind them. Ramseur's Division, now on the extreme left of Early's line, was completely unprepared for an attack from the west but still managed to offer some resistance that barely slowed the Federal onslaught. Within a matter of minutes, however, Sheridan's flanking force formed a junction with his other two corps, which were charging up the heights and over the Confederate works on Fisher's Hill. Early's line wavered, then crumbled, from west to east as Pegram's, Gordon's, and Wharton's Divisions gave way in succession. Units, disorganized remnants of units, and individuals first retreated, then ran wildly to the rear, as Sheridan's infantry swarmed over their positions. Confederates paid no heed to officers who pleaded with them to rally, and even less to those who threatened or cursed them as they raced south down the Valley Pike. The panic here, unlike that at Winchester, not only occurred before Early's soldiers had made any significant stand but also spread throughout the entire army, quickly becoming a stampede.

Meanwhile, elements of Fitzhugh Lee's cavalry clashed with Sheridan's horsemen and kept the line of retreat open long enough for the beaten and exhausted Confederates to make their escape in the gathering darkness. Early, in a series of retreats, eventually halted near Waynesboro, some twenty-five miles from Fisher's Hill and almost out of the Shenandoah.[61] Casualties were light, as might be expected from an action that saw little real combat. Sheridan's losses totaled about 500 killed and wounded, whereas Early's 1,200 casualties included nearly 1,000 men captured or missing, though many of the latter rejoined their commands in the days and weeks afterward. Early's losses in arms and equipment were relatively heavy, as twelve pieces of artillery and hundreds of rifles and other items were abandoned or thrown away in the confusion and the haste to escape.

Numerous members of the Army of the Valley, from the commanding general to his privates, later described the scene on Fisher's Hill. Early himself, writing Lee early the next morning, reported that Sheridan "succeeded in driving back the left of my line, which was defended by the cavalry, and throwing a force into the rear of the left of my infantry line, when the whole of the troops gave way in a panic and could not be rallied."[62] Many Confederates felt no obligation to report the details of the engagement but simply described how they and their fellow soldiers behaved when the Federal attack engulfed their lines. "I am sorry to say that our men were very much stampeded & did not keep cool or fight as well as they have heretofore done," Dodson Ramseur wrote his wife on 30 September.[63] Comments such as "the whole line gave way and was thrown into the greatest confusion," "our men would not rally and every man was for himselfe so you may beleive that was A stampeede of stampeeds," and "the skedaddle at Fishers Hill was worse than Winchester" reflected the prevailing mood in Early's army.[64] "Our whole line gave way toward the right, offering little or no resistance," Jedediah Hotchkiss noted in his diary; "most of our men went on, officers and all, at breakneck speed."[65] Some of Early's soldiers answered a comrade's pleas to fight with the remark, "No use for us to stand, go ahead and stop those ahead of us and when we get up there will be enough to make a stand."[66] Others retained their sense of humor, such as the North Carolina courier in Ramseur's Division who wrote his father the next day, "I hope to get out of this scrape but we are in a bad fix. . . . The Yanks can't catch me as long as my horse runs as fast as he did last night."[67]

One representative soldier who fled with the rest of the army and took his time straggling back to it was Green Clifton, a regimental musician in the 31st Georgia. Clifton and his brigade commander, Brig. Gen. Clem-

Sgt. George Cleveland Smith, Company C, 12th Georgia. Smith enlisted as a private in the Davis Rifles and was promoted to sergeant by October 1862; he was wounded at Cedar Creek in October 1864 but returned to his company and surrendered at Appomattox. (George M. Smith)

ent A. Evans, were old, prewar friends who had remained close in spite of the difference in their respective grades. The two met by chance a few days after Fisher's Hill, with Evans on his way back to the army after recuperating from a wound received at Monocacy and Clifton still absent from their brigade. Evans remarked in a letter home that Clifton had "*dispersed* himself but [was] bearing his brass horn gallantly on his shoulder. He told me that one half my brigade was cut off in the mountains, under Col. [Edmund N.] Atkinson [of the 26th Georgia, commanding the brigade in Evans's absence]. The balance being commanded by Col. [John H.] Lowe [of the 31st Georgia]." When Evans wrote his wife on 29 September, he mentioned that Clifton still had not reported for duty; a few days later he was passing on rumors that Clifton was in Charlottesville. On 11 October, some two and a half weeks after the stampede, Evans finally reported, "Green Clifton is here & well."[68] Henry P. Fortson, a second sergeant in Clifton's regiment, told a friend about his own escape into the mountains and his eventual return to the Army of the Valley:

> I went down the foot of the mountain opposite Edingburg, then I crossed the mountain into Loura [Luray] Valley. . . . The yankees were all around me. I was lucky enough to get through their lines safe. The mountain was full of men every man for himself. The roughest country. I had to go through the woods fraid to take a road. I was absent from the company four days. I got with the Army at Port Republic. You may know I was proud to get with the boys.[69]

Clifton's and Fortson's experiences were, if not typical, certainly common enough in the army after Fisher's Hill. Early complained to Lee in his report: "Very many of the missing in the infantry took to the mountains. A number of them have since come in and others are still out."[70]

Confederates who had the heart to do so ventured explanations of how such a debacle could have occurred so soon after Winchester and described their apprehensions for the future. Some officers and men blamed the troops for running without giving the Federals a battle, others criticized Early for placing them in such a precarious position in the first place, and still others believed both were at fault. Though many correspondents and diarists preferred not to speculate about the future of the army, others did so with insight if not with enthusiasm. On 23 September Lt. Micajah Woods, a Virginia artilleryman, wrote his father: "Of the prospects & condition of the army I forbear to speak. I can confidentially say to you that I regard its future career in the Valley with by no means hopeful anticipation."[71] A few days later Surgeon Charles W. Sydnor commented, "I fear this Army is very much demorilised and will require considerable time before it can be gotten in a fighting condition again." Sydnor then cautioned his fiancée, "this I say in confidence knowing you will not mention it to any one."[72] A Georgia sergeant who echoed Woods's and Sydnor's sentiments in simpler terms wrote to a friend, "I guess we were badly whip I hate to own it but it is best to tell the trouth."[73] Many veterans in the Army of the Valley whose confidence in their fellow soldiers and in themselves was already badly shaken after Winchester found that confidence strained to its limits after Fisher's Hill. Some would never again enter a battle without wondering when the Federals—especially the cavalry—might find a way to flank them or get in their rear.

Numerous soldiers, who thought that Early was primarily responsible for the defeat at Fisher's Hill, were somewhat more vigorous in assigning blame. Lt. Archibald Henderson of the 12th North Carolina, for example, asserted that "our defeat at Strasburg was a very unfortunate affair, due in no measure to the troops. Great blame is attached to Gen'l Early for his mismanagement there. . . . The men do not believe they were whipped but out-generalled badly."[74] One of Early's generals hoped that his commander might "profit by past sad experience and not risk too much in future." But Bryan Grimes did acknowledge that "our great danger lies in the fact that since our recent reverses the troops do not have that unbounded confidence in his judgment which is necessary for a successful Military leader—for without that he can hardly expect his men to act well their part."[75]

Grimes's gloomy assessment of the Army of the Valley's future combat effectiveness was both perceptive and persuasive. Even if the army's previous relationship with Early, who did not relate well to his subordinates or to the men in the ranks, had never been particularly close, it had still been characterized by respect. After Fisher's Hill, however, the soldiers began to doubt that he cared anything about them; more significantly, they began to mistrust his leadership. For example, an unidentified officer wrote Gov. William Smith of Virginia alleging that "his [Early's] appearance along the line excites no pleasure, much less enthusiasm and cheers. No salute is given. He is not greeted at all by private or officer, but is allowed to pass, and passes, neither receiving nor taking notice. The army once believed him a safe commander, and felt that they could trust to his caution, but unfortunately this has been proven a delusion and they cannot, do not, and will not give him their confidence." The anonymous officer called Winchester a surprise, blamed Fisher's Hill on the army's lack of confidence in Early, and claimed, "the good of the country requires that General Early should not be kept in command of this army." Moreover, "every officer with whom I have conversed upon the subject is of the same opinion, and I believe it is the sentiment of the army."[76] Smith, who agreed, forwarded the letter to Lee, who replied that he believed Early had done a creditable job so far in the Shenandoah Valley. "Of the care that he takes of his men and the estimation in which he is held by them," Lee continued, "I have no means of judging, except from what I witnessed when he was serving with me."[77] But such serious allegations, even if made by an unnamed correspondent and forwarded by someone who admitted "some little unfriendliness in my relations with General Early," might have some basis in fact and might well influence subsequent events in the valley.[78]

One of Early's brigadiers who had not been present at Winchester or Fisher's Hill repeated what he had heard in the army about the defeats. Clement Evans thought that they were "both due to our weak & cowardly cavalry mixed with some bad Generalship," concluding, "the whole affair is of the most distressing and mortifying kind and I am truly glad I did not witness it."[79] Several soldiers who wrote about Fisher's Hill, whether they blamed the stampede on the Confederate rank and file, the officers, or Early, also expressed feelings of shame at having to report another rout. "I have been too busy and too much mortified to write you for several days," one of Early's division commanders began a letter to his wife, and a Georgia sergeant admitted, "I should have writen before now but I have been so badly stampeded, I thought it would be useless to try to write."[80] One frank admission of shame was written by the surgeon of the 61st Alabama, discussing a much-anticipated furlough he hoped to receive by Christmas. "I do not want to go till we redeem ourselves a little," Abner Embry McGarity wrote his wife on 30 September. "I would hate to see My Love just after running so. We must do something before I go."[81]

McGarity and his comrades might eventually redeem themselves in their own eyes, but they would have a much more difficult task redeeming themselves in their commanding general's. Early believed that it was not his generalship, or lack of it, that lost the battles at Winchester and Fisher's Hill, but the poor performance of his army. Though he considered his cavalrymen primarily responsible, he also held the rest of his army accountable for his reverses. "The enemy's immense superiority in cavalry and the inefficiency of the greater part of mine has been the cause of all my disasters," he wrote Lee on 25 September. "My troops are very much shattered. . . . I shall do the best I can, and hope I may be able to check the enemy, but I cannot but be apprehensive of the result."[82] Lee, for his part, reassured Early as best he could. "One victory will put all things right," he replied. "You must do all in your power to invigorate your army." Gently pointing out some of Early's errors, such as fighting "more with divisions than with your concentrated strength," Lee reminded him that "I have given you all I can; you must use the resources you have so as to gain success." He further counseled Early, "Set all your officers to work bravely and hopefully, and all will go well."[83]

When Lee told Early that "I have given you all I can," he was referring to specific units—Kershaw's Division and Cutshaw's Battalion—that had been waiting for orders to proceed toward Richmond and Petersburg or to return to the Shenandoah Valley. One of Kershaw's men, the clerk of the 53d Georgia, thought on 21 September that there was "no doubt but that we are 'bound for' Petersburg. I don't like the idea much it is entirely too confining and then we cannot get vegetables and fruit as we could in the valley."[84] But circumstances dictated otherwise. Early ended the brief message of 23 September informing Lee of his latest defeat with the comment, "Kershaw's division had better be sent to my aid, through Swift Run Gap, at once."[85] Lee ordered the infantry and artillery back to the valley the same day. He also sent Brig. Gen. Thomas L. Rosser's small cavalry brigade, hoping that additional horsemen from the Army of Northern Virginia might add not only numbers but also some much-needed experience and discipline to the Valley cavalry.[86]

Aware that these reinforcements were on their way, some of Early's officers tried to bolster the morale of their troops by announcing the fact and by making speeches expressing hope for the future. "General Battle delivered two very good speeches, one to his brigade and one to General Grimes's," observed Capt. James Mercer Garnett of the division staff. "When General Ramseur alluded to General Rodes, in speaking to Battle's brigade, I could not refrain from tears, and there were many other wet eyes."[87] Kershaw's Division and Cutshaw's Battalion arrived on 26 September, increasing Early's force by some 3,500 troops. The army also gained twelve pieces of artillery that partially offset the loss of fifteen guns at Winchester and Fisher's Hill.[88] When Rosser's Brigade arrived on 5 October, it further increased the Army of the Valley by some 700 cavalrymen, for a grand total of about 14,000 men present for duty out of some 40,000 present and absent.[89]

In letters to their families, several members of Kershaw's Division described both the warm reception they received and the condition of Early's army when they rejoined it in the Shenandoah Valley. "We have had twelve days of hard marching to get back to the army we left," James Conner informed his mother. Conner, Kershaw's newest brigade commander, had briefly commanded Samuel McGowan's Brigade in the Third Corps while McGowan recuperated from a wound. He had just been assigned to lead Kershaw's old South Carolina brigade, which had had at least three different colonels since before the Wilderness. Conner also voiced an opinion common throughout the division, one undoubtedly shared by numerous Confederates who had suffered through Winchester and Fisher's Hill, when he wrote, "Had we been at Winchester, the defeat of Early would not have occurred. . . . Two thousand men to have met that cavalry [which routed Early's left flank late in the battle] would have secured a brilliant victory."[90]

One of Conner's soldiers was more concerned with the present and the immediate future than the immediate past. According to aide-de-camp Charles Kerrison, who described the scene on the evening of 26 September near Port Republic, "the air was made alive by the music of our bands—an order was sent round by our general to make as much noise as possible and as it does not take much to make a soldier noisy there was a great cheering till late of night." Kerrison reported that "great numbers of Earlys stragglers came in, they thought if Kershaws Div could be so hopeful and in such good spirits they had nothing to fear. . . . By tomorrow we will be straightened up, and I hope have an army worth something as before."[91]

Another member of the division, somewhat less optimistic than Conner or Kerrison, stressed his own weariness and the obvious discouragement among Early's exhausted troops. John L. G. Wood, a drummer in the 53d Georgia, wrote his father: "I am getting very tired of this war. It looks like it is to be an ever lasting war if we have got to have our independence I want us to get it shortly, and if we are to be subjugated, I want it to be shortly done, as I want peace." Turning his attention to the situation at hand, Wood observed: "I have some very bad news to write you at present. Gen. Early has been badly whipped, routed and his troops are completely demoralized. . . . The cause of this disaster, was by sending our Division to Gordonsville. As soon as the Yanks found out that Early's force was weakened they being reinforced, surprised our forces and by over-whelming numbers routed them." The musician, in spite of his relatively somber mood, still predicted that Early's newly reinforced army might succeed: "I think we will whip the Yankees here in the valley yet."[92]

Some officers and men in the Army of the Valley thought that these reinforcements would increase the likelihood of Early's success, if not guarantee it, in the near future. They believed they had already been through the worst part of the campaign in the Shenandoah Valley and hoped for better days to come, when they would defeat Sheridan, then return to Marse Robert and their comrades at Petersburg. These Confederates, while acknowledging the depth of their recent embarrassments, now took a slightly more positive view and in many instances attempted to reassure discouraged families and friends at home. One soldier whose correspondence after Fisher's Hill reflected this duality was Jonathan Coghill of North Carolina. When Coghill wrote his brother on 6 October he described the latest engagements at length, but when he wrote his sister four days later he saw no reason to go into detail. He remarked, somewhat philosophically, "wee cannot expect to gain every victory over the army that is opposing us [in] large and superior numbers to ours," then continued, "therefore wee should not be discouraged because the[y] repulsed and drove us from the field [at Winchester]. . . . they brag and bost over the victory for the onely perpose that it was the brag corps of the army of N.Va. which had never reallized A whipping before." Coghill, who observed, "I have already said more about the fight than I intended so I [will] not continue the horrible subject," ended his letter hoping "to get a furlough and return home to eat some good victuals and see you all."[93]

Others wrote in much the same vein, such as the Georgia brigadier who inspected his command a few days after Fisher's Hill. "You would have been amused to hear their assurances, 'We won't leave you, General.' 'Don't be uneasy about us, General.' 'We'll go with you, General.' 'We can whip them' &c &c.," he informed his wife. "My old invincible brigade is itself again." The next day, after noting that returning stragglers and reinforcements were welcome additions to the ranks of Early's army, Clement Evans wrote, "I expect our folks at home are very much disheartened on account of recent reverses. . . . This feeling of despondency is perfectly natural, but so long as it does not affect their resolve to be independent it will not materially affect our cause."[94] A sergeant in Evans's Brigade who described the disappointments at Winchester and Fisher's Hill in some detail concluded, "The boys are in good heart although they have had enough to dishearten them."[95]

Though many of Early's soldiers might well have been "in good heart," they had few officers of proper grade commanding them. "Our loss has been very heavy, especially in Offrs.," Dodson Ramseur wrote his wife on 25 September.[96] An inspection of the army a few days later dramatically confirmed Ramseur's statement when Maj. H. A. Whiting, inspector general of the division, commented, "The best and efficient officers in nearly every brigade have for the most part been either killed or wounded during this campaign, and some regiments and brigades are sadly deficient in this respect."[97] William R. Cox's North Carolina brigade, for example, had no regimental officers present above the grade of captain, and the 4th North Carolina was commanded by a second lieutenant. Ramseur's four brigades should have had nearly sixty field officers, but could only muster seven, with three colonels, three lieutenant colonels, and a major present; eight captains and a second lieutenant commanded regiments in three out of four brigades.[98] "Under these circumstances," Whiting reported, "it is impossible that discipline should be kept unimpaired or even efficient. Comparatively, the discipline of the division is fair, but much impaired by the recent disaster."[99] It was evident that the division, even when allowing for the small number of arms-bearing men present for duty—some 2,500 soldiers, out of a total of 12,500 present and absent—desperately needed qualified officers.[100]

Inspections of other units revealed similar deficiencies. The acting inspector general of John Pegram's old Virginia brigade, in Gordon's Division, blamed "The absence of Field and Company Officers, and the constant transfer of the Command of many Companies, & even regiments, to subaltern, *inexperienced*, and *inefficient* Officers" for "the loose discipline, so perceptible in some portions of this Brigade." Lt. W. B. McNuman proposed the temporary consolidation of understrength companies and "the assignment of Competent officers" in the brigade, which was commanded by a colonel, with its five regiments commanded by a lieutenant colonel and four captains.[101] Many other divisions, brigades, and regiments in the army—except, for the most part, the new arrivals—were just as hampered by their inability to retain good officers. Other problems that were having, and would continue to have, only slightly less deleterious effects on the army's performance were also identified in inspection reports.

One concern, which would manifest itself over time, was that some troops were not only growing less disciplined, but also were willfully so rather than through negligence. Inspector General McNuman reported that officers in his brigade allowed their soldiers to sell whatever Federal property they might capture or find, a practice in direct violation of regulations but one that was nevertheless widespread throughout the Confederate army. He believed that this behavior was having "a very demoralizing effect upon many of our once bravest and best soldiers," and that the troops' "great desire for plunder, in anticipation of *gain*, induce many men to swerve from their proper line of duty, leaving their comrades to do the duty that he would otherwise have assisted to do."[102] Some officers, including the commanding general, might have expected as much from the Valley cavalry, but it was another thing entirely for the army's infantrymen to engage in such large-scale plundering.

Another pressing issue was the relatively poor physical condition of many rank-and-file soldiers. "The men are much worn and exhausted by the fatigues of the campaign," one report noted, whereas another pointed out that "the scarcity of clothing, the active and constant duty this Brigade has performed, and the consequent bad condition of their worn and dirty clothing" kept the unit in question from receiving high marks in such categories as "Military Appearance" and "soldiery bearing."[103] Though Early wrote Lee on 9 October, "My infantry is now in good heart and condition," questions about his army's effectiveness still remained and would not be answered until its next battle with the Federals.[104]

Between Fisher's Hill and that next battle, however, Sheridan would contemplate leaving the Shenandoah Valley altogether, secure in the belief that Early and the Army of the Valley posed no real threat to him. The Federal commander, hoping to destroy the valley's usefulness to the Confederacy, sent his cavalrymen on a brief but intense period of devastation, known to the valley's residents as "the Burning." This methodical operation, much like the one pursued in August but over a wider territory and on a larger scale, evoked the same level of anger among Confederate correspondents and diarists. "The Yankees are at their fiendish work and thousands of dollars worth of property has been consigned to the flames," a Georgia brigadier wrote his wife on 4 October. A few days later he commented, "The role of both Sheridan and Early in the Valley is played. The smoking embers of five hundred barns tell how well Sheridan has performed his part."[105] A North Carolina private explained the destruction to his family on 17 October, after most of it had been completed. "While the yankees was on there raiding excursion they received special orders to burn and distroy everything that was in their power," Jonathan Fuller Coghill declared. "They carried out their orders in the most redicalous manner they burnt every barn and A good meny private buildings all now lyes in desolation wheat and meny other things . . . this is the fruits of warfare and especially in A country where the abolition foe is campying."[106]

The Confederate cavalry, especially after Thomas Rosser arrived in the Shenandoah Valley, responded to the Burning by harassing Sheridan's horsemen whenever possible. When Rosser joined Early he took command of Fitzhugh Lee's old division from Williams Wickham, who was leaving the army to take a seat in the Confederate Congress. Rosser, cooperating with Lomax, then set out to disrupt Federal operations, and the two were so annoying that Sheridan quickly ordered two of his cavalry divisions to crush the smaller Confederate force. Rosser and Lomax, who were miles from any infantry support, chose separate defensive positions near Tom's Brook, fought dismounted, and repulsed the first Federal attacks on 9 October. Eventually, however, Sheridan's cavalrymen turned first Rosser's, then Lomax's, flank, and the Valley cavalry broke, fleeing from yet another battlefield in an inglorious, panic-stricken rout. The Federals, who chased Rosser's and Lomax's troopers some twenty miles in what they dubbed "the Woodstock Races," also captured four pieces of artillery, numerous wagons, and other spoils.[107]

Early, appalled at this disgraceful performance, wrote Lee: "God knows I have done all in my power to avert the disasters which have befallen this command; but the fact is that the enemy's cavalry is so much superior to ours, both in numbers and equipment, and the country is so favorable to the operations of cavalry, that it is impossible for ours to compete with his." After listing several reasons for the failures of his horsemen, Early commented, "It would be better if they could all be put into the infantry; but if that were tried I am afraid they would all run off."[108] Dodson Ramseur, after describing the Valley cavalry's latest fiasco, remarked, "I declare I am sick at heart from these repeated disasters—but I hope this is the last."[109] Bryan Grimes seemed to be even more disgusted than Early and Ramseur, if such a thing was possible. In a letter to his wife the next day, he remarked:

> I had hoped that when Gen. Rosser came up here that he would inaugurate a change—but he also appears to have become demoralized—that must be something contagious in this atmosphere or in the Valley Cavalry for they cause everything to stampede that comes in association with them—If I had a dictum in this matter at least one hundred of them would have been suspended on gibbets this morning as a warning to others . . . perhaps they would then rather risk their chances in battle than to be hung.[110]

This catastrophe emphatically confirmed, if any observers in the army still needed to be convinced of the fact, that Early's cavalry was by far the weakest part of the Valley army, and that it simply could not be depended on.

Lee, meanwhile, though he admitted that it was "impossible at this distance to give definite instructions," continued to advise and sympathize with Early from afar.[111] "My regret is equal to your own at the reverses that occurred at Winchester and Fisher's Hill, but I hope our loss can be redeemed," he wrote him on 12 October, addressing concerns raised in Early's official report of the two battles and in their correspondence since. He advised Early to "keep your troops well together, to restore their confidence, improve their condition in every way you can, enforce strict discipline in officers and men, keep yourself well advised of the enemy's movements and strength, and endeavor to separate and strike them in detail." In discussing several possible Federal movements and corresponding Confederate responses in the Shenandoah Valley, Lee expressed the hope that if Sheridan attempted to reinforce Grant, Early might then be able to "move against him and endeavor to crush him." He then assured Early that he did not hold recent disappointments against him, telling him, "You must not be discouraged, but continue to try. I rely upon your judgment and ability, and the hearty co-operation of your officers and men." Lee reiterated his opinion of late September that Early overestimated Federal strength in the valley, cautioned that Sheridan's force was still formidable, and reminded Early once again that he needed any troops that the Army of the Valley could spare.[112] Early, with a relatively wide range of options available to him, decided to take the offensive and to risk another defeat in the hope that he might surprise the Federals and win a badly needed Confederate victory. His next move would be a critical one and might determine his ultimate success or failure in the Shenandoah Valley.

Sheridan, for his part, believed that Tom's Brook was only further proof that the Confederates in the area could not, or would not, continue to oppose him and that the campaign was over. The Federal commander moved the Army of the Shenandoah to the position it had held in August at Cedar Creek, between Strasburg and Middletown; made provisions to send one of his corps back to Grant and the Army of the Potomac; and waited to see what Early's intentions were. Sheridan did not have long to wait. Though he believed that Early was still far to his south, near Waynesboro, by 7 October the Confederates had slowly followed him back down the valley as far as New Market. The Army of the Valley left New Market on the twelfth, marched through Strasburg to the outskirts of Sheridan's camp on Cedar Creek, and conducted a reconnaissance in force the next day before retiring to Fisher's Hill. While the skirmish proved to Early that the Federals were posted in a strong position, it shattered any illusions that Sheridan might have had about the Confederates' whereabouts and persuaded him to keep all his troops close at hand for the moment.[113] At least one observer in the Army of the Valley thought that the brief engagement had demonstrated that "the general feeling in this army is to have one more good chance and if they do not amply retrieve the disgrace of Winchester and Fishers Hill, it is not for the want of fighting."[114]

Early, looking for his "one more good chance," was determined to make the most of whatever opportunity he was given, particularly after a reconnaissance from the top of nearby Massanutten Mountain revealed that the Federal left was vulnerable to a flanking maneuver. If Early could cross the Shenandoah River, march around the base of the mountain, and recross the river above Cedar Creek, he could surprise Sheridan's army in its camp and perhaps crush it. The plan called for John Gordon, with his own division, Ramseur's, and Pegram's, to start out on the night of 18 October and to be in position to attack the Federals from the east just before dawn the next morning. Kershaw, with his and Wharton's divisions, would launch an assault of his own from the south about the same time Gordon hit Sheridan's exposed flank. Early thought that "the chances of success would be greater from the fact that the enemy would not expect a move in that direction," and he was certainly right.[115]

Just after 5:00 on the morning of 19 October, while many unsuspecting Federals still slept in their tents, Early's Confederates dealt them a stunning blow. Gordon, with the bulk of the Valley army, swept through fog into Sheridan's camps while Kershaw crossed Cedar Creek and forced the Federals from their works. The separate Confederate assaulting columns then joined and drove two of Sheridan's corps in confusion, taking hundreds of prisoners and several pieces of artillery with relative ease. The momentum of Early's attack stalled during the morning, however, when a third Federal corps, which had been posted a short distance from the remainder of Sheridan's force, repulsed several Confederate attempts to dislodge it. By late morning the Federal infantry had withdrawn to a new position just north of the town and west of the Valley Pike, while Sheridan's dismounted cavalry held the pike itself and the ground to the east. In the meantime Sheridan himself, who had been conferring with superiors in Washington, had made a dramatic return to his army, rallying stragglers along the way. The Confederates, who had driven the Federals almost three miles, established a new line astride the pike, allowed the rest of their units time to come up, and waited.

Early, who believed that most of the fighting was over for the day and that the Federals would soon withdraw from the field in defeat, also recognized that his army was in little condition to press ahead. Many of his soldiers were exhausted from the difficult night march and the morning's battle; many others were missing from the ranks, having straggled into the Federal camps in search of whatever plunder they could find. A Confederate reconnaissance in force in the early afternoon, in which Early sent three divisions to probe Sheridan's lines, served only to put those units in a dangerously exposed position. As hours passed without substantial fighting on either side, Early's inactivity stood in direct contrast to Sheridan's aggressive preparations for a full-scale infantry and cavalry counterattack.

The Federal assault finally came about 4:00 P.M., when two infantry corps attacked Early's center and two cavalry divisions moved on his flanks. Gordon's Division, on the Confederate left, held its ground briefly but was soon driven back in confusion by Federal cavalrymen. The sudden appearance of Sheridan's cavalry precipitated a panic in the Confederate ranks, magnified by terrified soldiers shouting "we are flanked!" Kershaw's Division, to Gordon's right, soon collapsed as well and uncovered Ramseur's Division, in what had been the center of Early's line. Though Ramseur's troops and the Confederate artillery fought stubbornly, they were forced back and then gave way, fleeing with the troops to their left. Pegram's and Wharton's Divisions, on the end of Early's line to Ramseur's right, were then ordered to withdraw but broke when pressed by Sheridan's cavalry. The Confederates, blind to anything but visions of Federal horsemen riding over them and deaf to the appeals of their officers, sped down the Valley Pike in yet another shameful rout. For the third time in a month—this time after winning a brilliant, if incomplete, victory earlier in the day—Early's army disintegrated into a mob of individuals running for their lives. From that moment the Army of the Valley, for all practical purposes, ceased to be a threat to Federal operations in the Shenandoah. The Confederates, halting only briefly at Fisher's Hill, continued in the direction of New Market the next morning.[116]

Federal and Confederate casualties were comparable to those at Winchester, as Sheridan lost some 5,600 men killed, wounded, and captured, and Early lost about 2,900 troops and hundreds of wagons, ambulances, and other spoils. One striking indication of changing fortunes during the day was the number of artillery pieces captured and lost by each army; though the Confederates captured twenty pieces of Sheridan's artillery early in the battle, the Federals not only recaptured those but also took twenty-four of Early's guns during their counterattack.

Casualties among Confederate officers were just as devastating at Cedar Creek as they had been at Winchester. Early lost yet another division commander in the final phases of the battle when Dodson Ramseur was mortally wounded while rallying his division. Ramseur was later captured and died the next day in Federal hands. "I trust he may live and be restored to us," an Alabama lieutenant colonel observed a few days after the battle, before the news of Ramseur's death had reached the Army of the Valley. "No Maj Genl. ever handled a division with better skill & no soldier ever behaved more bravely than he did on that day."[117] In his report Bryan Grimes, Ramseur's friend and successor, called his death "not only a loss to this division but to his State and the country at large. No truer or nobler spirit has been sacrificed in this unjust and unholy war."[118] Other notable losses included Cullen A. Battle, seriously wounded while commanding his Alabama brigade early in the battle, and three out of four regimental commanders—two of them mortally wounded—in Simms's Brigade of Kershaw's Division.[119]

In the aftermath of their third major defeat, as Early's officers and men looked back on their performance at Cedar Creek, they contrasted their stunning victory of the morning with their shattering defeat that evening and expressed astonishment that such a reversal could have happened. A daring plan by Early and his subordinates, executed almost flawlessly by the troops, had seemed to erase the shame of Winchester and Fisher's Hill and to justify the risks taken to create the Army of the Valley. Charles Kerrison, an aide-de-camp in the 2d South Carolina, wrote his sister on the afternoon of 19 October while the Confederates and Federals watched each other. "The battle is still going on the enemy endeavoring to make a stand," he reported, "but I trust will not be able to do so." Kerrison, who had assisted Maj. Benjamin R. Clyburn of his regiment from the field after Clyburn was severely wounded, observed, "If our success continues we will drive Sheridan over the Potomac. God grant that we may."[120] In the late afternoon, however, the Federals were given time to reorganize their shaken troops as Sheridan massed his army for a counterattack, one in which his cavalry played the decisive role. Sgt. Daniel Boyd of the 7th South Carolina described what happened after Kershaw's Division was flanked: "We had to do Som of our best runing and the yankees after us their Was no Such a thing as ralleying our men they Went Swarming like bees they drove us back over the Same ground that We drove them in about as big a hury. . . . We had one of [the] greatest victories Won ov the War; if We cold of held it We had cut too corpse to peaces if our men had don their duty We cold hav Whipt them easy enough."[121] Many other correspondents and diarists characterized the battle in similar terms. "A great battle was there won and lost in one day," a lieutenant in the 12th North Carolina remarked, "by our army won by an admirably arranged and executed plan of battle and lost by want of discipline and its inevitable consequences."[122] Other observers called Cedar Creek "one of the most brilliant victories of the war turned into one of the most disgraceful retreats," "the worst stampede yet, and the harder to bear after our victory of the morning," or "the greatest victory of the war if we just could of helt it."[123]

Valley soldiers wrote at some length on the causes of their latest disaster. A few of them pointed to the long delay of the late morning and most of the afternoon as one reason for their defeat. Surgeon Robert P. Myers thought that the Confederates "foolishly rested on our Laurels until the afternoon—which rest proved very *weary* for us—for during our idleness the enemy recover'd and rec'd re-inforcements from Winchester."[124] But most observers believed that it was not the delay in and of itself but the troops' behavior during that delay that doomed the Army of the Valley. "Discipline is dead & our army is little better than a band of thieves & marauders," one disgusted staff officer asserted, referring to the remarkable breakdown of order when hundreds of Confederates either stopped during their advance or went back once the fighting slackened to loot the captured Federal camps.[125] Early's reasons for not continuing the engagement north of Middletown were threefold: "So many of our men had stopped in the camp to plunder (in which I am sorry to say that officers participated), the country was so open, and the enemy's cavalry so strong, that I did not deem it prudent to press farther."[126] He believed, with some justification, that the combination of plunder in the morning and panic in the afternoon had cost him a hard-won victory. "We had within our grasp a glorious victory," Early maintained, "and lost it by the uncontrollable propensity of our men for plunder, in the first place, and the subsequent panic among those who had kept their places."[127]

Numerous Confederates corroborated Early's claims of widespread plundering. Most, though not all, of them who wrote about the looting condemned the practice, believing that it contributed greatly to their defeat. Several observers referred to standing orders against straggling and plundering and blamed officers for not vigorously enforcing them; some noted that a few officers encouraged or even participated in the looting themselves. "If Genl Early's Orders had been carried out by Company Commanders, the result I am sure would have been quite different," Adjt. Samuel P. Collier of the 2d North Carolina wrote his father a few days later, "but instead of enforcing the order they acted to the contrary, and allowed their men to fall out of ranks to plunder the Yankee camps."[128] Such conduct, according to many Confederates, was much more than a simple disobedience of orders by both officers and men. It became, they insisted, the means of their defeat, because it unnecessarily weakened the

Army of the Valley at a critical moment in the battle. One North Carolina lieutenant noted, as if there was no need for elaboration, "While the battle in the evening was at its crisis the battlefield of the morning was filled with men from our army plundering."[129] Indeed, according to a Virginia cavalryman, "so many loaded themselves with the clothing & baggage the Yankees left, that our battle line was unable to stand the shock of the enemy's attack in the evening."[130]

Though the total number of stragglers and plunderers was unknown, immediate postbattle estimates were "a great many men," "about one-third of the army," "I reckon one half the army," or "a large proportion—probably a majority of the men."[131] "Many of those men I have no doubt had no idea that another battle would be fought," Lt. Archibald Henderson noted, "and in the loose state of discipline thought they were not doing much harm in securing blankets & tent sections for the winter, at least that could be their excuse."[132] But whatever the actual number might have been, the general perception was that Early and his officers had lost control of their men, who had in turn lost control of themselves. "The immense amount of plunder on the battlefield caused a great deal of straggling and proper steps were not taken to prevent it," one Georgia brigadier commented. "I have seldom seen a richer battlefield."[133]

A few of Early's soldiers admitted, without any particular emphasis on whether their conduct was right or wrong, that they had been greatly tempted by the immense quantities of food, clothing, and other supplies abandoned by the Federals. They seemed to believe that any "tricks" they captured were the natural rewards of victory over the enemy and that they were entitled to whatever they could carry away. To be sure, many Confederates plundered out of need rather than out of greed, especially when they picked up clothing, shoes, or blankets. Inspection reports that fall, both before and after Cedar Creek, revealed the pitiful condition to which some units had been reduced by the long campaign and the difficulties encountered in supplying the army over great distances. The inspector general of Grimes's Division reported shortly after the battle, for example, that "Many men are actually barefooted and a large number of shoes are badly worn. Many of the men are yet without Jackets or coats and very many need pants badly."[134] Some soldiers, even when they paused to grab a biscuit, some coffee, or a little tobacco from a Federal haversack, went on with their regiments and did their duty for the remainder of the day. Others, however, took advantage of their opportunity. "We soon whipped them and was master of the field," Pvt. Abel Crawford of the 61st Alabama wrote his wife on 21 October, "and our stragglers did fare sumptuously, for their camps was full of edibles of various kinds, I did not enjoy the feast for I do not claim myself to be a stragler though I got some of their crackers and pork." But Crawford did manage to take a few other items from the camp before he continued to advance with his brigade: "I also captured a blanket (something that I was very much needing for I had been without one for a month) two pair sock, paper and envelops and a silk handkerchief, besides other small articles."[135] One member of the 24th Georgia, writing his sister a few days later, said relatively little about the battle itself but made sure to mention, "well I captuerd me two good blankets and a fine capts haversack with some little tricks I will Send you a ring which I captured."[136]

Many Confederates, whether or not they believed plundering played a significant role in the battle, had definite opinions about the officers or men they held responsible for their defeat. Several members of the army blamed the troops rather than Early and his subordinates, pointing out that the soldiers' panic and resulting stampede negated not only a brilliant plan by the commanding general but also their own fine combat performance. Thomas Devereux alluded to this view in a letter to his grandfather on 23 October headed "Camp Stampede New Market." "I have not the heart to write about the army," Devereux observed, "you know enough to think we are all cowards—and it is nearly so."[137]

Other correspondents and diarists criticized the rank and file with words reminiscent of those describing Winchester and Fisher's Hill. "It is useless to disguise the fact that our army was completely stampeded," a Virginia artilleryman stated in a letter published in a Richmond newspaper a few days after the battle, and a North Carolina infantryman noted, "it was A disgracefull thing. I am sorry to say it but cannot help it."[138] Col. John R. Winston, of the 45th North Carolina, who commanded his regiment and the 43d North Carolina during the battle, reported, "My command acted well until the stampede began. With the co-operation of officers and men, should our army be disgraced with another stampede, under the direction of God, my command will not."[139] Still others, such as Lt. John T. Gay of the 4th Georgia, were even more emphatic in their denunciations of the army's conduct. "I have scarcely done anything since, but think, and O, what thoughts! enough to run any mind half crazy," Gay wrote his wife, continuing with a blistering indictment of the Army of the Valley. "Just to think that this, the 2d Corps of Lee's army, once the pride & admiration of the Confederacy, could have degenerated in so short a time as to merit the scorn and contempt of the whole world; and yet it is only just, that it should be so stigmatized, for such *dastardly cowardice* was never displayed on any battle field, as this corps exhibited on the afternoon of the 19th inst. I never believed that Southern troops could so degrade themselves." After acknowledging that many newspaper editors and civilians were saying "all sort of slanderous things" about Early after Cedar Creek, Gay remarked, "I cannot conceive that he or his Generals were atall to blame for the disaster unless it was for being too lenient [and not] enforcing a strict discipline."[140]

Though many other members of the Valley army, perhaps even most of them, had undoubtedly lost confidence in Early, relatively few expressed that opinion in their letters and diaries. Of those who did, some accused Early of outright mismanagement, claiming that his bad generalship cost the troops a victory they had already won, whereas others thought that his—and his subordinates'—inability to enforce strict discipline among the troops was the basis for the army's defeats throughout the campaign. "There was plundering done on this as on every other battle field," a Georgia brigadier in Gordon's Division conceded, but then claimed, "but it was Early's miserable Generalship which lost the battle. If history does not say so it will not speak the truth."[141] A North Carolina lieutenant observed that "to have a victory already won by good fighting and good generalship, in a few minutes snatched from your grasp . . . and to know that this is caused solely by want of discipline is enough to cause confidence to be lost in our commanding general."[142] One member of the army called for a thorough investigation of the campaign "so that honor could be given to whom honor is due, and likewise the blame," commenting, "I feel certain that most of the troops would come out all right, and General Early would then appear as he is—one of the ablest Generals in the service. The want of discipline is the greatest cause of all our misfortunes."[143]

All too aware that they had left a third battlefield in utter confusion, numerous Confederates were further humiliated and angered when a reprimand from their commander appeared in the Richmond newspapers. "I had hoped to have congratulated you on the splendid victory won by you on the morning of the 19th at Belle Grove, on Cedar Creek," Early's address began, "but I have the mortification of announcing to you that, by your subsequent misconduct, all the benefits of that victory were lost and a serious disaster occurred." This rebuke, in which Early placed all the blame for the defeat on the troops and accepted none himself, contained some stinging observations. "Many of you," Early claimed, "including some commissioned officers, yielding to a disgraceful propensity for plunder, deserted your colors." Regarding the army's flight, he declared, "under the insane dread of being flanked and a panic-stricken terror of the enemy's cavalry, you would listen to no appeal, threat or order."[144] Such language only widened the gulf that already existed between Early and his soldiers, many of whom considered it to be "very much out of taste," and created what one officer called "a new cause of bitter feeling": "I look for no further victories—no further glory to the old 2nd corps under its present leader."[145]

In an atmosphere charged with bitterness, mistrust, and apprehension, the Army of the Valley spent the remainder of October and the first half of November encamped at New Market. Many soldiers, as usual, speculated on what might happen next. "If they give us time to reorganize," one North Carolinian wrote optimistically, "we may still give Sheridan a lively time."[146] But most officers and men thought or hoped that the campaign was over and that winter weather would soon prohibit any action in the Shenandoah until the next spring. A South Carolina sergeant predicted, "I dont think that their wil be [a]ney mor fighting on the valley this Winter."[147]

Others, reflecting on the immediate past, took time to remember comrades who had been killed or mortally wounded during the campaign. The officers in the division commanded by Robert Rodes and then by Dodson Ramseur passed a series of resolutions in memory of their leaders, observing, "our cause has lost two brilliant officers; this Division two able and experienced leaders; and we personally two cultivated comrades and courteous and urbane instructors." When they asked permission to suspend routine duties for a day in order to hold a memorial service honoring Rodes and Ramseur, Early granted the request and added an appreciation of his own. After paying tribute to Rodes, Early could not resist the opportunity to remind his men that Ramseur, while many of them were fleeing from the field at Cedar Creek, had "rallied a small band and for one hour and a quarter held in check the enemy. . . . if his spirit could have animated those who left him thus battling, the 19th of October would have had a far different history." He concluded: "I join with the Division so well commanded by them, in honoring their memory. Let the Division be inspired by the example of these noble heroes, while lamenting their loss."[148]

Early and his subordinates, who could not assume that the campaign in the Shenandoah Valley had ended for the year, worked diligently to get their troops back into fighting trim. They reorganized and consolidated units as necessary; received new soldiers, both conscripts and men returning from various details; provided for appointed officers to fill vacancies; and attempted to create some semblance of discipline among the troops. Numerous observers believed that the only way to improve the army's combat effectiveness was to focus its attention on tasks such as drills or frequent inspections, or on minor details such as proper salutes and insignia of grade, which had become almost nonexistent during the campaign. "This Army is now undergoing the most rigid discipline," one North Carolina adjutant noted on 26 October, "and this I hope will continue for several weeks."[149] Another North Carolinian wrote his mother the next day, "We are still at New Market busy drilling and getting into something like a well organized army—and not an undisciplined mob—as we were after the battle of Cedar Creek."[150] Inspection reports for October and November revealed that the Valley army, which only numbered some 11,000 officers and men present for duty on 1 November, was benefiting greatly from close attention by its officers. "There is a more prompt and cheerful observance of Regulations than has been apparent for some past," Maj. H. A. Whiting observed after inspecting Grimes's Division on 31 October.[151] An officer who inspected the army wrote at the end of November, "In the last month, the improvement in the discipline of this army has been marked."[152]

Not all of Early's soldiers were as cheerful about the newly tightened discipline. Lt. John B. Evans of the 53d Georgia, still under arrest for a minor infraction and awaiting a court-martial any day, told his wife: "Mollie we have the tightest orders in camps that we have ever have had. If a man misses roll call he misses his rations the next day. It aint only a order but it is strickly caried out. One of our co missed roll call this evening and the Col said he should have no rations tomorrow."[153] Pvt. John J. Armfield of the 30th North Carolina, a new arrival in the ranks, described his daily routine to his wife. "We of the new recruits have to drill three times a day," Armfield observed on 9 November. "We will have to drill in a few minutes. I obey all commands, but I loathe everything that is warlike."[154]

The only significant operations undertaken by the Army of the Valley in the month after Cedar Creek occurred in mid-November, when Early conducted a large-scale reconnaissance in force intended to find Sheridan and the Army of the Shenandoah. After marching his troops from New Market some forty miles to Newtown, just south of Winchester, and discovering the Federals firmly entrenched there, Early retraced his steps up the valley. "As you have already seen in the papers," one North Carolinian wrote his brother after the expedition, "Gen'l Early took his customary monthly advance down the Valley, resulting in his customary monthly retreat up it."[155]

By this time it had become obvious that both Early and Sheridan had accomplished all they could in the Shenandoah, and their respective commanders began calling units back to the main armies at Petersburg. On 14 November a Georgian in Kershaw's Division complained: "I am getting extremely tired of the Valley I am willing to go back to Petersburg or anywhere else besides this place. I have pretty well lost confidence in Gen. Early and his troops."[156] The next day his division left the Shenandoah Valley to rejoin Lee and the Army of Northern Virginia. The three divisions—some cynical observers might have called them remnants—of the old Second Corps departed in the first two weeks of December and returned to Petersburg via Richmond under the command of John Gordon. Meanwhile, Early remained near Waynesboro to safeguard whatever interests the Confederacy still had in the Shenandoah Valley with a skeleton force consisting of Wharton's Division, Lomax's and Rosser's small divisions of cavalry, and four battalions of artillery.[157] A veteran lieutenant in the 4th Georgia, in Cook's Brigade of Grimes's Division, described the change not only in location but also in the soldiers' mood after the corps rejoined Lee. "When we left the valley," John Gay wrote his wife, "the snow was about eight or ten inc[h]es deep & the weather bitter cold—here it is quite different, the weather being mild & pleasant. So far the change is very pleasant & agreeable—our Corps has been placed in reserve, for the present and under the command of Genl Gordon, Genl Early having been left in the Valley."[158]

Gay and most of his fellow soldiers were all too happy to belong to the Second Corps of the Army of Northern Virginia again. When their comrades welcomed them back, some of them did so with the expectation that those who had remained behind might now be able to leave the trenches and participate in active campaigning of their own. The veterans of the First and Third Corps, of Beauregard's old command, which by this time had become part of a makeshift Fourth Corps, and of the Cavalry Corps had fought several battles of their own around Petersburg and Richmond since the first of August. Those battles, however, unlike the encounters in the Shenandoah, had been inconclusive, and numerous Confederates wanted an opportunity to engage Grant in a "fair fight" in the field. When Pvt. William D. Alexander, a hospital steward in the 37th North Carolina, saw a division of the Second Corps arriving on 8 December, he hurried to camp and heard a rumor that "all of the army in the front of Petersburg is to be relieved by Earleys command—the orders are to move in 'light fighting trimb.'" Alexander, hopeful that he might participate in some exciting maneuver or battle, wrote in his diary, "I think that a flank movement is on foot."[159]

As 1864 gave way to 1865, Lee's officers and men continued to search for whatever advantages they might obtain over the Federals. Many veterans did not realize just how much the Second Corps had been eroded by its hard campaign in the Shenandoah Valley or just how much the rest of the army had been weakened since August by an enemy whose continued pressure made it almost impossible to maneuver against him. By late 1864 the Army of Northern Virginia, which had previously achieved so much by retaining virtually unlimited mobility and an essentially offensive posture, had slowly been forced to adapt to a severely restricted mobility and an essentially defensive posture. Lee's soldiers, to be successful, would now have to win victories with fewer resources and against greater odds than ever before.

If the army could get a month's rest in the country,

with a little reorganization, it would shew itself to be

equal to more than it has ever done.

—*Lt. Col. W. J. Pegram*

Pegram / III Corps Artillery, to his sister, 5 October 1864

7

The Siege of Petersburg and the Richmond Front: Deep Bottom through Burgess Mill, August–November 1864

In the first few days of August 1864, while Early was entering the second phase of his campaign in the Shenandoah, the rest of the Army of Northern Virginia still occupied its position in the miles of trenches along the Petersburg-Richmond front. Many of Lee's soldiers, in the aftermath of the Crater, contemplated the significance of that remarkable explosion and the resulting battle while they wondered what might happen next. Several of them thought that the opposing armies might soon undertake wholesale mining operations under each other's lines, and a few anxious soldiers seemed to think of little else but the prospect of Federals and Confederates mining and countermining each other into oblivion. To cite one example, Federal officers who interviewed a deserter from the 2d

Maryland Battalion reported that "the enemy are afraid of other mines which they understand we are going to explode."[1]

No doubt such fears were influenced by the numerous reports and rumors surrounding current Confederate attempts to construct mines of their own under the Federals. Soldiers under the supervision of Capt. Hugh Thomas Douglas of the 1st Confederate Engineers had been working on several countermines since mid-July and increased their efforts after the Crater, hoping to forestall the construction or detonation of any other mines by Grant's troops. When one of Douglas's mines was charged on 1 August, the fuses would not burn and it failed to ignite. Another attempt several days later succeeded, but the explosion blasted a moderate amount of earth into the air and precipitated a short exchange of artillery fire, doing no real damage to the Federal lines and bringing on no engagement.[2] "A mine was sprung near the Yankee lines, which made the Yankees run," Capt. John A. F. Coleman of the 17th South Carolina observed in his diary on 5 August; the next day Maj. Matthew Love of the 25th North Carolina wrote his mother, "We did not do the Enemy much damage so far as we have learned."[3]

Both armies soon resumed the familiar routine of occasional sharpshooting, informal truces, and infrequent engagements that had previously characterized operations at Petersburg during June and July. The conventional nature of the siege's first weeks had helped shape the course of the Petersburg campaign far more than any unconventional ventures would. Early Federal offensives on the Weldon Railroad and near Deep Bottom, for instance, had attempted to disrupt Confederate transportation and supply lines but had been checked by Lee. The most recent Federal and Confederate failures at breaking the stalemate, though dramatic enough, were soon demonstrated to be truly insignificant as the campaign reverted to its previous pattern. "The springing of the mine the other day near Petersburg is still talked of," a member of Pickett's Division of the First Corps observed in a letter to the *Richmond Examiner*, "but no longer with apprehension. . . . Truly Grant's military experiments, like history, repeats itself, and he finds blowing up Confederate batteries as destructive to Yankee soldiers as charging Confederate fortifications. What will he try next?"[4]

Numerous observers in the army, such as the Alabama lieutenant who wrote that "nothing of interest has occured here since the battle on the 30th of July," remarked that any particular day along the lines was just like the day before it and would likely be followed by yet another day just like all the others.[5] One Texas private's diary entries for the first two weeks of

August consisted primarily of descriptions of the weather and the comment "no news."[6] A Georgia captain wrote his wife, "I have no changes to note and nothing of interest to write you. The positions of our armies are the same and no prospect of a move." Francis Marion Coker, adjutant of an artillery battalion in the Third Corps, continued in a somewhat melancholy vein: "I reckon it is all right, and that a just Providence will work it all for the best. The war seems to drag terribly slow to those who are suffering its hardships, separated from all that can give them happiness here below."[7]

During the late summer and early fall the war seemed "to drag terribly slow" indeed for Lee's soldiers, whether in the trenches at Petersburg, near Richmond, or at some points in between. Many of them, already weary of their relative inactivity, also protested that they were being neglected by Confederate civil and military authorities who could not or would not care for their needs. They complained about long-overdue or inadequate pay, scanty or inferior rations, shortages or poor workmanship in clothing and shoes, and other indignities, often airing their grievances in letters to the Richmond newspapers. Some soldiers claimed that officers were routinely allowed to take the best rations, clothing, and other issues for themselves before their men received anything. "The best hams and nicest flour are picked out and reserved for them, and, being allowed to purchase additional rations, they get a double share of any rarity sent to the army, such as vegetables, &c.," one veteran asserted in a letter to the *Richmond Examiner*.[8] Another of Lee's soldiers commented that when his regiment received new issues of clothing and shoes, officers quickly climbed into the wagon "picking out the best jackets, pants, shirts, shoes, &c, for their own use." The Confederate, who signed himself "A Ragged Private," continued, "There are scores of men in this army who are almost destitute of clothing, and would be glad of the commonest articles. But the private soldier is first and foremost in one thing only, and that is in battle."[9]

Others grumbled that detailed men serving with the quartermaster department were given an extra two dollars a day in addition to their standard private's pay of eighteen dollars a month. "The pay of a Second Lieutenant in the infantry is *eighty dollars per month and rations*," one soldier who signed himself "In The Trenches" observed in the *Examiner*. "Does the order mean to give a quartermaster's clerk better pay than a commanding officer who *fights* (not *writes*) for his country?" he asked.[10] Still other complaints concerned the poor quality of tobacco issued to the rank and file, which was described in such terms as "unfit to chew" or "as much rotten as if it had been in the farm yard under the feet of the stock all winter."[11] These and similar grievances only intensified the discouragement that was slowly increasing among the troops of the Army of Northern Virginia in the last half of 1864. "Some of our best military men think, above everything else, that this campaign in the trenches has tested the courage, endurance and patriotism of our soldiers," the colonel of the 6th Georgia observed in a brief history of his regiment written in August.[12]

The growing discouragement among Lee's officers and men gave rise to a corresponding increase in absences without leave and, more ominously, in desertions, which became markedly more pronounced after the Crater. On 10 August Lee issued a general order admonishing those soldiers guilty of such offenses to return to duty at once. The order asked men absent without leave to think of "the shame and disgrace they will bring upon themselves and their families if they shrink from the manful discharge of duty in the hour of their country's need" and warned deserters that "a prompt and voluntary return to duty alone can palliate their offense and entitle them to expect any clemency."[13] The next night, however, almost as if to underscore the futility of Confederate attempts to check the tide of desertions, a lieutenant and twenty-four enlisted men of the 9th Alabama left their camp near Petersburg. An officer in Sanders's Brigade reported the incident in a letter to his wife. "Since our arrival here a considerable number of our army has deserted," Lt. Elias Davis of the 10th Alabama observed on the thirteenth. "Night before last twenty five members of 9 Ala Regt. including one commissioned officer deserted. They did not go to the Yankees; are efforting to get home. Some of them had been good soldiers."[14] This case was only one of several in the first two weeks of August that prompted Lee to begin a letter to the secretary of war with the comment, "I regret to state that desertions are increasing in some of the regiments of this army." Lee mentioned several specific units in the Third Corps, including the 9th Alabama, in which desertions had risen considerably, then tried to explain some of the possible causes. "The troops are suffering much discomfort in the trenches," he noted, "which may in part account for these desertions, and the circular issued by the Washington authorities, promising immunity to deserters and exemption from military service, may also have had its effect." He reported that the Alabamians, for example, had deserted because one of their favorite officers had been dismissed during the winter and they planned to go home to Alabama and reenlist in cavalry units being organized there.[15]

Another, more fundamental reason was given for the recent surge in desertions. Numerous soldiers were giving in to feelings of hopelessness as the war continued—and intensified—without any indications that peace might be at hand. "I hope this will be the last year of the war & I believe it will," a division commander in the Third Corps remarked, "if our men will only fight with one half the spirit that they have heretofore. I Sometimes of late think that they are not quite so full of ardour & Spirit as they were the first two years of the war, and with the last few weeks we have [had a] good many desertions."[16]

Several Confederates who did not take the drastic step of desertion still registered their discontent with the war in letters to their families, to newspapers, and in some cases to the military or civil authorities. One such soldier was the North Carolinian who sent a remarkable letter to Gov. Zebulon B. Vance headed "Peters Burg Entrenchments" and signed "P.K.O.G. NC." "This is twice I have voated for you," he reminded Vance soon after he cast his vote for governor, "and if you dont seend out some procklamation now for peace and that soon I will cast one more [vote] or I shall want to cast one to put you out of thare." The miserable North Carolinian, turning his attention to the Confederate government's conduct of the war and the military's treatment of the men in the ranks, continued: "I understand very well the reason why peace cant be made it is on the account of the blacks I ashure you I one [own] some and before I will stay in this war and fight day and night I will give up the last one and if you ware hear presst down like I am you [would] doo so too or allmost any thing ellce for men is suffering death hear anyhow without being shot and then to stand all of this and have to be shot at last I cant stand it nor I shant." His letter closed with the comment, "I dont want you to take any offence at this atall for I saye just what I think nothing more at this time only I hope to hear of your good works soon." Vance's only reply, at least in writing, to this earnest—if anonymous—plea was the terse endorsement "File—ZBV."[17]

Despite widespread complaints, escalating desertions, and other signs of growing discontent, a number of observers believed that most of Lee's soldiers were still willing, if not eager, to fight the Federals. Several of them emphasized the physical condition of their units and contrasted it with the mood of the men. "The heat in the ditches has been intense," a contemporary historian observed in his sketch of a Georgia regiment. "Rations have been short. Many of the officers and men have been for six weeks without a change of clothing. Yet in spite of all, they are confident and in the very best of spirits."[18] One Alabamian stated, "I am much supprised at the desertions from our army now, as the campaign here is drawing to a close: and we are living better than we did at this time two years ago."[19] Though few men looked into the future with enthusiasm, many of them did so with determination, and a member of the 35th Georgia spoke for numerous soldiers in the Army of Northern Virginia when he remarked, "We are quietly reposing in our comfortless quarters, but whoever ventures to disturb our repose will bitterly repent it, for no lethargic sleep is upon us, and we are ready, willing, and anxious to again try the issue by the strength of arms, and thus end the strife."[20]

These soldiers and their comrades did not have to wait long for their chance to "again try the issue by the strength of arms," for the Federals soon launched yet another series of offensives intended to stretch Confederate resources to the breaking point. Grant's initial plan was similar to one that had failed just before the Crater, with one major difference. An attack north of the James River at Deep Bottom would threaten Richmond while it diverted Confederate attention from a subsequent attack south of the James, on the Weldon Railroad. It was also intended to prevent Lee from reinforcing Early in the Shenandoah Valley. By alternating his attacks between the Richmond and Petersburg fronts, Grant hoped to catch Lee off balance and defeat him somewhere along a defensive line that stretched for some thirty-five miles between the two cities.

This Federal offensive, undertaken by an infantry corps, two divisions of a second, and a cavalry division, began on 13 August. Though Lee's force at Deep Bottom was small—consisting of a division of the First Corps, a brigade of Beauregard's command, and a cavalry brigade from the Department of Richmond—it was quickly reinforced by four brigades of the Third Corps and a cavalry brigade from the Army of Northern Virginia. Operations began with skirmishes along the Charles City, Darbytown, and New Market roads southeast of Richmond on the fourteenth and fifteenth, but the major engagement took place on the Darbytown Road in the vicinity of Fussell's Mill on 16 August. The Federals enjoyed some early success there, driving several units back and taking hundreds of prisoners, but the Confederates launched vigorous counterattacks that captured hundreds of prisoners of their own and restored their lines by the late afternoon. When the day's fighting ended in the dense woods and thick underbrush, the two forces held essentially the same positions they had held that morning. Skirmishing continued for a few days but did not materially alter the situation, and Grant withdrew his forces to the south side of the river on the twentieth. Each side was able to claim some success from the action. Whereas the Federals had forced Lee to send reinforcements up from Petersburg and had kept him from sending additional infantry to Early, the Confederates had managed to hold the Richmond front and had prevented Grant from gaining any permanent advantage north of the James. Federal casualties over almost a week totaled some 3,000 troops, while Confederate losses were some 1,500 men killed, wounded, and captured.[21]

Many Confederate accounts of the battle at Deep Bottom emphasized, naturally enough, that the Federal assaults had eventually been beaten back and that no lasting harm had been done to Lee's defensive positions on the outskirts of Richmond. Some soldiers mentioned that Lee himself had been on the field and had witnessed the fighting. The next day Adjt. James McFall told his sister that "General Lee was over with us yesterday and was well pleased with the days work."[22] After describing "a splendid charge" made by his brigade, William Alexander of the 37th North Carolina recorded proudly in his diary, "Gen Lee compliments the Brig. he was an eye witness."[23] Numerous observers admitted that the initial enemy breakthrough created a minor crisis but noted that the Confederates responded swiftly and that their hard fighting canceled any Federal gains. "We skirmished with them all day through the thickets," Sgt. Edward Richardson Crockett of the 4th Texas wrote, recounting some of the obstacles his brigade faced during the fight: "We lost several men by Sun stroke or being over heated. Just after the fight we had a shower of rain. When night came on we were all nearly exhausted."[24] A South Carolina captain reported: "For awhile the foe held us in check, but our men were determined to recover the lost ground. . . . By 5 P.M., the enemy were driven from every point they had assaulted & our troops remained in possession of the entire field."[25]

Confederate casualties, though relatively few, were significant in an army that could ill afford any losses in officers or men. "Though the operations of the day were very successful for us," an officer in the Third Corps observed in his diary on the night of 16 August, "it was not without the loss of many noble spirits."[26] Two of Lee's brigadiers—John R. Chambliss and Victor J. B. Girardey—were among those "noble spirits" killed at Deep Bottom. Their deaths added still more names to the long list of general officers in the army killed, wounded, or captured since the opening of the 1864 campaign. Chambliss, while commanding a Virginia brigade in W. H. F. Lee's Division of the Cavalry Corps, fell in a clash on the Charles City Road on the morning of the sixteenth. He had been colonel of the 13th Virginia Cavalry for more than two years, had often been praised by his superior officers, and had won promotion to general at the end of 1863. Lee wrote Wade Hampton a few days later that Chambliss's death would be "felt throughout the army, in which, by his courage, energy, and skill, he had won for himself an honorable name."[27]

Girardey, commanding a Georgia brigade in William Mahone's Division of the Third Corps, was killed rallying his men near Fussell's Mill that afternoon. He, in marked contrast to Chambliss, had almost no experience leading troops in combat, for he had been a captain on Brig. Gen. Ambrose R. Wright's staff for most of the war and had commanded his men for less than two weeks. Girardey's superiors had recently recommended him for promotion to brigadier general under a law allowing temporary appointments of such officers. "During the current campaign," Mahone noted on 20 July, "no one under my observation has better earned such promotion," and A. P. Hill added, "The law was made to cover just such cases as this, and I know of none in which it can be applied with happier effect. The Brigade needs it, and the Country needs it."[28] Girardey's outstanding performance at the Crater—where he helped direct the vicious counterattack of Mahone's Division—only confirmed his superiors' high opinion of him, and he was appointed brigadier on 3 August, to date from 30 July. His death deprived the Army of Northern Virginia of yet another promising general officer, one whom Lee had recently described as "one of our boldest & most energetic officers."[29] All too many officers such as Chambliss and Girardey became casualties that summer, not only in major battles and engagements, but also in minor skirmishes, demonstrations, and other clashes that accomplished nothing at all.

Some of Lee's soldiers who encountered U.S. Colored Troops for the first time at Deep Bottom belittled the black Federals' performance there and cheerfully reported that hundreds of them had been killed. One officer in Wilcox's Division of the Third Corps wrote, "We moved on their left at a *double quick* and the *negroes* couldn't stand it, yes *negroes* for the first time we fought them was yesterday the woods is covered with them the yanks put them in front in every charge these days."[30] Such exaggerations as "many of the slain were negroes" or "seven or eight hundred negroes were killed in the fight" were typical in Confederate letters and diary entries after the battle, though total casualties in the black regiments numbered fewer than 150 men for the entire Deep Bottom operation.[31] A captain in the 1st South Carolina claimed that the blacks "had been faced to the front, & were terribly slaughtered"; another officer whose brigade was engaged but whose regiment did not participate in the battle quoted Federal prisoners as saying "a good many of the *kinkey* heads bit the dust."[32] The opinion expressed by Capt. W. H. Holcombe of the 1st South Carolina Rifles was shared by many in the Army of Northern Virginia. When on 17 August Holcombe declared, "we are now in good breastworks and if them *nigs* try us they will *catch it*," he displayed the disdain—if not the sheer hatred—that many Confederates felt toward blacks who dared to join the Federal army and oppose them in battle.[33]

Neither the black nor the white Federals made any further attempts to dislodge Lee's troops but crossed the James River and headed back toward Petersburg. Grant, after the Confederates moved substantial reinforcements in the direction of Richmond—just as he had hoped they would—acted quickly to take advantage of his far superior numbers south of the James. He ordered a corps south of Petersburg to take possession of a point along the Weldon Railroad and to destroy as much track as possible from that point south toward North Carolina. Meanwhile, Lee, whose presence at Deep Bottom had already demonstrated his concern for that portion of his lines, decided to move army headquarters north of the James to Chaffin's Bluff. Beauregard, for the time being, was given the responsibility for countering any enemy operations on the Petersburg front in Lee's absence.

On 18 August, the same day that Lee established headquarters north of the James, Beauregard learned that Federals were moving in force toward Globe Tavern, on the Weldon Railroad some six miles south of Petersburg. He ordered three brigades, elements of his own command and A. P. Hill's Third Corps, to join the Confederate cavalry brigade already near the railroad, to block the Federals' advance, and to drive them back. The Federals arrived at Globe Tavern in the late morning and deployed astride the railroad, sending one division south to tear up the track and two other divisions north toward the Petersburg defenses as a precautionary measure. When the Confederates reached the railroad early in the afternoon, they quickly formed across the tracks and attacked one of the two Federal divisions that had advanced toward Petersburg. Two infantry brigades, with a third in reserve, drove an isolated Federal brigade about a mile and took some 150 prisoners but withdrew in the early evening when enemy reinforcements arrived.

The Confederates, recognizing that Grant's attempt on the railroad was no mere raid, scrambled to put together a makeshift force to drive the Federals from Globe Tavern the next day. As a driving rain fell throughout 19 August, the Federals worked to concentrate their troops and to improve their defensive positions while the Confederates sent five brigades down from Petersburg to make another attempt at securing the railroad. The Confederate plan called for two brigades to attack the Federals in front while three others struck their right flank. When the assault finally came late in the afternoon, it scattered one division in confusion and took more than 2,500 prisoners but stalled after Federal reinforcements counterattacked and regained the lost ground. The Confederates withdrew toward Petersburg once again that evening, while the shaken Federals maintained their positions on the railroad.

Both forces spent 20 August preparing for a possible third engagement, the Federals working to consolidate their forces and strengthen their position, and the Confederates attempting to form yet another striking force with enough numbers to accomplish their task. By the evening the Federals had withdrawn a short distance south, nearer Globe Tavern, and were building earthworks, whereas the Confederates had spent most of the day shifting troops from the Petersburg trenches to the Weldon Railroad. Elements of Beauregard's command and the Third Corps were once again chosen to drive the Federals from the railroad, with two major differences. These Confederates were not only fresh troops replacing those that had participated in the operations of the eighteenth and nineteenth, but also numbered many more men than the earlier forces sent out from Petersburg. This force—nine brigades and a portion of a tenth—would attack straight down the railroad with three brigades while six others struck the Federals from the left rear. Beauregard and Lee hoped that a determined assault might finally succeed and force Grant back.

As soon as fighting began on the morning of 21 August, the Confederates discovered, to their dismay, that the Federals had faced a significant portion of their forces parallel to the Weldon Railroad. What had been intended as a flank attack had become a simple frontal assault against a strongly entrenched enemy with well-placed artillery. The first Confederate attack was repulsed with moderate casualties and the second, which came down the line of the railroad, fared no better. A third attempt, made by a single brigade of Beauregard's command, was made in the late morning and sought to flank the Federals but ended in disaster when the brigade was caught in an angle of the enemy's works and was virtually wrecked. Lee, whose concern for the railroad had prompted him to return to the Petersburg front, reached the field that afternoon and regretfully called off another proposed attack when reinforcements were late in arriving, conceding his inability to drive Grant from his strong position. Casualties over four days near Globe Tavern totaled some 4,300 Federal troops, whereas estimates of Confederate losses ranged from about 1,600 to 2,300 killed, wounded, and captured.[34]

Lee's officers and men were well aware that their failure to force the

Federals off the railroad had grave implications for the future security of Petersburg and, by extension, of Richmond. On the morning of 19 August, the adjutant of a Third Corps artillery battalion had written, "although we drove them a mile [on the eighteenth], we couldn't make them relinquish their hold on the road—being too weak for them. . . . today, I doubt not, we shall dislodge them, though it may cost a good many men."[35] After assaults on 19 and 21 August accomplished little except to cost the Confederates "a good many men," numerous correspondents and diarists described the intensity of the fighting and expressed their frustration at the disappointing results of the battle. "Heavy loss was inflicted on the enemy," a South Carolina captain noted in his diary on the night of 21 August, "but their position was too strongly fortified, & their numbers too much superior to those engaged on our side, for us to dislodge them."[36] Some of Lee's soldiers who were captured during the battle admitted that "everything they dared spare was taken from the lines to drive us off the Weldon railroad," in the words of one Federal officer who interviewed the prisoners.[37]

A member of Beauregard's staff, commenting on the relationship between Federal operations north of the James at Deep Bottom and south of the James at Globe Tavern, advanced the most compelling explanation for the Confederates' failure to retake the Weldon Railroad. "I fear that the Weldon RRd is now lost to us," Maj. Henry Bryan remarked, "as the Yankees entrenched themselves strongly there while Gen Lee was occupied on the north of the James River."[38] Lee explained to President Davis on 22 August that he could not have forced Grant back "even with additional troops, without a greater sacrifice of life than we can afford to make, or than the advantages of success would compensate for." Even if he had been able to drive the Federals from the railroad at Globe Tavern, they would have eventually taken hold of it somewhere else.[39]

The officers and men whose units had suffered heavily at the Weldon Railroad could have been pardoned for believing that those comrades killed, wounded, and captured were already "a greater sacrifice of life than we can afford to make."[40] One North Carolinian whose brigade lost many casualties in the first day's fighting wrote a pitiful letter to his family describing and lamenting losses among his fellow soldiers, friends, and relatives. James King Wilkerson of the 55th North Carolina wrote:

Oh mother the men we have lost on the road and made nothing for the yankees is well fortified. most of our brigade is killed and wounded also our Regiment and company. Pete Phillips was killed thursday and Stephen Sanford too and Jo Eritckes was missing surpose to be killed I saw cousin S. Sanford shot the ball went in his upper lip and went out back side of his head. Oh, I never saw search times in my life. . . . I am afraid we will have to go up on the road in a few days a gain to charge the yankees for all of us to get killed. . . . Our men have been fighting up on the road since friday but never accompliach much by chargeing the yankees work only lost men.[41]

The devastation caused by such losses was particularly acute in Brig. Gen. Johnson Hagood's South Carolina brigade, which made the third and final assault of the day on 21 August. The South Carolinians were ordered to attack what was presumed to be the Federal left flank and rear but instead found themselves advancing against "a very strong earth-work swarming with Yankees, while on both sides similar works flanked them, & rendered our men completely trapped."[42] Confusion reigned in front of the Federal works, as many of Hagood's men were captured or surrendered under a withering fire of musketry and artillery while others continued to fight. One noncommissioned officer, who was himself wounded, claimed a few days later, "Our men were at that time very near the Yankee works, & it was surrender or death."[43] When a Federal captain captured the flag of the 27th South Carolina and ordered the Confederates to surrender, Col. Peter C. Gaillard and many of his men wavered between "surrender or death." Hagood, sensing a crisis, ordered his men not to surrender, confronted the Federal captain and shot him, then led the remnants of his shattered brigade back to the main Confederate lines. "I succeeded in withdrawing the men with as little loss as could have been expected from the terrible fire to which we were exposed in retiring," he reported the next day.[44] Other members of the brigade described their withdrawal, and Hagood's part in it, in less euphemistic terms. "One of his orderlies picked up the flag, & the Genl. told the men to scatter & save themselves," a noncommissioned officer of the 25th South Carolina noted, seconded by a member of his regiment who described Hagood "calling to our men to save themselves as best they could."[45] Hagood himself called the battle "the hardest we have ever been in," and one of his South Carolinians observed, with considerable understatement, "Yesterday will be a day long remembered in the history of our brigade."[46]

Hagood's Brigade, which had already seen hard service that spring and summer in Beauregard's command, entered the battle with almost 750 officers and men and left the field with fewer than 300, losing 14 killed, 125 wounded, and 309 captured or missing.[47] When Maj. G. B. Lartigue of

Hagood's staff spoke of "the Brigade such as it is" the next day and 1st Sgt. Henry Greer of the 25th South Carolina, who would soon take command of Company B, referred to "the Company or rather what was left of it," they had ample justification for doing so.[48] In a poem written later that summer and titled "Charge of Hagood's Brigade. Weldon Railroad, August 21, 1864," Joseph Blyth Allston paid tribute to the dead officers and men of the brigade with these lines:

Ah, Carolina! well the tear
May dew thy cheek; thy clasped hands rear
In passion, o'er their tombless bier,
    Thy fallen chivalry![49]

Among the "fallen chivalry" was Capt. Patrick Kilbride Molony, the assistant adjutant general of the brigade and a longtime member of Hagood's staff, who was missing and presumed dead; his body was never recovered. "There was not a man more valued & liked in the Brigade than he was," one of Molony's friends and fellow staff officers wrote. "His like we will not meet again."[50] In a letter of condolence to Molony's brother, Johnson Hagood observed that "one of the men when he learned his fate seized my hand and leaning on my horses shoulder wept uncontrollably for minutes," then added his own tribute to Molony, concluding, "he came up more fully to my idea of a gentleman than any man I ever knew."[51] A friend of the family wrote: "The war, dear Col., has lasted too long, and the joy that comes with returning peace will be drowned in tears—bitter tears for the 'unreturning brave.' The noblest and the best are falling in the struggle."[52]

Grant, seeking to take full advantage of his success on the Weldon Railroad, allowed Lee's soldiers little time to grieve for their dead and even less time to rest or to prepare for another of his offensives along the Petersburg-Richmond front. He had ordered troops south from Deep Bottom even before the fighting ended near Globe Tavern, planning to employ them as reinforcements if needed but preferring to send them on another expedition along the Weldon Railroad. On 24 August Grant sent one corps, which had recently arrived from the north side of the James, to continue the destruction of track from Globe Tavern through Reams Station, some twelve miles from Petersburg.

Meanwhile, Confederate cavalry reconnaissances over the previous few days had alerted Lee to increased activity in the vicinity of Reams Station and persuaded him that the enemy corps there was vulnerable. He ordered a combined force of cavalry and infantry to attack the Federals destroying the railroad. Before dawn on 25 August two divisions of Confederate cavalry left Petersburg, followed a few hours later by six infantry brigades and a portion of a seventh from the Third Corps and one brigade from the First Corps. The Federals, who had torn up track as far as two miles below Reams Station, soon learned that a large enemy force was on its way south and returned to the station, hoping to improve their poorly constructed earthworks before the Confederates arrived.

Fighting began at Reams Station in the late morning, when Confederate cavalrymen drove in the Federal cavalry pickets with little resistance. The horsemen then encountered Federal infantry, which counterattacked but could neither drive the Confederates back nor flank them, and skirmishing continued until the early afternoon when the Confederate infantry came up. After two successive assaults by elements of the Third Corps were repulsed during the afternoon, the Confederates massed their troops for a third attempt against the Federal defenses. The last fighting of the day began about 5:30 P.M. after a Confederate artillery bombardment, when Lee's infantry and cavalry attacked the breastworks simultaneously from two directions. Though some Federal units held their ground, the majority of them fled or were captured in what threatened to become a full-scale rout. The Federals, after their faltering attempts to organize a counterattack failed, acknowledged their defeat and withdrew from Reams Station that night. Federal losses totaled some 2,700 soldiers, of whom more than 2,000 officers and men were captured, along with twelve flags and nine cannon. Confederate casualties, in contrast, numbered only about 800 troops killed, wounded, and captured.[53]

Such a complete tactical victory produced jubilation within the Army of Northern Virginia, both among the soldiers who had fought at Reams Station and those who only heard about the battle secondhand. A hastily assembled Confederate force had not only defeated a veteran Federal corps, but also had done so with a determined frontal assault over a fortified position. "Everything was accomplished that was intended & it is considered a brilliant thing," a North Carolina courier at Third Corps headquarters wrote his sister. A South Carolina captain whose brigade was held in reserve believed that "The plan of the battle reflected great credit upon the Generals who planned it, & also upon the actions of the gallant troops who were engaged."[54]

Three North Carolina brigades of the Third Corps led the decisive charge over the Federal breastworks and received most of the credit for the victory. All three brigades—John Rogers Cooke's and William MacRae's of Henry Heth's Division and James H. Lane's of Wilcox's Division, commanded in Lane's absence by James Conner—were veteran units and had distinguished themselves in several battles. "The fight was pretty severe while it lasted," one North Carolinian observed proudly, "but the gallant 'tar heels' made short work of it."[55] The units were warmly praised by Lee, who on 29 August wrote Gov. Zebulon B. Vance, "I have frequently been called upon to mention the services of North Carolina soldiers in this army, but their gallantry and conduct were never more deserving of admiration than in the engagement at Reams' Station, on the 25th instant."[56]

A few days after the battle James Conner remarked to his sister that "General Lee was in high spirits about it" and explained, "It was the first time in this campaign that we have taken breastworks, and our troops had begun to believe that they could not take them. They regarded storming works as belonging to an early period of the War and played out now." This victory gave the Confederates "great confidence in themselves, and the next time they are put at works they will take them at the first rush."[57] Capt. Benjamin Wesley Justice of MacRae's Brigade described the North Carolinians' final charge to his wife. "The men were ordered not to fire a gun, but to yell & rush forward until the top of the works should be gained," he wrote. "This order was obeyed. Once inside the works the victory was easy." Justice's account also noted the effect the Confederate victory had on the men in his brigade: "Numbers of our men are [or] were wearing the flashy uniforms of the yankee artillerists & the fine hats of officers a few days after the battle. I never saw men so much elated by any fight. They now think they can storm almost any yankee breastworks. The charge has been highly complimented by Gen. Lee, Gen. Hill, Gen. Heth, & all. No more gallant & daring charge has been made during the war."[58]

Another member of the brigade had a different view of the battle's aftermath. According to Chaplain Richard Stanford Webb of the 44th North Carolina, "The 'Tar Heels' did the fighting," and Reams Station was "one of the most complete victories of the campaign, but with the loss of many a noble soldier." Webb, in a letter to a cousin, emphasized the human cost of the battle more than the fruits of the victory and described the emotional scenes he had witnessed at a field hospital on the night of 25 August. "Some people speak of the glories of war," he commented, "but had they been spectators, or rather hearers at the hospital of Cooke's and MacRae's brigades, that night, they would not have imagined that there was mutch glory in it." The chaplain, who spent the night ministering to the physical and spiritual needs of wounded and dying Confederates, recalled that his emotions "would ebb and flow, in proportion to the spiritual condition of those I would address." He was particularly troubled by the memory of a dying colonel "who had been heard to say, when leaving Winter Quarters, that he did not believe that there was any such thing as genuine religion. All my efforts to get him to trust in Jesus was in vain, [the colonel] saying 'It was too late.'" The wounded officer died the next day without professing a belief in the possibility of eternal salvation. "Though I thus describe some of the horrors of war," Webb continued, echoing the general mood throughout the army after the battle, "I have never seen our boys in such fine spirits, being perfectly elated with their recent success."[59]

That "recent success" was an emphatic reminder to many Confederates—and to their foes in the Army of the Potomac—that Lee's soldiers could still be as formidable as they ever had been in spite of the lengthening odds against them. Reams Station's primary importance, however, was that it renewed confidence within the Army of Northern Virginia. From the Wilderness through the Weldon Railroad, the campaigns of 1864 had reinforced the belief that frontal assaults against fortified positions were doomed to failure. Though few of Lee's soldiers ever questioned their ability to withstand almost any such charges by the enemy, many, perhaps most, of them doubted that similar attempts of their own against Federal earthworks could succeed. If the Confederate victory at Reams Station proved to be a timely and welcome exception to that rule, the fact that such a renewal of confidence was necessary spoke volumes about the state of the Army of Northern Virginia in the last half of 1864. Lee now commanded an army that in many respects was far removed from the one he had led through 1862 and 1863.

Several correspondents and diarists, who paused throughout August and September to evaluate the army's performance since its arrival on the Petersburg-Richmond front, also took time to reflect on the vast changes that the war had produced among Lee's troops. One officer, writing in his diary the night after Reams Station, recalled the day when his company left home "to muster into the service of our Country for the defence of our homes, liberty & firesides." Capt. William Aiken Kelly of the 1st South Carolina had left Charleston as a private in August 1861 in a company that numbered eighty-seven men "All in the prime of life, many quite boys, & all full of hope & patriotism."[60] Kelly's unit, first named the "Carolina Light Infantry" and later designated Company L of the regiment, had a great deal in common with every other Confederate—or Federal—company organized early in the war. The typical Civil War company's volunteers might be brothers, cousins, or in-laws; they might be farmers, clerks, or merchants; and they might be neighbors, business acquaintances, or members of the same church congregations. They were, at first, a civilian extension of their home community, one that gradually became a military community unto itself, reinforced by the larger communities present at the regimental and brigade levels. This sense of community, which evolved through shared experiences in camp, on the march, and in battle, had over time bound men together as soldiers and as comrades. Such ties were most secure among men who had served together since the beginning of the war, but became almost as important among those who had joined the unit since and who had been accepted by its veterans. The bonds of affection and loyalty between a soldier and his comrades-in-arms often rivaled, and sometimes even surpassed, the bonds between the soldier and his family or friends back home.

This particular South Carolina company, like many others in Lee's army, had changed so dramatically in the past three years that it was barely recognizable as the group that left Charleston "full of hope & patriotism" in the summer of 1861. "Alas! What changes, & terrible scenes we have passed through during this short time," Kelly exclaimed. He owed his position as captain, for example, to the deaths of his two predecessors: Capt. C. D. Barksdale, first commander of the Carolina Light Infantry, who had been mortally wounded at Second Manassas in August 1862, and Capt. John W. Chambers, who had been killed on the retreat from Gettysburg in July 1863. The rank and file had fared no better. Only fifty-seven of the original eighty-seven soldiers belonging to the company were still on the rolls three years later. Of those fifty-seven men, Kelly counted only three officers and fifteen enlisted men present for duty on 26 August. "Ah! What horrors, sufferings, and sorrows, does cruel War cause," he declared. "God grant that it will soon end, that ere long our liberty & independence will, by our efforts be established." The South Carolina captain believed that the Confederacy could win its independence if his fellow soldiers and fellow citizens would persevere a little longer, observing: "Then will the blessings & comforts of home & independence be much greater appreciated by us, for the efforts it cost us to secure them. God grant that my life may be spared to see that happy day."[61]

While Kelly pondered the loss of his comrades since the beginning of the war, others pointed to the staggering numbers of casualties—and the individuals represented by those numbers—in the Army of Northern Virginia since the beginning of the year's campaigns. Capt. John D. Fain of the 33d North Carolina stated, "My company ("C" 33d) is terribly reduced and the reg't is but a fraction of what it once was." Fain, whose regiment was one of five belonging to Lane's Brigade of the Third Corps, continued, "We have had five Capts. killed and wounded since the opening of the campaign, and four 1st Lts. besides 2d. Lts wounded and captured."[62] Casualties for the entire brigade from the Wilderness through Reams Station numbered 149 officers and men killed, 766 wounded, and 587 captured or missing, for a total of 1,502 casualties in barely three months of fighting.[63] Losses in other units throughout the army were, of course, comparable to these casualties. Pvt. Robert Mabry of the 6th Virginia hoped that the war would end soon and believed that the 1864 presidential election in the North would be a decisive factor. "It must be clear to the mind of any outsider," Mabry wrote his wife, "that there has been Blood enough shed to settle any difficulty that Fighting could settle, here is Mahones skeleton of a Brigade numbering today less than Five Hundred Muskets, when she left Madison Run in May we had about Eighteen Hundred."[64]

Though such casualties had a marked effect on the army's performance, their impact on the army as a cohesive community was even greater. After the last day's fighting on the Weldon Railroad, a South Carolina staff officer reported that "Capts. Gordon, Sellers, & McKnall & Lieuts. Kennerly & Jim Ross are known to be killed," then reflected on the loss of men who were friends as well as comrades. "Poor Jim Ross, what a terrible blow to his poor mother," J. Adger Smyth wrote. "Sam Kennerly leaves a wife & one child. Poor fellow he was married about the same time we were. Oh I do feel so sad this morning, having lost so many friends, & our old Regiment being so much cut up."[65] The war was becoming more and more gloomy every day for many "old Regiments" and the soldiers who belonged to them.

A disturbing lack of efficiency, or incompetence, among some of Lee's officers revealed another major contrast between the army as it stood in the summer of 1864 and the army as it once had been. Numerous company, regimental, and even brigade officers were either unable or unwilling to discipline, care for, or properly command their troops, and their neglect gradually eroded both the army's performance and its morale. "What our officers most lack," Lee wrote Jefferson Davis in mid-August, "is the pains & labour of incubating discipline. It is a painful tedious process, & is not apt to win popular favour. Many officers have too many selfish views to promote to induce them to undertake the task of instructing & disciplining their Commands."[66] Lee's complaints were confirmed by inspection reports pointing out that "an officer is totally incompetent who can not command the respect & obedience of his men" or "the source of almost every evil existing in the army is due to the difficulty of having orders properly and promptly executed" and naming specific officers who neglected their responsibilities.[67] An August inspection report for one Georgia brigade in the First Corps, for example, noted, "In the *20th Ga* there is a general want of discipline among company officers who allow their men to disregard order and obedience." Capt. Heman H. Perry recommended that one captain and five lieutenants be brought before an examining board to determine their fitness for command. Perry did recognize "some officers in that Regt who are excellent ones" and thus concluded his report with the observation, "*Capt Mitchell* of the *20th* is recently in command of that Regt and promises to be an excellent officer. The 20th Ga has been unfortunate in the loss of Field officers which may in some measure account for poor discipline."[68] A South Carolina lieutenant near Petersburg described "upstarts Confederate officers doing nothing but riding out with the City girls, and look as if they have never been in the trenches, and did not care a strain for the Confederacy, [so long] as they have their fun."[69]

More serious offenses, such as cowardice or desertion, were relatively rare among Lee's officers but understandably attracted a great deal of attention when they did occur. One of the former cases during the late summer involved 2d Lt. James C. Otey, of the 13th Battalion Virginia Light Artillery, who was accused of cowardice during the battle of the Crater. Otey, who fled the battlefield, was court-martialed, found guilty, and sentenced to death by musketry. Capt. John Hampden Chamberlayne, of Otey's company, who had just been transferred and promoted to command the battery, commented on 19 August, "The Battery was raised in Lynchburg, is of fair material for soldiers, but mightily disorganized by long continued want of officers, a thing which made the men behave badly in the affair of 30th July [the Crater]."[70] Otey's execution, originally scheduled for early September, was delayed for a few days so that he could visit his family and say good-bye. Jefferson Davis, after reviewing the case, commuted Otey's death sentence to dismissal from the Confederate service. "Lt. Otey was not shot," First Corps chief of artillery Porter Alexander later remarked, "but his sentence was commuted to dismissal by the Pres.—a great shame when two poor *privates* are to be shot for it this very week."[71] Because units were only as reliable as their officers, the army's failure to maintain a full and dependable complement of company and field officers proved to be yet another troubling obstacle facing Lee in late 1864.

Many soldiers, pondering these and other changes in the army, expressed disappointment and frustration at their inability to win a decisive

Pvt. Levi David Bedingfield, Company G, 35th North Carolina. Bedingfield,
who served as a private in the Henderson Rifles, went home with several other
members of his company without leave in the spring of 1863 but was persuaded by
a lieutenant to return to his command; he was wounded in the Bermuda Hundred
campaign in May 1864 and surrendered at Appomattox. (Ruth Bedingfield).

victory over Grant and the Army of the Potomac. Such an achievement, they believed, would end the war and secure Confederate independence. "Neither side can achieve a complete victory; for if the opposing party is whipped ever so badly, they fall back to a perfect network of entrenchments, bristling with artillery and almost impregnable to the attacking party," one Virginia lieutenant observed.[72] Some men voiced their desire to leave the trenches of the Petersburg-Richmond front and march north, to take the war across the Potomac River and into Northern territory once again. "I would rejoice, & I doubt not the whole Army would share the same feeling, to see our columns heading again toward the Potomac," a South Carolina staff officer wrote in late August. "We are tired of this state of semi-inactivity. We all want to be moving again, & no direction holds out such allurements as the green vallies of Pennsylvania."[73] A member of the Washington Artillery, using the pseudonym "Fishback," wrote a similar letter to the *Richmond Whig* in early September. Calling the system of trenches surrounding Petersburg a "yellow line stretching in front of us like a huge serpent," the Louisianan claimed that "it is difficult to forget even momentarily the monotonous picture, unrelieved and unredeemed as it is by a single feature of interest." The artilleryman also informed the *Whig*'s readers: "The bulk of the army look back, I am inclined to think, with comparative envy upon the open field, with its rough marches and hardships, and would willingly risk again the fierce encounter for the pure air of the Valley or a sight of the Blue Ridge."[74]

Numerous members of the army, fearing that they were fated to spend the rest of 1864 watching the Federals and waiting for something to happen along the lines, expressed themselves in much the same way as the Alabama private who remarked, "this cruel war is going on and I am in it and cant help my self."[75] A lieutenant colonel of artillery in the Third Corps discounted rumors and hopes of an early end to the war, declaring in early September, "I do not believe that the war will end in less than two years—probably much longer."[76] About the same time Sgt. John F. Sale of the 12th Virginia cautioned: "If some strong, very strong signs of peace do not soon make their appearance I fear for the fortitude of our soldiers. Surely a soldiery who have borne so much in the cause of liberty as ours have during the continuance of this war deserve to be free."[77]

Other soldiers, more sanguine for the time being, hoped that the Democratic Party convention held during the last days of August might produce some "very strong signs of peace" in the form of a presidential candidate who could defeat Abraham Lincoln's bid for reelection. George B. McClellan was nominated on 29 August by the faction of the party that favored the prosecution of the war, with a peace candidate for his running mate. Rumors circulated through Lee's army that peace—or at the least, an armistice—might be at hand. "I heare a heap of talk heare about the army mistress not to fight no more for a surten length of time," a North Carolina private wrote his sister the day McClellan was nominated. "I hope they will have and army mistress, and it is hope they will come to some conclusion for an honorable peace. I am tired of this war."[78] After McClellan's nomination, but before he repudiated the peace plank of the Democratic platform, several Confederates speculated on the results of the convention. Sgt. Calvin Conner of the Palmetto Sharpshooters commented, "I do hope that an honourable peace may be brought about this fall for I am Sick and tired of camp and the teriable Slaughter of human Life which is going on from day to day."[79] At least one of Lee's soldiers hoped for an armistice for purely personal reasons. Sgt. Jacob Shook of the 15th Virginia wrote his sweetheart, "I hope we may have an armistice, then I can probably obtain leave of absence, and do myself the honor of visiting you."[80] In contrast, Capt. William Aiken Kelly believed that Confederate hopes for peace based on McClellan or the Democratic Party were "fatal ones, & if entertained by us, will lead us astray; weaken our efforts; & do our cause much harm." The South Carolinian's opinion was that "The only peace party upon whom we can rely for any good to ourselves, are our Armies in the field."[81]

Kelly's view of the war seemed to be borne out within a few days when word reached the army that Atlanta had at last fallen to Sherman on 2 September. The loss of this strategically vital city dashed many soldiers' hopes that the Confederacy might sue for peace in the near future and was a stunning blow to those who had believed that the Federal armies and the Northern people might be losing the will to continue the war. One officer remarked that the news "cast a sort of grim gloom over this whole army which is, I dare to say, a pretty good idea of its reception by the country at large."[82] Almost every soldier who mentioned the fall of Atlanta predicted that Sherman's victory would prolong the war and that the peace movement in the North would lose a great deal of momentum. A South Carolina sergeant called it "indeed mortifying to us to Loose Atlanta at this time when the peace party ware gaining ground So rapidly at the North and I feare it will have a tendancy to prolong the war but it is gone and we must make the most of it."[83]

The gloom among Lee's soldiers was felt even more deeply by the many Georgians in the army who feared for the safety of their families and their homes. "It falls on my mind like the doom of the Almighty," Frank

Coker wrote his wife on 5 September from Petersburg, "but my faith is as strong as ever that God is ruling, & that all will end right." Resigning himself to the thought that the Confederacy might not survive, Coker continued: "If we are to be crushed & slavery destroyed, so be it. It (the fall of Atlanta) don't take me by surprise at all. I only fear now that Hood will be powerless longer to control Sherman, and that he will overrun the balance of the State, release the prisoners [from Andersonville] &c; but let it come, we must bear the end whether it be shame and suffering, or glory and independence."[84] Five days later he wrote: "The peace element at the North, seems for the moment obscured & darkened by the great victory of the Capture of Atlanta. I have speculated on the future till I grow tired & sick of uncertainties, & feel sometimes disposed to '*let it rip.*'"[85]

Other members of the army who freely admitted that the fall of Atlanta was a Confederate disaster did not think that it would materially affect their own performance on the Petersburg-Richmond front. The observations of a young Virginian emphasized one reason for such thinking among Lee's soldiers, even those whose units had served with the army for only a short while. Lt. Frederick Fleet of the 26th Virginia quoted Northern claims that all of the Southern territory in Federal hands so far could be represented by the shape of an egg, then explained to his father: "Atlanta is the small end & Richmond is the big end. The little end is broken and with Richmond taken the shell falls to pieces. I don't think it can be done as easily as they can talk about it, however, as he [Grant] hasn't the Western army to fight here."[86]

Because Lee's veterans had even more confidence in themselves than the recent arrivals did, they often expressed that confidence in a general way that compensated for the negative impact of everyday events. One Virginia artillery captain remarked, "Old Mr Grant is still pegging away at us, first in one place then another. . . . Most armies would have been whipped by him, but the Army of N. Va. is of extraordinary quality, tho' we say it ourselves."[87] The depth of some soldiers' attachment to the army was demonstrated by one officer's comments on the assignment of general officers to new brigades. Brig. Gen. William W. Kirkland, who commanded a North Carolina brigade in Heth's Division of the Third Corps, was severely wounded at Cold Harbor in June and was succeeded by William MacRae, who was temporarily appointed brigadier. After MacRae proved to be an excellent choice both as a disciplinarian and as a combat officer, Lee was unwilling to remove him from command when Kirkland returned to duty in August. Kirkland, instead, was assigned to replace Brig. Gen. James G. Martin, who commanded a brigade in Hoke's

Division of Beauregard's command but whose ill health had made him unfit for duty in the field. "Gen. Kirkland is much chagrined at losing his brigade," Capt. Benjamin Wesley Justice told his wife. "He is now in Beauregard's army. This part of it he does not like, as every man who has ever served in Lee's army, is proud of it & unwilling to pass into any other."[88]

Other soldiers, either implicitly or explicitly comparing their generals and battlefield successes with generals and battlefield failures elsewhere—particularly in the Army of Tennessee—believed that they were the Confederacy's only hope for victory. Lt. Ezekiel Graham of the 6th Georgia predicted just after the fall of Atlanta that the Army of Northern Virginia would "sooner or later by its own unaided power win the independence of the Confederacy." One Virginian, writing his sister after a recent visit to see her, expressed concern that she was "in such bad spirits about the war" and tried to brighten her mood. Lt. Col. William Pegram of the Third Corps artillery, describing a conversation with his corps commander A. P. Hill, commented, "I met Gen. Hill on the cars going over to Richmond and he laughed very much when I told him that the people of Richmond were expecting Richmond and Petersburg to be evacuated."[89]

The troops' confidence in their own abilities, to be sure, was strengthened considerably by their faith in Lee's generalship and their gratitude for his efforts to care for his men. "I am satisfied, from what I see, that Gen. Lee has not the most remote idea of evacuating this place," Willy Pegram observed in the same letter that referred to his conversation with Hill. "If the President will only give everything into Genl. Lee's hands, I have no doubt but that, by the blessings of Providence, who has always assisted us when we have assisted ourselves, the whole situation will be changed by the winter."[90] Pvt. Thomas Walker Gilmer, a courier in the Third Corps, used less polished phrases to make the same point. "We will have a fine time after the war you must cheer up," Gilmer reassured his father in mid-September. "Old Bobie Lee will take care of the cuntry."[91]

Whether Lee could, in fact, take care of the Confederacy remained to be seen, but he could, and did, take care of his soldiers. His official and private correspondence always reflected his concern for the army's well-being, references that were more frequent and more explicit as the war continued into its fourth autumn. He was particularly distressed by casualties in his steadily weakening forces and was anxious to prevent unnecessary losses, commenting after Reams Station, "As usual we have to mourn the loss of brave men & officers, worth more to me than the whole Federal nation."[92] In late September Lee cautioned his troops that Federal artillery salutes intended to celebrate Sheridan's victories over Jubal Early in the Shenandoah might be fired from fully loaded guns instead of blank charges. "Gen. Lee is very careful of the lives of his men," a grateful sergeant in the 12th Battalion Virginia Light Artillery observed in his diary. "To-night he issued an order for the men to keep well under cover to-morrow, as he expected the Yankees to fire 'shotted' salutes in honor of Sheridan's success."[93]

Some officers and men referred to their affection and respect for Lee, not only as their commanding general, but also as a symbol of the Confederacy and its struggle for survival. A member of the Texas Brigade, signing himself "Trans-Mississippi," wrote a letter to the *Richmond Examiner* criticizing a proposal that every soldier who had not been absent from 1 April to 1 October would receive a one-hundred-dollar Confederate bond. The Texan observed that two-thirds of Lee's soldiers would prefer instead "a single strip of parchment in the shape of a certificate setting forth their good conduct and soldierly qualities, signed by General R. E. Lee. This would be a treasure, indeed, to keep in after years."[94] Lee's general officers were often as awed by their commander as the rank and file were. John Bratton, for example, had several opportunities to talk with Lee about the disposition of his South Carolina brigade north of the James River in August. A few days later Bratton wrote his wife, "Distance does not lend enchantment to the old fellows greatness I assure you. The nearer he comes the higher he looms up. It is plain, simple, unaffected greatness. It is just as natural and easy for him to be great as it is for me to be ordinary, and there is probably less affectation about it." Bratton enclosed a note he had received from Lee and explained, "I am sorry that it is in pencil and not in ink as you will, doubtless, like to preserve it. As I never expect to receive another from his own hand and with his own signature, you had better put it in a glass frame where it will be secured from rubbing and erasure."[95] The adjutant of a Virginia artillery battalion expressed the feelings of numerous soldiers when he wrote his mother, "Gen. Lee looms up grandly & more grandly still. May God preserve him & grant him the great blessing of living to see a country free, whose children will call him blessed."[96] Most of Lee's soldiers, whether they called him "General Lee," "Marse Robert," or "Old Bobie Lee," were more deeply devoted to him than ever before. In May 1863, just after his victory at Chancellorsville and just before his defeat at Gettysburg, Lee had written of his troops, "There never were such men in an army before. They will go anywhere and do anything if properly led."[97] The Army of Northern Virginia's willingness to continue fighting was to an increasingly great extent dependent on its soldiers' belief that Lee would lead them to final victory.

While Lee's soldiers remembered the past and anticipated the future, the stalemate of the present continued through September with few incidents of any consequence in the month after Reams Station. The most dramatic event, one that quickly captured the imagination of the army and the Confederate people, was a daring cavalry raid led by Wade Hampton that reminded many observers of Jeb Stuart's famous rides around the Army of the Potomac in 1862. The raid had its genesis in reports that Grant's wagon trains and supply depots were vulnerable to surprise. Lee wrote his cavalry commander on 3 September, "A sudden blow in that quarter might be detrimental to him."[98] Hampton received confirmation only two days later from a scout who reported that the Federal forces in the area were scattered and posed no real obstacle to a raid. The scout also noted that a herd of some 3,000 cattle was grazing at Coggins' Point, on the James River, and was loosely guarded by a small force of Federal soldiers and civilians. When Hampton proposed a bold plan to capture the cattle and provide the army with some badly needed meat, Lee quickly approved the scheme. The South Carolinian, commanding a force consisting of one entire division, a brigade each from his other two divisions, and a detachment from two additional brigades, left well before dawn on 14 September and reached the vicinity of a Federal camp south of the herd by midnight of the fifteenth. His orders for 16 September called for the division and one brigade to screen the raid from Federals to the west while the other brigade and the detachment attacked the small enemy force and blocked its way north. Everything worked according to plan on the morning of the sixteenth, as the Confederate horsemen quickly scattered or captured the Federals in their path and proceeded to Coggins' Point, where they routed the detachment guarding the herd. After taking nearly 2,500 head of cattle, 300 Federal prisoners, and several wagons, Hampton's triumphant cavalrymen rode south with their captures and fought off their pursuers, reaching the Army of Northern Virginia on the morning of 17 September.[99]

Hampton's expedition, which some wags soon dubbed "the Beefsteak Raid," was a remarkable success that was nowhere more appreciated than among Lee's hungry infantrymen and artillerymen on the Petersburg-Richmond front. Though some Confederates were inclined to doubt early reports of the raid, believing them to be nothing more than the usual exaggerated camp rumors, they were soon persuaded otherwise when

Hampton's cavalrymen led the cattle through the streets of Petersburg on their way to the army's commissary department. One noncommissioned officer who saw the herd remarked, "thay ware the best beeves that I ever Saw and its the opinion of all who saw them that thay will average five or six hundred pounds."[100] A private in the 17th South Carolina wrote his wife, "The beef is ordered to be given to the men every other day and will last the whole army 14 days So Says our Commissary Genl. and they have all been turned over to him."[101] Several members of the army mentioned the very welcome change in their rations, calling the meat "Hamptons beef" or "good Yankee beef" and describing it as "*very* fat and sweet."[102] A few days later Corp. Charles Baughman of the 13th Battalion Virginia Light Artillery gleefully told his mother, "I have just finished my dinner, and a remarkably huge one it was." After starting with sweet potatoes, Irish potatoes, biscuits, and butter, the highlight of Baughman's meal was "last but not by any means least some very nice beef steak which was originally intended for the gentlemen over the way but which through the instrumentality of a gentleman named Hampton (of whom you have doubtless heard) was transferred to this side of the lines, much to our satisfaction. Now you did not have much better than that at home did you?"[103] Lee's soldiers had little time to enjoy their new rations, however, for the relative inactivity of September was interrupted by another Federal offensive along the Petersburg-Richmond front. Grant, following the patterns of his attempts in June and August, would once again alternate attacks north and south of the James River to threaten Richmond and Petersburg while Lee was forced to shift troops to meet him at both points.

Grant's first move of the offensive was an attempt by Benjamin F. Butler's Army of the James to force through Confederate defenses a few miles southeast of Richmond and perhaps to take the city itself. Early on the morning of 29 September the Federals attacked the works at New Market Heights, initially surprising the small Confederate force there but suffering heavy casualties in the process. They occupied the works when the defenders withdrew to support Fort Harrison, part of the city's outer defenses a short distance west. Elements of the First Corps and the Department of Richmond, holding the lines at New Market Heights and Chaffin's Bluff, fought stubbornly but were unable to prevent the Federal capture of Fort Harrison and a section of the New Market lines. But they did manage to stabilize their positions enough to repulse several attacks during the afternoon, most notably at Fort Gilmer, north of Fort Harrison. When fighting ended on the evening of the twenty-ninth, Butler's troops still held the ground they had initially gained but had been unable to exploit their advantage further. Lee, who arrived that afternoon to supervise the defense of Richmond's outer lines, ordered considerable reinforcements up from the south side of the James and planned to retake Fort Harrison the next day.

The Confederate counterattack on the fort, made by a division of the First Corps and a division of Beauregard's command, did not begin until the early afternoon of 30 September. When it did occur, it was a piecemeal effort that lacked even the most simple coordination among the attacking units. Three brigades of the First Corps assaulted without adequate support and were repulsed with heavy casualties by the entrenched Federal defenders. When two brigades of Beauregard's command advanced a short time later, leaving the other three brigades of their division behind, they suffered the same fate. The fighting ended with the Federals firmly in control of the fort and the outer lines, while the Confederates established a strong second line a short distance to the west. Total casualties along the New Market lines for the two days numbered some 3,300 Federal losses, compared with about 1,700 Confederates killed, wounded, and captured.[104] Lee, though forced to concede the loss of Fort Harrison and a significant portion of the New Market lines, had little time to ponder the implications of the fighting there. As Grant and the Army of the Potomac were making a simultaneous thrust south of the James, they now demanded his immediate attention.

On the morning of 30 September, while the Confederates prepared to assault Fort Harrison, Federal infantry moved against Lee's cavalry south of Petersburg in an attempt to threaten that city and perhaps cut the Southside Railroad. An attack on the Confederate position along the Squirrel Level Road near Poplar Spring Church drove the cavalrymen from the field in the early afternoon. Later in the day four brigades of Confederate infantry from the Third Corps came up and counterattacked at Peebles Farm, forcing a Federal division back in confusion and reestablishing a defensive line close to its original position. Fighting ended there in the early evening after a second counterattack failed.

Anxious to regain their lost ground, the Confederates attacked on the morning of 1 October in yet another piecemeal assault that was repulsed with heavy casualties and failed to dislodge the Federals from the foothold they had gained on the Squirrel Level lines. Lee's troops then withdrew a short distance to the northwest, established a new defensive position there, and waited for the Federals to retake the initiative. Cavalry fighting to the south, which lasted for most of the day, ended with much the same result. Skirmishing continued throughout 2 October but did not materially alter the tactical or strategic situation, and both commanders seemed willing to suspend fighting in the vicinity of Poplar Spring Church. Federal forces south of the James had, much like those north of the river, taken a portion of the Confederate outer defenses and held them against several counterattacks. Federals casualties over three days of fighting numbered some 2,900 killed, wounded, and captured, while the Confederates lost about 1,300 troops.[105]

Both armies enjoyed a measure of tactical and strategic success during Grant's offensive. The Federals, at a cost of about 6,200 casualties for the period from 29 September through 2 October, were able to tighten their grip on the Petersburg-Richmond front along the New Market–Fort Harrison lines and the Squirrel Level Road–Poplar Spring Church lines. Though the Confederates, at a cost of some 3,000 men, had kept the Federals from taking either Petersburg or Richmond, they had been unable to prevent Grant from forcing them still closer to both cities. Lee's tactical victories, though significant for the moment, were no guarantee that the Federals could ultimately be driven away. By the fall of 1864 the Army of Northern Virginia had been so weakened in terms of manpower and leadership that it rarely took the initiative, most often reacting to situations imposed on it by an enemy who held the initiative itself.

Confederate accounts of the fighting were equally divided between those that emphasized success at beating the Federals back from the gates of Richmond and Petersburg and those that expressed concern at the ease with which Grant seemed to capture portions of Lee's defenses. Numerous soldiers were simultaneously relieved that they had checked yet another enemy offensive and optimistic that they could continue to do so. A brigadier in the Third Corps commented: "In this fight our troops gained a most decided victory with small loss but most heavy to the enemy. If we can gain such victories with what troops we have & against such odds what will we do when we get in all the detailed men[?]"[106] Several members of Lee's army wrote letters to reassure family members and friends who believed that the Federals might capture Richmond and Petersburg with another determined effort. On 1 October a North Carolina private wrote his wife, "my dear they have neather taken Petersburg nor Richmond yet but the Lord only noes what will be you must not listen to all the tales you hear," and on the third a Virginia private wrote a friend, "The Yankees have gained some advantage on both sides of the River tho' their losses are much heavier than ours. I must confess that (to me) things do not look so squally as some people seem to think."[107] A few days later Lt.

Col. William T. Poague admitted that Grant "got a little more of the Va. soil under his control" but asserted, "we killed and captured a considerable number of Yankees, and the account balances largely in our favor." Poague, commanding an artillery battalion in the Third Corps, thought that the ground lost was of little consequence. "There is a considerable margin of soil yet remaining that we can afford to give up, and still keep Ulysses Grant out of Richmond," he remarked.[108] Similar opinions were held by many of Lee's soldiers in the aftermath of these latest battles north and south of the James.

Other observers, recognizing that each new Federal offensive was gaining momentum if not actual ground, questioned the army's ability to withstand sustained blows at vulnerable points along its lines. Several of them pointed to the succession of piecemeal counterattacks and feeble thrusts made by numerous units, some argued that they could not hope to hold their positions indefinitely without the infusion of large numbers of reinforcements, and some believed that the troops on hand were simply not capable of duplicating the great offensive victories they had won earlier in the war. A few officers and men cited the lackluster performances of the recent battles as evidence to support their pessimistic views. The disastrous attempt to retake Fort Harrison on 30 September received a measure of well-deserved criticism. A South Carolina sergeant, writing his wife, thought that the attack failed "from the men behaveing badly and a misunderstanding amongst our officers"; the commander of the First Corps artillery observed, "Gen. Lee was more worried at this failure than I have ever seen him under similar circumstances."[109] Commenting that "the charge was not simultaneous by all the troops & degenerated into a most abortive attempt before reaching the Yankee works, & was easily repulsed," Porter Alexander advanced his theory for the troops' poor performance. "Our troops have fought so long behind breastworks that they have lost all spirit in attacking," he believed, "or they would have carried it easily."[110]

Some soldiers saw little to cheer them about either the immediate past or the immediate future. Those who had seen fierce, if ultimately inconclusive, combat on the outskirts of Richmond or Petersburg wondered if they would live to see the war's end. A Georgia private described "the hardest fight that we have ever bin in since the war" in a letter to his mother, declaring, "We had to charge the yankies 3 times . . . Ma it was the hotest fight that we have ever had it did look like that we would all get killed in Spite of all that could be done." John Everett thought that another battle would take place soon but hoped it would not, "for I tell you that we air all geting tired of this war and it will have to come to a close."[111] Pvt. James King Wilkerson of the 55th North Carolina, writing his parents after the battle at Peebles Farm on 1 October, exclaimed, "Oh it was and awful time Saturday chargeing the yankees in the rain through the woods and swamps and thickets, and the balls flying thick and fast in every direction and men getting killed and wounded hollowing all over the woods." Wilkerson asked his mother to "Save me all the good dram and things you have got untill I can ever come home, please god I ever live to come any more."[112]

Soldiers whose units had not participated in the latest fighting and whose outlooks were usually hopeful seemed to be almost as discouraged as Everett and Wilkerson. A Georgia captain who believed that the army's only pressing problem was *"inferiority in numbers"* explained, "Our lines being very long, they are necessarily very weak at some points if we make them strong at others, & then Grant with his strong force can hunt our weak places & dash against them." Frank Coker's deep religious faith prompted him to add, in an attempt to keep his spirits up, "It is all with a Higher Power, & will be all right."[113] Capt. John Coleman of the 17th South Carolina, writing in his diary on the evening of 2 October, declared: "I feel sad and depressed and fear that we are on the brink of some sad disaster. 'Lord prevent.' Let the enemy be driven from our land and peace once more established in our land."[114]

The commanding general himself gave the War Department a candid, even blunt, assessment of the situation on the Petersburg-Richmond front. He pointed out that Grant's superior numbers allowed the Federal commander to maintain his lines while extending past Lee's flanks and that understrength and exhausted Confederate divisions were in many instances facing full and fresh Federal corps. "We cannot fight to advantage with such odds," Lee warned Secretary Seddon on 4 October, "and there is the gravest reason to apprehend the result of every encounter." After discussing various ways to get as many arms-bearing men in the ranks as possible, Lee noted that he could not guarantee the results even if those efforts succeeded, remarking, "we may be able, with the blessing of God, to keep the enemy in check to the beginning of winter."[115] Such bleak statements from the usually reserved Lee underscored the continuing decline of the Army of Northern Virginia and, by extension, of Confederate fortunes in the Eastern theater.

The prevailing mood in the army, one that ranged somewhere between elation and dejection, was captured perfectly by a young artillery officer in the Third Corps who wrote to his sister in Richmond during the first week in October. William Pegram, who followed an account of the fighting at the Squirrel Level Road and Peebles Farm with an exceptionally astute appraisal of the state of Lee's army, was well qualified to judge the army's combat effectiveness. He had risen from second lieutenant of a Virginia battery in the spring of 1862 to lieutenant colonel of a battalion two years later, was a veteran of nearly all the army's battles, and had often earned the praise of his superior officers. Pegram, like many other officers and men, viewed the year's fighting so far as one long campaign, calling it "the most remarkable in the annals of history." His analysis combined equal measures of optimism and realism and concluded that the army's overall morale was high in spite of several months of almost constant fighting, marching, and fatigue duty. The Virginian admitted that Lee's soldiers did not "charge the enemy out of their works as they did in 1862" and did not always perform as well as expected, but he ventured the opinion that such failures were "not from the want of courage, but from the want of physical strength." Pegram described the troops' reaction when they were allowed a brief respite from the Petersburg trenches, observing, "It did my heart good last night to hear one of those old lusty yells ring from one end of the line to the other." His commentary on the state of the Army of Northern Virginia concluded: "I merely mention these facts in justice to this noble army, to shew you the reason why it does not achieve the brilliant feats, that characterized it in '62. If the army could get a month's rest in the country, with a little reorganization, it would shew itself to be equal to more than it has ever done."[116] Many soldiers of all grades, acutely aware of the army's many weaknesses in October 1864, were just as aware of its remaining strengths and hoped—like Pegram— that the winter of 1864–65 would give it an opportunity for the rest and reorganization it so desperately needed.

Before that opportunity presented itself, however, the army would fight three significant engagements that proved to be strikingly similar to those that had already taken place north and south of the James River since mid-June. The first battle, initiated by Lee, occurred on 7 October north of the James River and was a large-scale attempt to retake part of the Fort Harrison lines. Though carefully planned, the fight on the Darbytown Road ended in complete failure when a single division made the assault without the expected support of a second division and was repulsed with heavy casualties. Whereas Federal losses totaled some 400 men, the Confederates lost more than 1,300 killed, wounded, and captured. Lee, who resigned himself to the loss of the Fort Harrison lines and established new lines accordingly, was undoubtedly troubled by the continuing poor combat performance of some units and their commanders. Robert Hoke's Division of Beauregard's command, for example, seemed to present a particular—but by no means unique—problem in the army. When Charles W. Field's Division of the First Corps was repulsed on the Darbytown Road, it marked the third time since Cold Harbor that Hoke had neglected to support Field and had wrecked any chances of Confederate success in an engagement. The comments of the anonymous staff officer keeping the diary of the First Corps conveyed the disappointment felt at the day's defeat. "Field's attack fails," the diarist wrote. "Hoke cannot get at the enemy out of his trenches and does not move."[117]

The second and third battles of the fall, initiated by Grant on 27 October, represented yet another attempt to break Lee's lines by simultaneous offenses north and south of the James. These fights, which occurred on the Darbytown Road north of the river and at Burgess Mill south of it, ended in disappointment for the Federals. The first engagement was a small-scale affair that resulted in heavy Federal losses and minimal Confederate casualties; it was also notable for the performance of Field's and Hoke's Divisions, which cooperated to repulse several uncoordinated attacks.[118] The second engagement was a larger-scale battle reminiscent of Reams Station, in which the Third Corps and most of the Cavalry Corps blunted a Federal attack by three infantry corps and a cavalry division. The fight at Burgess Mill, which lasted for most of the day, inflicted moderate losses on both sides—some 1,700 Federals and more than 1,300 Confederates—but was still unquestionably a Confederate victory. These late October engagements provided ample evidence that the Army of Northern Virginia, despite its recent difficulties with offensive operations, was still effective when on the defensive and that Federal expectations to the contrary were groundless.[119] "This seems to have been an effort by the enemy to overlap our lines both on the right and on the left at the same time," Capt. Henry Chambers of the 49th North Carolina observed in his diary a few days later. "They did not gain a foothold on our left and they have been driven from their advantage on our right."[120]

Several changes were made in the assignment of commanders during October in an attempt to increase the efficiency of both officers and men. Among the most significant shifts were those involving officers commanding corps or larger units, such as the departure of P. G. T. Beauregard from the Petersburg-Richmond front and the return of James Longstreet to the First Corps. Beauregard, who had already been sent to Wilmington, North Carolina, in September to inspect the defenses there, was given command of a new Military Division of the West—embracing

Confederate territory from Georgia to Mississippi—early in the month. Longstreet, essentially but not completely recovered from his wounds received in the Wilderness, resumed command of his old corps on 19 October. Richard Anderson, who had performed creditably in Longstreet's stead since May, retained his temporary grade of lieutenant general and was given a new Fourth Corps consisting of the majority of Beauregard's old command.[121]

As necessary and as welcome as such changes were, they could not obscure—but instead helped to highlight—the single most critical issue facing the Army of Northern Virginia in late 1864, one that would shape its future as much as any other factor. That issue was, of course, the crippling lack of soldiers on hand and present for duty. Of some 120,000 men present and absent at the end of June 1864—or just after the army arrived at Petersburg and Early had been sent to the Shenandoah—Lee had been able to count about 50,000 present for duty. Almost two months later, on 10 September, field returns showed about 100,000 troops present and absent, of which some 38,000 were present for duty. Though Lee managed to gain some increase over the next month by restricting details and aggressively pursuing absentees and deserters, the numbers were still far below those needed to defend the Petersburg-Richmond front. On 31 October the army had a total strength of about 120,000 men present and absent, of which only some 47,000 troops were present for duty.[122] Though soldiers who had been wounded or captured increased the number of those absent, there were simply too many able-bodied soldiers still on the rolls who were not serving under arms.

Lee's troops, from the newest recruits to the most experienced veterans, had definite opinions about the shortage of men and the effect that shortage would have on the army's ability to defend its lines. One South Carolinian believed that the army's "Line of works encirkling Richmond" helped compensate—at least in part—for the scarcity of Confederate soldiers, commenting, "I do not think our Generals will venture to attact them out side with the number of troops we have here for thay [the Confederate generals] Should Save thair men as much as possiable."[123] Others noted that the enforcement of regulations abolishing most details brought some men into the ranks who had not been there for a long time, if at all. "You ought to see our soldiers who have been seeing easy times, taking muskets," a Georgia captain remarked. "Artillery drivers, supernumeraries, detailed men &c.; they do it very cheerfully but are made great sport of [by] the regular infantry."[124] Pvt. Alexander Fewell of the 17th South Carolina wrote that numerous men sent up to the front were not so cheerful and gave an explanation that underscored the acute need for infantrymen in Lee's army. "[T]hey have ordered all detailed men into the ditches," Fewell observed. "Some of them are not pleased with it but even Some of the Sick that looks as though they Should be in bed are Sent to the ditches."[125] One soldier sent back to the ranks took his new position somewhat more philosophically. "Every nerve is being strained to its utmost to get men," Ord. Sgt. James W. Albright of a Virginia artillery battalion reported in his diary. "All details revoked—all extra men in the artillery ordered to take muskets! Well, so we succeed in the end all will be satisfied. I am willing to do anything rather than be subjugated."[126]

The commanding general, in letters to Davis, Seddon, and other Confederate civilian authorities as well as to several military superiors and subordinates, emphasized over and over again that he could not protect the Petersburg-Richmond front without additional troops. Such warnings as "I fear it will be impossible to keep him [Grant] out of Richmond" or "We must drive them back at all costs" were typical of his comments during this period.[127] In late October, for example, Wade Hampton wrote Lee that his dismounted cavalrymen could attack an exposed flank of the enemy, but other men would then have to replace his troops in the trenches near Hatcher's Run. When Hampton suggested that A. P. Hill, whose Third Corps infantrymen shared the trenches with his cavalrymen, should be reinforced, Lee replied: "It would afford me great satisfaction if I could give General Hill the additional infantry to enable him to relieve your troops as you propose, as I can see that much benefit would result from it. But the difficulty is to get the men."[128] A week later, just after the engagement at Burgess Mill, Lee wrote Davis, "Unless we can obtain a reasonable approximation to his [Grant's] force I fear a great calamity will befall us. On last Thursday at Burgess' mill we had three brigades to oppose six divisions—On our left two divisions to oppose two corps—The inequality is too great."[129]

That inequality, as demonstrated by specific numbers in specific units, only confirmed the general feeling of unease throughout the Army of Northern Virginia. Regiments were often so reduced as to be half the size of decent companies, while companies might have fewer than ten men left or have ceased to exist altogether. In early October Capt. Henry T. Owen of the 18th Virginia, in Brig. Gen. Eppa Hunton's Brigade of Pickett's Division, observed, "My company is the largest in the whole Brigade and looks like a Battalion."[130] A few weeks later, when the assistant adjutant general of the First Corps relayed a routine order from Longstreet to Charles Field, the order requested Field to "so extend your line as to throw a good-sized regiment, say 300 men" into line as support for an adjacent unit, assuming that by 1864 standards a three-hundred man regiment was "good-sized."[131] About the same time Capt. Watson Dugat Williams of the 5th Texas wrote his fiancée, "There are 8 men in my Company for duty including Lt. McKinnon and myself. At inspection this morning there were 61 guns in the regiment."[132] In one of the most telling commentaries on the Confederates' waning ability to defend all points along their lines, a North Carolinian who deserted to the Federals told them that in his division, part of Beauregard's command stationed at Petersburg, "the men would make one good line, about elbow to elbow."[133]

Deserters such as that anonymous North Carolinian went over to the enemy in greater numbers than ever before; by the end of October the desertion rate in some units had increased to a few men a week, in extreme cases a man or more every night.[134] Some officers tried to minimize the effects of desertions by denouncing the culprits, such as the colonel of a Virginia brigade who lost three men from his command one night and reported, "three more useless, ignorant, and cowardly men never disgraced the rolls of any regiment."[135] Though deserters were often arrested, tried by courts-martial, and convicted, individual sentences varied so widely that their value as a deterrent was virtually nonexistent.

A few general orders of the Department of Northern Virginia published in late October illustrate the inconsistent sentences given to deserters in the same divisions, brigades, or even regiments. Most soldiers were sentenced to combinations of penalties such as forfeiting their pay and their right to a furlough, and wearing a ball and chain; or punishments intended to shame and humiliate them, such as wearing a placard marked "Deserter" and sitting in camp "riding" a wooden horse for a specified period. Relatively few deserters were sentenced "to be shot to death with musketry, at such time and place as the commanding General may direct," but their numbers increased in the last half of 1864 as desertions multiplied and the crisis within the army grew.[136] "It is now half after 3 oclock P.M. & one of Capt. Crumplers men (James Ray) is to be shot at 4 oclock," Capt. John Elmore Hall of the 59th Alabama wrote his father on the afternoon of 6 October. "His crime was desertion & cowardice. I am sorry for the boy for I do not really think he has any sense. He will be shot here in the trenches before the Regt. I would give almost any thing to be absent when it is done. Though he deserves death, I dont want to see him shot." Hall, who noted that Brig. Gen. Archibald Gracie was making last-minute efforts to postpone the execution, hoping for a reprieve, remarked, "I fear he will not succeed." A few minutes later, when the execution took place as scheduled, Hall and his regiment watched the deserter's death. "Father I have just witnessed a sight which I pray I may never again be called upon to see," he wrote, describing the grim scene: "Ray was shot to death by a detail of 15 men made for the purpose. A minister prayed with him & he was tied to a stake with his hands behind him a white cloth put over his face—& the order given the detail to fire upon him. Several balls to[ok] effect but a few moments later after life not being extinct entirely, he was again shot, the last trial finishing life. Twas a sad sight."[137]

Some deserters who were duly convicted and sentenced to death had their sentences reduced or remitted by military or civil authorities who took mitigating circumstances and past good conduct into account. One member of the 25th North Carolina who had deserted in October 1863 was court-martialed and sentenced to death nearly a year later but decided to make a personal appeal to Gov. Zebulon Vance for clemency. Pvt. James Fowler, who began his letter with an apology for writing the governor, admitted his "disobedience and transgression of the law that has plase me in this condition for which I am become quite penitent and ask forgivness and I hope I hav obtained pardon of God if I only can of man." Fowler explained the reasons for his desertion in a touching illustration of the extreme pressures faced by many of Lee's men. "I received a letter from my wife stating there condition and my two children was both at the point of Death and I made evry effort to get permission to go home honorably but failed in every effort." The North Carolinian's plea must have convinced either the governor or the commanding general, for Fowler returned to the ranks a few weeks later, only to be captured a few days before the end of the war.[138] Lee, his officers, and the Confederate authorities would all struggle to strike a balance between severity and leniency when dealing with deserters. The act of desertion, even in units that had formerly been distinguished for their discipline or among individuals who had served with distinction, would prove to be the greatest cause of the depletion of Lee's army and would only accelerate through the coming winter.

As October gave way to November, numerous members of the Army of Northern Virginia looked forward to the upcoming presidential election in the North with great anticipation, believing that it would have a decisive influence on the conduct of the war. "[T]here is a good deal of Speculation here in regards to who will be elected Lincoln or McClellen and which of them would be most Likely to be beneficiel to the South," a South Carolina sergeant wrote his wife a few days before the election. "Some perfer Lincoln and others McClellen but for my own part I do not have much choice but if I had any I would perfer McClellen as he seems to be the most honourable and would perhaps conduct the war uppon a more civilized principal than the other."[139] Some weary soldiers had high expectations for a Democratic victory followed by an early peace settlement. A Virginia captain reported that "Yankee deserters all say the yankees are tired of fighting and that a Peace President will be elected," and one of Lee's division commanders wrote his sister, "I earnestly hope that this may be the end of the war, should Lincoln be elected it may continue for years, but I cant believe it will. Should McClellan be elected I hope it will be brought to a speedy close & by our independence."[140]

Other Confederates thought that Lincoln would be reelected but said that they would rather continue the war against an administration that was a known quantity than try to make terms with an administration they knew nothing about. "In my opinion Old Abraham will come in again, and I believe it would be best for us," a South Carolina surgeon commented to his wife. "McClellan might have the Union restored, if elected. I should prefer to remain at war the rest of my life rather than to have any connection with the Yankees again."[141] One Georgia staff officer, who usually wrote his wife several times a week and whose letters had been generally cheerful until the fall of Atlanta, expressed a renewed optimism over the impending election in the North. "If Lincoln is elected," Capt. Frank Coker wrote on 4 November, "I believe the dissatisfaction in the North at the idea of carrying on the war will be so great that he will be forced to abandon his war policies and change his plans." Coker continued: "If McC. is elected I think other plans for restoring peace will be resorted to besides fighting which of course is independence to us. All we require is to get the fighting once stop'd. and our independence is certain."[142] The hopes and fears of many in the Confederacy, soldiers and civilians alike, seemed to hinge on the election. They believed that once Lincoln was reelected, or McClellan elected, the Federal strategy for the remainder of the war would reveal itself and they could then respond accordingly.

Though the fighting would indeed soon stop, it would do so because the armies facing each other across the Petersburg-Richmond front were going into winter quarters after almost five months of inconclusive battles, engagements, skirmishes, raids, and other forms of combat. As active campaigning ceased, Lee's most pressing concerns involved, not the presidential election or even Federal plans for the next spring, but the preservation of his dwindling forces. The greatest threat to the Army of Northern Virginia during the winter of 1864–65 would come not from Grant and the Army of the Potomac but from within.

We would not Complain of Rations or hardships

if there was a brighter prospect ahead.

—*Pvt. Alexander Faulkner Fewell*

17th South Carolina, to a friend, 1 January 1865

. . . .

The Petersburg-Richmond Front, Winter Quarters, and Hatcher's Run, November 1864–February 1865

As the Army of Northern Virginia continued to occupy its lines along the Petersburg-Richmond front in the first week of November 1864, Lee's officers and men viewed two upcoming, if unrelated, events with great anticipation. The first event, which occurred on 8 November and was the more significant of the two, was the reelection of Abraham Lincoln. The second, which took place later in the month and was undoubtedly of greater interest to most soldiers, was the end of active operations for the year and the establishment of the army's winter quarters. "This is the day that our enemies are to elect their next President for 4 years," a South Carolina captain observed in his diary on the eighth, "with every indication of Lincoln's reelection, which will have the appearance that they are determined to carry on the war for 4 more years."[1] Other soldiers, in the interval between the election and the confirmation of its results in the newspapers, commented on its implications for the Confederacy. A Georgia staff officer, for example, wrote his wife, "The Yankee election has come and gone:—whether for weal or woe of the people of this Continent, the thing is settled and done. With that, and in that election may have been decided the fate of the *Southern Confederacy*, and of thousands of brave and noble men."[2]

After the news reached the army that Lincoln had indeed been re-elected, many observers expressed the opinion that another four years of war was inevitable and that the Confederacy should resign itself to that fact. "I indulged the hope all fall that the election for president would bring about a change in [the] war but now I feel no prospect of it," a South Carolina sergeant wrote his wife in late November, "and I Suppose that we may as well make up our minds [to] fight untill our enemys Get tired of the war."[3] John Esten Cooke, the popular Virginia novelist and poet who was serving as a staff officer in the Cavalry Corps, recorded bluntly in his diary, "Lincoln elected: all right. More war—tedious but necessary," and a hospital steward in the 37th North Carolina commented, "Lincoln is elected no alternative but another four years of war."[4] Brig. Gen. Alfred Scales, who had long commanded a veteran North Carolina brigade in Wilcox's Division of the Third Corps, declared, "Lincoln is certainly elected & there is no telling when the war will end." Scales observed, "We must just determine to fight it out & look for the end when it comes," then noted, "I saw Genl Lee yesterday he was in fine spirits & more disposed to joke than I ever saw him."[5]

Several members of the army, perhaps as much to reassure themselves as to convince their families and friends, viewed a prolonged war as a necessity they could bear for the sake of Confederate independence. "Lincoln's Reelection is considered by most thinking men, as the best thing that could happen for the Confederate States," a young South Carolinian declared to his parents. Capt. Edward Laight Wells, who commanded the "Charleston Light Dragoons" of the 4th South Carolina Cavalry, continued, "We know him, & his party, & are ready, & willing to fight them, as long, as it may continue agreeable to them."[6] Such assessments of the election's importance, though by no means universal, reflected the predominant views of correspondents and diarists who commented on the subject. "We are in for four years more—Well, I can stand it, & on my own account dont dread it at all, but I do feel for the many in our country who will suffer from it," Capt. John Elmore Hall told his father, acknowledging the effect Lincoln's reelection was likely to have on many soldiers and civilians.[7]

Other Confederates, just as Hall had predicted, were discouraged by the realization that there would be no quick peace settlement and that the war was going to continue for the foreseeable future. "We are doomed to another four years war God forbid," Sgts. George Adams and Barzella McBride of the 1st North Carolina Cavalry exclaimed in a letter to Adams's parents.[8] One Georgian, who feared that Sherman might "distroy Every thing" in his home state, wrote his mother, "if I had the yanks all in my Power I would have an Earth quake and Kill the last one of them at once," explaining, "It looks like that we have got to fight them 4 years longer and I tell you the truth I dont think that we will bee able to Stand up to the War 4 years more for we have got our last army in the field and they can keep recruiting thair army all the time."[9] Still other soldiers took Lincoln's reelection and the prospect of an even longer war as their cue to desert. Some of them admitted as much to their comrades before leaving the lines or to their former enemies after going over to the Federals. A captain in Brig. Gen. William H. Wallace's South Carolina brigade, in Johnson's Division, reported in his diary that one private of the 23d South Carolina deserted because "A. Lincoln is elected for four more years. He could not stand the idea of hardship of four more long years of war."[10] Another deserter from Wallace's Brigade who went over to the Federals on 22 November was interviewed along with nineteen other Confederates from various units who deserted the same day. According to one Federal officer, the deserters' "principal reason for coming over [was] the fact of Mr. Lincoln's re-election and no prospect of the war ending."[11] Whereas numerous soldiers who were already inclined to give up found ample justification to do so after the election, many who had remained hopeful of an ultimate Confederate victory now began to doubt that it was possible.

If Lee's officers and men looked to the future with uncertainty, they also welcomed the end of active operations for the year and the chance to inhabit more substantial and more comfortable quarters than most of them had occupied since the previous winter. The adjutant of a Third Corps artillery battalion wrote sympathetically of the "poor fellows who for *five long months* have lain in the trenches and listened to the whistle and roar of bullets and shell above them." A few days later he observed: "The Army are preparing to go into Winter Quarters. A good portion of them already have their quarters up right along their trenches. Here they can listen to the whiz of the bullet and rush of the shell all the winter long."[12] Lee's soldiers, of course, hoped that they would not have to hear "the whiz of the bullet and rush of the shell" for a few months but would instead have an opportunity to rest before the campaign of 1865 opened. Many of them believed that their own officers would be content to suspend operations for the winter but feared that Grant's aggressiveness might force them to fight in spite of the season. A sergeant in the Palmetto Sharpshooters reported, "we are now buisey engaged in building of our winter Quarters and I hope we may be permitted to enjoy them untill the winter is over," and a private in the 11th North Carolina told his mother, "we have gone in winter quaters and ar very well prepared to stand the winter if the yankes will let us alone which I am in hop[e]s Ther want be much fiting don this campaign."[13] The prevailing mood in the army seemed to be one of cautious optimism as the soldiers began preparing for winter while keeping a wary eye toward the enemy. "I hope to be able to get out home Christmas, though there is no telling," Capt. Stephen Read of the 14th Virginia reflected. "War is uncertain and Genl. Grant may keep up the campaign all the Winter."[14]

Winter quarters varied in size and in construction, most often determined by whether a particular unit was on the front lines or in reserve, the diligence of the men building it, and the availability of materials. Some soldiers erected log houses that typically sheltered from four to eight men and measured about twelve or fourteen feet square, complete with a fireplace and a wood or tent roof. Others combined large tents with log walls and a fireplace or simply built a fireplace on one end of a tent. Additional types of quarters were those dug out of the sides of hills or trenches, which were often nothing more than bombproofs fitted with fireplaces, or those improvised by piling logs or pine boughs to form lean-to shelters. Soldiers whose units were in the trenches and regularly shifted from point to point along the lines did not have the luxury of substantial housing at first but were eventually able to construct something more permanent when the weather worsened. "[W]e dont anticipate another ingagement withe the yankees soon," Alfred Proffit of the 18th North Carolina observed on 20 November, "for we have been building winter quarters for the last few dayes with great rapidity we are building just in rear of our workes."[15] Though some units stayed in their tents for several weeks, the vast majority of the army had constructed and occupied winter quarters by the end of 1864, when Porter Alexander wrote his wife, "All remains quiet on our lines, & seems likely to stay so for a while at least, & the men are all in little huts or bombproofs along the line & quite comfortable."[16]

Lee's soldiers were grateful for protection from the frequent cold rains and slightly less frequent snows of a Virginia winter, and those who were unfortunate enough to be on picket duty that was exposed to the elements appreciated any shelter available when they returned to their camps. The most common complaints made about the weather were that numerous soldiers had too few overcoats or blankets and too little firewood to keep themselves warm. "Such material as our army is composed of has never before [been] seen," Maj. Giles B. Cooke of Lee's staff commented in his diary in late November, after a particularly cold and rainy night. "It is incomprehensible how they can stand so much exposure."[17]

The soldiers' ability to withstand that exposure, of course, was to a great extent determined by the quartermasters' success in keeping the army clothed, shod, and supplied with blankets during the winter months. As the production and transportation of goods in the Confederacy were haphazard at best, there was no way to guarantee an equitable distribution of clothing or other items throughout the entire army either in terms of quality or of quantity. These disparities were most common, and most striking, in the case of uniforms. Whereas the adjutant of a Virginia brigade in the Fourth Corps remarked in early November, "I fear there will be much suffering as many of the men are badly supplied with blankets, clothing, etc.," a hospital steward in a North Carolina regiment of the Third Corps commented a few days later, "The weather is growing quite cold—our men are *all* clothed & shod."[18] Several factors contributed to such differences within the army. Some units would be issued good jackets, pants, underwear, and hats on a regular basis, whereas others, when they obtained them at all, received inferior items that quickly fell into tatters. Because many soldiers neglected to care for their clothing, often selling, trading, or discarding items, and because they were not held responsible for such conduct by their officers, even those units that had been well supplied suffered chronic shortages. Poor communication between the army and the quartermaster-general's department in Richmond also hampered efforts to keep Confederates properly clothed.

The great disparity in clothing among Lee's soldiers is aptly illustrated by two letters written during the same week, one by a South Carolina cavalry captain and the other by a North Carolina infantry private. Capt. Zimmerman Davis, commanding the 5th South Carolina Cavalry, wrote headquarters on 17 November describing the poor conditions in his command. "My men are ragged," Davis wrote; "many have neither overcoats nor blankets, and numbers are obliged to shiver on picket, clad in tattered remnants of Jacket and Pantalons." He requested an essentially complete uniform—consisting of pants, jacket, shirt, and drawers—for more than 200 men in his regiment, which numbered about 375 soldiers. In late December, after Davis's letter worked its way through proper channels up to headquarters and through the same channels back to him, the captain

Pvt. Alfred Newton Proffit, Company D, 18th North Carolina. Proffit, who served as a private in the Robeson Rifle Guards, was slightly wounded in the arm at Sharpsburg in September 1862 and wounded in the forehead at the Wilderness in May 1864. (Charles W. Proffit)

was promised that the uniforms would be issued to his soldiers.[19] Pvt. Alfred Newton Proffit, on the other hand, wrote his sister proudly on 20 November that the 18th North Carolina had just been issued "a full suit of cloathing some of the prettist kind," stating, "all I lack is my over coat. If you can send it I would bee glad I do not want any blankets if you send any clothing but my coat let it bee a par of sockes."[20] Such varying conditions, even if one conceded in this case that cavalrymen on constant picket duty might be exposed to the elements more often than infantrymen or that the state of North Carolina made extraordinary efforts to ensure that its soldiers were properly clothed, were fairly common in the Army of Northern Virginia. For every Confederate who wrote that "we are sadly in need of clothes," there was a fellow soldier who reported, "the men are generally worse off for hats then any thing else."[21]

Though it could not have been said that Lee's troops were, as a rule, destitute, the comfort of a soldier in one unit could not compensate for the very real need felt by a member of another. An officer in the 26th Virginia, whose regiment was stationed near the Crater, reported in late November that his soldiers were required to spend twelve hours guarding their camp and twelve hours on picket out of every thirty-six-hour period. "The effect that one cold night has upon the boys is a little remarkable," Lt. Luther Rice Mills wrote his brother. "They are generally for *Peace on any terms* toward the close of a cold wet night but after the sun is up and they get warm they are in their usual spirits." Mills welcomed the recent arrival of shoes and blankets, commenting: "it is to be hoped that our men will do better. We have to carry some men to hospital for frostbites &c. Some have come in off picket crying from cold like children."[22]

The lack of adequate clothing, shoes, and blankets was often cited as a major reason for the increased number of desertions as winter set in and some soldiers went over to the enemy to acquire them. Others depended on their families to send them such articles from home or took what they could from Federal prisoners or deserters. Some men took more unusual steps to supply themselves. On one occasion, according to several deserters from Scales's Brigade of the Third Corps, sharpshooters made a night attack on a Federal picket line for no other reason than "it was expected a sufficient number of overcoats, shoes, and blankets would be captured to pay for the undertaking."[23] Still other Confederates resorted to stealing and robbery to get clothing or other items, either from their fellow soldiers or from the civilians near their camps. "There has been a great deal of stealing going on recently & every camp near ours has been robbed at night of provisions clothes boots &c.," one artillery officer wrote in late December. "A robbery of clothes now is quite a serious matter."[24] Though ragged and half-naked Confederates were still the exception rather than the rule in the Army of Northern Virginia, genuine want existed in enough units to induce a considerable number of soldiers to desert or steal to acquire adequate clothing for the winter.

If disparities in the quantity and quality of rations were generally not as great as those involving clothing, they were still pronounced enough to have an impact on the army as a whole and on many individuals in particular. Several of the same factors also frustrated the equitable distribution of daily rations to the troops, and commissary officers had the added burden of being responsible for what numerous soldiers considered to be the most important part of military life. A South Carolinian wrote his wife, "I do not mind the war as long as I can have plenty to eat and comfortable quarters," and a North Carolinian who had recently joined the army spoke for many of Lee's men when he observed, "They seem to think more about something to eat than they do about the danger of war."[25] Though few soldiers ever reported that they had enough to eat, many of them remarked that they could "make out" on what they were issued if they could rely on additional food they bought, foraged, or received in boxes sent from home.

Most objections to rations focused on the meat ration, which was ideally beef but almost as often bacon, and the bread ration, which was ideally uncooked flour but almost as often cornmeal or already-baked bread. Inspection reports and other communications throughout November and December alluded to the scanty and sometimes spoiled rations issued to several units, stated that the troops expressed more discontent over rations than over anything else, and blamed many recent desertions on that dissatisfaction. Commissary officers often responded to such reports with various explanations that were technically correct but displayed little sympathy for the plight of the soldiers in the ranks, further alienating many officers and men and giving the impression that the authorities did not care about them. The November inspection report of a Georgia brigade in the Third Corps, for example, noted, "The subject of rations requires notice on account of constant complaint heard among the men"; the brigade's meat ration was often spoiled with ashes or dirt, and the amount of bread (intended as a substitute for flour or meal) issued was not nearly enough. Lt. Col. H. E. Peyton, the army's inspector general, endorsed this report, stating that he had recently advised Lt. Col. Robert G. Cole, the army's chief commissary, that "the interests of the service as well as the comfort of the men required an increase of the flour and meat ration." Though Cole had told Peyton that an increase was "not practicable," the inspector general believed that "a larger quantity of meat & flour should be issued to the troops & it is possible." He argued: "This small ration and the inadequate supply of clothing—is doubtless promoting desertion among the men. These opinions are formed after abundant opportunity of ascertaining the general condition & sentiment of the army."[26] It was also the opinion of many observers that a ration sufficient for troops in camp was woefully insufficient for troops on picket duty or in the trenches, and that allowances should be made according to the duties that soldiers were required to perform. The commanding general endorsed a report informing him that sixty men had deserted from the Third Corps in one ten-day period with the comment, "Most of the men are supposed to have gone to the enemy. Scarce provisions, continuous duty in the trenches is probably the cause."[27]

Though numerous correspondents and diarists grumbled about their rations, others seemed to be making the best of things. "[E]verything Sells high here but we need not buy for we get plenty of meat & bread also good Coffee, Sufficient to make one Cup a day," one recent arrival from South Carolina wrote home in November. By late December Pvt. Alexander Fewell of the 17th South Carolina noted that his rations had been reduced somewhat but remarked: "Well I Cant say that we are hungry. I Can live on bread and water if they would only give us plenty of bread but if you will take one tinfull of flour & make it up with Cold water and bake it you will find it dont make much bread." Fewell did believe that "if the weather was moderate or we were not in the Cold we Could do Verry well on that even."[28] A few days later, writing, "I have eat but little for Some days," he explained, "not because I Could not have got it for I have money & Could buy but Our Rations is Verry Short and I am trying to see if I Cant live on them."[29] Soldiers were also skilled at improvising, such as the members of another company in Fewell's regiment who caught a rabbit and made a stew from it and whatever rations they had. Capt. John A. F. Coleman described the stew as "a pot filled with water, then a quanity of turnips, next the rabbit, and lastly an equal quanity of rice. . . . There is a little piece of bacon in the pot. The whole is to be eaten without bread, there being none on hand."[30] Whereas many Confederates used their money and their wits to supplement their meals and were in no danger of starving, many others could not—or would not—withstand the hardship of reduced or inferior rations. Just as with clothing, serious shortages of rations were common enough for numerous soldiers, conscripts and veterans alike, to desert or steal for the sake of them. The decline of the army's physical condition, whether from want of food, want of clothing, or exposure to the elements, would be a serious problem for Lee and his officers during the winter of 1864–65.

In contrast to these shortages, there was a slight improvement in the number of troops present for duty during November, as conscripts, detailed men, and veterans returning from sick or wounded furloughs swelled the ranks of badly depleted regiments. "All details between the ages of 18 and 45 are revoked and bombproofs are daily coming into us with musket and blanket," Sgt. Maj. Marion Hill Fitzpatrick of the 45th Georgia wrote his wife in early November. "This is a good thing and a great help."[31] The inspector general's report for the month, forwarded to the Adjutant and Inspector General's Department in Richmond, noted that the Third Corps had acquired some five thousand men, that Pickett's Division of the First Corps had gained significant numbers of troops, and that "the increase is specially noticed in the Va. and No.Ca. organizations." H. E. Peyton's report credited the efforts of Lee and the War Department to gain able-bodied men in the ranks and asserted that "the material thus added to the Army by the causes referred to is the best in the Army and the country." Several former company officers, who had been voted out of their positions when the army was reorganized in the spring of 1862, were now returning to their former units as enlisted men. They might well be commissioned once again in units that desperately needed "intelligent and efficient men, worthy of promotion and competent to command."[32]

Other observers corroborated these reports. Federal officers who interviewed deserters in late November noted that the Confederates were gaining conscripts daily, and that most deserters described regiments ranging from 150 to 300 troops, with regiments having as many as 300 men being the exception. "Conscripts and returned detailed men swell up the regiments considerably of late," one Federal report noted. "McGowan's brigade has received additions to the number of 300, and now musters 1,000 muskets."[33] About the same time Capt. John Fletcher Brabham, a member of the 1st South Carolina Rifles, wrote a friend: "Our regiment is recruiting very fast, wounded and sick returning and some few new numbers. After the battle of Fort Harrison, our regiment only numbered one hundred and ten muskets.—now it has two hundred and fifteen guns. I had in my Company ten guns after the charge at the same place, and this morning I reported twenty three." Brabham also described how two recent conscripts reacted to service in the trenches on the Richmond front, declaring, "They think the hardships awful, but I tell them they have not seen any thing, as we are doing better now than we have since the Campaign open[ed]."[34]

The army's strength returns demonstrated just how many conscripts, detailed men, and returning men had come in since the last serious engagements on the Petersburg-Richmond front. The 31 October returns reported 47,000 troops present for duty out of a total strength of about

120,000 men present and absent, whereas the 30 November returns showed some 62,000 troops present for duty out of a total strength of about 125,000 men present and absent. This represented an increase of about 15,000 men, not to mention the nearly 12,000 men of the Second Corps who would rejoin the army in the next few weeks.[35] These gains would not last, however, for though Lee tried to find a way to utilize his strengthened troops in offensive operations, he could not implement any plans before winter weather set in or before numbers of the newly arrived conscripts began deserting at their first opportunity.[36]

In spite of the ample reasons for dissatisfaction among the troops, numerous veterans belonging to the Army of Northern Virginia believed that most of Lee's soldiers were still willing to fight for as long as necessary and as long as possible. A. P. Hill wrote his sister that the army was "ready to do its duty, and men and officers in good spirits. I suppose now we shall, in addition to Grant, have Sherman on our hands too—Well, the Army of Northern Virginia is equal to it, and however much you task its powers, will always respond, and I hope successfully."[37] Several Confederates said that it was their faith in their commander and their identity as *Lee's* army that gave them confidence. "We are in a tight place—but I say stick up—and keep a bold front—and we are bound to win," a North Carolinian in the Second Corps wrote his sister. Pvt. Thomas Pollock Devereux, a courier in Bryan Grimes's old brigade who had seen hard service in the Shenandoah with Early, continued: "Gen Lee has 60000 of the best soldiers in the world and they have unbounded confidence in him—they know he will not tell them to go, where there is no necessity and when he says the word—we will storm Grant in his breastworks—if they were twice as strong as ours, and take them too—or die trying."[38] A Virginia staff officer in the Fourth Corps commented, "Whatever he [Lee] does we think it is all right, and whatever he neglects to do, we suppose is for our good."[39]

Many observers claimed that they were more discouraged by signs of despondency among the Confederate people—from politicians, to newspaper editors, to their families and friends at home—than by conditions in the army, and that they would prevail if the citizens would rally to their support. "There is no use talking about peace now," Charles Kerrison wrote his sister in early December, "we have got to fight it out, and the men who are fighting are perfectly willing to continue till they gain an *honorable* peace, all they ask is for the noncombatants and those who stay at home and wont fight, to let peace resolutions drop."[40] A fellow South Carolinian went so far as to excoriate "many at home who are destitute of boath honour and patriotisme . . . Shurly not fit to associate with those who have done thair duty . . . my candid opinion is that all Such men Should be debared the privilages of cittizens and treated as alien enemies."[41] Though many members of the army thought that its officers and men were in reasonably good spirits, most of them were realistic enough to recognize that their chances for an outright military victory and for the establishment of Confederate independence were waning with every day. In early December a Virginia lieutenant observed, "I think it is the desire of the Army at large to fight it out to the bitter end if we can remain united as we have been, if not let us give it up at once."[42]

There was a growing sense among Lee's soldiers, even those who wrote hopefully of the future, that the army's morale was considerably lower than it had ever been before and that it would be difficult, if not impossible, to recapture some of the old spirit of 1862 and 1863. Many members of the army who had previously been willing to endure shortages in clothing and rations for the sake of the country now questioned continued deficiencies that seemed to serve no purpose. They also entertained serious doubts that the Confederacy—not to mention their army— would survive the opening of the 1865 campaign. Such doubts, among veterans and conscripts alike, were clearly fueled by the downward spiral in Confederate fortunes that began with Sherman's capture of Atlanta and Sheridan's victories in the Shenandoah Valley, then accelerated through November and December with Sherman's march through Georgia and the virtual destruction of the Army of Tennessee at Franklin and Nashville. "I believe there is at this time more dissatisfaction in our army than I ever saw in it before," William Horace Phillips of the 14th Virginia commented on 26 November. "I raly believe there will be a general bash up in our army before next March."[43] The conscripts who complained of the hardships of military life were often joined by veterans weary of several years' service, such as those described by a South Carolina cavalryman in early December: "The spirit of the army is ever fluctuating, as the tide of the ocean. Kershaw's Division is low, awfully hacked from the whipping they got in the Valley."[44] A few days later Pvt. John Johnson of the 19th Georgia candidly informed his fiancée: "The 'morale' of the army is not as good as it was 2 years ago. I look for a good many to desert next spring for they are tired and can see no signs of a prospect of peace and neither can I."[45]

Other complaints, both tangible and intangible, undoubtedly contributed to the increasing despondency of many Confederates and were the subject of numerous letters to the Richmond newspapers during the last few weeks of the year. The soldiers, who signed their letters with such pseudonyms as "Buck Private," "The Soldiers," or "Many Sufferers," reported such indignities as the government's long-standing inability to pay the troops, the poor quality of tobacco or soap issued to them, or the condescending attitude displayed by staff officers, government officials, or civilians. Several privates in Bratton's Brigade of the First Corps observed on Christmas Eve that their officers had already been paid but that they had not, commenting: "We, though not so meritorious as they, would like to have our mite. The winter is growing cold, our clothes are getting threadbare, rations are also short, and we are sorely in need of our eighteen dollars per month."[46] A typical letter asking if Confederate soldiers deserved the disdain of staff or bureau officers sardonically assured the *Richmond Examiner*'s readers that its author was "far beneath the notice of authority" but asked for some respect for "the lowly world of privates, whose insignificant aid helps to support on giddy heights the fellow men who have the honour to provide and command."[47] Letters such as these became more and more frequent during the winter of 1864–65 as soldiers who believed that they had no other forum vented their frustration in the newspapers and hoped that public opinion might convince their military superiors and the civilian authorities to do something for them.

Descriptions of camp life became increasingly gloomy in late December as many veterans spent yet another Christmas and New Year's Day in the army and recent conscripts faced their first such holidays there. Pvt. Edward H. Steele of the 14th Tennessee conveyed this mood in a letter to a cousin on 17 December: "The Boys are all thinking pretty strongly about the approaching Christmas, all long for a 'rousing' dinner, but I fear will be disappointed, for everything is scarce around this place." Steele, whose regiment was one of the few Tennessee units in Lee's army, continued, "I had hoped myself, to have a 'big dinner,' and 'Egg Nog,' but know very well, it will be impossible to get at."[48] A few days later Lt. Fred Fleet, a Virginia staff officer whose parents lived at "Green Mount," the family plantation in King and Queen County northeast of Richmond, wrote wistfully: "I suppose you all are making preparations for Christmas, and I would like to be with you very much. I had hoped I would get something [from home] for a Christmas dinner, but it will be just as good any other time."[49] While few Confederates expected anything other than their regular rations and most resigned themselves to a quiet, cheerless holiday, others hoped that they might have something special to eat after all.

That hope was encouraged by the citizens of Richmond and the surrounding countryside, who were working diligently to give the army an immense holiday dinner in the trenches in appreciation of its sacrifices during the war. This meal, first suggested in late November and inspired by a similar dinner given to the Army of the Potomac, was originally planned as a Christmas gift to the Virginia units in the army that soon included the entire Army of Northern Virginia. When it became clear that this ambitious undertaking could not be completed in time for Christmas, the committee in charge of it proposed a New Year's Day dinner to be held on Monday, 2 January, as the first fell on a Sunday. The Richmond newspapers eagerly seized upon the idea, enlisting the aid of local citizens to donate their money, food, and time to the effort and filling their columns with daily reports about the progress of what was quickly dubbed "the soldiers' dinner." The editors of the *Richmond Examiner* declared, "Let the soldiers, while reminded of home and all its enjoyments, be admonished that, though cut off from these home festivities, there are those who appreciate their valour and devotion, and are willing to make their absence a pleasurable reminiscence."[50] Broadsides were printed and distributed announcing a "New Year's Dinner to Gen'l. Lee's Army," explaining, "As a slight token of gratitude to the Army of Gen. Lee, the citizens propose to give them a New Year's Dinner," and instructing those donating money or food to send it to Richmond by 29 December.[51] Maj. Henry Young of Lee's staff observed, "I hope they will get it up, for if ever men deserved the good things of the citizens these poor fellows do."[52]

Such a dinner would be especially appreciated by soldiers whose rations—particularly meat—had been dwindling in the first three weeks of December. It was becoming so difficult to obtain enough meat for the troops that on the fourteenth Lee reported: "Chief Commissary of this Army received notice yesterday from Richmond that there was no salt meat there to send him, but would forward preserved meat. He thinks he may get enough to last tomorrow."[53] Confederates frequently mentioned their increasingly meager rations and the effect they had on the army's morale, above all on Christmas Day. Walter Raleigh Battle of the 4th North Carolina wrote his mother: "It is the gloomiest Xmas that I ever saw. We not only miss the extras which we have had heretofore, but we have not got as much meat or bread as we can eat."[54] Creed Thomas Davis of the Richmond Howitzers described his Christmas ration of a half pound of pork and a pound of flour and observed sadly: "What a pity it is, that Santa Claus never visits the Confederate armies. We drew this morning a few grains of sugar and coffee, which the Government has kindly condescended, to issue in consideration of Christmas times. Our boys are very despondent to day."[55]

Inspection reports made at the end of the month noted that some brigades had been without meat for several days and that even if issued the amount "hardly suffices for men who are on duty every second or third night during cold weather."[56] On 30 December Capt. James Walker inspected a veteran Georgia brigade in the First Corps and noted, "for the past 4 days the Command has been without meat."[57] Several men who deserted to the Federals between Christmas and New Year's Day told much the same tale. One deserter who did so was 2d Lt. R. G. Redwood, of the 43d Alabama, who asserted that in his brigade fish was being issued instead of meat and that "swarms of deserters" would be arriving from the Confederate lines in the near future.[58] Bushrod Johnson, who commanded the division to which Redwood's brigade belonged, reported to Fourth Corps headquarters that twelve other members of the division had also deserted on Christmas Night. Lee's endorsement on Johnson's report observed that "scant fare, light clothing, constant duty, [and] no recruits" had discouraged many of his officers and men.[59]

Surrounded by such depressing scenes, Lee's troops read tantalizing details of the preparations being made for them and understandably had their expectations for the New Year's dinner raised to great heights. Some soldiers expressed concern that the commissaries or other officers might take the best food for themselves, that the troops around Petersburg might be neglected in favor of those nearer Richmond, or that units in the trenches might fare better than those in reserve. The newspaper editors, however, reassured them that all efforts were being made to ensure ample food for every member of the army.[60] The *Richmond Examiner* reported on 29 December that one of the capital's hotels had been selected to collect and prepare the meal; it called the dinner "the biggest barbecue ever gotten up on this continent."[61] The next day Corp. Simeon Gross of the 20th South Carolina, in a letter to his mother, remarked, "I here we is goin to have a big New Years dinner. They are thousands of chickens and turkeys in Richmond for us."[62] On New Year's Eve an article in the *Examiner* listed such items as "rounds of beef, saddles of mutton, venisons, whole shoats, hams, sausage of country make, rich with sage and redolent with pepper; turkies, geese, ducks, [and] chickens" and promised that the dinner would be one in which "the commonest private will be entitled to the first helping and the best."[63] Eagerly awaiting the dinner, numerous Confederates spent most of New Year's Day 1865 thinking about it. One Virginia artilleryman observed, "We are living in the hope of receiving and eating a large New Year's dinner, which the citizens of Virginia promise," and a Georgia surgeon commented, "Like Xmas the day with me is dull—no change in our diet which is the principal enjoyment of a 'reb'—tomorrow we are promised a treat in the shape of a New Years dinner a grateful offering from a grateful people."[64]

When the soldiers' dinner finally arrived along the lines—in many instances late on the evening of 2 January, or the next day, or the day after that—most hungry Confederates found that it was far short of what they had expected. Though the more fortunate units received a little turkey, chicken, ham, beef, or mutton, a few small loaves of bread, and some potatoes or other vegetables, some units obtained nothing but bread. "The citizens of Richmond and surrounding country made up a great New Year's dinner for this army," one North Carolina private informed his wife, "and when it was sent out to us it consisted of 3 or 4 bites of bread and 3 bites of meat and it was quite a snack for a feast." The disillusioned soldier then noted, "Somebody stole my part, but I did not grieve very much."[65] Surgeon Robert Pooler Myers of the 16th Georgia wrote in his diary, "the portion our Brigd got was quite small about 1/3 loaf bread and 1/3 the [usual] amt of cold meat or fowl—rather a poor treat the troops thought after the extensive preparations the papers led them to believe were being made."[66]

Other disappointed members of the army characterized the dinner in such terms as "a complete fizzle," a "Grand Farce," or "a most complete failure."[67] Lt. John T. Gay of the 4th Georgia, for example, was detailed to receive his brigade's share of the dinner on 2 January. After waiting all day, Gay took "a very limited supply of meat & bread & apple butter" back to his comrades; a few days later he wrote his wife: "The meat was very well cooked, and consisted of beef, mutton, chicken & turkey. When divided between each man, the quantity was so small that Eugenie [his daughter] would have pushed it aside with disdain as being too little for her dinner."[68] Estimates of the amounts issued to several other units were comparable. Porter Alexander noted that the share for some 1,500 men in the First Corps artillery was "182 lbs of meat—a little bread & four or five bushels of turnips & potatoes."[69] Pvt. Frank Lobrano of the famous Washington Artillery battalion of New Orleans complained that his company "did not get even a smell of any kind of meat" and that each man's entire New Year's dinner was about one-fourth of a loaf of bread.[70] Another member of Lobrano's battalion wrote scornfully, "if that is all they are going to give us let them keep it the 4th Company gave their Bread to the Orphans."[71] The soldiers of the Texas Brigade also donated their dinner to the poor and were praised by the newspapers for their "spirit of self-denial," when in fact Thomas McCarty of the 1st Texas explained, "I hardly think they would have done so if there had to have been sufficient [food] for the men to eat."[72] Several soldiers wrote the *Richmond Examiner* grumbling about "the grand dinner" and accusing the newspapers, organizers, and others of mismanagement or favoritism but were admonished by the editors: "The Committee who had the matter in charge did their best to feed all. . . . They could do no more."[73]

Other soldiers, who had looked forward to the dinner as much as any of their comrades, took a more philosophical view and praised those who had done their best. "I received my little piece of Turkey & mutton with as many thanks as if it had been plenty, knowing they did all in their power to give us a dinner," Grant Carter of the 2d Georgia Battalion explained to his mother on 4 January.[74] One South Carolinian in the First Corps called the dinner "Somewhat a falier" but "Sensible and thinking men do no[t] Say anything for it was a Large and difficult undertaking to prepair a dinner for So Large an army as this."[75] Edward Cook Barnes, a courier in Pickett's Division, observed, "Though the disappointment was exceedingly great, having been led to expect so much, the boys appreciated the difficulties in getting up such a gigantic affair, and the good motives & generosity of the contributors."[76]

Whether or not Lee's soldiers voiced their complaints, their disappointment in the New Year's dinner could not help but increase the misery felt throughout the army. Sitting in camp near Petersburg and writing to his parents on 4 January, one unhappy North Carolinian did not mention the dinner but said that it was "a pore chrismuss and new year's" and declared, "i think that we ar about gone up i dont [k]now what will becom of uss." Pvt. Riley Leonard of the 21st North Carolina concluded, "if th[ey] will quit feeding me i want stay hear that well mak me desert in[to] the cuntary quickery then anything elce you can cep this to yourselves if you pleas."[77] Such attitudes, though not yet widespread, were becoming more prevalent than ever in the first few days of 1865. "The past week has been one of some suffering to the troops in consequence of hard work & short rations," a Third Corps staff officer wrote his mother two days later. "These are times that try men's souls, and I am sorry so many prove fearful & faithless," Capt. Louis G. Young observed, then placed conditions in the army in a different light when he continued: "but I am glad of the test, and would be willing to see all the weak in spirit go to the enemy. Our country can spare them, and they serve it better by deserting to the enemy, than by remaining in our midst."[78] Though the sentiments of

Leonard at one end of the spectrum and Young at the opposite end were still atypical, their very expression did not bode well for the future of the Army of Northern Virginia.

Most observers who contemplated the year just behind them and looked anxiously into the year ahead believed that the devastation of 1864 had been unprecedented, agreed that 1865 would be the last year of the conflict, and differed primarily over the Confederacy's prospects for survival. As January and February wore on, even the most sanguine correspondents and diarists began to express doubts that the Army of Northern Virginia could sustain its previous reputation as the Confederacy's only truly successful fighting force. Many of them described miserable soldiers whose confidence was being shaken to their foundations by recent Federal victories in Georgia, Tennessee, and North Carolina, by the growing spirit of defeatism among the population, and by the hardships they were being asked to endure for a nation whose territory and resources were rapidly shrinking. "There is nothing pleasant or agreeable in a Soldiers life it is all hardships and troubles," an Alabama private remarked in a letter to his wife. "As for the war the Lord only knows when it will close . . . I dont think it can close to soon for the private Soldiers Judging from the way they all talk they are getting very tired of the war and would like to See it close."[79] The cumulative effect of those "hardships and troubles" was a burden that many weary Confederates were unwilling to bear. Over a four-day period in mid-January, for example, a Virginia artilleryman noted that rations were scarce and the prospect of more was "rather gloomy," that talk of a peace conference between Confederate commissioners and Federal authorities had fostered "a spirit of insubordination among the troops," and that the Federals had captured Fort Fisher and the Confederacy's last major seaport at Wilmington, North Carolina. Sgt. James Albright of the 12th Battalion Virginia Light Artillery called the latter event "sad & inexcusable," exclaiming, "Oh, how dark is our day! Every body is sad, & submission is even talked of by many!"[80]

Lee's soldiers often tried to balance such negative reports with expressions of hope that the army might prove itself equal to the crisis. "[W]e would not complain of Rations or hardships if there was a brighter prospect ahead," one South Carolina private assured a friend, and a Virginia lieutenant noted in late January, "The army has been quite low-spirited under our recent reverses, but I hope a reaction is taking place, and henceforth their spirits will rise."[81] Some soldiers who acknowledged their discouragement were careful to reassure their families and friends that they had not given up. Sgt. Will Montgomery of the 9th Georgia confessed, "I am getting somewhat tired of the business though not as bad whiped as a great many are," adding, "Our army is getting verry much out of heart."[82] A private in the 11th Georgia, whose regiment also belonged to Brig. Gen. George T. Anderson's Brigade of the First Corps, told his mother in January, "we air seeing Mity Hard times at this time . . . I tell you that things looks mity gloomy, it is all that the men can do to keep from derserting, but you need not think that I am going to dersert. I do love my contry too well to ever go to the yanks."[83]

Others thought that the general despondency in the army would be diminished if the soldiers ignored those at home who urged them to give up, shunned the discontented men in the ranks around them, and renewed their determination to do their duty. In early February Col. Fitz William McMaster of the 17th South Carolina admitted, "It is true that their sufferings have been great & that they are poorly clad & fed but they ought to nerve themselves up a few months longer & our cause would be won."[84] Some correspondents drew parallels between the American Revolution and the present war. The patriots of 1776 had persevered and were finally rewarded with their independence in spite of frequent battlefield defeats, the loss of vast stretches of territory, and the obstacles encountered by generals trying to hold their armies together, all challenges confronting the Confederacy in 1865. "Now we are truly fighting for our Independence as our fathers were," Capt. James Dewitt Hankins of the Surry Light Artillery observed in January. "O fainting heart and feeble faith, what chance was there for our fathers? And what was the light touch of the finger of English assumption compared with the loin-heavy weight of Yankee despotism and tyranny!"[85] A North Carolina courier in the Second Corps wrote, "we are no worse than our ancestors in the Revolution when they had no important town and no army in the field—they held out and were successful."[86] A few members of the army were even more emphatic about their will to continue the fight, declaring, for example, "Yankees may kill me, but they will never subjugate me" or "I am in for the War let it be long or Short if I never come home dont think the time long."[87] One such veteran was 3d Sgt. Henry Fortson of the "Muscogee Confederates," Company B of the 31st Georgia. Fortson, who had participated in all the army's major battles since the Seven Days' campaign, including Early's recent campaign in the Shenandoah Valley, wrote a friend, "I hope there is enough true men to give the yankees a thrashing when needed, or atleest when called on."[88] As the Army of Northern Virginia waited for spring, the perseverance and resiliency of Fortson and others like him stood in increasingly stark contrast to those men who faltered and were unable or unwilling to carry on.

The trickle of desertions that had plagued the army during 1864 swelled into a stream in the last few months of the year and then into a flood throughout January and February 1865. Comments such as "there is right smart Desertion here at this time" or "Our army is deserting very fast we loose more or less every day" became so commonplace in letters and diaries that many soldiers did not elaborate on the reasons for this latest wave of desertions but simply reported them.[89] "Many of the men who have been in the war ever since sixty one, are deserting and going to the yankees," Sgt. R. P. Scarbrough of Hurt's Battery wrote on the last day of January, and in mid-February Pvt. James King Wilkerson of the 55th North Carolina stated, "I have nearly lost all confidents in our men."[90] According to reports forwarded to army headquarters by division commanders, nearly 1,100 soldiers deserted in a single ten-day period in February, prompting Lee to comment, "These men generally went off in bands, taking arms and ammunition, and I regret to say that the greatest number of desertions have occurred among the North Carolina troops, who have fought as gallantly as any soldiers in the army."[91] One Tennessean in the Third Corps who deserted from Petersburg and made his way into the Shenandoah Valley told Federal officers that "Large numbers of Lee's army are deserting daily; sometimes as many as 200 a day. At least half would desert if they had an opportunity."[92]

These desertions were more often a response to conditions within the army or on the home front rather than to the military or political situation in the Confederacy at large, a response that reflected many soldiers' natural inclination to take matters into their own hands when they believed that they or their kin were being mistreated. One of the most obvious reasons given for the increase in desertions was the poor quality, and often poorer quantity, of rations. "I have no doubt that there is suffering for want of food," Lee reported to the War Department on 27 January. "The ration is too small for men who have to undergo so much exposure and labor as ours."[93] He enclosed several recent reports from company, regimental, brigade, and division commanders in the Third Corps verifying his opinion. Lt. Col. J. H. Duncan of the 16th Mississippi noted, "These desertions are becoming amazingly numerous," and stated flatly, "Our men do not get enough to eat"; the company officers of the 9th Florida observed that their soldiers' discontent over rations and pay was "now so general as to deserve serious consideration" and that desertions were increasing as a direct result.[94] Lee reminded the Confederate authorities:

"It will not answer to reduce the ration in order to make up for deficiencies in the subsistence department. . . . It may be that all is done that can be, but I am not satisfied that we cannot do more." He ended his letter with yet another plea for an increase in rations, expressing the hope that "no measure will be neglected that offers a chance of improvement."[95] In spite of such pressure, and in the face of overwhelming evidence that the Army of Northern Virginia was being wrecked by desertions attributable in part to slight rations, department officers—including Col. Lucius B. Northrop, the Confederate commissary-general of subsistence—continued to cite regulations and refused to authorize any increases.[96] Meanwhile, thousands of Lee's soldiers went hungry, and scores of them deserted every night to avoid facing yet another day without adequate food. "I get so hungry that it makes me sick," William Leak of the 22d South Carolina wrote his wife and children on 30 January. "I stand it much better than I thought I could, but don't know how long I will hold out at it. The reason they don't feed us any better may be thay can not getit. . . . Our men can not and will not stand it much longer."[97]

If other motives for desertion may have been less visceral, they were certainly no less real—and often much more significant—than motives based primarily on a soldier's physical condition. An individual Confederate's family or friends at home, those for whom the average soldier was fighting, were often the deciding factor when a man abandoned his comrades and left the army behind. "I know that many have a hard trial to stay in the war when they learn that their families are at home sufferering," one Alabamian observed to a cousin. "Well I have told you enough of this for my eyes will hardly refrain from tears when I think of it."[98] Others, who felt sympathy for their comrades who received letters pleading with them to abandon the army, condemned those who encouraged their husbands, fathers, sons, brothers, or friends to desert. "The desertions are becoming very numerous among the troops all proceeding from despondency created by the Croakers at home," Bryan Grimes wrote in late February regarding desertions from his division of the Second Corps. "[T]here were forty deserted from the 45th N.C.T. night before last, all from Rockingham county—they say that Tom Settle had written that the only way to have peace was for the troops to stop fighting and come home." Grimes angrily wrote of Settle, "I wish he were in my power for a short while you may be sure I would stop his mouth forever."[99] For all too many dispirited Confederates, however, pitiful letters begging them to come home were simply more than they could endure. On 24 February Lee reported to the War Department that some four hundred men of the Third Corps, most of them North Carolinians, had deserted in the past two weeks; he blamed "their friends at home, who appear to have become very despondent as to our success. . . . These desertions have a very bad effect on the troops who remain and give rise to painful apprehension."[100]

Numerous soldiers who still remained in the Army of Northern Virginia in January and February did so only for the moment, in some instances openly declaring their intention to desert when they could and in a few cases displaying insubordination that bordered on rebellion. "Some say the war will be over by spring," Pvt. John J. Armfield of the 30th North Carolina wrote his wife on 14 January, "and I intend to stop my part by the spring or before." By 31 January, amid hurried orders to cook a day's rations and be ready to march any moment, the discouraged North Carolinian speculated that his brigade might be going to Wilmington to reinforce the garrison at Fort Fisher. "We will not know until we get there," Armfield remarked, "but they better not take us into North Carolina especially by Greensboro for someone might go to see his family."[101] About the same time a Virginian in Pickett's Division of the First Corps wrote his sweetheart, "I have tride to git off to Come to see you an Cant So you Nead Not to rite to Me any More tell you here from Me A gin for I am going to leave her[e] I am going North soon." Pvt. James F. Ward of the 8th Virginia ended his letter with the hope that she would "Not think hard of Me for that for I Never Will Neavre forgit you and if I live till this ware ends I will be arond I want you to keep this rite to your self till you here from me A gin."[102]

As individuals like Armfield and Ward contemplated desertion, in some units groups of miserable soldiers banded together to encourage the spread of disloyalty. A Georgia brigade in Field's Division of the First Corps and a Virginia brigade in Evans's Division of the Second Corps, for example, were suspected of containing groups that either advocated or tolerated desertion. Though officers who investigated in mid-January found no firm evidence that these two units were engaged in such activities, it was widely feared that similar groups were at work in the army.[103] A corporal in the latter brigade observed, "The grumbling, disorganizing & treasonable talk of the men has increased so much that committees of officers have been appointed to report all such cases as occur," and warned, "This will add fuel to the flame."[104] Though deserters crippled the army by their absence, the behavior of dissatisfied individuals or groups had the potential to do greater harm by their presence, for they might represent the difference between success or failure when Lee's troops entered combat again.

When the army did fight the Federals for the first time in 1865, it would do so with slightly more troops present for duty than Lee had commanded during the battles and engagements of October 1864, but with considerably fewer men than those present for duty on the strength returns of 31 December. In spite of the welcome return of the Second Corps to the Petersburg-Richmond front, and in spite of the considerable temporary gains resulting from efforts to increase the number of able-bodied men in the army, only some 60,000 troops were present for duty on the last day of 1864, out of a total strength of about 150,000 present and absent. By the end of January the number present for duty had decreased to about 57,000 troops out of a total strength of about 140,000 present and absent, and an early February strength return reported only 50,000 soldiers present for duty out of about 135,000 present and absent.[105]

Though some units—most notably Hoke's Division of the Fourth Corps and Butler's Division of the Cavalry Corps—had been sent to North or South Carolina in December and January to aid Confederate forces there, their strength did not make up for the net losses in the number of troops present for duty.[106] "As all of our leading men are aware, the ranks of our army are very much depleted and thinned," a veteran in Phillips's Legion observed in the *Richmond Dispatch* in mid-February. "Can't something be done to strengthen our lines?"[107] His corps commander was among those officers who cautioned against attempting offensive operations with dwindling numbers and even admitted that they could not guarantee their troops' ability to hold their lines. James Longstreet kept up a steady correspondence with Lee in January and February that touched on many of the army's concerns and frequently on the lack of troops in his lines north of the James.[108] "When the time comes I think that we shall make as good a fight as the same number of men ever did," he observed on 1 February, "but I do not think that it would be prudent to risk a battle outside of our lines." A few days later Longstreet wrote Lee, "I shall endeavor so far as possible to execute your designs, but neither diligence nor skill nor valor can increase my number, and our present force cannot hold the line to the Chickahominy against a very determined attack." He assured his commander that if Grant attacked him, "we shall fight him, of course, as long as we have a man, but we should fight with much better heart if we could have better hope of results."[109]

Any substantive examination of the numbers available for combat revealed units so weakened by casualties, absenteeism, and desertions that brigades were often the size of regiments and regiments were the size of small companies. Some brigades had their full complement of colonels or a few lieutenant colonels commanding badly depleted regiments, but others, particularly in the Second Corps, had captains and lieutenants commanding regiments or consolidated remnants of them. Though several consolidations had already occurred out of sheer necessity—such as those in Edward Johnson's old division, shattered at Spotsylvania—Lee and others now proposed the wholesale consolidation of all understrength regiments and companies in the Confederate armies. Many officers and men who might have admitted the practical wisdom of such a measure still opposed it when an act authorizing consolidation was debated in the Confederate Congress, most often on the grounds that regiments that had served throughout the war would suddenly lose their identities. Longstreet, for example, suggested that regiments be reduced from ten companies to six, allowing them to retain their old designations rather than being merged with other understrength units. "When you break up a regiment," he wrote Lee in early January, "you destroy its prestige and its esprit de corps, which are the two most important elements in military organizations."[110]

Other officers and men voiced similar objections. The lieutenant colonel of the 6th North Carolina, acting on behalf of his soldiers, wrote Gov. Zebulon Vance: "We desire to protest against *any* consolidation which can effect our designation. . . . We have a history which it is desired to perpetuate and whatever of character this Regiment has made from first Manassas to the present should, in justice to our heroic dead, be preserved."[111] At the end of January another North Carolinian expressed the same sentiments in simpler terms: "I am afraid our company and regiment will lose their name after all the hard service which we have done since the commencement of the war."[112] Some observers thought that many regimental and company officers, who might lose their positions when their units were consolidated but who would then be given the option to choose other units or other branches of service, favored the bill for selfish reasons. One lieutenant in the First Corps described the plan to his wife with the comment, "I am compell to belive that it will have a bad affect and it will cause a greate dispondency in the army asspecially with the enlisted men, as for the officers a greate many of them are in favor of it."[113] If the consolidation bill was enacted and implemented in spite of such vocal opposition, it would give many soldiers yet another reason to complain that the civil and military authorities gave them no respect.

Many weary Confederates, from jaded veterans who had heard and passed on virtually every rumor imaginable, to unsuspecting conscripts who believed almost anything they were told, thought that a genuine chance for peace might finally be at hand in early 1865. Such ideas, which had considerable basis in fact, stemmed from a request by three official representatives of the Confederacy who asked to meet with Abraham Lincoln to discuss possible ways to end the war. After Confederate peace commissioners Vice President Alexander H. Stephens, Assistant Secretary of War John A. Campbell, and Senator Robert M. T. Hunter crossed into the Federal lines under a flag of truce on 25 January, soldiers and civilians alike waited for news of their mission and hoped to hear that terms had been reached. "There is great talk about peace in the army, and most of the soldiers think the war will end in the spring," one private remarked, "but I fear it is deception."[114] A captain who described the scene when the three commissioners left the Confederate lines near Petersburg was more optimistic, commenting, "These men were accompanied to our lines by Genl. Lee, in full uniform; also Genl. Hill & others. Great cheering on their passage. May our Heavenly Father speed and favour their Mission with an *honorable peace* as a result."[115] Numerous observers insisted that the only acceptable terms would be those guaranteeing an "honorable peace"—which to most Confederates meant a recognition of their independence—and that any other conditions would force them to continue fighting. Lt. John Evans of the 53d Georgia predicted, "when they get there old Abe will offer them submission or reconstruction of the union, which our people never will submit to, to think of liveing in the union with such a people is obnoxious."[116] After a few days of waiting Stephens, Campbell, and Hunter were escorted to Hampton Roads, where they met with Lincoln and Secretary of State William H. Seward on 3 February. The conference, which lasted several hours, ended in failure, for Lincoln refused to recognize the commissioners as representatives of a legitimate nation and insisted on Confederate surrender, the restoration of the Union, and acceptance of emancipation as the only possible terms.[117] "Our peace commissioners made a complete failure with Lincoln so it seems there is no peace for us but I still hope the Lord will look d[o]wn on us in mercy & give us peace soon," a disappointed Alabamian wrote after hearing the news.[118]

With their hopes for an early peace dashed, some of Lee's men followed the lead of Jefferson Davis, who proclaimed in a fiery speech in Richmond that "the true hope of the Confederacy was in brave soldiers in sufficient number to contest her claims in the military field."[119] One North Carolina cavalryman thought that "the uncompromising spirit of Lincoln & Co has had a fine effect upon the army"; a Virginia artillery officer called the peace conference "insults added to injuries. The army is stirred up as one man, and spurn with indignation the infamous propositions of Lincoln.

They accept war, protracted, never ending war, with all its evil and distress rather than yield themselves slaves to Yankeedom."[120] The Georgians in Thomas's Brigade of the Third Corps, meanwhile, passed a resolution characterizing Lincoln's conduct as "perfidious, unfeeling, and arrogant, and insulting in the highest degree to the people of the Southern Confederacy."[121] Though the failure of the peace mission rekindled the determination of many proud soldiers who vowed to remain at their posts, it just as certainly crushed many others who had rested all their hopes for peace on the shoulders of the three commissioners.

Within days of the Hampton Roads conference, two important administrative changes—one purely military and one essentially so—took place in the upper echelons of the Confederacy. The first, which was more symbolic than anything else, was Lee's appointment to the newly created position of general in chief of the Armies of the Confederate States, on 6 February. Neither Davis nor Lee truly believed the promotion necessary. Davis had resisted it for quite some time as an infringement on his capacity as commander in chief, and Lee had already expressed his doubts that he could hold such a position while retaining command of his own army. Those who had urged Lee's appointment hoped, with good reason, that his overall management of military affairs might improve the efficiency of the Confederate armies and that the announcement of his appointment could itself help to restore many soldiers' and civilians' confidence in the Confederacy.[122] The *Richmond Dispatch* hailed the new general in chief, declaring, "Providence raises up the man for the time, and a man for this occasion, we believe, has been raised up in Robert E. Lee, the Washington of the second American Revolution, upon whom, from the beginning, all thoughtful eyes have been fixed as the future Deliverer of his country."[123] Lee's soldiers, naturally enough, were even more enthusiastic in their praise of the new general in chief, and some units passed resolutions to that effect, such as the Georgia brigade in the First Corps which claimed, "our confidence is greatly heightened by the promotion of our noble chieftain, General Lee, to supreme command, and as in the past, so in the future, we'll follow where he leads."[124]

The second administrative change, which had slightly more significance but received much less attention throughout the Confederacy than the first one, was the appointment—on the same day that Lee was named general in chief—of Maj. Gen. John C. Breckinridge to replace James A. Seddon as Confederate secretary of war. Though at least one observer believed that Lee's and Breckinridge's appointments meant "we may reasonably expect the happiest results," it would remain to be seen whether administrative maneuverings would produce military victories.[125]

The first consequential engagement of the year took place just south of Petersburg that same week in February, as Grant tried yet again to stretch his lines past Lee's defenses and to cut vital Confederate supply routes from the south. Two Federal infantry corps and a cavalry division, seeking to threaten the Boydton Plank Road, arrived at Hatcher's Run near Burgess Mill—the scene of the last notable fight between the two armies—on the morning of 5 February. While the cavalry division screened their movements, Grant's infantrymen quickly established a defensive position and waited for the Confederate response, which was not long in coming. Lee dispatched elements of the Second and Third Corps to drive the Federals from their works, but a late afternoon assault against the entrenchments by two brigades accomplished nothing and the Confederates withdrew a short distance after dark. When a Federal division launched a reconnaissance in force in the early afternoon of 6 February just east of Burgess Mill, it struck a Confederate division from the Second Corps that had been sent on an identical mission. As additional troops joined the battle on both sides, first the Confederates and then the Federals fell back in some confusion; fighting ended just before night with the Confederates holding a slight advantage. Light skirmishing on the seventh, in a mixture of snow, sleet, and freezing rain, ended operations in the vicinity. About 1,000 Confederates were killed, wounded, and captured, most prominently Second Corps division commander John Pegram, who was killed on 6 February; the Federals suffered some 1,500 casualties.[126]

Each side could claim some success after Hatcher's Run, for though Grant had managed to extend his lines a short distance south, Lee had prevented him from making a permanent lodgment on the vital Boydton Plank Road. Nevertheless, within the Army of Northern Virginia the battle's real significance lay more in what it revealed about the morale of the Confederates who fought there than in its tactical or even strategic results. If most of the army's officers believed that their soldiers had fought as well as they ever had, many enlisted men declared that large numbers of Lee's troops were unable to defend their positions against enemy attacks and were unwilling to make the confident charges they had once made almost as a matter of course. Though such generalizations were often exaggerated and though some units succeeded at Hatcher's Run whereas others failed, the contrast between these two opinions was still striking. Col. William Henry Forney, for example, had commanded the Alabama brigade in Mahone's Division of the Third Corps since the previous November and would soon be promoted to brigadier general. He wrote with pride of his troops' performance on the evening of 6 February, noting: "My Brigade behaved just as well as I could wish.... I feel proud of the Alabamians and am rejoiced I can say they have lost none of their former spirit, 'tis all right with them—every man feels & knows that to gain our independence he must fight—and they do it cheerfully—willingly & bravely."[127]

Other members of the army, however, painted quite a different view of the battle and of the fighting spirit of Lee's troops. For instance, Pvt. Mebane Hinshaw of the 6th North Carolina was a Quaker who had managed to avoid military service until conscripted in late 1864. A few weeks earlier he had written his family, "I feal as tho I had lost all my frendes in airth I want thee to pray for god to forgive me for taking up armes.... it is rong to fite eny way in my opinion."[128] On 10 February 1865 Hinshaw, whose regiment belonged to William Gaston Lewis's Brigade in Pegram's Division of the Second Corps, informed his wife and children: "I have ben in a fite the other day and cum out with out gitting hurt.... The men dont want to fite eny more the privetes is willing to make peace on eny turms if they quit fiting they ar all Whipt and give up the cose."[129]

There was no reconciling Forney's and Hinshaw's views of their army, for whereas the former saw soldiers who fought "cheerfully—willingly & bravely," the latter saw men "willing to make peace on eny turms if they quit fiting." One North Carolina private who wrote his grandmother soon after Hatcher's Run observed: "No doubt this fighting here has blasted all hopes of peace for the present.... None of our troops are in high spirits, & it is said that they do not fight with the same resolution as they did the first year of the war; having done so much of it that they now have a distaste to it." The letter concluded, "All are anxiously awaiting for Spring to come, hoping that something may occur to bring about peace."[130] Those few words contained the hopes and fears of many soldiers in February 1865, as the Army of Northern Virginia looked toward the greatest challenge it had ever faced.

If we, the Army of Northern Virginia, are defeated, all is lost. We must bow in submission. I hope I have a chance to fight—I don't think I will surrender.
—*Orderly Sgt. James E. Whitehorne*
   12th Virginia, Diary, 2 April 1865

. . . .

The Petersburg-Richmond Front, Fort Stedman, Five Forks, Sailor's Creek, and Appomattox, February–April 1865

Whereas rumors of peace had been the dominant theme of numerous conversations, letters, and diary entries in Lee's army just before the Hampton Roads conference, they were soon replaced after the mission by the realization that the Federals would settle for nothing less than the surrender or destruction of all the Confederate armies. That realization, in turn, helped to spur a remarkable series of meetings in February throughout the Army of Northern Virginia in which several units drafted and passed resolutions reaffirming their devotion to the Confederacy and their scorn for the Union. Though a few units had organized such meetings in January, the movement did not gain momentum until after the failure of the peace conference, when regiments, battalions, and brigades sent their defiant proclamations to the Richmond

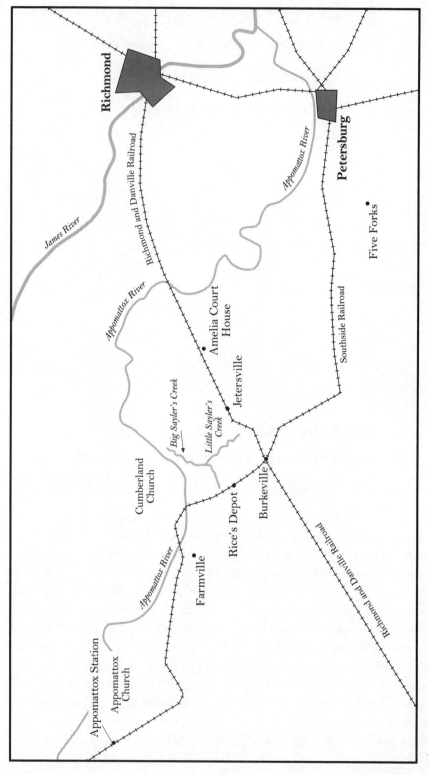

The Appomattox Campaign, 1865

newspapers, which published them under such headings as "The Spirit of the Army."[1] "As soon as the results of the peace mission were known," Lt. Col. William T. Poague of the Third Corps artillery, on 11 February, wrote, "my Batt'n passed unanimously resolutions indignantly rejecting the offered terms, renewing their vows of devotion to the great cause of Southern independence, etc."[2] Units often sent copies of their proceedings to newspapers in their home states, as well as to their representatives in the Confederate Congress, requesting that their resolutions be published for the benefit of the public.

Several recurring themes appeared in these resolutions: that the differences between the Confederacy and the Union were obviously irreconcilable; that most of the gloom and despair over the war was felt by civilians and not by Southern soldiers, who were confident that they would eventually succeed, just as their forefathers had in the American Revolution; and that the Army of Northern Virginia expected, with God's blessing and by General Lee's leadership, to win the battlefield victory that would establish Confederate independence. In fervent, and often florid, language, Lee's soldiers claimed that "all hopes for peace are false and hurtful, except those based on the triumph of our arms," or that "this army is ever ready to try the gauge of battle in defence of our homes and liberties," or that "we deem no sacrifice too great and no loss too heavy which will insure our eternal separation from the dominion of our hated foes."[3]

Capt. Charles Fenton James of the 8th Virginia described a representative meeting held in the winter camp of Hunton's Brigade of Pickett's Division. "After four years of bloody war—of hardships and privations," James wrote his sister, "the veteran soldiers of the invincible army of Northern Virginia, are speaking to the country." With encouragement from the commanding general, who was said to be "much gratified with the meetings which had been held and the resolutions adopted," Hunton and two of his colonels organized a joint meeting of the 8th Virginia, 18th Virginia, and Taylor's Battery that took place in the brigade chapel on 7 February. A regimental band entertained the Virginians while a committee drafted an appropriate preamble and resolutions, which the meeting then passed unanimously.[4] The lengthy preamble, published a few weeks later in the *Richmond Whig* along with the resolutions and a brief account of the meeting, claimed: "The army appreciates in its fullest sense the obligations resting upon them, and is prepared to discharge those obligations. It needs no appeals, nor does its patriotism require rekindling. It only asks to know that the 'loved at home' still uphold and sustain them in their struggle." These Confederates admitted that the fall of Atlanta,

defeats at Franklin and Nashville, and the fall of Savannah and Wilmington were "serious disasters and reverses" but compared the situation to
the spring of 1862, just after the fall of New Orleans, Memphis, and
Nashville, and just before the Seven Days' campaign that threatened Richmond. "The sky is not in reality as clouded as in 1862," they maintained.
"We have now a larger army than then; that army is better disciplined, and
has been tried in battle and learned to face its dangers. The officers, like
the men, have been improved by service—all have learned war." Several
short resolutions following the preamble asserted the Virginians' belief
that reunion was impossible, that the "independence, peace and prosperity
of our infant Republic" would soon be won, and that the Federal position
as stated at Hampton Roads was "a proposition so monstrous" that it
left the Confederacy "nothing worth living for unless secured to us by
independence."

The meeting continued with a two-hour speech by Representative
James W. Moore of Kentucky, followed by brief remarks from Hunton,
Col. Henry A. Carrington of the 18th Virginia, Col. Norborne Berkeley of
the 8th Virginia, and other members of the two infantry regiments.[5]
"When Berkely was called on," one account noted, "he said [he] could not
make a speech but he would give them a prophecy; 'That the Yankee
armies would be defeated in the next campaign and that the war would be
over by Christmas.'" Charlie James was so inspired by the meeting that
that night he wrote his sister: "I now feel as I felt in June/61 when I first
enlisted in this army—in February/62 when I reenlisted for two years or
the war—and in February/64 when I again reenlisted for the war.... I feel
as buoyant and hopeful and as confident of the result of this war as I ever
felt in the midst of the most brilliant successes."[6]

When newspaper editors claimed that the resolutions then being
drafted in the Army of Northern Virginia rang "like inspiring trumpet
tones on the air," they referred to such phrases as the Palmetto Battery's
"rather than submit to be the slaves of a Northern despot, we will fall with
our backs to the field and our faces to the foe" and the 15th Virginia's "we
have battled too long, shed too much good blood, and are engaged in too
holy and too glorious a cause ever to submit to a fanatical and vindictive
foe."[7] Other units' proceedings, whose language was not quite as refined
or as dramatic, were no less sincere. The 32d Virginia, for example, declared, "we are determined to follow wherever Jeff. Davis directs or General Lee leads.... as Virginians we mean to prove worthy of Virginia," and
an Alabama brigade in the Second Corps resolved, "relying on the justice

of our cause, we will do our whole duty, leaving the result to the God of battles, in whose hands are the destinies of men and nations."[8]

Some of the most original resolutions were those adopted by the 45th North Carolina, a veteran regiment in Grimes's Division of the Second Corps that had served with the army since just before Gettysburg and had been plagued by recent desertions. "We say to our people, cast off despondency, read history, and be quiet," the resolutions lectured; "liberty is not a swift-winged goddess, she frequently has to wade through blood to her throne." Col. John R. Winston's North Carolinians proceeded with a history lesson claiming that American liberty had been crowned by "the good, great and noble Washington . . . equalled by none save our own loved Lee," but that the same liberty had since been overthrown by Yankees. The Tar Heels concluded their resolutions with a warning that was both startling and ominous: "What desertion there is from the army is caused by the people at home; we soldiers tell you that you do this at your peril . . . should our army be disbanded, we will 'bushwhack;' or, at least, some of us will. . . . Almighty God helping us, we will never be conquered."[9] The editors of the *Richmond Dispatch*, commenting on the outpouring of resolutions drafted and passed by units throughout the Army of Northern Virginia, claimed, "it is the army which is the country. They have no thought of permitting all their labors, privations, perils, to go for naught, nor of suffering the blood of their fallen comrades to cry in vain from the ground. Whatever others may do, the heroes of the Confederacy neither intend nor desire to survive their country."[10] In the late winter of 1865, as resolutions proclaiming soldiers' willingness to fight for their homes and firesides were published almost daily, many Confederates and civilians received the impression that the cause could not possibly be hopeless.

Many members of these units did not endorse their resolutions, and many other units did not organize mass meetings and publish proceedings in the papers. Among the former were several members of Brig. Gen. William R. Terry's Virginia brigade in Pickett's Division who deserted to the enemy in late January and told the Federals, "these meetings are presided over by the colonels of regiments, resolutions are offered, and the men invited to give their votes, which is done for effect." The deserters also said: "The men are afraid to get up and declare their honest intentions, and the consequence is that it is taken for granted and declared by the officers that they are in favor of fighting it out. These resolutions are paraded in the papers for effect and to create a good state of feeling."[11]

Other members of the army were just as pessimistic about exhortations to fight "as long as the Southern Confederacy can furnish a cartridge or own an acre" or to "bear the Southern Cross through fire and blood till each star upon it shall glow and shine forever in the firmament of nations."[12] In mid-February one North Carolinian wrote his wife, "I believe the peace question is entirely dead and we have nothing before us but war war war, really a gloomy prospect before us, but I hope the Lord will deliver me out of it in some way."[13] Though attending meetings and adopting resolutions undoubtedly revived some soldiers' flagging spirits and helped restore confidence in the army, there were many others who saw no consolation in anything that seemed to prolong the war.

One of the most intense debates in Lee's army and throughout the Confederacy after the Hampton Roads conference, and one that found its way into numerous resolutions printed in the newspapers, concerned a proposal calling for the enlistment of black Confederate soldiers. Though similar schemes had been advanced as early as 1863, the vast majority of government and military leaders had then believed that the time for such a drastic measure had not yet arrived. Jefferson Davis had eventually suggested, in a November 1864 message to the Confederate Congress, that the army should employ slaves in noncombat roles to free able-bodied whites to serve in the ranks, and that such slaves should be freed by a gradual system of emancipation that compensated slaveowners. Though Davis received little political or popular support for his idea, it stimulated public and private discussion of the possibility that if the Federals could arm blacks to fight against the Confederacy, then the Confederacy might also arm blacks to help defend the South. By February 1865, as Grant's and Sherman's armies were crushing the life out of the Confederacy, and as both the Army of Northern Virginia and the Army of Tennessee were losing hundreds of men through desertion or straggling every day and night, it seemed as if the time had come to act. New companies or regiments of black troops would, some observers argued, add several thousand soldiers to the ranks and help turn the tide against the Federals.[14]

The dramatic and forceful statement of this position that ignited the debate was made by Secretary of State Judah Benjamin on 9 February at a public meeting in Richmond intended to rekindle the embers of Confederate patriotism. "War is a game that cannot be played without men," Benjamin told his audience. "Where are the men? . . . Look to the trenches below Richmond. Is it not a shame that men who have sacrificed all in our defence should not be reinforced by all the means in our power?" After citing statistics on the numbers of blacks fighting for the Union and against the Confederacy, Benjamin continued: "Let us say to every negro who wishes to go into the ranks on condition of being made free—'Go and fight; you are free.' . . . Let your Legislature pass the necessary laws, and we will soon have twenty thousand men down in those trenches fighting for the country."[15] A bill to that effect was introduced in the Confederate Congress the next day and aroused considerable debate, as did a similar bill presented in the Virginia legislature.

Benjamin, hoping to swing public opinion in favor of these measures, wrote Lee a few days later to explain that opponents of the plan were claiming that "it would disband the army by reason of the violent aversion of the troops to having negroes in the field with them." He asked the new general in chief to poll the Army of Northern Virginia on the question, observing, "we may yet be able to give you such a force as will enable you to assume the offensive when you think it best to do so."[16] Lee, who acknowledged that the creation of black units was an extreme step for the Confederate armies, had already privately expressed the opinion that it was a necessary step as well. He immediately passed Benjamin's request on to his corps and division commanders and in the meantime answered a similar letter from Representative Ethelbert Barksdale, of Mississippi, the sponsor of the bill then under consideration in the Confederate Congress. Lee's reply to Barksdale, written on 18 February, assessed the probable efficiency of black troops with the comment: "I think we could at least do as well with them as the enemy, and he attaches great importance to their assistance. Under good officers and good instructions, I do not see why they should not become soldiers."[17]

Several of Lee's officers and men had already begun registering their approval or disapproval of the scheme to enlist black Confederates, and others soon added their opinions to the debate through resolutions, official communications, or private letters. The attitudes expressed in numerous resolutions favored the plan, for most soldiers who were determined to persevere against formidable odds would be grateful for any assistance they could get. As one Georgia brigade in the First Corps phrased it, "We care not for the colour of the arm that strikes the invader of our homes."[18] The Texas Brigade believed that "the great peril of the country, and the extreme emergency, should prompt all friends of the cause to lay aside all prejudice," calling black soldiers "available and necessary for the furtherance of our ultimate object—independence and separate nationality."[19] Anticipating the argument that white soldiers might fear being subjected to the disgrace of serving with their intellectual, social, and moral inferiors, an artillery battery in the Department of Richmond insisted, "we would not feel any more degraded thereby than by ploughing in the same field or working the same shop, or that the humiliation was greater than seeing them made our equals by the edict of a Yankee Congress."[20]

Some resolutions were more cautious, such as those adopted by the 56th Virginia stressing that the regiment considered slavery "the normal condition of the negro—that the right of property in slaves is just and perfect," but conceding that if the crisis demanded it they were willing to accept black troops.[21] At least one meeting resulted in two different resolutions on the subject, revealing the fervor of the dialogue generated by the notion of black Confederate soldiers. One of several resolutions proposed by Col. Thomas H. Owen of the 3d Virginia Cavalry complained, "we contemplate with anxiety and apprehension the proposition to enlist negro troops in our armies, seriously doubting both its expediency and practicability, dreading its effect upon our social system, and earnestly desiring to see the independence of our country established by the strong arms of her white people, who have bravely resisted her enemies thus far." After "an animated and protracted discussion" on the merits of the resolution, a substitute resolution was suggested by Capt. James W. Hall, stating, "we are in favour of putting every man in the country between the ages of 17 and 45 in the army, and as many negroes, without changing their social status, as the Commander-in-chief may deem necessary." That resolution was passed and included in the proceedings of the meeting published in the *Richmond Examiner* on 25 February.[22]

When Lee asked his commanders to survey their troops he received a mixed response, even from the corps commanders themselves. John Gordon's report of the sentiments in the Second Corps, for example, was a positive one, stating that his soldiers were "decidedly in favor of the voluntary enlistment of the negroes as soldiers." Gordon remarked: "The aversion to the measure has in no instance been found strong. The opposition to it is now confined to a very few, and I am satisfied will soon cease to exist in any regiment of the corps."[23] Gordon, in a private letter of late February, observed: "We shall be compelled to have them [black troops] or be defeated—With them as volunteers fighting for their freedom we shall be successful. . . . If authority were granted to raise 200,000 of them it would greatly encourage the men & do much to stop desertions."[24] James Longstreet's circular to the division commanders in the First Corps, in contrast, was considerably more negative and stated that "the opinion of the lieutenant-general commanding is that the adoption of such a measure will involve the necessity of abolishing slavery entirely in the future, and that, too, without materially aiding us in the present."[25] Longstreet, skeptical that blacks would make good soldiers, asked Richard Ewell to send him one of the new black companies being organized in Richmond so it could be "tested" by his corps. "Their good behavior would do much to overcome a prejudice existing in the minds of many adverse to their employment as troops," explained one of the First Corps staff officers.[26]

Lee's troops seemed to be no less divided on the question than Gordon and Longstreet were. But the majority of them who expressed their opinions in resolutions, in official communications, and in private letters supported the proposal. Numerous officers and men concluded that if General Lee approved of the plan, it must be the best course for the Army of Northern Virginia and for the Confederacy. "The all absorbing topic here at present," Pvt. James B. Jones of the 1st Battalion North Carolina Sharpshooters wrote his brother and sister on 19 February, "is whether to put negroes in the army or not nine tenths of the Army is in favor of it. I am for one if Genl Lee thinks he can use them to any advantage which he says he can."[27] Meanwhile, Corp. Silas Chandler of the 55th Virginia remarked, "I believe there will be a majority for puting them in as Soldiers," explaining, "Gen. Lee is in favour of it I Shall cast my vote for it. I am in favour of giving him any thing that he wants in the way of gaining our independence for I look upon subjugation as being the next thing to death."[28] One Confederate, who wrote a letter to the *Richmond Dispatch* on the subject, believed that "this measure is now daily becoming more popular in the army" and that most of Lee's soldiers—including slaveowners—approved of the enlistment and emancipation of black troops; those who objected to the proposal "are not the slaveholders, but those who have never held such property, or are but slightly interested in negro property."[29]

Though many members of the army did indeed support the plan, that support indicated more about their determination to use any means possible to pursue the fading dream of Southern independence than it did about any positive sentiments toward the prospect of black Confederates. Those men who agreed with General Lee and the authorities in Richmond that the time had come did so recognizing that the measure was born out of necessity rather than choice. A staff officer's cryptic observation on a late February inspection report is a striking indication of the ambivalence felt by several soldiers over the issue of black troops. Lt. J. M. Young, ordnance officer of Brig. Gen. Dudley M. DuBose's Georgia brigade, offered his opinion that blacks should not be employed to drive the brigade's ordnance wagons because they would run away if exposed to musketry or shelling. "The negroe—not belonging to the army as a soldier, but merely as a laborer, does not expect to encounter the dangers of a battle field," Young argued. An endorsement on the inspection report placed Young's objections in context with a remark that was only slightly facetious: "Wait awhile old fellow, we will have negroe soldiers."[30] Seven members of the 18th North Carolina who deserted to the enemy gave credence to the belief that Lee's soldiers were not as enthusiastic about black Confederates as some believed, reporting that "the North Carolina troops voted against the employment of negro soldiers, while those from Georgia were in favor, and those from South Carolina were about equally divided."[31]

Gauging the breadth of the army's opposition to black troops is much more difficult than assessing its support for them, because those who still saw a chance for Confederate success in the face of daily signs to the contrary were more apt to put their views in writing than their less sanguine comrades. Extant evidence suggests, however, that there was widespread opposition to the proposal among Lee's officers and men. Many Confederates, from planters to poor whites, doubted that black troops would fight—despite ample proof otherwise—and feared that their enlistment would wreck the army to no good purpose and would lead to the unraveling of Southern society. Some voiced their disagreement emphatically in letters home, often warning plainly that "many soldiers," whether others in the abstract or including themselves in the here and now, would desert if the plan was implemented. Others expressed themselves more quietly but even more forcefully by simply leaving the army. Many officers and men bitterly resented the idea that former slaves might actually join the ranks of the Army of Northern Virginia and have the honor of serving under Lee with essentially the same rights as white soldiers. The Richmond newspapers, though preferring to publish resolutions and letters supporting the enlistment of black Confederates, occasionally printed comments such as those of an anonymous soldier who wrote that such an idea was "folly" because the government could not equip or care for the men already in uniform and because blacks would be "a very doubtful element" in the army. "Let us use every exertion to feed and clothe well those already enlisted, and enforce the immediate return to their commands of the hosts of 'absentees without leave,'" he urged; "if we then want more men, it will be time enough to extend conscription to our negroes."[32]

Other members of Lee's army expressed their objections to the plan in more basic and more emotional terms. "Thar is no fighting going on now," Daniel Abernathy of the 16th North Carolina remarked on 16 February in a literally if not figuratively correct statement. "[T]hay are holding elections to day on the negro question whether thay will Raise them in the army or not." Abernathy told his parents, "I thinke it is carr[y]ing that is thay are going to bring them oute in seperat Reg & brigads to them selvs and apinte [appoint] white ofesers over them which I thinke will end the war soon As the white men saye thay wante stay under such circum stances."³³ A member of Mahone's Division of the Third Corps who deserted to the enemy and was described as "an intelligent Georgian" told the Federals that there was "great dissatisfaction" in Lee's army over the question of black troops, that when the soldiers were asked their opinion, most did not vote, and that most of those who did vote favored the plan. "Hence, as he explains it," the Federal interviewer disclosed, "the unanimous vote reported to have been cast in some regiments for the arming of the negroes."³⁴ Many of Lee's troops, already discouraged by the course of the war in general and their miserable existence as soldiers in particular, viewed the possibility that blacks might fight beside them as proof that the Confederacy was no longer worth fighting and dying for. The debate in the Confederate Congress continued into March as Lee and his army waited for the decision that would have a profound impact on their future.

Less controversial measures were also taken to bring absentees and deserters back into the ranks. General Orders No. 2 of the Confederate States Army, issued on 11 February 1865, announced that men "who have abandoned their comrades in the hour of peril," whether they were absent without leave or deserters, would be pardoned if they reported to their commands within twenty days. The orders excluded those who had already deserted once and had been previously pardoned, as well as those who had deserted to the Federals, and sternly warned that this was the last chance for absentees and deserters to receive a pardon. "No general amnesty will again be granted," the orders stated, pointing out that soldiers who did not return to their commands in time, or those who left the army after the twenty-day deadline, would be shown no clemency. "Taking new resolution from the fate which our enemies intend for us," Lee observed, "let every man devote all his energies to the common defense."³⁵ General Orders No. 4 of the Army of Northern Virginia, issued a few days later, repeated the offer of amnesty and ordered that those enlisted men in the army who were under arrest, awaiting trial, or serving sentences for absence without leave or desertion should be immediately released and restored to duty.³⁶

Lee's veterans welcomed these directives and hoped that they would have the desired effect on absent members of the army. "Gen Lee's 'General Order No. 2,' calling on the soldiers & absentees is very fine," a Virginia artilleryman noted in his diary. "Hope it may bring many men back to the ranks."[37] A Virginia infantry officer in Pickett's Division discussed the order at some length in a letter to his sister. "This order has been looked for ever since Lee was made Commander in Chief," Capt. Charles Fenton James commented approvingly. "Many soldiers who left when the army and the people were depressed in spirits will be glad to avail themselves of the opportunity to return to their posts without being punished. . . . Our army will be heavily reinforced before Spring by veteran soldiers who have deserted in an hour of despondency or who have been enticed away by the allurements of home." A few days later, referring to his own company, James reported: "Elijah Bishop is at home—absent without leave. He went home on furlough. I wish Johnnie would try and get him to come back, under Lee's order. There are several others that he might notify."[38]

Other members of the army were not as sanguine, such as the North Carolinian who remarked enviously, "I suppose a great many will take advantage of this as they have had a pretty good furlough."[39] Lee's offer of amnesty did bring a few deserters back to the ranks; the Texas Brigade, for example, reported on 27 February that it had lost no soldiers by desertion in the previous ten-day period but that thirteen deserters had returned to the brigade under the provisions of the order.[40] For the most part, however, the order was ineffective both as an incentive for absentees and deserters to return without punishment and as a deterrent for those inclined to desert in the future. The inconsistent sentences given to convicted absentees or deserters and the likelihood that those sentences would be overturned, suspended, or reduced once they had been set, undoubtedly led many soldiers to believe that they had nothing to lose and everything to gain by leaving the army. Lee himself, only two weeks after issuing his order, commented on a case in which a deserter who was not eligible for the pardon had been convicted and sentenced to death but had had his sentence suspended by the authorities. "Hundreds of men are deserting nightly," Lee protested to Adjt. and Insp. Gen. Samuel Cooper, "and I cannot keep the army together unless examples are made of such cases."[41] His nephew Fitzhugh Lee, whose cavalrymen caught a total of twenty-two deserters from Pickett's Division and the Department of Richmond in the next two nights, would have agreed wholeheartedly with that assessment. The young Lee, telegraphing a quick report to First

Corps headquarters, recommended a swift and certain fate for these soldiers, advising, "Better have them hung at once."[42]

Two other general orders, issued in the face of Sherman's advance through the Carolinas and amid the collapse of transportation and communication routes between those states and the Petersburg-Richmond front, sought to reduce the likelihood that soldiers who left on leave or furlough would never return to the army. On 7 February Lee sent a circular to his corps commanders prohibiting leaves of absence or furloughs for soldiers wishing to go farther south or west than South Carolina. By the eighteenth, after the fall of Columbia and Charleston, a second circular suspended all leaves or furloughs for soldiers wishing to go farther than North Carolina and prohibited any additional requests for such leaves or furloughs.[43] Though these orders reflected Lee's desire to keep as many of his officers and men on duty as possible, they could not help but be resented by many soldiers, particularly those who had in some cases waited for several years for a short leave or furlough and who now found themselves unable to visit family or friends whose property and lives might be endangered by Federal armies. "Very much to my surprise a few nights ago, one of the boys handed me a letter from my beloved Father & mother," a Georgia sergeant wrote on 27 February. "[They] were looking for me home but no home for me. Gen Lee orders no furlows granted to go beyond N.C."[44]

The commanding general's untiring efforts to bring new and returning soldiers into the army during this period were complemented by his almost ceaseless concern for the troops already serving under him. Lee's frustration over the meager rations issued to his officers and men increased as the commissary-general demonstrated a petty reluctance to adapt to changing circumstances. When reports reached him that several units engaged at Hatcher's Run had suffered not only from exposure to rain, sleet, and snow, but also from three days without meat and with no better rations than cornbread, Lee wrote the War Department: "If some change is not made and the commissary department reorganized, I apprehend dire results. The physical strength of the men, if their courage survives, must fail under this treatment."[45] Breckinridge referred Lee's report to Davis, who angrily endorsed it, observing, "This is too sad to be patiently considered, and cannot have occurred without criminal neglect or gross incapacity."[46] A few days later deserters from Pegram's Division of the Second Corps, who had been at Hatcher's Run, told Federal officers that the army was "very much dispirited and starving, and that they know three-fourths of the men in ranks would make an unconditional surrender now." Moreover, "the two days' rations issued them every other day is so small that the men are so hungry when they get it as to eat it all up at one meal; it is only meat and flour."[47] Commissary-General Lucius Northrop, who offered only rationalizations and excuses when called to account by the new secretary of war, was quietly replaced by Brig. Gen. Isaac M. St. John on 16 February. "I am much gratified to learn that you are taking such prompt and vigorous measures to procure supplies for the army," Lee wrote St. John after learning of his plans for the commissary department.[48]

Though St. John's efforts did produce some improvements in the quantity and quality of rations, those improvements took time and had little impact on the troops until March. Still, at a time when any increase was welcome to Lee's discouraged troops, several observers expressed appreciation for whatever rations they received. In late February one North Carolina artilleryman acknowledged, "We have been drawing very short rations for the last week, pickled beef and corn meal, very little at that, but I have aplenty, if they do this well all the time I will never grumble." Of the "pickled beef" so maligned by many soldiers, he wrote: "It comes in red cans and it is made in London. There is no telling what it is made of. It is just as apt to be made of dogs as anything else. It is very good tho."[49] About the same time 2d Sgt. Henry Fortson of the 31st Georgia described typical rations drawn by his men, noting that his small company would draw rations of sorghum and apple brandy the next day, that they had recently drawn coffee and sugar, and that cornmeal was the staple of their diet. Fortson, temporarily commanding his company while its ranking officer—a second lieutenant—was sick at the brigade hospital, reported: "I gave my ration [of] coffee for 6 quarts of corn meal. we draw plenty of ration with the exception of bread. our meal is weighed to us for a pound but very seldom we get over 3/4 of a pound. I often cheet them [the commissary officers] by giving in more men than we have present."[50] Some Confederates masked their disgust or disappointment over poor rations with humor, such as the private in the 1st North Carolina Artillery who advised a friend whose son had been drafted and was coming to join his battery, "our Rations are very short tell Robert if he can bring with him some meat it will be best so he will not have to commence starving right away."[51]

Other members of Lee's army were not nearly as grateful for their rations or as ready to forgive those responsible for issuing them. "What is to become of this army without rations[?]—men cant fight on nothing to eat," a courier in the Second Corps wrote his father.[52] Inspection reports for late February revealed the magnitude of discontent in some units, such as in Kershaw's Division of the First Corps. On 27 February the commissary of DuBose's Brigade reported: "Sugar Coffee & Molasses (Sorghum) have been issued for (8) Eight days during the month in lieu of Meat— This creates much dissatisfaction among the troops. If for (3) three days rations we could draw (2) Two days rations of Meat, and (1) one day of Sugar and Coffee, it would be much better than that these substitutes should as heretofore be issued successively for 3 & 5 days."[53] Capt. R. N. Lowrance, assistant chief of subsistence for Kershaw's Division, gave further evidence of the great difficulties encountered in feeding the troops. Lowrance explained that standing orders in the First Corps prohibited commissaries from requesting rations for more than one day at a time because "it is unsafe to keep them on hand, the troops having taken by armed force the supplies of one of the C.S. [chiefs of subsistence] of the Div. during the month and several having indicated a disposition to do so."[54] Kershaw endorsed the inspection report and Lowrance's endorsement with the comment: "The amount allowed even when obtained is not sufficient for the men. . . . To these deficiencies of food I attribute the number of desertions daily occurring and a general feeling of depression existing."[55] Lee believed the situation so critical that on 9 March he warned Breckinridge: "Unless the men and animals can be subsisted, the army cannot be kept together, and our present lines must be abandoned. Nor can it be moved to any other position where it can operate to advantage without provisions to enable it to move in a body."[56]

The gloom felt throughout the army over rations, which had become more acute than ever in the first two months of the year, was alleviated somewhat in March as the new commissary-general supervised a much-improved system of acquisition and distribution. That system was based, in large part, on reports estimating that there were enough supplies in Virginia and North Carolina alone to feed Lee's army and that the Confederate government simply needed money to purchase them, transportation to carry them to the army, and enough local troops to guarantee their safety.[57] Such phrases as "rations are better than usual" began appearing in letters home, often accompanied by comments that the soldiers' morale was improving slightly as a direct result.[58] "We get plenty to eat now," Sgt. Henry Calvin Conner observed on 21 March, when he returned to the army after a furlough, "which I feared was not the case from the reports we got from the army while I was at home."[59] About the same time the chaplain of the 44th North Carolina remarked, "Our rations have been better, the soldiers are in better spirits, and what is better than all, we are now enjoying a refreshing shower of grace from the presence of the Lord."[60] Under the circumstances, the clergyman might even have excused those soldiers who thought that improved rations were a more vital comfort to them than the comfort of religion. Pvt. Edmund Jones, a new conscript in the 3d North Carolina Cavalry, wrote his father soon after arriving in camp, "We are drawing very good rations & the men are well satisfied." In a second letter a few days later Jones observed, "I have seen several men from Petersburg who say that our troops there are faring sumptuously & have stoped deserting, which I think is probable true for I know that we are faring very well, we get a third of a pound of meat a day & one pound of flour & sometimes one & a half."[61]

These and similar observations on the state of the army were more hopeful than accurate, however, for though the quantity and quality of rations had improved in some units, they had not in others. Furthermore, many of Lee's soldiers neither fared sumptuously nor stopped deserting in late February and throughout March. If anything, the rate of desertion had continued to increase after news of Sherman's advance through South Carolina and into North Carolina and after Lee's offer of amnesty to absentees and deserters who would return within twenty days. Numerous Carolinians, many of whom had been good soldiers throughout several campaigns, now deserted to look after their homes and families, which were in many instances threatened by Federal armies. Many other Confederates who deserted about this time believed that they could do so with impunity because they were convinced the authorities would soon issue another blanket pardon.

Lee's corps commanders began making regular reports of desertions in their commands, most often at ten-day intervals, and those reports were then compiled by headquarters staff and forwarded to Breckinridge and the War Department. Reports compiled from 15 February through 18 March revealed more than 3,000 desertions during the period.[62] The greatest number of desertions in any one division was in Pickett's Division of the First Corps, which had been reinforced throughout 1864 by large numbers of conscripts and had suffered from low morale for several months. The division lost more than 500 men in one ten-day period, and when it was ordered from Richmond to Petersburg soon afterward it was watched closely for fear large numbers of men would take advantage of the move to desert.[63] Lee dutifully informed the authorities on more than one occasion that "the alarming number of desertions" grew every day and night and acknowledged, "These desertions have a very bad effect upon the troops who remain and give rise to painful apprehension."[64]

Desertions were now so frequent that many soldiers took little notice of them in letters home. A private in the 61st Alabama observed, "the spirit of the army is very low desertion is getting to be a daily thing," while a private in the Palmetto Sharpshooters commented simply, "ther is A heap of our men Deserting an going to the yanks."[65] Other Confederates had definite opinions about the phenomenon. In early March Mebane Hinshaw of the 6th North Carolina declared: "they wous sum sixteen le[f]t this Brigade the other nite, the consequence I dont know. . . . The papers ses the soldiers is in good [s]perretes if that is so it is sum other parte of the armey I know that it is faltes [false] as well as I want to know."[66] About the same time Lt. Luther Mills of the 26th Virginia, in Johnson's Division of the Fourth Corps, stated bluntly: "It is useless to conceal the truth any longer. Many of our people at home have become so demoralized that they write to their husbands, sons and brothers that desertion *now* is not *dishonorable*."[67] Some members of Lee's army also wrote, spoke, or acted as if they believed that desertion was no longer dishonorable. On 15 March Capt. Benjamin Wesley Justice reported, "Fourteen left our Brigade last night & went over to the yankees. . . . numbers go over to the yankees every night." Justice then asserted, "And what speaks worse for the spirit of the army, is that the men on the picket line fire off their guns into the air & will not try to shoot down those who are in the act of deserting to the enemy."[68] Other soldiers could not believe that anyone would voluntarily return to the army from a furlough. "[W]hen I got Back the Boys Said to me what did you com back for all the other Boys has Runaway," Robert Hutspeth of the 3d North Carolina wrote in late March. "[T]ha has Runaway a bout 100 sence I lefte . . . it Seemes like tha air all a going to Runaway."[69]

It might have seemed as if Lee's soldiers were "all a going to Runaway" when desertion crippled even the best units, whose soldiers were equally renowned for their prowess in battle and for their discipline on the march and in camp. John Rogers Cooke's North Carolina brigade of the Third Corps, for instance, had long been considered one of the finest brigades in the Army of Northern Virginia. A recent inspection report had noted, "The discipline is, I venture to report, as good as any in the Army, and state of feeling, all things considered, cheerful."[70] When several of Cooke's veterans deserted on the night of 5 March, they still exhibited a touching respect for the soldiers they left behind. Nine members of Company H of the 48th North Carolina, on their way home to see about their families, wrote a note in which they explained their reasons for leaving, asked their comrades to forgive them, and said they intended "to take 60 days furlough" and return, assuring the rest of the regiment that they meant "no crime" by their actions. That night the colonel of the regiment observed in his diary, "Our cause looks gloomy in the extreme. . . . We have been decimated & more than decimated by desertion."[71]

A disturbing new element in the latest desertions was the increasing tendency for soldiers to organize among themselves, to engage in the open defiance of authority, and even, some officers feared, to threaten mutiny if attempts were made to stop deserters. In one plot to encourage and facilitate large numbers of desertions, men agreed to meet at points along the Petersburg lines and to desert in groups; discovered in late February, the scheme involved three North Carolina brigades of the Third Corps, a North Carolina brigade of the Fourth Corps, and a South Carolina brigade of the Fourth Corps.[72] Rumors of a plan in which a considerable number of men from Simms's Georgia brigade of the First Corps intended to desert "with their arms & fight their way home" in mid-March proved to be greatly exaggerated but prompted division headquarters to take the precaution of ordering the Georgians to stack their arms and of placing a guard over them for the night.[73] These rumors had grown out of an incident in another Georgia brigade in the corps in which virtually an entire company deserted with its arms and accoutrements one night, intending to go home and join local units being organized to arrest deserters in northern Georgia. A former captain in the 9th Georgia, who had been severely wounded and disabled in 1863, had written several members of his old company encouraging them to desert and join his company of disabled men and nonconscripts, assuring them that they "would be perfectly secure from any arrest or evil consequences." Brig. Gen. George T. Anderson, commanding the brigade, observed that many local companies had become "a fruitful source of desertion" from Lee's army and that "the very trifling punishments inflicted by some of our courts for this crime only offer a premium to bad men to desert whenever they wish to go home."[74]

Lee, hoping to address the growing problem of soldiers openly encouraging each other to desert, issued a general order soon after these episodes that observed, "the evil habit prevails with some in this army of proposing to their comrades in jest to desert and go home." General Orders No. 8 warned, "The penalty for advising or persuading a soldier to desert is death; and those indulging in such jests will find it difficult on a trial to rebut the presumption of guilt arising from their words," then specified that both this order and Article 23 of the Articles of War, which called for the death of any officer or man convicted of encouraging desertion, would be read to the army daily for three days and then once a week for the next month.[75] Though the general orders might not have acknowledged it explicitly, by March 1865 all too many conversations and schemes concerning desertion from Lee's army were anything but "jests." The Army of Northern Virginia was disintegrating daily, and nothing could be done to prevent it.

Several of Lee's veterans, many of whom had previously filled their letters and diaries with expressions of the army's good spirits and of their own patriotism and resolve, now described others'—and their own—uncertainty, despair, and weariness. One such Confederate, who might be considered representative of this type among the army's officer corps, was Col. Samuel Hoey Walkup of the 48th North Carolina. Walkup, as recently as January, had written cheerful descriptions of being sent "opossum, a pound cake and sweet cakes, sousage and Molasses" from home, or of such diversions as reading "books of romance and [Sir Walter] Scotts novels" and having a few drinks with the officers of the regiment to celebrate his birthday.[76] When the colonel returned to the army in February after a short furlough, however, the mood of his diary began to reflect the army's, and his own, growing dejection. Walkup recorded lists of men who had deserted from the 48th North Carolina rather than lists of the meats and pastries he enjoyed, and he outlined such disagreeable tasks as paying North Carolina newspapers to run advertisements listing deserters or drafting an order to his regiment on the subject of desertion rather than reading fiction or entertaining guests in his tent.[77] "We are forsaken by all the world & our friends deserting," he wrote in early March. "The enemy are exultant & numbers 5 or 6 to our one. An army against an unarmed, unorganized mob. The sea before us, the mountains on each side, behind us a mighty and desperate enemy. Where can we look for help but upwards[?]"[78]

A representative veteran among Lee's common soldiers was Pvt. Abel Crawford of the 61st Alabama. On 5 March Crawford observed, "it seems that the soldiers have become so tired of fighting that they are almost willing to give it up on most any terms," then admitted to his wife Dora, "I am *almost* tempted sometimes to take a french furlough when I think of being cut off from you and home, but I still have hopes of peace soon when I can meet with you never to part again." By the ninth the Alabamian described Lee's army as "fixing up for an active, though dreaded Campaign" and declared, "I shall go into it trusting to providence for a delivery through this war, I believe that this Campaign will close the war."[79]

Other members of the army—whether veterans or recent arrivals, volunteers or conscripts—added their voices to those of Walkup and Crawford during March. Benjamin Wesley Justice wrote his wife, "I look forward with shuddering & horror to the events of the campaign of this year. O that it were now over," while William Horace Phillips told his father, "I dont think this Southern Confedracey can stand much longer . . . I dont think there is any chance for us in the world."[80] Observations ranging from one North Carolinian's pitiful "may heven grant that peace may cum once more to this distress[ed] p[e]ople if I dont live to see it I want others to have peace" to another's lament that "there is no good place in the army and I long very much to be relieved of it but am almost ready to dispair" were also common.[81]

Many Confederates wrote anxiously about the opening of the spring campaign because they questioned their ability to hold their position—much less take one from the enemy—with an army that was literally fading away. Strength reports for the period 24 February–1 March revealed only 46,000 troops present for duty out of a total strength of some 116,000 men present and absent, and the numbers present for duty by the end of March were considerably fewer, due primarily to desertions from every unit in the army.[82] "We cannot hold any position long at a time," one Georgia staff officer predicted in early March, "but [will] depend on marching & *fighting only* when *advantages favour us*," and a North Carolina private wrote near the end of the month, "There are a good many of our soldiers deserting to the enemy, but I am in hopes we will have enough left to keep the Yankees in check on this line."[83] Engineers in the First Corps attempted to compensate for the relative scarcity of troops along one portion of the Richmond front with a resourceful, if unusual, plan to build a dam and flood the space between the opposing lines. If the Federals were unable to launch an attack in that immediate vicinity, the engineers believed, Confederate troops there might then be shifted for duty at more vulnerable points along the front lines. One Georgian whose regiment occupied the lines near the site of the proposed dam remarked to his sister, "You know we stand very much in need of men, and every device must and ought to be resorted to by our authorities."[84]

Some soldiers were so ready to end, if not win, the war that they listened to, and gave contributions to, a fraud by the name of R. O. Davidson who visited their camps throughout the winter of 1864–65. Davidson claimed to have invented a machine, called the "Artisavis" or "Bird of Art," that could win the war for the Confederacy in a matter of a few days. One noncommissioned officer who heard Davidson lecture on the machine's powers described it as "an artificial bird to go by steam through the air that can carry a man to guide it and a number of shells which the man can drop on the Yankees as he passes over them which will soon kill and scare them all away."[85] After the Confederate authorities refused to advance any money for the first Artisavis on a trial basis, Davidson took his case to the Army of Northern Virginia, holding lectures in its camps and trying to gain support from those who would supposedly benefit the most from his invention. He usually distributed a card announcing that he was soliciting funds from the army and that he would explain "how this invention may be employed to destroy or drive from our soil every hostile Yankee, and thus soon close the war."[86]

In late February and early March Davidson reported that he had received more than $1,500 in contributions from Lee's officers and men in various units and chided civilians for not helping to fund the Artisavis. "There may be something true and valuable in this invention," he declared, "why not aid in giving it a trial, at least at this juncture of our cause and country?"[87] When Davidson visited Simms's Brigade in the First Corps, he estimated the cost of the first "Bird of Art" at some $20,000 but told the soldiers that the Confederate government would certainly fund additional machines when the first one succeeded. He claimed that his invention might even end all wars, for as one skeptical observer reported his argument, "every nation should be furnished with them and they are so destructive that nations will prefer the settlement of all difficulties by Diplomacy rather than war with such terrible weapons." In mid-March James P. Simms's younger brother Benjamin, a clerk in the 53d Georgia, wrote his sister: "I should as soon look for perpetual motion to be invented as one of Davidson's Birds to rise and fly.... I never gave him anything, he received from the Brigade one hundred and twenty seven dollars—pretty liberal patronage for a humbug."[88] Simms's cheerful characterization of the would-be inventor—or perhaps his invention—as "a humbug" is a fitting conclusion to one of the more bizarre episodes in the history of Lee's army.

About this time there were, of course, realistic plans under consideration that enjoyed much greater support and had a far greater chance to make a positive impact on the army than did Davidson's outlandish scheme. These proposals, intended to strengthen the Army of Northern Virginia by improving the efficiency of its existing units or by adding significant numbers of troops to its ranks, were finally passed by the Confederate Congress in late February and early March. When the act authorizing the consolidation of companies, battalions, and regiments

Lt. Jesse Levi Furgurson, Company C, 32d North Carolina. Furgurson, who enlisted as a sergeant, was elected as a lieutenant in July 1862; he was wounded at Petersburg, 2 April 1865, as the Federals broke Lee's lines and was in a Danville hospital when the army surrendered the next week. (Ernest B. Furgurson)

was referred to Lee for his opinion, the commanding general replied, on 15 March: "This army is in close proximity to the enemy, and active operations may commence any day. It would be extremely hazardous at this time, in my opinion, to begin a general consolidation of the regiments." He suggested that the War Department might announce its authority to consolidate units but leave the timing of the actual consolidations up to the discretion of army commanders.[89]

A second measure, which had slightly more impact on Lee's officers and men and generated considerably more discussion among them, was the act "to increase the military force of the Confederate States," which finally authorized the enlistment of black Confederate troops on 13 March.[90] Though the act did not provide for the emancipation of slaves who enlisted, general orders issued from the adjutant and inspector general's office on 23 March made it clear that any blacks who served in the Confederate army would do so as free men.[91] Lee, whose support of the plan had removed many soldiers' and civilians' objections to it, believed that companies of black Confederates should be organized and trained as soon as possible, commanded by white commissioned officers but including black noncommissioned officers. "I should prefer on the whole at the commencement to receive them by companies, and to attach the companies when formed, to such of the present Regts as desired them, from the same state," Lee observed. "In this way I think we should the sooner get them into service, and secure their fidelity." This proposal to integrate the army had one major practical advantage over the system of separate black regiments as formed in the U.S. Army, for Lee's plan allowed veteran Confederate regiments to gain a substantial number of troops while the new black companies would benefit from the experience of the veterans.[92]

The Army of Northern Virginia's reaction to these developments, as might be expected, was mixed. Individuals and units that supported the enlistment of black Confederates were enthusiastic. The 49th Georgia, in Wilcox's Division of the Third Corps, submitted a proposal to recruit black troops in its home counties, with the new recruits filling up existing understrength companies. These Georgians declared that they "did not consider it disgraceful to labor with negroes in the field or at the same work bench" before the war, and that they would not consider it disgraceful to fight in the same companies with them "when an end so glorious as our independence is to be achieved."[93] When some of Lee's soldiers— including numerous enlisted men, many field and company officers, and at least one brigadier general—expressed a desire to raise or command black units ranging in size from companies to divisions, their names were forwarded to the secretary of war.[94] An officer's commission in one of the new units, furthermore, was promised to any man in the First Corps who would prevent a comrade from deserting to the enemy and who could bring the offender to trial. Longstreet recommended four of his men for commissions in late March after they exposed plots made by would-be deserters in their brigades.[95] Maj. James West Pegram, who was one of the first Confederate officers authorized to raise a black company, went to work immediately, recruiting soldiers within a few days of the announcement and marching them through the streets of Richmond on at least one occasion. "You made a lucky hit, in being the first to make the start," Pegram's younger brother, Col. Willy Pegram of the Third Corps artillery, wrote on 17 March. "I have heard several officers say the same, and it seems to meet with general approbation in the army. . . . I understand that a large number of the best officers in the army are trying to get commands in the '*Corps D'Afrique.*'"[96]

Some members of Lee's army, who had always opposed the idea of black Confederates and hoped that the Confederate Congress would not pass the bill authorizing their enlistment, thought that the Confederacy was gambling its future away for a desperate hope. On 16 March one Virginia artilleryman in the trenches near Petersburg noted in his diary, "The *first order* to raise negro troops appears in to-day's papers—from to-day, I date the history of our downfall as a nation."[97] Pvt. William Horace Phillips of the 14th Virginia registered a particularly strong protest against black Confederate soldiers in a letter to his father a few days later, claiming, "this bringing the Negroes in the army is certainly going to ruin us if nothing else dont for they are going to fight and in Six months after they are brought in the field there will be more of them in the woods all mixed up with white men than you ever see in your life."[98] Though the comprehensive consolidation of existing units and the large-scale enlistment and training of black Confederate units were undoubtedly subjects of great interest throughout the army, subsequent events would soon overtake any attempts to implement either plan and make both issues irrelevant.

While many of Lee's soldiers deserted or straggled and many others agonized about the army's—and their own—future, there were some who managed to keep up their spirits in spite of overwhelming evidence that the Confederate cause was waning. Numerous officers and men still displayed that powerful combination of pride in past accomplishments and confidence that they could still repeat or surpass those achievements that had long made the Army of Northern Virginia such an effective fighting force. The writings of these men, who had few—if any—illusions that the

1865 campaign would be anything but a desperate fight for survival, combined realistic assessments of the odds they faced with expressions of determination to do their duty. Pvt. John Everett of the 11th Georgia, for example, on 16 March admitted to his mother, "I am Dreading this Springs campaign but thair is no use in it I have got to take it or else take Worse and I dont feel like takeing any worse." After noting that seventy-five Georgians had deserted from his brigade the night before—including twenty-eight men from his company alone—Everett took heart and observed, "I am as tired of this War as any Boddy can be, and I tell you the fact if Every man in our Army had as little use for the yanks as I have they would not any more of them Desert and go to them."[99] Other soldiers expressed similar sentiments, from the Virginia artilleryman who set words to the tune of "Annie Laurie" titled "We'll fight until we die!" to the North Carolina cavalryman who insisted, "in every engagement we are going to whip them severely."[100] Ord. Sgt. James W. Albright of Sturdivant's Battery included his patriotic song in his diary entry for 1 March, opening, "The clash of arms is ringing / All o'er our Southern land, / But, 'round brave Lee is clinging / A fine devoted band," and ending with words to inspire his fellow Confederates: "Then, boys, let's do our duty, / In this the hour of need— / Ne'er forsake this glorious cause / Until our land is freed."[101] Capt. Cadwallader J. Iredell of the 1st North Carolina Cavalry, on 8 March wrote his wife, "Our Army is strengthening, and the men are in fine spirits and determined," declaring two days later, "We are going to whip every fight hereafter. Grant is 'trembling in his shoes,' already."[102]

Some soldiers believed, not without reason, that the Southern people were giving up more readily and in proportionately larger numbers than they actually were, and that the Confederate armies—most notably the Army of Northern Virginia—were in fact the embodiment of the Confederate nation. "Every one whom I have seen in this army, is cheerful & hopeful," Col. William Pegram claimed in mid-March. "Certainly the spirit & opinion of the army is worth more than that of the people of Richmond, or of people out of it."[103] To his wife Mollie, Lt. John B. Evans admitted that "a greate many persons think that we had better go back into the union than to do worst" but called those people "so chickin hearted that they think we are whiped, but let me tell you that will not dow we had better stick our heads in the fire at once than do this awfull thing. this war may last four years longer, I hope not, if it dos I am regular in for the hole time."[104] Though Lee commanded considerably fewer men "regular in for the hole time" at the end of March than he had at the beginning of 1865, there were still many officers and men left who would fight whenever and wherever he led them into battle.

The next battle for many Confederates occurred on 25 March, as Lee attempted to break through and capture a portion of Grant's lines near Petersburg in the hope that he could then detach troops to reinforce Johnston's tiny army, facing Sherman in North Carolina. When a reconnaissance by Second Corps commander John Gordon identified Fort Stedman, just east of the city, as a possible vulnerable point near the Federal left, Lee approved a plan calling for a surprise attack. Gordon, commanding his own corps, two brigades each from the Third and Fourth Corps, and a division from the Cavalry Corps, would attempt to capture the fort and several smaller works nearby. If he succeeded, most of his infantry would then secure their foothold in the Federal lines while selected groups of Confederates captured works farther to the rear and the cavalry rode to cut off Grant's communications.

Gordon's troops, who began their assault about 4:00 on the morning of the twenty-fifth, overpowered Grant's startled pickets, took Fort Stedman and three adjacent batteries with relative ease, and held on to their gains while the specially chosen squads searched for the forts in the rear. For the next few hours large segments of both armies milled in and around Fort Stedman in confusion, with Gordon's troops unable to locate the Federal forts to the rear and Grant's troops unable to organize a decisive counterstroke. The Federals, however, slowly rallied, concentrated several batteries on the Confederates within their lines, and massed units to drive Gordon from his position. The Second Corps commander, realizing that his force would soon be destroyed if he remained in the Federal lines, ordered a withdrawal about 8:00 A.M. Most of the Confederate casualties suffered during the battle occurred in this phase, as many soldiers were either killed or wounded while retreating to their own lines or were taken prisoner where they were. A large number of those captured had refused to withdraw under the severe musketry and artillery fire and preferred surrender to what they believed was certain death.[105] The battle cost the Federals about 1,500 troops killed, wounded, and captured, whereas the Confederates suffered nearly 4,000 casualties, with nearly half of that number taken prisoner. Lee's failure to gain a lasting advantage at Fort Stedman both wrecked the Army of Northern Virginia's best chance for a tactical victory over Grant and made the Confederate evacuation of Petersburg and Richmond inevitable.

Most Confederates who described or mentioned the fight for Fort Sted-man in their letters and diaries contrasted the initial success of Gordon's assault with the spectacle of Lee's soldiers running a gauntlet of fire back to their lines and the great disappointment felt after the battle. A North Carolina captain claimed that the Federals were "dumb-founded" and called the early morning attack "sudden, vigorous, [and] unlooked for," while a Virginia surgeon in the Second Corps reported, "Genl Gordon made an attack upon the Enemys fortifications compleatly supprising and routing him capturing three lines of their works."[106] Virtually all of these accounts went on to say that the Confederates were eventually forced from the enemy's works by large numbers of Federal reinforcements and suf-fered heavy casualties in the process. "The batteries and lines taken had to be abandoned eventually, at which time we lost many men," a lieutenant in the 31st Virginia noted in a typical diary entry.[107] "To retreat under the concentrated fire of all the enemy's batteries and rifles within range, looked like almost certain destruction," Capt. Henry Chambers of the 49th North Carolina observed. "But try it we must. . . . Good God what a time!" Chambers continued: "Many were wounded and as their unhurt comrades passed them would beg piteously to be carried out. The hearts of many failed them and they did not start at all."[108] One soldier who did start back toward the Confederate lines and who reached them safely was a North Carolina private in his first battle. Henry London, who had just joined the army as a courier in the Second Corps, wrote his father later that day, "I have heard the shells shriek and the minnie balls whistle and I can assure you, it is rather unpleasant." London escaped "by running as hard as I could a quarter of a mile through an open field swept by their fire, expect-ing every moment to be knocked over . . . and I can assure you I drew a long breath of relief when I jumped into our works, for it was a miracle almost that I got through safe."[109]

For numerous observers, whether they participated in the battle or heard about it secondhand, Fort Stedman confirmed their fears that the Army of Northern Virginia might not be able to prevent the capture of Petersburg and Richmond, or even to save itself. Some criticized Lee's aggressiveness, such as the South Carolina sergeant who remarked, "I do think that the days has past for hurling men aganst brest works when we have Scarcely men enough to act uppon the defencive but General Lee has always beene a Great Gambler in human life and is not the man to Save his men that Johnston is."[110] Others blamed no one for the defeat but simply expressed regret, such as the member of Lee's staff who commented a few days later, "I regard the contingency we have fearfully anticipated [the evacuation of Petersburg and Richmond] as a foregone conclusion. . . . I say nothing of our fight. 'Twas gallantly done as far as it went."[111]

The initiative now passed from Lee to Grant, who took steps to force the Army of Northern Virginia from the Petersburg-Richmond front by once again threatening the Southside Railroad and attempting to turn the vulnerable Confederate right flank in the vicinity of Hatcher's Run. On 29 March the Federal commander ordered Philip Sheridan toward Five Forks, a strategic crossroads several miles west of Petersburg, with three divisions of cavalry reinforced by two infantry corps. Sheridan, who had just joined Grant after defeating Jubal Early and scattering the remnants of the Army of the Valley at Waynesboro, moved quickly, reaching Dinwiddie Court House by nightfall. Lee hastily dispatched a combined force of his own to counter the Federal advance, consisting of Pickett's Division of the First Corps, elements of the Fourth Corps, and most of the Cavalry Corps—now commanded by Fitzhugh Lee—all under Pickett's overall command. Skirmishing on 29 and 30 March on the Boydton Plank Road, White Oak Road, and at Dinwiddie Court House slowed but did not halt Sheridan's push toward Five Forks. On the night of the thirty-first the Confederates withdrew to the crossroads, where during the next morning and early afternoon Pickett established a defensive position with his infantry and a division of cavalry though he did not believe that an attack was imminent. Meanwhile, Sheridan's cavalry arrived near Five Forks and deployed, skirmishing with the Confederate cavalry while waiting for the Federal infantry to come up and join it in an assault on the hastily built works.

The battle began in earnest about 4:00 P.M. as the Federals attacked with mounted and dismounted cavalry and several divisions of infantry, quickly breaking Pickett's lines from the front, on the left flank, and in the rear. Those Confederates who were not captured scattered in confusion before Sheridan's cavalry and infantry, leaving Lee's flank and the Southside Railroad virtually unprotected.[112] Total casualties numbered fewer than 1,000 Federals lost and some 3,000 to 4,000 Confederates killed, wounded, and captured, the vast majority of them taken prisoner. That night a North Carolina captain who was wounded in the melee wrote in his diary: "The contagion spread as this made its way up the line. The cowardly ran, the timid were dumbfounded, the brave, alone, could not withstand the vastly superior force of the enemy."[113]

Lee responded to the disaster at Five Forks by ordering Longstreet from the Richmond front to the south side of the James River with a division of the First Corps, and by sending Richard Anderson toward the Southside Railroad with three brigades of the Fourth Corps. Richard Ewell's small force from the Department of Richmond, along with a division of the First Corps, remained in position defending the capital. The Second and Third Corps still held onto the Petersburg front, where Grant was massing troops for a final assault all along the lines on 2 April.[114] It was becoming increasingly evident to many Confederates—and to even more Federals—that the Army of Northern Virginia was on its last legs. Col. Samuel Hoey Walkup of the 48th North Carolina, in Heth's Division of the Third Corps, added a gloomy postscript to a letter he had begun on 30 March, writing on 1 April: "You need not send my clothes, nor flour, nor anything else to me, my dearest, we will either be killed or captured or the road will be destroyed before this letter reaches you. . . . Be prepared for bad news from Lee's army. There is no reasonable prospect of good news."[115]

The final week of the army's existence began before dawn on 2 April with a series of vigorous Federal assaults that broke through the thinly held Confederate lines on Lee's extreme right near Hatcher's Run and farther north on the Boydton Plank Road. Grant's offensive quickly overwhelmed two divisions of the Third Corps, isolated the remnants of those units from the rest of Lee's army, and cost the Confederates one of their best-known and most accomplished combat officers when corps commander A. P. Hill was killed attempting to rally his troops. By midmorning the only Confederate troops of any note between the Federals and Petersburg were elements of Wilcox's Division and a brigade of Mahone's Division, whose stubborn defense of Fort Gregg west of the city prevented the collapse of Lee's entire line. To Breckinridge, Lee admitted, "I see no prospect of doing more than holding our position here till night. I am not certain that I can do that." He advised the Confederate authorities to evacuate Richmond immediately, notified them that he would have to abandon Petersburg to save his army, and ordered Ewell to leave the capital that night.[116] A determined Federal attack on Fort Gregg that afternoon sustained heavy casualties but eventually succeeded, inflicting proportionately high casualties on the defenders and forcing most of the rest to surrender. Federal losses numbered some 700 casualties, while the Confederates lost a staggering 250 men killed and wounded out of a total force of some 300 defenders, whose stand gave the rest of their army enough time to organize a withdrawal from the city during the night of 2 April.[117] "O, how sad I felt to think so noble a little city should so soon be in Yankee hands!" one Virginia artilleryman exclaimed in his diary the next morning. "I shall ever remember this 10 months siege."[118]

Lee, intending to make his way southwest toward Danville and a possible junction with Johnston, ordered a concentration of troops at Amelia Court House, a junction on the Richmond and Danville Railroad some thirty-five miles northwest of Petersburg and some forty miles southwest of Richmond. He believed that rations were being forwarded to this point to await the arrival of his reunited army, which now consisted of the force immediately under his command, elements of units detached elsewhere or isolated from the army that morning, and Ewell's troops from Richmond.[119] About 8:00 P.M. the main portion of the army, with Longstreet commanding his own and the Third Corps and Gordon leading the Second Corps, began the march across the Appomattox River and northwest from Petersburg. Orderly Sgt. James E. Whitehorne, of the 12th Virginia, who had begun a diary on 30 March both to occupy his spare time and in anticipation of the campaign about to open, wrote on the night of 2 April, "We cannot hold out longer. I am afraid Grant will destroy this army if we have to fall back far." Whitehorne, a native of Hicksford, in Greensville County, had not yet turned twenty-one when he enlisted as a corporal in Company F, the "Huger Greys," in the summer of 1861. He had been promoted to first sergeant later that year, had been severely wounded in both legs by a shell at Gettysburg in July 1863, and had been wounded again at the Crater in July 1864. By the spring of 1865 he had become orderly sergeant of his regiment. "The moon has just risen clear and calm," he recorded in his diary. "If we, the Army of Northern Virginia, are defeated, all is lost. We must bow in submission. I hope I have a chance to fight—I don't think I will surrender. I'll never see the calm moon again without remembering this sad night."[120]

A few hours later Ewell's troops started from Richmond but were slowed by confusion on all sides, a great deal of it caused by fires that had been started by Confederate authorities seeking to keep warehouses out of Federal hands. Those fires quickly burned out of control and threatened to engulf the city during the night. The last Confederate soldiers to leave Richmond as an organized body of troops did so on the morning of 3 April and crossed the James River, making their way southwest toward their rendezvous with Lee at Amelia Court House. One South Carolina cavalryman described the scene in his diary as "a sight that will never be forgotten thousands of Ladies weeping & wringing their hands as they saw their last hope departing would that every one of the army could of seen it."[121]

Lee's officers and men had few opportunities to write during the retreat. Most who did contented themselves with either brief notes letting family and friends know they were safe or short diary entries recording a few details of the march and describing the profound fatigue, hunger, and gloom felt by almost every Confederate. More diaries than letters seem to survive from the Army of Northern Virginia for the week of 2–9 April, due as much to the rapid progression of events as to the fragile state of Confederate communications. "I have never been in a real retreat before," one Virginian commented, "but this looks like a disorderly one to me."[122] Such phrases as "I never laid down during the night," "We have not had a thing to eat for two days," "I never was so tired in my life," and "Have never seen such confusion. Feel like I was 'going up'" were common in diaries written on the retreat.[123] In a typical entry dated 2 April but updated on 9 April, Capt. John A. F. Coleman of the 17th South Carolina wrote: "After a great deal of cautious traveling we got with the remnant of our army and wagon train in full retreat towards Lynchburg. From the 3rd till the 9th we had a fight every day, marching almost constantly day and night. I never was so near worn out in my life."[124]

The separated elements of the Army of Northern Virginia, some 35,000 to 40,000 troops in all, marched quickly and made more than twenty miles from their respective starting points by the evening of 3 April. They were aided to some extent by Grant's pursuit, which at this stage was led by his cavalry corps under Sheridan, who was ordered to cut off the Confederate avenue of retreat down the Richmond and Danville Railroad. When Lee, with the van of his army, recrossed to the south side of the Appomattox River and reached Amelia Court House on the morning of 4 April, he was stunned to discover that the rations supposed to be waiting for his hungry soldiers were nowhere to be found. He appealed to the local farmers for provisions and sent wagons to collect whatever the citizens would give the army, then telegraphed to Danville with an urgent request for rations. The entire army—now including not only Longstreet's combined First and badly depleted Third Corps and Gordon's Second Corps, but also Fitzhugh Lee's Cavalry Corps, the remnants of Anderson's Fourth Corps and of various other units, and Ewell's command—soon arrived in the vicinity, and Lee spent 4 April and half of the fifth waiting for or searching for food for men and horses. When it became evident that rations were not to be had in the area and that several corps of Federal infantry were rapidly approaching from the east, he started his troops from Amelia Court House. Finding his way southwest blocked by Sheridan's cavalry at Jetersville, Lee turned west toward Farmville, hoping to find provisions there before continuing on to Danville. The march began late on 5 April and proceeded through the night with Longstreet in the lead, followed by Anderson, Ewell, and Gordon.[125] At virtually every step along the way from Amelia Court House to Farmville, weary and hungry Confederates fell out of the ranks, prompting at least one commander to caution a subordinate on the morning of the sixth, "Every effort must be made to get up all stragglers, and all such men as have fallen asleep by the camp-fires or by the wayside."[126]

While Longstreet's troops marched west toward the Southside Railroad and Farmville that morning, Sheridan's cavalry harassed and skirmished with the army's wagon trains, which were between Ewell and Gordon in the line of march. When Anderson and Ewell halted near Sayler's Creek to let the wagon trains pass ahead of them but neglected to notify Longstreet that they had stopped, the consolidated First and Third Corps continued toward the railroad station at Rice's Depot, leaving a sizable gap between Longstreet and Anderson. Ewell, meanwhile, decided to divert the wagons to another road altogether about midday but did not alert Gordon, whose Second Corps was already being hard pressed by Grant's infantry and who followed the wagons instead of coming up behind Ewell's troops. Ewell's and Anderson's blunders not only isolated their commands but also left them completely exposed to attacks from the advancing Federal infantry and cavalry late on the afternoon of 6 April. Though Ewell held his own against several assaults from an infantry corps, his line was ultimately enveloped and overwhelmed, while Anderson had even less success defending his position against a cavalry division a short distance to the south. Joseph B. Kershaw, whose veteran division of the First Corps had been assigned to Ewell's command before the evacuation of Richmond, reported a few months later, "On no battle-field of the war have I felt a juster pride in the conduct of my command."[127]

If many individuals and units fought as bravely as Lee's soldiers ever had, they were doomed by their generals' mistakes and by the aggressiveness of Federal commanders, whose men significantly outnumbered the available Confederate force. Casualties in Ewell's and Anderson's commands totaled nearly 6,000 men—most of them captured—including eight general officers; Ewell's entire command was surrounded and taken prisoner, while about half of Anderson's command scattered and escaped the field. The most effective resistance offered by the Confederate infantry during the day was that led by Gordon—who fought a rear-guard action to protect Lee's wagons at the confluence of Big Sayler's Creek and Little Sayler's Creek—but he still suffered more than 1,500 casualties, most of them prisoners. Elements of Confederate cavalry also clashed with a small

Federal force of infantry and a few companies of cavalry where the South-side Railroad crossed the Appomattox River on the High Bridge; their brief fight secured the vital escape route and resulted in the surrender of a few hundred Federal prisoners. The day's combat in the vicinity of Sayler's Creek had cost Lee more than 7,500 men—almost a quarter of his total force—and dealt a near-fatal blow to the dwindling Army of Northern Virginia.[128]

That night the army continued toward Farmville, a few miles to the west. Longstreet's command left Rice's Depot while Gordon's command—now including the remaining troops from Ewell's, Anderson's, and other commands broken up by Five Forks and Sailor's Creek—crossed the Appomattox at the High Bridge. "The army continued its march during the night," Lee reported a few days later, "and every effort was made to reorganize the divisions which had been shattered by the day's operations; but the men being depressed by fatigue and hunger, many threw away their arms, while others followed the wagon trains and embarrassed their progress."[129] On the night of 6 April a veteran of the famous Washington Artillery of New Orleans wrote in his diary: "the Yanks are following us closely Started from Amelia at 3 P.M. we are to march all night. I tell you I am tired but there is no help for it."[130] It was now only a matter of time until the rest of the army—or what was left of it—would be forced to either make a stand or surrender.

The Confederates, followed closely by Federal cavalry and infantry, reached Farmville on the morning of 7 April. Adequate if not abundant rations for Lee's famished soldiers, who had not enjoyed a substantial meal in several days, had been collected at the depot by the commissary-general's department and were waiting for them there. But the Army of Northern Virginia barely had time to begin cooking its meals before the enemy came into view from the east, forcing it to resume its retreat once more. The remaining rations were sent ahead to Appomattox Station, some twenty-five to thirty miles west on the Southside Railroad, and the Confederates were marched north over the Appomattox River and then west toward that point. Though Lee still hoped to retreat by way of Danville, his immediate goal was to reach Appomattox Station ahead of the Federals, supply his troops there, and proceed to Lynchburg. Skirmishes occurred at Farmville and at Cumberland Church north of the town, where Lee's rearguard held off the Federals and allowed the rest of the army to continue west in yet another forced march through the afternoon and late into the night.[131] At every step of the way men fell out of the ranks, many from fatigue and hunger and many others from sheer hopelessness. A Louisiana artilleryman reported that "a great many Virginians in the army are deserting every day—& are not willing to leave the state," referring to Lee's attempt to make his way to North Carolina.[132] A Virginia infantryman described his struggle to keep up with the retreating army. "It has been raining a little all day and I am right wet and my leg aches," he jotted in his diary, "but I will lie down to get some sleep. Have not slept for about three days and nights. I am very hungry, have not eaten anything since early yesterday."[133]

Grant, who spent the night of 7 April at Farmville, sent a short note to Lee that began, "The result of the last week must convince you of the hopelessness of further resistance on the part of the Army of Northern Virginia," then asked the Confederate commander to surrender. Lee replied that he did not think his predicament was hopeless but expressed a desire "to avoid useless effusion of blood" and asked Grant what terms he might expect if he did surrender.[134] His retreating Confederates halted just after midnight a short distance from Appomattox Court House, a crossroads two miles northeast of the station that bore the same name. Their pursuers were not far behind.

Saturday, 8 April, was a relatively quiet day for Lee's officers and men as some of them made their way toward Appomattox Court House and the army's wagon train beyond the courthouse at Appomattox Station, while many others straggled or deserted along the roadside. "The roads are in an undescribable condition and it is still raining," one veteran reported. "I fear General Lee will have to abandon or burn all transportation—we have passed hundreds of wagons stuck or broken. We have been marching steadily since midnight without halts except for the wagons to catch up. I scribble in this diary to take my mind off food."[135] With Grant's infantry a short distance to their rear and Sheridan's cavalry still on their left but displaying slightly less inclination to press them, Lee's exhausted men marched or straggled west with less interference from the Federals than they had had for several days. The chief of the First Corps artillery, finishing a letter to his wife begun on 3 April, commented, "Today we are not pressed & are rolling along toward Lynchburg rapidly & in fine spirits—at least I am," and a hospital steward in the 37th North Carolina noted in his diary, "we have herd no firing today so far it is the first quiett days travell that we have had."[136]

Numerous Confederates ate the rations issued to them at Farmville, foraged in the area on their own, or received rations during the day, all the while speculating about their probable fate. Though many soldiers, including some high-ranking officers, believed that continuing to fight could serve no real purpose, others were more sanguine—or at least managed to keep up appearances; still others ventured the hope that they might reach Danville after all. Most of the army had reached the vicinity of Appomattox Court House by nightfall, with Longstreet and the rear-guard a few miles to the rear. The only action of any consequence occurred that night when Sheridan's cavalry attacked the Confederate wagon train and artillery reserve at Appomattox Station, capturing most of it and scattering the rest.[137]

A note from Grant arrived that evening in response to Lee's request for a clarification of possible surrender terms. The Federal commander succinctly stated, "there is but one condition I would insist upon, viz, that the men and officers surrendered shall be disqualified for taking up arms against the Government of the United States until properly exchanged." Lee, who was still unwilling to concede that a formal surrender to Grant was necessary, replied, "To be frank, I do not think the emergency has arisen to call for the surrender of this army" but proposed a meeting with Grant between the lines the next morning so that the two might discuss the general situation as it applied to the Army of Northern Virginia and how Grant's proposal of terms might "tend to the restoration of peace."[138] As Lee waited for an answer, he conferred with his principal commanders—Longstreet, Gordon, and Fitzhugh Lee—and made plans for the next day. "During the night," he wrote President Davis a few days later, "there were indications of a large force massing on our left and front." Fitzhugh Lee and Gordon were instructed to test the Federals in their front early on the morning of 9 April. If the troops blocking the army's escape were only cavalry, the two corps commanders might force their way through them and allow the army to continue its retreat, pursued by Federal infantry in their rear. If, however, Sheridan's cavalrymen were supported by Grant's infantry, then the Federals had Lee trapped and there was no alternative but surrender.[139]

In the meantime Lee's officers and men waited for morning and wondered what would become of them. James Whitehorne resumed his diary entry from the morning of the eighth but interrupted it to observe, "Oh, Good News! I hear we are going to draw rations. Must stop and go see." On returning, the orderly sergeant reported: "I have just eaten the best supper of my life. We drew one days rations of meal and bacon. Allen, Davis and myself soon had the flour made up and baked. We made up the flour in an oilcloth and baked it on a hot rock." Turning his attention to the army, Whitehorne continued: "I feel ready for more marching or fighting. . . . Rumors are everywhere. . . . Must close for some sleep because there will be plenty fighting tomorrow."[140]

Fighting began early on the morning of Sunday, 9 April, as Fitz Lee's cavalrymen and Gordon's infantrymen clashed with Sheridan between the courthouse and Appomattox Station, driving the Federals back a short distance and raising faint hopes that the Confederates might make their escape. That morning James Whitehorne, whose brigade was part of the army's rearguard, reported in his diary: "Heard heavy firing in several directions. Just before we halted all the firing suddenly ceased. All the men were jubilant as we concluded we had whipped the enemy and put their guns out of commission. The road seemed clear."[141] Yet all too soon those hopes were crushed by the discovery that Grant's infantry was deployed in force behind his cavalry, with two full Federal corps and a division of a third ready for battle. Fitz Lee, under an arrangement made with the commanding general the night before, broke off the fight and withdrew to avoid the now-inevitable surrender, hoping to join Johnston's force somewhere south. Meanwhile, Gordon continued skirmishing with the enemy cavalry and watched as the Federals massed their infantry for a full-scale assault on his corps. The rearguard of the army fared no better than the advance, as Longstreet, near New Hope Church on the road east of Appomattox Court House, had to contend with two full corps of Federal infantry threatening to overwhelm his depleted command. Neither Gordon nor Longstreet had enough troops to hold their own positions, much less support each other's corps, and they reported that assessment to headquarters. Gordon withdrew to the vicinity of the courthouse, Longstreet remained in place to the east, and Lee, who had still not received a reply to his note of the night before, rode to keep his appointment with the Federal commander.[142]

Lee heard from Grant soon after passing through the Federal lines under a flag of truce. Grant's reply, which cancelled their proposed meeting, reminded Lee that he had no authority from the Federal government to discuss peace in general terms. He added, however, that he believed if the South would simply stop fighting, it could "hasten that most desirable event" and expressed his hope that "all our difficulties may be settled without the loss of another life." Hours passed while the two generals exchanged notes. Lee's first response asked for "an interview in accordance with the offer contained in your letter of yesterday"; a second message requested "a suspension of hostilities pending the adjustment of the terms of the surrender of this army"; and a third note, sent in case the second failed to reach Grant, proposed a meeting "to discuss the terms of the surrender of this army." A preliminary truce was in effect sometime between 11:00 A.M. and noon, though sporadic skirmishing and firing continued until all units on both sides were informed of it. Grant, who received Lee's first note shortly before noon, immediately notified his longtime adversary that he was making his way to the front to meet him and sent a member of his staff to escort the Confederate commander.[143] In the early afternoon Lee rode into the village of Appomattox Court House and proceeded to the home of Wilmer McLean—whose house had been chosen as the best place for the meeting—to wait for Grant.

Lee's soldiers knew instinctively that something was amiss when they received orders to cease firing and saw Federal officers within their lines talking freely with Confederate officers. But few of them were prepared to accept the stunning news that came later that afternoon—that "Marse Robert" had met with Grant, that the Army of Northern Virginia had been surrendered to their old foe, and that the war, at least for them, was over.[144] Some soldiers refused to believe that Lee's army would ever surrender to Yankees, doubting that such a thing was even possible. Lt. William G. Hinson of the 7th South Carolina Cavalry was startled by the "peculiar voice & oaths" of his brigade commander Brig. Gen. Martin W. Gary, who cursed a Federal officer for presuming to be in his lines and talking about a surrender. Hinson, who could not make out what Gary was saying, wondered what the "excited dispute" meant, then saw a flag of truce and understood instantly: "Oh horror of horrors it flashes through the command that Lee had surrendered. My pencil almost refuses to write the disgrace, many an iron souled veteran burst in to tears, which could not of been wrung by 'the rack' & were willing to sacrifice life at any moment for the cause."[145]

Many other veterans, once they were persuaded that Lee had indeed surrendered them, also recorded their shock and despair in diaries. A Virginia artillery lieutenant who wrote a brief matter-of-fact description of his battalion's reaction to the surrender proclaimed *"The saddest day of my life"* at the end of his diary entry for 9 April, and a North Carolina private declared, " 'The life of the 'C.S.' is gon' when Gen Lee and his army surrendered."[146] Adjt. James E. Hall of the 31st Virginia thought: "How strange! The Grand old Army of Northern Virginia—the heroes of a hundred victories, and of world wide fame, surrendering to the enemy! But the Grand old Army is not here. It is dead!"[147] Capt. Henry A. Chambers of the 49th North Carolina wrote an impassioned diary entry: "Who would have ventured to prophesy this two years, aye, twelve or six or three or even one month ago! Oh! but it is a bitter, bitter humiliation. All our hopes of independence blasted! . . . Can it be? can it be? . . . Oh, God! our burden is almost too heavy to be borne."[148]

The emotions expressed by James Whitehorne were typical, if more fully and more eloquently stated than most. "We did not know what to think," he wrote. "I was thunderstruck, but was soon convinced for General Weisiger himself said it was certainly so." As the realization slowly sank in that he would soon be a civilian again and would be returning to his parents' farm in Greensville County, Virginia, Whitehorne declared: "Lord! The war has been going on so long I can't realize what a man would do now it's over. All I know is to drill, and march, and fight. How can we get interested in farming or working in a store or warehouse when we have been interested day and night for years in keeping alive, whipping the invaders, and preparing for the next fight?" He wondered what those officers and men who had been killed fighting under Lee might think of them now. "What would Jackson, or Stuart, or—any of them say about us?" Whitehorne admitted that "It is humiliating in the extreme. I never expected to see men cry as they did this morning. All the officers cried and most of the privates broke down and wept like little children and Oh, Lord! I cried too. I wish General Lee had called on Mahone's Division to make that attack this morning." The young Virginian closed with a description of the evening moon and a comment on his new status, writing, "The moon, watery and pale, is up. Last night we were free soldiers of the Southern States; tonight, we are defeated men, prisoners of war of the Northern States."[149]

A few veterans displayed more bitterness and anger than sadness and acceptance over their defeat. "Excitement among the officers and men is intense," wrote Chaplain John Paris of the 54th North Carolina as rumors swept through the ranks in the afternoon, before the terms of the army's surrender had been announced to the troops. "Many propose to fight [it] out to the bitter end, rather than to Surrender. Others are determined to take to the bushes and thus take care of themselves." Paris, who was initially one of those planning "to take to the bushes" rather than endure the disgrace of surrendering, told his brigade commander about his plans and asked for advice. William Gaston Lewis replied that his brigade, including the 54th North Carolina, was still considered part of the Army of Northern Virginia and that Paris was honor-bound to abide by the terms agreed upon by Generals Lee and Grant. "I yielded to his suggestions," Paris noted, observing that "a better feeling seemed to prevail" once Second Corps commander John Gordon explained Grant's terms to the troops.[150]

Many of Lee's officers and men who had feared that they would be sent to Northern prisons were relieved to hear that they would soon be paroled and would be free to go home. They were also grateful that the Federals began issuing them ample rations, that most of Grant's troops kept their distance, and that those who did come into their camps were usually careful not to offend them by exulting over their surrender. Several veterans were impressed by Federal soldiers who shared rations or money with them and carried on pleasant, and sometimes friendly, conversations about the end of the war. Maj. Richard Watson Jones of the 12th Virginia was visited by a Federal officer he had known before the war when they attended the same college. One of Jones's men described the scene when the Federal entered the Confederate camp. "We saw him come up and hold out his hand—the Major did nothing for so long it was painful," James Whitehorne reported. "Then he took the offered hand and I had a feeling the war was really over." Whitehorne, for his part, declared, "After all, I never hated any one Yankee. I hated the spirit that was sending them to invade the south."[151] Numerous Confederates spent the next two days making out final company rolls or paroles, visiting with each other or their former enemies, enjoying the luxuries of abundant food and occasional drink, and waiting to begin the trip home. "We are still in suspense not knowing when we will get off," a North Carolina infantryman observed on 11 April; a Virginia artilleryman spent the day "Lying in camp near Appomattox C.H. with nothing to do but eat—which latter can be enjoyed as we suffered terribly with hunger while on the retreat from Richmond."[152]

Several formalities now needed to be handled, either by Lee and his officers, by Grant and his officers, or by the joint commission appointed by the two commanders to work out the details of the surrender. Lee asked his aide Charles Marshall to draft a farewell order to the army, which Marshall began on the night of 9 April and finished the next morning; the order was issued and read to the troops on the tenth and eleventh. "After four years of arduous service, marked by unsurpassed courage and fortitude," General Orders No. 9 began, "the Army of Northern Virginia has been compelled to yield to overwhelming numbers and resources." Lee explained that he had surrendered because he saw no other alternative, expressed "an increasing admiration of your constancy and devotion to your country," and thanked his soldiers for the "kind and generous considerations" they had always shown him, closing, "I bid you all an affectionate farewell."[153] Many officers and some enlisted men made their own copies of the order and took them to headquarters for Lee's autograph so they might have a keepsake of their service with him, something they and their descendants could treasure in the years to come.

The final and most symbolic detail still undone was the actual surrender of the army to the Federals. The first provision of the agreement made by the joint commission on 10 April called for such a capitulation, in which the Confederates would "march by brigades and detachments to a designated point, [and] stack their arms, deposit their flags, sabers, pistols, &c."[154] Though many of Lee's soldiers had hoped to simply stack their arms in their camps and disband their units, Grant's commissioners insisted that there be a formal ceremony in which the Confederates marched in front of the Federals and surrendered to them. The proceedings took place on 12 April with John B. Gordon at the head of the Second Corps, followed by the remnants of the Fourth Corps, then by the Third Corps, and last by the First Corps.[155] "At Sunrise we were all moved off in order of march by Brigades and divisions," one North Carolinian noted in his diary. "We took our arms and stacked them at Appomattox C. House in the presence of the Yankee divisions, and from thence at half past 8 Oclock struck off for home by Brigades."[156] A Virginian described the surrender in somewhat more detail, observing, "Had to march between two columns of the enemy, one on each side. They did not look at us, did not look defiant, did not make disrespectful remarks. Our men marched up boldly and stacked arms and did not seem to mind any more than if they had been going on dress parade."[157]

The Army of Northern Virginia had ceased to exist, except in the memory of its veterans and its adversaries, and took with it the last flickering hopes of Confederate independence. When Col. William Preston Johnston of Jefferson Davis's staff wrote Mrs. Davis the same day, "The loss of an army is not the loss of the cause," and predicted, "There is a great deal of fight in us yet," he could not have been more wrong.[158] Though other Southern armies were still in the field, most notably the Army of Tennessee and the forces in the Trans-Mississippi Department, the word "Appomattox"—and all it represented—eventually came to signify the end of the Civil War.

After the surrender ceremony Orderly Sgt. James Whitehorne marched back to camp with the rest of the 12th Virginia and waited to be paroled. A few minutes after he went to sleep that night a lieutenant woke him, told him the blank paroles were ready, and said that if Whitehorne would help fill them out for the regiment, the commanding officer could sign them that night and the men could start for home the next morning. "I needed no persuasion," the young Virginian wrote, "so up I jumped and borrowed a pen and bottle of ink from one of the men. Some one found a scrap of tallow candle and we improvised a candlestick in the shape of an old bayonet stuck in the soft soil. The lieutenant and myself fell to work and in little time had them all ready to go." Maj. Richard W. Jones signed the men's paroles and Whitehorne soon had his in his pocket, marveling, "Two signatures on a piece of paper—one in the spring of 1861 which made me a soldier—the other in the spring of 1865 which makes me——."[159]

The Last Hope of the South:
The Army of Northern Virginia's
Last Year in Retrospect

The Army of Northern Virginia passed from reality into memory, history, and legend when its officers and men filed through the village of Appomattox Court House, marched past their longtime foes in the Army of the Potomac, and laid down their weapons and banners in surrender. The army's last year had been unlike any other in its brief existence, not only in terms of the extraordinary demands made by the changing face of the war. There was also an increasingly heavy burden placed on it by the expectations of those who believed that General Lee and his soldiers represented the Confederacy's only real chance for victory. When a Georgia lieutenant wrote in September 1864 that "the Army of Northern Virginia alone" was "the last hope of the South, to say nothing of what may be done elsewhere," he only articulated what many others in and out of the army were thinking.[1]

A similar opinion of the army's unique position among Confederate forces has been adopted—whether consciously or not—by many writers since 1865, from Confederate veterans to journalists, from academic historians to armchair generals, and from biographers to novelists. Hundreds of books and articles have helped instill in the popular consciousness the reputations of the Army of Northern Virginia as *the* Confederate Army, Robert E. Lee as the ranking Confederate general for the entire war, and Appomattox as the place where the Civil War ended. That distinction is not undeserved, for as Gary Gallagher reminds us: "By the third year of the war, Lee and his soldiers personified the Confederacy for many fellow citizens who expected bad news from almost every other theater. So long as the Army of Northern Virginia remained in the field, it was possible to believe the southern experiment in nation-building retained viability."[2] Such observations underscore the truth that Lee's army was indeed "the last hope of the South" and point toward an examination of its last year as a profitable contribution to the literature.[3]

Though this study essentially follows the army from the Wilderness to Appomattox, several topics naturally present themselves for further review. A retrospective look at the period should add light, shadow, depth, and focus to the portrait already drawn and should add context as well by addressing itself to existing scholarship on the Army of Northern Virginia, the campaigns of 1864–65, Civil War soldier life, the Southern home front, and the causes of Confederate defeat. Such an approach may also be helpful, to paraphrase Bell Wiley, in identifying additional roads down which historians might profitably go.

A useful point of departure for this retrospective, and one that might normally be neglected in favor of a more standard frame of reference, is a brief critical assessment of the major sources consulted for this portrait of life in the Army of Northern Virginia in the last year of the war. These sources, which are, of course, indispensable for their contemporary descriptions of life in a specific Confederate army, also merit attention for less apparent reasons. A careful reading of thousands of unpublished and published letters, diaries, and other papers written by Lee's officers and men from May 1864 to April 1865—and, indeed, years of reading similar Confederate sources written from April 1861 through April 1864 as well—has identified several defining characteristics. Those shared qualities are themselves an indirect commentary on the events these sources describe and on the morale of the soldiers who wrote them. An introduction to the nature of these personal narratives as texts in the literary sense may provide another intriguing perspective from which to gauge the army's response to the fortunes of its last year.

The ever-changing course of the war had a profound impact on a soldier's ability, or even willingness, to write accounts of his daily experiences.[4] More detailed letters and diary entries survive from the first six or eight weeks of the 1864 campaigns than from any other comparable period during the year. Though many of Lee's officers and men had already predicted that the intensity and importance of these campaigns would surpass those of previous years, they could hardly have imagined what lay ahead from the first week of May to the end of June. From the Wilderness to Cold Harbor and on to Petersburg, they found themselves in almost constant contact, and often in daily combat, with their counterparts in the Army of the Potomac.

The seemingly unrelenting pressure of what the soldiers themselves viewed as one long battle rather than a rapid succession of several battles is often apparent in letters and diaries painting the period as an unprecedented chapter in the army's, and in all likelihood the Confederacy's, history. Soldiers' narratives included, of course, the usual accounts of marches, skirmishes, and full-scale battles, some written in great detail and others in a more matter-of-fact style. But now many letters and diaries also included frequent expressions of frustration or resignation reflecting their authors' attempts to describe, much less come to grips with, what they were experiencing, while many other Confederate narratives included perceptive observations that this campaign was quite unlike earlier campaigns. Expressions of astonishment at the staggering numbers of dead, wounded, and missing in both armies, and at the determination with which Lee and Grant continued to face each other after such losses, for example, were so common and so similar as to be almost standard during this period. Such language often gave these accounts a more generally somber tone than in most previous letters and diaries. Though speculations about the future ranging from the plausible to the impossible were always frequent, many members of the Army of Northern Virginia were now convinced that they were describing the one great decisive battle that would end the war at last.

By the time the army had settled into its trenches near Petersburg in late June, however, and as the summer wore on, it was clear to most of Lee's soldiers that the end was nowhere in sight. They soon settled into a routine in which they spent most of their time watching and waiting, often shooting at and occasionally fraternizing with an enemy who occupied a line of trenches within sight, earshot, and musket range of them. Only occasionally would they and their units leave the lines for a few days to rest or to carry out operations intended to break the developing stalemate. Their letters and diaries from the early summer, naturally enough, began to reflect the gradual evolution of the war being waged by the Army of Northern Virginia and the Army of the Potomac, one in which long stretches of relative inactivity were periodically broken by episodes of brief excitement. Most accounts written from the Petersburg-Richmond front between the summer of 1864 and the spring of 1865 are every bit as ordinary as the events they describe.

Once the intensity of close combat and forced marches gave way to the monotony of a siege, many Confederates were also less frequent and regular correspondents and diarists than before. They often observed, by way of justification or explanation, that they saw no real reason for writing long letters and diary entries when there was so little news to write about. When they did write, furthermore, they usually discussed such ordinary subjects as the weather, camp life, rations, their opinion that family and friends did not write them often enough, or their ever-present desire to return home, and even then discussed them only briefly. Descriptions of sharpshooting, artillery bombardments, and other routine small-scale actions up and down the lines were usually mentioned only in passing unless the writer or his unit was directly involved. Though the larger-scale and less routine actions from the Crater at the end of July 1864 through Fort Stedman at the end of March 1865 received more general notice throughout the army, these operations—and most soldiers' accounts of them— were exceptions rather than the rule. Moreover, the Army of Northern Virginia seemed to play a supporting role rather than its accustomed leading role and to be less directly involved in most of the pivotal events during the second half of 1864 and into 1865. Each new major Confederate defeat or setback elsewhere, from Atlanta to Fort Fisher, prompted many correspondents and diarists to adopt a more philosophical perspective. Many soldiers now devoted less attention to simple descriptions of events around them than to more candid, and often perceptive, assessments of what those events might mean for the future.

Many officers and men spent the summer and fall of 1864 in the Shenandoah with the Army of the Valley instead of in the trenches with the Army of Northern Virginia. They marched, fought, and saw a great deal more than the Confederates along the Petersburg and Richmond lines during the same period. In spite of the basic differences between their experiences and those of their fellow soldiers with Lee, the letters and diaries written from the Shenandoah Valley are most notable for their commonplace qualities. The members of Early's little army spent so much time marching, countermarching, and engaging the enemy in numerous minor actions that they had few opportunities and little inclination to write in great detail about what they had done, were doing, or expected to do. In that respect the frequency and format, though not the concrete facts, of their accounts are much like those provided by the comrades they left behind with Lee. Though the raid into Maryland and to the outskirts of Washington in July produced a little of the old anticipation many Confederates had felt when crossing the Potomac in 1862 or 1863, hopes for a dramatic strategic victory were never realized. The middle phase of the campaign, which took up most of July, August, and September and saw very little action of any note, was seen as proof that operations in the Shenandoah Valley were now of secondary importance.

The three climactic battles of September and October, in which the army suffered progressively disastrous routs at Winchester, Fisher's Hill, and Cedar Creek, not only proved such predictions badly mistaken but also had a tremendous impact on the ways Confederates viewed their experiences in the Shenandoah Valley. The letters and diary entries written after each battle are striking indications of the mood within the Army of the Valley as such bitter defeats successively weakened, and in many instances shattered, the morale and confidence of the officers and men who survived them. Most of these accounts share the same reflective tone of letters and diaries from the Petersburg-Richmond front during the same period. Yet their descriptions and interpretations often convey a depth of personal and emotional involvement with their subjects that is missing from the writings of those who did not participate or were less directly involved in such combat. The members of the Valley army, most of them veterans of Stonewall Jackson's old Second Corps, were proud of the reputation they had won on so many battlefields since the beginning of the war. They were also painfully aware that when they fled panic-stricken from the field at Winchester, it was the first time in the war that elements of Lee's army had done so on a mass scale. The routs they suffered at Fisher's Hill and at Cedar Creek were even more humiliating and acutely affected the way they wrote about the campaign, their commanders, and themselves. Some officers and men were so disheartened that they barely wrote anything at all. Others vividly expressed the shame they felt or vented their frustration and anger at those they blamed for the defeats, and still others pondered what would happen to them next. One sentiment shared by virtually all of these soldiers, a view expressed most forcefully in the aftermath of Cedar Creek, was their wish to leave the Shenandoah Valley and return to General Lee and the rest of the Army of Northern Virginia.

Throughout the winter of 1864–65 and into the first few days of spring, members of the now-reunited army along the Petersburg-Richmond front described the slow disintegration of its ranks by desertion and debated such proposals as the enlistment of black soldiers in the Confederate armies or the consolidation of understrength units. Some of these soldiers declared their determination to persevere in spite of the odds against them and expressed surprise that the Confederacy seemed to have so little support from its civilians. Almost all of Lee's officers and men looked forward to the opening of the 1865 campaign with both anticipation and dread, for they knew that it would finally decide the outcome of a longer and bloodier war than most observers had predicted four years earlier.

Once that brief campaign actually began, however, the tide of successive engagements, withdrawals, retreats, and forced marches rolled over the army with such force that most Confederates found precious little time to stop and write even the briefest summaries of what was happening. Letters were outdated as soon as they were sent, even if they did make their way to their intended recipients, and seem to have been less common than diary entries, which were usually confined to a few lines outlining a day's or several days' events. Most officers and men spent considerably more time after 2 April concerning themselves with survival than with leaving an account of their experiences for posterity, though several unpublished and published diaries are impressive chronicles of the death throes of the Army of Northern Virginia.

Historians have long mined the rich vein of Civil War personal narratives for nuggets to enrich their works, from sweeping general histories to the most meticulous biographies, unit histories, and battle narratives. Though these sources have an intrinsic value apart from their worth as descriptions of people, places, and events in the past, most scholars have been content to cite them or quote from them and leave it at that. Few historians have seriously considered these sources—particularly the wartime letters and diaries—as a genre, a type of writing emanating from a particular time, place, and circumstance. Bell Wiley's two magnificent volumes on the Union and Confederate common soldier, for example, confine any discussion of personal narratives to their role as a function of a soldier's everyday existence. Wiley describes such writing primarily in terms of poor grammar and spelling, exciting or mundane subjects, and stock or colorful expressions; he does not address the ways in which the form, structure, content, and language of many soldiers' writings evolved over time.[5] Though Michael Barton's sociological study of the character of Civil War soldiers, based on published letters and diaries, does touch on some of these points, it does not progress much beyond a rather sterile quantification of key words and phrases such as "kind," "noble," "gentleman," "brave," and "gallant." Union and Confederate soldiers, whether as members of military organizations or as individuals, have rarely been rendered so lifeless.[6]

The recent revival of interest in Civil War soldiers, however, as demonstrated by several fine books published in the last few years, has encouraged further assessments of their personal narratives. Most of these works have exhibited varying degrees of interest in the shared qualities of wartime soldiers' writings, and several of them subject these sources to some preliminary textual analysis.[7] Two of the latter are Joseph T. Glatthaar's *The March to the Sea and Beyond* and Larry J. Daniel's *Soldiering in the Army of Tennessee*, which focus on specific armies. Because it was possible for Glatthaar and Daniel to follow individual soldiers over time and to identify patterns in what they wrote, their books allow an analysis—albeit primarily implicit rather than explicit—of letter writing and diary keeping that more general studies of Civil War soldiers usually do not.[8]

Two recent books by James M. McPherson approach Civil War soldiers and their writings from a fresh perspective. *What They Fought For, 1861–1865*, published in 1994, is an introduction to an understanding of soldiers' motivations and how the war itself fundamentally changed the ways in which its participants expressed themselves about it. *What They Fought For* was followed in 1997 by *For Cause and Comrades*, McPherson's more comprehensive study of Civil War soldiers and why they fought, based on his examination of more than 25,000 letters and more than 250 diaries of Union and Confederate soldiers. *For Cause and Comrades* includes an especially valuable evaluation of Civil War soldiers' letters and diaries and of the context in which they were written, for as McPherson observes, "these documents bring us closer to the real thoughts and emotions of those men than any other kind of surviving evidence." Earl J. Hess's *The Union Soldier in Battle: Enduring the Ordeal of Combat*, another recent work that analyzes the experiences of Civil War soldiers through a close examination of their writings, appeared just as this book was going to press.[9]

If an evaluation of selected Confederate letters and diaries as texts is preliminary at best and an unorthodox but insignificant exercise at worst, the same cannot be said of an examination of several topics vital to an understanding of the Army of Northern Virginia between May 1864 and April 1865. Many conclusions drawn from a close study of the personal narratives reinforce assessments already made by authorities on Union and Confederate soldiers or on the army and its campaigns. Other conclusions differ to some lesser or greater extent with these assessments, and still others may offer new insights on how the war affected some of the men who fought in it.

Many Confederate soldiers who endured the Overland campaign observed that its six or seven weeks represented a dramatic departure from the pattern so familiar in most previous campaigns between the Army of Northern Virginia and the Army of the Potomac. Most of their contemporaries—including family members and friends, newspaper correspondents and editors, Confederate soldiers in other theaters, the military and civilian authorities, as well as their Union counterparts—agreed with them. Scholars since then have tended to follow the participants' lead in stressing the unique nature of the campaign from the Wilderness through Cold Harbor.[10] Such observations as Douglas Southall Freeman's contention that "In all the bloody fighting of the two armies there had never been such a struggle as this," James McPherson's description of "a seven-week campaign of movement and battle whose brutal intensity was unmatched in the war," and Noah Andre Trudeau's comment on "a scale of combat that surpassed understanding" are representative.[11] Charles Royster remarks in *The Destructive War*, his study of how Americans transformed the conduct of the war and how the conduct of the war in turn transformed them, that though "the images of battle were not new . . . soldiers in both armies and civilians following events at a distance felt themselves in a different kind of war. Combat on a scale that once would have been thought a single great climax of the war went on for weeks, and nothing seemed to change, except the armies' positions and the length of the casualty lists."[12] The ample testimony of letters and diaries written in the Army of Northern Virginia throughout May and June 1864 confirms such assessments.

The Overland campaign was indeed an exceptional one, one that had an enduring impact on almost every facet of the war's last year in the East. Civil War specialists and other military historians have long emphasized the wartime evolution of essentially Napoleonic infantry tactics and the resulting impact that such a development had first on combat performance and then, by extension, on strategy. That process, brought about by the sheer firepower of the rifled musket and the gradually more sophisticated use of field fortifications, was well under way, if not essentially complete, by the opening of the 1864 campaigns. Though many officers and men had at first objected to the construction of battlefield works on the grounds that fighting from behind protection was somehow unmanly—believing, as Grady McWhiney and Perry Jamieson observe, that "There was no glory to be gained from fighting out of a hole in the ground"—most such objections were eventually overcome by the recognition that entrenching often meant the difference between successfully defending a position and being driven from it.[13]

Field fortifications also served a psychological purpose as well as a tangible one, boosting the confidence of the men defending them and heightening the apprehension and fears of the men attacking them.[14] Paddy Griffith, a British military historian who has studied Civil War infantry tactics in some detail, speculates that by 1864 the simple act of entrenching was itself "a symbolic staking of a claim," and that soldiers "learned to dig in automatically wherever they halted, as much to warn the enemy not to try anything foolish as to give themselves physical protection from shot and shell."[15] Furthermore, entrenchments began to play an increasingly important role in the tactical offensive, as they not only improved the odds that a unit would hold a particular position but also kept one's lines as close to the enemy as possible, providing a forward point from which an attack might be launched.[16]

The campaign from the Wilderness to Petersburg further refined the practice of field fortification in what Edward Hagerman calls "a final testing and problem-solving phase for the tactics of trench warfare," observing that the opposing armies in Virginia mutually "established the brutal reality of the new era of entrenched positional warfare."[17] The gradual acceptance of that "entrenched positional warfare" throughout the Army of Northern Virginia began during the month of bloody fighting from the Wilderness to Cold Harbor and matured during the nine-and-one-half months the army occupied its extensive system of earthworks along the Petersburg-Richmond front. Entrenchments—some of them hastily improvised on the spot, others ordered by company, regimental, or brigade commanders, and still others painstakingly laid out by engineers under instructions from division, corps, or army headquarters—helped define life in the army after the 1864 campaign began. Officers and men alike frequently referred to such works in their letters, diaries, official correspondence, and reports, but most often did so in terms of day-to-day life in and around the trenches rather than their positive or negative impact on tactics or strategy. In contrast, most historians of the army or its campaigns have focused their attention on the effect these earthworks, log breastworks, abatis, chevaux de frise, and other obstructions had on the ebb and flow of particular military operations.[18]

While such tactical and strategic considerations helped establish the boundaries for concluding the war in the East, a pair of even more fundamental considerations governed virtually all operations during the same period. The success or failure of almost any offensive or defensive action undertaken, no matter how complex or simple it might be, no matter how large or small, was often determined by two basic criteria: the performance of battlefield commanders and the extent of unit cohesion. In this, at least, the Civil War was no different from any other war in which the outcome of a battle depends primarily on men rather than materiel.

These criteria have rarely been more significant or more powerfully demonstrated than when applied to the campaigns of the Army of Northern Virginia between May 1864 and April 1865. From the first few days of the Overland campaign it was evident that the year 1864 would cost the army an unprecedented number of experienced officers killed, wounded, captured, or otherwise rendered unfit for duty. Generals such as Longstreet, Ewell, and Stuart, whose careers were synonymous with the history of the army, might be succeeded in command but could never truly be replaced. Hundreds of other Confederate officers, many of whom had served with the army since well before the Seven Days' campaign, were also literally or figuratively left behind along the way from the Wilderness to Petersburg. These men, from major generals to third lieutenants, were typical Civil War officers. Many of them were professional soldiers, and countless others had at least received some military education or practical experience. Most officers, whether professionals or amateurs, had learned and refined their leadership skills on the battlefield, on the march, and in camp. The best of them learned not only how to maneuver their troops and lead them in combat, but also how to keep them in the best possible physical condition and how to turn citizen volunteers into soldiers the equal of most nineteenth-century professionals. Yet the same qualities that helped make these officers such successful commanders also motivated them to take enormous personal risks in combat and often cost them their lives. Though the army had almost always produced acceptable officers to succeed those who had been killed, wounded, captured, or found wanting during the campaigns of 1862 and 1863, the number of potential candidates for promotion or even temporary appointment was now dwindling rapidly.

By the time Lee's army arrived at Petersburg in mid-June 1864, numerous units from corps down to company level were commanded by officers who were at best unproven and at worst unqualified for their new positions. Lee, who took a great personal interest in finding the best possible officers for his troops, kept in close contact with his subordinates and with the authorities in Richmond on the proper candidates for advancement. Some officers managed quite well under emergency conditions, and numerous others performed adequately. All too many of them, however, were promoted or assigned to positions beyond their capabilities and simply could not fill the vacuum left by the loss of their predecessors. The army underwent a gradual transformation in which the cumulative effect of the siege at Petersburg, the campaign in the Shenandoah Valley, and an ever-lengthening list of critical vacancies often frustrated the best efforts of its officers in the second half of 1864 and into 1865. Confederate inspection reports during this period often included remarks on officers lost since the last report and candid observations on the strengths and weaknesses of the surviving officers at almost every level of command. Moreover, the practical experience and leadership of noncommissioned officers became more and more indispensable as regiments and companies continued to suffer catastrophic losses among their commissioned officers.[19]

A persuasive case has long been made for the view that internal pressures on the Army of Northern Virginia after the Wilderness were every bit as critical as the more obvious external pressures brought to bear on it by its Federal opponents. Douglas Southall Freeman advances a central feature of this interpretation in *R. E. Lee*, suggesting that the army was crippled by its inability to retain anything like an adequate number of experienced officers. He observes that the command structure of the army was shaken as early as the summer of 1863, just after Gettysburg, but that it was wrecked beyond repair by the time Lee and his soldiers occupied their trenches on the Petersburg-Richmond front almost a year later. His assessment of the Overland campaign concludes: "the sombre fact remained: troops were no longer led as they had been in the period from Second Manassas through Chancellorsville. In the largest sense, only Lee and the men in the ranks still made the army terrible in battle."[20]

Freeman develops this argument further in the final volume of *Lee's Lieutenants*, as his study in command becomes a study in the collapse of command. "A student who has become acquainted with the general officers of the Army of 1863," he comments, "will have the sense of being in the company of strangers after the Battle of the Crater."[21] As Freeman chronicles the fortunes of the army from Petersburg to Appomattox, he often pauses to highlight the stark contrast between the generally outstanding combat performance of Lee's officers before the 1864 campaigns and the all-too-frequently lackluster combat performance of officers once those campaigns were under way. Though his focus is primarily on general officers, Freeman also acknowledges the devastating effects of casualties among the army's field and company officers and alludes to the still-more devastating collapse of command that such losses produced during the last year of the war.[22]

Gary Gallagher, in a valuable examination of the army's high command through the first four weeks of the Overland campaign, reinforces this assessment by adding concrete details and insightful analysis. In doing so, he demonstrates even more emphatically than Freeman that effective corps and divisional command, long a hallmark of the Army of Northern Virginia, had all but disintegrated by the end of May 1864. "In slightly more than three weeks of campaigning," Gallagher points out, "the structure of command weakened and then fractured. Casualties, failures of health, and incompetence forced Lee to adjust constantly, often in the midst of crises on the battlefield."[23]

Lee adjusted then, and thereafter, by personally assuming more and more of the immediate burden of command in addition to the ultimate responsibility for its results. This response manifested itself most memorably in the "Lee to the rear" incidents in the Wilderness and at Spotsylvania, but there were many other occasions when the commanding general attempted to inspire his troops or to rally shattered and shaken units on battlefields from Petersburg to Sailor's Creek.[24] Emory Thomas, Lee's most recent biographer, writes: "No longer could he trust his subordinates to react in battle as he desired. Lee believed that he had to take charge and take action himself."[25] At such moments the special bond that Lee and his soldiers had always shared became more apparent than ever. Thomas Nelson Page mentions these incidents in the Wilderness and at Spotsylvania not so much to describe them in heroic terms as to explain their effect on the Confederate rank and file: "the fact that he had felt it necessary to place himself at their head called forth new efforts from the jaded soldiers and stirred them to redoubled valor."[26] It almost seemed as if General Lee and his men were the *real* Army of Northern Virginia—that their relationship was often akin to that of a father and his sons—and that most of the generals, staff officers, and even field and company officers in between them were somehow more administrators than active participants.[27]

Lee's faith in his men, and their faith in him, was central to that élan and esprit de corps that made the army successful on so many battlefields. As one Virginia private put it so well in a letter to the *Richmond Sentinel* in the summer of 1864, "what 'Marse Robert' says is gospel in this squad—the A.N.V."[28] Soon afterward an Alabama private wrote home, "we are not a frade of the yankees while we have old Generel Lee to lead us in the fites."[29] Many of Lee's soldiers, well aware that many other Southerners viewed them as the men who would settle the question of Confederate independence on the battlefield, were both proud of their hard-earned reputation and confident of their continued success and eventual victory. But as the war dragged on with no end in sight, some—and eventually, perhaps, most—members of the army who managed to persevere seemed to be fighting as much for Lee himself as for the Confederate government, for the idea of a Southern nation, or even for their families and homes. In June 1864, just as the opposing armies settled into a siege at Petersburg, the *Richmond Examiner* described the dream a veteran of Pickett's Division had about the end of the war. The unidentified Virginian dreamed that he went to sleep for twenty years, "seven more than old Rip Van Winkle snoozed," and that when he "awoke" within his dream he found himself somewhere near Hanover, Pennsylvania, with "General Lee in front of him, with a corporal and four men, waving his sword and crying out, 'Come on men, let's finish up this fight to-day anyhow.'"[30] Eight months later, near the end of February 1865, Sgt. Henry P. Fortson of the 31st Georgia wrote—but in all seriousness rather than in jest—"I have resolved to fight as long as Moss Robert has a corporals guard, or until he says give up. [H]e is the man that I shall follow or die in the attempt."[31] With seemingly little else to fight for, the more steadfast soldiers good-naturedly, even proudly, called themselves "Lee's Miserables" and owed their principal loyalty to "Marse Robert."[32]

Lee did not leave the command of such troops to chance. He resorted to more direct supervision of his subordinates by written and verbal orders and by his presence on the scene of minor tactical operations as well as more important operations. His almost constant anxiety for the future success of the army was also demonstrated by his increasingly frequent displays of anger directed at subordinate commanders and staff officers when they did not perform to his expectations. Furthermore, the challenge of incorporating numerous unfamiliar officers and units from other Confederate departments, and of compensating for the absence of officers and units detached to the Shenandoah Valley, compounded the difficulty of Lee's task. With Longstreet absent wounded, Ewell commanding the Department of Richmond, his successor Early in the Shenandoah commanding the Army of the Valley, Hill ailing much of the time, and Hampton and Fitzhugh Lee often sharing command of the cavalry, Lee spent most of the second half of 1864 without an experienced corps commander. When Longstreet resumed command of the First Corps in October, he also resumed his role as Lee's most trusted subordinate and was given responsibility for a significant portion of the Richmond front. Even Longstreet's welcome return, however, could not obscure the fact that the Army of Northern Virginia was now literally *Lee's* army in fact as well as in the popular imagination.[33]

The extent of unit cohesion was often directly related to the success or failure—or even the presence—of a particular unit's officers. Many units, even the renowned ones, often struggled without their full complement of officers, wavered in confusion on the field when their best officers were killed or wounded, and deteriorated under the direction of indifferent or inferior commanders. One new brigadier general, after only a few weeks in command of his South Carolina brigade—both of them recent arrivals in Virginia—wrote his wife in July 1864 that he expected to "succeed if the war lasts two or more years longer in getting at least one reliable officer in each company that is unless they are killed sooner or I. Those companies that have good officers do well," Stephen Elliott explained. "The others do not."[34] A veteran sergeant major in the 5th Texas was more blunt: "I am tired of being ordered around by every little squirt of a 2nd Lieut who can work around and get himself elected by a Company of backwards soldiers. . . . There are plenty of officers in our Brigade and Army who are perfect numbskulls."[35]

Some of the most critical promotions in this or any other Civil War army were those made for brigade commanders, who were responsible for the basic functional unit of the war, one that was theoretically large enough and strong enough to carry out important assignments on a battlefield and that often affected the course of a particular battle. "The brigade is really the unit organization of the army, and reflects the character and qualifications of its commander," the army's inspector general wrote in the fall of 1864. "Indeed, the brigadier makes the brigade. . . . If he holds his colonels to a strict accountability, the colonels will look to their captains, the captains to their lieutenants, the commissioned to the noncommissioned officers. . . . The illustration might be extended to show that an army with good brigadiers will have good discipline and that without them the best troops deteriorate."[36] Richard J. Sommers, whose massive *Richmond Redeemed: The Siege at Petersburg* is both a tactical history and a contextual analysis of Grant's fifth offensive on the Petersburg-Richmond front, highlights one of the typical late-war challenges facing Lee's army. "Brigadier and brigade had been together nearly three years," Sommers writes, describing the advance of Anderson's Brigade against Fort Harrison in September 1864, "yet attrition had so gutted the lower echelon of command that the general discovered himself as lacking a medium through which to exert his will over troops in motion as if he were still at the head of the untrained volunteers of '61. All he could do was go along with his armed mob and hope for the best."[37] Though Brig. Gen. George T. Anderson's Georgia brigade did not boast a reputation to rival that of more renowned units in the army such as the Stonewall Brigade or Hood's Texans, Anderson was nevertheless a reliable officer and his men—many of them veterans of the heady victory at First Manassas—were as steady as any other soldiers in the Army of Northern Virginia.

Even if the army had been able to find enough qualified officers to command its units in the last year of the war, it still would have been paralyzed by its inability to keep enough dependable soldiers in the ranks and present for duty. Casualties occurred almost daily, from full-scale pitched battles such as the Wilderness or Cedar Creek, to middle-level battles such as Monocacy or the Weldon Railroad, to minor actions such as the North Anna or Hatcher's Run, and in the frequent skirmishing and sharpshooting between the lines. But they were only the most conspicuous cause of the steady depletion of Confederate manpower. Disease, the most efficient killer of the war, cost Lee's army thousands of men dead, discharged due to medical disabilities, absent in field or general hospitals, or ill in camp. Hundreds more, some of them unable to withstand service in the trenches or on an active campaign but many others able-bodied, were detailed as cooks, wagon masters, hospital stewards, pioneers, couriers, signal operators, or in other noncombat roles. Those soldiers who were absent without permission, furthermore, were a constant drain on the army's effective strength and were never more so than during the last year of the war, when they numbered well into the thousands. Though many simply straggled or overstayed their furloughs and eventually returned to duty, more and more men, weary of the war and their role in it, deserted their comrades altogether and went home or across the lines to the Federals. Increases in the army's strength did occur periodically when new units were assigned to it, conscripts were placed in the ranks of existing units, or veterans rejoined their comrades after extended absences. Though such arrivals were, of course, welcome, they were only a temporary gain and did nothing to offset the growing number of soldiers leaving the army on a daily and nightly basis.[38]

After the army reached Petersburg, Lee devoted increasingly more of his correspondence with President Jefferson Davis and the Confederate authorities to the problems of keeping his force together. Even before the winter of 1864–65 he warned his superiors in Richmond that the Federals' war of attrition against the Confederacy was succeeding. In July Lee asked his son Custis, who was an aide to the president, "Where are we to get sufficient troops to oppose Grant?"; in August he warned Secretary of War James A. Seddon, "Without some increase of our strength, I cannot see how we are to escape the natural military consequences of the enemy's numerical superiority"; in September he promised Gen. Braxton Bragg, "I will hold my position as long as I can retain the men in it"; and in November he informed Davis, "I always find something to correct on the lines, but the great necessity I observed yesterday, was the want of men."[39] As most of his soldiers spent the winter watching and waiting for something to happen that would somehow end the war, Lee continued to caution the authorities. By early 1865 he wrote candidly, "you must not be surprised if calamity befalls us."[40] Furloughs, already curtailed in the Army of Northern Virginia in an attempt to keep its units intact, were most often limited to one for every one hundred soldiers present for duty or promised to men who brought a new recruit into the ranks. They were prohibited altogether to any point south or west of South Carolina in February 1865 and to any point beyond North Carolina by the end of that month. The risk was simply too great that men given an opportunity to see their "families and firesides" might never return.

Many units, facing such disastrous shortages in both officers and men, eventually reached a critical stage beyond which they simply could not function. This collapse was perhaps most ominous in the basic tactical units such as brigades and regiments, though countless companies and even a few whole divisions declined in much the same manner. These failures occurred most often and most alarmingly in combat, but indicators of a unit's potential breakdown were usually also present in the physical condition of its soldiers, their clothing, arms and equipment, and their camps. Though some of the better-led units subsequently regained at least some of their former effectiveness after such failures, others never recovered from them.[41] The eventual collapse of the army in 1865 was in many ways a direct result of the decline of its component units.

If the constant weight of physical and psychological stress endured by the officers and men in the Army of Northern Virginia during this period was a significant factor in the collapse of unit cohesion, it contributed even more directly to a steady deterioration in the morale of individual soldiers. Men who not only risked death, wounds, or capture on the battlefield but also faced persistent hunger and prolonged exposure to the elements without adequate clothing or shoes often wavered or broke under the constant strain. These burdens, singly or in combination, drove hundreds of weary soldiers to straggle, absent themselves without leave, or desert, either toward home or to the enemy. Their comrades frequently acknowledged that a Confederate's morale was often subject to his ability to survive the next fight relatively unscathed and the extent of the army's ability to feed, clothe, support, and protect him. One member of Lee's headquarters staff called the army's experience in its last year "the most wearysome, fatiguing & trying summer, autumn & winter that I expect men have ever been called on to endure."[42]

Countless Confederates, who seldom gave much thought to the old Union, the institution of slavery, the prospect of an independent Confederacy, or even battles being won and lost in Virginia or elsewhere, began to base their relationship to the army almost entirely on their physical wants and needs, and to abandon it when they believed that those wants and needs outweighed any other considerations.[43] Men willing, or at least able, to bear physical hardships were often much less disposed to accept what they considered shabby treatment from their military superiors and the civilian authorities. Many of them deeply resented being paid late if at all; chafed at waiting many months, often a year or longer, for a furlough; were offended by the proposal to create black Confederate companies and regiments; and questioned the plan to consolidate understrength units. While thousands of soldiers took such grievances to heart, hundreds—and eventually thousands—of others took them across the lines or home.[44] Whether men bore their misery in silence or voiced their disaffection in writing or conversation, the cumulative effect of life in the Confederate army operated impartially on veteran and conscript alike and prompted widespread despair throughout 1864 and into 1865.

For numerous members of the Army of Northern Virginia, however, there was no separating the various physical and psychological factors affecting their morale. A soldier's will to persevere was often determined as much by his response to events unfolding around him and at a distance as by his ability and willingness to withstand the adversity or frustration of army life. After the Crater, as it became increasingly evident that Lee and his men bore most of the burden for the waning Confederate cause, each successive disappointment in the East—from the frustrations of a prolonged siege on the Petersburg-Richmond front to embarrassing battlefield defeats in the Shenandoah Valley—only loomed larger and larger. Many members of Lee's army began to question the wisdom, or even the necessity, of continuing to oppose the vast Federal army facing them. "I am so low spirited about this war that I can't write a letter," Pvt. Abel Crawford of the 61st Alabama confessed to his wife at the end of an uncharacteristically short letter. "I am hardly able to write anything at all, therefore you *must* excuse me for not writing any more."[45] As one North Carolina veteran put it, "a good many say the Confederacy has 'gone up' (as they term it), and that we are whipped. I have never seen the men so discouraged before."[46]

While numerous Confederates expressed such fears in their letters and diaries, hundreds of others discussed them in conversations in camp or on the march. "Pore soldiers they want peace so bad," a conscript observed. "I herde two this morning talking that has ben in the war the most [of] the time since the beg[inn]ing and they sed they wod not go in a nother such a fite for all the nigros in the confederacy."[47] Still others kept to themselves, saying little or nothing about the war and its possible outcome. Many soldiers were simply weary of fighting Yankees. "None of our troops are in high spirits," Pvt. James B. Jones of the 1st Battalion North Carolina Sharpshooters wrote in early 1865, "& it is said that they do not fight with the same resolution as they did the first year of the war; having done so much of it that they now have a distaste to it."[48] It became increasingly difficult for Lee's soldiers—whatever their mode of expression—to endure personal sacrifices or accept enormous losses in Southern lives and property as the necessary price of Confederate independence when they had no confidence that they would ever see it achieved. One young Georgian spoke for many of his comrades when he admitted, "I Wish this War would come to a Close and I dont care how all I want is Peace."[49]

Though such views were more common in the army after mid-1864 than before, the same kinds of doubts had long been held, and often publicly expressed, by many of the folks at home. "The Civil War was not conducted in isolation from the societies that sent men, money, and supplies to wage it," Bill Cecil-Fronsman observes of the close relationship between home front and battlefield. "The values of the common whites, on whom Confederate hopes rested, would shape the conduct of the war."[50] As late as the summer of 1864, with Grant and Sherman seemingly bogged down in Virginia and Georgia, indications might have appeared to point toward the possibility of a military stalemate that could eventually force the war-weary Union to sue for peace on terms acceptable to the Confederacy. But by November, crushing battlefield defeats at Atlanta and in the Shenandoah Valley, further reinforced by Lincoln's reelection and the likelihood of another four years of war, then followed closely by Sherman's all-but-unopposed March to the Sea, hastened a further collapse of Southern morale. These last great blows to the collective will of the Confederate people gave an already-creeping hopelessness added momentum through the end of 1864 and into 1865 and made the end result inevitable. For many white Southerners, their fading hopes for good news clashed with and usually gave way to growing feelings of resignation. In February 1865, for example, as Sherman's Federals neared Columbia, South Carolina, Caroline Jones wrote her mother-in-law from Augusta, Georgia, exclaiming, "Oh, for a victory! But that seems to be a forgotten word with us."[51] There were still some newspaper editors, politicians, and citizens at home who bravely tried to make the best of things, but as Paul Escott points out, "mere words lacked the power to banish reality, and despondency spread throughout the Confederacy. . . . Thousands of private citizens in the South began to prepare themselves in their own ways for the end"—an end that would not be long in coming.[52]

Though this mood had certainly been accelerated by the avalanche of one battlefield defeat after another, it was nevertheless due almost as much to the isolation, economic hardship, and social dislocation of life behind the lines. "Behind the battle lines," Emory Thomas comments, "the Southern nation underwent a disintegration parallel to that taking place on its battlefields."[53] By 1865 that disintegration, in a society that was never as unified in support of the war as many had believed, had spared almost no county, parish, city, town, neighborhood, crossroads, plantation, or farmstead in the Confederacy. The gradual erosion and even collapse of the accepted standards of everyday life—of physical needs met, of personal relationships shared, of government's ability to protect persons and property—was to most white Southerners beyond even their wildest imaginings of what defeat might bring. The war had literally come home to them, and they were not prepared for the often brutal lessons it brought to their doorsteps. By this point the gloomy mood on the home front was beginning to have a disastrous effect on the already declining morale within the dwindling Confederate armies. Many at home made no secret of their feelings when they wrote to their family members and friends still in the field. "The armies had not yet surrendered," one recent study of Southern defeat notes, "but the people were beaten."[54]

Several recent Southern community studies, some of them focusing entirely or primarily on the war years and others covering periods before, during, and after the Confederate experience totaling as many as thirty or forty years, are valuable for their portrayals of specific families and communities in the midst of a war they no longer wanted.[55] Historians from Steven Hahn to Drew Gilpin Faust chronicle, often in some depth, the feelings of alienation, doubt, and hostility felt by many Southern civilians toward their state and central governments, the army, and the Confederate cause itself, in some cases from the start of the war and in countless more by the beginning of 1865. They agree that disaffected Southerners were naturally inclined to place their families' immediate needs above the rapidly dying dream of an independent Confederate nation. These scholars acknowledge that such sentiments were not only communicated to, but often shared by, the soldiers who represented their kin in the field and who would return to them at war's end whether in victory or defeat.[56] "Perhaps nothing struck the Confederacy as deep an internal wound, or provoked such social tension, or revealed as much about the values and priorities of the common people, as did developments on the home front," Hahn points out.[57]

Lee's soldiers, who were keenly sensitive to those developments, certainly recognized the close ties between morale at home and in the army. Many, perhaps most, Southerners who had volunteered in 1861 and later had gone to war on behalf of those people at home, for their "families and firesides," as they often phrased it when explaining what they were fighting for. They believed that they were defending their wives and children, their parents and siblings, and their neighbors and were protecting their houses, property, and communities from the Yankee invaders. Countless other Confederates, who were often reluctant conscripts rather than enthusiastic volunteers, still shared these sentiments. The South Carolina veterans of McGowan's Brigade expressed it as plainly as possible in early 1865, when they passed resolutions explaining, "nearly four years ago, we took up arms in defence of the right to govern ourselves, and to protect our country from invasion, our homes from desolation and our wives and children from insult and outrage."[58] Though few soldiers ever literally fought for their own families and firesides, they represented their hometowns, their counties, districts, or parishes, and their states in waging war against a common enemy and sometimes found it necessary to remind their fellow countrymen and women that they did so.[59] "We hereby say to our mothers, our wives and our sisters, cheer up, we fight for you," one Tar Heel regiment urged those at home, asking them for "your prayers, your letters, and your sweet messages."[60] Some Confederates needed no more motivation than that to keep fighting their enemies.

A soldier's reactions to the course of the war, furthermore, were often based on fears of the effect a particular campaign might have on his loved ones at home. Virginians, of course, were ubiquitous throughout the army, from the commanding general and many of his most prominent generals down to thousands of privates in the ranks, and had always been a predominant and defining element in shaping the army's unique character. Many men from the Old Dominion, much nearer their homes than their counterparts from other states, were torn between the temptation to leave the ranks to visit their families and the recognition that they were defending their native soil against an enemy that had helped transform Virginia into a vast battlefield. Other Confederates, whose more distant homes had felt little of the dangers and destruction of war before 1864 but whose families were now in the path of advancing Federal armies, were subjected to even greater fears and temptations than the Virginians. As Sherman's veterans made their frequently destructive way from Atlanta to Savannah, from Savannah to Columbia, and from Columbia to Raleigh between November 1864 and March 1865, most of the Georgians, South Carolinians, and North Carolinians who comprised a considerable percentage of the troops in the Army of Northern Virginia found it almost impossible to obtain leave or to get timely or accurate information from home. Still other Confederates, whose homes from Florida to Texas might have been less exposed to immediate harm in the last year of the war, fared no better and often fared far worse.

Those men who did hear from their kith and kin were more likely to get bad news than any other kind. Throughout the fall of 1864 and the winter of 1864–65 numerous members of Lee's army referred to "the people" in their letters and diaries. Staunch Confederates often blamed the "faint hearts" behind the lines for tolerating or encouraging the rampant defeatism spreading throughout Southern towns and communities and swaying the men still facing the enemy. Many civilians, terrified in a world that seemed to be disintegrating all around them, wrote emotional letters to their absent husbands, fathers, sons, brothers, and other relations. Confederates often read letters or newspaper stories repeating lurid accounts of Yankee "outrages" and of deserters, draft dodgers, and other "stay-at-homes" who avoided military service with apparent impunity. Though many soldiers were encouraged to remain at their posts, many others received pitiful pleas begging them to leave the army and tend to their families, homes, property, and communities. A headquarters clerk in the 53d Georgia described the effect of such letters in early 1865. "Friends write, imprudently they communicate their despondent feelings to friends in the army and you see the legitimate result—desertion," he wrote his sister. "People at home have done more harm by discouraging the army than they have any idea."[61]

Such heart-wrenching appeals, in which loved ones and friends sought both physical protection from the Yankees or the war's other hardships and psychological reassurance that things would be all right in the end, were often enough to make even the best of soldiers go home to stay. As Reid Mitchell states so succinctly, "Love of one's family and hatred of the invader could be a potent reason for Confederate service; it could also be the reason for desertion."[62] Mitchell elaborates on this point in an essay on "Domesticity and Confederate Defeat," part of the afterword to his study of Federal soldiers and their home communities. "After 1864," he comments, "some Confederates saw the war as likely to end in defeat; others saw it unlikely to end at all. Not surprisingly, more of them chose their duty to their families over their duty to the Confederacy, even over their duty to their fellow soldiers."[63] For many, it was an easy decision to make, a choice between a wretched existence in the army for no compelling reason and an uncertain future that at least represented a better chance for survival.

By the winter of 1864–65, as scores of miserable men crept away from the lines almost daily, desertion had all but destroyed the Confederate armies and made their final defeat a matter of time. Both the act itself and the stigma associated with the label of deserter had long ceased to mean as much as they once had, and the never-clear distinction between soldiers who were absent without leave and those who had truly deserted their commands had been almost completely lost as well. The Army of Northern Virginia was no exception. "The morale of this army is not so good as it was last fall," one lieutenant colonel commented in a masterpiece of understatement in early 1865, while a private wrote more frankly of Confederates "runing a way and deserting every day and night our army are be coming wearker and weaker."[64] Though many soldiers and civilians of the day and numerous historians since have portrayed most deserters either as unwilling conscripts snared by the draft after the war was virtually lost or as men who left the ranks because they feared combat, conscripts and cowards were not numerous enough to account for all, or even most, men who deserted from the Confederate armies during the critical months from November 1864 to the end. For every observer who wrote scornfully of those "ready to bring eternal disgrace on themselves & country by their ignominious conduct," there was another who wrote regretfully that "to hear so frequently of the desertion of men who have been among the best soldiers serves to unnerve me."[65] General Lee himself confessed, "I do not know what can be done to put a stop to it."[66]

Though it is not possible—or even desirable—to rank the many factors contributing to the last great wave of desertion in the Army of Northern Virginia, it may be worthwhile to note the major reasons advanced at the time by officers and men who sought to explain the behavior of their wayward comrades. Evidence from Lee's frequent correspondence with the Confederate authorities, from reports by unit commanders to superiors or army headquarters, and from inspection reports emphasizes an administrative interpretation of desertion. Combat and staff officers at levels from corps to regiments or battalions seemed reluctant to acknowledge the role of war weariness and other psychological factors in prompting men to leave the army. They reported that many soldiers deserted because they could not or would not accept chronic shortages in food, clothing, shoes, shelter, or other necessities, and that many others did so because they believed that the government and the army had not honored promises made to them concerning pay or furloughs. These observers viewed the tangible causes of desertion as simple physical hardships that might conceivably be eliminated or at least alleviated by commissaries, quartermasters, and other support services of the army. In the winter of 1864 Capt. James Walker, inspector general of a Georgia brigade in the First Corps, asserted that "nothing has a greater tendency to create discontent and dissatisfaction than the want of the usual quantity of nourishment."[67] Lee, reporting to Richmond on the likely causes of desertion in early 1865, offered his opinion that "the insufficiency of food and non-payment of the troops have more to do with the dissatisfaction among the troops than anything else. All commanding officers concur in this opinion."[68]

The personal correspondence of officers down to company level and of vast numbers of enlisted men, on the other hand, provides a more humanistic interpretation of desertion. Correspondents more readily admitted the influence of doubt and despair in an individual's decision to abandon the army. According to them, many soldiers deserted because they believed that the war was already lost or that their families needed them more than the Confederacy did. Many correspondents and diarists viewed the intangible causes of desertion as complex trials of the spirit that could only be confronted—if at all—by renewed determination on the part of soldiers and civilians alike. "Our Army generally is in the lowest spirits I have ever seen it since the commencement of the war," Sgt. R. P. Scarbrough of Hurt's Battery commented on the last day of January 1865.

"The facilities of the Yankees for carry[ing] on the war is so much better than ours that I cannot for my life see how we can hold out with them much Longer. They already have an army mch Larger than ours . . . while our army is decresing faster than we can recruit in spite of all we can do."[69]

By early 1865 many officers now openly discussed motives for desertion that previously they had acknowledged only in private conversation or to themselves. One brigade inspector reported that during February thirty-one Virginians in Pegram's Brigade deserted toward homes or to the enemy; he speculated that the two leading causes of desertion were "first: tired of fighting—2nd: discouragement at the situation of our affairs." Capt. R. N. Wilson observed, "I know of no remedy for the desertions in this Brigade—I believe that the success of our arms would stop it."[70] Lee, writing about the same time, expressed his opinion that the four hundred soldiers who deserted from his army in a two-week period had been "influenced very much by the representations of their friends at home, who appear to have become very despondent as to our success." He admitted, referring not only to this evidence of declining morale throughout the Confederacy but also to the act of desertion itself, "I do not know what can be done to prevent this evil."[71]

Soldiers often wrote candidly to their families or friends about discouraged Confederates who threatened to desert, many of whom made those threats good during the winter of 1864–65. "A great many of them swears that they cant stand it, they will run away before they will stand it," commented William Horace Phillips of the 14th Virginia.[72] Other soldiers wrote of their own plans to abandon the army as soon as they had the opportunity or by the time the campaigns of 1865 opened, if not before. John J. Armfield of the 30th North Carolina, who had tried for weeks to get a furlough, was torn between a desperate desire to make his way home and a gnawing fear that he might not succeed in the attempt. In January Armfield wrote bravely, "I intend to make the effort and take the consequences," but in March he admitted, "I have been disappointed so many times it has made a coward of me and I am afraid to do anything but I feel like the time is fast approaching when I must act in a decisive way."[73] Armfield, a recent conscript, never made it back to his wife in Brunswick County. He was captured at Farmville only three days before the surrender and died in a prison camp at Point Lookout, Maryland, in June, nearly two months after Appomattox.[74] Armfield's poignant letters convey the complex emotions shared by thousands of otherwise silent Confederates, many of whom gave in to despair and left the Army of Northern Virginia in the last months of the war.

Soldiers who deserted after mid-1864 often did so because they believed that it was the only way they could escape the risks and responsibilities of soldier life, because they saw that desertion was tolerated both along the lines and on the home front, and perhaps most of all because they doubted that any military or civilian power could or would punish them for leaving a forlorn hope. The amnesty proposed by Lee and approved by Davis in early 1865, offering deserters and other absentees a final opportunity to rejoin their commands within twenty days without being punished, brought in a few soldiers but was generally ignored. Though the proclamation warned that there would be no more amnesties or pardons for those convicted of desertion or absence without leave, some Confederates took it as an excuse to leave the army for a time before returning while others considered it proof that nothing would be done to them even if they were caught. The comments of Lt. John B. Evans of the 53d Georgia, in an early 1865 letter home regarding a recent deserter in his company, suggest the depth and breadth of the phenomena throughout the Confederate armies. "When Rich Thaxton comes back here if he ever dos," Evans wrote his wife Mollie, "he will be apt to be punished for he has run away so many times that it will go pretty hard with him."[75] For every soldier who believed that deserters should be tried by courts-martial and shot or hanged if convicted—and there is evidence that executions for desertion were carried out as late as the day before Petersburg and Richmond were evacuated—there were dozens who sympathized with deserters and their desire to escape the army. By March, at least one company officer was ordered to go on picket duty with a musket and ten cartridges and to be prepared to shoot deserters himself because his men would not. "The men seem to think desertion no crime & hence never shoot a deserter when he goes over," explained 2d Lt. Luther Rice Mills of the 26th Virginia. "They always shoot but never hit."[76] When desertion was widely condoned and even encouraged, potential deserters gave little or no thought to picket guards, the guardhouse, or a court-martial, or even to the threat of death by a firing squad or the gallows.

Some men who deserted from the Army of Northern Virginia in early 1865 made their decision to do so because they objected to bold plans, or rumors of such plans, being made to change the character of the army. As the enlistment of black Confederates was first proposed, then debated at length, and finally implemented, discontented soldiers who might have otherwise remained left the army in protest. A private in the 44th North Carolina wrote his parents, "I suppose that they are going to put in the negroes in the army I think that will not do for the White Soldiers they say that they wont stay here"; a captain in the 59th Alabama who deserted to the Federals also reported that "the soldiers will not stand the enlistment of colored troops."[77] Many of Lee's soldiers agreed with the North Carolinian who commented, "Mother I did not volunteer my services to fight for A free negroes free country but to fight for A free white mans free country & I do not think I love my country well enough to fight with black soldiers."[78]

Meanwhile, persistent rumors circulated through the ranks that Lee was going to leave the Army of Northern Virginia in order to concentrate on his position as general in chief or to take command of the beleaguered Army of Tennessee, and that Joe Johnston was returning to command the army he had left in the spring of 1862. Numerous Confederates from enlisted men to officers believed that such a step was at least possible, and some did not think they loved their country well enough to fight for any general but "Marse Robert." A few of them went so far as to desert on the strength of such rumors. Pvt. John A. Johnson, of the 7th Tennessee, who left the lines near Petersburg in late January and made his way to the Shenandoah Valley, told the Federals who interviewed him, "The report that Lee is to leave the army causes great discontent. The men say they never will fight under any other commander."[79] Some men, looking skeptically toward a future in which the Army of Northern Virginia might have black soldiers and a new commander, decided that such an army was too revolutionary for them.

Whereas there is no doubt that desertion was a decisive factor in the collapse of the Confederate armies, there is somewhat less agreement on its deeper meaning among those historians who have sought to enumerate and explain its causes, from Civil War historians to scholars focusing on the impact of the war on Southern communities.[80] Earlier studies are generally more critical of desertion than recent studies but are also more critical of desertion as a widespread problem than they are of deserters as individuals. "It is one thing to catalog the hardships that burdened the army as a whole," Richard Bardolph remarks, "but it is quite another thing to pass judgment upon a particular soldier whose resolution broke under the strain."[81] Though such historians express regret or even condemnation at the waves of desertion that doomed the Confederate armies, they almost as often express sympathy and understanding for the plight of deserters as men stretched beyond their limits. "Desertion from the Southern armies rose disastrously with the mounting fury of the war," Charles Roland observes in a typical example. "Cowards fled from the constant prospect of death, and the weak broke under the indescribable hardships and privations of the field."[82] Douglas Southall Freeman, referring specifically to desertion in the Army of Northern Virginia during the winter of 1864–65, calls it a "sickening and bewildering" spectacle but characterizes the deserters themselves as "weak, hungry and half-frozen" soldiers.[83]

Other scholars, though as reluctant to condemn individual soldiers, have advanced the view that because Confederate desertion undoubtedly hastened the end of the war, it should be considered in the final analysis a positive rather than a negative phenomenon.[84] "Since the South could not achieve nationhood without an army," Paul D. Escott notes in his study of the failure of Confederate nationalism, "the decision which common soldiers made with their feet sealed the fate of the Confederacy."[85] Reid Mitchell observes, even more pointedly: "The men who answered their wives' calls and went home were hardly cowards, nor were the realists who saw the handwriting on the wall. Their good sense took away from Jefferson Davis and Robert E. Lee the means of prosecuting the war."[86]

Even in late 1864 and early 1865, however, all was not despair, defeat, disaffection, and desertion in the camps of Lee's army, for there were still stalwart Confederates, more optimistic than most, who believed that the cause was not yet lost if the Southern people would only support the armies in the field. Douglas Southall Freeman writes, "If hundreds deserted, there were thousands who had resolved that neither hunger nor cold, neither danger nor the bad example of feebler spirits could induce them to leave 'Marse Robert.'"[87] Officers and men of the 31st Virginia passed a resolution referring to "our week-kneed, desponding brethren, both citizens and soldiers, (if there are any such soldiers,)" and admonished them to "'be of good cheer'; do but half your duty to your God, your country and yourselves, and all will be well."[88] Numerous soldiers writing home to their families and friends or in their diaries expressed themselves in much the same terms, some conceding sympathy for those behind the lines and others scolding them for losing hope. "I understand the people are allmost whipped at home am sorry to hear it," a South Carolina adjutant wrote his sister in January, in a typical letter. "Shall we submit quietly, and go back into the union & be ruled by Abraham or shall we fight it out[?] The people must make up their mind to do one or the other. . . . We are a ruined people if we give up. There is a chance if we all do our duty."[89]

Though sympathetic to the undeniable sacrifices made and apprehensions felt by their families and friends at home, many soldiers believed that their own sacrifices were far greater than those of the civilian population and feared that if the people gave up, then they were risking everything in vain, and their dead, wounded, and imprisoned comrades had suffered for nothing. "They particularly felt it unfair," Robert Kenzer observes, "that civilians, who were far from the front and ignorant of military matters, should decide whether the war continued."[90] Men who had shared and endured so much together in the Army of Northern Virginia often experienced a disturbing sense of alienation from the people whom they were presumably fighting for. One North Carolinian, a conscript who had been in the ranks for only a few months, wrote his family that the veterans in his regiment who had gone home for furloughs in the winter of 1864–65 had "becum like town folk they ar not satisfide unless they ar in the armey to gether or a grate meney of them they say when they go home they is no boddy thear and they feal so lonsom they want [to go] back."[91] Such feelings, often difficult for soldiers to express and even harder for them to fully understand, made some Confederates more determined than ever. As Reid Mitchell points out, "The military experience created loyalty in the soldier to those who suffered by his side, whether officers or common soldiers, and a corresponding distance from those civilians who stayed at home."[92]

Pvt. John A. Everett of the 11th Georgia, a veteran of almost four years' service who had "seen the elephant" at First Manassas soon after he enlisted, was one of those staunch Confederates who displayed and expressed a fierce loyalty to his comrades, both living and dead. Everett had ample reason to feel that he and his family had done their fair share for the cause, for though his father J. H. and brother T. H. had also joined the "Houston Volunteers" that first summer of the war, he was the only one of the three still in the ranks at the beginning of 1865. His father had died of disease in Richmond in December 1861, and his brother had been captured in the Wilderness. Everett himself had been wounded several times. His mother Patience, at home in Haynesville, Georgia, with two small children, wrote him complaining that he and his fellow Georgians should not be defending Virginia soil when "the yanks was all over Ga." John answered, "it is not Right for the Ga. Soldiers to Stay hear but we cant Help our Selves if every man would Stick together and go Home in thair one State and fight we could all Stay thair but men cant Stay at Home." Patience Everett had gone so far as to advise her son to leave the ranks and make his way back to Houston County but now read his indignant reply:

you stated in youre letter that you was now willing for me to Desert and go home you ought not to write any Such thing as that Supose all the Pepel at Home were to write to thair Sons in the army to Desert and go Home and they did so what would be the circumstances[?] why they could not feel like they had done thair Deuty as Soldiers after fighting 4 years then Desert it is more than I can bear on my Sholders. If Peace was made in Six months after I did so . . . why I would feel worse than a Sheep Killing Dog after I have Stade in this war 4 years and have bin in So many fights.

Everett cautioned his anxious mother, "Now let me beg [you] to write no more Such nuse," then reassured her, "I am all ways glad to hear from you But dont write any more Such letters as it was for I tell you in Plain talk that I never will Desert." When Everett hastened to add that he was staying in the army "not because I love to fight so well for I do Hate that Part of a Soldiers Buisness," his mother probably wondered why anyone would want to remain true to a cause that had already cost her a husband and perhaps another son as well.[93]

In two subsequent letters Everett emphasized his determination to do his duty. In mid-February he declared, "we have got to whip the Yanks or Submit to them and I had Rather be a Gard Dog in Some Good mans yard than to be a Rebel and Submit to the Yanks." A month later he wrote hopefully, "If I am Spaird to Survive this cruel war I expect to be in the Eleventh Ga. Regt. untill it is disbanded then I can face any man and Say to him that I did my Deuty while in the Noble Armey of Northern Va."[94] Larry Logue's recent study of Civil War soldiers analyzes the view of Everett and men like him who remained in the army. "Deserting a doomed cause was one thing," Logue observes, "but abandoning comrades, the only people who truly understood what soldiers had endured, was unthinkable. And so men made agonizing choices between conflicting ways of surviving, conflicting duties, and conflicting loyalties."[95]

Statements such as John Everett's have led many historians to conclude that until the very end there were probably more soldiers willing to persevere on behalf of the Confederacy than there were civilians. "It was the home front that gave way first," one study concludes, "and many brave soldiers sensed it."[96] Some scholars praise stalwarts who "still believed they could win where they did not face impossible odds," who fought "with valor steadfast to the last," or "still distinguished themselves during that final season of combat."[97] Bell Wiley calls these men "gray-clad heroes who remained firm amid a sea of defection."[98] Other historians, though agreeing that such Confederates existed in the last few months and weeks of the war, view them, and their complex motives for staying in the army, quite differently. Reid Mitchell makes an often-overlooked point when he observes: "If Lee's army was pitifully small when he surrendered to Grant, it was still bigger than the Confederate government had any right to expect. The Confederate soldier endured the crisis of the Old South with more loyalty than the Confederacy deserved."[99] Charles Royster sees the major difference between those men who remained in the army to the end and those who did not in terms of the former's determination to continue fighting the enemy no matter what happened. "Both groups could see Confederate defeat coming," he explains. "One resolved to fight it out, while the other went home or to the enemy. If the nation inhered in the army, it did so primarily as a desperate hope." Royster also argues that in the end "fighting Yankees, though it was a prerequisite for Confederate nationhood, could not alone define or create nationality. The South could not vindicate with its armies' combat a belief in the nation's future it could not sustain among civilians or soldiers. . . . The Confederate army outlived the purpose for which it had been created."[100] It outlived most dreams of an independent Southern nation because many soldiers in 1864 and 1865 believed in and fought for their communities or comrades more than they did their country or cause.

Any assessment of the Army of Northern Virginia in the last year of the war must consider the ways in which Confederate perceptions of the siege on the Petersburg-Richmond front shaped both Lee's generalship and the performance of the army itself. "We must destroy this army of Grant's before he gets to James River," Lee told Jubal Early in June 1864, just before the siege of Petersburg began. "If he gets there, it will become a siege, and then it will be a mere question of time."[101] About the same time, and in remarkably similar language, he wrote to another corps commander: "We shall be obliged to go out and prevent the enemy from selecting such positions as he chooses. If he is allowed to continue that course we shall be at last obliged to take refuge behind the works of Richmond and stand a siege, which would be but a work of time."[102] Lee's soldiers often made similar comments about the siege and about their chances of success against the Federals facing them. "I see nothing but lying here in the trenches & terrible fighting in the end," a Georgia captain predicted early that summer, and by fall a North Carolina private wrote, "This is certainly the most cruel war that has ever been waged & instead of getting better it gets worse every day it lasts."[103] Several uneasy Confederates marveled at Grant's perseverance and feared that the weight of Federal numbers would ultimately prove to be the deciding factor as long as Lee was tied to a defensive position. "There has been many lives lost in the Battles around Petersburg which seems to have resulted in but little good to us, as Grants position today is such as to trouble us more than at any former time," one veteran commented, "and I am one of the few who believe that Grant will finally if sustained by the Administration at Washington take Richmond and Petersburg."[104]

Some members of the Army of Northern Virginia were convinced that the campaign would not end—indeed, *could* not end—without a conventional battle to decide the fate of the opposing armies and the cities they sought to capture or defend. "Skirmishing, sharpshooting and cannonading have been constant but that cannot be called a fight," Capt. Francis Marion Coker of Cutts's Battalion insisted soon after the siege of Petersburg began.[105] After several more weeks passed without a major battle, Ordnance Sgt. James W. Albright of the 12th Battalion Virginia Light Artillery reported in his diary, "A great fight is hourly anticipated. I believe, it will be a decisive one—perhaps *the* battle of the war."[106] Numerous jaded Confederates saw little or no good being accomplished by sitting day after day in their earthworks watching an enemy only yards away who seemed content to do the same.

Students of the Eastern theater often cite such observations to support the generally accepted view of the siege—that Lee recognized the damage that a prolonged and largely static campaign would wreak upon his army's combat effectiveness, physical condition, and morale; that he recognized the effect that such a siege would have on the Confederacy's chances for ultimate victory; and that he believed the end result would be disastrous for both.[107] Douglas Southall Freeman's influential *Lee's Lieutenants* describes the army as "chained down and unable to employ the offensive strategy that had won it many battles," and Richard Sommers argues that "the very loss of strategic mobility resulting from being pinned in place was itself a major contributing factor to the decline of the Army of Northern Virginia."[108] This standard interpretation of the campaign paints a familiar portrait of both the army and its commander, one that depicts Lee's army wasting away in the Petersburg-Richmond trenches between mid-June 1864 and the end of March 1865, losing not only its strength but its hope as well. Such a view also features an aggressive Lee, frustrated because he had to defend an essentially fixed position rather than operating freely as he had done in 1862, 1863, and the first half of 1864, anxious instead to force Grant to fight him in a large-scale Napoleonic battle of maneuver that might prove to be decisive. This analysis, which has considerable merit, leaves little doubt that, as J. F. C. Fuller writes, "From the date Grant began to lay siege to Petersburg, the end of the Confederacy, like a gathering storm cloud, loomed over the horizon of the war, daily growing greater and more leaden."[109]

A simple either/or interpretation of the situation facing the Army of Northern Virginia after mid-1864, however, is so overshadowed by the fact of Confederate defeat that it may ultimately owe as much to the hindsight of historians as it does to the foresight of Robert E. Lee or the realities of the war in the Eastern theater. Another, equally plausible view, one also supported by Lee's own words and by his reactions to the siege, has recently been addressed by several historians seeking to evaluate the campaign from Petersburg to Appomattox.[110] In March 1865, a month to the day before he surrendered to Grant, Lee wrote a confidential letter to Secretary of War John C. Breckinridge that spoke volumes. "While the military situation is not favorable," he candidly admitted, "it is not worse than the superior numbers and resources of the enemy justified us in expecting from the beginning. Indeed, the legitimate military consequences of that superiority have been postponed longer than we had reason to anticipate."[111]

Though Lee certainly grasped the implications of a long siege, he also knew—even if he did not often publicly or privately acknowledge it—that the same field fortifications that he resented as an obstacle to his preferred method of waging war were also a formidable obstacle to an enemy hoping to destroy his army.[112] More and more of his soldiers, meanwhile, came to appreciate the impact of those lines on the course of the war. "Our men have never known the value of intrenchments," one staff officer observed early in the siege, "until the commencement of the present campaign."[113] Lt. James M. Simpson, of the 13th Alabama, who characterized life in the trenches as "very disagreeable," still concluded that "these things are bearable if we can only keep Grant and his Vandals from taking their long sought prize and there is no doubt in the world that we [can] hold it as long as he can keep his army together."[114] Capt. William Aiken Kelly of the 1st South Carolina, recalling Grant's promise to Washington that he would "fight it out on this line if it takes all summer," wrote in his diary at the end of August that the Federals were "doomed to disappointment, for the brave & determined hearts & strong arms of Rebels stood in their way, & with such leaders as Lee & Beauregard, the minions under Grant could accomplish nothing."[115] Many of Lee's officers and men believed that every day the Yankees sat across from them looking longingly toward Petersburg and Richmond was another day closer to the time when Grant, Lincoln, and the Northern people would decide that they could not take those cities and could not win the war.

An alternative, more balanced, and more nuanced assessment of the campaign refines the standard view by pointing out ways by which a stalemate benefited Lee, his army, and the Confederate war effort. In his history of the Confederacy, Emory Thomas sides with those scholars who see the siege as an insurmountable obstacle to Lee and his soldiers, calling Richmond—and, by extension, Petersburg as well—"a military millstone around Lee's neck. . . . every day the Confederates remained in their trenches, they were accepting a war of attrition—and such a war they could not hope to win."[116] Thomas's recent biography of Lee, in striking contrast, recognizes the indisputable challenges of the 1864–65 campaign but points out that the siege prolonged the life of the Army of Northern Virginia—and of the Confederacy—beyond reasonable expectations. "He had to keep his men in the trenches in order to protect his army, his government, and his country," Thomas concedes, then asserts: "the Army of Northern Virginia depended upon its trenches to compensate for its inferiority in men and material vis-à-vis the Army of the Potomac. . . . Trenches precluded maneuver and compelled Lee to fight a war of attrition. But those same trenches kept Lee's army alive and intact against overwhelming odds. . . . Lee was holding a wolf by the ears."[117] According to James McPherson, the siege was a campaign of attrition "by Lee's choice, not Grant's. The Union commander's purpose was to maneuver Lee into an open field for a showdown; Lee's purpose was to prevent this by entrenching an impenetrable line to protect Richmond and his communications. Lee was hoping to hold out long enough and inflict sufficient casualties on attacking Union forces to discourage the people of the North and overturn the Lincoln administration in the 1864 election."[118] However, events elsewhere that summer and fall—at Atlanta and in the Shenandoah Valley—held far greater importance for the election and the Confederate cause than those on the Petersburg-Richmond front.

Perhaps the best argument to support the view of the siege as extending rather than shortening the life of the Army of Northern Virginia comes from the performance of a significant element of the army in the Shenandoah Valley. When Jubal Early's little Army of the Valley—which had as its nucleus the old Second Corps, including many of Lee's best officers and men—attempted to push the Federals out of the Shenandoah, it employed the familiar Napoleonic methods of maneuver and combat favored by most Civil War generals. For almost five months Early's Confederates, operating not only in the Shenandoah Valley but also as far north as the very outskirts of Washington, commanded the attention of an enemy that usually outnumbered them by almost three to one. But ultimately they were soundly beaten by Sheridan in successive engagements at Winchester, Fisher's Hill, and Cedar Creek. Questions of generalship aside, there is ample evidence that these veterans, both officers and men, were being asked to do the impossible. Many units, understrength and without experienced commanders, worn down by the physical demands of marching and countermarching up and down the valley without adequate rations, clothing, or shoes, and with little confidence in their commanding general or themselves, broke under the strain, whether by degrees over time or all at once in panic on the battlefield. Meanwhile, the Army of Northern Virginia faced many of the same disadvantages as the Army of the Valley but managed to hold onto the Petersburg-Richmond front without fighting that one climactic battle, a battle that would not come until Grant broke through its lines just before the end. Perhaps it was just as well, for Lee's troops were in no condition to make the kind of sweeping maneuvers and slashing attacks that had made them the Confederacy's most successful soldiers. By the second half of 1864 the result of such an attempt, even one led by "Marse Robert" himself, would very likely have been something more like Cedar Creek than Chancellorsville.

The immediate crisis that doomed the army in the first week of April 1865 was the evacuation of Petersburg and Richmond. This forced Lee to stake everything on reaching Gen. Joseph E. Johnston and the remnants of the Army of Tennessee more than a hundred miles away in North Carolina. The evacuation was caused more than anything else by the army's inability to hold the miles and miles of lines defending the two cities, a predicament due primarily to the daily desertion of Confederates either toward their homes or to the enemy in the first three months of the year. When Grant's Federals broke through the thin Confederate lines in several places on 2 April, Lee patched together a defensive perimeter that held just long enough to cover his retreat that night. Noah Andre Trudeau, in a recent essay on Lee's generalship from the Wilderness to Appomattox, observes that "it was not an insubstantial force that left the Richmond-Petersburg trenches on 2 April. . . . What failed was the structure of command within this mass of men. While some units preserved discipline and morale, many others trudged along more by instinct than conviction."[119] Some units barely existed at all, and many individual soldiers who were unable or unwilling to carry on for more than a few hours or a few miles simply stopped trying. Edward A. Pollard, the irascible wartime editor of the *Richmond Examiner*, aptly summed up the retreat from Petersburg and Richmond with the observation that "Lee's whole army had almost ran through his fingers" before he reached Appomattox.[120] Though there were still those who persevered, from officers grimly commanding skeleton units to men wearily putting one foot in front of the other, the army was doomed and most of its soldiers knew it.

Mr. James E. Whitehorne—Sergeant Whitehorne no longer—wasted no time leaving Appomattox Court House behind the day after the surrender ceremony, walking home to Greensville County, Virginia, with a few members of his now-disbanded company. "It is needless to say I rose at break of day and started for home," he began his diary entry for 13 April.[121] The veterans managed to travel several miles each day, camping along the road or stopping at houses along the way. They found a mule and a lame horse, foraged cornmeal and persuaded local citizens to bake bread for them, and bought or begged such delectables as ham and buttermilk. Whitehorne kept his diary faithfully, describing each day's travels and meals and sometimes adding a few lines referring to the end of the war and the uncertain future ahead. "The sun rose beautifully and we rose with it in the highest spirits of a week," he noted on 16 April. "Expect to reach home today. . . . Just one week today since the tragedy at Appomattox. The memory hurts like an open wound."

One by one the group parted company as each man neared his home, and soon Whitehorne and Sidney Bass were the only ones left. After Bass, who had been a private in Whitehorne's old Company F, parted with him just three miles from "Pleasant Shade," Whitehorne worried about his appearance when he finally reached his parents' house. "Lord! I wish I was wearing shoes and my pants held together better," he wrote, then added when he first caught sight of the farm, "Well, I never expected to see these familiar lanes again. There's the house."[122]

When Whitehorne had started his little diary on 30 March, he had written, "I had just as well set everything down as it is, be it for or against us."[123] The final entry, composed soon after his return home, is striking for what it reveals about his character and, by extension, the character of many officers and men who had belonged to Lee's army. The transition from soldier to civilian would be a difficult but by no means impossible one for most men who had marched and fought under "Marse Robert," and James Whitehorne was no exception:

> April 22nd—Saturday
> Back home and pleased to be with all my folks. Haven't written anything for a week as there seems to be nothing doing worth writing. Plenty work to make a crop before we all starve to death. Lord! Food is

almost as scarce here as it was in the army. Bass just rode by on his way back from town. Said a Yankee by name of Simeon Parsons of Boston had come to town and was going to open a store. The Masonic Lodge will be reorganized and start meetings soon. All the church bells were melted down for cannons, but the preachers are back from the army and services as usual tomorrow. Bass also said the boys were going to get together tonight and form a Confederate Veterans Organization. My ears keep straining for big guns to open up suddenly, but it seems I'm a veteran and . . . . suppose I'll attend the meeting. I wish General Lee (may heaven bless him forever) had ordered our (Mahone's) brigade to bust through the invaders back in Appomattox. So endeth this scribbling.[124]

And so life in the army gave way to life among one's family and friends once again. Whitehorne's determination to go on, particularly when set in the context of a war whose final year surpassed anything imaginable in 1861, is remarkable but not unique. Countless men who had endured the confusion of the Wilderness, the horrors and numbing fatigue of Spotsylvania, the tedium of the trenches at Petersburg, the ferocity of the Crater, the alternating exhilaration and despair of the Shenandoah Valley campaign, and the grim retreat toward Appomattox returned home and went immediately back to work, just as the twenty-five-year-old Whitehorne did. Though all too many of Lee's troops never had the opportunity to rebuild their lives and to contribute to a new, postwar society, the vast majority of those who did survive neither dwelt on the war nor forgot the sacrifices they and their comrades made during it. Those who persevered from the Wilderness to Appomattox and called themselves "Lee's Miserables" set a standard that is a fitting testament to the resiliency of the human spirit, that quality that above all others made the Army of Northern Virginia such a cohesive community of men and such a formidable body of soldiers.

Notes

ABBREVIATIONS

AAP   Auburn University, Auburn, Ala.

A-Ar   Alabama Department of Archives and History, Montgomery

A&IGO   Adjutant and Inspector General's Office, Confederate States Army

ANV   Army of Northern Virginia

F   Florida State Archives, Tallahassee

G-Ar   Georgia Department of Archives and History, Atlanta

GEU   Emory University, Atlanta, Ga.

GHi   Georgia Historical Society, Savannah

GO   General Orders

GU   University of Georgia, Athens

HQ   Headquarters

LC   Library of Congress, Washington, D.C.

LHA   Louisiana Historical Association

LNT   Tulane University, New Orleans, La.

Ms-Ar   Mississippi Department of Archives and History, Jackson

NA   National Archives, Washington, D.C.

Nc-Ar   North Carolina Division of Archives and History, Raleigh

NcD   Duke University, Durham, N.C.

NcGG   Friends Historical Collection, Guilford College, Greensboro, N.C.

NcU   Southern Historical Collection, University of North Carolina, Chapel Hill

OR   U.S. War Department, *The War of the Rebellion: A Compilation of the Official Records of the Union and Confederate Armies*. 128 vols. Washington: Government Printing Office, 1880–1901. *OR* citations take the following form: volume number (part number, where applicable): page number(s). Unless otherwise noted, all citations are to series 1.

PNB   Petersburg National Battlefield, Petersburg, Va.

RNBP   Richmond National Battlefield Park, Richmond, Va.

ScC   Charleston Library Society, Charleston, S.C.

ScCC   College of Charleston, Charleston, S.C.

ScCoAH   South Carolina Department of Archives and History, Columbia

ScHi   South Carolina Historical Society, Charleston

ScU   South Caroliniana Library, University of South Carolina, Columbia

SO   Special Orders

T   Tennessee State Library and Archives, Nashville

TxHiC   Confederate Research Center, Hill Junior College, Hillsboro, Tex.

TxU   University of Texas, Austin

UDC	United Daughters of the Confederacy
Vi	Library of Virginia, Richmond
ViHi	Virginia Historical Society, Richmond
ViRC	Museum of the Confederacy, Richmond, Va.
ViU	University of Virginia, Charlottesville
V-vol	Virginia Typescript/Photocopy Volumes, Fredericksburg-Spotsylvania National Military Park, Fredericksburg, Va.

PREFACE

1. *Richmond Whig,* 19 May 1864.

2. McMurry, *Two Great Rebel Armies,* 2.

3. Freeman, *R. E. Lee* and *Lee's Lieutenants.* "For any book on the Army of Northern Virginia," Clifford Dowdey wrote in 1960, "the work of the late Douglas Southall Freeman is the alphabet and the grammar." Dowdey, *Lee's Last Campaign,* 387. Freeman's focus in these two studies, of course, was on Lee and on his subordinate commanders respectively, not on the field, staff, and company officers or the enlisted men. Though *Lee's Lieutenants* is perhaps the most read and most influential work ever written on the Army of Northern Virginia, it is, as its subtitle states, *A Study in Command,* and not a history of the army per se. In his foreword (1:xvii), Freeman himself pointed out that he considered *Lee's Lieutenants* "a review of the command of the Army of Northern Virginia, rather than a history of the Army itself."

4. Donald, *Lincoln Reconsidered,* 82; Dowdey, *Lee's Last Campaign,* 379.

5. See also Wiley's *Plain People of the Confederacy* and *The Road to Appomattox.*

6. For examples before 1985, see Donald, "The Confederate as a Fighting Man"; Maslowski, "A Study of Morale"; and Barton, *Goodmen.*

7. Marvin R. Cain's "A 'Face of Battle' Needed" helped usher in a period—beginning in the mid-1980s and showing no signs of slowing down in the late 1990s—during which many significant studies of Civil War soldiers have appeared and have often been cited as examples of what is sometimes known as "the new military history." See Glatthaar, *March to the Sea;* Linderman, *Embattled Courage;* Mitchell, *Civil War Soldiers;* James I. Robertson Jr., *Soldiers Blue and Gray;* Jimerson, *The Private Civil War,* which also includes ample evidence from civilians; Hess, *Liberty, Virtue, and Progress;* Glatthaar, *Forged in Battle;* Daniel, *Soldiering in the Army of Tennessee;* Mitchell, *The Vacant Chair;* McPherson, *What They Fought For* and *For Cause and Comrades;* Logue, *To Appomattox and Beyond;* and Hess, *The Union Soldier in Battle.*

8. Hess, review of Rosenblatt and Rosenblatt, *Hard Marching Every Day,* and of Sutherland, *Reminiscences of a Private.*

9. Wiley, "Historians and the National Register," 326–27.

10. Gallagher, "Home Front and Battlefield," 161. This essay includes a valuable evaluation of the most significant scholarship on the Army of Northern Virginia in the 1980s. A simple list of the recent and forthcoming books detailing

the army's battles or campaigns, not to mention the recent and forthcoming biographies of the army's personalities, would run to several pages. See also Glatthaar's excellent " 'New' Civil War History," which is a more comprehensive assessment of the Civil War scholarship of the 1970s and 1980s, and Sutherland's "Getting the 'Real War' into the Books." Reviews published since 1990 in *Civil War History*, the *Journal of Southern History*, the *Journal of American History*, the *American Historical Review*, *Reviews in American History*, the *New York Times Book Review*, the *New York Review of Books*, and various state historical journals attest even more dramatically to the continuing vitality of and considerable readership for Civil War history. Two recent collections of essays that include insightful observations on the current state of Civil War historiography are McPherson's *Drawn with the Sword* and Castel's *Winning and Losing*.

11. Gallagher, "Home Front and Battlefield," 161.

12. Gary W. Gallagher, " 'Upon Their Success Hang Momentous Interests': Generals," in *Why the Confederacy Lost*, ed. Boritt, 94; his "Another Look at the Generalship of R. E. Lee," a revised and somewhat expanded version of this essay focusing solely on Lee, appears in Gallagher, *Lee The Soldier*, 275–89.

13. Several recent works, some of them controversial, debate the causes for Confederate defeat—or Union victory. Primarily military interpretations include McWhiney and Jamieson, *Attack and Die*; Hattaway and Jones, *How the North Won*; Hagerman, *The American Civil War*; Griffith, *Battle Tactics*; Boritt, *Why the Confederacy Lost*; and Jones, *Civil War Command and Strategy*. More general studies include Beringer et al., *Why the South Lost*, and McPherson, *Battle Cry of Freedom*.

14. Walt Whitman, *Specimen Days* (Philadelphia: D. McKay, 1882–83), quoted in *". . . The Real War Will Never Get in the Books": Selections from Writers during the Civil War*, ed. Louis P. Masur (New York: Oxford University Press, 1993), 281.

15. The footnotes and bibliography demonstrate the diversity of grades and units represented in the manuscript (and published) sources. The letters and diaries examined, for example, were written by more than four hundred officers and enlisted men, a significant cross section of the Army of Northern Virginia for the period May 1864–April 1865. A few specific observations about these sources may be of interest. Common soldiers—that is, enlisted men—and to a lesser extent, company-level officers, are more numerous in the sample than those holding higher grades. Evidence from field, staff, and general officers, however, provides some of the most valuable information available on the men in the ranks and on conditions in particular units or the army as a whole. Furthermore, most officers and men cited are from Virginia, North Carolina, Georgia, and South Carolina not only because more of these soldiers' papers survive in public collections, but also because these four states furnished most of the units in the army. Inspection reports, Federal interviews with prisoners and deserters, and major Confederate newspapers are other valuable—and often underutilized—sources on the army.

16. Freeman, *The South to Posterity*, 170 (first phrase), 172.

17. Michael Schudson observes, "Imagine the historian as a sculptor, facing a slab of marble. This sculptor-historian can make that marble into a variety of shapes, but not an infinite variety. The sculptor has freedom to interpret as he or she chooses, but the freedom is limited. The sculptor cannot with that marble slab and a finite set of tools, create a sculpture of greater mass than the slab available at the beginning. The sculptor cannot make a sculpture of wood or brass or Styrofoam. The sculptor cannot make a piece that will keep critics from comparing it and judging it by the standards of other marble sculpture nor can the sculptor do very much to make the piece one the critics will think to compare to sculptures of fabric or ice. The sculptor, and the historian, are at once free and constrained." Schudson, *Watergate in American Memory: How We Remember, Forget, and Reconstruct the Past* (New York: Basic Books, 1992), 219. See also Gene Wise's admonition in his *American Historical Explanations: A Strategy for Grounded Inquiry*, 2d ed., rev. (Minneapolis: University of Minnesota Press, 1980), 78: "Documents *aren't* the experience, or at least they're not the exact experience they refer to. If we can keep this clear in our minds, we have a better case for taking books in the field seriously, but never confusing what historians have said with the original historical experience."

18. David Hackett Fischer, "Preface: An Idea of Cultural History," *Albion's Seed: Four British Folkways in America* (New York: Oxford University Press, 1989), vii–xi. For a more in-depth explication of his concept, see Fischer's "The Braided Narrative: Substance and Form in Social History," in *The Literature of Fact: Selected Papers from the English Institute*, ed. Angus Fletcher (New York: Columbia University Press, 1976).

19. For additional identification of soldiers and units, see the footnotes and bibliography in J. Tracy Power, "From the Wilderness to Appomattox: Life in Lee's Army of Northern Virginia, May 1864–April 1865" (Ph.D. diss., University of South Carolina, 1993). Unless otherwise identified, units mentioned in this volume are infantry regiments: e.g., the 16th Georgia. Confederate artillery battalions, brigades, and divisions were designated by the names of their commanders, unlike equivalent Federal units, which were most often designated by numbers. The notation 26th North Carolina/MacRae/Heth/III Corps, e.g., refers to the 26th North Carolina Infantry, MacRae's Brigade, Heth's Division, Third Corps. When a brigade or division commander was assigned temporarily, the permanent commander's name appears first, with the actual commander's name in parentheses: e.g., Kershaw (Kennedy). In addition, significant bodies of troops technically were not part of the Army of Northern Virginia but operated with it in 1864 and 1865. They are considered to be part of the army in the present study. The most notable of these organizations were from the Department of North Carolina and Southern Virginia, the Department of Richmond, and the Valley District. Troops from the Department of North Carolina and Southern Virginia, under Gen. P. G. T. Beauregard, were assigned to the defenses of Petersburg

under Lee's supervision from June to October 1864, then became the nucleus of the new Fourth Corps. Their army or administrative designation is Beauregard for the earlier period and IV Corps afterward. Units from the Department of Richmond also shared trenches and assignments with the Army of Northern Virginia in the last year of the war, most often under Lt. Gen. Richard S. Ewell. Their army designation is Richmond. The Army of the Valley, which operated in the Shenandoah Valley from June to December 1864 under Lt. Gen. Jubal A. Early, contained the Army of Northern Virginia's Second Corps and other units assigned to the vicinity. Their army designation is Valley.

20. For example, the first note would read Pvt. James Wesley Williams, Company C, 16th Georgia, to his wife, 15 May 1864, James Wesley Williams Papers, GEU; a second reference would be J. W. Williams to his wife, 15 May 1864, Williams Papers, GEU.

21. Lt. Col. William Ransom Johnson Pegram, Pegram/III Corps Artillery, to his sister, 5 October 1864, in James I. Robertson Jr., "'The Boy Artillerist,'" 248–49.

22. Lee to "General," 31 July 1865, in J. William Jones, *Personal Reminiscences of . . . Lee*, 180, and Lee to Walter H. Taylor, 31 July 1865, in Taylor, *General Lee*, 309.

23. Castel, "The Civil War and the Quest for Originality." See also Castel's "Afterword: Civil War History and the Quest for Originality," which revises and expands some of the themes of this review, in his *Winning and Losing*, 199–204.

PROLOGUE

1. 3d Lt. Robert P. Tutwiler, Company B, 15th Virginia Cavalry, to his aunt, 24 April 1864, Mrs. Thomas Chalmers McCorvey Papers, NcU.

2. Col. William Ruffin Cox, 2d North Carolina, "Sketch of the 2nd North Carolina Troops," 2 February 1864, George Holland Collection, Nc-Ar.

3. Ord. Sgt. Thomas J. Gardner, Company I, 3d North Carolina Cavalry, to his cousin, 22 April 1864, Caroline Gardner Papers, NcD.

4. Col. Gilbert Jefferson Wright, Cobb's Legion Cavalry, to his wife, 29 April 1864, Gilbert Jefferson Wright Papers, ViHi.

5. See, e.g., Capt. Henry Clay Albright, Company G, 26th North Carolina, to his brother, 10 April 1864, Henry Clay Albright Papers, Nc-Ar; Lt. Col. William Murdoch Parsley, 3d North Carolina, to his sister, 12 April 1864, Eliza Hall Parsley Papers, NcU; and Pvt. Charles Kerrison, Aide-de-Camp, 2d South Carolina, to his brother, 24 April 1864, ScU.

6. 1st Sgt. John F. Sale, Company H, 12th Virginia, to his aunt, 22 April 1864, John F. Sale Papers, Vi.

7. Pvt. Andrew Boyd, Company D, 7th South Carolina, to his father, 22 April 1864, Boyd Papers, ScU.

8. See, e.g., Capt. Reuben Allen Pierson, Company C, 9th Louisiana, to his father, 22 March 1864, Rosemonde E. and Emile Kuntz Collection, LNT; Sgt.

W. H. Strayhorn, Company K, 2d North Carolina Cavalry, to his cousin, 24 April 1864, Craig Papers, NcD; and Maj. Gen. Wade Hampton, Hampton/Cavalry Corps, to Mrs. Richard Singleton, 24 April 1864, Hampton Family Papers, ScU.

9. GO 26, A&IGO, 1 March 1864, *OR*, ser. 4, 3:178–83.

10. Capt. Asbury Hull Jackson, Commissary, Doles/Rodes/II Corps, to his sister, 11 February 1864, Harden Family Papers, NcD.

11. Sgt. Jacob E. Patton, Company F, 14th North Carolina, to his father, 21 February 1864, Patton Family Papers, NcU. See also Maj. Hunter Holmes McGuire, Medical Director, II Corps, to his mother, 3 February 1864, Hunter Holmes McGuire Papers, ViHi.

12. GO 14, ANV, 3 February 1864, *OR* 33:1145. Typical resolutions of Congress thanking units that reenlisted are in 33:1149–50, 1181–82, 1183–84, and 36(2):1019.

13. Sgt. Christopher Hackett, Company B, 45th North Carolina, to his parents, 25 February 1864, John C. Hackett Papers, NcD.

14. GO 1, ANV, 1 January 1864, *OR* 33:1059.

15. Hunter McGuire to his mother, 3 February 1864, McGuire Papers, ViHi.

16. Lee to Davis, 19 January 1864, *OR* 33:1097; Lee to Seddon, 15 February 1864, 33:1174.

17. GO 15, ANV, 7 February 1864, *OR* 33:1150; *Regulations for the Army of the Confederate States, 1863: Corrected and Enlarged with a Revised Index. [The Only Correct Edition.]* (Richmond: J. W. West, 1863) (hereafter cited as *Army Regulations*), 407.

18. Capt. William R. Redding Jr., Company E, 13th Georgia, to his wife, 8 April 1864, W. R. Redding Papers, NcU.

19. Pvt. Daniel Abernathy, Company C, 16th North Carolina, to his parents, 22 March 1864, Daniel Abernathy Papers, NcD.

20. James D. Richardson, ed., *A Compilation of the Messages and Papers of the Confederacy, Including Diplomatic Correspondence, 1861–1865*, 2 vols. (Nashville: U.S. Publishing Co., 1905), 2:413.

21. GO 23, ANV, 30 March 1864, Orders and Circulars Issued by the Army of the Potomac and the Army and Dept. of Northern Virginia, Confederate States Army, 1861–65, War Dept. Collection of Confederate Records, Record Group 109, NA, microfilm publication M921, roll 1 (hereafter cited as ANV Orders and Circulars, NA, with microfilm roll number).

22. 3d Lt. Harry Lewis, Company K, 16th Mississippi, to his mother, 6 April 1864, Harry Lewis Papers, NcU.

23. Pvt. Jesse M. Frank, Company B, 48th North Carolina, to his family, 26 April 1864, Alexander Frank Papers, NcD.

24. W. R. Redding to his wife, 8 April 1864, Redding Papers, NcU.

25. *Richmond Dispatch*, 6 April 1864.

26. Ibid., 11 April 1864.

27. Ibid., 7 April 1864.

28. Ibid., 11 April 1864.

29. Lee to Col. Lucius B. Northrop, Commissary Gen., Confederate States Army, 5 January 1864, *OR* 33:1065. For the standard ration, see *Army Regulations*, 191.

30. Lee to Seddon, 22 January 1864, *OR* 33:1114.

31. GO 7, ANV, 22 January 1864, *OR* 33:1117. See also Lee to Northrop, 5 January 1864, 33:1064–65; Lee to Davis (with endorsements), 11 January 1864, 33:1076–80; Lee to Seddon, 21 January 1864, 33:1113–14; and Lee to Seddon (with endorsements), 22 January 1864, 33:1114–16.

32. For Lee's concern over numerous desertions in Hays/Early/II Corps, attributed to dissatisfaction over rations, see Lee to Lt. Gen. Richard S. Ewell, II Corps, 18 February 1864, George Washington Campbell Papers, LC, and Lee to Seddon on the same date, *OR* 33:1187.

33. Christopher Hackett to his parents, 26 March 1864, Hackett Papers, NcD; Christopher Hackett, 45th [North Carolina] Infantry, War Dept. Collection of Confederate Records, Record Group 109, NA, microfilm publication M270, roll 444 (hereafter cited as Compiled Service Records, NA, with unit, state, and microfilm roll number).

34. *Army Regulations*, 410.

35. GO 17 (March 1864), GO 19 (8 March 1864), GO 22 (26 March 1864), Dept. of Northern Virginia, ANV Orders and Circulars, NA, roll 1.

36. Lee to Davis, 13 April 1864, in Freeman, *Lee's Dispatches*, 156.

37. Col. Bryan Grimes, 4th North Carolina, to Lt. Col. Walter H. Taylor, Asst. Adjt. Gen., HQ, ANV, 25 April 1864, Bryan Grimes Papers, NcD.

38. 2d Lt. Jesse L. Henry, Company K, 26th North Carolina, to his brother, April [undated] 1864, J. L. Henry Papers, NcD.

39. Lt. Thomas Frederick Boatwright, Company C, 44th Virginia, to his wife, 15 April 1864, Thomas Frederick Boatwright Papers, NcU.

40. GO 27, ANV, 5 April 1864, ANV Orders and Circulars, NA, roll 1. See also GO 32, ANV, 19 April 1864, ibid.

41. Pvt. Powell Benton Reynolds, Company K, 50th Virginia, to "Dear Sir," 13 April 1864, V-vol.

42. 5th Sgt. Marion Hill Fitzpatrick, Company K, 45th Georgia, to his wife, 14 April 1864, in Hammock, *Letters to Amanda*, 127; *Richmond Sentinel*, 23 April 1864.

43. Pvt. Thomas Pollock Devereux, Courier, Daniel/Rodes/II Corps, to his mother, 15 April 1864, Thomas Pollock Devereux Papers, Nc-Ar.

44. Circular, ANV, 7 April 1864, *OR* 33:1266–67.

45. T. F. Boatwright to his wife, 15 April 1864, Boatwright Papers, NcU.

46. P. B. Reynolds to "Dear Sir," 13 April 1864, V-vol.

47. W. H. Strayhorn to his cousin, 24 April 1864, Craig Papers, NcD.

48. W. M. Parsley to his sister, 12 April 1864, Parsley Papers, NcU.

49. See, e.g., Surg. Charles W. Sydnor, II Corps, to his fiancée, 3 April 1864,

Charles W. Sydnor Papers, NcU; Col. James Conner, Military Court/III Corps, to his mother, 3 April 1864, in Moffett, *Letters of General James Conner*, 122; Lt. Col. Alexander Swift Pendleton, Asst. Adjt. Gen., II Corps, to "Lella," 4 April 1864, William Nelson Pendleton Papers, NcU; H. C. Albright to his brother, 10 April 1864, Albright Papers, Nc-Ar; and Pvt. Robert C. Mabry, Company K, 6th Virginia, to his wife, 18 April 1864, Robert C. Mabry Papers, Nc-Ar. For the sake of clarity, this study will hereafter refer to Grant as if he were the official as well as the de facto commander of the Army of the Potomac.

50. *OR* 33:1191, 1233–34.

51. *OR* 33:1297–98, adding an estimate of First Corps strength derived from 32(2):721. At this time the strength of the Army of the Potomac was some 166,000 present and absent, of which only about 103,000 were present and fit for duty; see 33:1036.

52. Gen. Samuel Cooper, Adjt. & Insp. Gen., Confederate States Army, to Longstreet, 7 April 1864, *OR* 32(3):756.

53. Andrew Boyd to his father, 22 April 1864, Boyd Papers, NcD.

54. Charles Kerrison to his brother, 24 April 1864, Kerrison Family Papers, ScU. See also Capt. John William McLure, Quartermaster, Palmetto Sharpshooters, to his wife, 24 April 1864, McLure Family Papers, ScU, for a description of his visit to Stonewall Jackson's grave in Lexington.

55. *Charleston Mercury*, 25 May 1864.

56. Pvt. David Hugh Crawford, Signal Corps/Courier, Kershaw (Kennedy)/Kershaw/I Corps, to his mother, 30 April 1864, Crawford Family Papers, ScU. See also Brig. Gen. Edward Porter Alexander, Chief of Artillery, I Corps, to his wife, 2 May 1864, Edward Porter Alexander Papers, NcU.

57. Sgt. Arthur Benjamin Simms, Company E, 53d Georgia, to his sister, 4 May 1864, in Peacock, "A Georgian's View of War," 105. See also Col. John Bratton, 6th South Carolina, to his wife, 3 May 1864, John Bratton Papers, ScCoAH.

58. M. H. Fitzpatrick to his wife, 29 April 1864, in Hammock, *Letters to Amanda*, 132–33.

CHAPTER 1

1. Pvt. Thomas L. McCarty, Company L, 1st Texas, Diary, 2 May 1864, Thomas L. McCarty Papers, TxU.

2. E. P. Alexander to his wife, 2 May 1864, Alexander Papers, NcU. See also Capt. Benjamin Wesley Justice, Commissary, Kirkland/Heth/III Corps, to his wife, 4, 9 May 1864, Benjamin Wesley Justice Papers, GEU.

3. T. L. McCarty, Diary, 3 May 1864, McCarty Papers, TxU; John Bratton to his wife, 3 May 1864, Bratton Papers, ScCoAH.

4. John Bratton to his wife, 3 May 1864, Bratton Papers, ScCoAH.

5. Sgt. Isaac Lefevers, Company K, 46th North Carolina, to his wife, 3 May 1864, Isaac Lefevers Papers, Nc-Ar.

6. Wade Hampton to his sister, 6 May 1864, in Cauthen, *Family Letters*, 104.

7. R. C. Mabry to his wife, 5 May 1864, Mabry Papers, Nc-Ar.

8. See also A. B. Simms to his sister, 4 May 1864, in Peacock, "A Georgian's View of War," 105.

9. Lee to Seddon, 5 May 1864, *OR* 36(1):1028. See also Longstreet's and Ewell's reports, 36(1):1054, 1070.

10. Lt. Elias Davis, Company B, 10th Alabama, to his wife, 4 May 1864, Elias Davis Papers, NcU.

11. For an excellent overview of the campaign from the Wilderness to Petersburg (often referred to as the Overland campaign, and including the fighting at the Wilderness, Spotsylvania, the North Anna, Bethesda Church, and Cold Harbor), see Trudeau, *Bloody Roads South*; from the point of view of the Army of Northern Virginia for the same period, see Freeman's valuable *Lee's Lieutenants*, 3:342–514, and Dowdey's dated but still useful *Lee's Last Campaign*. Frassanito's *Grant and Lee* is a fascinating analysis of camp and battlefield pictures taken by various photographers from May 1864 to April 1865. Noah Andre Trudeau's "'A Mere Question of Time': Robert E. Lee from the Wilderness to Appomattox Court House," in *Lee The Soldier*, ed. Gallagher, 523–58, is a thoughtful and worthwhile commentary on Lee's generalship in the last year of the war.

12. Lee to Seddon, 5–6 May 1864, *OR* 36(1):1028; reports of corps and subordinate commanders, 36(1):1038–41, 1061–71, 1076–78, 1081, 1084–85, 1090–91. See also reports of Federal commanders, *OR* 36(1). Secondary accounts include Rhea, *Battle of the Wilderness*; Steere, *Wilderness Campaign*; Trudeau, *Bloody Roads South*, 41–116; Dowdey, *Lee's Last Campaign*, 83–176; and Freeman, *Lee's Lieutenants*, 3:342–72.

13. Capt. George P. Ring, Company K, 6th Louisiana, to his wife, 6 May 1864, ANV Papers, Louisiana Historical Association Collection, LNT.

14. Capt. Andrew Jackson McBride, Company E, 10th Georgia, to his wife, 6 May 1864, Andrew Jackson McBride Papers, NcD; Capt. Charles Minor Blackford, Judge Advocate Gen., I Corps, to his wife, 5 [6] May 1864, in Blackford and Blackford, *Letters from Lee's Army*, 243; Longstreet's report, *OR* 36(1):1055.

15. Capt. James Hays, Asst. Adjt. Gen., Harris/Anderson (Mahone)/III Corps, to his mother, 7 May 1864, James Hays Papers, ViHi.

16. Surg. Spencer Glasgow Welch, 13th South Carolina, to his wife, 7 May 1864, in Welch, *A Confederate Surgeon's Letters*, 95.

17. Brig. Gen. Goode Bryan, Bryan/Kershaw/I Corps, report, *OR* 36(1):1064.

18. Col. James R. Hagood, 1st South Carolina, *OR* 36(1):1068. See also reports of Brig. Gen. Joseph B. Kershaw, Kershaw/I Corps, 36(1):1061–62, and Brig. Gen. John B. Gordon, Gordon/Early/II Corps, 36(1):1077–78.

19. C. M. Blackford to his wife, 6 May 1864, in Blackford and Blackford, *Letters From Lee's Army*, 245; E. P. Alexander to his wife, 19 May 1864, Alexander Papers, NcU. See also Corp. Joseph Mullen Jr., Company F, 27th North Carolina, Diary, 6 May 1864, Joseph Mullen Papers, ViRC, and Pvt. Samuel Finley Harper, Courier, III Corps, to his father, 6 May 1864, Samuel Finley Harper Papers, Nc-Ar.

20. Lt. Col. J. W. McGill, 18th North Carolina, report of the Wilderness, James H. Lane Papers, AAP; J. F. Sale, Diary, 6 May 1864, Sale Papers, Vi.

21. Brig. Gen. William Nelson Pendleton, Chief of Artillery, report, *OR* 36(1):1040.

22. E. P. Alexander to his father, 29 May 1864, Alexander Papers, NcU.

23. Capt. Jesse Hartwell Heath, Asst. Quartermaster, 4th Virginia Cavalry, to his wife, 8 May 1864, James Payne Beckwith Jr., Papers, NcU.

24. S. F. Harper to his father, 6 May 1864, Harper Papers, Nc-Ar.

25. 2d Lt. James E. Green, Company I, 53d North Carolina, Diary, 6 May 1864, James E. Green Papers, NcU. See also Elias Davis to his wife, 9 May 1864, Davis Papers, NcU; Adjt. Francis Atherton Boyle, 32d North Carolina, Diary, 6 May 1864, in Thornton, "Prison Diary," 59; and J. R. Hagood, report, *OR* 36(1):1068.

26. G. P. Ring to his wife, 6 May 1864, ANV Papers, LHA Collection, LNT.

27. Pvt. John G. LaRoque, Company E, 4th Georgia, to his wife, 7 May 1864, LaRogue [LaRoque] Collection, GU.

28. S. F. Harper to his father, 6 May 1864, Harper Papers, Nc-Ar. See also Pvt. George W. Pearsall, Company G, 55th North Carolina, to his wife, 11 May 1864, George W. Pearsall Papers, Nc-Ar; Pvt. James A. Reynolds, Company K, 16th Georgia, Diary, 6 May 1864, James A. Reynolds Papers, RNBP; and J. W. McGill's report, Lane Papers, AAP.

29. G. W. Pearsall to his wife, 11 May 1864, Pearsall Papers, Nc-Ar.

30. T. L. McCarty, Diary, 6 May 1864, McCarty Papers, TxU.

31. A. J. McBride to his wife, 6 May 1864, McBride Papers, NcD.

32. Capt. Louis Gourdin Young, Asst. Adjt. Gen., Kirkland / Heth / III Corps, to his uncle, 7 May 1864, Robert Newman Gourdin Papers, GEU.

33. Isaac Lefevers to his wife, 20 May 1864, Lefevers Papers, Nc-Ar. See also A. J. McBride to his wife, 6 May 1864, McBride Papers, NcD, and D. H. Crawford to his mother, 16 May 1864, Crawford Family Papers, ScU.

34. J. F. Sale, Diary, 6 May 1864, Sale Papers, Vi.

35. G. W. Pearsall to his wife, 7 May 1864, Pearsall Papers, Nc-Ar.

36. B. W. Justice to his wife, 4, 9 May 1864, Justice Papers, GEU.

37. J. H. Heath to his wife, 8 May 1864, Beckwith Papers, NcU.

38. B. W. Justice to his wife, 4, 9 May 1864, Justice Papers, GEU; G. W. Pearsall to his wife, 7 May 1864, Pearsall Papers, Nc-Ar; Bryan Grimes to his wife, 6–7 May 1864, Grimes Papers, NcU; Capt. Cadwallader Jones Iredell, Company E, 1st North Carolina Cavalry, to his wife, 7 May 1864, Cadwallader J. Iredell Papers, NcU; Maj. William Edgeworth Bird, Quartermaster, Benning (DuBose) / Field / I Corps, to his wife, 6 May 1864, in Rozier, *Granite Farm Letters*, 165.

39. L. G. Young to his uncle, 7 May 1864, Gourdin Papers, GEU.

40. Bryan Grimes to his wife, 6–7 May 1864, Grimes Papers, NcU. For examples of criticism in official reports, see Lee to Seddon, 6 May 1864, *OR* 36(1):1028; Longstreet's report, 36(1):1054–55; Kershaw's report, 36(1):1061; Bryan's re-

port, 36(1):1063; J. R. Hagood's report, 36(1):1069; Ewell's report, 36(1):1070; and John B. Gordon's report, 36(1):1076. See also G. P. Ring to his wife, 6 May 1864, ANV Papers, LHA Collection, LNT; J. G. LaRoque to his wife, 7 May 1864, LaRogue [LaRoque] Collection, GU; and Pvt. B. L. Wynn, Signal Corps, II Corps, Diary, 6 May 1864, B. L. Wynn Papers, Ms-Ar.

41. See, e.g., Sgt. Henry Calvin Conner, Company G, Palmetto Sharpshooters, to his wife, 7 May 1864, Henry Calvin Conner Papers, ScU; James Hays to his mother, 7 May 1864, Hays Papers, ViHi; C. J. Iredell to his wife, 7 May 1864, Iredell Papers, NcU; and J. H. Heath to his wife, 8 May 1864, Beckwith Papers, NcU.

42. C. J. Iredell to his wife, 7 May 1864, Iredell Papers, NcU.

43. Maj. Gen. Cadmus M. Wilcox, Wilcox/III Corps, to his sister-in-law, 21 May 1864, Cadmus M. Wilcox Papers, LC.

44. For a description and analysis of the "Lee to the rear" incidents that occurred in the Wilderness and at Spotsylvania, see Chapter 2.

45. B. W. Justice to his wife, 4, 9 May 1864, Justice Papers, GEU; W. E. Bird to his wife, 6 May 1864, in Rozier, *Granite Farm Letters*, 164.

46. Bryan Grimes to his wife, 7, 6–7 [two letters], May 1864, Grimes Papers, NcU.

47. J. G. LaRoque to his wife, 7 May 1864, LaRogue [LaRoque] Collection, GU; S. F. Harper to his father, 6 May 1864, Harper Papers, Nc-Ar.

48. J. A. Reynolds, Diary, 6 May 1864, Reynolds Papers, RNBP.

49. Surg. Abner Embry McGarity, 61st Alabama, to his wife, 7 May 1864, in Burnett, "Letters of a Confederate Surgeon," December 1945, 237. See also J. H. Heath to his wife, 8 May 1864, Beckwith Papers, NcU, and the history of the 18th Georgia in Folsom, *Heroes and Martyrs of Georgia*, 19–20.

50. B. L. Wynn, Diary, 6 May 1864, Wynn Papers, Ms-Ar.

51. James Hays to his mother, 7 May 1864, Hays Papers, ViHi.

52. Both armies gained additional support after the Wilderness. Grant's reinforcements partially offset his losses, giving the Army of the Potomac a total strength of some 111,000 troops; Lee's reinforcements slightly outnumbered his losses, giving the Army of Northern Virginia a total strength of some 63,000 troops just before Spotsylvania.

53. Folsom, *Heroes and Martyrs of Georgia*, 122, in his history of Thomas/ Wilcox/III Corps.

54. Lee to Seddon, 8 (2 letters), 10, 12, 16 May 1864, *OR* 36(1):1028–30; reports of corps and subordinate commanders, 36(1):1042–46, 1065–67, 1069, 1071–73, 1078–80, 1081–84, 1086–88, 1091–94; diary of I Corps, 36(1):1056–58; itinerary of Hardaway/II Corps Artillery, 36(1):1089–90. See also reports of Federal commanders, *OR* 36(1). Secondary accounts include Rhea, *Battles for Spotsylvania Court House*; Matter, *If It Takes All Summer*; Trudeau, *Bloody Roads South*, 117–213; Dowdey, *Lee's Last Campaign*, 179–248; and Freeman, *Lee's Lieutenants* 3:373–410, 437–41.

55. 3d Sgt. Edward Richardson Crockett, Company F, 4th Texas, Diary, 9–10

May 1864, Edward Richardson Crockett Papers, TxU. See also T. L. McCarty, Diary, 8–12 May 1864, McCarty Papers, TxU, and Jedediah Hotchkiss, Topographic Engineer, II Corps, Diary, 10 May 1864, in McDonald, *Make Me a Map of the Valley*, 203.

56. Lee to Ewell, 10 May 1864, Campbell Papers, LC.

57. E. R. Crockett, Diary, 11 May 1864, Crockett Papers, TxU. See also J. E. Green, Diary, 8–20 May 1864, Green Papers, NcU; J. F. Sale, Diary, 10–20 May 1864, Sale Papers, Vi; and Pvt. Creed Thomas Davis, Company K, 1st Virginia Artillery, Diary, 11–17 May 1864, Creed Thomas Davis Papers, ViHi.

58. B. W. Justice to his wife, 11 May 1864, Justice Papers, GEU.

59. G. W. Pearsall to his wife, 11, 13–14 May 1864, Pearsall Papers, Nc-Ar.

60. M. H. Fitzpatrick to his wife, 19 May 1864, in Hammock, *Letters to Amanda*, 137. See also Pvt. Walter Raleigh Battle, Company F, 4th North Carolina, to his parents, 14, 17 May 1864, in Lee, *Forget-Me-Nots*, 113–18; Pvt. Francis Asbury Wayne Jr., Company L, 1st South Carolina, to his mother, 17 May 1864, Mrs. E. K. Atkinson Collection, NcU; Brig. Gen. Alfred Moore Scales, Scales/Wilcox/III Corps, to his wife, 20 May 1864, Alfred M. Scales Papers, Nc-Ar; and Pvt. John H. Hartman, Company D, 1st North Carolina Artillery, to his wife, 25 May 1864, John H. Hartman Papers, NcD.

61. S. G. Welch to his wife, 13 May 1864, in Welch, *A Confederate Surgeon's Letters*, 96; B. L. Wynn, Diary, 12 May 1864, Wynn Papers, Ms-Ar; John Bratton, report, *OR* 36(1):1066; Brig. Gen. Samuel McGowan, McGowan/Wilcox/III Corps, report, 36(1):1094.

62. J. F. Sale, Diary, 12 May 1864, Sale Papers, Vi.

63. W. R. Battle to his parents, 14 May 1864, in Lee, *Forget-Me-Nots*, 116.

64. W. R. Battle to his mother, 17 May 1864, in ibid., 118.

65. Pvt. Charles E. Whilden, Color Bearer, 1st South Carolina, to his brother, 14 May 1864, Charles E. Whilden Papers, ScHi.

66. T. L. McCarty, Diary, 12 May 1864, McCarty Papers, TxU; J. E. Green, Diary, 15 May 1864, Green Papers, NcU.

67. Samuel McGowan's report, *OR* 36(1):1094; Brig. Gen. Nathaniel H. Harris, Harris/Mahone/III Corps, report, 36(1):1092. The stump of the tree is now on display at the National Museum of American History, part of the Smithsonian Institution in Washington, D.C. See also app. C, "The Oak Stump of Spotsylvania," in Matter, *If It Takes All Summer*, 373.

68. Lt. Charles E. Denoon, Company K, 41st Virginia, to his parents, 15 May 1864, Denoon Family Papers, Vi.

69. T. L. McCarty, Diary, 10 May 1864, McCarty Papers, TxU.

70. M. H. Fitzpatrick to his wife, 15 May 1864, in Hammock, *Letters to Amanda*, 136. See also A. H. Jackson to his wife, 11 May 1864, Harden Family Papers, NcD, and P. B. Reynolds to "Dear Sir," 19 May 1864, V-vol.

71. Isaac Lefevers to his wife, 11 May 1864, Lefevers Papers, Nc-Ar.

72. Pvt. William H. Slater, Company A, 1st South Carolina (Hagood's), to his son, 20 May 1864, Barkley Family Papers, NcU.

73. B. W. Justice to his wife, 16 May 1864, Justice Papers, GEU.

74. Samuel McGowan's report, *OR* 36(1):1094.

75. *Charleston Courier*, 28 May 1864.

76. F. A. Wayne to his mother, 17 May 1864, Atkinson Collection, NcU. See also Frank A. Wayne Jr., 1st (McCreary's) [South Carolina] Infantry (1st Provisional Army), Compiled Service Records, NA, microcopy M267, roll 134.

77. Philip H. Force, 1st (McCreary's) [South Carolina] Infantry (1st Provisional Army), Compiled Service Records, NA, microcopy M267, roll 128.

78. *Charleston Mercury*, 25 May 1864; "Obituary: The Young and The Brave," *Charleston Mercury*, *Charleston Courier*, 4 June 1864.

79. Quoted in "The Young and The Brave," *Charleston Mercury*, 4 June 1864.

80. Capt. William Aiken Kelly, Company L, 1st South Carolina, Diary, 8 August 1864, William Aiken Kelly Papers, ScCC. See also William Aiken Kelly, 1st (McCreary's) [South Carolina] Infantry (1st Provisional Army), Compiled Service Records, NA, microcopy M267, roll 130.

81. F. A. Wayne to his mother, 17 May 1864, Atkinson Collection, NcU.

82. Bryan Grimes to his wife, 14 May 1864, Grimes Papers, NcU.

83. W. R. Battle to his mother, 17 May 1864, in Lee, *Forget-Me-Nots*, 118.

84. J. E. Green, Diary, 12 May 1864, Green Papers, NcU; T. P. Devereux to his family, 13 May 1864, Devereux Papers, Nc-Ar. See also T. L. McCarty, Diary, 12 May 1864, McCarty Papers, TxU; G. P. Ring to his wife, 15 May 1864, ANV Papers, LHA Collection, LNT; and F. A. Wayne to his mother, 17 May 1864, Atkinson Collection, NcU.

85. Col. George H. Sharpe, Deputy Provost-Marshal-Gen., Army of the Potomac, to Maj. Gen. Andrew A. Humphreys, Chief of Staff, Army of the Potomac, 17 May 1864, *OR* 36(2):842.

86. Joseph Mullen, Diary, 13 May 1864, Mullen Papers, ViRC.

87. G. P. Ring to his wife, 15 May 1864, ANV Papers, LHA Collection, LNT.

88. W. R. Battle to his parents, 14 May 1864, in Lee, *Forget-Me-Nots*, 116.

89. W. R. Battle to his mother, 17 May 1864, in ibid., 118. See also E. R. Crockett, Diary, 13 May 1864, Crockett Papers, TxU.

90. B. W. Justice to his wife, 16 May 1864, Justice Papers, GEU; David Fort, 14th [North Carolina] Infantry, Compiled Service Records, NA, microcopy M270, roll 224. Fort was mortally wounded less than a month later, spent a few days in a hospital in Richmond, and died in Wake County, N.C., in July 1864.

91. Quartermaster Sgt. William Young Mordecai, 1st Virginia Artillery, to his mother, 19 May 1864, William Young Mordecai Papers, ViHi.

92. S. F. Harper to his sister, 21 May 1864, Harper Papers, Nc-Ar. See also E. R. Crockett, Diary, 12 May 1864, Crockett Papers, TxU, and C. M. Wilcox to his sister-in-law, 21 May 1864, Wilcox Papers, LC.

93. Pvt. Joseph F. Shaner, Rockbridge Artillery, to his parents, 17 May 1864, V-vol.

94. W. H. Slater to his son, 20 May 1864, Barkley Family Papers, NcU. See also D. H. Crawford to his mother, 16 May 1864, Crawford Family Papers, ScU.

95. Capt. Watson Dugat Williams, Company F, 5th Texas, to his sister, 18 May 1864, Watson Dugat Williams Papers, Confederate Research Center, TxHiC.

96. T. P. Devereux to his family, 13 May 1864, Devereux Papers, Nc-Ar. See also Pvt. Abel H. Crawford, Company A, 61st Alabama, to his wife, 19 May 1864, Abel H. Crawford Papers, NcD, and 1st Lt. John Hampden Chamberlayne, Company C, 13th Battalion Virginia Light Artillery, to his mother, 21 May 1864, in Chamberlayne, *Ham Chamberlayne*, 222.

97. *Richmond Examiner*, 16 May 1864.

98. Adjt. Robert Stiles, Cabell/I Corps Artillery, to his mother and sister, 15 May 1864, Robert Augustus Stiles Papers, ViHi.

99. F. A. Wayne to his mother, 17 May 1864, Atkinson Collection, NcU. See also W. R. Battle to his parents, 14 May 1864, in Lee, *Forget-Me-Nots*, 113–14, and M. H. Fitzpatrick to his wife, 19 May 1864, in Hammock, *Letters to Amanda*, 137.

100. C. E. Denoon to his parents, 15 May 1864, Denoon Family Papers, Vi; W. H. Slater to his son, 20 May 1864, Barkley Family Papers, NcU. See also B. W. Justice to his wife, 14 May 1864, Justice Papers, GEU.

101. Lt. Col. Charles S. Venable, Aide-de-Camp, HQ, ANV, to his wife, 15 May 1864, Charles S. Venable Papers, NcU.

102. Pvt. James Wesley Williams, Company C, 16th Georgia, to his wife, 18 May 1864, James Wesley Williams Papers, GEU. See also Pvt. William Ross Stillwell, Courier, Bryan/Kershaw/I Corps, to his wife, 16 May 1864, William Ross Stillwell Papers, G-Ar, and Pvt. William L. Wilson, Company B, 12th Virginia Cavalry, to his mother, 27 May 1864, in Summers, *A Borderland Confederate*, 80–81.

103. C. E. Whilden to his brother, 14 May 1864, Whilden Papers, ScHi.

104. Maj. Alfred D. Kelly, 21st Virginia, to his brother, 25 May 1864, Williamson Kelly Papers, NcD.

105. G. P. Ring to his wife, 15 May 1864, ANV Papers, LHA Collection, LNT.

106. P. B. Reynolds to "Dear Sir," 19 May 1864, V-vol. There was also a widespread belief in the rest of the army that only a fierce defensive stand had prevented Grant from gaining a significant advantage, and that the emergency was caused by faulty defensive positions and an unfortunate tendency of some units (including those in other divisions) to break under pressure. See also J. E. Green, Diary, 10–13 May 1864, Green Papers, NcU, and Pvt. Virgil E. Lucas, Company C, 26th Georgia, to John J. Dillard, 20 May 1864, John J. Dillard Papers, NcD.

107. C. T. Davis, Diary, 11, 13–14 May 1864, Davis Papers, ViHi.

108. B. W. Justice to his wife, 20 May 1864, Justice Papers, GEU.

109. J. W. Williams to his wife, 15 May 1864, Williams Papers, GEU. See also

Isaac Lefevers to his wife, 20 May 1864, Lefevers Papers, Nc-Ar, and A. J. McBride to his wife, 29 May 1864, McBride Papers, NcD.

110. Bryan Grimes to his wife, 14 May 1864, Grimes Papers, NcU.

111. A. E. McGarity to his wife, 17 May 1864, in Burnett, "Letters of a Confederate Surgeon," December 1945, 238; F. A. Wayne to his mother, 17 May 1864, Atkinson Collection, NcU.

112. J. F. Shaner to his parents, 17 May 1864, V-vol.

113. W. R. Stillwell to his wife, 16 May 1864, Stillwell Papers, G-Ar; William D. Curry, 50th [Georgia] Infantry, Compiled Service Records, NA, microcopy M266, roll 506.

114. B. W. Justice to his wife, 20 May 1864, Justice Papers, GEU.

CHAPTER 2

1. J. H. Hartman to his wife, 25, 29 May 1864, Hartman Papers, NcD.

2. See, e.g., Bryan Grimes to his wife, 6 May 1864, Grimes Papers, NcU; G. W. Pearsall to his wife, 11 May 1864, Pearsall Papers, Nc-Ar; W. D. Williams to his sister, 18 May 1864, Williams Papers, TxHiC; Elias Davis to his wife, 20 May 1864, Davis Papers, NcU; Corp. Jonathan Fuller Coghill, Company G, 23d North Carolina, to his brother, 25 May 1864, Jonathan Fuller Coghill Papers, AAP, and to his parents, 29 May 1864, James O. Coghill Papers, NcD; and Capt. Council A. Bryan, Company C, 5th Florida, to his wife, 25 May 1864, Council A. Bryan Papers, F.

3. See, e.g., T. L. McCarty, Diary, 1–31 May 1864, McCarty Papers, TxU; J. E. Green, Diary, 1–31 May 1864, Green Papers, NcU; J. F. Sale, 4–31 May 1864, Sale Papers, Vi; J. A. Reynolds, Diary, 4 May–5 June 1864, Reynolds Papers, RNBP; and Pvt. William D. Alexander, Hospital Steward, 37th North Carolina, Diary, 5–22 May 1864, William D. Alexander Papers, NcU.

4. James Hays to his mother, 7 May 1864, Hays Papers, Vi.

5. C. M. Blackford to his wife, 19 May 1864, in Blackford and Blackford, *Letters from Lee's Army*, 245.

6. J. W. Williams to his wife, 15 May 1864, Williams Papers, GEU.

7. J. F. Coghill to his brother, 25 May 1864, Coghill Papers, AAP.

8. A. M. Scales to his wife, 20 May 1864, Scales Papers, Nc-Ar. See also Elias Davis to his wife, 20 May 1864, Davis Papers, NcU, and A. J. McBride to his wife, 20 May 1864, McBride Papers, NcD.

9. W. H. Slater to his son, 20 May 1864, Barkley Family Papers, NcU; J. G. LaRoque to his wife, 7 May 1864, LaRogue [LaRoque] Collection, GU. See also B. W. Justice to his wife, 4, 9 May 1864, Justice Papers, GEU, and F. A. Wayne to his mother, 17 May 1864, Atkinson Collection, NcU.

10. J. F. Coghill to his parents, 29 May 1864, Coghill Papers, NcD; A. J. McBride to his wife, 29 May 1864, McBride Papers, NcD.

11. Pvt. Charles L. Burn, Company G, 1st South Carolina, to his father, 11 May 1864, Burn Family Papers, ScU

12. W. R. Battle to his parents, 14 May 1864, in Lee, *Forget-Me-Nots*, 113–16.

13. A. E. McGarity to his wife, 17 May 1864, in Burnett, "Letters of a Confederate Surgeon," December 1945, 239.

14. S. G. Welch to his wife, 17 May 1864, in Welch, *A Confederate Surgeon's Letters*, 98.

15. B. W. Justice to his wife, 14 May 1864, Justice Papers, GEU.

16. A. J. McBride to his wife, 20 May 1864, McBride Papers, NcD.

17. Generals killed or mortally wounded in the two battles were Brig. Gens. Junius Daniel, Micah Jenkins, John M. Jones, Abner M. Perrin, and Leroy A. Stafford; those wounded were Lt. Gen. James Longstreet and Brig. Gens. Henry L. Benning, John Rogers Cooke, Harry T. Hays, Robert D. Johnston, Samuel McGowan, John Pegram, Edward A. Perry, Henry H. Walker, and James A. Walker; those captured were Maj. Gen. Edward Johnson and Brig. Gen. George H. Steuart. Maj. Gen. J. E. B. Stuart and Brig. Gen. James B. Gordon of the Cavalry Corps were mortally wounded at Yellow Tavern on 11 and 12 May, respectively, but are not included in the totals for the Wilderness and Spotsylvania.

18. Lee to Seddon, 5–6, 10, 12 May 1864, *OR* 36(1):1028–30; Lee to his wife, 16 May 1864, in Dowdey and Manarin, *Wartime Papers*, 731.

19. B. W. Justice to his wife, 14 May 1864, Justice Papers, GEU; W. E. Bird to his wife, 6 May 1864, in Rozier, *Granite Farm Letters*, 164.

20. A. E. McGarity to his wife, 17 May 1864, in Burnett, "Letters of a Confederate Surgeon," December 1945, 238. See also Maj. Thomas Claybrook Elder, Commissary, Perry/Anderson (Mahone)/III Corps, to his wife, 13 May 1864, Thomas Claybrook Elder Papers, ViHi; J. F. Shaner to his parents, 17 May 1864, V-vol.; and Bryan Grimes to his wife, Grimes Papers, NcU, 17 May 1864.

21. J. M. Frank to his father, 19 May 1864, Frank Papers, NcD.

22. T. L. McCarty, Diary, 6 May 1864, McCarty Papers, TxU.

23. E. R. Crockett, 6 May 1864, Crockett Papers, TxU.

24. Joseph Mullen Jr., Diary, 6 May 1864, Mullen Papers, ViRC.

25. J. F. Sale, Diary, 31 May 1864, Sale Papers, Vi.

26. Bryan Grimes to his wife, 6–7 May 1864, Grimes Papers, NcU; D. H. Crawford to his mother, 16 May 1864, Crawford Family Papers, ScU. See also Joseph Mullen Jr., Diary, 6 May 1864, Mullen Papers, ViRC; S. F. Harper to his father, 6 May 1864, Harper Papers, Nc-Ar; and B. W. Justice to his wife, 4, 9 May 1864, Justice Papers, GEU.

27. *Richmond Sentinel*, 25 May 1864. Similar incidents occurred at Spotsylvania on 10 May, when Lee's staff kept him from riding into the battle with George P. Doles's Georgia brigade of the Second Corps, and on 12 May, when Lee attempted to lead Nathaniel H. Harris's Mississippi brigade of the Third Corps.

28. Lt. Col. William T. Poague, Poague/III Corps Artillery, to his father, 1 June 1864, in Cockrell, *Gunner With Stonewall*, 135.

29. *Richmond Whig*, 17 May 1864.

30. *Richmond Dispatch*, 18 May 1864.

31. Davis to Lee, 15 May 1864, *OR* 51(2):933.

32. *Richmond Examiner*, 9 May 1864.

33. *Richmond Dispatch*, 18 May 1864.

34. Bryan Grimes to his wife, 17 May 1864, Grimes Papers, NcU; James Conner to his mother, 25 May 1864, in Moffett, *Letters of General James Conner*, 130.

35. G. P. Ring to his wife, 15 May 1864, ANV Papers, LHA Collection, LNT. See also A. J. McBride to his wife, 6 May 1864, McBride Papers, NcD; T. P. Devereux to his family, 11 May 1864, Devereux Papers, Nc-Ar; and J. E. Green, Diary, 10, 12 May 1864, Green Papers, NcU.

36. H. C. Conner to his wife, 7 May 1864, Conner Papers, ScU.

37. B. W. Justice to his wife, 11 May 1864, Justice Papers, GEU; E. R. Crockett, Diary, 6 May 1864, Crockett Papers, TxU.

38. G. W. Pearsall to his wife, 7 May 1864, Pearsall Papers, Nc-Ar. See also J. G. LaRoque to his wife, 7 May 1864, LaRogue [LaRoque] Collection, GU; 1st Lt. John B. Evans, Company I, 53d Georgia, to his wife, 12 May 1864, John B. Evans Papers, NcD; and W. H. Slater to his son, 20 May 1864, Barkley Family Papers, NcU.

39. A. J. McBride to his wife, 6 May 1864, McBride Papers, NcD.

40. A. H. Jackson to his mother, 11–12 May 1864, Harden Family Papers, NcD. See also J. W. Williams to his wife, 11 May 1864, Williams Papers, GEU; W. D. Williams to his sister, 18 May 1864, Williams Papers, TxHiC; and A. D. Kelly to his brother, 25 May 1864, Kelly Papers, NcD.

41. Kershaw's report, *OR* 36(1):1062. See also Ewell's report, 36(1):1074.

42. W. R. Stillwell to his wife, 16 May 1864, Stillwell Papers, G-Ar.

43. Ibid. Pvt. James A. Stephens would be captured in the Shenandoah Valley in the fall of 1864 and would die in a Federal prison at Elmira, N.Y. John W. and James A. Stephens, 53d [Georgia] Infantry, Compiled Service Records, NA, microcopy M266, roll 524. See also S. F. Harper to his father, 6 May 1864, Harper Papers, Nc-Ar; G. P. Ring to his wife, 6 May 1864, ANV Papers, LHA Collection, LNT; and V. E. Lucas to J. J. Dillard, 20 May 1864, Dillard Papers, NcD.

44. V. E. Lucas to J. J. Dillard, 20 May 1864, Dillard Papers, NcD.

45. C. E. Denoon to his parents, 15 May 1864, Denoon Family Papers, Vi.

46. Pvt. John A. Everett, Company K, 11th Georgia, to his mother, 4, 7 May 1864, John A. Everett Papers, GEU. See also L. G. Young to Robert Newman Gourdin, 7 May 1864, Gourdin Papers, GEU; C. E. Whilden to his brother, 14 May 1864, Whilden Papers, ScHi; Elias Davis to his wife, 9, 20 May 1864, Davis Papers, NcU; and J. F. Coghill to his parents, 29 May 1864, Coghill Papers, NcD.

47. E. P. Alexander to his wife, Alexander Papers, 19 May 1864, NcU.

48. Bryan Grimes to his wife, 17 May 1864, Grimes Papers, NcU.

49. J. W. Williams to his wife, 18 May 1864, Williams Papers, GEU.

50. M. H. Fitzpatrick to his wife, 23–24 May 1864, in Hammock, *Letters to*

Amanda, 138–39. See also Fitzpatrick to his wife, 19 May 1864, in ibid., 137; E. R. Crockett, Diary, 6–20 May 1864, Crockett Papers, TxU; D. H. Crawford to his mother, 21 May 1864, Crawford Family Papers, ScU; A. D. Kelly to his brother, 25 May 1864, Kelly Papers, NcD; and W. R. Battle to his mother, 25 May 1864, in Lee, *Forget-Me-Nots*, 119–20.

51. T. C. Elder to his wife, 20 May 1864, Elder Papers, ViHi; J. F. Shaner to his parents, 17 May 1864, V-vol.

52. A. M. Scales to his wife, 20 May 1864, Scales Papers, Nc-Ar.

53. Sgt. Thomas E. Nimmo, Company B, 15th Virginia, to "Dear Sir," 24 May 1864, Munford-Ellis Family Papers, NcD.

54. C. W. Sydnor to his fiancée, 29 May 1864, Sydnor Papers, NcU.

55. C. A. Bryan to his wife, 23 May 1864, Bryan Papers, F.

56. J. M. Frank to his father, 25 May 1864, Frank Papers, NcD.

57. C. T. Davis, Diary, 17 May 1864, Davis Papers, Vi.

58. M. H. Fitzpatrick to his wife, 19 May 1864, in Hammock, *Letters to Amanda*, 137; A. J. McBride to his wife, 29 May 1864, McBride Papers, NcD.

59. James Conner to his mother, 14 May 1864, in Moffett, *Letters of General James Conner*, 127; Isaac Lefevers to his wife, 20 May 1864, Lefevers Papers, Nc-Ar.

60. W. H. Slater to his son, 20 May 1864, Barkley Family Papers, NcU. See also V. E. Lucas to J. J. Dillard, 20 May 1864, Dillard Papers, NcD, and A. J. McBride to his wife, 20 May 1864, McBride Papers, NcD.

61. A. M. Scales to his wife, 20 May 1864, Scales Papers, Nc-Ar; V. E. Lucas to J. J. Dillard, 20 May 1864, Dillard Papers, NcD.

62. *Richmond Examiner*, 23 May 1864.

63. A. D. Kelly to his brother, 25 May 1864, Kelly Papers, NcD.

64. Pvt. Samuel P. Lockhart, Company G, 27th North Carolina, to his cousin, 30 May 1864, Hugh Conway Browning Papers, NcD.

65. B. W. Justice to his wife, 25–26, 29 May 1864, Justice Papers, GEU.

66. Lee to Seddon, 20 May 1864, *OR* 36(3):800.

67. Lee to Davis, 22 May 1864, in Freeman, *Lee's Dispatches*, 191–92.

68. M. H. Fitzpatrick to his wife, 23 May 1864, in Hammock, *Letters to Amanda*, 138.

69. Lee to Seddon, 21 May 1864, *OR* 36(3):812; Charles Venable to Richard H. Anderson, 21 May 1864, 36(3):814; Lee to Anderson, 21 May 1864 (two messages), 36(3):814–15; Lee to Seddon, 22 May 1864, 36(3):823; Lt. Col. Charles Marshall, Aide-de-Camp, HQ, to Anderson, 22 May 1864, 36(3):823–24; W. H. Taylor to Anderson, 22 May 1864, 36(3):824.

70. C. A. Bryan to his wife, 23 May 1864, Bryan Papers, F. See also W. D. Alexander, Diary, 21–22 May 1864, Alexander Papers, NcU; E. R. Crockett, Diary, 21–22 May 1864, Crockett Papers, TxU; and D. H. Crawford to his mother, 21 May 1864, Crawford Family Papers, ScU.

71. E. R. Crockett, Diary, 24 May 1864, Crockett Papers, TxU.

72. J. M. Frank to his father, 25 May 1864, Frank Papers, NcD.

73. J. F. Coghill to his brother, 25 May 1864, Coghill Papers, AAP.

74. C. E. Denoon to his parents, 28 May 1864, Denoon Family Papers, Vi.

75. W. N. Pendleton's report, *OR* 36(1):1046–48; diary of I Corps, 21–26 May 1864, 36(1):1058; Bratton's report, 36(1):1067; J. R. Hagood's report, 36(1):1069; Lee to Seddon, 23 May 1864, 36(3):825, and 24 May 1864, 36(3):827. See also T. E. Nimmo to "Dear Sir," 24 May 1864, Munford-Ellis Family Papers, NcD; J. M. Frank to his father, 25 May 1864, Frank Papers, NcD; and T. L. McCarty, Diary, 23–27 May 1864, McCarty Papers, TxU. Secondary accounts include Miller, *North Anna Campaign*; Trudeau, *Bloody Roads South*, 220–46; Dowdey, *Lee's Last Campaign*, 255–66; and Freeman, *Lee's Lieutenants*, 3:496–99.

76. Lee to Seddon, 26 May 1864, *OR* 36(3):834, 27 May 1864, 36(3):835; W. H. Taylor to Richard H. Anderson, 27 May 1864 (three messages), 36(3):837–38; C. S. Venable to Anderson, 27 May 1864, 36(3):838; Lee to Seddon, 28 May 1864, 36(3):843.

77. J. E. Green, Diary, 27 May 1864, Green Papers, NcU.

78. M. H. Fitzpatrick to his wife, 23 May 1864, in Hammock, *Letters to Amanda*, 138; J. H. Hartman to his wife, 25 May 1864, Hartman Papers, NcD.

79. A. M. Scales to his wife, 25 May 1864, Scales Papers, Nc-Ar; J. M. Frank to his father, 25 May 1864, Frank Papers, NcD.

80. C. M. Blackford to his wife, 30 May 1864, in Blackford and Blackford, *Letters From Lee's Army*, 249. See also 1st Lt. John T. Gay, Company B, 4th Georgia, to his wife, 25 May 1864, Mary Barnard Nix Collection, GU, and A. J. McBride to his wife, 29 May 1864, McBride Papers, NcD.

81. W. R. Stillwell to his wife, 29 May 1864, Stillwell Papers, G-Ar.

82. E. P. Alexander to his wife, 28 May 1864, Alexander Papers, NcU.

83. Adjt. James M. McFall, Palmetto Sharpshooters, to his sister, 25 May 1864, William McFall Papers, GEU.

84. SO 122, ANV, 7 May 1864, *OR* 36(2):967; SO 123, ANV, 8 May 1864, 36(2):974; Lee to Ewell, 8 May 1864, 51(2):902–3; SO 126, ANV, 14 May 1864, 36(2):1001; SO 128, 21 May 1864, 36(3):814; SO 134, 29 May 1864, 36(3):846.

85. Compare the list of general officers killed, mortally wounded, or captured in n. 17 above with the table of organization in *OR* 36(1):1021–27 and with the special orders cited in n. 84 above.

86. Lee to Anderson, 30 May 1864, *OR* 36(3):851.

87. McGowan's report, *OR* 36(1):1094; Benjamin T. and J. K. Brockman, 13th [South Carolina] Infantry (roll 262), William Lester, 13th [South Carolina] Infantry (roll 266), and Joseph N. Brown, 14th [South Carolina] Infantry (roll 270), Compiled Service Records, NA, microcopy M267.

88. *OR* 36(1):1023; G. P. Ring to his wife, 15 May 1864, ANV Papers, LHA Collection, LNT.

89. P. B. Reynolds to "Dear Sir," 19 May 1864, V-vol.; SO 126, ANV, 14 May 1864, *OR* 36(2):1001; SO 128, ANV, 21 May 1864, 36(3):813–14.

90. Adjt. Henry Francis Jones, Cobb's Legion Cavalry, to his sister, 1 June 1864, UDC Typescripts, vol. 2, G-Ar.

91. W. L. Wilson to his mother, 27 May 1864, in Summers, *A Borderland Confederate*, 80. See also C. T. Davis, Diary, 1 June 1864, Davis Papers, ViHi.

92. SO 126, ANV, 14 May 1864, *OR* 36(2):1001.

93. GO 44, ANV, 20 May 1864, *OR* 36(3):800.

94. Lee to Davis, 4 May 1864, in Dowdey and Manarin, *Wartime Papers*, 720; Lee to Davis, 13 May 1864, *OR* 51(2):925.

95. See, e.g., Lee to Davis, 23, 25, 28 May 1864, Lee to Gen. Braxton Bragg, Armies of the Confederate States, 29 May 1864, and Lee to Davis, 29–30 May 1864, in Dowdey and Manarin, *Wartime Papers*, 747–48, 750, 754–57; Gen. P. G. T. Beauregard, Dept. of North Carolina and Southern Virginia, Memorandum, 18 May 1864, *OR* 36(2):1021–22; Bragg to Seddon, 19 May 1864 (enclosing Beauregard to Bragg, 14 May 1864, and Bragg to Davis, 19 May 1864), 36(2):1023–25; Beauregard to Davis, 21 May 1864, 36(3):818–19; Beauregard to Bragg, 23 May 1864, 36(3):826; and Beauregard to Davis, 29 May 1864, 36(3):849.

96. Lee to Bragg, 4 May 1864, *OR* 51(2):887; SO 117, A&IGO, 20 May 1864, 36(3):799; Bragg to Samuel Cooper, 20 May 1864, 36(3:808); diary of I Corps, 36(1):1058; Davis to Lee, 20 May 1864, 51(2):951.

97. 2d Lt. Henry M. Talley, Company G, 14th Virginia, to his mother, 23 May 1864, Henry C. Brown Papers, Nc-Ar.

98. Lee to Breckinridge, 14 May 1864, *OR* 37(1):735, 16 May 1864, 37(1):738, and 18 May 1864, 37(1):742; Charles Marshall to Breckinridge (with enclosures), 20 May 1864, 37(1):744–45; Breckinridge to Lee, 18 May 1864, 51(2):943; Davis to Lee, 20 May 1864, 51(2):951; Lee to Breckinridge, 24 May 1864, 51(2):957; D. H. Crawford to his mother, 20, 22 May 1864, Crawford Family Papers, ScU; Corp. Henry Clay Krebs, Company H, 13th Virginia, to "My dear Lizzie," 22 May 1864, Henry Clay Krebs Papers, NcD.

99. *OR* 36(1):1027; SO 121, A&IGO, 25 May 1864, 36(3):831–32; Col. Hugh K. Aiken, 6th South Carolina Cavalry, to Col. John B. Sale, Military Secretary to Bragg, 30 May 1864 (with enclosures), 36(3):852–54.

100. Sgt. E. O. Harkins, Company C, 4th South Carolina Cavalry, to James Earle Hagood, 24 May 1864, James Earle Hagood Papers, ScU.

101. Pvt. Hugh Lide Law, Company I, 6th South Carolina Cavalry, to his father, 31 May 1864, Thomas Cassells Law Papers, ScU. See also Law to his brother, 27 May 1864, ibid., and Pvt. James Michael Barr, Company I, 5th South Carolina Cavalry, to his wife, 23, 27, 29, 31 May 1864, in McDaniel, *War Correspondence of . . . Barr*, 237–45.

102. SO 113, A&IGO, 16 May 1864, *OR* 36(2):1012; SO 125, A&IGO, 30 May 1864, 36(3):850; Lee to Davis, 31 May 1864, in Freeman, *Lee's Dispatches*, 365 (app.); Col. Lawrence M. Keitt, Kershaw (Keitt)/Kershaw/I Corps, to his wife, 31 May 1864, Lawrence Massillon Keitt Papers, NcD; D. H. Crawford to his mother,

1 June 1864, Crawford Family Papers, ScU; Adjt. John A. Wilson, 20th South Carolina, to Susan Keitt, 8 June 1864, Keitt Papers, NcD; and Daniel Boyd to his sisters, 9 June 1864, Boyd Papers, NcD.

103. L. M. Keitt to his wife, 31 May 1864, Keitt Papers, NcD. See also Pvt. J. W. Tindall, Company D, 20th South Carolina, to his wife, 29, 31 May 1864, J. W. Tindall Papers, ScU.

104. E. R. Crockett, Diary, 29–31 May 1864, Crockett Papers, TxU. See also diary of I Corps, 29–31 May 1864, *OR* 36(1):1058.

105. S. P. Lockhart to his cousin, 30 May 1864, Browning Papers, NcD.

106. J. E. Green, Diary, 29–30 May 1864, Green Papers, NcU.

107. W. H. Taylor to his fiancée, 30 May 1864, in Tower, *Lee's Adjutant*, 164.

108. Lee to Anderson, 30 May 1864 (two messages), *OR* 36(3):851; Early to Lee, 30 May 1864, 36(3):854; Early's report, 51(1):244–45; Early to Lee, 31 May 1864, 51(2):975. Secondary accounts include Trudeau, *Bloody Roads South*, 252–59; Dowdey, *Lee's Last Campaign*, 279–81; and Freeman, *Lee's Lieutenants*, 3:502.

109. Early's report, *OR* 51(1):245; James B. Terrill, Compiled Service Records of Confederate General and Staff Officers, and Nonregimental Enlisted Men, War Dept. Collection of Confederate Records, Record Group 109, NA, microfilm publication M331, roll 244 (hereafter cited as Compiled Service Records of General and Staff Officers, NA, with microfilm roll number); Davis to Lee, 31 May 1864, *OR* 51(2):973; Edward Willis, 12th [Georgia] Infantry, Compiled Service Records, NA, microcopy M266, roll 275; Edward Willis, Compiled Service Records of General and Staff Officers, NA, microcopy M331, roll 269.

110. Lee to Davis, 31 May 1864, in Freeman, *Lee's Dispatches*, 364 (app.).

111. Pvt. Marcus Hefner, Company E, 57th North Carolina, to his wife, 1 June 1864, Marcus Hefner Papers, Nc-Ar.

112. Lee to Davis, 30 May 1864, *OR* 36(3):850.

113. Beauregard to Bragg, 30 May 1864, Bragg to Beauregard, 30 May 1864, SO 16, Dept. of North Carolina and Southern Virginia, 30 May 1864, and SO 126, A&IGO, 30 May 1864, *OR* 36(3):857.

114. Diary of I Corps, 31 May 1864, *OR* 36(1):1058; Field Return of Hoke/Beauregard, 21 May 1864, 36(3):817; Taylor to Anderson, 31 May 1864 (second message), 36(3):858; Fitzhugh Lee to Lee, 31 May 1864, 36(3):858; Anderson to Lee, 31 May 1864, 51(2):974; Hoke to Taylor, 31 May 1864, 51(2):975.

115. Brig. Gen. Stephen Dodson Ramseur, Early (Ramseur)/II Corps, to his wife, 31 May 1864, Stephen Dodson Ramseur Papers, NcU.

116. E. P. Alexander to his father, 29 May 1864 (fragment), Alexander-Hillhouse Family Papers, NcU; S. P. Lockhart to his cousin, 30 May 1864, Browning Papers, NcD.

117. Lee to Seddon, 1–3 June 1864, *OR* 36(1):1031–32; reports of corps and subordinate commanders, 36(1):1049–51, 1064, 1090, 36(3):864, 51(2):976–83; diary of the I Corps, 1–3 June 1864, 36(1):1058–59; Lee to Davis, 3 June 1864, in Dowdey and Manarin, *Wartime Papers*, 763. See also reports of Federal com-

manders, *OR* 36(1). Secondary accounts include Baltz, *Battle of Cold Harbor*; Maney, *Marching to Cold Harbor*; Trudeau, *Bloody Roads South*, 261–99; Dowdey, *Lee's Last Campaign*, 284–98; and Freeman, *Lee's Lieutenants*, 3:504–8.

118. J. E. Green, Diary, 7 June 1864, Green Papers, NcU.

119. E. R. Crockett, Diary, 1 June 1864, Crockett Papers, TxU.

120. Pvt. John G. Hall, Company G, 51st North Carolina, to his father, 3 June 1864, W. P. Hall Collection, Nc-Ar.

121. D. H. Crawford to his mother, 1 June 1864, Crawford Family Papers, ScU. See also Charles Kerrison to his sister, 31 May–1 June 1864, Kerrison Family Papers, ScU; J. A. Wilson to Susan Keitt, 8 June 1864, Keitt Papers, NcD; and diary of the First Corps, *OR* 36(1):1059.

122. W. R. Stillwell to his brother, 14 June 1864, Stillwell Papers, G-Ar.

123. C. M. Blackford to his wife, 2 June 1864, in Blackford and Blackford, *Letters From Lee's Army*, 250.

124. See, e.g., Capt. William H. S. Burgwyn, Staff, Clingman / Hoke / Beauregard, Diary, 1 June 1864, William Hyslop Sumner Burgwyn Papers, Nc-Ar; J. G. Hall to his father, 3 June 1864, Hall Collection, Nc-Ar; and Col. David Lang, 8th Florida, to his cousin, 7 June 1864, in Groene, "Civil War Letters of . . . Lang," 363.

125. M. H. Fitzpatrick to his wife, 4 June [misdated 4 May] 1864, Hammock, *Letters to Amanda*, 134.

126. Capt. Francis Marion Coker, Adjutant, Cutts / III Corps Artillery, to his wife, 7 June 1864, Florence Hodgson Heidler Collection, GU. See also, e.g., J. L. Henry to his brother, 2 June 1864, Henry Papers, NcD; Maj. Gen. S. D. Ramseur, Ramseur / II Corps, to his wife, 4 June 1864, Ramseur Papers, NcU; and Pvt. W. H. Brotherton, Company K, 23d North Carolina, to his parents, 4 June 1864, William H. Brotherton Papers, NcD.

127. Daniel Boyd to his sisters, 9 June 1864, Boyd Papers, NcD.

128. A. E. McGarity to his wife, 3 June 1864, in Burnett, "Letters of a Confederate Surgeon," December 1945, 240. For estimates of the number of Federal assaults, see J. G. Hall to his father, 3 June 1864, Hall Collection, Nc-Ar; Early's report, *OR* 51(1):245; W. H. Brotherton to his parents, 8 June 1864, Brotherton Papers, NcD; D. H. Crawford to his mother, 4 June 1864, Crawford Family Papers, ScU; and diary of the I Corps, 3 June 1864, *OR* 36(1):1059.

129. 2d Lt. Virgil Duc, Company E, 25th South Carolina, to his father, 10 June 1864, Virgil Duc Papers, ScU.

130. Elias Davis to his wife, 5 June 1864, Davis Papers, NcU.

131. W. H. Brotherton to his parents, 8 June 1864, Brotherton Papers, NcD.

132. Grant to Lee, 5 June 1864, and Lee to Grant, 5 June 1864, *OR* 36(3):600: Grant to Lee, 6 June 1864 (two letters), and Lee to Grant, 6 June 1864 (two letters), 36(3):638–69; Grant to Lee, 7 June 1864 (two letters), and Lee to Grant, 7 June 1864, 36(3):666–67.

133. Elias Davis to his wife, 5 June 1864, Davis Papers, NcU.

134. Pvt. Grant Davis Carter, Company C, 2d Georgia Battalion, to his brother, 11 June 1864, UDC Typescripts, vol. 2, G-Ar. See also T. L. McCarty, Diary, 6–7 June 1864, McCarty Papers, TxU; J. A. Reynolds, Diary, 7 June 1864, Reynolds Papers, RNBP; and W. D. Williams to his fiancée, 7 June 1864, Williams Papers, TxHiC.

135. John Bratton to his wife, [5 June 1864], Bratton Papers, ScCoAH.

136. Pvt. John S. Anglin, Company A, 4th North Carolina, to his parents, 4 June 1864, John S. Anglin Papers, LC.

137. Chap. Richard Stanford Webb, 44th North Carolina, to his cousin, 10 June 1864, Webb Family Papers, NcU; Pvt. Marshall Elton Decker, Company E, 9th Virginia Cavalry, to his wife, 5 June 1864, Decker Family Papers, Vi. See also J. G. Hall to his father, 3 June 1864, Hall Collection, Nc-Ar; A. H. Crawford to his wife, 5 June 1864, Crawford Papers, NcD; and W. D. Williams to his fiancée, 7 June 1864, Williams Papers, TxHiC.

138. A. B. Simms to his sister, 4 June 1864, in Peacock, "A Georgian's View of War," 108; C. A. Bryan to his wife, 10 June 1864, Bryan Papers, F.

139. Capt. N. A. Ramsey, Company D, 61st North Carolina, to Gov. Zebulon B. Vance, 8 June 1864, Governor's Papers, Nc-Ar.

140. Virgil Duc to his father, 10 June 1864, Duc Papers, ScU. See also W. H. Brotherton to his parents, 4, 8 June 1864, Brotherton Papers, NcD, and J. W. Tindall to his wife, 6 June 1864, Tindall Papers, ScU.

141. J. B. Evans to his wife, 6 June, 12 May 1864, Evans Papers, NcD; James A. Evans, 14th [Georgia] Infantry, Compiled Service Records, NA, microcopy M266, roll 284.

142. D. H. Crawford to his mother, 4 June 1864, Crawford Family Papers, ScU. See also 1st Sgt. James M. McClelland, Company I, 44th Georgia, to Mrs. N. E. Cushing, 3 June 1864, J. M. McClelland Papers, G-Ar; Elias Davis to his wife, 9 June 1864, Davis Papers, NcU; Grant Davis Carter to his brother, 11 June 1864, UDC Typescripts, vol. 2, G-Ar; and Sgt. William Horace Phillips, Company F, 14th Virginia, to his parents, 13 June 1864, William Horace Phillips Papers, NcD.

143. Lt. James M. Simpson, 13th Alabama, to his wife, 11 June 1864, Allen and Simpson Family Papers, NcU.

CHAPTER 3

1. W. H. Brotherton to his parents, 4 June 1864, Brotherton Papers, NcD.

2. A. B. Simms to his sister, 4 June 1864, in Peacock, "A Georgian's View of War," 108.

3. Circular, ANV, 3 June 1864, in Dowdey and Manarin, *Wartime Papers*, 762–63.

4. Circular, ANV, 3 June 1864, *OR* 36(3):869.

5. Circular, ANV, 5 June 1864, ANV Orders and Circulars, NA, roll 1.

6. SO 38, ANV, 4 June 1864, *OR* 36(3):873–74. See also Ewell to Lee, 1 June

1864, 36(3):863; Lee to Samuel Cooper, 12 June 1864, 36(3):897–98; S. D. Ramseur to his wife, 4 June 1864, Ramseur Papers, NcU; and Brig. Gen. Bryan Grimes, Grimes/Rodes/II Corps, to his wife, 8 June 1864, Grimes Papers, NcU.

7. J. T. Gay to his wife, 5 June 1864, Nix Collection, GU.

8. J. M. McClelland to Mrs. N. E. Cushing, 3 June 1864, McClelland Papers, G-Ar.

9. J. T. Gay to his wife, 5 June 1864, Nix Collection, GU.

10. J. M. McClelland to Mrs. N. E. Cushing, 3 June 1864, McClelland Papers, G-Ar.

11. F. M. Coker to his wife, 3 June 1864, Heidler Collection, GU.

12. Daniel Boyd to his sisters, 9 June 1864, Boyd Papers, NcD.

13. F. M. Coker to his wife, 7 June 1864, Heidler Collection, GU.

14. E. P. Alexander to his wife, 10 June 1864, Alexander Papers, NcU.

15. Daniel Boyd to his sisters, 9 June 1864, Boyd Papers, NcD.

16. W. H. Phillips to his parents, 13 June 1864, Phillips Papers, NcD; G. D. Carter to his brother, 11 June 1864, UDC Typescripts, vol. 2, G-Ar. See also J. E. Green, Diary, 4–12 June 1864, Green Papers, NcU; J. A. Reynolds, Diary, 5–12 June 1864, Reynolds Papers, RNBP; Charles Kerrison to his sister, 6 June 1864, Kerrison Family Papers, ScU; and C. A. Bryan to his wife, 7, 10 June 1864, Bryan Papers, F.

17. *Richmond Examiner*, 13 June 1864.

18. T. L. McCarty, Diary, 8 June 1864, McCarty Papers, TxU; C. T. Davis, Diary, 10 June 1864, Davis Papers, ViHi; C. A. Bryan to his wife, 6 June 1864, Bryan Papers, F; Anonymous Soldier, Stonewall Brigade, to Mrs. Fanny Haralson Gordon, 5 June 1864, Gordon Family Papers, GU.

19. D. H. Crawford to his mother, 4 June 1864, Crawford Family Papers, ScU; E. R. Crockett, Diary, 4 June 1864, Crockett Papers, TxU.

20. D. H. Crawford to his mother, 4 June 1864, Crawford Family Papers, ScU; W. D. Williams to his fiancée, 7 June 1864, Williams Papers, TxHiC.

21. E. R. Crockett, Diary, 4, 9 June 1864, Crockett Papers, TxU.

22. W. H. Brotherton to his father, 8 June 1864, Brotherton Papers, NcD.

23. W. H. Phillips to his parents, 13 June 1864, Phillips Papers, NcD; Elias Davis to his wife, 9 June 1864, Davis Papers, NcU. See also *Richmond Examiner*, 6 June 1864, and J. F. Shaner to his parents, 12 June 1864, V-vol.

24. Virgil Duc to his father, 10 June 1864, Duc Papers, ScU; C. A. Bryan to his wife, 10 June 1864, Bryan Papers, F. A possible explanation for the increase in rations—particularly in vegetables—can be found in a Confederate prisoner's statement to the Federals who captured him. According to this soldier, the vegetables came from a Federal wagon train—three hundred wagons—recently taken by Confederates near Gordonsville. See Col. G. H. Sharpe, Deputy Provost-Marshal-Gen., Army of the Potomac, to Maj. Gen. A. A. Humphreys, Chief of Staff, Army of the Potomac, 11 June 1864, *OR* 36(3):747.

25. Lee to Seddon, 10 June 1864, *OR* 36(3):888.

26. J. F. Shaner to his parents, 12 June 1864, V-vol.

27. *Richmond Dispatch*, 8 June 1864; *Richmond Examiner*, 9 June 1864.

28. *Richmond Examiner*, 11 June 1864; *Richmond Dispatch*, 17 June 1864. See also *Dispatch*, 8 June 1864, and *Examiner*, 9–10, 13, 15, 18 June 1864.

29. *Richmond Dispatch*, 17 June 1864.

30. Maj. Gen. John B. Gordon, Gordon/II Corps, to his wife, 11 June 1864, Gordon Family Papers, GU. In addition to the Richmond newspapers cited above, see also C. T. Davis, Diary, 9 June 1864, Davis Papers, ViHi, and E. R. Crockett, Diary, 12 June 1864, Crockett Papers, TxU. For complaints from Beauregard's soldiers about their inability to donate to the poor and about the poor quality and quantity of their rations, particularly when compared to those issued to Lee's soldiers, see *Richmond Examiner*, 15 June 1864, and Maj. Gen. Robert Ransom, Ransom/Beauregard, to Bragg (with endorsements), 12 June 1864, *OR* 36(3): 898–900.

31. A. E. McGarity to his wife, 3–4 June 1864, in Burnett, "Letters of a Confederate Surgeon," December 1945, 239.

32. E. P. Alexander to his wife, 10 June 1864, Alexander Papers, NcU.

33. W. N. Pendleton to E. P. Alexander, and Alexander to Pendleton, 10 June 1864 (written on the reverse of the title page of M. E. Braddon, *Eleanor's Victory: A Novel* [Richmond: Ayres and Wade, 1864]), Pendleton Papers, NcU; Pendleton to Lt. Col. Briscoe G. Baldwin, Chief of Ordnance, 10 June 1864 (with endorsements), *OR* 36(3):888–89.

34. W. N. Pendleton to B. G. Baldwin, 10 June 1864 (with endorsements), *OR* 36(3):888–89.

35. E. R. Crockett, Diary, 12 June 1864, Crockett Papers, TxU.

36. A. E. McGarity to his wife, 12 June 1864, in Burnett, "Letters of a Confederate Surgeon," December 1945, 243.

37. W. H. Brotherton to his father, 8 June 1864, Brotherton Papers, NcD.

38. J. W. Tindall to his wife, 6 June 1864, Tindall Papers, ScU.

39. See, e.g., A. H. Crawford to his wife, 5 June 1864, Crawford Papers, NcD; Charles Kerrison to his sister, 6 June 1864, Kerrison Family Papers, ScU; and W. D. Williams to his fiancée, 7 June 1864, Williams Papers, TxHiC.

40. Lee to Hill, June [undated] 1864, *OR* 40(2):702–3.

41. J. S. Anglin to his parents, 4 June 1864, Anglin Papers, LC.

42. A. E. McGarity to his wife, 12 June 1864, in Burnett, "Letters of a Confederate Surgeon," December 1945, 243. See also S. P. Lockhart to his mother and sister, 9 June 1864, Browning Papers, NcD, and J. M. Simpson to his wife, 11 June 1864, Allen and Simpson Family Papers, NcU.

43. James Conner to his mother, 5 June 1864, in Moffett, *Letters of General James Conner*, 134.

44. See, e.g., C. A. Bryan to his wife, 3 June 1864, Bryan Papers, F; John Bratton to his wife, 5 June 1864, Bratton Papers, ScCoAH; and J. T. Gay to his wife, 10 June 1864, Nix Collection, GU.

45. J. T. Gay to his wife, 10 June 1864, Nix Collection, GU.

46. A. B. Simms to his mother, 9 June 1864, in Peacock, "A Georgian's View of War," 109.

47. Capt. Edward A. T. Nicholson, Asst. Adjt. Gen., Lane / Wilcox / III Corps, to his niece, 16 June 1864, Mary E. Grattan Papers, NcU.

48. G. D. Carter to his brother, 11 June 1864, UDC Typescripts, vol. 2, G-Ar; J. T. Gay to his wife, 5 June 1864, Nix Collection, GU; A. B. Simms to his mother, 9 June 1864, in Peacock, "A Georgian's View of War," 109. See also Elias Davis to his wife, 5 June 1864, Davis Papers, NcU; S. P. Lockhart to his mother and sister, 9 June 1864, Browning Papers, NcD; and W. R. Stillwell to his wife, 14 June 1864, Stillwell Papers, G-Ar.

49. David Lang to his cousin, 7 June 1864, in Groene, "Civil War Letters of . . . Lang," 364.

50. J. L. Henry to his brother, 2 June 1864, Henry Papers, NcD.

51. A. E. McGarity to his wife, 7 June 1864, in Burnett, "Letters of a Confederate Surgeon," December 1945, 241.

52. Virgil Duc to Antoinette, 12 June 1864, Duc Papers, ScU. See also Duc to his father, 10 June 1864, Duc Papers, ScU.

53. L. M. Keitt to his wife, 31 May 1864, Keitt Papers, NcD.

54. Pvt. George W. Boatwright, Company E, 12th Battalion Georgia Light Artillery, to his girlfriend, 4 June 1864, George W. Boatwright Papers, RNBP.

55. C. A. Bryan to his wife, 3 June 1864, Bryan Papers, F.

56. E. R. Crockett, Diary, 3 June 1864, Crockett Papers, TxU.

57. See Maj. Edward Clifford Anderson Jr., 7th Georgia Cavalry, to his mother, 5 June 1864, Wayne-Stiles-Anderson Families Papers, Georgia Historical Society, Savannah.

58. Hampton's report, *OR* 36 (1):1095–98; Fitzhugh Lee to Lee, 13 June 1864, 51(2):1009; Lee to Seddon, 13 June 1864, 36(1):1035; Hampton to Lee, 14 June 1864, 51(2):1014; reports of Federal commanders, 36(1). Secondary accounts include Freeman, *Lee's Lieutenants* 3:516–22, and Dowdey, *Lee's Last Campaign*, 306–9. See also Swank, *Battle of Trevilian Station*; Pvt. Noble John Brooks, Company E, Cobb's Legion Cavalry, Diary, 11–13 June 1864, Noble John Brooks Papers, NcU, and Pvt. Beverley K. Whittle, Company C, 2d Virginia Cavalry, to his father, 13 June 1864, Stafford Gorman Whittle Papers, ViU.

59. Hampton to Lee, 14 June 1864, *OR* 51(2):1014.

60. J. W. McLure, Quartermaster Dept., Field / I Corps, to his wife, 15 June 1864, McLure Family Papers, ScU.

61. Lee's endorsement, 11 June 1864, on Breckinridge to Bragg, 10 June 1864, *OR* 51(2):1003; Lee to Davis, 14 June 1864, in Dowdey and Manarin, *Wartime Papers*, 777; Early to Lee, 14 June 1864, *OR* 51(2):1012–13; Early to Breckinridge, 15 June 1864, 37(1):761; Lee's report, 37(1):346. Secondary accounts include Vandiver, *Jubal's Raid*, and Cooling, *Jubal Early's Raid*.

62. Jedediah Hotchkiss, Topographic Engineer, Valley, Diary, 13 June 1864, in

McDonald, *Make Me a Map of the Valley*, 211; V. E. Lucas to J. J. Dillard, 16 June 1864, Dillard Papers, NcD. See also Lt. William Beavans, Company D, 43d North Carolina, Diary, 12–13 June 1864, William Beavans Papers, NcU, and J. E. Green, Diary, 12–13 June 1864, Green Papers, NcU.

63. Lee to Seddon, 13–15 June 1864, *OR* 36(1):1035; Lee to Davis, 14 June 1864 (two messages), in Dowdey and Manarin, *Wartime Papers*, 777–79; Pendleton's report, *OR* 36(1):1051–52; diary of the I Corps, 13–15 June 1864, 36(1): 1059–60; Lt. Col. G. Moxley Sorrel, Asst. Adjt. Gen., I Corps, to I Corps Division and Artillery Commanders, 13 June 1864, 40(2):647; Abstract of Field Return, ANV, 30 June 1864, 40(2):707. See also reports of Federal commanders, 40(1).

64. E. R. Crockett, Diary, 13 June 1864, Crockett Papers, TxU.

65. J. M. Frank to his father, 16 June 1864, Frank Papers, NcD. See also E. R. Crockett, Diary, 13–16 June 1864, Crockett Papers, TxU; Corp. Joseph Pryor Fuller, Company B, 20th Georgia, Diary, 16 June 1864, Joseph Pryor Fuller Papers, NcU; J. A. Reynolds, Diary, 13–15 June 1864, Reynolds Papers, RNBP; and Elias Davis to his wife, 14 June 1864, Davis Papers, NcU.

66. Beauregard to Bragg, 8 June 1864, *OR* 51(2):996, and 9 June 1864 (ten messages), 36(3):884–86; Bragg to Lee, 9 June 1864 (with enclosures), 51(2):997; Seddon, endorsement on Thomas H. Wynne to Davis, 9 June 1864, 51(2):999–1000; Beauregard to Bragg, 10 June 1864, 36(3):889; Maj. Gen. D. H. Hill, Aide-de-Camp, Beauregard, to Beauregard, 11 June 1864 (with Beauregard's endorsement), 36(3):896; Beauregard to Bragg, 14 June 1864 (three messages), 40(2): 652–53; Beauregard to Lee, 14 June 1864, 40(2):653; Bragg to Beauregard, 14 June 1864, 40(2):653; Beauregard to Bragg, 15 June 1864 (eleven messages), 40(2):655–57; Beauregard to Lee, 15 June 1864, 40(2):657; Orders, Dept. of North Carolina and Southern Virginia, 15 June 1864, 40(2):657; Beauregard to Bragg, 21 June 1864, 40(2):675–78; Field Return, ANV, 30 June 1864, 40(2):707. Secondary accounts of the first phases of the Petersburg campaign include William Glenn Robertson, *Petersburg Campaign*, and Howe, *Petersburg Campaign*. See also Trudeau, *The Last Citadel*—which in many respects is the most satisfactory overview of the siege of Petersburg and the fighting on the Petersburg-Richmond front between the summer of 1864 and the spring of 1865—3–55; Dowdey, *Lee's Last Campaign*, 317–51; and Freeman, *Lee's Lieutenants*, 3:528–38.

67. Beauregard to Bragg, 14 June 1864, *OR* 40(2):652, and 15 June 1864 (two messages), 40(2):655.

68. Beauregard's report, *OR* 36(2):199–204; reports of subordinate commanders, 36(2):210–18, 235–64. See also reports of Federal commanders, 36(2). Among the secondary accounts of the Bermuda Hundred campaign (including the battles at Port Walthall Junction, Swift Creek, and Drewry's Bluff) are William Glenn Robertson, *Back Door to Richmond*, and Schiller, *Bermuda Hundred Campaign*; see also Freeman, *Lee's Lieutenants*, 3:450–95.

69. Virgil Duc to Antoinette, 26 May 1864, Duc Papers, ScU.

70. Virgil Duc to Antoinette, 12 June 1864, ibid.; Virgil Duc, 25th [South

Carolina] Infantry, Compiled Service Records, NA, microcopy M267, roll 344; Hagood's report, *OR* 36(2):252.

71. 2d Sgt. John Washington Calton, Company I, 56th North Carolina, to his father, 24 May 1864, John Washington Calton Papers, Nc-Ar. See also, e.g., 1st Sgt. Henry I. Greer, Company B, 25th South Carolina, to his parents, 18 May 1864, Henry I. and Robert Greer Papers, LC; Capt. Patrick Kilbride Molony, Assistant Adjutant General, Hagood/Hoke/Beauregard, to Constance Ryan, 19 May 1864, Molony-Ryan Families Papers, Private Collection of Barnwell R. Linley, Columbia, S.C.; Pvt. Robert G. Hutson, Company G, 11th South Carolina, to his father, 23 May 1864, Robert G. Hutson Papers, NcD; 2d Lt. Luther Rice Mills, Company K, 26th Virginia, to his brother, 24, 27 May 1864, in Harmon, "Letters of . . . Mills," 298–300; and 2d Lt. Samuel Catawba Lowry, Company F, 17th South Carolina, Diary, 26 May 1864, Samuel Catawba Lowry Papers, ScU.

72. Pvt. William C. Leak, Company F, 22d South Carolina, to his wife and children, 25 May 1864, William Leak Papers, PNB.

73. H. I. Greer to his parents, 18 May 1864, Greer Papers, LC. See also P. K. Molony to Constance Ryan, 19 May 1864, Molony-Ryan Families Papers, Private Collection of Barnwell Rhett Linley, Columbia, S.C.; Lt. William Mason Smith, Adjt., 27th South Carolina, to his mother, 24 May 1864, in Smith, Smith, and Childs, *Mason Smith Family Letters*, 92–93; and Virgil Duc to Antoinette, 26 May 1864, Duc Papers, ScU.

74. L. R. Mills to his brother, 27 May 1864, in Harmon, "Letters of . . . Mills," 299. See also, e.g., Lt. Col. Theodore Gaillard Trimmier, 41st Alabama, to his wife, 8 May 1864, Trimmier Collection, T; Pvt. Benjamin Mason, Company F, 60th Alabama, to his wife, 8 May 1864, Benjamin Mason Papers, AAP; S. C. Lowry, Diary, 25 May 1864, Lowry Papers, ScU; H. I. Greer to his mother, 26 May 1864, Greer Papers, LC; and Brig. Gen. Stephen Elliott Jr., Elliott/Johnson/Beauregard, to his wife, 30 May 1864, Elliott Family Papers, ScU.

75. T. G. Trimmier to his wife, 31 May 1864, Trimmier Collection, T. For opinions of Lee's army on Beauregard's troops, see J. H. Chamberlayne to his mother, 21 May 1864, in Chamberlayne, *Ham Chamberlayne*, 222, and Abel H. Crawford to his wife, 5 June 1864, Crawford Papers, NcD.

76. S. C. Lowry, 10 June 1864, Lowry Papers, ScU.

77. L. R. Mills to his brother, 6 June 1864, in Harmon, "Letters of . . . Mills," 300.

78. Stephen Elliott to his wife, 1 June 1864, Elliott Family Papers, ScU; Stephen Elliott, Compiled Service Records of General and Staff Officers, NA, microcopy M331, roll 85.

79. Maj. Henry Bryan, Adjt. & Insp. Gen., Beauregard, to R. N. Gourdin, 10 June 1864, Gourdin Papers, GEU.

80. See, e.g., Bragg to Lee, 9 June 1864 (with enclosures), *OR* 51(2):997; Seddon, endorsement on T. H. Wynne to Davis, 9 June 1864, 51(2):999–1000; and Bragg to Beauregard, 14 June 1864, 40(2):653.

81. Ord. Sgt. James W. Albright, Company A, 12th Battalion Virginia Light Artillery, Diary, 11, 14, 16 June 1864, James W. Albright Papers, NcU. See also 1st Sgt. John W. Knight, Company B, 26th South Carolina, to his father, June 1864 [undated, but after 8 June], John N. [W.] Knight Papers, ScU, and Bvt. 2d Lt. Alexander Frederick Fleet, Company I, 26th Virginia, to his parents, 6 June 1864, in Fleet and Fuller, *Green Mount*, 327–28.

82. Lee to Davis, 15 June 1864 (first quotation); Lee to Bragg, 15 June 1864 (second quotation), in Dowdey and Manarin, *Wartime Papers*, 780–81.

83. Lee to Beauregard, 16 June 1864 (three messages), *OR* 40(2):659.

84. Beauregard to Lee, 16–17 June 1864, *OR* 51(2):1078–79.

85. E. R. Crockett, Diary, 16–17 June 1864, Crockett Papers, TxU; T. L. McCarty, Diary, 17 June 1864, McCarty Papers, TxU. See also Lee to Davis, 17 June 1864 (two messages), *OR* 40(1):749; diary of the I Corps, 16–17 June 1864, 40(1):760; Lee to Anderson, 17 June 1864, in Harrison, *Pickett's Men*, 130–31; Anderson to Lee, 17 June 1864, *OR* 51(2):1019–20; and *Richmond Examiner*, 18 June 1864.

86. F. M. Coker to his wife, 17 June 1864, Heidler Collection, GU.

87. James Conner to his mother, 17 June 1864, in Moffett, *Letters of General James Conner*, 137.

88. W. C. Leak to his wife and children, 20 June 1864, Leak Papers, PNB.

89. T. G. Trimmier to his wife, 21 June 1864, Trimmier Collection, T. See also Pendleton's report, *OR* 40(1):755–56; diary of the I Corps, 17 June 1864, 40(1):760; Beauregard to Bragg, 16 June 1864, 40(2):660, and 17 June 1864 (two messages), 40(2):666; Instructions, Dept. of North Carolina and Southern Virginia, 17 June 1864, 40(2):666; Beauregard to Lee, 16 June 1864 (two messages), 51(2):1078–79, and 17 June 1864 (two messages), 51(2):1079.

90. E. R. Crockett, Diary, 18 June 1864, Crockett Papers, TxU; Lee to Bragg, 18 June 1864, *OR* 40(2):667; Beauregard to Bragg, 18 June 1864, 40(2):668.

91. T. L. McCarty, Diary, 18 June 1864, McCarty Papers, TxU.

92. J. P. Fuller, Diary, 18 June 1864, Fuller Papers, NcU.

93. F. M. Coker to his wife, 20 June 1864, Heidler Collection, GU.

94. J. W. Albright, Diary, 18 June 1864, Albright Papers, NcU.

95. Stephen Elliott to his wife, 18 June 1864, Elliott Family Papers, ScU.

96. W. D. Alexander, Diary, 19 June 1864, Alexander Papers, NcU.

97. B. W. Justice to his wife, 27 June 1864, Justice Papers, GEU.

98. C. M. Blackford to his wife, 18 June 1864, in Blackford and Blackford, *Letters From Lee's Army*, 257–58.

99. S. P. Lockhart to his sister, 26 June 1864, Browning Papers, NcD.

100. Stephen Elliott to his wife, 26 June 1864, Elliott Family Papers, ScU; A. B. Simms to his sister, 22 June 1864, in Peacock, "A Georgian's View of War," 111–12; Elias Davis to his wife, 20 June 1864, Davis Papers, NcU; F. M. Coker to his wife, 19 June 1864, Heidler Collection, GU.

101. E. P. Alexander to his wife, 19 June 1864, Alexander Papers, NcU.

102. J. P. Fuller, Diary, 20 June 1864, Fuller Papers, NcU.

103. Pvt. Ira Traweek, Jeff Davis Battery, to his sister, 20 June 1864, Ira Traweek Papers, Confederate Microfilm Miscellany, GEU.

104. Lee to his wife, 19 June 1864, in Dowdey and Manarin, *Wartime Papers*, 793.

105. Lee to Seddon, 21 June 1864 (first quotation), *OR* 40(2):672, and 26 June 1864 (second quotation), 40(2):690. See also Seddon to Lee, 24 June 1864, 40(2): 684–85, and 25 June 1864, 40(2):686–87.

106. Lee to Davis, 21 June 1864, in Freeman, *Lee's Dispatches*, 254.

107. Lee to Early, 18 June 1864, *OR* 40(2):667.

108. Early to Lee, 30 June 1864, *OR* 51(2):1029.

CHAPTER 4

1. 1st Lt. Robert Emory Park, Co. F, 12th Alabama, Diary, 13 June 1864, in Park, "Diary," May 1876, 373; J. E. Green, Diary, 13 June 1864, Green Papers, NcU. See also Vandiver, *Jubal's Raid*, 1–24; Cooling, *Jubal Early's Raid*, 1–29; and Freeman, *Lee's Lieutenants*, 3:524–27.

2. J. E. Green, Diary, 13 June 1864, Green Papers, NcU.

3. V. E. Lucas to J. J. Dillard, 16 June 1864, Dillard Papers, NcD.

4. William Beavans, Diary, 17 June 1864, Beavans Papers, NcU; J. S. Anglin to his parents, 28 June 1864, Anglin Papers, LC.

5. Bryan Grimes to his wife, 18 June 1864, Grimes Papers, NcU.

6. Early to Breckinridge, 16 June 1864, *OR* 37(1):763, 16 June 1864 (four additional messages), 37(1):763–64, and 17 June 1864, 37(1):765. See also J. E. Green, Diary, 17 June 1864, Green Papers, NcU; William Beavans, Diary, 17–18 June 1864, Beavans Papers, NcU; and Brig. Gen. Clement A. Evans, Evans/Gordon/Valley, to his wife, 18 June 1864, in Stephens, *Intrepid Warrior*, 420–21.

7. Early to Lee, 19, 22 June 1864, *OR* 37(1):160; Lee to Seddon, 19 June 1864, 37(1):766; Jedediah Hotchkiss, Diary, 17–19 June 1864, in McDonald, *Make Me A Map of the Valley*, 211–12; William Beavans, Diary, 19–22 June 1864, Beavans Papers, NcU; J. S. Anglin to his parents, 27 June 1864, Anglin Papers, LC; Brig. Gen. William Gaston Lewis, Lewis/Ramseur/Valley, to his wife, 27 June 1864, William Gaston Lewis Papers, NcU.

8. R. E. Park, Diary, 21 June 1864, in Park, "Diary," May 1876, 374.

9. J. S. Anglin to his parents, 27 June 1864, Anglin Papers, LC.

10. William Beavans, Diary, 15 June 1864, Beavans Papers, NcU; Bryan Grimes to his wife, 16 June 1864, Grimes Papers, NcU. See also V. E. Lucas to J. J. Dillard, 16 June 1864, Dillard Papers, NcD.

11. J. S. Anglin to his parents, 28 June 1864, Anglin Papers, LC.

12. J. E. Green, Diary, 14, 17 June 1864, Green Papers, NcU.

13. Early to Lee, 22 June 1864, *OR* 37(1):160; A. S. Pendleton to Breckinridge, 23 June 1864, 37(1):766; Jedediah Hotchkiss's report, 43(1):1019 (app.); Hotchkiss, Diary, 22–24 June 1864, in McDonald, *Make Me a Map of the Valley*, 213.

14. Capt. Cary Whitaker, Company D, 43d North Carolina, Diary, 25 June 1864, Cary Whitaker Papers, NcU.

15. B. L. Wynn, Diary, 24 June 1864, Wynn Papers, Ms-Ar.

16. W. G. Lewis to his wife, 27 June 1864, Lewis Papers, NcU.

17. Lee to Davis, 29 June 1864, *OR* 37(1):769–70; GO, Valley, 27 June 1864, 37(1):768.

18. GO, Valley, 27 June 1864, *OR* 37(1):768.

19. R. E. Park, Diary, 28 June 1864, in Park, "Diary," May 1876, 375.

20. Hotchkiss's report, *OR* 43(1):1019 (app.).

21. J. S. Anglin to his parents, 27 June 1864, Anglin Papers, LC.

22. Early to Lee, 30 June 1864, *OR* 51(2):1028–29.

23. A. E. McGarity to his wife, 30 June 1864, in Burnett, "Letters of a Confederate Surgeon," December 1945, 246.

24. R. E. Park, Diary, 29 June 1864, in Park, "Diary," May 1876, 376.

25. Hotchkiss's report, *OR* 43(1):1019–20 (app.); Hotchkiss, Diary, 3–4 July 1864, in McDonald, *Make Me a Map of the Valley*, 213; William Beavans, Diary, 1–5 July 1864, Beavans Papers, NcU; A. H. Jackson to his mother, 5 July 1864, Harden Family Papers, NcD; R. E. Park, Diary, 1–5 July 1864, in Park, "Diary," May 1876, 376–77; C. A. Evans, Diary, 1–5 July 1864, in Stephens, *Intrepid Warrior*, 423–24.

26. 3d Sgt. William H. Aycock, Company E, 13th Georgia, to W. R. Redding, 23 July 1864, Redding Papers, NcU. See also 2d Sgt. Henry P. Fortson, Company B, 31st Georgia, to Mrs. N. A. Barnes, 19 July 1864, Barnes Family Papers, ViU.

27. William Beavans, Diary, 5 July 1864, Beavans Papers, NcD.

28. Hotchkiss's report, *OR* 43(1):1020 (app.); H. P. Fortson to Mrs. R. A. Barnes, 19 July 1864, Barnes Family Papers, ViU; W. H. Aycock to W. R. Redding, 23 July 1864, Redding Papers, NcU; W. H. Brotherton to his family, 5 July 1864, Brotherton Papers, NcD; William Beavans, Diary, 6 July 1864, Beavans Papers, NcU.

29. Early to Breckinridge, 5 July 1864, and GO, Valley, 5 July 1864, *OR* 37(2):592.

30. GO, Valley, 5 July 1864, *OR* 37(2):592.

31. A. H. Jackson to his mother, 5 July 1864, Harden Family Papers, NcD.

32. Gordon's report, *OR* 37(1):352.

33. Early's report, *OR* 37(1):347–48; Gordon's report 37(1):350–52; Hotchkiss's report, 43(1):1020–21 (app.). See also reports of Federal commanders, 37(1), as well as Vandiver, *Jubal's Raid*, 104–24; Cooling, *Jubal Early's Raid*, 61–81; and Freeman, *Lee's Lieutenants*, 3:560–64.

34. Early's report, *OR* 37(1):348.

35. W. G. Lewis to his wife, 18 July 1864, Lewis Papers, NcU; Jedediah Hotchkiss, Diary, 9 July 1864, in McDonald, *Make Me a Map of the Valley*, 25; William Beavans, Diary, 9 July 1864, Beavans Papers, NcU. See also B. L. Wynn, Diary, 9 July 1864, Wynn Papers, Ms-Ar, and R. E. Park, Diary, 9 July 1864, in Park, "Diary," May 1876, 378–79.

36. W. H. Aycock to W. R. Redding, 23 July 1864, Redding Papers, NcU.

37. J. B. Gordon to his wife, 11 July 1864, Gordon Family Papers, GU.

38. Gordon's report, *OR* 37(1):352.

39. J. B. Gordon to his wife, 11 July 1864, Gordon Family Papers, GU.

40. William Beavans, Diary, 10 July 1864, Beavans Papers, NcU. See also B. L. Wynn, Diary, 10 July 1864, Wynn Papers, Ms-Ar.

41. Early's report, *OR* 37(1):348.

42. B. L. Wynn, Diary, 10 July 1864, Wynn Papers, Ms-Ar.

43. A. S. Pendleton, Asst. Adjt. Gen., Valley, to Breckinridge, 10 July 1864, *OR* 37(2):594.

44. Early's report, *OR* 37(1):348.

45. B. L. Wynn, Diary, 11 June 1864, Wynn Papers, Ms-Ar.

46. William Beavans, Diary, 11 July 1864, Beavans Papers, NcU. See also Early's report, *OR* 37(1):348.

47. Early's report, *OR* 37(1):348. See also Hotchkiss's report, 43(1):1021 (app.).

48. J. B. Gordon to his wife, 11 July 1864, Gordon Family Papers, GU.

49. Early's report, *OR* 37(1):348. See also Hotchkiss's report, 43(1):1021 (app.).

50. B. L. Wynn, Diary, 12 July 1864, Wynn Papers, Ms-Ar.

51. William Beavans, Diary, 12 July 1864, Beavans Papers, NcU.

52. Early's report, *OR* 37(1):348–49; Hotchkiss's report, 43(1):1021 (app.); reports of Federal commanders, 37(1). See also William Beavans, Diary, 12–14 July 1864, Beavans Papers, NcU, and B. L. Wynn, Diary, 13–14 July 1864, Wynn Papers, Ms-Ar, as well as the secondary accounts in Cooling, *Jubal's Early's Raid*, 83–204; Vandiver, *Jubal's Raid*, 122–74; and Freeman, *Lee's Lieutenants*, 3:564–67.

53. R. E. Park, Diary, 12 July 1864, in Park, "Diary," May 1876, 380.

54. S. D. Ramseur to his wife, 15 July 1864, Ramseur Papers, NcU. See also John B. Gordon to his wife, 11 July 1864, Gordon Family Papers, GU, and E. A. T. Nicholson, Asst. Adjt. Gen., Lomax/Cavalry/Valley, to his niece, 23 August 1864, Grattan Papers, NcU.

55. W. G. Lewis to his wife, 18 July 1864, Lewis Papers, NcU.

56. H. P. Fortson to Mrs. R. A. Barnes, 19 July 1864, Barnes Family Papers, ViU.

57. Lee to Seddon, 20 July 1864, *OR* 37(1):346, and 23, 26, 28 July 1864, 37(1):347; Rodes's report, 37(1):353–54; Hotchkiss's report, 43(1):1021–23 (app.). See also reports of Federal commanders, 37(1), as well as Freeman, *Lee's Lieutenants*, 3:568–71. For a useful introduction to the second and climactic phase of the Shenandoah Valley campaign of 1864, see Wert, *From Winchester to Cedar Creek*, and Gallagher, *Struggle for the Shenandoah*.

58. Jedediah Hotchkiss, Diary, 4–31 August 1864, in McDonald, *Make Me a Map of the Valley*, 220–26; Hotchkiss's report, *OR* 43(1):1021–26 (app.).

59. A. E. McGarity to his wife, 27 July 1864, in Burnett, "Letters of a Confederate Surgeon," December 1945, 247.

60. W. H. Aycock to W. R. Redding, 23 July 1864, Redding Papers, NcU.

61. J. E. Green, Diary, 21 July 1864, Green Papers, NcU. See also J. S. Anglin to his sisters, 1 August 1864, Anglin Papers, LC; E. A. T. Nicholson to his niece, 23 August 1864, Grattan Papers, NcU; and T. P. Devereux to his sister, 28 August 1864, Devereux Papers, Nc-Ar.

62. Maj. Edward Moore, Insp. Gen., Gordon / Valley, Inspection Report, 21 August 1864, *OR* 43(1):609.

63. E. A. T. Nicholson to his niece, 23 August 1864, Grattan Papers, NcU.

64. A. H. Jackson to his mother, 5 July 1864, Harden Family Papers, NcD; H. P. Fortson to Mrs. R. A. Barnes, 19 July 1864, Barnes Family Papers, ViU. See also W. H. Aycock to W. R. Redding, 23 July 1864, Redding Papers, NcU, and T. P. Devereux to his sister, 28 August 1864, Devereux Papers, Nc-Ar.

65. W. H. Aycock to W. R. Redding, 23 July 1864, Redding Papers, NcU.

66. E. A. T. Nicholson to his niece, 23 August 1864, Grattan Papers, NcU.

67. J. E. Green, Diary, 8, 18, 20 August 1864, Green Papers, NcU; see also 20 July–26 August 1864.

68. B. L. Wynn, Diary, 31 July 1864, Wynn Papers, Ms-Ar.

69. S. D. Ramseur to his wife, 23 July 1864 (second letter), Ramseur Papers, NcU.

70. G. P. Ring to his wife, 27 July 1864, ANV Papers, LHA Collection, LNT.

71. A. E. McGarity to his wife, 8 August 1864, in Burnett, "Letters of a Confederate Surgeon," December 1945, 249. See also McGarity to his wife, 20 August 1864 (December 1945, 251–52) and 28 August 1864 (March 1946, 35–36), in ibid.; W. H. Brotherton to his family, 10 August 1864, Brotherton Papers, NcD; and W. R. Redding, to his wife, 14 August 1864, Redding Papers, NcU.

72. W. H. Brotherton to his father, 6 August 1864, Brotherton Papers, NcD.

73. Maj. Seaton Gales, Asst. Adjt. Gen., Cox / Rodes / Valley, to his wife, 14 August 1864, Gales Family Papers, Nc-Ar.

74. 1st Lt. James Manning Goldsmith, Company K, 60th Georgia, to his father, 28 August 1864, UDC Typescripts, vol. 2, G-Ar.

75. S. D. Ramseur to his wife, 15 July, 23 July (second letter) 1864, Ramseur Papers, NcU.

76. B. L. Wynn, Diary, 24, 27 July 1864, Wynn Papers, Ms-Ar.

77. A. E. McGarity to his wife, 8, 28 August 1864, in Burnett, "Letters of a Confederate Surgeon," December 1945, 249; March 1946, 35–36.

78. E. L. Moore, Inspection Report, Gordon / Valley, *OR* 43(1):609.

79. Lt. Col. H. E. Peyton, Asst. Adjt. & Insp. Gen., ANV, Endorsement, 10 September 1864, *OR* 43(1:610). See also Capt. Randolph I. Barton, Asst. Insp. Gen., York / Gordon / Valley, Inspection Report, 19 August 1864, Records of the Adjutant & Inspector General's Dept., War Dept. Collection of Confederate Rec-

ords, Record Group 109, NA; NA microfilm publication M935, roll 10 (hereafter cited as Inspection Reports, NA, with inspecting officer, unit, date, and microfilm roll number).

80. E. L. Moore, Inspection Report, Gordon/Valley, 21 August 1864, and H. E. Peyton, Endorsement, 10 September 1864, *OR* 43(1):609–10.

81. S. D. Ramseur to his wife, 23 July 1864 (first letter), 23 July 1864 (second letter), Ramseur Papers, NcU. See also Ramseur to David Schenck, 20 August 1864, ibid.

82. J. F. Coghill to his brother, 23 July 1864, Coghill Papers, AAP.

83. Rodes to Ewell, 12 September 1864, *OR* 37(1):353–54. For Ewell's orders, see SO 137, A&IGO, 13 June 1864, 40(2):646.

84. Bryan Grimes to his wife, 15 August 1864, Grimes Papers, NcU.

85. Ibid.

86. J. F. Coghill to his brother, 23 July 1864, Coghill Papers, AAP.

87. J. S. Anglin to his parents, 27 June 1864, Anglin Papers, LC.

88. W. G. Lewis to his wife, 27 June 1864, Lewis Papers, NcU.

89. W. H. Brotherton to his family, 10 August 1864, Brotherton Papers, NcD. See also Brotherton to his brother, 6 August 1864, ibid.; William Beavans, Diary, 26–27 June, 2 July 1864, Beavans Papers, NcU; and J. M. Goldsmith to his father, 28 August 1864, UDC Typescripts, vol. 2, G-Ar.

90. A. E. McGarity to his wife, 30 June, 8 August 1864, in Burnett, "Letters of a Confederate Surgeon," December 1945, 246, 249.

91. William Beavans, Diary, 26 June 1864, Beavans Papers, NcU.

92. R. E. Park, Diary, 4 July 1864, in Park, "Diary," May 1876, 377.

93. J. S. Anglin to his sisters, 1 August 1864, Anglin Papers, LC.

94. J. S. Anglin to his sisters, 28 June 1864, ibid. See also Anglin to his parents, 27 June 1864, and to his sisters, 1 August 1864, ibid.; William Beavans, Diary, 26–27, 29 June 1864, Beavans Papers, NcU; and W. H. Brotherton to his family, 10 August 1864, Brotherton Papers, NcD.

95. J. S. Anglin to his sisters, 28 June 1864, Anglin Papers, LC. See also A. H. Jackson to his mother, 5 July 1864, Harden Family Papers, NcD, and Capt. Ruffin Barnes, Company C, 43d North Carolina, to his wife, 2 August 1864, in Johnston, "Confederate Letters," 99.

96. Cary Whitaker, Diary, 30 July 1864, Whitaker Papers, NcU. See also J. S. Anglin to his sisters, 28 June 1864, Anglin Papers, LC, and William Beavans, Diary, 5 July 1864, Beavans Papers, NcU.

97. W. G. Lewis to his wife, 27 June 1864, Lewis Papers, NcU.

98. William Beavans, Diary, 3–4, 17 July 1864, Beavans Papers, NcU. See also Beavans, Diary, 12 June–19 July 1864, ibid., and Cary Whitaker, Diary, 1 August 1864, Whitaker Papers, NcU.

99. W. G. Lewis to his wife, 27 June 1864, Lewis Papers, NcU.

100. J. S. Anglin to his sisters, 1 August 1864, Anglin Papers, LC.

101. W. R. Battle to his mother, 30 August 1864, in Lee, *Forget-Me-Nots*, 121;

Walter Raleigh Battle, 4th [North Carolina] Infantry, Compiled Service Records, NA, microcopy M270, roll 136.

102. Ruffin Barnes to his wife, 2 August 1864, in Johnston, "Confederate Letters," 99.

103. Lee to Davis, 29 June 1864, *OR* 37(1):769–70.

104. Lee to Seddon, 19 July 1864, *OR* 37(1):346.

105. Lee to Davis, 4 August 1864, *OR* 42(2):1161; Lee to Early, 8 August 1864, 43(1):990; Lee to Anderson, 43(1):995; Lee to Hampton, 11 August 1864, 43(1): 996; Lee to Davis, 43(1):996–97; Lee to Anderson, 15 August 1864, 43(1):997; diary of the I Corps, 6–18 August 1864, 42(1):873–74.

106. A. B. Simms, Clerk, 53d Georgia, to his sister, 15 August 1864, in Peacock, "A Georgian's View of War," 119.

107. W. R. Redding to his wife, 14 August 1864, Redding Papers, NcU. See also R. E. Park, Diary, 18 August 1864, in Park, "Diary," June 1876, 431.

108. T. P. Devereux to his sister, 28 August 1864, Devereux Papers, Nc-Ar.

109. Daniel Boyd to his father, 10 August 1864, Boyd Papers, NcD. See also Capt. Francis Warrington Dawson, Asst. Chief of Ordnance, I Corps, to his mother, 7 August 1864, in Dawson, *Reminiscences*, 200–201, and Charles Kerrison to his sister, 17 August 1864, Kerrison Family Papers, ScU.

110. 2d Lt. Harvey Judson Hightower, Company G, 20th Georgia, to his sister, 2 August 1864, Harvey Hightower Papers, G-Ar.

CHAPTER 5

1. F. M. Coker to his wife, 16–17 July 1864, Heidler Collection, GU.

2. T. L. McCarty, Diary, 22 June 1864, McCarty Papers, TxU.

3. Daniel Boyd to his father, 7 July 1864, Boyd Papers, NcD.

4. Pvt. William Thomas Casey, Company K, 34th Virginia, to his brother, 30 June 1864, William Thomas Casey Papers, ViHi.

5. H. I. Greer to his father, 28 June 1864, Greer Papers, LC. See also Brig. Gen. John C. C. Sanders, Sanders/Mahone/III Corps, to his father, 20 June 1864, William Henry Sanders Papers, A-Ar; Ira Traweek to his sister, 20 June 1864, Traweek Papers, Confederate Microfilm Miscellany, GEU; and Elias Davis to his wife, 20 June 1864, Davis Papers, NcU.

6. B. W. Justice to his wife, 27 June 1864, Justice Papers, GEU.

7. J. P. Fuller, Diary, 3–4 July 1864, Fuller Papers, NcU.

8. T. L. McCarty, Diary, 4 July 1864, McCarty Papers, TxU. See also Adjt. O. D. Cooke, 24th North Carolina, to William J. Clarke, 3 July 1864, William J. Clarke Papers, NcU; F. M. Coker to his wife, 4 July 1864, and to J. W. Furlow, 4 July 1864, Heidler Collection, GU; and *Richmond Examiner*, 4 July 1864.

9. S. P. Lockhart to his mother, 19 June 1864, Browning Papers, NcD. See also F. M. Coker to his wife, 19 June 1864, Heidler Collection, GU, and Elias Davis to his wife, 20 June 1864, Davis Papers, NcU.

10. F. M. Coker to his wife, 4 July 1864, Heidler Collection, GU.

11. Pvt. Thomas Lafayette Alexander, Company C, 37th North Carolina, to his wife, 6 July 1864, T. J. [T. L.] Alexander Papers, PNB. See also W. D. Williams to his fiancée, 4, 16 July 1864, Williams Papers, TxHiC; T. G. Trimmier to his wife, 9, 15 July 1864, Trimmier Collection, T; and Sgt. Maj. J. Mark Smither, 5th Texas, to his mother, 17 July 1864, J. Mark Smither Papers, TxHiC.

12. Pvt. Henry Ferrell, Company H, 31st North Carolina, to Sidney Horton, 14 July 1864, Willis Horton Papers, NcD. See also Maj. William Sammons Grady, 25th North Carolina, to his wife, 7 July 1864, Henry Woodfin Grady Papers, GEU, and W. J. Pegram to his sister, 21 July 1864, Pegram-Johnson-McIntosh Family Papers, ViHi.

13. J. W. McLure to his wife, 29 June 1864, McLure Family Papers, ScU.

14. S. G. Welch to his wife, 6 July 1864, in Welch, *A Confederate Surgeon's Letters*, 102.

15. Capt. Heman H. Perry, Quartermaster, Benning (DuBose)/Field/I Corps, to H. L. Benning, 22 July 1864, Henry Lewis Benning Papers, NcU. See also M. H. Fitzpatrick to his wife, 10 July 1864, in Hammock, *Letters to Amanda*, 147–48, and J. M. Smither to his uncle, 24 July 1864, Smither Papers, TxHiC.

16. J. W. Albright, Diary, 28 July 1864, Albright Papers, NcU.

17. F. M. Coker to his wife, 21 July 1864, Heidler Collection, GU.

18. T. L. Alexander to his wife, 6 July 1864, Alexander Papers, PNB.

19. J. F. Sale, Diary, 13 July 1864, Sale Papers, Vi.

20. John Bratton's report, *OR* 40(1):767. See also Pvt. Timothy Morgan, Company F, 49th Alabama, to his wife and children, 1 July 1864, Timothy Morgan Papers, PNB; Pvt. James H. Lee, Company C, 43d Alabama, to his wife, 7 July 1864, James H. Lee Papers, GEU; S. C. Lowry, Diary, 18 July 1864, Lowry Papers, ScU; 1st Sgt. R. P. Scarbrough, Hurt's Battery, to his cousin, 22 July 1864, Confederate Miscellany, GEU; and H. C. Conner to his wife, 28 July 1864, Conner Papers, ScU.

21. B. W. Justice to his wife, 11–12, 14 July 1864, Justice Papers, GEU.

22. W. E. Bird to his wife, 17 July 1864, in Rozier, *Granite Farm Letters*, 176. Bird's "Capt. Jones" was Capt. A. M. Jones of Company K, the "Webster Confederate Guards," of the 17th Georgia. The private in the 2d Georgia has not been identified. A. M. Jones, 17th [Georgia] Infantry, Compiled Service Records, NA, microcopy M266, roll 305.

23. H. H. Perry to H. L. Benning, 22 July 1864, Benning Papers, NcU.

24. B. R. Johnson's report, 16 July 1864, *OR* 40(1):781; Johnson's daily reports, 1–29 July 1864, 40(1):773–86, esp. 17–23 and 26 July 1864, 40(1):773–85. See also O. D. Cooke to W. J. Clarke, 3 July 1864, Clarke Papers, NcU; W. S. Grady to his wife, 7 July 1864, Grady Papers, GEU; and W. T. Casey to his brother, 7 July 1864, Casey Papers, ViHi.

25. S. C. Lowry, Diary, 18 July 1864, Lowry Papers, ScU.

26. J. P. Simms's report, *OR* 40(1):768.

27. J. B. Evans to his wife, 3 July 1864, Evans Papers, NcD. See also W. S.

Grady to his wife, 7 July 1864, Grady Papers, GEU; Daniel Boyd to his father, 7 July 1864, Boyd Papers, NcD; and R. P. Scarbrough to his cousin, 22 July 1864, Confederate Miscellany, GEU.

28. E. P. Alexander to his wife, 1 July 1864, Alexander Papers, NcU.

29. Timothy Morgan to his wife and children, 1 July 1864, Morgan Papers, PNB.

30. B. W. Justice to his wife, 11–12, 14 July 1864, Justice Papers, GEU.

31. B. R. Johnson's daily report, 15 July 1864, *OR* 40(1):780–81.

32. B. W. Justice to his wife, 11–12, 14 July 1864, Justice Papers, GEU.

33. W. T. Casey to his brother, 7 July 1864, Casey Papers, ViHi.

34. W. S. Grady to his wife, 7, 12 July 1864, Grady Papers, GEU. Grady, who was mortally wounded at the Crater on 30 July and died on 20 October, was the father of Henry W. Grady, who later became the editor of the *Atlanta Constitution* and the leading spokesman for the New South movement in the postwar South.

35. Ibid.

36. John Bratton's report, *OR* 40(1):767.

37. E. P. Alexander to his wife, 1 July 1864, Alexander Papers, NcU; J. A. Reynolds, Diary, 7–8, 12 July 1864, Reynolds Papers, RNBP; B. W. Justice to his wife, 27 June 1864, Justice Papers, GEU.

38. E. R. Crockett, Diary, 30 June 1864, Crockett Papers, TxU. See also Timothy Morgan to his wife and children, 1 July 1864, Morgan Papers, PNB.

39. S. G. Welch to his wife, 6 July 1864, in Welch, *A Confederate Surgeon's Letters*, 102.

40. Lee to Seddon, 22, 24 June 1864, *OR* 40(1):749–50; diary of the I Corps, 22–23 June 1864, 40(1):761; Richard H. Anderson to Lee, 22 June 1864, 52(2): 1025; A. P. Hill to W. H. Taylor, 22 June 1864, 52(2):1025–26; William Mahone to Hill, 22 June 1864, 52(2):1026; Hill to Lee, 23 June 1864, 52(2):1027; Hill to Taylor, 24 June 1864, 52(2):1028.

41. Surg. William Henry Sanders, 11th Alabama, to his father, 7 July 1864, W. H. Sanders Papers, A-Ar. See also J. A. Reynolds, Diary, 22 June 1864, James A. Reynolds Papers, RNBP, and J. C. C. Sanders to his mother, 28 June 1864, W. H. Sanders Papers, A-Ar.

42. Lee to Seddon, 24–25 June 1864, *OR* 40(1):750–51; diary of the I Corps, 23–24 June 1864, 40(1):761; R. F. Hoke's report (with endorsements), 40(1:)796–99; Johnson Hagood's report, 40(1):802–5.

43. T. L. McCarty, Diary, 24 June 1864, McCarty Papers, TxU; H. I. Greer to his father, 28 June 1864, Greer Papers, LC. See also H. I. Greer to his parents, 24 June 1864, Greer Papers, LC; J. P. Fuller, Diary, 24 June 1864, Fuller Papers, NcU; and F. M. Coker to his wife, 24, 26 June 1864, Heidler Collection, GU.

44. F. M. Coker to his wife, 26 June 1864, Heidler Collection, GU. See also W. J. Pegram to his sister, 28 June 1864, Pegram-Johnson-McIntosh Family Papers, ViHi.

45. Lee's undated endorsement to Hoke's report, *OR* 40(1):799.

46. Pendleton's report, *OR* 40(1):759; diary of the I Corps, 27–28 July 1864, 40(1):762; Ewell's report, 40(1):805–6; Lee to Anderson, 27 July 1864, 40(3):809; Ewell to Kershaw, 27 July 1864 (three messages), 40(3):810–11; and Ewell to Lee, 28 July 1864, 40(3):813.

47. Reports of Lt. Col. J. W. McGill, 18th North Carolina, 29 July 1864; Capt. J. G. Harris, 7th North Carolina, 29 July 1864; and Capt. W. J. Callais, 33d North Carolina, 29 July 1864, all in Lane Papers, AAP. See also reports of Lt. Col. W. H. A. Speer, 28th North Carolina, 31 July 1864, and Maj. J. L. Bost, 37th North Carolina, 3 August 1864, ibid.

48. Pvt. Augustin E. Shore, Company I, 33d North Carolina, to his brother and sister, 2 August 1864, Augustin E. Shore Papers, GEU.

49. John Bratton to his wife, 9 July 1864, Bratton Papers, ScCoAH; J. P. Fuller, Diary, 8 July 1864, Fuller Papers, NcU.

50. T. L. McCarty, Diary, 8 June 1864, McCarty Papers, TxU.

51. John Bratton to his wife, 9 July 1864, Bratton Papers, ScCoAH.

52. Diary of the I Corps, 8 July 1864, *OR* 40(1):761. See also E. R. Crockett, Diary, 8 July 1864, Crockett Papers, TxU, and *Richmond Sentinel*, 15 July 1864.

53. See, e.g., J. P. Simms's report, *OR* 40(1):768; B. R. Johnson's daily reports, 30 June 1864, 40(2):703–4, and 1–14, 22 July 1864, 40(1):773–80, 783–84; Lee to Anderson, 4 July 1864, 40(2):713; Johnson to Col. John T. Goode, Wise (Goode)/Johnson/Beauregard, 12 July 1864, 40(3):770; Johnson to Col. Paul F. Faison, Ransom (Faison)/Johnson/Beauregard, 14 July 1864, 40(3):775.

54. W. S. Grady to his wife, 12 July 1864, Grady Papers, GEU.

55. J. P. Fuller, Diary, 30 June 1864, Fuller Papers, NcU.

56. H. H. Perry to H. L. Benning, 22 July 1864, Benning Papers, NcU.

57. B. W. Justice to his wife, 11–12, 14 July 1864, Justice Papers, GEU.

58. Lee to Anderson, 4 July 1864, *OR* 40(2):713.

59. J. M. Smither to his uncle, 24 July 1864, Smither Papers, TxHiC.

60. John Bratton to his wife, 2–3 July 1864, Bratton Papers, ScCoAH. See also Stephen Elliott to his wife, 26 June 1864, Elliott Family Papers, ScU; W. S. Grady to his wife, 7 July 1864, Grady Papers, GEU; and B. R. Johnson's daily report, 5 July 1864, *OR* 40(1):775–76.

61. Stephen Elliott to his wife, 26 June 1864, Elliott Family Papers, ScU.

62. Lee to his wife, 26 June 1864, in Dowdey and Manarin, *Wartime Papers*, 808.

63. J. W. Calton to his brother, 6 July 1864, Calton Papers, Nc-Ar.

64. 2d Lt. E. Harleston Barton, 2d South Carolina Rifles, to J. E. Hagood, 6 July 1864, Hagood Papers, ScU.

65. J. M. Smither to his sister, 15 July 1864, Smither Papers, TxHiC. See also E. P. Alexander to "Will," 27 June 1864, Alexander Papers, NcU, and B. W. Justice to his wife, 27 June 1864, Justice Papers, GEU.

66. F. M. Coker to his wife, 9 July 1864, Heidler Collection, GU; S. C. Lowry,

Diary, 18 July 1864, Lowry Papers, ScU; H. C. Conner to his wife, 19 July 1864, Conner Papers, ScU; J. B. Evans to his wife, 13 July 1864, Evans Papers, NcD.

67. J. H. Chamberlayne to his sister, 13 July 1864, in Chamberlayne, *Ham Chamberlayne*, 243.

68. T. L. McCarty, Diary, 19 July 1864, McCarty Papers, TxU; J. A. Reynolds, Diary, 19 July 1864, Reynolds Papers, RNBP.

69. A. B. Simms to his sister, 19 July 1864, in Peacock, "A Georgian's View of War," 114. See also E. R. Crockett, Diary, 18–19 July 1864, Crockett Papers, TxU, and F. M. Coker to his wife, 21 July 1864, Heidler Collection, GU.

70. T. L. McCarty, Diary, 24 July 1864, McCarty Papers, TxU.

71. O. D. Cooke to W. J. Clarke, 20 July 1864, Clarke Papers, NcU.

72. F. M. Coker to his wife, 25 July 1864, Heidler Collection, GU. See also E. R. Crockett, Diary, 24 July 1864, Crockett Papers, TxU.

73. B. R. Johnson's daily report, 19 July 1864, *OR* 40(3):784.

74. H. C. Conner to his wife, 19 July 1864, Conner Papers, ScU.

75. John Bratton's report, *OR* 40(1):766.

76. J. B. Evans to his wife, 3 July 1864, Evans Papers, NcD.

77. T. G. Trimmier to his wife, 6 July 1864, Trimmier Collection, T.

78. J. H. Lee to his wife, 7 July 1864, J. H. Lee Papers, GEU.

79. J. W. McLure to his wife, 24 July 1864, McLure Family Papers, ScU.

80. Hoke to Capt. John M. Otey, Asst. Adjt. Gen., Beauregard, 27 June 1864, General Order and Letter Book (1864), Robert F. Hoke Papers, Nc-Ar.

81. H. I. Greer to his father, 28 June 1864, Greer Papers, LC; Henry I. Greer, 25th [South Carolina] Infantry, Compiled Service Records, NA, microcopy M267, roll 345; Johnson Hagood's report, *OR* 36(2):255.

82. H. I. Greer to his father, 13 July 1864, Greer Papers, LC.

83. S. P. Lockhart to his sister, 18 July 1864, Browning Papers, NcD.

84. J. A. Everett to his mother, 7 July 1864, Everett Papers, GEU. See also B. R. Johnson's daily report, 28 July 1864, *OR* 40(1):786; J. W. Calton to his brother, 6 July 1864, Calton Papers, Nc-Ar; E. H. Barton to J. E. Hagood, 6 July 1864, Hagood Papers, ScU; and H. H. Perry to H. L. Benning, 22 July 1864, Benning Papers, NcU.

85. Henry Ferrell to Willis Horton, 14 July 1864, Horton Papers, NcD.

86. Timothy Morgan to his wife and children, 1 July 1864, Morgan Papers, PNB; Pvt. John L. G. Wood, Drummer, 53d Georgia, to his father, 20 July 1864, UDC Typescripts, vol. 4, G-Ar.

87. W. C. Leak to his wife and children, 17 July 1864, Leak Papers, PNB. See also F. M. Coker to his wife, 9 July 1864, Heidler Collection, GU; *Richmond Sentinel*, 15 July 1864; and H. C. Conner to his wife, 28 July 1864, Conner Papers, ScU.

88. S. C. Lowry, Diary, 18 July 1864, Lowry Papers, ScU.

89. T. L. Alexander to his wife, 6 July 1864, Alexander Papers, PNB.

90. Daniel Boyd to his father, 7 July 1864, Boyd Papers, NcD.

91. J. C. C. Sanders to his father, 25 July 1864, Sanders Papers, A-Ar. See also J. P. Fuller, Diary, 7 July 1864, Fuller Papers, NcU.

92. Chaplain John Cowper Granbery, III Corps, to his wife, 21 June 1864, John Cowper Granbery Papers, ViU. See also T. L. McCarty, Diary, 24 July 1864, McCarty Papers, TxU, and E. R. Crockett, Diary, 24 July 1864, Crockett Papers, TxU.

93. J. W. Albright, Diary, 10 July 1864, Albright Papers, NcU. See also Lee to his wife, 10 July 1864, in Dowdey and Manarin, *Wartime Papers*, 818.

94. J. A. Reynolds, Diary, 10 July 1864, Reynolds Papers, RNBP.

95. S. P. Lockhart to his sister, 26 June 1864, Browning Papers, NcD.

96. H. C. Conner to his wife, 28 July 1864, Conner Papers, ScU. See also W. T. Casey to his brother, 7 July 1864, Casey Papers, ViHi.

97. Elias Davis to his wife, 13 July 1864, Davis Papers, NcU.

98. M. H. Fitzpatrick to his wife, 10 July 1864 (first quotation), 18 July 1864 (second quotation), in Hammock, *Letters to Amanda*, 147–49.

99. John C. Babcock, Provost-Marshal-Gen.'s Dept., Army of the Potomac, to Maj. Gen. A. A. Humphreys, Chief of Staff, Army of the Potomac, 11 July 1864, *OR* 40(3):148–49.

100. C. M. Blackford to his wife, 17 July 1864, in Blackford and Blackford, *Letters From Lee's Army*, 267.

101. Orders, Dept. of Virginia and North Carolina, U.S. Army, 5 July 1864, enclosing GO 64, Adjutant-General's Office, U.S. War Dept., 18 February 1864; quoted in Lee to Samuel Cooper, 19 July 1864, *OR* 40(3):782–83.

102. Col. G. H. Sharpe, Deputy Provost-Marshal-Gen., Army of the Potomac, to Maj. Gen. A. A. Humphreys, Chief of Staff, Army of the Potomac, 1 July 1864, *OR* 40(2):564; J. C. Babcock, Provost-Marshal-Gen.'s Dept., Army of the Potomac, to Humphreys, 17 July 1864, 40(3):294.

103. Col. G. H. Sharpe, Provost-Marshal-Gen., Army of the Potomac, to Maj. Gen. A. A. Humphreys, Chief of Staff, Army of the Potomac, 1 July 1864, *OR* 40(2):564.

104. Col. George H. Sharpe, Provost-Marshal-Gen., Army of the Potomac, to Maj. Gen. A. A. Humphreys, Chief of Staff, Army of the Potomac, 18 July 1864, *OR* 40(3):315; see also J. C. Babcock to Humphreys, 17 July 1864, 40(3):294, and Sharpe to Humphreys, 19 July 1864, 40(3):334. For other examples of Federal interviews with deserters in July 1864, see Babcock to Humphreys, 8 July 1864, 40(3):75–76; Babcock to Humphreys, 13 July 1864, 40(3):209–10; and Maj. Gen. Winfield S. Hancock, II Army Corps/Army of the Potomac, to Humphreys, 29 July 1864, 40(3):598.

105. Maj. Gen. W. S. Hancock, II Corps/Army of the Potomac, to Maj. Gen. A. A. Humphreys, Chief of Staff, Army of the Potomac, 29 July 1864, 40(3):598. See also Maj. Gen. Ambrose E. Burnside, IX Army Corps/Army of the Potomac, to Brig. Gen. Seth Williams, Asst. Adjt. Gen., HQ, Army of the Potomac, 17 July 1864, *OR* 40(3):300–301. For letters and diaries from North Carolinians who *did* vote—for Vance—see also J. W. Albright, Diary, 28 July 1864, Albright Papers,

NcU; W. D. Alexander, Diary, 29 July 1864, Alexander Papers, NcU; 3d Corp. Benjamin H. Freeman, Company K, 44th North Carolina, to his parents, 29 July 1864, in Wright, *Confederate Letters*; and A. M. Scales to his wife, 2 August 1864, Scales Papers, Nc-Ar.

106. J. A. Everett to his mother, 7 July 1864, Everett Papers, GEU.

107. J. C. Granbery to his wife, 14 July 1864, Granbery Papers, ViU.

108. O. D. Cooke to William J. Clarke, 20 July 1864, Clarke Papers, NcU.

109. Stephen Elliott to his wife, 10 July 1864, Elliott Family Papers, ScU.

110. J. B. Evans to his wife, 13 July 1864, Evans Papers, NcD.

111. S. P. Lockhart to his sister, 18 July 1864, Browning Papers, NcD.

112. James Farrow to J. E. Hagood, 25 July 1864, Hagood Papers, ScU.

113. W. D. Williams to his fiancée, 16 July 1864, Williams Papers, TxHiC. See also F. M. Coker to his wife, 25 July 1864, Heidler Collection, GU, and J. W. McLure to his wife, 28 July 1864, McLure Family Papers, ScU.

114. W. J. Pegram to his sister, 14 July 1864, Pegram-Johnson-McIntosh Family Papers, ViHi.

115. J. P. Fuller, Diary, 17 July 1864, Fuller Papers, NcU.

116. E. R. Crockett to his wife, 15 July 1864, Crockett Papers, TxU. See also Pvt. Thomas E. Jackson, Company E, Cobb's Legion Cavalry, to his cousin, 11 July 1864, Harden Family Papers, NcD; J. M. Smither to his sister, 15, 17 July 1864, Smither Papers, TxHiC; and S. C. Lowry, Diary, 18 July 1864, Lowry Papers, ScU.

117. F. M. Coker to his wife, 16 July 1864, Heidler Collection, GU. See also T. G. Trimmier to his wife, 15 July 1864, Trimmier Collection, T; W. E. Bird to his wife, 17 July 1864, in Rozier, *Granite Farm Letters*, 176; and James Conner to his mother, 30 July 1864, in Moffett, *Letters of General James Conner*, 144–45.

118. Stephen Elliott to his wife, 14 July 1864, Elliott Family Papers, ScU. See also Elliott to his wife, 16 July 1864, ibid.

119. H. I. Greer to his father, 13 July 1864, Greer Papers, LC.

120. T. G. Trimmier to his wife, 15 July 1864, Trimmier Collection, T; W. E. Bird to his wife, 18 July 1864, in Rozier, *Granite Farm Letters*, 178; F. M. Coker to his wife, 21 July 1864, Heidler Collection, GU.

121. C. M. Blackford to his wife, 17 July 1864, in Blackford and Blackford, *Letters from Lee's Army*, 267.

122. M. H. Fitzpatrick to his wife, 18 July 1864, in Hammock, *Letters to Amanda*, 150.

123. Lee to Davis, 12 July 1864, in Dowdey and Manarin, *Wartime Papers*, 821.

124. Stephen Elliott to his wife, 21 July 1864, Elliott Family Papers, ScU. See also J. W. McLure to his wife, 24 July 1864, McLure Family Papers, ScU, and F. M. Coker to his wife, 25 July 1864, Heidler Collection, GU.

125. E. R. Crockett, Diary, 24 July 1864, Crockett Papers, TxU; Elias Davis to his wife, 27 July 1864, Davis Papers, NcU.

126. F. M. Coker to his wife, 25 July 1864, Heidler Collection, GU. See also

J. M. Smither to his uncle, 24 July 1864, Smither Papers, TxHiC, and J. W. McLure to his wife, 24 July 1864, McLure Family Papers, ScU.

127. H. C. Conner to his wife, 28 July 1864, Conner Papers, ScU. See also J. H. Chamberlayne to his mother, 28 July 1864, in Chamberlayne, *Ham Chamberlayne*, 246, and B. H. Freeman to his parents, 29 July 1864, in Wright, *Confederate Letters*, 48.

128. L. G. Young to his mother, 29 July 1864, Gourdin Papers, GEU.

129. J. W. Albright, Diary, 20 July 1864, Albright Papers, NcU. See also daily reports and orders of Capt. Hugh Thomas Douglas, Company F, 1st Confederate Engineers, to Col. Walter H. Stevens and various staff officers, 13–29 July 1864, *OR* 40(3):772, 774, 776–81, 784–85, 789–92, 795, 797, 801, 806–8, 813, 816.

130. J. W. Albright, Diary, 28 July 1864, Albright Papers, NcU.

131. Pvt. Dorsey N. Binion, Company K, 48th Georgia, to his sister, 1 August 1864, Confederate Miscellany, GEU.

132. Lee to Seddon, 30 July 1864 (two messages), 1 August 1864, *OR* 40(1): 752–53; reports of corps and subordinate commanders, 40(1):759–60, 787–93, 795, 799–800, 819–20. See also reports of Federal commanders, 40(1). Secondary accounts of the fighting at the Crater include Cavanaugh and Marvel, *Petersburg Campaign*; Trudeau, *The Last Citadel*, 99–127; and Freeman, *Lee's Lieutenants*, 3:542–44.

133. J. C. C. Sanders to his father, 3 August 1864, Sanders Papers, A-Ar.

134. Sgt. William Russell, Company H, 26th Virginia, Diary, 30 July 1864, William Russell Papers, PNB.

135. B. R. Johnson's report, *OR* 40(1):788, 792.

136. Daniel Boyd to his father, 10 August 1864, Boyd Papers, NcU.

137. Capt. Henry A. Chambers, Company C, 49th North Carolina, Diary, 30 July 1864, in Pearce, *Diary of ... Chambers*, 209. See also Capt. John Alfred Feister Coleman, Company B, 17th South Carolina, Diary, 3 August 1864, Confederate Miscellany I, GEU; Lt. C. C. Haile, 23d South Carolina, report, *OR* 40(1):799–800; and Sgt. A. H. Smyth, Company F, 1st Confederate Engineers, to Capt. H. T. Douglas, 30 July 1864, 40(1):820.

138. R. C. Mabry to his wife, 1 August 1864, Mabry Papers, Nc-Ar.

139. Folsom, *Heroes and Martyrs*, 95.

140. Elias Davis to his wife, 3 August 1864, Davis Papers, NcU. See also Thomas Claybrook Elder to his wife, 30 July 1864, Elder Papers, ViHi; J. F. Sale, Diary, 30 July 1864, Sale Papers, Vi; W. J. Pegram to his sister, 1 August 1864, in James I. Robertson Jr., "'The Boy Artillerist,'" 242–44; D. N. Binion to his sister, 1 August 1864, Confederate Miscellany, GEU; and J. C. C. Sanders to his father, 3 August 1864, Sanders Papers, A-Ar.

141. Lee to Seddon, 13 August 1864 (with endorsement and enclosure), *OR* 40(1):753–54. See also Lee to his wife, 31 July 1864, in Dowdey and Manarin, *Wartime Papers*, 828.

142. W. J. Pegram to his sister, 1 August 1864, in James I. Robertson Jr., "'The Boy Artillerist,'" 244.

143. H. A. Chambers, Diary, 30 July 1864, in Pearce, *Diary of . . . Chambers,* 209–10.

144. Folsom, *Heroes and Martyrs,* 96.

145. Maj. Matthew Norris Love, 25th North Carolina, to his mother, 6 August 1864, PNB; H. A. Chambers, Diary, 30 July 1864, in Pearce, *Diary of . . . Chambers,* 209–10; J. C. C. Sanders to his father, 3 August 1864, Sanders Papers, A-Ar.

146. D. N. Binion to his sister, 1 August 1864, Confederate Miscellany, GEU; 2d Corp. Thomas W. G. Inglet, Company C, 28th Georgia, to his wife, 31 July 1864, Thomas W. G. Inglet Papers, LNT. See also E. R. Crockett, Diary, 30 July 1864, Crockett Papers, TxU; Folsom, *Heroes and Martyrs,* 95; E. C. Anderson to his mother, 1 August 1864, Wayne-Stiles-Anderson Families Papers, GHi; A. M. Scales to his wife, 2 August 1864, Scales Papers, Nc-Ar; and J. A. F. Coleman, Diary, 3 August 1864, Confederate Miscellany I, GEU.

147. W. J. Pegram to his sister, 1 August 1864, in James I. Robertson Jr., "'The Boy Artillerist,'" 243. See also J. F. Sale to his aunt, 24 August 1864, Sale Papers, Vi.

148. Pvt. Andrew J. Perkins, Company B, 7th Georgia Cavalry, to his uncle, 2 August 1864, Perkins Papers, G-Ar.

149. D. N. Binion to his sister, 1 August 1864, Confederate Miscellany, GEU; J. W. Albright, Diary, 30 July 1864, Albright Papers, NcU; Daniel Abernathy to his father, 7 August 1864, Abernathy Papers, NcD. See also N. J. Brooks, Diary, 30 July 1864, Brooks Papers, NcU; R. C. Mabry to his wife, 1 August 1864, Mabry Papers, Nc-Ar; *Richmond Dispatch,* 2 August 1864; and J. L. G. Wood to his father, 5 August 1864, UDC Typescripts, vol. 4, G-Ar.

150. E. R. Crockett, Diary, 30 July 1864, Crockett Papers; A. B. Simms to his sister, 31 July 1864, in Peacock, "A Georgian's View of War," 115.

151. D. N. Binion to his sister, 1 August 1864, Confederate Miscellany, GEU.

152. M. N. Love to his mother, 6 August 1864, Love Papers, PNB.

153. A. B. Simms to his sister, 1 August 1864, in Peacock, "A Georgian's View of War," 115. See also R. C. Mabry to his wife, 1 August 1864, Mabry Papers, Nc-Ar, and A. J. Perkins to his uncle, 2 August 1864, Perkins Papers, G-Ar.

154. W. J. Pegram to his sister, 1 August 1864, in James I. Robertson Jr., "'The Boy Artillerist,'" 243–44.

155. T. C. Elder to his wife, 30 July 1864, Elder Papers, ViHi; Elias Davis to his wife, 3 August 1864, Davis Papers, NcU.

156. N. J. Brooks, Diary, 30 July 1864, Brooks Papers, NcU.

157. F. M. Coker to his wife, 1 August 1864, Heidler Collection, GU.

158. Daniel Boyd to his father, 10 August 1864, Boyd Papers, NcD; Dorsey Binion to his sister, 1 August 1864, Confederate Miscellany, GEU. See also William Russell, Diary, 30 July 1864, Russell Papers, PNB; Lee to his wife, 31 July

1864, in Dowdey and Manarin, *Wartime Papers*, 820; W. J. Pegram to his sister, 1 August 1864, in James I. Robertson Jr., "'The Boy Artillerist,'" 244; and J. L. G. Wood to his father, 5 August 1864, UDC Typescripts, vol. 4, G-Ar.

159. T. W. G. Inglet to his wife, 31 July 1864, Inglet Papers, LNT.

160. Lee to Davis, 4 August 1864, *OR* 42(2):1161.

CHAPTER 6

1. A. E. McGarity to his wife, 20 August 1864, in Burnett, "Letters of a Confederate Surgeon," December 1945, 251–52.

2. B. L. Wynn, Diary, 2 September 1864, Wynn Papers, Ms-Ar.

3. Daniel Boyd to his father, 9 September 1864, Boyd Papers, NcD.

4. A. E. McGarity to his wife, 20 August 1864, in Burnett, "Letters of a Confederate Surgeon," December 1945, 252; A. B. Simms, to his sister, 2 September 1864, in Peacock, "A Georgian's View of War," 120; Lt. Archibald Erskine Henderson, Company B, 12th North Carolina, to his brother, 7 September 1864, Archibald Erskine Henderson Papers, NcD. See also B. L. Wynn, Diary, 13 August, 4 September 1864, Wynn Papers, Ms-Ar; Capt. James Mercer Garnett, Chief of Ordnance, Rodes/Valley, in Garnett, "Diary," 2, and T. P. Devereux to his sister, 28 August 1864, Devereux Papers, Nc-Ar.

5. Col. David G. Cowand, Grimes (Cowand)/Grimes/II Corps, report, *OR* 43(1):604. See Wert, *From Winchester to Cedar Creek*, 29–45, for background on the campaign throughout August and into the first weeks of September 1864.

6. R. E. Park, Diary, 31 August 1864, in Park, "Diary," June 1876, 433.

7. R. E. Park, Diary, 17 August 1864, in ibid., May 1876, 386.

8. Daniel Boyd to his father, 23 August 1864, Boyd Papers, NcD. See also Jedediah Hotchkiss, Diary, 17, 28 August, 9 September 1864, in McDonald, *Make Me a Map of the Valley*, 222, 225, 228.

9. Diary of the I Corps, 21, 24–25, 29 August, 1–5 September 1864, *OR* 42(1):874–75; Lee to Seddon, 20 August 1864, 43(1):552; Cowand's report, 43(1):604; J. H. Wartman to the Editor of the *Richmond Whig*, 9 August 1864, in 43(1):991; Early to Breckinridge, 10 August 1864, 43(1):993; Early to Anderson, 19 August 1864, 43(1):1001; Breckinridge to Early, 24 August 1864, 43(1):1005; Early to Anderson, 28 August 1864, 43(1):1007; Hotchkiss's report, 43(1):1023–27 (app.); Early to Anderson, 2 September 1864, 43(2):862; A. S. Pendleton to Breckinridge, 7 September 1864, 43(2):864; Hotchkiss, Diary, 5 August–5 September 1864, in McDonald, *Make Me a Map of the Valley*, 220–27.

10. Bryan Grimes to his wife, 10 September 1864, Grimes Papers, NcU. See also B. L. Wynn, Diary, 4 August–4 September 1864, Wynn Papers, Ms-Ar; Daniel Boyd to his father, 23 August 1864, and to his sisters, 9 September 1864, Boyd Papers, NcD; Charles Kerrison to his sister, 28 August 1864, Kerrison Family Papers, ScU; J. L. G. Wood to his father, 9 September 1864, UDC Typescripts, vol. 4, G-Ar.

11. Brig. Gen. Bradley T. Johnson, Johnson/Valley Cavalry, report, *OR* 43(1):7.

12. B. L. Wynn, Diary, 24 August 1864, Wynn Papers, Ms-Ar.

13. Lee to Early, 8 August 1864, *OR* 43(1):990; Davis to Lee, 9 August 1864, 43(1):990; Lee to Davis, 9 August 1864, 43(1):990; SO 188, A&IGO, 10 August 1864, 43(1):993; Lee to Hampton, 11 August 1864, 43(1):996; Lee to Early, 11 August 1864, 43(1):996; Lee to Anderson, 12 August 1864, 43(1):997; Lee to Hampton, 14 August 1864, 43(1):999; Early to Anderson, 19 August 1864, 43(1):1001; Robert Ransom to Samuel Cooper, 22 August 1864, 43(1):1003–4; Braxton Bragg to Early, 29 August 1864, 43(1):1008.

14. Bragg to Early, 29 August 1864, *OR* 43(1):1008; Col. John B. Sale, Military Secretary, HQ, C.S. Army, Endorsement, 20 December 1864, on Robert Ransom to Samuel Cooper, 22 August 1864, 43(1):1004.

15. J. H. Wartman to the Editor of the *Richmond Whig*, 9 August 1864, in *OR* 43(1):991. See also B. T. Johnson's report, 43(1):4–8; Lee to Davis, 9 August 1864, 43(1):990; Lee to Seddon, 11 August 1864, 43(1):551; and Johnson to T. H. Wynne, 11 August 1864, 43(1):994.

16. B. T. Johnson's report, *OR* 43(1):8.

17. Jedediah Hotchkiss, Diary, 10 August 1864, in McDonald, *Make Me a Map of the Valley*, 221; W. H. Brotherton to his family, 10 August 1864, Brotherton Papers, NcD.

18. Early to Breckinridge, 10 August 1864, *OR* 43(1):993.

19. Early to Anderson, 28 August 1864, *OR* 43(1):1007.

20. Charles Kerrison to his sister, 28 August 1864, Kerrison Family Papers, ScU.

21. Daniel Boyd to his father, 1 September 1864, Boyd Papers, NcD. See also diary of the I Corps, 26 August 1864, *OR* 42(1):874, and Early to Anderson, 28 August 1864, 43(1):1007.

22. Jedediah Hotchkiss, Diary, 25 August 1864, in McDonald, *Make Me a Map of the Valley*, 224; D. G. Cowand's report, *OR* 43(1):604; T. P. Devereux to his sister, 28 August 1864, Devereux Papers, Nc-Ar; J. M. Garnett, Diary, 22, 31 August 1864, in Garnett, "Diary," 2–3; B. L. Wynn, Diary, 21, 26 August 1864, Wynn Papers, Ms-Ar.

23. Jedediah Hotchkiss, Diary, 17 August–6 September 1864, in McDonald, *Make Me a Map of the Valley*, 222–27; D. G. Cowand's report, *OR* 43(1):604; Early to Breckinridge, 18 August 1864, 43(1):1000–1001; Early to Anderson, 19 August 1864, 43(1):1001; Maj. Gen. Fitzhugh Lee, Fitz Lee/Valley Cavalry, to G. M. Sorrel, 23 August 1864, 43(1):1005; Lee to Seddon, 25 August 1864, 43(1): 1006; Early to Anderson, 28 August 1864, 43(1):1007; Breckinridge to Rodes, 2 September 1864, 43(2):861; Early to Anderson, 2 September 1864, 43(2):862; A. S. Pendleton to Breckinridge, 3 September 1864, 43(2):863; diary of the I Corps, 25 August–14 September 1864, 42(1):874–75; R. E. Park, Diary, 18

August–13 September 1864, in Park, "Diary," June 1876, 430–35; J. M. Garnett, Diary, 4 September 1864, in Garnett, "Diary," 3; B. L. Wynn, Diary, 3–4, 8 September 1864, Wynn Papers, Ms-Ar.

24. T. P. Devereux to his sister, 28 August 1864, Devereux Papers, Nc-Ar; A. E. Henderson to his brother, 7 September 1864, Henderson Papers, NcD.

25. Jedediah Hotchkiss, Diary, 14 September 1864, in McDonald, *Make Me a Map of the Valley*, 228; diary of the I Corps, 15 September 1864, *OR* 42(1):875; Lee to Early, 26 August 1864, 43(1):1006; Strength report of the Army of the Valley, 31 August 1864, 43(1):1011, estimating a strength of 500 for Cutshaw's three batteries; Early to Anderson, 2 September 1864, 43(2):862; Lee to Early, 17 September 1864, 43(2):873–74; Lee to Anderson, 17 September 1864, 43(2):875–76.

26. Bryan Grimes to his wife, 17 September 1864, Grimes Papers, NcU.

27. Early to Breckinridge, 17 September 1864, *OR* 43(2):875.

28. Early's report, *OR* 43(1):554; L. L. Lomax's report, 43(1):610; Jedediah Hotchkiss's report, 43(1):1027 (app.); Early to Breckinridge, 17 September 1864, 43(2):875; Hotchkiss, Diary, 17–18 September 1864, in McDonald, *Make Me a Map of the Valley*, 229; R. E. Park, Diary, 17–18 September 1864, in Park, "Diary," June 1876, 437; B. L. Wynn, Diary, 17–18 September 1864, Wynn Papers, Ms-Ar.

29. Lee to Seddon, 20 September 1864, *OR* 43(1):552; Early's report, 43(1): 554–55; Early to Lee, 25 September 1864, 43(1):557–58; reports of subordinate commanders, 43(1):604–5, 610–11. See also reports of Federal commanders, 43(1), as well as Wert, *From Winchester to Cedar Creek*, 47–99, and Freeman, *Lee's Lieutenants*, 3:577–82.

30. Bryan Grimes to his wife, 20 September 1864, Grimes Papers, NcU.

31. T. P. Devereux to his mother, 20 September 1864, Devereux Papers, Nc-Ar.

32. J. F. Coghill to his brother, 6 October 1864, Coghill Papers, NcD.

33. Sgt. Maj. Samuel P. Collier, 2d North Carolina, to his parents, 21 September 1864, Samuel P. Collier Papers, Nc-Ar; G. P. Ring to his wife, 21 September 1864, ANV Papers, LHA Collection, LNT.

34. S. D. Ramseur to his brother-in-law, 10 October 1864, Ramseur Papers, NcU.

35. J. F. Coghill to his brother, 6 October 1864, Coghill Papers, NcD. See also S. D. Ramseur to his wife, 25, 30 September 1864, Ramseur Papers, NcU.

36. T. P. Devereux to his mother, 20 September 1864, Devereux Papers, Nc-Ar. See also R. E. Park, Diary, 19 September 1864, in Park, "Diary," July 1876, 25–27, and J. M. Garnett, Diary, 21 September 1864, in Garnett, "Diary," 5–6.

37. D. G. Cowand's report, *OR* 43(1):605.

38. G. P. Ring to his wife, 21 September 1864, ANV Papers, LHA Collection, LNT.

39. Ibid.

40. J. M. Garnett, Diary, 21 September 1864, in Garnett, "Diary," 6; S. D. Ramseur to his wife, 30 September 1864, Ramseur Papers, NcU.

41. S. P. Collier to his parents, 21 September 1864, Collier Papers, Nc-Ar.

42. J. M. Garnett, Diary, 21 September 1864, in Garnett, "Diary," 7. See also C. W. Sydnor to his fiancée, 26 September 1864, Sydnor Papers, NcU.

43. Early's report, *OR* 43(1):555.

44. G. P. Ring to his wife, 21 September 1864, ANV Papers, LHA Collection, LNT.

45. Ibid. See also B. L. Wynn, Diary, 19 September 1864, Wynn Papers, Ms-Ar, and S. D. Ramseur to his brother-in-law, 10 October 1864, Ramseur Papers, NcU.

46. S. P. Collier to his parents, 21 September 1864, Collier Papers, Nc-Ar; A. E. McGarity to his wife, 20 September 1864, in Burnett, "Letters of a Confederate Surgeon," March 1946, 41.

47. R. E. Park, Diary, 19 September 1864, in Park, "Diary," July 1876, 27.

48. J. M. Garnett, Diary, 21 September 1864, in Garnett, "Diary," 7. See also 1st Lt. Micajah Woods, Charlottesville Artillery, to his father, 23 September 1864, Micajah Woods Papers, ViU.

49. A. E. McGarity to his wife, 20 September 1864, in Burnett, "Letters of a Confederate Surgeon," March 1946, 41; J. F. Coghill to his brother, 6 October 1864, Coghill Papers, NcD. See also 2d Lt. Leonidas Lafayette Polk, Company I, 43d North Carolina, to his wife, 24 September 1864, Leonidas Lafayette Polk Papers, NcU.

50. S. P. Collier to his parents, 21 September 1864, Collier Papers, Nc-Ar.

51. G. P. Ring to his wife, 21 September 1864, ANV Papers, LHA Collection, LNT.

52. R. E. Park, Diary, 19 September 1864, in Park, "Diary," July 1876, 26; A. E. McGarity to his wife, 20 September 1864, in Burnett, "Letters of a Confederate Surgeon," March 1946, 42. See also Early's report, *OR* 43(1):555; Jedediah Hotchkiss, Diary, 19–20 September 1864, in McDonald, *Make Me a Map of the Valley*, 229–30; Bryan Grimes to his wife, 20 September 1864, Grimes Papers, NcU; and T. P. Devereux to his mother, 20 September 1864, Devereux Papers, Nc-Ar.

53. Lee to Seddon, 20 September 1864, *OR* 43(1):552; Wood Bouldin, Asst. Insp. Gen., Patton/Wharton/Valley, Inspection Report, 29 September 1864, 43(1):597; B. L. Wynn Diary, 19 September 1864, Wynn Papers, Ms-Ar; R. E. Park, Diary, 19 September 1864, in Park, "Diary," July 1876, 29; G. P. Ring to his wife, 21 September 1864, ANV Papers, LHA Collection, LNT. Patton was the grandfather of Gen. George S. Patton, commander of the Third Army in World War II.

54. Wood Bouldin, Patton/Wharton/Valley, Inspection Report, 29 September 1864, *OR* 43(1):597.

55. See L. L. Polk to his wife, 24 September 1864, Polk Papers, NcU.

56. Samuel Cooper to Early, 19 September 1864, *OR* 43(2):876; GO__, Valley, 20 September 1864, 43(2):877; Jedediah Hotchkiss, Diary, 20–21 September 1864, in McDonald, *Make Me a Map of the Valley*, 230; J. M. Garnett, Diary, 21

September 1864, in Garnett, "Diary," 7; B. L. Wynn, Diary, 22 September 1864, Wynn Papers, Ms-Ar; S. D. Ramseur to his brother-in-law, 10 October 1864, Ramseur Papers, NcU; Lee to Anderson, 20 September 1864 (two messages), *OR* 43(2):877, and 22 September 1864, 43(2):878.

57. B. L. Wynn, Diary, 20 September 1864, Wynn Papers, Ms-Ar; G. P. Ring to his wife, 21 September 1864, ANV Papers, LHA Collection, LNT.

58. J. F. Coghill to his brother, 6 October 1864, Coghill Papers, NcD.

59. C. A. Evans to his wife, 26 September 1864, in Stephens, *Intrepid Warrior*, 455.

60. Early's report, *OR* 43(1):556.

61. Lee to Seddon, 23 September 1864, *OR* 43(1):552, and 29 September 1864, 43(1):552; Early's report, 43(1):555–56; Early to Lee, 23 September 1864, 43(1):557, and 25 September 1864, 43(1):558; reports of subordinate commanders, 43(1):605, 611. See also reports of Federal commanders, 43(1), as well as Wert, *From Winchester to Cedar Creek*, 108–34, and Freeman, *Lee's Lieutenants*, 3:583–85.

62. Early to Lee, 23 September 1864, *OR* 43(1):557.

63. S. D. Ramseur to his wife, 30 September 1864, Ramseur Papers, NcU.

64. B. L. Wynn, Diary, 22 September 1864, Wynn Papers, Ms-Ar; J. F. Coghill to his brother, 6 October 1864, Coghill Papers, NcD; H. P. Fortson to Mrs. R. A. Barnes, 11 October 1864, Barnes Family Papers, ViU.

65. Jedediah Hotchkiss, Diary, 22 September 1864, in McDonald, *Make Me a Map of the Valley*, 230–31.

66. B. L. Wynn, Diary, 22 September 1864, Wynn Papers, Ms-Ar.

67. T. P. Devereux to his father, 23 September 1864, Devereux Papers, Nc-Ar. See also B. L. Wynn, Diary, 22 September 1864, Wynn Papers, Ms-Ar; Micajah Woods to his father, 23 September 1864, Woods Papers, ViU; S. D. Ramseur to his wife, 30 September 1864, and to his brother-in-law, 10 October 1864, Ramseur Papers, NcU; and J. F. Coghill to his sister, 11 October 1864, Coghill Papers, NcD.

68. C. A. Evans to his wife, 26 September 1864 (second letter), 29 September 1864 (first letter), 8, 11 October 1864, in Stephens, *Intrepid Warrior*, 452, 459, 466–67.

69. H. P. Fortson to Mrs. R. A. Barnes, 11 October 1864, Barnes Family Papers, ViU.

70. Early's report, *OR* 43(1):556.

71. Micajah Woods to his father, 23 September 1864, Woods Papers, ViU.

72. C. W. Sydnor to his fiancée, 26 September 1864, Sydnor Papers, NcU.

73. H. P. Fortson to Mrs. R. A. Barnes, 11 October 1864, Barnes Family Papers, ViU. See also B. L. Wynn, Diary, 22 September 1864, Wynn Papers, Ms-Ar, and J. F. Coghill to his brother, 6 October 1864, Coghill Papers, NcD.

74. A. E. Henderson to his brother, 29 September 1864, Henderson Papers, NcD.

75. Bryan Grimes to his wife, 3 October 1864, Grimes Papers, NcU. See also S. D. Ramseur to his brother-in-law, 10 October 1864, Ramseur Papers, NcU.

76. Unidentified Officer, Valley, to William Smith, 2 October 1864, in William Smith to Lee, 6 October 1864, "Inclosure No. 1," in Lee to Seddon, 14 October 1864, *OR* 43(2):894.

77. Lee to Smith, 10 October 1864, "Inclosure No. 2," in Lee to Seddon, 14 October 1864, *OR* 43(2):895.

78. Smith to Lee, 6 October 1864, "Inclosure No. 1," in Lee to Seddon, 14 October 1864, *OR* 43(2):894. See also Smith to Lee, 12 October 1864, and Lee to Smith, 14 October 1864, "Inclosure No. 1" and "No. 2," in Lee to Seddon, 14 October 1864, 43(2):895–98; endorsements by Seddon, 17 October 1864, and Davis, 18 October 1864, 43(2):893.

79. C. A. Evans to his wife, 26 September 1864 (first letter), 26 September 1864 (third letter), in Stephens, *Intrepid Warrior*, 450, 455–56. See also Evans to his wife, 23 September 1864 (second letter) and 26 September 1864 (second letter), in ibid., *Intrepid Warrior*, 448, 452.

80. S. D. Ramseur to his wife, 30 September 1864, Ramseur Papers, NcU; H. P. Fortson to Mrs. R. A. Barnes, 11 October 1864, Barnes Family Papers, ViU.

81. A. E. McGarity to his wife, 30 September 1864, in Burnett, "Letters of a Confederate Surgeon," March 1946, 44.

82. Early to Lee, 25 September 1864, *OR* 43(1):558.

83. Lee to Early, 27 September 1864, *OR* 43(1): 558–59.

84. A. B. Simms to his sister, 21 September 1864, in Peacock, "A Georgian's View of War," 122.

85. Early to Lee, 23 September 1864, *OR* 43(1):557; Lee to Anderson, 23 September 1864, 43(2):878; Lee to Early, 23 September 1864, 43(2):878; diary of the I Corps, 24 September 1864, 42(1):875.

86. Lee to Early, 17 September 1864, *OR* 43(2):874–75; Early to Lee, 25 September 1864, 43(1):558; Lee to Early, 25 September 1864, 43(2):879, 26 September 1864, 43(2):879, and 27 September 1864, 43(1):558–59.

87. J. M. Garnett, Diary, 26 September 1864, in Garnett, "Diary," 10.

88. Jedediah Hotchkiss, Diary, 26 September 1864, in McDonald, *Make Me a Map of the Valley*, 232–33; J. M. Garnett, Diary, 26 September 1864, in Garnett, "Diary," 10; Brig. Gen. James Conner, Conner/Kershaw/Valley, to his mother, 29 September 1864, in Moffett, *Letters of General James Conner*, 155.

89. Jedediah Hotchkiss, Diary, 4–5 October 1864, in McDonald, *Make Me a Map of the Valley*, 232, 234–35; A. E. McGarity to his wife, 9 October 1864, in Burnett, "Letters of a Confederate Surgeon," March 1946, 46. See also *OR* 43(2): 882–83, 903, 911.

90. James Conner to his mother, 29 September 1864, in Moffett, *Letters of General James Conner*, 155.

91. Charles Kerrison to his sister, 27 September 1864, Kerrison Family Papers, ScU.

92. J. L. G. Wood to his father, 29 September 1864, UDC Typescripts, vol. 4, G-Ar.

93. J. F. Coghill to his sister, 10 October 1864, Coghill Papers, NcD.

94. C. A. Evans to his wife, 28 September 1864 (first quotation), 29 September 1864 (second quotation), in Stephens, *Intrepid Warrior*, 458.

95. H. P. Fortson to Mrs. R. A. Barnes, 11 October 1864, Barnes Family Papers, ViU. See also S. D. Ramseur to his wife, 25, 30 September, 2 October 1864, and to his brother-in-law, 10 October 1864, Ramseur Papers, NcU; B. K. Whittle to his sister, 29 September 1864, Whittle Papers, ViU; and A. E. McGarity to his wife, 9 October 1864, in Burnett, "Letters of a Confederate Surgeon," March 1946, 46.

96. S. D. Ramseur to his wife, 25 September 1864, Ramseur Papers, NcU.

97. Maj. H. A. Whiting, Asst. Adjt. & Insp. Gen., Ramseur/Valley, Inspection Report, 30 September 1864, *OR* 43(1):601.

98. Ibid.; Organization of the Army of the Valley, 30 September 1864, 43(2):884.

99. H. A. Whiting, Ramseur/Valley, Inspection Report, 30 September 1864, *OR* 43(1):601.

100. *OR* 43(2):882.

101. 1st Lt. W. B. McNuman, Acting Insp. Gen., Pegram (Hoffman)/Gordon/Valley, 30 September 1864, Inspection Reports, NA, microcopy M935, roll 10. See also 1st Lt. Henry G. Cannon, Brig. Insp., Smith/Wharton/Valley, Inspection Report, 29 September 1864, *OR* 43(1):595–96, and Wood Bouldin, Patton/Wharton/Valley, Inspection Report, 29 September 1864, 43(1):597.

102. W. B. McNuman, Pegram (Hoffman)/Gordon/Valley, 30 September 1864, Inspection Reports, NA, microcopy M935, roll 10.

103. Henry G. Cannon, Smith/Wharton/Valley, Inspection Report, 29 September 1864, *OR* 43(1):596; W. B. McNuman, Pegram (Hoffman)/Gordon/Valley, 30 September 1864, Inspection Reports, NA, microcopy M935, roll 10. See also H. A. Whiting, Ramseur/Valley, Inspection Report, 30 September 1864, 43(1):600–601.

104. Early to Lee, 9 October 1864, *OR* 43(1):560.

105. C. A. Evans to his wife, 4, 7 October 1864, in Stephens, *Intrepid Warrior*, 463–64.

106. J. F. Coghill to his parents and sister, 17 October 1864, Coghill Papers, NcD. See also Jedediah Hotchkiss, Diary, 29, 30 September, 4, 6 October 1864, in McDonald, *Make Me a Map of the Valley*, 234–35; James Conner to his mother, 9 October 1864, in Moffett, *General James Conner*, 157; Early to Lee, 9 October 1864, *OR* 43(1):560; and Lee to Early, 12 October 1864, 43(2):892.

107. Lee to Seddon, 9 October 1864, *OR* 43(1):552–53; Early to Lee, 9 October 1864, 43(1):559; Lomax's report, 43(1):612–13; Lee to Early, 12 October 1864, 43(2):891. See also reports of Federal commanders, 43(1), as well as Wert, *From Winchester to Cedar Creek*, 161–64, and Freeman, *Lee's Lieutenants*, 3:596–97.

108. Early to Lee, 9 October 1864, *OR* 43(1):559.

109. S. D. Ramseur to his brother-in-law, 10 October 1864, Ramseur Papers, NcU.

110. Bryan Grimes to his wife, 10 October 1864, Grimes Papers, NcU. See also S. D. Ramseur to his brother-in-law, 10 October 1864, Ramseur Papers, NcU, and Jedediah Hotchkiss, Diary, 9 October 1864, in McDonald, *Make Me a Map of the Valley*, 235.

111. Lee to Early, 12 October 1864, *OR* 43(2):892.

112. Ibid., 891–92. See also Lee to Early, 27 September 1864, 43(1):559.

113. Early's report, *OR* 43(1):561; Jedediah Hotchkiss, Diary, 30 September–13 October 1864, in McDonald, *Make Me a Map of the Valley*, 234–37; J. M. Garnett, Diary, 15 October 1864, in Garnett, "Diary," 12–13; C. A. Evans to his wife, 7, 12, 14 October 1864, in Stephens, *Intrepid Warrior*, 464–65, 468–70.

114. G. P. Ring to his wife, 14 October 1864, ANV Papers, LHA Collection, LNT. See also C. A. Evans to his wife, 14 October 1864, in Stephens, *Intrepid Warrior*, 469–70, and Pvt. William E. Lightfoot, Company B, 6th Alabama, to his cousin, 15 October 1864, in Burnett, "Letters of Three Lightfoot Brothers," 89.

115. Early's report, *OR* 43(1):564; J. P. Simms's report, 43(1):590–91; Bryan Grimes's report, 43(1):598; D. G. Cowand's report, 43(1):606.

116. Lee to Seddon, 20–21 October 1864, *OR* 43(1):553; Early to Lee, 20–21 October 1864, 43(1):560; Early's report, 561–64; reports of subordinate commanders, 43(1):590–91, 593–95, 598–600, 606–9; W. N. Pendleton's report, 42(1):864–65. See also reports of Federal commanders, 43(1). Secondary accounts include Mahr, *Battle of Cedar Creek*; Wert, *From Winchester to Cedar Creek*, 172–238; and Freeman, *Lee's Lieutenants*, 3:597–612.

117. Lt. Col. Edwin Lafayette Hobson, Battle (Hobson)/Grimes/Valley, to his wife, 23 October 1864, Hobson Family Papers, ViHi. See also Early to Lee, 20 October 1864, *OR* 43(1):560; Lee to Seddon, 20 October 1864, 43(1):553; Early's report, 43(1):562; A. H. Crawford to his wife, 21 October 1864, Crawford Papers, NcD; S. P. Collier to his parents, 22 October 1864, and to his father, 26 October 1864, Collier Papers, Nc-Ar; and Pvt. Levi A. Lockman, Company K, 23d North Carolina, to Thomas Brotherton, 23 October 1864, Brotherton Papers, NcD.

118. Bryan Grimes's report, *OR* 43(1):600.

119. Ibid., 598; E. L. Hobson to his wife, 23 October 1864, Hobson Family Papers, ViHi; J. P. Simms's report, 43(1):591; A. B. Simms to his sister, 21 October 1864, in Peacock, "A Georgian's View of War," 125.

120. Charles Kerrison to his sister, 20 [19] October 1864, Kerrison Family Papers, ScU.

121. Daniel Boyd to his father, 25 October 1864, Boyd Papers, NcD.

122. A. E. Henderson to his wife, 22 October 1864, Henderson Papers, NcD.

123. Jedediah Hotchkiss, Diary, 19 October 1864, in McDonald, *Make Me a Map of the Valley*, 240; J. M. Garnett, Diary, 26 October 1864, in Garnett, "Diary," 13; J. B. Evans to his wife, 24 October 1864, Evans Papers, NcD. See also R. P.

Myers, Diary, 19 October 1864, Myers Papers, ViRC; Commissary Sgt. Richard Woolfolk Waldrop, 21st Virginia, to his father, 21 October 1864, Richard Wool-folk Waldrop Papers, NcU; A. H. Crawford to his wife, 21 October 1864, Craw-ford Papers, NcD; and J. F. Coghill to his parents and sister, 22 October 1864, Coghill Papers, NcD.

124. R. P. Myers, Diary, 19 October 1864, Myers Papers, ViRC. See also Jedediah Hotchkiss, Diary, 23 October 1864, in McDonald, *Make Me a Map of the Valley*, 243, and D. G. Cowand's reports, *OR* 43(1):606–7.

125. R. W. Waldrop to his father, 21 October 1864, Waldrop Papers, NcU.

126. Early's report, *OR* 43(1):562.

127. Ibid., 563.

128. S. P. Collier to his father, 26 October 1864, Collier Papers, Nc-Ar. See also R. W. Waldrop to his father, 21 October 1864, Waldrop Papers, NcU, and *Rich-mond Dispatch*, 29 October 1864.

129. A. E. Henderson to his brother, 22 October 1864, Henderson Papers, NcD.

130. W. L. Wilson to his mother and aunt, 23 October 1864, in Summers, *A Borderland Confederate*, 83.

131. A. E. Henderson to his brother, 30 October 1864, Henderson Papers, NcD; *Richmond Dispatch*, 29 October 1864; T. P. Devereux to his grandfather, 23 October 1864, Devereux Papers, Nc-Ar; R. W. Waldrop to his father, 21 October 1864, Waldrop Papers, NcU. See also S. P. Collier to his father, 22 October 1864, Collier Papers, Nc-Ar, and J. B. Evans to his wife, 24 October 1864, Evans Papers, NcD.

132. A. E. Henderson to his brother, 30 October 1864, Henderson Papers, NcD.

133. C. A. Evans to his wife, 21 October 1864, in Stephens, *Intrepid Warrior*, 483.

134. H. A. Whiting, Grimes/Valley, 31 October 1864, Inspection Reports, NA, microcopy M935, roll 11. See also H. A. Whiting, Rodes (Ramseur)/Valley), Inspection Report, 30 September 1864, *OR* 43(1):600–601, and Inspection Re-ports, NA, microcopy M935, for: W. B. McNuman, Pegram (Hoffman)/Gordon/Valley, 30 September 1864, roll 10; 1st Lt. Thomas F. Roche, Acting Insp. Gen., Wharton (Otey)/Wharton/Valley, 28 October 1864, roll 11; E. L. Moore, Valley, November 1864, roll 12; Col. Abner Smead, Insp. Gen., Valley, 1 November 1864, roll 11; T. F. Roche, Wharton (Otey)/Wharton/Valley, 28 November 1864, roll 12; 1st Lt. R. B. Smith, Asst. Adjt. & Insp. Gen., York (Peck)/Gordon/Valley, 29 November 1864, roll 12; and 1st Lt. Richard V. Jones, Cook (Peebles)/Grimes/Valley, 30 November 1864, roll 12.

135. A. H. Crawford to his wife, 21 October 1864, Crawford Papers, NcD.

136. Pvt. Gardner O. Megarity, Company B, 24th Georgia, to his sister, 29 October 1864, Megarity Family Papers, G-Ar. See also Charles Kerrison to his sister, 20 [19] October 1864, Kerrison Family Papers, ScU, and J. L. G. Wood to his father, 23 October 1864, UDC Typescripts, vol. 4, G-Ar.

137. T. P. Devereux to his grandfather, 23 October 1864, Devereux Papers, Nc-Ar.

138. *Richmond Dispatch*, 29 October 1864; J. F. Coghill to his parents and sister, 22 October 1864, Coghill Papers, NcD.

139. Col. John R. Winston, 45th North Carolina, report, *OR* 43(1):609.

140. J. T. Gay to his wife, 25 October 1864, Nix Collection, GU. See also R. P. Myers, Diary, 19 October 1864, Myers Papers, ViRC; E. L. Hobson to his wife, 23 October 1864, Hobson Family Papers, ViHi; Daniel Boyd to his father, 25 October 1864, Boyd Papers, NcD; and Pvt. Augustus Clewell, Company B, 1st Battalion North Carolina Sharpshooters, to his sister, 29 October 1864, Augustus Clewell Papers, Nc-Ar.

141. C. A. Evans to his wife, 5 November 1864, in Stephens, *Intrepid Warrior*, 497. See also Evans to his wife, 20–23, 30 October (two letters), in ibid., 482–96.

142. A. E. Henderson to his brother, 30 October 1864, Henderson Papers, NcD. See also S. P. Collier to his parents, 22 October 1864, Collier Papers, Nc-Ar.

143. *Richmond Whig*, 25 November 1864.

144. "An Address from Gen. Early to His Troops," 22 October 1864, in *Richmond Enquirer*, 27 October 1864.

145. C. A. Evans to his wife, 30 October 1864 (two letters), in Stephens, *Intrepid Warrior*, 491, 493.

146. T. P. Devereux to his grandfather, 23 October 1864, Devereux Papers, Nc-Ar.

147. Daniel Boyd to his father, 25 October 1864, Boyd Papers, NcD. See also G. O. Megarity to his sister, 29 October 1864, Megarity Family Papers, G-Ar.

148. "Tribute to the Memory of Maj. Generals Rodes and Ramseur," *Richmond Whig*, 8 November 1864. See also J. T. Gay to his wife, 1 November 1864, Nix Collection, GU, and J. M. Garnett, Diary, 3 November 1864, in Garnett, "Diary," 14.

149. S. P. Collier to his father, 26 October 1864, Collier Papers, Nc-Ar.

150. T. P. Devereux to his mother, 27 October 1864, Devereux Papers, Nc-Ar. See also Bryan Grimes, Grimes/Valley, to his wife, 25 October 1864, Grimes Papers, NcU; A. E. Henderson to his brother, 30 October 1864, Henderson Papers, NcD; Brig. Gen. Robert D. Johnston, Johnston/Pegram/Valley, to Col. Henry E. Coleman, 12th North Carolina, 5 November 1864, Robert D. Johnston Papers, NcD; *Richmond Dispatch*, 7 November 1864; and *Richmond Sentinel*, 10 November 1864.

151. H. A. Whiting, Grimes/Valley, 31 October 1864, Inspection Reports, NA, microcopy M935, roll 11.

152. E. L. Moore, Army of the Valley, November 1864, Inspection Reports, NA, microcopy M935, roll 12. See also T. F. Roche, Wharton (Otey)/Wharton/Valley, 28 October 1864, ibid., roll 11; Maj. John H. New, Asst. Adjt. & Insp. Gen., Pegram/Valley, 31 October 1864, ibid., roll 11; and Abner Smead, 1 November 1864, ibid., roll 11.

153. J. B. Evans to his wife, 8 November 1864, Evans Papers, NcD.

154. Pvt. John J. Armfield, Company C, 30th North Carolina, to his wife, 9 November 1864, John J. Armfield Papers, Nc-Ar.

155. A. E. Henderson to his brother, 15 November 1864, Henderson Papers, NcD. See also J. J. Armfield to his wife, 15 November 1864, Armfield Papers, Nc-Ar; J. B. Evans to his wife, 15 November 1864, Evans Papers, NcD; Lee to Seddon, 13 November 1864, *OR* 43(1):553–54; and C. A. Evans to his wife, 9 November, 11 November (two letters), 12–14 November 1864, in Stephens, *Intrepid Warrior*, 508–12.

156. A. B. Simms to his sister, 14 November 1864, in Peacock, "A Georgian's View of War," 126.

157. Lee to Davis, 6 December 1864, *OR* 43(2):936; Early to Bryan Grimes, 13 December 1864, 43(2):938; Lee to Davis, 14 December 1864, 43(2):938, and 17 December 1864, 43(2):940; Jedediah Hotchkiss, Diary, 15 November, 6, 8–9, 14 December 1864, in McDonald, *Make Me a Map of the Valley*, 244, 246–47. See also Organization of the Army of the Valley District, 30 November 1864, 43(2):927–29, and 31 December 1864, 43(2):951; Lee to Seddon, 7, 26 December 1864, in Dowdey and Manarin, *Wartime Papers*, 874, 879.

158. J. T. Gay to his wife, 20 December 1864, Nix Collection, GU. See also A. E. Henderson to his brother, 12 December 1864, Henderson Papers, NcD, and T. P. Devereux to his sister, 21 December 1864, Devereux Papers, Nc-Ar.

159. W. D. Alexander, Diary, 8 December 1864, Alexander Papers, NcU.

CHAPTER 7

1. Col. G. H. Sharpe, Deputy Provost-Marshal-Gen., Army of the Potomac, to Maj. Gen. A. A. Humphreys, Chief of Staff, Army of the Potomac, 5 August 1864, *OR* 42(2):54. See also Maj. Gen. Edward O. C. Ord, XVIII Army Corps/Army of the James, to Brig. Gen. Hiram Burnham, First Division/XVIII Army Corps/Army of the James, and Brig. Gen. Adelbert Ames, Second Division/XVIII Army Corps/Army of the James, 2 August 1864, 42(2):24–25.

2. H. T. Douglas, reports, *OR* 42(2):1155, 1158–60, 1162–63; Beauregard to Cooper, 6 August 1864, 42(2):1163; B. R. Johnson's daily reports, 2–7 August 1864, 42(1):883–86.

3. J. A. F. Coleman, Diary, 5 August 1864, Confederate Miscellany I, GEU; M. N. Love to his mother, 6 August 1864, Love Papers, PNB.

4. *Richmond Examiner*, 12 August 1864.

5. Elias Davis to his wife, 8 August 1864, Davis Papers, NcU.

6. T. L. McCarty, Diary, 1–12 August 1864, McCarty Papers, TxU.

7. F. M. Coker to his wife, 13 August 1864, Heidler Collection, GU. See also E. R. Crockett, Diary, 1–13 August 1864, Crockett Papers, TxU; J. M. Simpson to his wife, 4 August 1864, Allen and Simpson Family Papers, NcU; M. N. Love to his mother, 6 August 1864, Love Papers, PNB; and *Richmond Sentinel*, 6 August 1864.

8. *Richmond Examiner*, 1 August 1864.

9. Ibid., 5 August 1864. See also 12 August 1864.

10. Ibid., 2 August 1864. See also 12 August 1864.

11. Ibid., 1 August 1864.

12. Col. John T. Loftin, 6th Georgia, "Sixth Georgia Regiment," 14 August 1864, in Folsom, *Heroes and Martyrs*, 31.

13. GO 54, ANV, 10 August 1864, *OR* 42(2):1169.

14. Elias Davis to his wife, 13 August 1864, Davis Papers, NcU.

15. Lee to Seddon, 14 August 1864, *OR* 42(2):1175. See also Seddon to Lee, 17 August 1864, 42(2):1182–83.

16. C. M. Wilcox to his sister-in-law, 15 August 1864, Wilcox Papers, LC. See also Adjt. William Barr Lowrance, 34th North Carolina, to "Harriet," 8 August 1864, William Barr Lowrance Papers, ScU. For reports by Federals who interviewed Confederate deserters in the first two weeks of August, see, in addition to the reports cited above, Capt. John McEntee, Asst. Provost-Marshal, Provost-Marshal-Gen.'s Dept., Army of the Potomac, to Maj. Gen. A. A. Humphreys, Chief of Staff, Army of the Potomac, 1–2, 4, 6, 13 August 1864, *OR* 42(2):4–5, 17, 41, 66, 141–42; Col. G. H. Sharpe, Deputy Provost-Marshal-Gen., Army of the Potomac, to Humphreys, 5 August 1864 (two reports), 42(2):53–54; and J. C. Babcock, Provost-Marshal Gen.'s Dept., Army of the Potomac, to Humphreys, 8, 11 August 1864, 42(2):85–86, 114–15.

17. "P.K.O.G. NC" [Unidentified North Carolinian] to Gov. Zebulon B. Vance, 6 August 1864, Governor's Papers, Nc-Ar.

18. Folsom, *Heroes and Martyrs*, 40, in his history of the 19th Georgia.

19. Elias Davis to his wife, 13 August 1864, Davis Papers, NcU.

20. Folsom, *Heroes and Martyrs*, 143, in his history of the 35th Georgia. See also H. C. Conner to his wife, 4 August 1864, Conner Papers, ScU; M. N. Love to his mother, 6 August 1864, Love Papers, PNB; Capt. John Hampden Chamberlayne, Company C, 13th Battalion Virginia Light Artillery, to his mother, 10 August 1864, in Chamberlayne, *Ham Chamberlayne*, 252; and Capt. John D. Fain, Company C, 33d North Carolina, to his cousin, 12 August 1864, Henderson Papers, NcD.

21. Lee to Seddon, 16 August 1864 (two messages), *OR* 42(1):850; reports of subordinate commanders, 42(1):878–79, 935, 937–38; Lee to C. W. Field, 14 August 1864 (four messages), 42(2):1176–77; Lee to Wade Hampton, 14 August 1864, 42(2):1177; W. H. Taylor to E. C. Anderson, 14 August 1864, 42(2):1177; Davis to Field, 15 August 1864, 42(2):1179; Taylor to Field, 15 August 1864, 42(2):1180; Lee to Davis, 16 August 1864, 42(2):1180; Lee to Seddon, 22 August 1864, 42(2):1194. See also reports of Federal commanders, 42(1). A secondary account of the fighting at Deep Bottom, the Weldon Railroad, and Reams Station is John Horn, *Petersburg*; for Deep Bottom, see 1–53. See also Trudeau, *The Last Citadel*, 150–70, and Freeman, *Lee's Lieutenants*, 3:588.

22. J. M. McFall to his sister, 17 August 1864, McFall Papers, GEU.

23. W. D. Alexander, Diary, 16 August 1864, Alexander Papers, NcU.

24. E. R. Crockett, Diary, 16 August 1864, Crockett Papers, TxU. See also W. A. Kelly, Diary, 14–17 August 1864, Kelly Papers, ScCC.

25. W. A. Kelly, Diary, 16 August 1864, Kelly Papers, ScCC. See also T. L. McCarty, Diary, 16 August 1864, McCarty Papers, TxU; Lee to Seddon (two messages), *OR* 42(1):850; Capt. W. H. Holcombe, Company A, 1st South Carolina Rifles, to J. E. Hagood, 17 August 1864, Hagood Papers, ScU; and J. M. McFall to his sister, 17 August 1864, McFall Papers, GEU.

26. W. A. Kelly, Diary, 16 August 1864, Kelly Papers, ScCC.

27. Lee to Hampton, 19 August 1864, *OR* 42(2):1189.

28. William Mahone to Samuel Cooper, 20 July 1864, and A. P. Hill, endorsement on Mahone to Cooper, 20 July 1864, Victor J. B. Girardey, Compiled Service Records of General and Staff Officers, NA, microcopy M331, roll 107.

29. Lee's endorsement, 11 July 1864, on William Mahone to Samuel Cooper, 7 July 1864, Victor J. B. Girardey, Compiled Service Records of General and Staff Officers, NA, microcopy M331, roll 107. See also Davis to Lee, 2 August 1864, *OR* 42(2):1156–57, and C. M. Blackford to his wife, 17 August 1864, in Blackford and Blackford, *Letters From Lee's Army*, 272–73.

30. W. H. Holcombe to J. E. Hagood, 17 August 1864, Hagood Papers, ScU.

31. E. R. Crockett, Diary, 16 August 1864, Crockett Papers, TxU; T. G. Trimmier to his wife, 19 August 1864, Trimmier Collection, T. For a return of casualties in the U.S. Colored Troops at Deep Bottom, see *OR* 42(1):120.

32. W. A. Kelly, Diary, 16 August 1864, Kelly Papers, ScCC; J. M. McFall to his sister, 17 August 1864, McFall Papers, GEU.

33. W. H. Holcombe to J. E. Hagood, 17 August 1864, Hagood Papers, ScU.

34. Lee to Seddon, 18, 20–21 August 1864, *OR* 42(1):850–51; Beauregard to Lee, 18 August (four messages), 19 August 1864, 42(1):857–58; Beauregard to Seddon, 20 August 1864, 42(1):858; reports of subordinate commanders, 42(1): 858, 936–37, 939–40; Beauregard to Lee, 18 August 1864 (fifth message), 19 August 1864 (second message), 20 August 1864 (three messages), 42(2):1187, 1190–92; Lee to Seddon, 22 August 1864, 42(2):1194–95; Col. R. L. Walker, III Corps Artillery, to W. N. Pendleton, 22 August 1864, 42(2):1195–96. See also reports of Federal commanders, 42(1), as well as Horn, *Destruction of the Weldon Railroad*, 54–113; Trudeau, *The Last Citadel*, 161–74; and Freeman, *Lee's Lieutenants*, 3:588–89.

35. F. M. Coker to his wife, 19 August 1864, Heidler Collection, GU. See also Robert Stiles to his mother, 21 August 1864, Stiles Papers, ViHi.

36. W. A. Kelly, Diary, 21 August 1864, Kelly Papers, ScCC. See also J. W. Albright, Diary, 21 August 1864, Albright Papers, NcU; Lt. Col. T. G. Trimmier, 41st Alabama, to his wife, 22 August 1864, Trimmier Collection, T; and Pvt. Edward H. Steele, 14th Tennessee, to his cousin, 26 August 1864, Munford-Ellis Family Papers, NcD.

37. Col. G. H. Sharpe, Deputy Provost-Marshal-Gen., Army of the Potomac, to Lt. John I. Davenport, Bureau of Information, Dept. of Virginia and North Carolina, 23 August 1864, *OR* 42(2):437.

38. Henry Bryan to R. N. Gourdin, 23 August 1864, Gourdin Papers, GEU.

39. Lee to Davis, 22 August 1864, in Dowdey and Manarin, *Wartime Papers*, 842. See also Davis to Lee, 23 August 1864, *OR* 42(2):1197–98, and Seddon to Lee, 23 August 1864, 42(2):1199.

40. The most notable casualty of the fighting at Globe Tavern was Brig. Gen. John C. C. Sanders, who was killed on 21 August. Sanders, who was only twenty-four, had long been colonel of the 11th Alabama. He had commanded Sanders/Mahone/III Corps for barely two months but had already been recognized by his superiors for his outstanding performance at the Crater. See, e.g., T. G. Trimmier to his wife, 22 August 1864, Trimmier Collection, T, and John C. C. Sanders, Compiled Service Records of General and Staff Officers, NA, microcopy M331, roll 218.

41. Pvt. James King Wilkerson, Company K, 55th North Carolina, to his family, 23 August 1864, James King Wilkerson Papers, NcD. See also Pvt. A. L. P. Vairin, Company B, 2d Mississippi, Diary, 18 August 1864, A. L. P. Vairin Papers, Ms-Ar; 3d Lt. William W. England, Company E, 25th North Carolina, to his father, 22 August 1864, Alexander England Family Papers, Nc-Ar; and James Hays's report, *OR* 42(1):939.

42. Quartermaster Sgt. J. Adger Smyth, 25th South Carolina, to his wife, 22 August 1864, Adger-Smyth Family Papers, ScHi.

43. H. I. Greer to his father, 24 August 1864, Greer Papers, LC.

44. Johnson Hagood's report, *OR* 42(1):936.

45. H. I. Greer to his father, 24 August 1864, Greer Papers, LC; J. A. Smyth to his wife, 22 August 1864, Adger-Smyth Family Papers, ScHi.

46. Brig. Gen. Johnson Hagood, Hagood/Hoke/Beauregard, to J. J. Ryan, 24 August 1864, Molony-Ryan Families Papers, Private Collection of Barnwell Rhett Linley, Columbia, S.C.; J. A. Smyth to his wife, 22 August 1864, Adger-Smyth Family Papers, ScHi.

47. Johnson Hagood's report, *OR* 42(1):936–37.

48. Maj. G. B. Lartigue, Asst. Quartermaster, Hagood/Hoke/Beauregard, to J. J. Ryan, 22 August 1864, Molony-Ryan Families Papers, Private Collection of Barnwell Rhett Linley, Columbia, S.C.; H. I. Greer to his father, 24 August 1864, Greer Papers, LC.

49. [Joseph Blyth Allston], "Charge of Hagood's Brigade: Weldon Railroad, August 21, 1864," in William Gilmore Simms, ed., *War Poetry of the South* (New York: Richardson and Co., 1867), 357.

50. G. B. Lartigue to J. J. Ryan, 22 August 1864, Molony-Ryan Families Papers, Private Collection of Barnwell Rhett Linley, Columbia, S.C. See also Patrick K. Molony, 1st (Hagood's) [South Carolina] Infantry, Compiled Service Records, NA, microcopy M267, roll 123.

51. Johnson Hagood to J. J. Ryan, 24 August 1864, Molony-Ryan Families Papers, Private Collection of Barnwell Rhett Linley, Columbia, S.C.

52. S. P. Hay to J. J. Ryan, 1 September 1864, Molony-Ryan Families Papers, Private Collection of Barnwell Rhett Linley, Columbia, S.C.

53. Lee to Seddon, 26 August 1864, *OR* 42(1):851; reports of subordinate commanders, 42(1):940–44; Brig. Gen. Rufus Barringer, Barringer/W. H. F. Lee/Cavalry Corps, to Maj. Gen. Matthew C. Butler, Butler/Cavalry Corps, 24 August 1864, 51(2):1037; Lee to Hampton, 24 August 1864, 42(2):1202, and 26 August 1864, 42(2):1204–5; Lee to Gov. Zebulon B. Vance of North Carolina, 29 August 1864, 42(2):1206–7. See also reports of Federal commanders, 42(1), as well as Horn, *Destruction of the Weldon Railroad*, 114–76; Trudeau, *The Last Citadel*, 176–91; and Freeman, *Lee's Lieutenants*, 3:589.

54. S. F. Harper to his sister, 26 August 1864, Harper Papers, Nc-Ar; W. A. Kelly, Diary, 25 August 1864, Kelly Papers, ScCC. See also A. L. P. Vairin, Diary, 25 August 1864, Vairin Papers, Ms-Ar; H. C. Conner to his wife, 26 August 1864, Conner Papers, ScU; and T. L. McCarty, Diary, 27 August 1864, McCarty Papers, TxU.

55. S. F. Harper to his sister, 26 August 1864, Harper Papers, Nc-Ar.

56. Lee to Vance, 29 August 1864, *OR* 42(2):1207. See also Lee to his wife, 28 August 1864, in Dowdey and Manarin, *Wartime Papers*, 847.

57. James Conner to his sister, 3 September 1864, in Moffett, *Letters of General James Conner*, 149.

58. B. W. Justice to his wife, 30 August 1864, Justice Papers, GEU. For unpublished reports of 28 August 1864 from regimental commanders in Lane (Conner)/Wilcox/III Corps, see Capt. J. G. Harris, 7th North Carolina; Capt. B. F. Rinaldi, 18th North Carolina; Maj. S. N. Stowe, 28th North Carolina; Capt. W. J. Callais, 33d North Carolina; and Maj. J. L. Bost, 37th North Carolina, all in Lane Papers, AAP.

59. R. S. Webb to his cousin, 31 August 1864, Webb Family Papers, NcU. The "colonel" was almost certainly Lt. Col. Francis Wilder Bird, of the 11th North Carolina, the only field officer in either brigade killed or mortally wounded at Reams Station; he was "shot in the head and died the next morning." See also B. W. Justice to his wife, 30 August 1864, Justice Papers, GEU.

60. W. A. Kelly, Diary, 26 August 1864, Kelly Papers, ScCC.

61. Ibid. See also Compiled Service Records, C. D. Barksdale, John W. Chambers, and William Aiken Kelly, 1st (McCreary's) [South Carolina] Infantry (1st Provisional Army), Compiled Service Records, NA, microcopy M267, rolls 126, 127, and 130, respectively.

62. J. D. Fain to his cousin, 12 August 1864, Henderson Papers, NcD.

63. "List of Casualties in Lane's Brigade from May 5th 1864 to Oct 1st 1864" [ca. 1864], Lane Papers, AAP.

64. R. C. Mabry to his wife, 27 August 1864, Mabry Papers, Nc-Ar.

65. J. A. Smyth to his wife, 22 August 1864, Adger-Smyth Family Papers, ScHi. See also C. E. Whilden to Miss S. E. Alston, 23 August 1864, Whilden Papers, ScHi.

66. Lee to Davis, 13 August 1864, in Freeman, *Lee's Dispatches*, 369 (app.).

67. Capt. H. H. Perry, Asst. Adjt. Gen., Benning (DuBose)/Field/I Corps, 9

August 1864, Inspection Reports, NA, microcopy M935, roll 10; H. E. Peyton, Inspection Report, Army of Northern Virginia, 23 September 1864 [covering August and September 1864], *OR* 42(2):1276.

68. H. H. Perry, Benning (DuBose)/Field/I Corps, 9 August 1864, Inspection Reports, NA, microcopy M935, roll 10. See also 1st Lt. D. H. Pope, Acting Insp. Gen., Wright (Gibson)/Mahone/III Corps, 28 September 1864, Inspection Reports, ibid.

69. 1st Lt. Henry Duplessis Wells, Company I, 23d South Carolina, to his sister, 5 September 1864, Henry D. Wells Papers, PNB.

70. J. H. Chamberlayne to his mother, 19 August 1864, in Chamberlayne, *Ham Chamberlayne*, 258.

71. E. P. Alexander to his wife, 15 September 1864, Alexander Papers, NcU. See also Alexander to his wife, 28 August, 5 September 1864, ibid., and Pvt. William C. McFall, Company C, Palmetto Sharpshooters, to his mother and sister, 4 September 1864, McFall Papers, GEU.

72. Brevet 2d Lt./2d Lt. Alexander Frederick Fleet, Company I, 26th Virginia, to his father, 29 September 1864, in Fleet and Fuller, *Green Mount*, 341.

73. J. W. McLure to his wife, 23 August 1864, McLure Family Papers, ScU.

74. *Richmond Whig*, 6 September 1864.

75. Pvt. Benjamin Mason, Company F, 60th Alabama, to his wife and children, 1 September 1864, Benjamin Mason Papers, AAP.

76. W. J. Pegram to his sister, 1 September 1864, Pegram-Johnson-McIntosh Family Papers, ViHi.

77. J. F. Sale, Diary, 6 September 1864, Sale Papers, Vi. See also H. M. Talley to his mother, 5 September 1864, Brown Papers, Nc-Ar, and Lt. Col. John L. Harris, 24th North Carolina, to W. J. Clarke, 12 September 1864, Clarke Papers, NcU.

78. J. K. Wilkerson to his sister, 29 August 1864, Wilkerson Papers, NcD.

79. H. C. Conner to his wife, 3 September 1864, Conner Papers, ScU.

80. Sgt. Jacob Shook, Company G, 15th Virginia, to Miss Julia Deane, 4 September 1864, Julia Deane Papers, NcD.

81. W. A. Kelly, Diary, 31 August 1864, Kelly Papers, ScCC.

82. John Bratton to his wife, 5 September 1864, Bratton Papers, ScCoAH.

83. H. C. Conner to his wife, 9 September 1864, Conner Papers, ScU. See also H. D. Wells to his sister, 5 September 1864, Wells Papers, PNB; H. M. Talley to his mother, 5 September 1864, Brown Papers, Nc-Ar; and T. C. Elder to his wife, 11 September 1864, Elder Papers, ViHi.

84. F. M. Coker to his wife, 5 September 1864, Heidler Collection, GU.

85. F. M. Coker to his wife, 10 September 1864, ibid.

86. A. F. Fleet to his father, 13 September 1864, in Fleet and Fuller, *Green Mount*, 338–39. See also T. G. Trimmier to his wife, 7 September 1864, Trimmier Collection, T, and T. C. Elder to his wife, 11 September 1864, Elder Papers, ViHi.

87. J. H. Chamberlayne to Mrs. Sally Grattan, 19 August 1864, in Chamberlayne, *Ham Chamberlayne*, 259.

88. B. W. Justice to his wife, 1 September 1864, Justice Papers, GEU. See also Justice to his wife, 30 August 1864, ibid., and H. E. Peyton, ANV, Inspection Report, 23 September 1864, *OR* 42(2):1274–75.

89. Jr. 2d Lt. Ezekiel Dunagan Graham, Company B, 6th Georgia, to Miss Laura Mann, 14 September 1864, UDC Typescripts, vol. 2, G-Ar; W. J. Pegram to his sister, 24 September 1864, Pegram-Johnson-McIntosh Family Papers, ViHi. See also *Richmond Dispatch*, 12 September 1864; *Richmond Examiner*, 13 September 1864; and *Richmond Whig*, 13 September 1864.

90. W. J. Pegram to his sister, 24 September 1864, Pegram-Johnson-McIntosh Family Papers, ViHi.

91. Pvt. Thomas Walker Gilmer, Courier, III Corps Artillery, to his father, 18 September 1864, Gilmer Family Papers, Private Collection of Walker Gilmer Petroff, Beaufort, S.C. See also W. A. Kelly, Diary, 31 August 1864, Kelly Papers, ScCC; T. C. Elder to his wife, 11 September 1864, Elder Papers, ViHi; and J. W. Albright, Diary, 23 September 1864, Albright Papers, NcU.

92. Lee to his wife, 28 August 1864, in Dowdey and Manarin, *Wartime Papers*, 847.

93. J. W. Albright, Diary, 23 September 1864, Albright Papers, NcU. See also E. R. Crockett, Diary, 25 September 1864, Crockett Papers, TxU, and E. P. Alexander to his wife, 25 September 1864, Alexander Papers, NcU.

94. *Richmond Examiner*, 19 August 1864.

95. John Bratton to his wife, 21 August 1864, Bratton Papers, ScCoAH.

96. R. A. Stiles to his mother, 21 August 1864, Stiles Papers, ViHi.

97. Lee to Maj. Gen. John B. Hood, Hood/I Corps, 21 May 1863, in Dowdey and Manarin, *Wartime Papers*, 490.

98. Lee to Hampton, 3 September 1864, *OR* 42(2):1233.

99. Sgt. George D. Shadburne, Scout, Jeff Davis Legion, to Hampton, 5 September 1864, *OR* 42(2):1235–36; Lee to Hampton, 9 September 1864, 42(2):1242; Lee to Seddon, 17 September 1864, 42(1):852; Hampton's report, 42(1):944–47; GO 11, Cavalry Corps, ANV, 18 September 1864, 42(1):952. See also reports of Federal commanders, 42(1). Secondary accounts include Boykin, *Beefsteak Raid*, and Trudeau, *The Last Citadel*, 192–201.

100. H. C. Conner to his wife, 19 September 1864, Conner Papers, ScU.

101. Pvt. Alexander Faulkner Fewell, Company E, 17th South Carolina, to his wife, 18 September 1864, in Mackintosh, *"Dear Martha,"* 137–38.

102. W. D. Alexander, Diary, 20 September 1864, Alexander Papers, NcU; M. H. Fitzpatrick to his wife, 24 September 1864, in Hammock, *Letters to Amanda*, 158; A. F. Fleet to his mother, 20 September 1864, in Fleet and Fuller, *Green Mount*, 340.

103. Corp. Charles C. Baughman, Company A, 13th Battalion Virginia Light Artillery, to his mother, 28 September 1864, Charles C. Baughman Papers, ViRC. See also F. M. Coker to his wife, 18 September 1864, Heidler Collection, GU; Pvt.

Edward Stuart, Signal Corps, W. H. F. Lee/Cavalry Corps, to his father, 18 September 1864, Oscar J. E. Stuart Papers, Ms-Ar; and Pvt. Hugh Y. Spence, Company D, 18th South Carolina, to Martin V. Barkley, 23 September 1864, Barkley Family Papers, NcU.

104. Lee to Seddon, 29 September 1864, *OR* 42(2):1301; W. H. Taylor to Samuel Cooper, 29 September 1864, 42(2):1301; Lee to Bragg, 29 September 1864 (two messages), 42(2):1302; Lee to Ewell [undated, but 29 September 1864], 42(2):1302; Ewell to Bragg, 29 September 1864 (six messages), 42(2): 1303–4; Lee to Ewell, 29 September 1864, 42(2):1304; Taylor to Brig. Gen. John Gregg, Texas (Gregg)/Field/I Corps, 29 September 1864, 42(2):1305; Lee to Seddon, 30 September 1864, 42(2):1306; Seddon to Davis, 1 October 1864, 42(3):1130; reports of subordinate commanders, 42(1):859, 879–80, 934, 938; diary of the I Corps, 29–30 September 1864, 42(1):875–76. See also reports of Federal commanders, 42(1).

105. Lee to Seddon, 1 October 1864, *OR* 42(1):852; Seddon to Davis, 1 October 1864, 42(3):1130; reports of subordinate commanders, 42(1):859, 870, 941–42, 947–48. See also reports of Federal commanders, 42(1). For unpublished reports from regimental commanders in Lane/Wilcox/III Corps, see Maj. T. J. Wooten, Sharpshooters, 7 October 1864; Lt. Col. W. L. Davidson, 7th North Carolina, 6 October 1864; Lt. Col. J. W. McGill, 18th North Carolina, 6 October 1864; Capt. G. G. Holland, 28th North Carolina, 2 October 1864; Col. R. V. Cowan, 33d North Carolina, 3 October 1864; and Maj. J. L. Bost, 37th North Carolina, 6 October 1864, all in Lane Papers, AAP. A remarkably detailed and valuable study of Grant's Fifth Offensive (including fighting at New Market Heights, Fort Harrison, the Squirrel Level Road, and Poplar Spring Church) is Sommers, *Richmond Redeemed*; see also Trudeau, *The Last Citadel*, 202–17, and Freeman, *Lee's Lieutenants*, 3:590–93.

106. A. M. Scales to his wife, 9 October 1864, Scales Papers, Nc-Ar.

107. T. L. Alexander to his wife, 1 October 1864, Alexander Papers, PNB; Pvt. Willis Michael Parker, Company K, 9th Virginia, to Peter Guerrant Jr., 3 October 1864, Guerrant Family Papers, ViHi.

108. W. T. Poague to his mother, 5 October 1864, in Cockrell, *Gunner With Stonewall*, 139. See also T. L. McCarty, Diary, 29 September 1864, McCarty Papers, TxU; E. R. Crockett, Diary, 29 September 1864, Crockett Papers, TxU; W. D. Alexander, Diary, 30 September 1864, Alexander Papers, NcU; and Adjt. Alexander Smith Webb, 44th North Carolina, to his mother, 6 October 1864, Webb Family Papers, NcU.

109. H. C. Conner to his wife, 3 October 1864, Conner Papers, ScU; E. P. Alexander to his wife, 3 October 1864, Alexander Papers, NcU.

110. E. P. Alexander to his wife, 3 October 1864, Alexander Papers, NcU. See also W. H. S. Burgwyn, Diary, 30 September 1864, Burgwyn Papers, Nc-Ar, and J. A. Everett to his mother, 9 October 1864, Everett Papers, GEU.

111. J. A. Everett to his mother, 9 October 1864, Everett Papers, GEU.

112. J. K. Wilkerson to his parents, 5 October 1864, Wilkerson Papers, NcD. See also a second letter of the same date to his mother, ibid.

113. F. M. Coker to his wife, 5 October 1864, Heidler Collection, GU. See also J. F. Sale, Diary, 1 October 1864, Sale Papers, Vi; J. A. F. Coleman, Diary, 2 October 1864, Confederate Miscellany I, GEU; and T. C. Elder to his wife, 6 October 1864, Elder Papers, ViHi.

114. J. A. F. Coleman, Diary, 2 October 1864, Confederate Miscellany I, GEU. See also J. F. Sale, Diary, 1 October 1864, Sale Papers, Vi.

115. Lee to Seddon, 4 October 1864, *OR* 42(3):1134.

116. W. J. Pegram to his sister, 5 October 1864, in James I. Robertson Jr., "'The Boy Artillerist,'" 248–49.

117. Diary of the I Corps, 7 October 1864, *OR* 42(1):876.

118. See, e.g., H. C. Conner to his wife, 29 October 1864, Conner Papers, ScU, and J. A. Everett to his mother, 29 October 1864, Everett Papers, GEU.

119. For the 7 October engagement on the Darbytown Road, see Lee to Seddon, 7–8 October 1864, *OR* 42(1):852; reports of subordinate commanders, 42(1):859, 881, 938–39; and diary of the I Corps, 7 October 1864, 42(1):876. See also reports of Federal commanders, 42(1), as well as Freeman, *Lee's Lieutenants*, 3:592–93. For the 27 October engagements on the Darbytown Road and at Burgess Mill, see Lee to Seddon, 27 October 1864 (two messages), 42(1):853, 28 October 1864, 42(1):853–54, and 29 October 1864, 42(1):854; and reports of subordinate commanders, 42(1):860, 871–72, 877; 949–50. See also reports of Federal commanders, 42(1), as well as Trudeau, *The Last Citadel*, 223–51, and Freeman, *Lee's Lieutenants*, 3:615–16. The most notable Confederate casualty of these operations was Brig. Gen. John Gregg, of the Texas Brigade, Field/I Corps, who was killed on 7 October. Gregg, who had been severely wounded at Chickamauga in the fall of 1863, had returned to the army in time for the Wilderness and had commanded his famous brigade through all of the 1864 campaigns. See, e.g., T. L. McCarty, Diary, 7, 9 October 1864, McCarty Papers, TxU, and E. R. Crockett, Diary, 7, 9 October 1864, Crockett Papers, TxU.

120. H. A. Chambers, Diary, 29 October 1864, in Pearce, *Diary of . . . Chambers*, 227. See also Maj. L. H. Hunt, Insp. Gen., Wilcox/III Corps, 30 October 1864, Inspection Reports, NA, microcopy M935, roll 11; H. L. Law to his mother, 29 October 1864, Law Papers, ScU; and J. M. Frank to his father, 30 October 1864, Frank Papers, NcD.

121. On Beauregard's departure, see Zebulon B. Vance to Lee, 5 September 1864, and Lee's endorsement, 10 September 1864, *OR* 42(2):1235; Lee to Davis, 19 September 1864, 39(2):846; and SO 235, A&IGO, 4 October 1864, 42(3):1134. On Longstreet's return, see Longstreet's report, undated, 42(1):871; Longstreet to W. H. Taylor, 7 October 1864, 42(3):1140; and Longstreet to Lee, 20 October 1864, 42(3):1155. For one officer's reaction to Longstreet's return, see Capt. John Fletcher Brabham, Company C, 1st South Carolina, to "Jube," 26 October 1864,

Brabham Family Papers, ScU. On Anderson's assignment to lead the new Fourth Corps (most often referred to in the army as "Anderson's Corps"), see Field Return, ANV, 20 October 1864, 42(3):1156; Monthly Return, ANV, 31 October 1864, 42(3):1186–87; and Organization of the ANV, 31 October 1864, 42(3):1190. At this time Hoke's Division was temporarily attached to the First Corps, leaving Anderson with Johnson's Division and the artillery from Beauregard's old command.

122. Field Returns, ANV, 30 June 1864, *OR* 40(2):707; 10 September 1864, 42(2):1243; and 31 October 1864, 42(3):1186–87. On 31 October Ewell's troops in the Department of Richmond added another 3,000 men present for duty, out of a total strength of 8,700 present and absent; abstract from Field Return, Richmond, 31 October 1864, 42(3):1197.

123. H. C. Conner to his wife, 18 October 1864, Conner Papers, ScU.

124. F. M. Coker to his wife, 18 October 1864, Heidler Collection, GU.

125. A. F. Fewell to his wife, 16 October 1864, in Mackintosh, *"Dear Martha,"* 148.

126. J. W. Albright, Diary, 14 October 1864, Albright Papers, NcU.

127. Lee to Samuel Cooper, 10 October 1864, *OR* 42(3):1144; Lee to A. P. Hill, 10 October 1864, 42(3):1145.

128. Lee to Hampton, 26 October 1864, *OR* 42(3):1176. See also Hampton to Lee, 24 October 1864, 42(3):1161–62.

129. Lee to Davis, 2 November 1864, in Freeman, *Lee's Dispatches,* 305.

130. Capt. Henry Thweat Owen, Company C, 18th Virginia, to his wife, 9 October 1864, Henry T. Owen Papers, Vi. Owen's reference to his company looking "like a Battalion" was in comparison with the other companies in Hunton's Brigade.

131. G. M. Sorrel to C. W. Field, 26 October 1864, *OR* 42(3):1177.

132. W. D. Williams to his fiancée, 20 October 1864, TxHiC. See also T. C. Elder to his wife, 13 October 1864, Elder Papers, ViHi; F. M. Coker to his wife, 18 October 1864, Heidler Collection, GU; and Sgt. Maj. Marion Hill Fitzpatrick, 45th Georgia, to his wife, 3 November 1864, in Hammock, *Letters to Amanda,* 169.

133. Maj. Gen. W. S. Hancock, II Army Corps / Army of the Potomac, to Maj. Gen. A. A. Humphreys, Chief of Staff, Army of the Potomac, 2 October 1864, *OR* 42(3):38–39.

134. See, e.g., the daily reports of B. R. Johnson, 10, 15, 18–19, 22, 27 September 1864, 19, 24 October 1864, *OR* 42(1):890, 892–93, 895–97, 903, 905.

135. Col. John T. Goode, Wise (Goode) / Johnson / Beauregard, quoted in B. R. Johnson's daily report, 15 September 1864, *OR* 42(1):892. See also Johnson's daily report, 19 October 1864, 42(1):903.

136. See, e.g., for Dept. of Northern Virginia, GO 62, 21 October 1864; GO 63, 22 October 1864; and GO 64, 31 October 1864, all in ANV Orders and Circulars, NA, microcopy M921, roll 1.

137. J. E. Hall to his father, 6 October 1864 (two letters), Hall Family Papers, A-Ar.

138. Pvt. James C. Fowler, Company C, 25th North Carolina, to Gov. Zebulon B. Vance, 6 October 1864, Governor's Papers, Nc-Ar. See also James C. Fowler, 25th [North Carolina] Infantry, Compiled Service Records, NA, microcopy M270, roll 315.

139. H. C. Conner to his wife, 4 November 1864, Conner Papers, ScU.

140. H. T. Owen to his wife [undated, but October/November 1864], Owen Papers, Vi; C. M. Wilcox to his sister-in-law, 18 October 1864, Wilcox Papers, LC.

141. S. G. Welch to his wife, 3 November 1864, in Welch, *A Confederate Surgeon's Letters*, 114. See also Adjt. Crenshaw Hall, Gracie/Johnson/IV Corps, to his father, 24 October 1864, Hall Family Papers, A-Ar.

142. F. M. Coker to his wife, 4 November 1864, Heidler Collection, GU.

CHAPTER 8

1. J. A. F. Coleman, Diary, 8 November 1864, Confederate Miscellany I, GEU. See also H. C. Conner to his wife, 9 November 1864, Conner Papers, ScU.

2. F. M. Coker to his wife, 10 November 1864, Heidler Collection, GU.

3. H. C. Conner to his wife, 24 November 1864, Conner Papers, ScU.

4. Capt. John Esten Cooke, Asst. Insp. Gen., Cavalry Corps Artillery, Diary, 15 November 1864, John Esten Cooke Papers, NcD; W. D. Alexander, Diary, 17 November 1864, Alexander Papers, NcU.

5. A. M. Scales to his wife, 12 November 1864, Scales Papers, Nc-Ar.

6. Capt. Edward Laight Wells, Company K, 4th South Carolina Cavalry, to his parents, 17 November 1864, in Smith, Smith, and Childs, *Mason Smith Family Letters*, 148. See also J. M. Smither to his sister, 12 November 1864, Smither Papers, TxHiC, and 2d Lt. Alexander Frederick Fleet, Asst. Adjt. Gen., Wise/Johnson/IV Corps, to his sister, 26 November 1864, in Fleet and Fuller, *Green Mount*, 348.

7. J. E. Hall to his father, 10 November 1864, Hall Family Papers, A-Ar.

8. Sgts. George F. Adams and Barzella C. McBride, Company D, 1st North Carolina Cavalry, to Adams's parents, 16 November 1864, Alfred Adams Papers, NcD.

9. J. A. Everett to his mother, 27 November 1864, Everett Papers, GEU.

10. J. A. F. Coleman, Diary, 16 November 1864, Confederate Miscellany I, GEU.

11. Capt. John McEntee, Provost Marshal Gen.'s Dept., Army of the Potomac, to Maj. Gen. A. A. Humphreys, Chief of Staff, Army of the Potomac, 22 November 1864, *OR* 42(3):681. The deserters were from MacRae/Heth/III Corps, Lane/Wilcox/III Corps, Finegan/Heth/III Corps, Washington Artillery/III Corps Artillery, Wallace/Johnson/IV Corps, and Ransom/Johnson/IV Corps.

12. F. M. Coker to his wife, 4, 16 November 1864, Heidler Collection, GU. See also T. L. McCarty, Diary, 17, 20–21, 25–26 November 1864, T. L. McCarty Papers, TxU; Capt. Stephen P. Read, Company F, 14th Virginia, to his sister, 20 November 1864, Mabry Papers, Nc-Ar; and W. H. Phillips to his parents, 21 November 1864, Phillips Papers, NcD.

13. H. C. Conner to his wife, 24 November 1864, Conner Papers, ScU; Pvt. Bellfield King, Company G, 11th North Carolina, to his mother, 28 November 1864, Willis H. King Papers, NcD. See also Pvt. Alfred Newton Proffit, Company D, 18th North Carolina, to his sister, 20 November 1864, Proffit Family Papers, NcU.

14. S. P. Read to his sister, 20 November 1864, Mabry Papers, Nc-Ar.

15. A. N. Proffit to his sister, 20 November 1864, Proffit Family Papers, NcU.

16. E. P. Alexander to his wife, 25 December 1864, Alexander Papers, NcU. For descriptions of winter quarters, see A. F. Fewell to his wife, November 1864 (undated fragment), 10 December 1864, in Mackintosh, *"Dear Martha,"* 159, 168; J. J. Armfield to his wife, 22, 31 December 1864, Armfield Papers, Nc-Ar; and A. E. Henderson to his brother, 31 December 1864, Henderson Papers, NcD.

17. Maj. Giles B. Cooke, Asst. Adjt. Gen., HQ, Diary, 22 November 1864, Giles Buckner Cooke Papers, ViHi. For other descriptions of the rain and snow during November and December, see Cooke, Diary, 12 December 1864, Cooke Papers, ViHi; Pvt. J. B. Sanders, Company C, 2d South Carolina Rifles, to J. E. Hagood, 21 November 1864, Hagood Papers, ScU; and S. P. Read to his sister, 11 December 1864, Mabry Papers, Nc-Ar.

18. A. F. Fleet to his father, 10 November 1864, in Fleet and Fuller, *Green Mount*, 347; W. D. Alexander, Diary, 17 November 1864, Alexander Papers, NcU.

19. Capt. Zimmerman Davis, 5th South Carolina Cavalry, to W. H. Taylor, (with endorsements), 17 November 1864, Orders, Company D, 5th South Carolina Cavalry, ScCoAH.

20. A. N. Proffit to his sister, 20 November 1864, Proffit Family Papers, NcU.

21. Anonymous Private, Bedford [Virginia] Light Artillery, "Soldiers' Pay," *Richmond Dispatch*, 1 December 1864; A. F. Fewell to his wife, 18 December 1864, in Mackintosh, *"Dear Martha,"* 176–77. See also Walter Harrison, Asst. Adjt. & Insp. Gen., Pickett/I Corps, Reports of Clothing Issued, November–December 1864, Confederate Inspection Book, NcU; Brig. Gen. A. R. Lawton, Quartermaster Gen., Confederate States Army, to Lt. Col. J. L. Corley, Chief Quartermaster, ANV, 12 December 1864, *OR* 42(3):1268–69; Col. William H. Peebles, Cook (Peebles)/Grimes/II Corps, to Maj. J. A. Whiting, Asst. Adjt. Gen., Grimes/II Corps, 27 December 1864, Grimes Papers, Nc-Ar; and the inspection reports of various units for November–December 1864, NA, microcopy M935, rolls 11–14.

22. L. R. Mills to his brother, 26 November 1864, in Harmon, "Letters of . . . Mills," 303–4.

23. J. C. Babcock, Bureau of Information, Army of the Potomac, to Brig. Gen. Seth Williams, Asst. Adjt. Gen., Army of the Potomac, 31 December 1864, *OR* 42(3):1107. See also Babcock to Maj. Gen. A. A. Humphreys, Chief of Staff, Army of the Potomac, 19 November 1864, 42(2):660, and Babcock to Maj. Gen. George G. Meade, Army of the Potomac, 14 December 1864, 42(2):995.

24. E. P. Alexander to his wife, 25 December 1864, Alexander Papers, NcU. See also GO 71, ANV, 12 December 1864, *OR* 42(3):1270; G. B. Cooke, Diary,

13 December 1864, Cooke Papers, ViHi; and J. A. F. Coleman, Diary, 20 December 1864, Confederate Miscellany I, GEU.

25. S. G. Welch to his wife, 3 November 1864, in Welch, *A Confederate Surgeon's Letters to His Wife*, 115; J. J. Armfield to his wife, 22 December 1864, Armfield Papers, Nc-Ar.

26. Capt. H. H. Perry, Adjt. & Insp. Gen., Sorrel/Mahone/III Corps, 30 November 1864; H. E. Peyton, Endorsement, 12 December 1864, Inspection Reports, NA, microcopy M935, roll 13. See also inspection reports of various units for November–December 1864, NA, microcopy M935, rolls 11–14. For comments by soldiers on the poor quality and quantity of their rations during this period, especially in late December, see also J. J. Armfield to his wife, 22 December 1864, Armfield Papers, Nc-Ar; C. T. Davis, Diary, 25 December 1864, Davis Papers, ViHi; and *Richmond Examiner*, 28 December 1864.

27. Lee's endorsement, 1 December 1864, on A. P. Hill to W. H. Taylor, 1 December 1864, *OR* 42(3):1249.

28. A. F. Fewell to his wife, November [undated], 22 December 1864, in Mackintosh, *"Dear Martha,"* 159–60, 178.

29. A. F. Fewell to his wife, 25 December 1864, in ibid., 179–80.

30. J. A. F. Coleman, Diary, 26 November 1864, Confederate Miscellany I, GEU. For comments by soldiers on the fair-to-good quality and quantity of their rations during this period, see G. F. Adams and B. C. McBride to Adams's parents, 16 November 1864, Adams Papers, NcD; W. H. Phillips to his parents, 21 November 1864, Phillips Papers, NcD; H. C. Conner to his wife, 14 December 1864, Conner Papers, ScU; W. C. McFall to his mother, 19 December 1864, McFall Papers, GEU; J. J. Armfield to his wife, 31 December 1864, Armfield Papers, Nc-Ar; and A. E. Henderson to his brother, 31 December 1864, Henderson Papers, NcD.

31. M. H. Fitzpatrick to his wife, 3 November 1864, in Hammock, *Letters to Amanda*, 169.

32. H. E. Peyton, ANV, 29 November 1864, Inspection Reports, NA, microcopy M935, roll 11. See also Walter Harrison, Pickett/I Corps, 30 November 1864, Inspection Reports, NA, microcopy M935, roll 13, and inspection reports of various units for November–December 1864, NA, microcopy M935, rolls 11–14.

33. J. C. Babcock, Provost Marshal Gen.'s Dept., Army of the Potomac, to Maj. Gen. G. G. Meade, Army of the Potomac, 28 November 1864, *OR* 42(3):727. See also Babcock to Maj. Gen. A. A. Humphreys, Chief of Staff, Army of the Potomac, 6, 10 November 1864, 42(3):530, 583, and to Meade, 11, 29 December 1864, 42(3):956, 1092; and Capt. John McEntee, Provost Marshal Gen.'s Dept., Army of the Potomac, to Humphreys, 22 November 1864, 42(3):681.

34. J. F. Brabham to "Jube," 25 November 1864, Brabham Family Papers, ScU.

35. Field Return, ANV, 31 October 1864, *OR* 42(3):1186–87; Field Return, ANV, 30 November 1864, 42(3):1236–37. On 30 November Ewell's troops in the Department of Richmond added another 6,000 men present for duty, out of a total

strength of 17,000 present and absent; Abstract from Field Return, Richmond, 30 November 1864, 42(3):1248.

36. For examples of Lee's plans in November and December, see Lee to Hampton, 21 November 1864 (two letters), *OR* 42(3):1223; Longstreet to Lee, 22 November 1864, 42(3):1224, and 24 November 1864, 42(3):1227; Longstreet to C. S. Venable, 6 December 1864, 42(3):1256; and Longstreet to Lee, 9 December 1864 (two letters), 42(3):1260–61. For reports of recent conscripts deserting to the Federals, see Maj. Gen. A. A. Humphreys, II Army Corps, Army of the Potomac, to Maj. Gen. G. G. Meade, Army of the Potomac, 11 December 1864, 42(3):961, and J. C. Babcock, Provost Marshal Gen.'s Dept., Army of the Potomac, to Meade, 11 December 1864, 42(3):1008.

37. A. P. Hill to his sister, 17 December 1864, Ambrose Powell Hill Papers, ViHi.

38. T. P. Devereux to his sister, 29 December 1864, Devereux Papers, Nc-Ar.

39. A. F. Fleet to his father, 9 December 1864, in Fleet and Fuller, *Green Mount*, 350. See also L. R. Mills to his brother, 5 December 1864, in Harmon, "Letters of . . . Mills," 305, and A. B. Simms to his sister, 7 December 1864, in Peacock, "A Georgian's View of War," 128.

40. Charles Kerrison to his sister, 3 December 1864, Kerrison Family Papers, ScU.

41. H. C. Conner to his wife, 14 December 1864, Conner Papers, ScU. See also A. F. Fleet to his sister, 21 December 1864, in Fleet and Fuller, *Green Mount*, 351–52, and "The Spirit of Virginia," *Richmond Dispatch*, 24 December 1864.

42. L. R. Mills to his brother, 5 December 1864, in Harmon, "Letters of . . . Mills," 305.

43. W. H. Phillips to his father, 26 November 1864, Phillips Papers, NcD.

44. Pvt. W. T. [or W. G.] Field, Company K, 6th South Carolina Cavalry, to J. E. Hagood, 3 December 1864, Hagood Papers, ScU.

45. J. A. Johnson to his fiancée, 15 December 1864, Johnson Papers, NcU.

46. "Privates Bratton's Brigade," *Richmond Examiner*, 24 December 1864.

47. "The Soldiers," ibid., 28 December 1864. See also the letters by "Buck Private" and "Fourteenth Tennessee," 21 December 1864; "A Member of the Seventh Ga. Cavalry," 28 December 1864; "A Private" and "Many Sufferers," 30 December 1864; and "A Virginian Officer," 31 December 1864, ibid.

48. E. H. Steele to his cousin, 17 December 1864, Munford-Ellis Family Papers, NcD.

49. A. F. Fleet to his sister, 21 December 1864, in Fleet and Fuller, *Green Mount*, 351.

50. "The Proposed Dinner to General Lee's Army Postponed to New Year's Day," *Richmond Examiner*, 22 December 1864. See also "Christmas Dinner for the Soldiers," *Richmond Whig*, 25 November 1864; "The Soldiers' Christmas Dinner," *Richmond Examiner*, 20 December 1864; "The Soldiers' Dinner," *Richmond Exam-*

iner, 21 December 1864; and various other articles and advertisements in the *Richmond Dispatch, Examiner, Sentinel*, and *Whig*, 22–31 December 1864.

51. *New Year's Dinner*. The only known copy of this unique broadside is in the collection of the Boston Athenaeum, Boston, Mass. Several versions of the text were published in advertisements in the Richmond newspapers; the most complete version appears in the *Richmond Whig*, 29 December 1864.

52. Maj. Henry Edward Young, Asst. Adjt. Gen., HQ, to his mother, 23 December 1864, Gourdin Papers, GEU.

53. Lee to Davis, 14 December 1864, in Freeman, *Lee's Dispatches*, 307–8.

54. W. R. Battle to his mother, 25 December 1864, in Lee, *Forget-Me-Nots*, 123.

55. C. T. Davis, Diary, 25 December 1864, Davis Papers, ViHi.

56. Capt. James Lowndes, Asst. Adjt. & Insp. Gen., Wallace/Johnson/IV Corps, 29 December 1864, Inspection Reports, NA, microcopy M935, roll 11.

57. Capt. James Walker, Adjt. & Insp. Gen., Simms/Kershaw/I Corps, 30 December 1864, Inspection Reports, NA, microcopy M935, roll 13. For discussion of the bread ration, see also Walter Harrison, Pickett/I Corps, 30 December 1864, ibid.

58. J. C. Babcock, Bureau of Information, Army of the Potomac, to Maj. Gen. G. G. Meade, Army of the Potomac, 26 December 1864, *OR* 42(3):1077. For Redwood's identity, see B. R. Johnson to Richard H. Anderson, 26 December 1864, 42(3):1311. See also Maj. Gen. Orlando B. Willcox, IX Army Corps, Army of the Potomac, to Brig. Gen. Seth Williams, Asst. Adjt. Gen., Army of the Potomac, 31 December 1864, 42(3):1112.

59. Lee's endorsement, 27 December 1864, on B. R. Johnson to Richard H. Anderson, 26 December 1864, *OR* 42(3):1311.

60. See, e.g., "Fourteenth Tennessee," *Richmond Examiner*, 18 December 1864; *Richmond Examiner*, 28 December 1864; and "The Soldiers' Dinner," *Richmond Dispatch*, 2 January 1865.

61. "Preparing the Soldiers' Dinner," *Richmond Examiner*, 29 December 1864.

62. Corp. Simeon Gross, Company K, 20th South Carolina, to his mother, 30 December 1864, in Smith, *Rebel Yell*.

63. "Virginia's New Year's Greeting to the Army of Northern Virginia," *Richmond Examiner*, 31 December 1864.

64. Corp. Harry C. Townsend, 1st Company, Richmond Howitzers, Diary, 1 January 1865, in Townsend, "Townsend's Diary," 99; R. P. Myers, Diary, 1 January 1865, Myers Papers, ViRC. See also 5th Sgt. Will F. Montgomery, Company B, 9th Georgia, to his fiancée, 1 January 1865, UDC Typescripts, vol. 2, G-Ar; A. H. Jackson to his mother, 1 January 1865, Harden Family Papers, NcD; and W. D. Williams to his fiancée, 1 January 1865, Williams Papers, TxHiC.

65. J. J. Armfield to his wife, 10 January 1865 [misdated 1864], Armfield Papers, Nc-Ar.

66. R. P. Myers, Diary, 3 January 1865, Myers Papers, ViRC.

67. E. P. Alexander to his wife, 3 January 1865, Alexander Papers, NcU; Surg.

Richard V. Leach, 2d North Carolina Battalion, to his sister, 4 January 1865, James H. C. Leach Papers, NcD; Pvt. Edward Cook Barnes, Courier, Company G, 11th Virginia, to his mother, 12 January 1865, Barnes Family Papers, ViU.

68. J. T. Gay to his wife, 7 January 1865, Nix Collection, GU.

69. E. P. Alexander to his wife, 3 January 1865, Alexander Papers, NcU.

70. Pvt. Frank Lobrano, Washington Artillery, Diary, 4 January 1865, Civil War Papers, LHA Collection, LNT.

71. Pvt. Alexander C. Jones, 4th Company, Washington Artillery, Diary, 4 January 1865, Civil War Papers, LHA Collection, LNT. For other complaints about the dinner, see John Bratton to his wife, 2 January 1865, Bratton Papers, ScCoAH; Sgt. Maj. Richard S. Ellis Jr., 21st Virginia/Terry/Evans/II Corps, to his brother, 5 January 1865, Munford-Ellis Family Papers, NcD; and "A.B.C.," 1st Virginia, "The Soldiers' New-Year's Dinner," *Richmond Dispatch*, 6 January 1865.

72. "An Example," *Richmond Whig*, 10 January 1865; T. L. McCarty to his sister, 26 January 1865, McCarty Papers, TxU.

73. *Richmond Examiner*, 5 January 1865. See also ibid., 3 January 1865, and "The New Year's Dinner to the Army," ibid., 9 January 1865.

74. G. D. Carter to his mother, 4 January 1865, UDC Typescripts, vol. 2, G-Ar.

75. H. C. Conner to his wife, 4 January 1865, Conner Papers, ScU. See also T. L. McCarty to his sister, 26 January 1865, McCarty Papers, TxU.

76. E. C. Barnes to his mother, 12 January 1865, Barnes Family Papers, ViU.

77. Pvt. Riley W. Leonard, Company A, 21st North Carolina, to his parents, 4 January 1865, Riley Leonard Papers, Nc-Ar.

78. L. G. Young to his mother, 6 January 1865, Gourdin Papers, GEU.

79. Benjamin Mason to his wife, 21 January 1865, Mason Papers, AAP.

80. J. W. Albright, Diary, 15–17 January 1865, James W. Albright Papers, NcU. See also R. S. Ellis to his brother, 11 January 1865, Munford-Ellis Family Papers, NcD; Capt. Joseph F. Sessions, Company K, 18th Mississippi, to his uncle, 19 January 1865, Oscar J. E. Stuart Papers, Ms-Ar; Corp. Silas Chandler, Company B, 55th Virginia, to his wife, 25 January 1865, Silas Chandler Papers, PNB; R. H. Hutspeth to his aunt, 26 January 1865, Hutspeth Papers, Nc-Ar; Capt. Charles Fenton James, Company F, 8th Virginia, to his sister, 13 February 1865, Charles Fenton James Papers, NcU; and North Carolina Officers in the Army of Northern Virginia to William Alexander Graham, 27 February 1865, in Williams, *Papers of William Alexander Graham*, 258.

81. A. F. Fewell to W. A. Quinton, 1 January 1865, in Mackintosh, *"Dear Martha,"* 182; A. F. Fleet to his mother, 23 January 1865, in Fleet and Fuller, *Green Mount*, 356.

82. W. F. Montgomery to his fiancée, 1 January 1865, UDC Typescripts, vol. 2, G-Ar.

83. J. A. Everett to his mother, 10 January 1865, Everett Papers, GEU. See also Everett to his mother, 7 February 1865, Everett Papers, GEU; T. L. McCarty to his sister, 26 January 1865, McCarty Papers, TxU; A. H. Crawford to his wife,

17 February 1865, Crawford Papers, NcD; and H. P. Fortson to Mrs. R. A. Barnes, 27 February 1865, Barnes Family Papers, ViU.

84. Col. Fitz William McMaster, 17th South Carolina, to his wife, 10 February 1865, Fitz William McMaster Papers, ScU. See also J. M. McFall to his sister, 23 January 1865, McFall Papers, GEU.

85. Capt. James Dewitt Hankins, Surry Light Artillery, to unknown correspondent, January [undated] 1865, Hankins Family Papers, ViHi.

86. T. P. Devereux to his sister, 7 January 1865, Devereux Papers, Nc-Ar.

87. M. H. Fitzpatrick to his wife, 1 January 1865, in Hammock, *Letters to Amanda*, 177; J. A. Everett to his mother, 18 February 1865, Everett Papers, GEU.

88. H. P. Fortson to Mrs. R. A. Barnes, 27 February 1865, Barnes Family Papers, ViU. See also T. P. Devereux to his father, 20 February 1865, Devereux Papers, Nc-Ar.

89. Pvt. Robert M. Hannah, Company C, 45th North Carolina, to his cousin, 8 January 1865, John C. Hackett Papers, NcD; A. H. Crawford to his wife, 17 February 1865, Crawford Papers, NcD.

90. R. P. Scarbrough to his cousin, 31 January 1865, Confederate Miscellany, GEU; J. K. Wilkerson to his sister, 14 February 1865, Wilkerson Papers, NcD. See also R. S. Ellis to his brother, 11 January 1865, Munford-Ellis Family Papers, NcD; W. R. Battle to his mother, 15 January 1865, in Lee, *Forget-Me-Nots*, 125–26; and 2d Lt. J. F. Sale, Company H, 12th Virginia, to his father, 20 January 1865, J. F. Sale Papers, Vi.

91. Lee to Secretary of War John C. Breckinridge, 28 February 1865, *OR* 46(2):1265.

92. Statement of Pvt. John Johnson, Company A, 7th Tennessee, 3 February 1865, *OR* 46(2):387.

93. Lee to Seddon, 27 January 1865, *OR* 46(2):1143.

94. Lt. Col. J. H. Duncan, 16th Mississippi, to Brig. Gen. Joseph H. Finegan, Mahone (Finegan)/III Corps, 21 January 1865 (with endorsements), Company Officers, 9th Florida, to Lt. B. F. Parker, Adjt., 9th Florida, 22 January 1865 (with endorsements), and enclosures in Lee to Seddon, 27 January 1865, *OR* 46(2): 1144–45. See also various additional enclosures in Lee to Seddon, 27 January 1865, 46(2):1143–50.

95. Lee to Seddon, 27 January 1865, *OR* 46(2):1143.

96. See, e.g., Seddon to Lee, 12 January 1865 (with enclosures), *OR* 46(2): 1039–40; Lee to Seddon, 16 January 1865 (with enclosure), 46(2):1074–75, and 8 February 1865 (with endorsements), 46(1):381–82; and Col. Lucius B. Northrop, Commissary-Gen. of Subsistence, Confederate States Army, to J. C. Breckinridge, 9 February 1865 (with enclosures), 46(2):1211–25.

97. W. C. Leak to his wife and children, 30 January 1865, Leak Papers, PNB. See also Maj. Gen. G. K. Warren, V Army Corps, Army of the Potomac, to Maj.

Gen. A. S. Webb, Chief of Staff, Army of the Potomac, 15 February 1865, *OR* 46(2):564–65.

98. R. P. Scarbrough to his cousin, 31 January 1865, Confederate Miscellany, GEU.

99. Bryan Grimes to his wife, 28 February 1865, Grimes Papers, NcU. See also T. G. Trimmier to his wife, 6 February 1865, Trimmier Collection, T; C. F. James to his sister, 13 February 1865, James Papers, NcU, and North Carolina Officers in the ANV to W. A. Graham, 27 February 1865, in Williams, *Papers of William Alexander Graham*, 258.

100. Lee to Breckinridge, 24 February 1865, *OR* 46(2):1254; see also Lee to Breckinridge, 28 February 1864, 46(2):1265.

101. J. J. Armfield to his wife, 14 January 1865 [misdated 1864], 31 January 1865 [misdated 1864], Armfield Papers, Nc-Ar.

102. Pvt. J. F. Ward, Company K, 8th Virginia, to his sweetheart, 28 January 1865, Jacob B. Click Papers, NcD. Ward's Compiled Service Record, which contains no definite information on his possible desertion, does note that he was at Guyandotte, W.Va. in April 1865, presumably taking the oath of allegiance to the United States and being paroled. Compiled Service Record, James F. Ward, 8th [Virginia] Infantry, Compiled Service Records, NA, microcopy M324, roll 474.

103. C. W. Field to James Longstreet, 23 January 1865 (with endorsements), *OR* 46(2):1125–26; R. S. Ellis to his brother, 16 January 1865, Munford-Ellis Family Papers, NcD. See also P. A. Oliver, Bureau of Information, Army of the Potomac, to Maj. Gen. J. G. Parke, IX Army Corps, Army of the Potomac, 30 January 1865, *OR* 46(2):299; and C. J. Iredell to his wife, 3 February 1865, Iredell Papers, NcU.

104. R. S. Ellis to his brother, 16 January 1865, Munford-Ellis Family Papers, NcD.

105. Strength Return, ANV, 31 December 1864, *OR* 42(3):1362; Abstracts from Field Returns, ANV, 10 January 1865, 46(1):383–84; 26–31 January 1865, 46(1):384–85; 10 February 1865, 46(1):386–87.

106. Longstreet to Lee, 19 December 1864, *OR* 42(3):1280; Davis to Bragg, 20 December 1864, 42(3):1283; Maj. Osmun Latrobe, Asst. Adjt. Gen., I Corps, to Ewell, 21 December 1864, 42(2):1288; SO 8, Cavalry Corps, 19 January 1865, 46(2):1101. See also Latrobe to J. B. Kershaw, 3 January 1865, 46(2):1008–9, for the detachment of Kennedy / Kershaw / I Corps to South Carolina.

107. "Omega," Phillips's Legion, "Furloughs for Getting Recruits," *Richmond Dispatch*, 13 February 1865.

108. See, e.g., Longstreet to Lee, 10 January, 1–2, 4, 6, 10, 14 February 1865, *OR* 46(2):1032–33, 1188–89, 1203, 1206, 1228, 1233–34.

109. Longstreet to Lee, 1, 4 February 1865, *OR* 46(2):1189, 1203.

110. Longstreet to Lee, 10 January 1865, *OR* 46(2):1033; Lee to Longstreet, 7 January 1865, Army of Northern Virginia HQ Papers, R. E. Lee Papers, ViHi.

111. Lt. Col. Samuel McDowell Tate, 6th North Carolina, to Gov. Zebulon B. Vance, 10 January 1865, Governor's Papers, Nc-Ar.

112. W. R. Battle to his parents, 29 January 1865, in Lee, *Forget-Me-Nots*, 128. See also J. M. Goldsmith to his father, 6 January 1865, UDC Typescripts, vol. 2, G-Ar; "Officer," *Richmond Examiner*, 11 January 1865; and "Soldier," *Richmond Examiner*, 17 January 1865.

113. J. B. Evans to his wife, 11 January 1865, Evans Papers, NcD. For comments by representative officers who favored consolidation, see J. F. Sessions to his uncle, 19 January 1865, Stuart Papers, Ms-Ar, and Brig. Gen. Rufus Barringer, Barringer/W. H. F. Lee/Cavalry Corps, to W. A. Graham, 25 January 1865, in Williams, *Papers of William Alexander Graham*, 221.

114. J. J. Armfield to his wife, 31 January 1865, Armfield Papers, Nc-Ar.

115. F. M. Coker to his wife, 1 February 1865, Heidler Collection, GU.

116. J. B. Evans to his wife, 4 February 1865, Evans Papers, NcD. For other opinions on the mission, see B. H. Freeman to his father, 1 February 1865, in Wright, *Confederate Letters*, 58; A. B. Simms to his sister, 2 February 1865, in Peacock, "A Georgian's View of War," 130; T. G. Trimmier to his wife, 2 February 1865, Trimmier Collection, T; and H. C. Conner to his wife, 4 February 1865, Conner Papers, ScU.

117. Alexander H. Stephens, John A. Campbell, and Robert M. T. Hunter to Lt. Gen. U. S. Grant, Armies of the United States, 30 January 1865, *OR* 46(2):297; Secretary of War Edwin M. Stanton to Maj. Gen. Edward O. C. Ord, Army of the James, 30 January 1865, 46(2):302; Grant to Stephens, Campbell, and Hunter, 31 January 1865, 46(2):312; Grant to Stanton, 1 February 1865, 46(3):342–43; Stephens, Hunter, and Campbell to Davis, 5 February 1865, and Davis to the House of Representatives and Senate of the Confederate States, 6 February 1865, in *Richmond Dispatch*, 7 February 1865.

118. Benjamin Mason to his wife, 10 February 1865, Mason Papers, AAP.

119. *Richmond Enquirer*, 9 February 1865.

120. Pvt. William Robert Webb, Company K, 2d North Carolina Cavalry, to his mother, 12 February 1865, Webb Family Papers, NcU; W. T. Poague to his mother, 11 February 1865, in Cockrell, *Gunner With Stonewall*, 148. See also C. F. James to his sister, 7 February 1865, James Papers, NcU, and Orderly Sgt. James E. Whitehorne, 12th Virginia, to his sister, 11 February 1865, J. E. Whitehorne Papers, Vi.

121. Resolutions of Thomas/Wilcox/III Corps, *Richmond Examiner*, 18 February 1865.

122. General Assembly of Virginia to Davis, 17 January 1865, *OR* 46(2):1084; Davis to Lee, 18 January 1865, 46(2):1091; Davis to the General Assembly of Virginia, 18 January 1865, 46(2):1091–92; Lee to Davis, 19 January 1865, in Freeman, *Lee's Dispatches*, 322–23; Samuel Cooper to Lee, 1 February 1865, *OR* 46(2):1188; Lee to Cooper, 4 February 1865, 46(2):1199; GO 3, A&IGO, 6 Febru-

ary 1865, 46(2):1205; GO 1, Confederate States Army, 9 February 1865, 46(2): 1226–27; Lee to Davis, 9 February 1865, 51(2):1082–83.

123. *Richmond Dispatch*, 7 February 1865.

124. Resolutions, Anderson/Field/I Corps, 10 February 1865, in "Spirit of the Army: Anderson's Brigade," *Richmond Examiner*, 16 February 1865. See also Resolutions, Palmetto Battery, in "Spirit of the Army: Palmetto Battery," ibid., 18 February 1865, and Resolutions, 3d Virginia Cavalry, in "Spirit of the Army: Third Regiment Virginia Cavalry," ibid., 25 February 1865.

125. C. F. James to his sister, 9 February 1865, James Papers, NcU.

126. Lee to Seddon, 5–6, 8 February 1865 (two messages), *OR* 46(1):381–82; reports of subordinate commanders, 46(1):390–92. See also reports of Federal commanders, 46(1), as well as Trudeau, *The Last Citadel*, 312–22.

127. Col. William Henry Forney, Sanders (Forney)/Mahone/III Corps, to his wife, 8 February 1865, William Henry Forney Papers, NcU. See also J. E. Whitehorne to his sister, 11 February 1865, J. E. Whitehorne Papers, Vi; Crenshaw Hall to his father, 17 February 1865, Hall Family Papers, A-Ar; and "The Fighting at Burgess's Mill," *Richmond Dispatch*, 11 February 1865.

128. Pvt. Mebane Hinshaw, Company B, 6th North Carolina, to his family, 22 January 1865, Hinshaw Papers, NcD. See also Hinshaw to his family, 11 January 1865, ibid.

129. Mebane Hinshaw to his family, 10 February 1865, ibid. See also Hinshaw to his family, 16, 22 February 1865, ibid.; Chaplain John Paris, 54th North Carolina, Diary, 6 February 1865, John Paris Papers, NcU; J. K. Wilkerson to his mother, 9 February 1865, Wilkerson Papers, NcD; J. C. Babcock, Bureau of Information, Army of the Potomac, to Maj. Gen. G. G. Meade, Army of the Potomac, 9 February 1865, *OR* 46(2):499; and Maj. Gen. G. K. Warren, V Army Corps, Army of the Potomac, to Bvt. Maj. Gen. A. S. Webb, Chief of Staff, Army of the Potomac, 11 February 1865, 46(2):531.

130. Pvt. James B. Jones, Company A, 1st Battalion North Carolina Sharpshooters, to his grandmother, 16 February 1865, Jones Family Papers, NcU.

CHAPTER 9

1. For examples of the late January–early February resolutions before the news of the Hampton Roads conference had reached the army, see "Spirit of the Army," *Richmond Whig*, 27 January 1865; "The Soldiers," *Richmond Sentinel*, 28 January 1865; "Meeting of the Thirty-first Virginia Regiment, of Pegram's Brigade," *Richmond Dispatch*, 4 February 1865; and "Resolution of the Fifty-second Virginia Regiment," *Richmond Dispatch*, 4 February 1865.

2. W. T. Poague to his mother, 11 February 1865, in Cockrell, *Gunner With Stonewall*, 148–49.

3. "Spirit of the Army: Palmetto Battery," "Spirit of the Army: Hurt's Alabama Battery, Chew's Maryland Battery, and Price's Virginia Battery," and "Spirit of

the Army: Second Regiment Virginia Cavalry," *Richmond Examiner*, 18 February 1865.

4. C. F. James to his sister, 7, 9 February 1865, James Papers, NcU. For an example of Lee's encouragement, see Lee to Brig. Gen. Henry A. Wise, Wise/Johnson/IV Corps, 4 February 1865, in "Letter from General Lee," *Richmond Dispatch*, 17 February 1865.

5. Resolutions, 8th Virginia, 18th Virginia, and Taylor's Battery, in "Spirit of the Army," *Richmond Whig*, 24 February 1865.

6. C. F. James to his sister, 9 February, 7 February 1865, James Papers, NcU.

7. "Spirit of the Army," *Richmond Dispatch*, 28 February 1865; "Spirit of the Army: Palmetto Battery," *Richmond Examiner*, 18 February 1865; Resolutions, Companies B, G, and I, 15th Virginia, in "Spirit of the Army," *Richmond Dispatch*, 14 February 1865.

8. Resolutions, 32d Virginia, "Spirit of Our Soldiers," *Richmond Dispatch*, 22 February 1865; Resolutions, Battle (Pickens)/Grimes/II Corps, in "Spirit of the Army," *Richmond Whig*, 16 February 1865.

9. "Spirit of the Army: Forty-Fifth North Carolina Regiment," *Richmond Examiner*, 25 February 1865.

10. "Spirit of the Army," *Richmond Dispatch*, 28 February 1865. For examples of the February resolutions, see the *Richmond Dispatch*, *Examiner*, *Sentinel*, and *Whig*, February–March 1865.

11. P. A. Oliver, Bureau of Information, Army of the Potomac, to Maj. Gen. J. G. Parke, IX Army Corps, Army of the Potomac, 30 January 1865, *OR* 46(2):299. See, e.g., the editorial "The Soldiers," *Richmond Sentinel*, 28 January 1865, in which the editors praised "the voices that are now coming from our heroes" and claimed, "Pickett's whole division is said to be afire!"

12. Resolutions, 53d Virginia, in "Spirit of the Army," *Richmond Whig*, 27 January 1865.

13. J. J. Armfield to his wife, 13 February 1865, Armfield Papers, NcU.

14. For secondary accounts of this proposal and the debate over it in late 1864 and early 1865, see Durden, *The Gray and the Black*; Preisser, "The Virginia Decision to Use Negro Soldiers"; Roark, *Masters Without Slaves*, 101–3; Emory M. Thomas, *The Confederate Nation*, 292–99; Rable, *The Confederate Republic*, 287–97; "The Confederate Debate over Arming Slaves"; and Jordan, *Black Confederates and Afro-Yankees*, 232–51.

15. *Richmond Dispatch*, 10 February 1865.

16. Secretary of State Judah P. Benjamin to Lee, 11 February 1865, *OR* 46(2):1229.

17. Lee to Rep. Ethelbert Barksdale, 18 February 1865, in "Letter from General Lee on the Negro Enlistment," *Richmond Dispatch*, 24 February 1865. For Lee's earlier correspondence with State Sen. Andrew Hunter of Virginia, see Hunter to Lee, 7 January 1865, and Lee to Hunter, 11 January 1865, *OR*, ser. 4, 3:1008, 1012–13.

18. "Spirit of the Army: Anderson's Brigade," *Richmond Examiner*, 16 February 1865.

19. Resolutions, Texas (Bass)/Field/I Corps, "Spirit of the Army," in *Richmond Dispatch*, 24 February 1865. See also, e.g., Resolutions, 1st Virginia, in "Spirit of the Army," *Richmond Whig*, 18 February 1865; "Spirit of the Army: Thomas' Brigade," *Richmond Examiner*, 18 February 1865; "Spirit of the Army. Peeple's Battery," *Richmond Examiner*, 23 February 1865; Resolutions, Company A, 18th Battalion Virginia Artillery, in "Spirit of the Army," *Richmond Dispatch*, 24 February 1865; and "Storkes' Light Artillery," *Richmond Examiner*, 25 February 1865.

20. "Spirit of the Army: Peeple's Battery," *Richmond Examiner*, 23 February 1865.

21. Resolutions, 56th Virginia, in "Spirit of the Army," *Richmond Whig*, 23 February 1865.

22. "Spirit of the Army: Third Regiment Virginia Cavalry," *Richmond Examiner*, 25 February 1865.

23. J. B. Gordon to W. H. Taylor, 18 February 1865, *OR* 51(2):1063.

24. Gordon to unidentified major, 26 February 1865, Gordon Family Papers, GU.

25. Osmun Latrobe, Circular to Division Commanders, I Corps, 16 February 1865, *OR* 46(2):1236.

26. Osmun Latrobe to Ewell, 17 February 1865, *OR* 46(2):1238.

27. J. B. Jones to his brother and sister, 19 February 1865 [misdated 1864], Jones Family Papers, NcU.

28. Silas Chandler to his wife, 21 February 1865, Chandler Papers, PNB.

29. "A. T." [Unidentified Soldier, Terry/Pickett/I Corps], *Richmond Dispatch*, 22 February 1865. For other expressions of support during February, see "Sentiment of the Army," *Richmond Sentinel*, 27 February 1865; F. M. Coker to his wife, 17 February 1865, Heidler Collection, GU; T. G. Trimmier to his wife, 17 February 1865, Trimmier Collection, T; T. P. Devereux to his father, 20 February 1865, Devereux Papers, Nc-Ar; and Maj. William Starr Basinger, 18th Georgia Battalion, to his mother, 23 February 1865, William Starr Basinger Papers, NcU.

30. H. E. Young, Remarks on Lt. J. M. Young, Acting Ordnance Officer, DuBose/Kershaw/I Corps, Endorsement, 27 February 1865, Capt. J. T. Hackett, Asst. Adjt. & Insp. Gen., DuBose/Kershaw/I Corps, 26 February 1865, Inspection Reports, NA, microcopy M935, roll 15.

31. Maj. Gen. H. G. Wright, VI Army Corps, Army of the Potomac, to Bvt. Maj. Gen. A. S. Webb, Chief of Staff, Army of the Potomac, 21 February 1865, *OR* 46(2):640.

32. Unidentified Soldier, ANV, *Richmond Examiner*, 24 February 1865.

33. Daniel Abernathy to his parents, 16 February 1865, Abernathy Papers, NcD.

34. Maj. Gen. H. G. Wright, VI Army Corps, Army of the Potomac, to Bvt.

Brig. Gen. A. S. Webb, Chief of Staff, Army of the Potomac, 23 February 1865, *OR* 46(2):660. See also Pvt. Joseph Francis Maides, Company I, 27th North Carolina, to his mother, 18 February 1865, J. Francis Maides Papers, NcD; Maj. Gen. G. G. Meade, Army of the Potomac, to Lt. Gen. U. S. Grant, Armies of the United States, 21 February 1865, *OR* 46(2):610; and B. H. Freeman to his parents and sisters, 26 February 1865, in Wright, *Confederate Letters*, 60.

35. GO 2, Confederate States Army, 11 February 1865, *OR* 46(2):1230. See also Lee to Davis, 9 February 1865, 51(2):1082–83; Davis to Lee, 10 February 1865, 46(2):1228; and GO 4, ANV, 16 February 1865, ANV Orders and Circulars, NA, microcopy M921, roll 1.

36. GO 4, ANV, 16 February 1865, ANV Orders and Circulars, NA, microcopy M921, roll 1.

37. J. W. Albright, Diary, 13 February 1865, Albright Papers, NcU.

38. C. F. James to his sister, 13, 18 February 1865, James Papers, NcU.

39. J. B. Jones to his brother and sister, 19 February 1865 [misdated 1864], Jones Family Papers, NcU.

40. 2d Lt. John I. Shotwell, Acting Asst. Adjt. Gen., Texas (Bass)/Field/I Corps, to Maj. Leander Masters, Asst. Adjt. Gen., Field/I Corps, 27 February 1865, ANV HQ Papers, R. E. Lee Papers, ViHi.

41. Lee to Cooper, 25 February 1865, *OR* 46(2):1258.

42. Fitzhugh Lee to Osmun Latrobe, 28 February 1865, ANV HQ Papers, R. E. Lee Papers, ViHi. The ultimate fate of these deserters is unknown.

43. Circular, W. H. Taylor to James Longstreet, J. B. Gordon, and A. P. Hill, 7 February 1865, Fairfax Papers, ViHi; Circular, Taylor to Longstreet, Gordon, and Hill, 18 February 1865, *OR* 46(2):1240.

44. H. P. Fortson to Mrs. R. A. Barnes, 27 February 1865, Barnes Family Papers, ViU. See also Sgt. Berry Greenwood Benson, Company A, Sharpshooter Battalion/McGowan/Wilcox/III Corps, to his father, 27 February 1865, Berry Benson Papers, NcU. For other measures intended to improve the efficiency of the army during this period, see GO 4, Grimes/II Corps, 20 February 1865, Brown Papers, Nc-Ar; Circular, ANV, 22 February 1865, *OR* 46(2):1247–48; and GO 4, ANV, 22 February 1865, 46(2):1249–50.

45. Lee to Seddon, 8 February 1865 (with endorsements), *OR* 46(1):382. See also W. H. Forney to his wife, 9 February 1865, Forney Papers, NcU.

46. Davis's endorsement, undated, on Lee to Seddon, 8 February 1865, *OR* 46(1):382.

47. Maj. Gen. G. K. Warren, V Army Corps, Army of the Potomac, to Bvt. Maj. Gen. A. S. Webb, Chief of Staff, Army of the Potomac, 15 February 1865, *OR* 46(2):564–65.

48. Lee to Brig. Gen. Isaac M. St. John, Commissary-Gen., Confederate States Army, 21 February 1865, *OR* 46(2):1246. See also Northrop to Breckinridge, 9 February 1865 (with enclosures), 46(2):1211–25, and Lee to Longstreet, 22 February 1865, 46(2):1250.

49. Pvt. John H. Stewart, Company C, 1st North Carolina Artillery, to his mother, 28 February 1865, John H. Stewart Papers, NcD.

50. H. P. Fortson to Mrs. R. A. Barnes, 27 February 1865, Barnes Family Papers, ViU.

51. Pvt. Nathan Mathewson, Company A, 1st North Carolina Artillery, to "Dr. Sills," 17 February 1865, Howell Collection, Nc-Ar.

52. T. P. Devereux to his father, 20 February 1865, Devereux Papers, Nc-Ar.

53. Lt. H. W. Bell, Acting Asst. Chief of Subsistence, DuBose/Kershaw/I Corps, Remarks, 27 February 1865, on Capt. J. T. Hackett, 26 February 1865, Inspection Reports, NA, microcopy M935, roll 15.

54. Capt. R. N. Lowrance, Chief of Subsistence, Kershaw/I Corps, Endorsement, 1 March 1865, to Maj. E. L. Costin, Asst. Adjt. & Insp. Gen., Kershaw/I Corps, 28 February 1865, Inspection Reports, NA, microcopy M935, roll 15.

55. J. B. Kershaw, Endorsement, 1 March 1865, on Maj. E. L. Costin, Kershaw/I Corps, 28 February 1865, Inspection Reports, NA, microcopy M935, roll 15.

56. Lee to Breckinridge, 9 March 1865, *OR* 46(2):1295.

57. Maj. S. B. French, Commissary of Subsistence, Subsistence Dept., Confederate States Army, to I. M. St. John, 10 March 1865, *OR* 46(2):1297–98; T. G. Williams, Subsistence Dept. to St. John, 10 March 1865, 46(2):1298; Maj. J. H. Claiborne, Commissary of Subsistence, Office of Chief Commissary for Virginia, to St. John, 10 March 1865, 46(2):1298–99; Capt. John M. Strother, Asst. Commissary of Subsistence, Subsistence Dept., to St. John, 11 March 1865, 46(2):1302.

58. Surg. A. E. McGarity, 3d North Carolina Cavalry, to his wife, 21 March 1865, in Burnett, "Letters of a Confederate Surgeon," March 1946, 64–65. See also F. M. Coker to his wife, 6, 17 March 1865, Heidler Collection, GU.

59. H. C. Conner to his wife, 21 March 1865, Conner Papers, ScU.

60. R. S. Webb to his cousin, 23 March 1865, Webb Family Papers, NcU.

61. Pvt. Edmund Jones, Company F, 3d North Carolina Cavalry, to his father, 5, 14 March 1865, Edmund Walter Jones Papers, NcU.

62. Lee to Breckinridge, 28 February 1865, *OR* 46(2):1265; W. H. Taylor, Report of Desertions for Ten Days Ending 8 March 1865, 46(2):1293; Lee to Breckinridge, 27 March 1865, 46(3):1353.

63. Osmun Latrobe to W. H. Taylor, 21 March 1865, *OR* 46(3):1332; Latrobe to Taylor, 24 March 1865, 46(3):1341; Longstreet to Taylor, 24 March 1865, 46(3):1341; Latrobe to Maj. Erasmus Taylor, Chief Quartermaster, I Corps, 24 March 1865, 46(3):1342–43; Lee to Breckinridge, 27 March 1865, 46(3):1353.

64. Lee to Breckinridge, 24 February 1865, *OR* 46(2):1254; see also Lee to Breckinridge, 27 March 1865, 46(3):1353.

65. A. H. Crawford to his wife, 5 March 1865, Crawford Papers, NcD; Pvt. G. S. Killbury, Company B, Palmetto Sharpshooters, to J. E. Hagood, 11 March 1865, Hagood Papers, ScU. See also J. A. F. Coleman, Diary, 1 March 1865, Confederate Miscellany I, GEU; A. N. Proffit to his family, 4 March 1865, Proffit

Family Papers, NcU; and B. W. Justice to his wife, 22 March 1865, Justice Papers, GEU.

66. Mebane Hinshaw to his wife, 1 March 1865, Hinshaw Papers, NcD. For further evidence that the campaign in the Carolinas and the recent Confederate States Army and Army of Northern Virginia general orders (GO 2, 11 February, and GO 4, 16 February, respectively, cited in n. 35 above) influenced desertions in late February, see Maj. John H. New, Asst. Adjt. & Insp. Gen., Johnston / II Corps, 28 February 1865, Inspection Reports, NA, microcopy M935, roll 15.

67. L. R. Mills to his brother, 2 March 1865, in Harmon, "Letters of . . . Mills," 307.

68. B. W. Justice to his wife, 15 March 1865, Justice Papers, GEU.

69. R. H. Hutspeth to his aunt, 22 March 1865, Hutspeth Papers, Nc-Ar.

70. Maj. R. J. Wingate, Adjt. & Insp. Gen., III Corps, 31 January 1865, Inspection Reports, NA, microcopy M935, roll 15.

71. Col. Samuel Hoey Walkup, 48th North Carolina, Diary, 5 March 1865, Samuel Hoey Walkup Papers, NcU.

72. B. R. Johnson's daily report, 26 February 1865, *OR* 46(2):1261–62.

73. Col. Peter Alexander Selkirk McGlashan, Simms (McGlashan) / Kershaw / I Corps, to Maj. James Monroe Goggin, Asst. Adjt. Gen., Kershaw / I Corps, 19 March 1865, and Goggin to Osmun Latrobe, 19 March 1865 (two messages), ANV HQ Papers, R. E. Lee Papers, ViHi.

74. Brig. Gen. George T. Anderson, Anderson / Field / I Corps, to Maj. Leander Masters, Asst. Adjt. Gen., Field / I Corps, 25 March 1865, enclosure in Lee to Breckinridge, 27 March 1865, *OR* 46(3):1355. See also A. B. Simms to his sister, 15, 21 March 1865, in Peacock, "A Georgian's View of War," 133–34.

75. GO 8, ANV, 28 March 1865, *OR* 46(3):1357.

76. S. H. Walkup, Diary, 1–3, 22 January 1865, Walkup Papers, NcU.

77. Ibid., 27 January, 16–22 February, 3–5 March 1865.

78. Ibid., 6 March 1865.

79. A. H. Crawford to his wife, 5, 9 March 1865, Crawford Papers, NcD.

80. B. W. Justice to his wife, 15 March 1865, Justice Papers, GEU; W. H. Phillips to his father, 25 March 1865, Phillips Papers, NcD.

81. Mebane Hinshaw to his family, 1 March 1865, Hinshaw Papers, NcD; J. J Armfield to his wife, 9 March 1865, Armfield Papers, Nc-Ar.

82. Abstract from Field Return, ANV, 24 February–1 March 1865, *OR* 46(1): 388–90. On 28 February Ewell's troops in the Department of Richmond added another 4,500 men present for duty, out of a total strength of 9,700 present and absent; Abstract from Field Return, Richmond, 28 February 1865, 46(2): 1274.

83. F. M. Coker to his wife, 3 March 1865, Heidler Collection, GU; W. R. Battle to his mother, 23 March 1865, in Lee, *Forget-Me-Nots*, 132.

84. A. B. Simms to his sister, 15, 21 March 1865, in Peacock, "A Georgian's View of the War," 131. See also L. R. Mills, 9 March 1865, in Harmon, "Letters

of . . . Mills," 308, and H. P. Fortson to Mrs. R. A. Barnes, 17 March 1865, Barnes Family Papers, ViU.

85. M. H. Fitzpatrick to his wife, 8 December 1864, in Hammock, *Letters to Amanda*, 174.

86. [Davidson], *The artisavis*. The only known copy of this unique card is in the collection of the Rare Book Room, NcD.

87. R. O. Davidson, "Artisavis," *Richmond Whig*, 27 February 1865; see also Davidson, "Artisavis," *Richmond Dispatch*, 7 March 1865.

88. A. B. Simms to his sister, 15 March 1865, in Peacock, "A Georgian's View of War," 132–33.

89. Lee to Breckinridge, 15 March 1865, ser. 4, 3:1143–44.

90. "An act to increase the military force of the Confederate States," approved March 23, 1865, *OR*, ser. 4, 3:1161. See also Lee to Davis, 10 March 1865, in Freeman, *Lee's Dispatches*, 373–74 (app.), and Davis to Lee, 13 March 1865, *OR* 46(2):1308. For a similar act passed by the Virginia General Assembly on 6 March, see Bell Smith, Aide-de-Camp to Gov. William Smith, to Davis, 16 March 1865, 46(3):1315.

91. GO 14, A&IGO, 23 March 1865, *OR*, ser. 4, 3:1161–62.

92. Lee to Breckinridge, 14 March 1865, ANV HQ Papers, R. E. Lee Papers, ViHi. See also W. H. Taylor, Endorsement, 27 March 1865, to Officers of the 49th Georgia to Taylor, 15 March 1865, *OR* 46(2):1317, and Lee to Davis, 27 March 1865, 46(3):1356–57.

93. Officers of the 49th Georgia to W. H. Taylor, 15 March 1865 (with endorsements), *OR* 46(2):1316.

94. "List of Officers who ask authority to raise or be assigned to the command of Negro Troops," 14 March 1865, enclosure in Lee to Breckinridge, 14 March 1865, ANV HQ Papers, R. E. Lee Papers, ViHi; John W. Riely, Asst. Adjt. Gen., A&IGO, Confederate States Army, to Maj. J. W. Pegram and Maj. Thomas P. Turner, Dept. of Richmond, 15 March 1865, *OR* 46(2):1318; Riely to Capt. George P. Ring, 28 March 1865, ser. 4, 3:1193.

95. Osmun Latrobe to J. B. Kershaw, 28 March 1865, *OR* 46(3):1361; Longstreet to W. H. Taylor, 30 March 1865, 46(3):1367.

96. Col. William J. Pegram, Pegram/III Corps Artillery, to Maj. James West Pegram, 17 March 1865, Pegram-Johnson-McIntosh Family Papers, ViHi.

97. J. W. Albright, Diary, 16 March 1865, Albright Papers, NcU.

98. W. H. Phillips to his father, 25 March 1865, Phillips Papers, NcD. See also B. H. Freeman to his parents and sisters, 15 March 1865, in Wright, *Confederate Letters*, 61.

99. J. A. Everett to his mother, 16 March 1865, Everett Papers, GEU.

100. J. W. Albright, Diary, 1 March 1865, Albright Papers, NcU; C. J. Iredell to his wife, 8 March 1865, Iredell Papers, NcU.

101. J. W. Albright, Diary, 1 March 1865, Albright Papers, NcU.

102. C. J. Iredell to his wife, 8, 10 March 1865, Iredell Papers, NcU.

103. W. J. Pegram to his sister, 14 March 1865, in James I. Robertson Jr., "'The Boy Artillerist,'" 257.

104. J. B. Evans to his wife, 30 March 1865, John B. Evans Papers, NcD. See also W. D. Alexander, Diary, 18 March 1865, Alexander Papers, NcU; F. M. Coker to his wife, 21 March 1865, Heidler Collection, GU; and B. W. Justice to his wife, 22 March 1865, Justice Papers, GEU.

105. Lee to Breckinridge, 25 March 1865, *OR* 46(1):382–83; Lee to Davis, 26 March 1865, in Freeman, *Lee's Dispatches*, 341–46; C. A. Evans's report, in Stephens, *Intrepid Warrior*, 534–36. See also reports of Federal commanders, 46(1), as well as Trudeau, *The Last Citadel*, 333–54, and Freeman, *Lee's Lieutenants*, 3:644–54.

106. H. A. Chambers, Diary, 25 March 1865, in Pearce, *Diary of . . . Chambers*, 253; C. W. Sydnor to his wife, 27 March 1865, Sydnor Papers, NcU. See also T. P. Devereux to his father, 25 March 1865, Devereux Papers, Nc-Ar; John Paris, Diary, 25 March 1865, Paris Papers, NcU; and Bryan Grimes to his wife, 25, 29 March 1865, Grimes Papers, NcU.

107. 3d Lt. James E. Hall, Company H, 31st Virginia, Diary, 25 March 1865, in Dayton, *Diary of a Confederate Soldier*, 129. See also A. C. Jones, Diary, 25, 27 March 1865, Civil War Papers, LHA Collection, LNT; J. W. Albright, Diary, 25 March 1865, Albright Papers, NcU; and C. W. Sydnor to his wife, 27 March 1865, Sydnor Papers, NcU.

108. H. A. Chambers, Diary, 25 March 1865, in Pearce, *Diary of . . . Chambers*, 253.

109. Pvt. Henry Armand London, Courier, Grimes/II Corps, to his father, 25 March 1865, Henry Armand London Papers, NcU.

110. H. C. Conner to his wife, 27 March 1865, Conner Papers, ScU.

111. Taylor to his fiancée, 27 March 1865, in Tower, *Lee's Adjutant*, 238–39. See also S. H. Walkup, Diary, 27 March 1865, Walkup Papers, NcU.

112. Lee to Breckinridge, 29 March 1865, *OR* 46(1):1263; Lee to Davis, 30 March 1865 (p. 352), Lee to Breckinridge, 31 March 1865 (pp. 355–56), and Lee to Davis, 1 April 1865 (pp. 358–60), all in Freeman, *Lee's Dispatches*; Lee to Breckinridge, 1 April 1865, *OR* 46(1):1264; Lee to Davis, 2 April 1865, in Dowdey and Manarin, *Wartime Papers*, 927–28; reports of subordinate commanders, *OR* 46(1):1286–88, 1298–1300. See also reports of Federal commanders, 46(1). A secondary account of the fighting at Five Forks is Bearss and Calkins, *Battle of Five Forks*. For a secondary account of the entire period from April 1–9, see Burke Davis, *To Appomattox*; for Five Forks, see pp. 41–51, 54–49. See also Freeman, *Lee's Lieutenants*, 3:655–74.

113. H. A. Chambers, Diary, 1 April 1865, in Pearce, *Diary of . . . Chambers*, 258. See also J. A. F. Coleman, Diary, 1 April 1865, Confederate Miscellany I, GEU.

114. Longstreet to Lee, 1 April 1865, *OR* 46(3):1372; Osmun Latrobe to C. W. Field, 1 April 1865, 46(3):1373–74; Latrobe to J. B. Kershaw, 1 April 1865,

46(3):1375; John W. Riely to Ewell, 1 April 1865, 46(3):1375; Latrobe to Ewell, 1 April 1865, 46(3):1376.

115. S. H. Walkup to his wife, 30 March, 1 April 1865, Walkup Papers, NcU.

116. Lee to Breckinridge, 2 April 1865 (first message), *OR* 46(1):1264.

117. Lee to Breckinridge, 2 April 1865, *OR* 46(1):1265; reports of subordinate commanders, 46(1):1280, 1285; Lee to Henry Heth, 2 April 1865 (p. 925), and Lee to Davis, 2 April 1865 (p. 928), in Dowdey and Manarin, *Wartime Papers*. See also Trudeau, *The Last Citadel*, 356–97; Davis, *To Appomattox*, 63–86; and Freeman, *Lee's Lieutenants*, 3:675–83.

118. J. W. Albright, Diary, 2 April 1865, Albright Papers, NcU. See also W. D. Alexander, Diary, 2 April 1865, Alexander Papers, NcU; A. C. Jones, Diary, 2 April 1865, Civil War Papers, LHA Collection, LNT; Adjt. James E. Hall, 31st Virginia, Diary, 2–3 April 1865, in Dayton, *Diary of a Confederate Soldier*, 132–33; J. E. Whitehorne, Diary, 2 April 1865, Whitehorne Papers, NcU; and John Paris, Diary, 2 April 1865, Paris Papers, NcU.

119. Lee to Breckinridge, 2 April 1865 (third message), *OR* 46(1):1265; reports of subordinate commanders, 46(1):1280–81, 1283, 1293–94, 1296; W. H. Taylor, Circular, to James Longstreet, J. B. Gordon, and R. S. Ewell, 2 April 1865, 46(3):1379; Lee to Ewell, 2 April 1865 (second message), 46(3):1380; Taylor to Ewell, 2 April 1865, 46(3):1380.

120. J. E. Whitehorne, Diary, 2 April 1865, Whitehorne Papers, NcU. See also Whitehorne, Diary, 31 [30] March–1 April 1865, ibid.; and James E. Whitehorne, 12th [Virginia] Infantry, Compiled Service Records, NA, microcopy M324, roll 533.

121. 2d Lt. William G. Hinson, Company G, 7th South Carolina Cavalry, Diary, 2–3 April 1865, William G. Hinson Papers, ScC.

122. J. E. Whitehorne, Diary, 3 April 1865, Whitehorne Papers, NcU.

123. John Paris, Diary, 3 April 1865, Paris Papers, NcU; A. C. Jones, Diary, 5 April 1865, Civil War Papers, LHA Collection, LNT; J. E. Whitehorne, Diary, 5 April 1865, Whitehorne Papers, NcU; J. W. Albright, Diary, 6 April 1865, Albright Papers, NcU. See also E. P. Alexander to his wife, 3, 8 April 1865, E. P. Alexander Papers, NcU; W. G. Hinson, Diary, 3–6 April 1865, Hinson Papers, ScC; W. D. Alexander, Diary, 3–6 April 1865, W. D. Alexander Papers, NcU; and Frank Lobrano, Diary, 3–6 April 1865, Civil War Papers, LHA Collection, LNT.

124. J. A. F. Coleman, Diary, 2–9 April 1865, Confederate Miscellany I, GEU.

125. Lee to Davis, 12 April 1865, *OR* 46(1):1265; reports of subordinate commanders, 46(1):1281, 1283, 1285–86, 1289, 1292, 1294, 1296, 1301–2; Lee to Ewell, 3 April 1865, 46(3):1382; W. H. Taylor, Circular to Corps Commanders, 4 April 1865, 46(3):1384; Lee to Ewell, 4 April 1865, 46(3):1384–85; Taylor, Circular to Corps Commanders, 5 April 1865, 46(3):1385; Lee to Davis, 6 April 1865, 46(3):1386; Lee to Gordon, 46(3):1387.

126. Osmun Latrobe to C. M. Wilcox, 6 April 1865, *OR* 46(3):1386.

127. J. B. Kershaw's report, *OR* 46(1):1284.

128. Lee to Davis, 12 April 1865, *OR* 46(1):1265–66; reports of subordinate commanders, 1283–84, 1289–90, 1292, 1294–98, 1302; Breckinridge to Davis, 8 April 1865, 46(3):1389. See also reports of Federal commanders, 46(1). Secondary accounts include Calkins, *Thirty-Six Hours before Appomattox*; Trudeau, *Out of the Storm*, 106–16; Davis, *To Appomattox*, 242–71; and Freeman, *Lee's Lieutenants*, 3:698–711. The name of the stream and of the battle has variously been spelled "Sayler's Creek" and "Sailor's Creek." The Commonwealth of Virginia, seeking to settle the matter, has recently decreed that the name of the battle and of the state park on the battlefield is officially "Sailor's Creek," whereas the name of the creek retains the spelling "Sayler's."

129. Lee to Davis, 12 April 1865, *OR* 46(1):1266.

130. A. C. Jones, Diary, 6 April 1865, Civil War Papers, LHA Collection, LNT.

131. Lee to Davis, 12 April 1865, *OR* 46(1):1266; reports of subordinate commanders, 46(1):1281–82, 1286, 1291, 1303; Breckinridge to Davis, 8 April 1865, 46(3):1389.

132. Frank Lobrano, Diary, 7 April 1865, Civil War Papers, LHA Collection, LNT.

133. J. E. Whitehorne, Diary, 7 April 1865, Whitehorne Papers, NcU.

134. Grant to Lee, 7 April 1865, and Lee to Grant, 7 April 1865, *OR* 46(3):619.

135. J. E. Whitehorne, Diary, 8 April 1865, Whitehorne Papers, NcU.

136. E. P. Alexander to his wife, 3, 8 April 1865, E. P. Alexander Papers, NcU; W. D. Alexander, Diary, 8 April 1865, W. D. Alexander Papers, NcU.

137. Lee to Davis, 12 April 1865, *OR* 46(1):1266; W. N. Pendleton's report, 46(1):1282. See also Calkins, *Appomattox Station and Appomattox Court House*, 28–44.

138. Grant to Lee, 8 April 1865, and Lee to Grant, 8 April 1865, *OR* 46(3):641.

139. Lee to Davis, 12 April 1865, *OR* 46(1):1266.

140. J. E. Whitehorne, Diary, 8 April 1865, Whitehorne Papers, NcU.

141. Ibid., 9 April 1865.

142. Lee to Davis, 12 April 1865, *OR* 46(1):1266–67; W. N. Pendleton's report, 46(1):1282; Fitzhugh Lee's report, 46(1):1303–4; Lee to Davis, 20 April 1865, in Dowdey and Manarin, *Wartime Papers*, 938–39. See also Calkins, *Appomattox Station and Appomattox Court House*, 55–131.

143. Grant to Lee, 9 April 1865, Lee to Grant, 9 April 1865 (three messages), and Grant to Lee, 9 April 1865 (second message), *OR* 46(3):664–65. See also Meade to Lee, 9 April 1865, 46(3):666.

144. Though the precise number of Confederate troops ready for battle on 9 April cannot be determined, statistics are available for the number of troops properly belonging to the Army of Northern Virginia that surrendered over the next few days. Some 28,000 officers and men were paroled at Appomattox, and an additional 4,000 or so at Farmville or Lynchburg, for a total estimate of 32,000 soldiers. See, e.g., "Tabular Statement of Officers and Men of the Confederate Army Paroled at Appomattox Court-House," *OR* 46(1):1277–79, and Calkins's

meticulous and persuasive discussion of the strength of the Army of Northern Virginia just before the evacuation of Petersburg and Richmond and the likely effective strength of the army in and around Appomattox at the time of the surrender, in *The Final Bivouac*, app. 3, "The Numbers Involved in the Appomattox Campaign," 201–21.

145. W. G. Hinson, Diary, 9 April 1865, Hinson Papers, ScC.

146. 2d Lt. Kena King Chapman, Company A, 19th Battalion Virginia Light Artillery, Diary, 9 April 1865, Kena King Chapman Papers, NcU; W. D. Alexander, Diary, 9 April 1865, Alexander Papers, NcU.

147. J. E. Hall, Diary, 9 April 1865, in Dayton, *Diary of a Confederate Soldier*, 136.

148. H. A. Chambers, Diary, 9 April 1865, in Pearce, *Diary of . . . Chambers*, 262.

149. J. E. Whitehorne, Diary, 9 April 1865, Whitehorne Papers, NcU.

150. John Paris, Diary, 9 April 1865, Paris Papers, NcU. See also H. A. Chambers, Diary, 10–12 April 1865, in Pearce, *Diary of . . . Chambers*, 262–64.

151. J. E. Whitehorne, Diary, 11 April 1865, Whitehorne Papers, NcU.

152. W. D. Alexander, Diary, 11 April 1865, Alexander Papers, NcU; K. K. Chapman, Diary, 11 April 1865, Chapman Papers, NcU. See also W. D. Alexander, Diary, 10 April 1865, Alexander Papers, NcU; K. K. Chapman, Diary, 10 April 1865, Chapman Papers, NcU; John Paris, Diary, 10–11 April 1865, Paris Papers, NcU; and H. A. Chambers, Diary, 10–11 April 1865, in Pearce, *Diary of . . . Chambers*, 262–63.

153. GO 9, ANV, 10 April 1865, in Dowdey and Manarin, *Wartime Papers*, 934–35.

154. "Agreement Entered Into This Day in Regard to the Surrender of the Army of Northern Virginia to the United States Authorities," *OR* 46(3):685.

155. See Calkins, *The Final Bivouac*, 6–43.

156. John Paris, Diary, 12 April 1865, Paris Papers, NcU. See also K. K. Chapman, Diary, 12 April 1865, Chapman Papers, NcU, and W. D. Alexander, Diary, 12 April 1865, Alexander Papers, NcU.

157. J. E. Whitehorne, Diary, 12 April 1865, Whitehorne Papers, NcU.

158. Col. William Preston Johnston, Aide-de-Camp, to Mrs. Varina Howell Davis, 12 April 1865, *OR* 46(3):1393.

159. J. E. Whitehorne, Diary, 12 April 1865, Whitehorne Papers, NcU.

CHAPTER 10

1. E. D. Graham to Miss Laura Mann, 14 September 1864, UDC Typescripts, vol. 2, G-Ar. For similar comments about the same time, see John Bratton to his wife, 5 September 1864, Bratton Papers, ScCoAH; *Richmond Examiner*, 12 September 1864; "The Army of Northern Virginia," *Richmond Whig*, 13 September 1864; and Charles Kerrison to his uncle, 19 September 1864, Kerrison Family Papers, ScU.

2. Gallagher, "Building a Legend," 428.

3. Gallagher, "Home Front and Battlefield," 156–68, "'Upon Their Success Hang Momentous Interests': Generals," in *Why the Confederacy Lost*, ed. Boritt, 81–108, "Another Look at the Generalship of R. E. Lee," in *Lee the Soldier*, ed. Gallagher, 275–89, and "Building a Legend," 428; McMurry, *Two Great Rebel Armies*; Royster, *The Destructive War*, 187.

4. Faust's observation in "Christian Soldiers" (p. 84) is particularly appropriate to Confederate soldiers' personal narratives written in 1864 and 1865: "Twentieth-century scholars have often commented on the seeming failure of the Civil War soldier to grapple with the emotional significance of his experience. . . . Yet in their own way and in their own particular idiom, Confederate soldiers were just as expressive as their World War I counterparts. Southerners were very articulate, for example, about their *inability* to portray what they had witnessed . . . their silences are eloquent. Their speechlessness was part of a process of numbing, of the denial that is a widespread human response to stress."

5. See, e.g., Wiley, *The Life of Johnny Reb*, chap. 11, "Dear Folks," 192–216, and bibliographical notes, 421–23, and *The Life of Billy Yank*, 183–90, and bibliographical notes, 438–41. Neither study really considers diaries as a much less common—yet distinct—form of soldiers' writing. James I. Robertson's *Soldiers Blue and Gray*, intended as a "supplement" to Wiley's pioneering works and based primarily on published material, takes much the same view of letters; see, e.g., pp. 104–10. Wiley's 1955 presidential address to the Southern Historical Association touches on the subject of Civil War letters and diaries as a genre to some extent, certainly more than he does in *The Life of Johnny Reb* and *The Life of Billy Yank*; see also Wiley, "A Time of Greatness."

6. See Barton, *Goodmen*, esp. chap. 2, "The Values of Civil War Soldiers," 23–33; chap. 3, "The Character of Civil War Soldiers," 35–44; and chap. 4, "The Style of Character," 45–56. Barton's exceedingly brief chap. 5, "The Experience of Character," 57–62, is in many ways the most useful part of the book. For a more detailed and more convincing examination of this theme, see Barton's earlier article, "Painful Duties." A later essay, "Did the Confederacy Change Southern Soldiers? Some Obvious and Some Unobtrusive Measures," in *The Old South in the Crucible of War*, ed. Owens and Cooke, pp. 65–79, addresses some of the same themes as *Goodmen*.

7. For a brief but useful introduction to this type of analysis, see, e.g., Jimerson, *The Private Civil War*, 3–6.

8. Glatthaar, *March to the Sea*, esp. 87–90; Daniel, *Soldiering in the Army of Tennessee*, esp. 140–47.

9. McPherson, *For Cause and Comrades*, 12. See not only *For Cause and Comrades*, passim, but also McPherson, *What They Fought For*, esp. 1, 13–18, 24–25, 35–37, 42, 68–69. McPherson forcefully disagrees with Bell Wiley's often-cited observations about Confederate soldiers, in *The Life of Johnny Reb* (p. 309), that "it is doubtful whether many of them either understood or cared about the Constitutional issue at stake," and about Union soldiers, in *The Life of Billy Yank* (pp. 39–

40), that "While the men in blue were not so irreverent toward high-sounding appeals to patriotic sentiments as were their khaki-clad descendants in World War II, yet American soldiers of the 1860s appear to have been about as little concerned with ideological issues as were those of the 1940s." McPherson's research in over 25,000 letters and over 100 diaries has also convinced him that the almost-as-often-cited sociological study of American GIs in World War II— Samuel A. Stouffer et al., *The American Soldier*, 4 vols. (Princeton: Princeton University Press, 1949)—has little if any relevance to the motivations of Civil War soldiers.

10. See—in addition to the soldiers' letters, diaries, and other papers cited throughout Chapters 1–3 above—Steere, *Wilderness Campaign*, 459–60, 463–64, and Rhea, *Battle of the Wilderness*, 271, 430–31, 441, 446–47, on the immediate impact of the battle in the Wilderness; and Freeman, *Lee's Lieutenants*, 3:352, 372, 407–8, 555–56; Trudeau, *Bloody Roads South*, 181–82, 187; Hattaway and Jones, *How the North Won*, 561–62, 570–71, 590–93; Beringer et al., *Why the South Lost*, 317–20; McPherson, *Battle Cry of Freedom*, 725–42; and Hagerman, *The American Civil War*, 244–45, 254–65, for assessments of particular battles or general statements on the Overland campaign. Bruce Catton's *A Stillness at Appomattox*, the last volume of his classic trilogy on the Army of the Potomac, includes the battle of the Crater when he sums up "one continuous battle, a battle three months long," commenting, "All that had gone before was no more than prelude. . . . The war had taken on a new magnitude, and perhaps it was no longer the kind of struggle anybody could win" (p. 253).

11. Freeman, *Lee's Lieutenants*, 3:407; McPherson, *Battle Cry of Freedom*, 741; Trudeau, *Bloody Roads South*, 187.

12. Royster, *The Destructive War*, 333.

13. McWhiney and Jamieson, *Attack and Die*, 191. See, to cite only a few notable examples, some of them emphasizing the campaigns of 1864 and 1865: John K. Mahon, "Civil War Infantry Assault Tactics," *Military Affairs* 25 (1961), reprinted in *Military Analysis of the Civil War: An Anthology by the Editors of Military Affairs* (Millwood, N.Y.: KTO Press, 1977), esp. 255; Edward Hagerman, "From Jomini to Dennis Hart Mahan: The Evolution of Trench Warfare and the American Civil War," *Civil War History* 31 (September 1967), reprinted in *Battles Lost and Won*, ed. Hubbell, esp. 51–53; McWhiney and Jamieson, *Attack and Die*, 73–76, 102–11; Hattaway and Jones, *How the North Won*, 692–93; Beringer et al., *Why the South Lost*, 468–70; Linderman, *Embattled Courage*, 142–45; Hagerman, *The American Civil War*, xi–xii, 253–74; McPherson, *Battle Cry of Freedom*, 475–77; and Archer Jones, *Civil War Command and Strategy*, 38, 103, 249–50. The most controversial—and debatable—opinion expressed by Paddy Griffith in his *Battle Tactics* disputes the standard view of the profound impact of the rifled musket on Civil War tactics (pp. 73–90). Though his argument that the undisputed psychological advantages of entrenchments outweighed their tactical advantages is of some interest, it is not entirely convincing. See, e.g., pp. 123–35.

14. McWhiney and Jamieson, *Attack and Die*, 102–11; Hagerman, *The American Civil War*, 254–66, 270–71; Griffith, *Battle Tactics*, 123–35; Jones, *Civil War Command and Strategy*, 38, 193.

15. Griffith, *Battle Tactics*, 132.

16. Hagerman, *The American Civil War*, 254; Jones, *Civil War Command and Strategy*, 38.

17. Hagerman, *The American Civil War*, 254, 274.

18. See, e.g., Freeman, *Lee's Lieutenants*, 3:389, 392–94, 506–7, 538, 541, 615–16; Dowdey, *Lee's Last Campaign*, 119, 175, 195, 197–98, 215, 261, 263, 267–68, 300, 350, 355; Steere, *Wilderness Campaign*, 281–83; Trudeau, *The Last Citadel*, 84–86, 165, 170, 232, 286, 288–89, 333–52, 356–57, 360–65, 368, 379–81; Trudeau, *Out of the Storm*, 51–53, 61–64; Rhea, *Battle of the Wilderness*, 105, 124–25, 145, 183, 225, 276, 281, 323, 376, 379–80, 390, 393–97; Matter, *If It Takes All Summer*, 95, 103, 106–8, 128; and Sommers, *Richmond Redeemed*, 14–15.

19. See the letters, diaries, and other papers cited throughout Chapters 1–9 above, but particularly the Inspection Reports, August 1864–February 1865, NA, microcopy M935, rolls 10–15, cited in Chapters 4 and 6–9. For examples of excellent modern unit histories that address this collapse of command in tactical-level units, see James I. Robertson Jr., *The Stonewall Brigade*, 218–28, 233, 240–41, and Terry L. Jones, *Lee's Tigers* 206, 208, 213, 219. For a useful introduction to the nature of command at the field and company level in the Civil War, see Richard M. McMurry, "Civil War Leaders," in *Leadership during the Civil War*, ed. Heleniak and Hewitt, 171–85.

20. Freeman, *R. E. Lee*, 3:447; see also 427, 437, 509.

21. Freeman, *Lee's Lieutenants*, 3:xiv.

22. Ibid., 3:xiii–xiv, xxi, 410, 432, 441, 449, 508–9, 512–14, 550, 556, 610, 614, 625–34. Even the chapter titles of this volume reflect Freeman's emphasis on the collapse of command after the Wilderness—and, indeed, after Gettysburg: chap. 18, "The Wilderness Takes Its Toll"; chap. 22, "The Debits and Credits of May"; chap. 25, "The End of the Old Organization"; chap. 27, "Toward Immobilized Command"; chap. 28, "Attrition in a Changed Army"; chap. 30, "The Darkening Autumn of Command"; chap. 31, "Discipline and Desertion"; and chap. 34, "The Collapse of Command," which leads inevitably to chap. 37, "Appomattox: Exeunt Omnes."

23. Gallagher, "The Army of Northern Virginia in May 1864," 108. See also Gallagher's pointed comments in his "Home Front and Battlefield," 166–67.

24. In addition to the discussion of the "Lee to the rear" incidents in the Wilderness and at Spotsylvania in Chapter 2 above, see the modern secondary accounts in Freeman, *R. E. Lee*, 3:286–88, 313, 317–21, and *Lee's Lieutenants*, 3:357–58, 405–6; Emory M. Thomas, *Robert E. Lee*, 332–33; and Trudeau, "'A Mere Question of Time,'" in *Lee the Soldier*, ed. Gallagher, 528, 531, 538.

25. Emory M. Thomas, *Robert E. Lee*, 332. See also the analyses in Freeman, *R. E. Lee* 3:286–88, 313, 317–21, 501–4, 508–9, 4:84–86, and *Lee's Lieutenants*,

3:357–58, 405–6, 711, 716; Rhea, *Battle of the Wilderness*, 293, 299–301; Matter, *If It Takes All Summer*, 164, 201–2, 211; Gallagher, "The Army of Northern Virginia in May 1864," 110–11; Sommers, *Richmond Redeemed*, 146–47; and Trudeau, " 'A Mere Question of Time,' " 533–34, 538.

26. Page, *Robert E. Lee*, 205–6.

27. See, e.g., *Richmond Examiner*, 5, 23 May 1864; T. E. Nimmo to "Dear Sir," 24 May 1864, Munford-Ellis Family Papers, NcD; W. L. Wilson to his mother, 27 May 1864, in Summers, *A Borderland Confederate*, 80–81; "Gen. Lee and the Army," *Richmond Dispatch*, 1 June 1864; John Tyler Jr. to Maj. Gen. Sterling Price, 7 June 1864, *OR* 41(2):994–95; James Farrow to J. E. Hagood, 25 July 1864, J. E. Hagood Papers, ScU; "A Soldier on Finance," *Richmond Examiner*, 19 August 1864; T. W. Gilmer to his father, 18 September 1864, Gilmer Family Papers, Private Collection of Walker Gilmer Petroff, Beaufort, S.C.; A. F. Fleet to his father, 10 November 1864, 9 December 1864, Fleet and Fuller, *Green Mount*, 347, 350; T. P. Devereux to his sister, 29 December 1864, Devereux Papers, Nc-Ar; and H. P. Fortson to Mrs. R. A. Barnes, 27 February 1865, Barnes Family Papers, ViU. M. E. Bradford makes the often-overlooked point that the Confederate army as a whole "was an extension of the region's social character, not the embodiment of a separate and antiseptic military 'profession' or martial juggernaut," and that its generals "were more patriarchs than imitations of Napoleon or Frederick the Great." As a specific example, he cites "Lee in the Wilderness that day when his men refused to let him assume a position in the line of fire and tugged at the bridle of Traveler until they had turned him aside." Bradford, "Not in Memoriam, But in Affirmation," in *Why the South Will Survive: Fifteen Southerners Look at Their Region a Half Century after I'll Take My Stand*, ed. Clyde N. Wilson (Athens: University of Georgia Press, 1981), 215.

28. Anonymous Private, Pickett/I Corps, to the *Richmond Sentinel*, 10 July 1864, "Army Correspondence of the Sentinel," *Richmond Sentinel*, 15 July 1864.

29. Pvt. James Preston Crowder, Company I, 47th Alabama, to his family, 9 August 1864, James Preston Crowder Papers, GEU.

30. *Richmond Examiner*, 24 June 1864.

31. H. P. Fortson to Mrs. R. A. Barnes, 27 February 1865, Barnes Family Papers, ViU.

32. See also Gallagher, "Another Look at the Generalship of R. E. Lee," 275–89.

33. See, e.g., W. J. Pegram to his sister, 28 June 1864, Pegram-Johnson-McIntosh Family Papers, ViHi, and W. H. Taylor to his fiancée, 15 August 1864, 18 December 1864, in Tower, *Lee's Adjutant*, 182, 212. See also—in addition to the letters, diaries, and other papers cited throughout Chapters 1–9 above—Freeman, *R. E. Lee*, 3:357–59, 367–68, 508–11, 513; and *Lee's Lieutenants*, 3:xiv, 449, 497–98, 593–94, 613, 627, 711; Charles P. Roland, "The Generalship of Robert E. Lee," in *Grant, Lee, Lincoln and the Radicals*, ed. Grady McWhiney, (Evanston, Ill.: Northwestern University Press, 1964), reprinted in Gallagher, *Lee the Soldier*,

179; Dowdey, *Lee's Last Campaign*, 302–3; Gallagher, "The Army of Northern Virginia in May 1864," 108, 113, 115–16; Sommers, *Richmond Redeemed*, 51, 117, 137, 148, 210, 439–40; and Emory M. Thomas, *Robert E. Lee*, 350–53.

34. Stephen Elliott to his wife, 21 July 1864, Elliott Family Papers, ScU.

35. J. M. Smither to his uncle, 24 July 1864, Smither Papers, TxHiC.

36. H. E. Peyton, Inspection Report, Army of Northern Virginia, 23 September 1864 [covering August–September 1864], *OR* 42(2):1276.

37. Sommers, *Richmond Redeemed*, 139–40.

38. See, in addition to the returns and official correspondence cited in the prologue and Chapters 1–9 above, Freeman, *R. E. Lee*, 3:332, 359, 385, 443, 446, 459, 496–97, 516–18, 541–42, and *Lee's Lieutenants*, 3:555–56, 581, 584–85, 590, 611, 615, 618–19, 623–25, 628, 651–52; Trudeau, *The Last Citadel*, 418; Sommers, *Richmond Redeemed*, 9–10, 34, 114, 420–21; and Wert, *From Winchester to Cedar Creek*, 26, 135, 139, 240, 247–48.

39. Lee to G. W. C. Lee, 24 July 1864; to Seddon, 23 August 1864; to Bragg, 12 September 1864; and to Davis, 2 November 1864, in Dowdey and Manarin, *Wartime Papers*, 825, 844, 852, and 868, respectively.

40. Lee to Seddon, 8 February 1865, *OR* 46(1):382.

41. See, in addition to the letters, diaries, and other papers (particularly the Inspection Reports, August 1864–February 1865, NA, microcopy M935, rolls 10–15) cited in Chapters 4 and 6–9 above, Freeman, *Lee's Lieutenants* 3:434–35, 506, 542, 555–56, 558, 570, 580–81, 584, 591, 596–97, 607–8, 616, 625, 650–51, 671; Dowdey, *Lee's Last Campaign*, 275; Trudeau, *The Last Citadel*, 172–73, 316, 375, 396–97; Sommers, *Richmond Redeemed*, 15, 116, 139–40, 145–49, 212–13, 441; and Wert, *From Winchester to Cedar Creek*, 95–98, 123–26, 163–65, 234–36.

42. H. E. Young to his mother, 23 December 1864, Gourdin Papers, GEU.

43. For examples from late 1864 and early 1865, see W. H. Phillips to his father, 26 November 1864, Phillips Papers, NcD; J. J. Armfield to his wife, 22 December 1864, 14 January 1865 [misdated 1864], Armfield Papers, Nc-Ar; J. F. Sale to his aunt, 31 December 1864, Sale Papers, Vi; Pvt. J. R. Brown, Company H, 7th Georgia Cavalry, to his wife, 1 January 1865, J. R. Brown Papers, NcD; R. W. Leonard to his parents, 4 January 1865, Leonard Papers, Nc-Ar; G. B. Cooke, Diary, 4 January 1865, Cooke Papers, ViHi; W. R. Battle to his sister, 18 January 1865, in Lee, *Forget-Me-Nots*, 127; F. W. McMaster to his wife, 10 February 1865, McMaster Papers, ScU; and R. H. Hutspeth to his aunt, 15 February 1865, Hutspeth Papers, Nc-Ar.

44. For examples from late 1864 and early 1865, see R. H. Hutspeth to his aunt, 30 October 1864, 15 February 1865, Hutspeth Papers, Nc-Ar; Sgt. John R. Clements, Company G, 11th North Carolina, to Gov. Zebulon B. Vance, 19 December 1864, and Pvt. William W. Bramble, Company A, 52d North Carolina, to Vance, 25 December 1864, Governor's Papers, Nc-Ar; W. R. Battle to his parents, 29 January 1865, in Lee, *Forget-Me-Nots*, 128; Benjamin Mason to his wife, 10

February 1865, Mason Papers, AAP; Daniel Abernathy to his parents, 16 February 1865, Abernathy Papers, NcD; J. F. Maides to his mother, 18 February 1865, Maides Papers, NcD; and B. H. Freeman to his parents and sisters, 27 February 1865, in Wright, *Confederate Letters*, 60.

45. A. H. Crawford to his wife, 9 March 1865, Crawford Papers, NcD.

46. W. R. Battle to his mother, 15 January 1865, in Lee, *Forget-Me-Nots*, 125.

47. Mebane Hinshaw to his family, 22 February 1865, Hinshaw Papers, NcD.

48. J. B. Jones to his grandmother, 16 February 1865, Jones Family Papers, NcU. For other examples from early 1865, see W. F. Montgomery to his fiancée, 1 January 1865, UDC Typescripts, vol. 2, G-Ar; L. G. Young to his mother, 6 January 1865, Gourdin Papers, GEU; J. F. Sale to his aunt, 6 January 1865, Sale Papers, Vi; Benjamin Mason to his wife, 21 January 1865, Mason Papers, AAP; Silas Chandler to his wife, 25 January 1865, Chandler Papers, PNB; A. F. Fewell to his wife, 27 January 1865, in Mackintosh, *"Dear Martha,"* 190; W. C. Leak to his wife and children, 30 January 1865, Leak Papers, PNB; H. C. Conner to his wife, 4 February, 27 March 1865, Conner Papers, ScU; and A. H. Crawford to his wife, 5 March 1865, Crawford Papers, NcD.

49. J. A. Everett to his mother, 29 December 1864, Everett Papers, GEU. See also Corp. Jefferson Hedrick, Company B, 48th North Carolina, to his sister, 31 December 1864, Frank Family Papers, NcU; R. S. Ellis Jr. to his brother, 11 January 1865, Munford-Ellis Family Papers, NcD; Mebane Hinshaw to his wife, 11 January 1865, Hinshaw Papers, NcD; and J. J. Armfield to his wife, 17 February 1865, Armfield Papers, Nc-Ar.

50. Cecil-Fronsman, *Common Whites*, 204. Two recent articles that are particularly valuable and innovative examinations of the complex relationship between Confederate soldiers and their home communities, each of them focusing on specific counties and the units they raised, are Smith, "'Georgians Seem to Suffer More," and McKaughan, "'Few Were the Hearts.'"

51. Caroline S. Jones to her mother-in-law, 14 February 1865, in Myers, *Children of Pride*, 1252.

52. Escott, *After Secession*, 219–20.

53. Emory M. Thomas, *The Confederate Nation*, 284.

54. Beringer et al., *Why the South Lost*, 335. See also Eaton, *History of the Southern Confederacy*, 224; Wiley, *Plain People of the Confederacy*, 64–69, and *The Road to Appomattox*, 71–76; and Escott, *After Secession*, 216–21. In the last few years there has been a spirited debate among Civil War historians who have asked whether Southerners *lacked* the will to win their war for independence from the very beginning, or whether they had at one time possessed that will but *lost* it once it became evident that military victory was impossible. See the arguments advanced by Beringer et al., *Why the South Lost*, esp. 299–335, and McPherson, *Battle Cry of Freedom*, 854–58, and "Why Did the Confederacy Lose?," *Drawn with the Sword*, 113–36, a revision of his "American Victory, American Defeat" in *Why the Confederacy Lost*, ed. Boritt, 15–42.

55. See, e.g.—to cite several recent studies that are useful for their portrayal both of elements of the Southern home front and of the home front's effect on morale in the Confederate armies—Cecil-Fronsman, *Common Whites*; Hahn, *The Roots of Southern Populism*; Escott, *Many Excellent People*; Harris, *Plain Folk and Gentry*; McMillan, *Disintegration of a Confederate State*; Kenzer, *Kinship and Neighborhood*; Rable, *Civil Wars*; Bynum, *Unruly Women*; Whites, *The Civil War as a Crisis in Gender*; Sutherland, *Seasons Of War*; and Faust, *Mothers Of Invention*.

56. See Hahn, *The Roots of Southern Populism*, 116, 119–25; Escott, *Many Excellent People*, 32, 35–36, 40, 65, 69; Harris, *Plain Folk and Gentry*, 178–80; McMillan, *Disintegration of a Confederate State*, 127–28; Kenzer, *Kinship and Neighborhood*, 80–83, 90–91; Rable, *Civil Wars*, 57–58, 87–90, 214–15; Bynum, *Unruly Women*, 133–35, 140–43, 149–50; Cecil-Fronsman, *Common Whites*, 203–4, 211–16; Whites, *The Civil War as a Crisis in Gender*, 102, 107–9; and Faust, *Mothers of Invention*, 238–41, 243. See also the useful articles by Ambrose, "Yeoman Discontent in the Confederacy"; Escott, "'The Cry of the Sufferers'"; Archie K. Davis, "'She Disdains to Pluck One Laurel'"; Auman, "Neighbor Against Neighbor"; Escott and Crow, "The Social Order and Violent Disorder"; Wynne and Harrison, "'Plain Folk' Coping in the Confederacy"; Faust, "Altars of Sacrifice"; and Inscoe, "Coping in Confederate Appalachia."

57. Hahn, *The Roots of Southern Populism*, 124.

58. *Resolutions Adopted by McGowan's Brigade*.

59. See, e.g., Bessie Martin, *Desertion of Alabama Troops*, 149–50, 155–58; Coulter, *The Confederate States of America*, 465–66; Hahn, *The Roots of Southern Populism*, 116; Mitchell, *Civil War Soldiers*, 3–4, 177; Jimerson, *The Private Civil War*, 23–25; Cecil-Fronsman, *Common Whites*, 211–16; McPherson, *What They Fought For*, 18–21; and Whites, *The Civil War as a Crisis in Gender*, 107–9.

60. "Spirit of the Army: Forty-fifth North Carolina Regiment," *Richmond Examiner*, 25 February 1865.

61. A. B. Simms to his sister, 15, 21 March 1865, in Peacock, "A Georgian's View of War," 133–34.

62. Mitchell, *Civil War Soldiers*, 177.

63. Mitchell, *The Vacant Chair*, 162.

64. T. G. Trimmier to his wife, 17 February 1865, Trimmier Collection, T; J. K. Wilkerson to his sister, 14 February 1865, Wilkerson Papers, NcD.

65. F. W. McMaster to his wife, 10 February 1865, McMaster Papers, ScU; J. F. Sale to his aunt, 6 January 1865, Sale Papers, Vi. For other examples of those who condemned deserters, see L. G. Young to his mother, 6 January 1865, Gourdin Papers, GEU; R. M. Hannah to his cousin, 8 January 1865, Hackett Papers, NcD; "Desertion," *Richmond Whig*, 25 January 1865; and H. P. Fortson to Mrs. R. A. Barnes, 27 February 1865, Barnes Family Papers, ViU. For other examples of those who were more sympathetic, see also R. W. Leonard to his parents, 4 January 1865, Leonard Papers, Nc-Ar; William Leak to his wife and children, 30 January 1865, Leak Papers, PNB; R. P. Scarbrough to his cousin, 31 January 1865,

Confederate Miscellany, GEU; and A. H. Crawford to his wife, 5 March 1865, Crawford Papers, NcD.

66. Lee to Breckinridge, 27 March 1865, *OR* 46(3):1353.

67. Capt. James Walker, Bryan (Simms)/Kershaw/I Corps, 30 December 1864, Inspection Reports, NA, microcopy M935, roll 13.

68. Lee to Seddon, 27 January 1865, *OR* 46(2):1143. For examples after November 1864, see also Lee's endorsement on A. P. Hill to W. H. Taylor, 1 December 1864, *OR* 42(3):1249; Lee's endorsement on B. R. Johnson to Maj. R. P. Duncan, Asst. Adjt. Gen., IV Corps, 27 December 1864, 42(3):1311; Lee to Seddon (with enclosures), 27 January 1865, 46(2):1143, and Lee to Breckinridge, 9 March 1865, 46(2):1295; reports and correspondence of unit commanders, 42(3):1249, 1311, 46(2):1125–26, 1143–50, 1261–62; and Capt. H. H. Perry, Sorrel/Mahone/III Corps, 30 November 1864; Capt. James Walker, Bryan (Simms)/Kershaw/I Corps, 30 December 1864; Capt. J. T. Hackett, DuBose/Kershaw/I Corps, 26 February 1865, and Maj. E. L. Costin, Kershaw/I Corps, 28 February 1865, Inspection Reports, NA, microcopy M935, rolls 13, 15. Private correspondence cites physical hardship as a major factor in desertion; for only a few such examples, see J. J. Armfield to his wife, 21 December 1864, Armfield Papers, Nc-Ar; W. R. Battle to his sister, 18 January 1865, in Lee, *Forget-Me-Nots*, 127; and F. W. McMaster to his wife, 10 February 1865, McMaster Papers, ScU.

69. R. P. Scarbrough to his cousin, 31 January 1865, Scarbrough Papers, Confederate Miscellany, GEU. For examples after November 1864, see J. A. Johnson to his fiancée, 15 December 1864, Johnson Papers, NcU; W. F. Montgomery to his fiancée, 1 January 1865, UDC Typescripts, vol. 2, G-Ar; R. S. Ellis to his brother, 11 January 1865, Munford-Ellis Family Papers, NcD; A. F. Fewell to his wife, 27 January 1865, in Mackintosh, *"Dear Martha,"* 190–91; W. C. Leak to his wife and children, 30 January 1865, Leak Papers, PNB; H. C. Conner to his wife, 4 February 1865, Conner Papers, ScU; T. G. Trimmier to his wife, 6 February 1865, Trimmier Collection, T; C. F. James to his sister, 13 February 1865, James Papers, NcU; J. F. Maides to his mother, 18 February 1865, Maides Papers, NcD; Bryan Grimes to his wife, 28 February 1865, Grimes Papers, NcU; L. R. Mills to his brother, 2 March 1865, in Harmon, "Letters of . . . Mills," 307; and A. H. Crawford to his wife, 5 March 1865, Crawford Papers, NcD. Official correspondence and reports also cite psychological stress as a major factor in desertion; for only a few such examples, see Lee to Breckinridge, 24 February 1865, *OR* 46(2):1254, and 28 February 1865, 46(2):1265; Capt. E. T. Nicholson, Lane (Cowan)/Wilcox/III Corps, 28 November 1864, and Capt. R. N. Wilson, Pegram (Kasey)/Johnston/II Corps, 26 February 1865, Inspection Reports, NA, microcopy M935, rolls 12, 15.

70. Capt. R. N. Wilson, Pegram (Kasey)/Johnston/II Corps, 26 February 1865, Inspection Reports, NA, microcopy M935, roll 15.

71. Lee to Breckinridge, 24 February 1865, *OR* 46(2):1254; see also Lee to Breckinridge, 28 February 1865, 46(2):1265.

72. W. H. Phillips to his parents, 26 November 1864, Phillips Papers, NcD. See also J. A. Johnson to his fiancée, 15 December 1864, Johnson Papers, NcU, and W. R. Battle to his sister, 18 January 1865, in Lee, *Forget-Me-Nots*, 127.

73. J. J. Armfield to his wife, 31 January 1864 [1865], 10 March 1865, Armfield Papers, Nc-Ar. See also R. H. Hutspeth to his aunt, 30 October 1864, 15 February 1865, Hutspeth Papers, Nc-Ar, and J. F. Ward to his sweetheart, 28 January 1865, Click Papers, NcD.

74. John J. Armfield, 30th [North Carolina] Infantry, Compiled Service Records, NA, microcopy 270, roll 355.

75. J. B. Evans to his wife, 11 January 1865, Evans Papers, NcD.

76. L. R. Mills to his brother, 2 March 1865, in Harmon, "Letters of . . . Mills," 307; see also B. W. Justice to his wife, 15 March 1865, Justice Papers, GEU. For evidence of last-minute executions of convicted deserters, see J. B. Evans to his wife, 30 March 1865, Evans Papers, NcD, and R. P. Myers, Diary, 1 April 1865, Myers Papers, ViRC.

77. B. H. Freeman to his parents and sisters, 26 February 1865, in Wright, *Confederate Letters*, 60; Maj. Gen. G. G. Meade, Army of the Potomac, to Lt. Gen. U. S. Grant, Armies of the United States, 21 February 1865, *OR* 46(2):610.

78. J. F. Maides to his mother, 18 February 1865, Maides Papers, NcD.

79. Statement of Pvt. John A. Johnson, Company A, 7th Tennessee, to Federal officers at Winchester, 3 February 1865, *OR* 46(2):387. See also H. C. Townsend, Diary, 28 January 1865, in Townsend, "Townsend's Diary," 99–100; W. H. Taylor to his fiancée, 20 February 1865, in Tower, *Lee's Adjutant*, 225; S. P. Collier to his parents, 21 February 1865, Collier Papers, Nc-Ar; A. C. Jones, Diary, 23, 26 February 1865, Civil War Papers, LHA Collection, LNT; and F. M. Coker to his wife, 25 February 1865, Heidler Collection, GU.

80. See, e.g., Lonn, *Desertion during the Civil War*; Martin, *Desertion of Alabama Troops*, 147–50, 155–58; Wiley, *The Life of Johnny Reb*, 143–45, 210, and *The Road to Appomattox*, 71–73; Coulter, *The Confederate States of America*, 465–66; Eaton, *History of the Southern Confederacy*, 251, 260–62; Roland, *The Confederacy*, 128, 145; Ambrose, "Yeoman Discontent in the Confederacy," 266–68; Bardolph, "Inconstant Rebels," in which the explication of the almost countless motives for Confederate desertion (172–74) is especially useful; Escott, *After Secession*, 125–28; Reid, "A Test Case"; Hattaway and Jones, *How the North Won*, 671; Beringer et al., *Why the South Lost*, 327, 334, 434–35, 439; Escott and Crow, "The Social Order and Violent Disorder," 393–95; McMillan, *Disintegration of a Confederate State*, 127; Jimerson, *The Private Civil War*, 233–35; McPherson, *Battle Cry of Freedom*, 820–21, 844; Bardolph, "Confederate Dilemma"; Rable, *Civil Wars*, 87–90; Mitchell, "The Perseverance of the Soldiers," in *Why the Confederacy Lost*, ed. Boritt, 126–28, 130, as well as a slightly revised version in *The Vacant Chair*, 161–63, 165; and Faust, *Mothers of Invention*, 243.

81. Bardolph, "Inconstant Rebels," 172.

82. Roland, *The Confederacy*, 145. See also, e.g., Lonn, *Desertion during the Civil*

War, 123; Freeman, *Lee's Lieutenants*, 3:623; Wiley, *The Life of Johnny Reb*, 143–45, 210, and *The Road to Appomattox*, 71–73; Eaton, *History of the Southern Confederacy*, 251, 260–61; Bardolph, "Inconstant Rebels," 167, 172–74; and Johnson, *Division and Reunion*, 155.

83. Freeman, *Lee's Lieutenants*, 3:623.

84. See, e.g., Lonn, *Desertion during the Civil War*, 124; Escott, *After Secession*, 128; Beringer et al., *Why the South Lost*, 34; Jimerson, *The Private Civil War*, 235; and esp. Reid Mitchell's arguments in his "The Perseverance of the Soldiers," in *Why the Confederacy Lost*, ed. Boritt, 126–28, 130, and in *The Vacant Chair*, 161–63, 165.

85. Escott, *After Secession*, 128.

86. Mitchell, *The Vacant Chair*, 165, which differs slightly—but significantly—from his assertion in "The Perseverance of the Soldiers": "I can only rejoice that their good sense took away from Jefferson Davis and Robert E. Lee the means of prosecuting an immoral war" (p. 130).

87. Freeman, *R. E. Lee* 3:542.

88. Resolutions, 31st Virginia/Pegram (Hoffman)/Pegram/II Corps, in "Meeting of the Thirty-first Virginia Regiment, of Pegram's Brigade," *Richmond Dispatch*, 4 February 1865. See also Resolutions, Companies B, G, and I, 15th Virginia/Corse/Pickett/I Corps, in "The Spirit of the Army," *Richmond Dispatch*, 14 February 1865.

89. J. M. McFall to his sister, 23 January 1865, McFall Papers, GEU. See also J. D. Hankins to his sister, January [undated] 1865, Hankins Family Papers, ViU; G. B. Cooke, Diary, 11 January 1865, Cooke Papers, ViHi; E. C. Barnes to his mother, 12 January 1865, Barnes Family Papers, ViU; C. F. James to his sister, 7 February 1865, 9, 13, 18 February 1865, James Papers, NcU; J. E. Whitehorne to his sister, 11 February 1865, Whitehorne Papers, Vi; J. B. Jones to his grandmother, 16 February 1865, Jones Family Papers, NcU; W. H. Taylor to his fiancée, 24 February 1865, in Tower, *Lee's Adjutant*, 227–28; L. R. Mills to his brother, 2 March 1865, in Harmon, "Letters of . . . Mills," 307; and W. J. Pegram to his sister, 14 March 1865, in James I. Robertson Jr., "'The Boy Artillerist,'" 257.

90. Kenzer, *Kinship and Neighborhood*, 81.

91. Mebane Hinshaw to his family, 14 March 1865, Hinshaw Papers, NcD. See also H. C. Conner to his wife, 14 December 1864, Conner Papers, ScU; J. A. Johnson to his fiancée, 15 December 1864, Johnson Papers, NcU; A. F. Fewell to his wife, 22 December 1864, in Mackintosh, *"Dear Martha,"* 178; M. H. Fitzpatrick to his wife, 1 January 1865, in Hammock, *Letters to Amanda*, 177; E. C. Barnes to his mother, 12 January 1865, Barnes Family Papers, ViU; T. L. McCarty to his sister, 26 January 1865, McCarty Papers, TxU; J. B. Evans to his wife, 4 February 1865, Evans Papers, NcD; J. K. Wilkerson to his sister, 14 February 1865, Wilkerson Papers, NcD; *Richmond Whig*, 25 February 1865; W. J. Pegram to his sister, 14 March 1865, in James I. Robertson Jr., "'The Boy Artillerist,'" 257; and J. E. Hall, Diary, 23 March 1865, in Dayton, *Diary of a Confederate Soldier*, 128.

92. Mitchell, *Civil War Soldiers*, 172.

93. J. A. Everett to his mother, 7 February 1865, Everett Papers, GEU. See also John A. Everett, J. H. Everett, and T. H. Everett, 11th [Georgia] Infantry, Compiled Service Records, NA, microcopy 266, roll 261.

94. J. A. Everett to his mother, 18 February, 16 March 1865, Everett Papers, GEU. See also Everett to his mother, 29 December 1864, 10 January 1865, ibid.

95. Logue, *To Appomattox and Beyond*, 81. See, in addition to the soldiers' letters cited in n. 91 above, Coulter, *The Confederate States of America*, 465–66; Kenzer, *Kinship and Neighborhood*, 80–81; Mitchell, *Civil War Soldiers*, 172–73; Rable, *Civil Wars*, 88; Cecil-Fronsman, *Common Whites*, 216; and Whites, *The Civil War as a Crisis in Gender*, 102, 107–9.

96. Coulter, *The Confederate States of America*, 466.

97. Freeman, *Lee's Lieutenants* 3:619; Henry, *The Story of the Confederacy*, 449; Emory M. Thomas, *The Confederate Nation*, 287. See also Coulter, *The Confederate States of America*, 466; Wiley, *The Road to Appomattox*, 73; Ambrose, "Yeoman Discontent in the Confederacy," 268; Bardolph, "Inconstant Rebels," 163, 167; and Thomas, *The Confederate Nation*, 289, 299.

98. Wiley, *The Road to Appomattox*, 73. Wiley acknowledges in *The Life of Johnny Reb* (p. 145) that "months before Appomattox the Confederacy's doom was plainly written in the ever swelling tide of men who were unpatriotically taking leave of their comrades-in arms," then adds, "But in the midst of all the defection that cursed the Confederacy, and in the face of increasing hardship, there were a large number of Rebs whose spirit remained strong. It is pleasant to turn from the woeful subject of evasion to consideration of those who stood firm at their posts of duty."

99. Mitchell, *Civil War Soldiers*, 179. See also Mitchell, *The Vacant Chair*, 160–62, 165; Escott, *After Secession*, 128; Jimerson, *The Private Civil War*, 235–37; Royster, *The Destructive War*, 187–88; and Logue, *To Appomattox and Beyond*, 80–81.

100. Royster, *The Destructive War*, 187–88.

101. Jubal A. Early, "The Campaigns of Gen. Robert E. Lee: An Address by Lieut. General Jubal A. Early, before Washington and Lee University, January 19th, 1872," cited in J. William Jones, *Personal Reminiscences . . . of Lee*, 40.

102. Lee to an unidentified corps commander [probably A. P. Hill], undated [June 1864], *OR* 40(2):703. See also Lee to Davis, 21 June 1864, in Freeman, *Lee's Dispatches*, 254–55. For representative comments by officers and men who expressed much the same opinion, see C. M. Blackford to his wife, 16 June 1864, in Blackford and Blackford, *Letters From Lee's Army*, 256; R. C. Mabry to his wife, 3 July 1864, Mabry Papers, Nc-Ar; and T. C. Elder to his wife, 6 October 1864, Elder Papers, ViHi.

103. F. M. Coker to his wife, 16 July 1864, Heidler Collection, GU; J. F. Maides to his mother, 23 September 1864, Maides Papers, NcD.

104. R. C. Mabry to his wife, 27 August 1864, Mabry Papers, Nc-Ar. See also

F. M. Coker to his wife, 26 June, 13 August 1864, Heidler Collection, GU; W. J. Pegram to his sister, 1 September 1864, Pegram-Johnson-McIntosh Family Papers, ViHi; and Pvt. William A. Boyle, Company K, Hampton Legion Cavalry/ Aiken/Butler/Cavalry Corps, to his mother, 23 November 1864, Boyle Papers, LC.

105. F. M. Coker to his wife, 4 July 1864, Heidler Collection, GU.

106. J. W. Albright, Diary, 23 August 1864, Albright Papers, NcU. See also, e.g., F. M. Coker to his wife, 16 July 1864, Heidler Collection, GU, and H. H. Perry to H. L. Benning, 22 July 1864, Benning Papers, NcU.

107. For the most notable examples, see Fuller, *Grant and Lee*, 228; Freeman, *R. E. Lee* 3:425, 496 n. 33, and *Lee's Lieutenants* 3:541; Coulter, *The Confederate States of America*, 362; Dowdey, *Lee*, 486; Emory M. Thomas, *The Confederacy as a Revolutionary Experience*, 51, and *The Confederate Nation*, 270, 274 (though Thomas's recent assessment of Lee's generalship in 1864–65 in his *Robert E. Lee*, cited below, differs dramatically from these earlier views); Sommers, *Richmond Redeemed*, 207, 423–24; Royster, *The Destructive War*, 285–86; Glatthaar, *Partners In Command*, 210; Nolan, *Lee Considered*, 85–86, 112–33; Vandiver, *Blood Brothers*, 171, 176; Woodworth, *Davis and Lee at War*, 299–327; Roland, *Reflections On Lee*, 73; and Trudeau, "'A Mere Question of Time,'" 545, 548.

108. Freeman, *Lee's Lieutenants*, 3:541; Sommers, *Richmond Redeemed*, 423.

109. Fuller, *Grant and Lee*, 228.

110. For the most notable recent examples, see Beringer et al., *Why the South Lost*, 320; Hagerman, *The American Civil War*, 274; Jones, *Civil War Command and Strategy*, 227; Gallagher, "Home Front and Battlefield" (pp. 166–67), "The Army of Northern Virginia in May 1864" (p. 118), "'Upon Their Success Hang Momentous Interests'" (p. 98), and "Another Look at the Generalship of Robert E. Lee" (pp. 285–86); Emory M. Thomas, *Robert E. Lee*, 339–40, 342; and McPherson, "Grant's Final Victory," *Drawn with the Sword*, 171.

111. Lee to Breckinridge, 9 March 1865, *OR* 46(2):1295. See also Breckinridge to Lee, 8 March 1865, *OR* 46(2):1292.

112. There is some evidence to support the view that Lee's spoken and written comments on the siege, particularly those expressing his desire to conduct operations against Grant without the limitations imposed on him by the trenches around Petersburg and Richmond, were not always the most accurate reflection of his thinking. Cf. William C. Davis, "Lee and Jefferson Davis," in *Lee the Soldier*, ed. Gallagher, 304. "I would like to have this kind of warfare broken up, and get to field fighting once more," Lt. Col. William J. Pegram wrote his sister in the summer of 1864 and proudly described a conversation with Lee in which the commanding general told him "that there was nothing he desired now more than a 'fair field fight,' and that if Grant would meet him on equal ground, he would give him *two to one*." Pegram, who was anxious for a decisive battle, never stopped to consider that Lee might have made this and similar statements out of his sense

of duty to his army, to Davis, and to the Confederate people because he believed that he was expected to do so. W. J. Pegram to his sister, 14 July 1864, Pegram-Johnston-McIntosh Family Papers, ViHi.

113. B. W. Justice to his wife, 11–12, 14 July 1864, Justice Papers, GEU.

114. J. M. Simpson to his wife, 4 August 1864, Allen and Simpson Family Papers, NcU.

115. W. A. Kelly, Diary, 31 August 1864, Kelly Papers, ScCC. See also, e.g., Stephen Elliott to his wife, 23 June 1864, Elliott Family Papers, ScU; E. P. Alexander to "Will," 27 June 1864, Alexander Papers, NcU; W. D. Williams to his fiancée, 4 July 1864, Williams Papers, TxHiC; T. G. Trimmier to his wife, 9 July 1864, Trimmier Collection, T; H. C. Conner to his wife, 18 October 1864, Conner Papers, ScU; J. H. Chamberlayne to his mother, 31 October 1864, in Chamberlayne, *Ham Chamberlayne*, 289; and Longstreet to Lee, 1 February 1865, *OR* 46(2):1189. For Grant's famous vow, which was widely quoted in Northern and Southern newspapers that spring and summer, see his message to Maj. Gen. H. W. Halleck, Chief of Staff, Armies of the United States, 11 May 1864, *OR* 36(2): 627.

116. Emory M. Thomas, *The Confederate Nation*, 270.

117. Emory M. Thomas, *Robert E. Lee*, 339–40.

118. McPherson, "Grant's Final Victory," 171.

119. Trudeau, "'A Mere Question of Time,'" 549.

120. Pollard, *Southern History of the War*, 507.

121. J. E. Whitehorne, Diary, 13 April 1865, Whitehorne Papers, NcU.

122. Ibid., 16 April 1865.

123. Ibid., 31 [30] March 1865.

124. Ibid., 22 April 1865.

Bibliography

PRIMARY SOURCES

MANUSCRIPTS
Alabama
Alabama Department of Archives and History, Montgomery
    Hall Family Papers
        Col. Bolling Hall, 59th Alabama
        Adjt. Crenshaw Hall, Gracie/Johnson/Beauregard, Gracie/Johnson/IV
            Corps, and Moody/Johnson/IV Corps
        Capt. John Elmore Hall, Company B, 59th Alabama
    William Henry Sanders Papers
        Col./Brig. Gen. John Caldwell Calhoun Sanders, 11th Alabama and
            Sanders/Mahone/III Corps
        Surgeon William Henry Sanders, 11th Alabama
Auburn University, Auburn
    Jonathan Fuller Coghill Papers
        Corp. Jonathan Fuller Coghill, Company G, 23d North Carolina
    James H. Lane Papers
        Col. John D. Barry, Lane (Barry)/Wilcox/III Corps
        Capt. J. G. Harris, 7th North Carolina
        Lt. Col. J. W. McGill, 18th North Carolina
    Benjamin Mason Papers
        Pvt. Benjamin Mason, Company F, 60th Alabama
Florida
Florida State Library, Tallahassee
    Council A. Bryan Papers
        Capt. Council A. Bryan, Company C, 5th Florida
Georgia
Emory University, Atlanta
    Confederate Microfilm Miscellany
        Pvt. Ira Traweek, Jeff Davis Battery
    Confederate Miscellany I
        Dorsey Binion Papers
            Pvt. Dorsey N. Binion, Company K, 48th Georgia
        John Alfred Feister Coleman Papers
            Capt. John Alfred Feister Coleman, Company B, 17th South Carolina
        R. P. Scarbrough Papers
            1st Sgt. Robert P. Scarbrough, Hurt's Battery
    James Preston Crowder Papers
        Pvt. James Preston Crowder, Company I, 47th Alabama

John A. Everett Papers

    Pvt. John A. Everett, Company K, 11th Georgia

Robert Newman Gourdin Papers

    Maj. Henry Bryan, Adjt. & Insp. Gen., Beauregard

    Brig. Gen. G. W. C. Lee, G. W. C. Lee / Richmond

    Maj. Henry Edward Young, Judge Advocate Gen., HQ

    Capt. Louis Gourdin Young, Asst. Adjt. Gen., Kirkland / Heth / III Corps
        and MacRae / Heth / III Corps

Henry Woodfin Grady Papers

    Maj. William Sammons Grady, 25th North Carolina

Benjamin Wesley Justice Papers

    Capt. Benjamin Wesley Justice, Commissary, Kirkland / Heth / III Corps
        and MacRae / Heth / III Corps

James H. Lee Papers

    Pvt. James H. Lee, Company C, 43d Alabama

William McFall Papers

    Adjt. James M. McFall, Palmetto Sharpshooters

    Pvt. William McFall, Company C, Palmetto Sharpshooters

Augustin E. Shore Papers

    Pvt. Augustin E. Shore, Company I, 33d North Carolina

James Wesley Williams Papers

    Pvt. James Wesley Williams, Company C, 16th Georgia

Georgia Department of Archives and History, Atlanta

    Abner R. Cox Papers

        2d Lt. Abner R. Cox, Company L, Palmetto Sharpshooters

    Harvey Hightower Papers

        2d Lt. Harvey Judson Hightower, Company G, 20th Georgia

    J. M. McClelland Papers

        1st Sgt. James M. McClelland, Company I, 44th Georgia

    Megarity Family Papers

        Pvt. Gardner O. Megarity, Company B, 24th Georgia

    Andrew J. Perkins Papers

        Pvt. Andrew J. Perkins, Company B, 7th Georgia Cavalry

    Charles L. Ross Papers

        5th Sgt. Charles Lewellyn Ross, Company C, 2d Georgia Battalion

    Alexander H. Stephens Museum Collection

        Walter H. Taylor Papers

            Lt. Col. Walter H. Taylor, Asst. Adjt. Gen., HQ

        James D. Williams Papers

            Pvt. James D. Williams, Company D, 16th Georgia

    William Ross Stillwell Papers

        Pvt. William Ross Stillwell, Courier, Bryan / Kershaw / I Corps

United Daughters of the Confederacy, Georgia Division, Typescripts

Volume 2

Pvt. Grant Davis Carter, Company C, 2d Georgia Battalion

Jr. 2d Lt. Horatio J. David, Company B, 16th Georgia

1st Lt. James Manning Goldsmith, Company K, 60th Georgia

Jr. 2d Lt. Ezekiel Dunagan Graham, Company B, 6th Georgia

Adjt. Henry Francis Jones, Cobb's Legion Cavalry

5th Sgt. Will F. Montgomery, Company B, 9th Georgia

Volume 4

Pvt. John L. G. Wood, Drummer, 53d Georgia

Volume 8

3d Sgt. James B. May, Company I, 21st Georgia

Volume 9

Pvt. Jesse Mercer Wellborn, Company D, 3d Georgia

Georgia Historical Society, Savannah

Joseph Hilton Papers

Capt. Joseph Hilton, Asst. Adjt. Gen., Evans/Gordon/Valley

Wayne-Stiles-Anderson Families Papers

Maj. Edward Clifford Anderson Jr., 7th Georgia Cavalry

Brig. Gen. Matthew C. Butler, Butler/Cavalry Corps

Maj. Gen. Wade Hampton, Cavalry Corps

University of Georgia, Athens

Baber-Blackshear Families Papers

1st Lt. George D. Smith, Company B, 18th Georgia Battalion

Gordon Family Papers

Anonymous Soldier, Stonewall/Gordon/II Corps

Mrs. Fanny Haralson Gordon

Maj. Gen. John B. Gordon, Gordon/II Corps, Gordon/Valley, and II
Corps

Florence Hodgson Heidler Collection

Capt. Francis Marion Coker, Adjt., Cutts/III Corps Artillery

LaRogue [LaRoque] Collection

Pvt. John G. LaRoque, Company E, 4th Georgia

Mary Barnard Nix Collection

1st Lt. John T. Gay, Company B, 4th Georgia

Louisiana

Tulane University, New Orleans

Thomas W. G. Inglet Papers

2d Corp. Thomas W. G. Inglet, Company C, 28th Georgia

Rosemonde E. and Emile Kuntz Collection

Capt. Reuben Allen Pierson, Company C, 9th Louisiana

— Louisiana Historical Association Papers

    Pvt. Alexander C. Jones, 4th Company, Washington Artillery

    Pvt. Frank Lobrano, Washington Artillery

    Army of Northern Virginia Papers

       Capt. George P. Ring, Company K, 6th Louisiana

Mississippi

Mississippi Department of Archives and History, Jackson

  Oscar J. E. Stuart Papers

    Capt. Joseph F. Sessions, Company K, 18th Mississippi

    Pvt. Edward Stuart, Signal Corps/W. H. F. Lee/Cavalry Corps

  A. L. P. Vairin Papers

    Pvt. A. L. P. Vairin, Company B, 2d Mississippi

  B. L. Wynn Papers

    Pvt. B. L. Wynn, Signal Corps/II Corps and Signal Corps/Valley

North Carolina

Duke University, Durham

  Daniel Abernathy Papers

    Pvt. Daniel Abernathy, Company C, 16th North Carolina

  Alfred Adams Papers

    Sgts. George F. Adams and Barzella C. McBride, Company D, 1st North Carolina Cavalry

  William B. G. Andrews Papers

    2d Lt. William B. G. Andrews, Company C, 10th Battalion Virginia Heavy Artillery

  F. A. Bleckley Papers

    Pvt. William L. Bleckley, Company I, 49th North Carolina

  Eli Whitney Bonney Papers

    Lt. Usher Parsons Bonney, 7th South Carolina Cavalry

  Alexander R. Boteler Papers

    Maj. Gen. J. E. B. Stuart, Cavalry Corps

  Robert Boyd Papers

    Pvt. Andrew Boyd, Company D, 7th South Carolina

    Sgt. Daniel Boyd, Company D, 7th South Carolina

  William H. Brotherton Papers

    Pvt. William H. Brotherton, Company K, 23d North Carolina

    Pvt. Levi A. Lockman, Company K, 23d North Carolina

  J. R. Brown Papers

    Pvt. J. R. Brown, Company H, 7th Georgia Cavalry

  Hugh Conway Browning Papers

    Pvt. William R. Clark, Company E, 31st North Carolina

    Pvt. Samuel P. Lockhart, Company G, 27th North Carolina

  Jacob B. Click Papers

    Pvt. J. F. Ward, Company K, 8th Virginia

James O. Coghill Papers
    Corp. Jonathan Fuller Coghill, Company G, 23d North Carolina
Mary E. Craig Papers
    Sgt. W. H. Strayhorn, Company K, 2d North Carolina Cavalry
Abel H. Crawford Papers
    Pvt. Abel H. Crawford, Company A, 61st Alabama
John N. Cummings Papers
    Pvt. John N. Cummings, Company C, 5th South Carolina Cavalry
Julia Deane Papers
    Sgt. Jacob Shook, Company G, 15th Virginia
John J. Dillard Papers
    Pvt. Virgil E. Lucas, Company C, 26th Georgia
John B. Evans Papers
    1st Lt. John B. Evans, Company I, 53d Georgia
Alexander Frank Papers
    Pvt. Jesse M. Frank, Company B, 48th North Carolina
Caroline Gardner Papers
    Ord. Sgt. Thomas J. Gardner, Company I, 2d North Carolina Cavalry
Bryan Grimes Papers
    Col. Bryan Grimes, 4th North Carolina
John C. Hackett Papers
    Sgt. Christopher Hackett, Company B, 45th North Carolina
    Pvt. Robert M. Hannah, Company C, 45th North Carolina
Harden Family Papers
    Capt. Asbury Hull Jackson, Commissary, Doles/Rodes/II Corps,
        Cook/Rodes/II Corps, and Cook/Rodes/Valley
    Pvt. Thomas E. Jackson, Company E, Cobb's Legion Cavalry
John H. Hartman Papers
    Pvt. John H. Hartman, Company D, 1st North Carolina Artillery
Archibald Erskine Henderson Papers
    Capt. John D. Fain, Company C, 33d North Carolina
    Lt. Archibald Erskine Henderson, Company B, 12th North Carolina
J. L. Henry Papers
    2d Lt. Jesse L. Henry, Company K, 26th North Carolina
Mebane Hinshaw Papers
    Pvt. Mebane Hinshaw, Company B, 6th North Carolina
Willis Horton Papers
    Pvt. Henry Ferrell, Company H, 31st North Carolina
Robert G. Hutson Papers
    Pvt. Robert G. Hutson, Company G, 11th South Carolina
Robert D. Johnston Papers
    Brig. Gen. Robert D. Johnston, Johnston/Pegram/Valley

Lawrence Massillon Keitt Papers
      Col. Lawrence Massillon Keitt, Kershaw (Keitt)/Kershaw/I Corps
      Adjt. John A. Wilson, 20th South Carolina
Williamson Kelly Papers
      Maj. Alfred D. Kelly, 21st Virginia
Willis H. King Papers
      Pvt. Bellfield King, Company G, 11th North Carolina
Henry Clay Krebs Papers
      Corp. Henry Clay Krebs, Company H, 13th Virginia
Hannah Lawrence Papers
      Pvt. Jesse L. Moffett, Company H, 44th North Carolina
James H. C. Leach Papers
      Surgeon Richard V. Leach, 2d North Carolina Battalion
Andrew J. McBride Papers
      Capt. Andrew Jackson McBride, Company E, 10th Georgia
James F. [Joseph Francis] Maides Papers
      Pvt. Joseph Francis Maides, Company I, 27th North Carolina
Munford-Ellis Family Papers
      Sgt. Maj./Corp. Richard S. Ellis Jr., 21st Virginia and Company E, 21st
         Virginia
      Capt. Jesse S. Jones, Company B, 3d Virginia Cavalry
      1st Lt. B. W. Lacy, Company F, 3d Virginia Cavalry
      Sgt. Thomas E. Nimmo, Company B, 15th Virginia
      Pvt. Edward H. Steele, 14th Tennessee
      Capt. William Steptoe, Company B, 2d Virginia Cavalry
William Horace Phillips Papers
      Sgt. William Horace Phillips, Company F, 14th Virginia
John H. Stewart Papers
      Pvt. John H. Stewart, Company C, 1st North Carolina Artillery
James King Wilkerson Papers
      Pvt. James King Wilkerson, Company K, 55th North Carolina
Friends Historical Collection, Guilford College, Greensboro
      Reverend John Bacon Crenshaw Papers
            Pvt. John R. Beckerdite, Company A, 6th North Carolina
            Pvt. William F. Bell, Company A, 6th North Carolina
            Pvt. W. A. Burgess, Company I, 18th North Carolina
            George Caudle, Mount Nebo, Yadkin County, North Carolina
            Pvt. Lewis Caudle, Company C, 13th North Carolina
            Pvt. William F. Folson, Company I, 15th North Carolina
            Pvt. William T. Hales, Company B, 34th North Carolina
            Pvt. Joshua A. Hill, Company F, 27th North Carolina
            Pvt. Seth W. Laughlin, Company F, 27th North Carolina

Pvt. Clark Millikan, Company A, 6th North Carolina

Pvt. Henry Stuart, Company A, 6th North Carolina

North Carolina Division of Archives and History, Department of Cultural
Resources, Raleigh

Henry Clay Albright Papers

Capt. Henry Clay Albright, Company G, 26th North Carolina

Capt. Austin R. Johnson, Company G, 26th North Carolina

John J. Armfield Papers

Pvt. John J. Armfield, Company C, 30th North Carolina

Henry C. Brown Papers

2d Lt. Henry M. Talley, Company G, 14th Virginia

John B. Brown Papers

Capt. John Badger Brown, 1st & 3d North Carolina (Consolidated)

Capt. H. A. Whiting, Asst. Adjt. Gen., Grimes/II Corps

William Hyslop Sumner Burgwyn Papers

Capt. William H. S. Burgwyn, Aide-de-Camp,
Clingman/Hoke/Beauregard

John Washington Calton Papers

2d Sgt. John Washington Calton, Company I, 56th North Carolina

William Bailey Clement Papers

Maj. William Bailey Clement, 10th Virginia Cavalry

Augustus Clewell Papers

Pvt. Augustus Clewell, Company B, 1st Battalion North Carolina
Sharpshooters

Samuel P. Collier Papers

Sgt. Maj. Samuel P. Collier, 2d North Carolina

Thomas Pollock Devereux Papers

Pvt. Thomas Pollock Devereux, Courier, Daniel/Rodes/II Corps,
Grimes/Rodes/Valley, Grimes/Ramseur/Valley, Grimes
(Cowand)/Grimes/Valley, and Grimes (Cowand)/Grimes/II Corps

Alexander England Family Papers

3d Lt. William W. England, Company E, 25th North Carolina

Gales Family Papers

Maj. Seaton Gales, Asst. Adjt. Gen., Cox/Rodes/Valley

Governor's Papers: Gov. Zebulon B. Vance

Pvt. William W. Bramble, Company A, 52d North Carolina

Sgt. John R. Clements, Company G, 11th North Carolina

Pvt. J. W. Cole, Company K, 7th South Carolina Cavalry

Adjt. O. D. Cooke, 24th North Carolina

Pvt. James C. Fowler, Company C, 25th North Carolina

Maj. Gen. Henry Heth, Heth/III Corps

Pvt. B. T. Person, Company D, 2d North Carolina Cavalry

Capt. Frederick Phillips, Asst. Q.M., 30th North Carolina

"P. K. O. G." [Unidentified North Carolinian, ANV or Beauregard]

Capt. N. A. Ramsey, Company D, 61st North Carolina

Maj. C. L. Randolph, Q.M., Johnson/IV Corps

Capt. John A. Sloan, 27th North Carolina

Lt. Col. Samuel McDowell Tate, 6th North Carolina

Bryan Grimes Papers

2d Lt. Robert E. Ballard, Company K, 32d North Carolina

Col. William H. Peebles, Cook (Peebles)/Grimes/II Corps

W. P. Hall Collection

Pvt. John G. Hall, Company G, 51st North Carolina

Samuel Finley Harper Papers

Pvt. Samuel Finley Harper, Courier, III Corps

Marcus Hefner Papers

Pvt. Marcus Hefner, Company E, 57th North Carolina

Robert F. Hoke Papers

Maj. Gen. Robert F. Hoke, Hoke/Beauregard

George Holland Collection

Col. William Ruffin Cox, 2d North Carolina

Roy Vernon Howell Collection

Pvt. Nathan Mathewson, Company A, 1st North Carolina Artillery

Lt. David N. Sills, Company B, 66th North Carolina

Pvt. J. G. Sills, Company B, 66th North Carolina

Robert H. Hutspeth Papers

Pvt. Robert H. Hutspeth, Company I, 3d North Carolina

Hugh Buckner Johnston Collection

Pvt. William Henry Edwards, Company H, 4th North Carolina Cavalry

Isaac Lefevers Papers

Sgt. Isaac Lefevers, Company K, 46th North Carolina

E. J. Lentz Papers

Pvt. Elias J. Lentz, Company C, 48th North Carolina

Riley Leonard Papers

Pvt. Riley W. Leonard, Company A, 21st North Carolina

Robert C. Mabry Papers

Pvt. Robert C. Mabry, Company K, 6th Virginia

Capt. Stephen P. Read, Company F, 14th Virginia

B. F. Medley Papers

Pvt. Benjamin Frank Medley, Company C, 14th North Carolina

George W. Pearsall Papers

Pvt. George W. Pearsall, Company G, 55th North Carolina

Alfred M. Scales Papers

Brig. Gen. Alfred M. Scales, Scales/Wilcox/III Corps

Mrs. Louis Polk Sherman Collection

    Pvt. James E. R. Yancey, Company B, 12th North Carolina

Southern Historical Collection, University of North Carolina, Chapel Hill

  James W. Albright Papers

    Ord. Sgt. James W. Albright, Company A, 12th Battalion Virginia Light
      Artillery

  Alexander-Hillhouse Family Papers

    Brig. Gen. Edward Porter Alexander, Chief of Artillery, I Corps

  Edward Porter Alexander Papers

    Brig. Gen. Edward Porter Alexander, Chief of Artillery, I Corps

  William D. Alexander Papers

    Pvt. William D. Alexander, Hospital Steward, 37th North Carolina

  Allen & Simpson Family Papers

    2d Lt. James M. Simpson, Company F, 13th Alabama

  Mrs. E. K. Atkinson Collection

    Pvt. Francis Asbury Wayne Jr., Company L, 1st South Carolina

  Barkley Family Papers

    Sgt. Daniel Dendy, Company C, 7th South Carolina Cavalry

    Pvt. William H. Slater, Company A, 1st South Carolina (Hagood's)

    Pvt. Hugh Y. Spence, Company D, 18th South Carolina

  William Starr Basinger Papers

    Maj. William Starr Basinger, 18th Georgia Battalion

  William Beavans Papers

    Lt. William Beavans, Company D, 43d North Carolina

  James Payne Beckwith Jr., Papers

    Capt. Jesse Hartwell Heath, Asst. Q.M., 4th Virginia Cavalry

  Henry Lewis Benning Papers

    Capt. Heman H. Perry, Q.M., Benning (DuBose)/Field/I Corps

  Berry Benson Papers

    Sgt. Berry G. Benson, Company A, South Carolina Sharpshooter Battalion

    Capt. Henry C. Lindsey, 47th Alabama

  Thomas Frederick Boatwright Papers

    Lt. Thomas Frederick Boatwright, Company C, 44th Virginia

  Noble John Brooks Papers

    Pvt. Noble John Brooks, Company E, Cobb's Legion Cavalry

  Henry A. Chambers Papers

    Capt. Henry A. Chambers, Company C, 49th North Carolina

  Kena King Chapman Papers

    2d Lt. Kena King Chapman, Company A, 19th Battalion Virginia Light
      Artillery

  William J. Clarke Papers

    Adjt. O. D. Cooke, 24th North Carolina

    Lt. Col. John L. Harris, 24th North Carolina

Jesse A. Clement Papers
  Capt. Baxter C. Clement, Company M, 7th Confederate Cavalry
Confederate Inspection Book
  Capt. Walter Harrison, Adjt. & Insp. Gen., Pickett/I Corps
Elias Davis Papers
  Lt. Elias Davis, Company B, 10th Alabama
William Henry Forney Papers
  Col. William Henry Forney, Sanders (Forney)/Mahone/III Corps
Frank Family Papers
  Corp. Jefferson Hedrick, Company B, 48th North Carolina
Joseph Pryor Fuller Papers
  2d Corp. Joseph Pryor Fuller, Company B, 20th Georgia
Mary E. Grattan Papers
  Capt. Charles Grattan, Chief of Ordnance, Cavalry Corps
  Pvt. Peter M. Grattan, Company I, 1st Virginia Cavalry
  Capt. Edward A. T. Nicholson, Asst. Adjt. Gen., Lane/Wilcox/III Corps
    and Lomax/Cavalry/Valley
James E. Green Papers
  2d Lt. James E. Green, Company I, 53d North Carolina
Bryan Grimes Papers
  Col./Brig. Gen./Maj. Gen. Bryan Grimes, 4th North Carolina, Grimes/
    Rodes/II Corps, Grimes/Rodes/Valley, and Grimes/II Corps
Cadwallader J. Iredell Papers
  Capt. Cadwallader J. Iredell, Company E, 1st North Carolina Cavalry
Charles Fenton James Papers
  Capt. Charles Fenton James, Company F, 8th Virginia
John Johnson Papers
  Pvt. John A. Johnson, Company C, 19th Georgia
Jones Family Papers
  Pvt. James B. Jones, Company A, 1st Battalion North Carolina
    Sharpshooters
Edmund Walter Jones Papers
  Pvt. Edmund Jones, Company F, 3d North Carolina Cavalry
Harry Lewis Papers
  3d Lt. Harry Lewis, Company K, 16th Mississippi
William Gaston Lewis Papers
  Brig. Gen. William Gaston Lewis, Lewis/Ramseur/Valley
Henry Armand London Papers
  Pvt. Henry Armand London, Company I, 32d North Carolina, and
    Courier, Grimes/II Corps
Mrs. Thomas Chalmers McCorvey Papers
  3d Lt. Robert P. Tutwiler, Company B, 15th Virginia Cavalry

John Paris Papers
 Chaplain John Paris, 54th North Carolina
Eliza Hall Parsley Papers
 Lt. Col. William Murdoch Parsley, 3d North Carolina, and 1st & 4th
  North Carolina (Consolidated)
Patton Family Papers
 Sgt. Jacob E. Patton, Company F, 14th North Carolina
William Nelson Pendleton Papers
 Brig. Gen. Edward Porter Alexander, Chief of Artillery, I Corps
 Lt. Col. Alexander Swift Pendleton, Asst. Adjt. Gen., II Corps
 Brig. Gen. William Nelson Pendleton, Chief of Artillery
Leonidas Lafayette Polk Papers
 Maj. R. C. Bridges, Judge Advocate Gen., Grimes/Valley
 Capt. R. T. Hall, 43d North Carolina
 2d Lt. Leonidas Lafayette Polk, Company I, 43d North Carolina
 Capt. Cary Whitaker, 43d North Carolina
 Col. John R. Winston, 43d North Carolina
Proffit Family Papers
 Pvt. Alfred Newton Proffit, Company D, 18th North Carolina
Stephen D. Ramseur Papers
 Brig. Gen./Maj. Gen. Stephen Dodson Ramseur, Ramseur/II Corps and
  Ramseur/Valley
John Andrew Ramsay Papers
 2d Lt. Francis C. Schaefer, Company D, 1st North Carolina Artillery
W. R. Redding Papers
 3d Sgt. William H. Aycock, Company E, 13th Georgia
 Col. John Harris Baker, 13th Georgia
 Capt. William R. Redding Jr., Company E, 13th Georgia
 C. W. Yates, Sperryville, Rappahannock County, Virginia
Charles W. Sydnor Papers
 Surgeon Charles W. Sydnor, II Corps and Valley
Charles S. Venable Papers
 Brig. Gen. Edward Porter Alexander, Chief of Artillery, I Corps
 Lt. Col. Charles Scott Venable, Aide-de-Camp, HQ
Richard Woolfolk Waldrop Papers
 Commissary Sgt. Richard Woolfolk Waldrop, 21st Virginia
Samuel Hoey Walkup Papers
 Col. Samuel Hoey Walkup, 48th North Carolina
Webb Family Papers
 Adjt. Alexander Smith Webb, 44th North Carolina
 Chaplain Richard Stanford Webb, 44th North Carolina
 Pvt. William Robert Webb, Company K, 2d North Carolina Cavalry

Cary Whitaker Papers
> Capt. Cary Whitaker, Company D, 43d North Carolina

J. E. Whitehorne Papers
> Orderly Sgt. James E. Whitehorne, Company F, 12th Virginia

Oregon

Private Collection of Edwin Thomas Sims, Salem
> Sims Family Papers
>> Pvt. Harry Farnandis, Company E, Hampton Legion Cavalry
>> Capt. Joseph Banks Lyle, Asst. Adjt. & Insp. Gen., Bratton / Field / I Corps
>> Capt. Isaac Going McKissick, Company C, 7th South Carolina Cavalry
>> Pvt. Charles Sims, Company E, Hampton Legion Cavalry

South Carolina

Charleston Library Society, Charleston
> William G. Hinson Papers
>> 2d Lt. William G. Hinson, Company G, 7th South Carolina Cavalry

College of Charleston, Charleston
> William Aiken Kelly Papers
>> Capt. William Aiken Kelly, Company L, 1st South Carolina

Private Collection of Sebron Hood Jr., Myrtle Beach
> McLeod Family Papers
>> Capt. Marcus D. L. McLeod, Company C, 1st North Carolina Cavalry

Private Collection of Barnwell R. Linley, Columbia
> Molony-Ryan Families Papers
>> Brig. Gen. Johnson Hagood, Hagood / Hoke / Beauregard
>> Maj. G. B. Lartigue, Asst. Q.M., Hagood / Hoke / Beauregard
>> Capt. Patrick Kilbride Molony, Asst. Adjt. Gen., Hagood / Hoke / Beauregard

Private Collection of Walker Gilmer Petroff, Beaufort
> Gilmer Family Papers
>> Pvt. Thomas Walker Gilmer, Courier, III Corps Artillery

South Carolina Department of Archives and History, Columbia
> John Bratton Papers
>> Col. / Brig. Gen. John Bratton, 6th South Carolina, and Bratton / Field / I Corps
> Company D, 5th South Carolina Cavalry Papers
>> Capt. Zimmerman Davis, 5th South Carolina Cavalry

South Carolina Historical Society, Charleston
> Adger-Smyth Family Papers
>> Q.M. Sgt. J. Adger Smyth, 25th South Carolina
> Charles E. Whilden Papers
>> Pvt. Charles E. Whilden, Color Bearer, Company I, 1st South Carolina

South Caroliniana Library, University of South Carolina, Columbia
> Richard Heron Anderson Papers
>> Lt. Gen. Richard Heron Anderson, I Corps

Box Family Papers

Pvt. William J. Box, Company C, 3d South Carolina

Brabham Family Papers

Capt. John Fletcher Brabham, Company C, 1st South Carolina

Pvt. George W. Platts, Company C, 1st South Carolina

Burn Family Papers

Pvt. Charles L. Burn, Company G, 1st South Carolina

Henry Calvin Conner Papers

Sgt. Henry Calvin Conner, Company G, Palmetto Sharpshooters

Crawford Family Papers

Pvt. David Hugh Crawford, Signal Corps/Courier, Kershaw
(Kennedy)/Kershaw/I Corps, and Company A, Hampton Legion
Cavalry

Capt. Robert A. Fishburne Jr., Company I, 2d South Carolina

Virgil Duc Papers

2d/1st Lt. Virgil Duc, Company E, 25th South Carolina

Elliott Family Papers

Col./Brig. Gen. Stephen Elliott Jr., Holcombe Legion, and
Elliott/Johnson/Beauregard

James Earle Hagood Papers

2d Lt. E. Harleston Barton, 2d South Carolina Rifles

James Farrow, Laurens District, South Carolina

Pvt. W. T. [or W. G.] Field, Company K, 6th South Carolina Cavalry

Sgt. J. B. Hester, Company C, 6th South Carolina Cavalry

Capt. William H. Holcombe, Company A, 1st South Carolina Rifles

Pvt. J. B. Sanders, Company C, 2d South Carolina Rifles

Capt. Charles H. A. Woodin, Company A, 20th South Carolina

Wade Hampton Papers

Maj. Gen. Wade Hampton, Hampton/Cavalry Corps

Kerrison Family Papers

Pvt. Charles Kerrison Jr., Aide-de-Camp, 2d South Carolina

John N. [W.] Knight Papers

1st Sgt. John W. Knight, Company B, 26th South Carolina

Thomas Cassells Law Papers

Pvt. Hugh Lide Law, Company I, 6th South Carolina Cavalry

James Blackman Ligon Papers

1st Lt. James Blackman Ligon, Company I, Hampton Legion Cavalry

T. M. Logan Papers

Col. Thomas Muldrup Logan, Hampton Legion Cavalry

William Barr Lowrance Papers

Adjt. William Barr Lowrance, 34th North Carolina

Samuel Catawba Lowry Papers

2d Lt. Samuel Catawba Lowry, Company F, 17th South Carolina

McLure Family Papers
    Capt. John William McLure, Q.M., Palmetto Sharpshooters, and Q.M.
        Dept., Field/I Corps
Fitz William McMaster Papers
    Col. Fitz William McMaster, 17th South Carolina
Thomas John Moore Papers
    1st Lt. Thomas John Moore, Company A, Holcombe Legion
Thomson Family Papers
    1st Lt. T. N. Appleton, Company E, 48th Alabama
J. W. Tindall Papers
    Pvt. J. W. Tindall, Company D, 20th South Carolina

Tennessee

Tennessee State Library and Archives, Nashville
    Trimmier Collection
        Lt. Col. Theodore Gaillard Trimmier, 41st Alabama

Texas

Confederate Research Center, Hill Junior College, Hillsboro
    J. Mark Smither Papers
        Sgt. Maj. J. Mark Smither, 5th Texas
    Watson Dugat Williams Papers
        Capt. Watson Dugat Williams, Company F, 5th Texas
University of Texas, Austin
    Edward Richardson Crockett Papers
        3d Sgt. Edward Richardson Crockett, Company F, 4th Texas
    Thomas L. McCarty Papers
        Pvt. Thomas L. McCarty, Company L, 1st Texas

Virginia

Fredericksburg-Spotsylvania National Military Park, Fredericksburg
    Virginia Typescript/Photocopy Volumes
        1st Lt. William A. Miller, Company F, 18th Virginia
        Pvt. Powell Benton Reynolds, Company K, 50th Virginia
        Pvt. Joseph F. Shaner, Rockbridge Artillery
Museum of the Confederacy, Richmond
    Charles C. Baughman Papers
        Corp. Charles C. Baughman, Company A, 13th Battalion Virginia Light
          Artillery
    Joseph Mullen Papers
        Corp. Joseph Mullen Jr., Company F, 27th North Carolina
    Robert P. Myers Papers
        Asst. Surgeon Robert Pooler Myers, 16th Georgia
Petersburg National Battlefield, Petersburg
    T. J. [T. L.] Alexander Papers
        Pvt. Thomas Lafayette Alexander, Company C, 37th North Carolina

Mrs. William Cameron Scrapbook
Gen. R. E. Lee
Silas Chandler Papers
Corp. Silas Chandler, Company B, 55th Virginia
William Leak Papers
Pvt. William C. Leak, Company F, 22d South Carolina
Matthew N. Love Papers
Maj. Matthew Norris Love, 25th North Carolina
Theophilus Moore Papers
Pvt. Theophilus Moore, Company C, 30th North Carolina
Timothy Morgan Papers
Pvt. Timothy Morgan, Company F, 49th Alabama
William Russell Papers
Sgt. William Russell, Company H, 26th Virginia
Henry D. Wells Papers
1st Lt. Henry Duplessis Wells, Company I, 23d South Carolina
Richmond National Battlefield Park, Richmond
George W. Boatwright Papers
Pvt. George W. Boatwright, Company E, 12th Battalion Georgia Light
Artillery
James A. Reynolds Papers
Pvt. James A. Reynolds, Company K, 16th Georgia
Willis Family Papers
Pvt. E. R. Willis, Company A, 3d South Carolina
University of Virginia, Charlottesville
Barnes Family Papers
Pvt. Edward Cook Barnes, Company G, 11th Virginia, and Courier,
Terry/Pickett/I Corps
2d Sgt. Henry P. Fortson, Company B, 31st Georgia
John Cowper Granbery Papers
Chaplain John Cowper Granbery, III Corps
Asa Holland Papers
2d Lt. Marcus D. Holland, Company D, 2d Virginia Cavalry
Rawlings Family Papers
Pvt. James Minor Rawlings, Rockbridge Artillery
Stafford Gorman Whittle Papers
Pvt. Beverley K. Whittle, Company C, 2d Virginia Cavalry
Micajah Woods Papers
1st Lt. Micajah Woods, Charlottesville Horse Artillery
Virginia Historical Society, Richmond
William Thomas Casey Papers
Pvt. William Thomas Casey, Company K, 34th Virginia
Giles Buckner Cooke Papers
Maj. Giles Buckner Cooke, Asst. Adjt. Gen., HQ

Creed Thomas Davis Papers
  Pvt. Creed Thomas Davis, Company K, 1st Virginia Artillery
Thomas Claybrook Elder Papers
  Maj. Thomas Claybrook Elder, Commissary, Finegan/Mahone/III Corps
John Walter Fairfax Papers
  Gen. R. E. Lee
  Capt. Dunlop Scott, Acting Provost Marshal, Field/I Corps
  Lt. Col. Walter H. Taylor, Asst. Adjt. Gen., HQ
Guerrant Family Papers
  Pvt. Willis Michael Parker, Company K, 9th Virginia
Hankins Family Papers
  Capt. James Dewitt Hankins, Surry Light Artillery
James Hays Papers
  Capt. James Hays, Asst. Adjt. Gen., Harris/Anderson (Mahone)/III Corps
Ambrose Powell Hill Papers
  Lt. Gen. A. P. Hill, III Corps
Hobson Family Papers
  Lt. Col. Edwin Lafayette Hobson, Battle (Hobson)/Grimes/Valley
Robert Edward Lee Papers
  Headquarters Papers, Army of Northern Virginia
      Col. William A. Jackson Brown, Anderson (Brown)/Field/I Corps
      Maj. Gen. Charles W. Field, Field/I Corps
      Maj. James Monroe Goggin, Asst. Adjt. Gen., Kershaw/I Corps
      Maj. Gen. Joseph B. Kershaw, Kershaw/I Corps
      Maj. Gen. Fitzhugh Lee, Fitz Lee/Cavalry Corps
      Gen. R. E. Lee
      Col. Peter Alexander Selkirk McGlashan, Simms
          (McGlashan)/Kershaw/I Corps
      Col. William Flank Perry, Law (Perry)/Field/I Corps
      2d Lt. John I. Shotwell, Acting Asst. Adjt. Gen., Texas (Bass)/Field/
          I Corps
      Capt. A. C. Sorrel, Asst. Adjt. Gen., Bratton/Field/I Corps
      Lt. Col. Walter H. Taylor, Asst. Adjt. Gen., HQ
      Maj. Henry Edward Young, Judge Advocate, Gen., HQ
Hunter Holmes McGuire Papers
  Maj. Hunter Holmes McGuire, Medical Director, II Corps
Miller Family Papers
  Pvt. Samuel R. Miller, Company F, 63d Tennessee
William Young Mordecai Papers
  Q.M. Sgt. William Young Mordecai, 1st Virginia Artillery
Pegram-Johnson-McIntosh Family Papers
  Lt. Col./Col. William Ransom Johnson Pegram, Pegram/III Corps
      Artillery

Robert Augustus Stiles Papers
    Adjt. Robert Augustus Stiles, Cabell / I Corps Artillery
Franklin Stringfellow Papers
    2d Lt. Franklin Stringfellow, Signal Corps
Gilbert Jefferson Wright Papers
    Col. Gilbert Jefferson Wright, Cobb Legion Cavalry
Library of Virginia, Richmond
    Decker Family Papers
        Pvt. Marshall Decker, Company E, 9th Virginia Cavalry
    Denoon Family Papers
        Lt. Charles E. Denoon, Company K, 41st Virginia
    Grimsley Family Papers
        Maj. Daniel Amon Grimsley, 6th Virginia Cavalry
    L. Robert Moore Papers
        Pvt. L. Robert Moore, Company C, 1st Battalion Virginia Light Artillery
    Henry T. Owen Papers
        Capt. Henry Thweat Owen, Company C, 18th Virginia
    Rives Family Papers
        1st Lt. Charles C. Harrison, Company I, 46th Virginia
    John F. Sale Papers
        1st Sgt. / 2d Lt. John F. Sale, Company H, 12th Virginia
    J. E. Whitehorne Papers
        1st Sgt. / Orderly Sgt. James E. Whitehorne, Company F, 12th Virginia

Washington, D.C.
Library of Congress
    John S. Anglin Papers
        Pvt. John S. Anglin, Company A, 4th North Carolina
    William A. Boyle Papers
        Pvt. William A. Boyle, Company K, Hampton Legion Cavalry
    George Washington Campbell Papers
        Gen. R. E. Lee
        Col. Charles Marshall, Aide-de-Camp, HQ
    Henry I. and Robert Greer Papers
        1st Sgt. Henry I. Greer, Company B, 25th South Carolina
        Pvt. Robert Greer, Company B, 25th South Carolina
    Habersham Family Papers
        Pvt. Richard W. Habersham, Milledge's Battery
    Cadmus M. Wilcox Papers
        Lt. Col. Osmun Latrobe, Chief of Staff, I Corps
        Maj. Gen. Cadmus M. Wilcox, Wilcox / III Corps
National Archives
    Record Group 109: War Department Collection of Confederate Records
        Orders and Circulars Issued by the Army of the Potomac and the Army
            and Department of Northern Virginia, C.S.A., 1861–1865

General Orders, April 1864–April 1865

Circulars, May 1864–February 1865

Records of the Adjt. & Insp. Gen.'s Department

Inspection Reports & Related Records Received by the Inspection
Branch

Benning (DuBose)/Field/I Corps, 9 August 1864

Barton (Aylett)/Pickett/I Corps, 10 August 1864

Davis/Heth/III Corps, 16 August 1864

Heth/III Corps, 18 August 1864

York/Gordon/Valley, 19 August 1864

Gordon/Valley, 21 August 1864

Pickett/I Corps, 29 August 1864

Field/I Corps, 30 August 1864

Benning (DuBose)/Field/I Corps, 8 September 1864

McGowan/Wilcox/III Corps, 27 September 1864

Wright (Gibson)/Mahone/III Corps, 28 September 1864

Pegram (Hoffman)/Gordon/Valley, 30 September 1864

Rodes (Grimes)/Valley, 30 September 1864

Hagood/Hoke/IV Corps, 26 October 1864

Wharton (Otey)/Wharton/Valley, 28 October 1864

Benning (DuBose)/Field/I Corps, 29 October 1864

Lane (Cowan)/Wilcox/III Corps, 29 October 1864

Lt. Col. H. E. Peyton (Insp. Gen.'s Report), 29 October 1864

Finegan/Mahone/III Corps, 30 October 1864

Johnson/IV Corps, 30 October 1864

Wilcox/III Corps, 30 October 1864

Texas (Bass)/Field/I Corps, 31 October 1864

Grimes/Valley, 31 October 1864

Pegram/Valley, 31 October 1864

Wright (Gibson)/Mahone/III Corps, 31 October 1864

Army of the Valley, 1 November 1864

Cavalry Corps, 13 November 1864

Hagood/Hoke/IV Corps, 26 November 1864

Lane (Cowan)/Wilcox/III Corps, 28 November 1864

Texas (Bass)/Field/I Corps, 28 November 1864

Wharton (Otey)/Wharton/Valley, 28 November 1864

Lt. Col. H. E. Peyton (Insp. Gen.'s Report), 29 November 1864

York (Peck)/Gordon/Valley, 29 November 1864

Cook (Peebles)/Grimes/Valley, 30 November 1864

Corse/Pickett/I Corps, 30 November 1864

Field/I Corps, 30 November 1864

Pickett/I Corps, 30 November 1864

Sorrel/Mahone/III Corps, 30 November 1864

Wilcox/III Corps, 30 November 1864
Hoke/IV Corps, November 1864
Horse Artillery/Cavalry Corps, 1 December 1864
Perry/Field/I Corps, 27 December 1864
Terry/Evans/II Corps, 29 December 1864
Wallace/Johnson/IV Corps, 29 December 1864
Pickett/I Corps, 30 December 1864
Simms/Kershaw/I Corps, 30 December 1864
Wilcox/III Corps, 31 December 1864
Thomas (Simmons)/Wilcox/III Corps, 26 January 1865
McGowan/Wilcox/III Corps, 27 January 1865
Terry/Evans/II Corps, 28 January 1865
Lewis/Pegram/II Corps, 29 January 1865
Evans (Lowe)/Evans/II Corps, 30 January 1865
Pickett/I Corps, 30 January 1865
Simms (Dickey)/Kershaw/I Corps, 30 January 1865
I Corps, 31 January 1865
II Corps, 31 January 1865
III Corps, 31 January 1865
DuBose/Kershaw/I Corps, 26 February 1865
Battle (Pickens)/Grimes/II Corps, 26 February 1865
Pegram (Kasey)/Johnston/II Corps, 26 February 1865
Evans (Baker)/Evans/II Corps, 27 February 1865
Johnston (Lea)/Johnston/II Corps, 27 February 1865
Lewis/Johnston/II Corps, 27 February 1865
Johnston/II Corps, 28 February 1865
Kershaw/I Corps, 28 February 1865
McGowan/Wilcox/III Corps, 28 February 1865
Bratton/Field/I Corps, February 1865
Compiled Service Records of Confederate General and Staff Officers and Nonregimental Enlisted Men
Compiled Service Records of Confederate Soldiers Who Served in Organizations from the State of Georgia
Compiled Service Records of Confederate Soldiers Who Served in Organizations from the State of North Carolina
Compiled Service Records of Confederate Soldiers Who Served in Organizations from the State of South Carolina
Compiled Service Records of Confederate Soldiers Who Served in Organizations from the State of Virginia

PUBLISHED SOURCES

Blackford, Susan Leigh, comp., and Charles Minor Blackford III, ed. *Letters from Lee's Army; Or, Memoirs of Life in and out of the Army in Virginia during the War between the States.* New York: Charles Scribner's Sons, 1947.

Burnett, Edmund Cody, ed. "Letters of Barnett Hardeman Cody and Others, 1861–1864, Part II." *Georgia Historical Quarterly* 23, no. 4 (December 1939): 362–80.

——, ed. "Letters of a Confederate Surgeon: Dr. Abner Embry McGarity, 1862–1865 . . ." *Georgia Historical Quarterly* 29, no. 4 (December 1945): pt. 3, 222–53; 30, no. 1 (March 1946): pt. 4, 35–70.

——, ed. "Letters of Three Lightfoot Brothers, 1861–1864, Part II." *Georgia Historical Quarterly* 26, no. 1 (March 1942): 65–90.

Cauthen, Charles E., ed. *Family Letters of the Three Wade Hamptons, 1782–1901.* Columbia: University of South Carolina Press, 1953.

Chamberlayne, C. G., ed. *Ham Chamberlayne—Virginian: Letters and Papers of an Artillery Officer in the War for Southern Independence.* Richmond: Press of the Dietz Printing Co., 1932.

Cockrell, Monroe F., ed. *Gunner With Stonewall: Reminiscences of William Thomas Poague: Lieutenant, Captain, Major, and Lieutenant Colonel of Artillery, Army of Northern Virginia, CSA, 1861–65: A Memoir Written for His Children in 1903.* Jackson, Tenn.: McCowat-Mercer Press, 1957.

[Davidson, R. O.] *The artisavis: The undersigned is engaged in soliciting contributions from the officers and soldiers of the Army of Northern Virginia, to construct the above machine, (Bird of Art.) He will address the Regiment at o'clock to-day and explain how this invention may be employed to destroy or drive from our soil every hostile Yankee, and thus soon close the war.* N.p., n.d. [ca. 1865].

Dawson, Francis Warrington. *Reminiscences of Confederate Service, 1861–1865.* Charleston: *News and Courier* Book Presses, 1882. Reprint, Baton Rouge: Louisiana State University Press, 1980.

Dayton, Ruth Woods, ed. *The Diary of a Confederate Soldier: James E. Hall.* Charleston, W.Va.: N.p., 1961.

Dowdey, Clifford, ed., and Louis H. Manarin, associate ed. *The Wartime Papers of R. E. Lee.* Boston: Little, Brown, 1965.

Fleet, Betsy, and John D. P. Fuller, eds. *Green Mount: A Virginia Plantation Family during the Civil War: Being the Journal of Benjamin Robert Fleet and Letters of His Family.* Lexington: University of Kentucky Press, 1962.

Folsom, James Madison. *Heroes and Martyrs of Georgia: Georgia's Record in the Revolution of 1861.* Macon, Ga.: Burke, Boykin and Co., 1864.

Freeman, Douglas Southall, ed. *Lee's Dispatches: Unpublished Letters of General Robert E. Lee, C.S.A. to Jefferson Davis and the War Department of the Confederate States of America, 1862–1865.* From the private collection of Wymberley Jones de Renne of Wormsloe, Ga. New York: G. P. Putnam's Sons, 1915. New ed. with additional dispatches and a foreword by Grady McWhiney, New York: G. P. Putnam's Sons, 1957.

Garnett, James Mercer. "Diary of Captain James M. Garnett, Ordnance Officer Rodes's Division, 2d Corps, Army of Northern Virginia, From August 5th to

November 30th, 1864, Covering Part of General Early's Campaign in the Shenandoah Valley." *Southern Historical Society Papers* 27 (1899): 1–16.

Groene, Bertram H., ed. "Civil War Letters of Colonel David Lang." *Florida Historical Quarterly* 54, no. 3 (January 1976): 340–66.

Hammock, Henry Mansell, ed. *Letters to Amanda from Sergeant Major Marion Hill Fitzpatrick, Co. K, 45th Georgia Regiment, Thomas' Brigade, Wilcox' Division, Hill's Corps, CSA to His Wife Amanda Olive Elizabeth Fitzpatrick, 1862–1865.* Culloden, Ga.: N.p., 1976. Reprint, Nashville: Champion Resources, n.d.

Harmon, George D., ed. "Letters of Luther Rice Mills—A Confederate Soldier." *North Carolina Historical Review* 4, no. 3 (July 1927): 285–310.

Harrison, Walter. *Pickett's Men: A Fragment of War History.* New York: D. Van Nostrand, 1870.

Harwell, Richard Barksdale, ed. *A Confederate Diary of the Retreat from Petersburg, April 3–20, 1865.* Emory Sources and Reprints, Series 8:1. Atlanta: Emory University Library, 1953.

Johnston, Hugh Buckner Jr., ed. "The Confederate Letters of Ruffin Barnes of Wilson County." *North Carolina Historical Review* 31, no. 1 (January 1954): 75–99.

Jones, J. William. *Personal Reminiscences, Anecdotes, and Letters of General Robert E. Lee.* New York: D. Appleton, 1874.

Lane, James Henry. "Glimpses of Army Life in 1864: Extracts from Letters Written by Brigadier General J. H. Lane." *Southern Historical Society Papers* 18 (1890): 406–22.

Lee, Laura Elizabeth, ed. *Forget-Me-Nots of the Civil War: A Romance, Containing Reminiscences and Original Letters of Two Confederate Soldiers.* St. Louis: Press A. R. Fleming Printing Co., 1909.

Lewis, Richard. *Camp Life of a Confederate Boy, of Bratton's Brigade, Longstreet's Corps, C.S.A.: Letters Written by Richard Lewis, of Walker's Regiment, to His Mother, during the War. Facts and Inspirations of Camp Life, Marches, &c.* Charleston, S.C.: *News and Courier* Book Presses, 1883.

McDaniel, Ruth Barr, ed. *Confederate War Correspondence of James Michael Barr and Wife Rebecca Ann Dowling Barr.* Taylors, S.C.: Faith Printing Co., 1963.

McDonald, Archie P., ed. *Make Me a Map of the Valley: The Civil War Journal of Stonewall Jackson's Topographer.* Dallas: Southern Methodist University Press, 1973.

Mackintosh, Robert Harley Jr., ed. *"Dear Martha . . .": The Confederate War Letters of a South Carolina Soldier: Alexander Faulkner Fewell.* Columbia, S.C.: R. L. Bryan Co., 1976.

Moffett, Mary C., ed. *Letters of General James Conner, C.S.A.* Columbia, S.C.: R. L. Bryan Co., 1950.

Myers, Robert Manson, ed. *Children of Pride: A True Story of Georgia and the Civil War.* New Haven: Yale University Press, 1973.

New Year's Dinner to Gen'l. Lee's Army: To the People of Virginia. . . . [Richmond: N.p., 1864].

Park, Robert Emory. "Diary of Robert E. Park, Macon, Georgia, Late Captain Twelfth Alabama Regiment, Confederate States Army." *Southern Historical Society Papers* 1, no. 5 (May 1876): 370–86; 1, no. 6 (June 1876): 430–37; 2, no. 1 (July 1876): 25–31.

Peacock, Jane Bonner, ed. "A Georgian's View of War in Virginia: The Civil War Letters of A. B. Simms." *Atlanta Historical Journal* 23, no. 2 (Summer 1979): 90–136.

Pearce, T. H., ed. *Diary of Capt. Henry A. Chambers.* Wendell, N.C.: Broadfoot's Bookmark, 1983.

Polley, J. B. *A Soldier's Letters to Charming Nellie.* New York: Neale Publishing Co., 1908.

Resolutions Adopted by Bratton's Brigade, South Carolina Volunteers, January 30th, 1865. [Richmond: N.p., 1865].

Resolutions Adopted by Co. "H," "I," and "K" Thirteenth Virginia Infantry, January 28, 1865. [Richmond: N.p., 1865].

Resolutions Adopted by Humphrey's Mississippi Brigade, Army of Northern Virginia, February 3, 1865. [Richmond: N.p., 1865].

Resolutions Adopted by McGowan's Brigade, South Carolina Volunteers. [Richmond: N.p., 1865].

Resolutions Adopted by the Officers and Men of the 57th Virginia Regiment. [Richmond: N.p., 1865].

Resolutions Adopted by the Staunton Artillery, February 1st, 1865. [Richmond: N.p., 1865].

Resolutions Adopted by Sturdivant's Artillery Battalion, Army Northern Virginia, Expressive of Their Determination to Continue Their Efforts for Independence. [Richmond: N.p., 1865].

Resolutions Passed at a Meeting of the Fourteenth Regiment of Virginia Infantry, in Relation to the Condition of the Country and the Conduct of the War. [Richmond: N.p., 1865].

Resolutions Passed at a Meeting of the Ninth Virginia Infantry, January 25, 1865. [Richmond: N.p., 1865].

Resolutions of the Texas Brigade, Camp Texas Brigade, January 26th, 1865. [Richmond: N.p., 1865].

Robertson, James I. Jr., ed. " 'The Boy Artillerist': Letters of Col. William Pegram, C.S.A." *Virginia Magazine of History and Biography* 98, no. 2 (April 1990): 221–60.

Rozier, John, ed. *The Granite Farm Letters: The Civil War Correspondence of Edgeworth and Sallie Bird.* Athens: University of Georgia Press, 1988.

Smith, Daniel E. Huger, Alice R. Huger Smith, and Arney R. Childs, eds. *Mason Smith Family Letters, 1860–1868.* Columbia: University of South Carolina Press, 1950.

Smith, W. C., ed. *Rebel Yell: 20th South Carolina Infantry* (quarterly newsletter of 20th South Carolina Volunteer Infantry, Reenactors, Lexington), vol. 3, no. 2, March 1989.

Stephens, Robert Grier, ed. *Intrepid Warrior: Clement Anselm Evans, Confederate General from Georgia: Life, Letters, and Diaries of the War Years.* Dayton, Ohio: Morningside Press, 1992.

Stevens, Robert J. *Captain Bill: The Records and Writings of Captain William Henry Edwards (And Others), Company A, 17th Regiment, South Carolina Volunteers, Confederate States of America.* Richburg, S.C.: Chester District Genealogical Society, 1985.

Summers, Festus P., ed. *A Borderland Confederate.* Pittsburgh: University of Pittsburgh Press, 1962.

Taylor, Walter H. *General Lee: His Campaigns in Virginia, 1861–1865.* Norfolk: Press of Braunworth, 1906.

Thomas, John P. *Career and Character of Gen. Micah Jenkins, C.S.A.* Columbia, S.C.: State Co., 1903.

Thornton, Mary Lindsay, ed. "The Prison Diary of Adjutant Francis Atherton Boyle, C.S.A." *North Carolina Historical Review* 39, no. 1 (Winter 1962): 58–84.

Tower, R. Lockwood, ed. *Lee's Adjutant: The Wartime Letters of Colonel Walter Herron Taylor, 1862–1865.* Columbia: University of South Carolina Press, 1995.

Townsend, Harry C. "Townsend's Diary—January–May, 1865: From Petersburg to Appomattox, Thence to North Carolina to Join Johnston's Army." *Southern Historical Society Papers* 34 (1906): 99–127.

U.S. War Department. *The War of the Rebellion: A Compilation of the Official Records of the Union and Confederate Armies.* 128 vols. Washington: Government Printing Office, 1880–1901.

Welch, Spencer Glasgow. *A Confederate Surgeon's Letters to His Wife: By Spencer Glasgow Welch, Surgeon, Thirteenth South Carolina Volunteers, McGowan's Brigade.* New York: Neale Publishing Co., 1911.

White, Max E., ed. "The Thomas G. Jordan Family during the War between the States." *Georgia Historical Quarterly* 59 (Supplement, 1975): 134–40.

Williams, Max R., ed. *The Papers of William Alexander Graham.* Vol. 6, 1864–65. Raleigh: North Carolina Department of Cultural Resources, Division of Archives and History, 1976.

Wright, Stuart T., ed. *The Confederate Letters of Benjamin H. Freeman.* Hicksville, N.Y.: Exposition Press, 1974.

NEWSPAPERS

Charleston Courier, May–June 1864
Charleston Mercury, May–June 1864
Richmond Dispatch, April 1864–March 1865

Richmond Examiner, March 1864–February 1865
Richmond Sentinel, April 1864–January 1865
Richmond Whig, May 1864–February 1865

SECONDARY SOURCES

BOOKS
Military Studies

Baltz, Louis J. *The Battle of Cold Harbor, May 27–June 13, 1864.* Virginia Civil War Battles and Leaders Series. Lynchburg: H. E. Howard, 1994.

Barton, Michael. *Goodmen: The Character of Civil War Soldiers.* University Park: Pennsylvania State University Press, 1981.

Bearss, Edwin C., and Chris M. Calkins. *The Battle of Five Forks.* Virginia Civil War Battles and Leaders Series. Lynchburg: H. E. Howard, 1987.

Boykin, Edward. *Beefsteak Raid.* New York: Funk and Wagnalls, 1960.

Calkins, Chris M. *The Battles of Appomattox Station and Appomattox Court House.* Virginia Civil War Battles and Leaders Series. 2d ed. Lynchburg: H. E. Howard, 1987.

———. *The Final Bivouac: The Surrender Parade at Appomattox and the Disbanding of the Armies, April 10–May 20, 1865.* Virginia Civil War Battles and Leaders Series. 2d ed. Lynchburg: H. E. Howard, 1987.

———. *Thirty-Six Hours before Appomattox: The Battles of Sayler's Creek, High Bridge, Farmville, and Cumberland Church.* 2d printing. Farmville, Va.: *Farmville Herald*, 1989.

Catton, Bruce. *A Stillness at Appomattox.* Garden City, N.Y.: Doubleday, 1953.

Cauble, Frank P. *The Surrender Proceedings, April 9, 1865: Appomattox Court House.* Virginia Civil War Battles and Leaders Series. 3d ed. Lynchburg: H. E. Howard, 1987.

Cavanaugh, Michael A., and William Marvel. *The Petersburg Campaign: The Battle of the Crater: "The Horrid Pit," June 25–August 6, 1864.* Virginia Civil War Battles and Leaders Series. Lynchburg: H. E. Howard, 1989.

Cooling, B. Franklin. *Jubal Early's Raid on Washington, 1864.* Baltimore: Nautical and Aviation Publishing Co. of America, 1989.

Daniel, Larry J. *Soldiering in the Army of Tennessee: A Portrait of Life in a Confederate Army.* Chapel Hill: University of North Carolina Press, 1991.

Davis, Burke. *To Appomattox: Nine April Days, 1865.* New York: Rinehart, 1959.

Dowdey, Clifford. *Lee.* Boston: Little, Brown, 1965.

———. *Lee's Last Campaign: The Story of Lee and His Men against Grant, 1864.* Boston: Little, Brown, 1960.

Frassanito, William. *Grant and Lee: The Virginia Campaigns, 1864–1865.* New York: Charles Scribner's Sons, 1983.

Freeman, Douglas Southall. *Lee's Lieutenants: A Study in Command.* 3 vols. New York: Charles Scribner's Sons, 1942–44.

——. *R. E. Lee: A Biography.* 4 vols. New York: Charles Scribner's Sons, 1934–35.

Fuller, J. F. C. *Grant And Lee: A Study in Personality and Generalship.* New York: Charles Scribner's Sons, 1933. Reprint, Civil War Centennial Series, Bloomington: Indiana University Press, 1957.

Gallagher, Gary W., ed. *Lee The Soldier.* Lincoln: University of Nebraska Press, 1996.

——, ed. *Struggle for the Shenandoah: Essays on the 1864 Valley Campaign.* Kent, Ohio: Kent State University Press, 1991.

Glatthaar, Joseph T. *Forged In Battle: The Civil War Alliance of Black Soldiers and White Officers.* New York: Free Press, 1990.

——. *The March to the Sea and Beyond: Sherman's Troops in the Savannah and Carolinas Campaigns.* American Social Experience Series. New York: New York University Press, 1985.

——. *Partners In Command: The Relationships between Leaders in the Civil War.* New York: Free Press, 1994.

Griffith, Paddy. *Battle Tactics of the Civil War.* New Haven: Yale University Press, 1989.

Hagerman, Edward. *The American Civil War and the Origins of Modern Warfare: Ideas, Organization, and Field Command.* Bloomington: Indiana University Press, 1988.

Hattaway, Herman, and Archer Jones. *How the North Won: A Military History of the Civil War.* Urbana: University of Illinois Press, 1983.

Heleniak, Roman J., and Lawrence L. Hewitt, eds. *Leadership during the Civil War: The 1989 Deep Delta Civil War Symposium: Themes in Honor of T. Harry Williams.* Shippensburg, Pa.: White Mane Publishing Co., 1992.

Hess, Earl J. *The Union Soldier in Battle: Enduring the Ordeal of Combat.* Modern War Studies. Lawrence: University Press of Kansas, 1997.

Horn, John. *The Petersburg Campaign: The Destruction of the Weldon Railroad: Deep Bottom, Globe Tavern, and Reams Station, August 14–25, 1864.* Virginia Civil War Battles and Leaders Series. Lynchburg: H. E. Howard, 1991.

Howe, Thomas J. *The Petersburg Campaign: Wasted Valor, June 15–18, 1864.* Virginia Civil War Battles and Leaders Series. Lynchburg: H. E. Howard, 1989.

Hubbell, John T., ed. *Battles Lost and Won: Essays from Civil War History.* Contributions in American History, no. 45. Westport, Conn.: Greenwood Press, 1975.

Jones, Archer. *Civil War Command and Strategy: The Process of Victory and Defeat.* New York: Free Press, 1992.

Jones, Terry L. *Lee's Tigers: The Louisiana Infantry in the Army of Northern Virginia.* Baton Rouge: Louisiana State University Press, 1987.

Linderman, Gerald F. *Embattled Courage: The Experience of Combat in the American Civil War.* New York: Free Press, 1987.

Logue, Larry M. *To Appomattox and Beyond: The Civil War Soldier in War and Peace*. American Ways Series. Chicago: Ivan R. Dee, 1996.

Lonn, Ella. *Desertion during the Civil War*. New York: Century Co., 1928. Reprint, Gloucester, Mass.: Peter Smith, 1968.

McMurry, Richard M. *Two Great Rebel Armies: An Essay in Confederate Military History*. Chapel Hill: University of North Carolina Press, 1989.

McPherson, James M. *For Cause and Comrades: Why Men Fought in the Civil War*. New York: Oxford University Press, 1997.

——. *What They Fought For, 1861–1865*. Walter Lynwood Fleming Lectures in Southern History. Baton Rouge: Louisiana State University Press, 1994.

McWhiney, Grady, and Perry D. Jamieson. *Attack And Die: Civil War Military Tactics and the Southern Heritage*. University, Ala.: University of Alabama Press, 1982.

Mahr, Theodore C. *The Battle of Cedar Creek: Showdown in the Shenandoah, October 1–30, 1864*. Virginia Civil War Battles and Leaders Series. Lynchburg: H. E. Howard, 1992.

Maney, R. Wayne. *Marching to Cold Harbor: Victory and Failure, 1864*. Shippensburg, Pa.: White Mane Publishing Co., 1995.

Martin, Bessie. *Desertion of Alabama Troops from the Confederate Army: A Study in Sectionalism*. Studies in History, Economics, and Public Law, no. 378. New York: Columbia University Press, 1932.

Matter, William D. *If It Takes All Summer: The Battle of Spotsylvania*. Chapel Hill: University of North Carolina Press, 1988.

Maurice, Sir Frederick. *Robert E. Lee the Soldier*. Boston: Houghton Mifflin, 1925.

Military Analysis of the Civil War: An Anthology by the Editors of Military Affairs. Millwood, N.Y.: KTO Press, 1977.

Miller, J. Michael. *The North Anna Campaign: "Even to Hell Itself," May 21–26, 1864*. Virginia Civil War Battles and Leaders Series. Lynchburg: H. E. Howard, 1989.

Mitchell, Reid. *Civil War Soldiers: Their Expectations and Their Experiences*. New York: Viking, 1988.

——. *The Vacant Chair: The Northern Soldier Leaves Home*. New York: Oxford University Press, 1993.

Page, Thomas Nelson. *Robert E. Lee the Southerner*. New York: Charles Scribner's Sons, 1908.

Pollard, Edward A. *The Southern History of the War*. 2 vols in 1. New York: C. B. Richardson, 1866.

Rhea, Gordon C. *The Battle of the Wilderness, May 5–6, 1864*. Baton Rouge: Louisiana State University Press, 1994.

——. *The Battles for Spotsylvania Court House and the Road to Yellow Tavern*. Baton Rouge: Louisiana State University Press, 1997.

Robertson, James I. Jr. *Soldiers Blue and Gray*. American Military History Series. Columbia: University of South Carolina Press, 1988.

——. *The Stonewall Brigade*. Baton Rouge: Louisiana State University Press, 1962, 1977.

Robertson, William Glenn. *Back Door to Richmond: The Bermuda Hundred Campaign, April–June 1864*. Wilmington: University of Delaware Press, and Toronto: Associated University Presses, 1987.

——. *The Petersburg Campaign: The Battle of Old Men and Young Boys, June 9, 1864*. Virginia Civil War Battles and Leaders Series. Lynchburg: H. E. Howard, 1989.

Roland, Charles P. *Reflections On Lee: A Historian's Assessment*. Mechanicsburg, Pa.: Stackpole Books, 1995.

Royster, Charles. *The Destructive War: William Tecumseh Sherman, Stonewall Jackson, and the Americans*. New York: Alfred A. Knopf, 1991.

Schiller, Herbert M. *The Bermuda Hundred Campaign*. Dayton, Ohio: Morningside Press, 1988.

Sommers, Richard J. *Richmond Redeemed: The Siege at Petersburg*. Garden City, N.Y.: Doubleday, 1981.

Steere, Edward. *The Wilderness Campaign*. Harrisburg, Pa.: Stackpole Co., 1960.

Swank, Walbrook D. *Battle of Trevilian Station: The Civil War's Bloodiest and Greatest All Cavalry Battle, with Eyewitness Memoirs*. Civil War Heritage Series, vol. 4. Shippensburg, Pa.: Burd Street Press, 1994.

Thomas, Emory M. *Robert E. Lee: A Biography*. New York: W. W. Norton, 1995.

Trudeau, Noah Andre. *Bloody Roads South: The Wilderness to Cold Harbor, May–June 1864*. Boston: Little, Brown, 1989.

——. *The Last Citadel: Petersburg, Virginia, June 1864–April 1865*. Boston: Little, Brown, 1991.

——. *Out of the Storm: The End of the Civil War*. Boston: Little, Brown, 1994.

Vandiver, Frank E. *Jubal's Raid: General Early's Famous Attack on Washington in 1864*. New York: McGraw-Hill, 1960.

Wert, Jeffry D. *From Winchester to Cedar Creek: The Shenandoah Valley Campaign of 1864*. Carlisle, Pa.: South Mountain Press, 1987.

Wiley, Bell Irvin. *The Life of Billy Yank: The Common Soldier of the Union*. Indianapolis: Bobbs-Merrill, 1952.

——. *The Life of Johnny Reb: The Common Soldier of the Confederacy*. Indianapolis: Bobbs-Merrill, 1943.

Woodworth, Steven E. *Davis and Lee at War*. Modern War Studies. Lawrence: University Press of Kansas, 1995.

General Histories and Social / Political Studies

Ayers, Edward L., and John C. Willis, eds. *The Edge of the South: Life in Nineteenth-Century Virginia*. Charlottesville: University Press of Virginia, 1991.

Beringer, Richard E., Herman Hattaway, Archer Jones, and William N. Still Jr. *Why the South Lost the Civil War*. Athens: University of Georgia Press, 1986.

Boritt, Gabor S., ed. *Why the Confederacy Lost*. New York: Oxford University Press, 1992.

Bynum, Victoria. *Unruly Women: The Politics of Social and Sexual Control in the Old South*. Gender and American Culture Series. Chapel Hill: University of North Carolina Press, 1992.

Cecil-Fronsman, Bill. *Common Whites: Class and Culture in Antebellum North Carolina*. Lexington: University Press of Kentucky, 1992.

Coulter, E. Merton. *The Confederate States of America, 1861–1865*. Vol. 7 of *A History of the South*, edited by Wendell Holmes Stephenson and E. Merton Coulter. Baton Rouge: Louisiana State University Press, 1950.

Donald, David. *Lincoln Reconsidered: Essays on the Civil War Era*, 2d ed., enlarged. New York: Vintage Books, 1960.

Durden, Robert F. *The Gray and the Black: The Confederate Debate on Emancipation*. Baton Rouge: Louisiana State University Press, 1972.

Eaton, Clement. *A History of the Southern Confederacy*. New York: Free Press, 1956, 1965.

Escott, Paul D. *After Secession: Jefferson Davis and the Failure of Confederate Nationalism*. Baton Rouge: Louisiana State University Press, 1978.

——. *Many Excellent People: Power and Privilege in North Carolina, 1850–1890*. Fred W. Morrison Series in Southern Studies. Chapel Hill: University of North Carolina Press, 1985.

Faust, Drew Gilpin. *Mothers Of Invention: Women of the Slaveholding South in the American Civil War*. Fred W. Morrison Series in Southern Studies. Chapel Hill: University of North Carolina Press, 1996.

Hahn, Steven. *The Roots of Southern Populism: Yeoman Farmers and the Transformation of the Georgia Upcountry, 1850–1890*. New York: Oxford University Press, 1983.

Harris, J. William. *Plain Folk and Gentry in a Slave Society: White Liberty and Black Slavery in Augusta's Hinterlands*. Middletown, Conn.: Wesleyan University Press, 1985.

Henry, Robert Selph. *The Story of the Confederacy*. New and rev. ed., New York: Grosset and Dunlap, 1936.

Hess, Earl J. *Liberty, Virtue, and Progress: Northerners and Their War for the Union*. American Social Experience Series. New York: New York University Press, 1988.

Jimerson, Randall C. *The Private Civil War: Popular Thought during the Sectional Conflict*. Baton Rouge: Louisiana State University Press, 1988.

Johnson, Ludwell H. *Division and Reunion: America, 1848–1877*. American Republic Series. New York: John Wiley and Sons, 1978.

Jordan, Ervin L., Jr. *Black Confederates and Afro-Yankees in Civil War Virginia*. A Nation Divided: New Studies in Civil War History. Charlottesville: University Press of Virginia, 1995.

Kenzer, Robert. *Kinship and Neighborhood in a Southern Community: Orange County, North Carolina, 1849–1881*. Knoxville: University of Tennessee Press, 1987.

McMillan, Malcolm C. *The Disintegration of a Confederate State: Three Governors and Alabama's Wartime Home Front, 1861–1865*. Macon, Ga.: Mercer University Press, 1986.

McPherson, James M. *Battle Cry of Freedom: The Civil War Era*. The Oxford History of the United States Series. New York: Oxford University Press, 1988.

Mohr, Clarence L. *On the Threshold of Freedom: Masters and Slaves in Civil War Georgia*. Athens: University of Georgia Press, 1986.

Owens, Harry P., and James J. Cooke, eds. *The Old South in the Crucible of War*. Jackson: University Press of Mississippi, 1983.

Rable, George C. *Civil Wars: Women and the Crisis of Southern Nationalism*. Women in American History Series. Urbana: University of Illinois Press, 1989.

——. *The Confederate Republic: A Revolution against Politics*. Civil War America. Chapel Hill: University of North Carolina Press, 1994.

Roark, James L. *Masters Without Slaves: Southern Planters in the Civil War and Reconstruction*. New York: W. W. Norton, 1977.

Roland, Charles P. *An American Iliad: The Story of the Civil War*. Lexington: University Press of Kentucky, 1991.

——. *The Confederacy*. The Chicago History of American Civilization. Chicago: University of Chicago Press, 1960.

Sutherland, Daniel E. *Seasons Of War: The Ordeal of a Confederate Community, 1861–1865*. New York: Free Press, 1995.

Thomas, Emory M. *The Confederacy as a Revolutionary Experience*. New Insights in History Series. Englewood Cliffs, N.J.: Prentice-Hall, 1971.

——. *The Confederate Nation, 1861–1865*. The New American Nation Series. New York: Harper and Row, 1979.

Vandiver, Frank E. *Blood Brothers: A Short History of the Civil War*. Texas A&M University Military History Series, no. 26. College Station: Texas A&M University Press, 1992.

——. *Their Tattered Flags: The Epic of the Confederacy*. New York: Harper's Magazine Press, 1970.

Vinovskis, Maris. *Toward a Social History of the American Civil War: Explanatory Essays*. Cambridge: Cambridge University Press, 1990.

Whites, Lee Ann. *The Civil War as a Crisis in Gender: Augusta, Georgia, 1860–1890*. Athens: University of Georgia Press, 1995.

Wiley, Bell Irvin. *The Plain People of the Confederacy*. Baton Rouge: Louisiana State University Press, 1943.

——. *The Road to Appomattox*. Memphis: Memphis State College Press, 1956.

Civil War Historiography

Castel, Albert. *Winning and Losing in the Civil War: Essays and Stories*. Columbia: University of South Carolina Press, 1996.

Freeman, Douglas Southall. *The South to Posterity: An Introduction to the Writing of Confederate History*. New York: Charles Scribner's Sons, 1939.

McPherson, James M. *Drawn with the Sword: Reflections on the American Civil War*. New York: Oxford University Press, 1996.

Nolan, Alan T. *Lee Considered: General Robert E. Lee and Civil War History*. Chapel Hill: University of North Carolina Press, 1991.

ARTICLES

Military Studies

Bardolph, Richard. "Confederate Dilemma: North Carolina Troops and the Deserter Problem." *North Carolina Historical Review* 66, no. 1 (January 1989): 61–86; 66, no. 2 (April 1989): 179–210.

——. "Inconstant Rebels: Desertion of North Carolina Troops in the Civil War," *North Carolina Historical Review* 41, no. 2 (April 1964): 163–89.

Barton, Michael. "Painful Duties: Art, Character, and Culture in Confederate Letters of Condolence." *Southern Quarterly: A Journal of the Arts in the South* 17, no. 2 (Winter 1979): 123–34.

Donald, David. "The Confederate as a Fighting Man." *Journal of Southern History* 25, no. 2 (May 1959): 178–93.

Faust, Drew Gilpin. "Christian Soldiers: The Meaning of Revivalism in the Confederate Army." *Journal of Southern History* 53, no. 1 (February 1987): 63–90.

Gallagher, Gary W. "The Army of Northern Virginia in May 1864: A Crisis of High Command." *Civil War History* 36, no. 2 (June 1990): 101–18.

McKaughan, Joshua. " 'Few Were the Hearts . . . That Did Not Swell with Devotion': Community and Confederate Service in Rowan County, North Carolina, 1861–1862." *North Carolina Historical Review* 73, no. 2 (April 1996): 156–83.

McMurry, Richard M. "Confederate Morale in the Atlanta Campaign of 1864." *Georgia Historical Quarterly* 54, no. 2 (Summer 1970): 226–43.

McNeill, William J. "A Survey of Confederate Soldier Morale during Sherman's Campaigns through Georgia and the Carolinas." *Georgia Historical Quarterly* 55, no. 1 (Spring 1971): 1–25.

McWhiney, Grady. "Who Whipped Whom? Confederate Defeat Reexamined." *Civil War History* 11, no. 1 (March 1965): 5–26.

Maslowski, Pete. "A Study of Morale in Civil War Soldiers." *Military Affairs* 34, no. 4 (December 1970): 122–26.

Preisser, Thomas M. "The Virginia Decision to Use Negro Soldiers in the Civil War." *Virginia Magazine of History and Biography* 83, no. 1 (January 1975): 98–113.

Reid, Richard. "A Test Case of the 'Crying Evil': Desertion among North Carolina Troops during the Civil War." *North Carolina Historical Review* 58, no. 3 (July 1981): 234–62.

Smith, David G. " 'Georgians Seem to Suffer More Than Any Troops in the

Service': A Profile of Two Companies of Madison County Confederates."
Georgia Historical Quarterly 79, no. 1 (Spring 1995): 169–91.

Wiley, Bell Irvin. "A Time of Greatness." *Journal of Southern History* 22, no. 1
(February 1956): 3–35.

Social / Political Studies

Ambrose, Stephen E. "Yeoman Discontent in the Confederacy." *Civil War History*
8, no. 3 (September 1962): 259–68.

Auman, William T. "Neighbor Against Neighbor: The Inner Civil War in the
Randolph County Area of Confederate North Carolina." *North Carolina
Historical Review* 61, no. 1 (January 1984): 59–92.

Davis, Archie K. " 'She Disdains to Pluck One Laurel from a Sister's Brow':
Disloyalty to the Confederacy in North Carolina." *Virginia Magazine of
History and Biography* 88, no. 2 (April 1980): 131–47.

Dillard, Philip D. "The Confederate Debate over Arming Slaves: Views from
Macon and Augusta Newspapers." *Georgia Historical Quarterly* 79, no. 1
(Spring 1995): 117–46.

Escott, Paul D. " 'The Cry of the Sufferers': The Problem of Welfare in the
Confederacy." *Civil War History* 23, no. 3 (September 1977): 228–40.

Escott, Paul D., and Jeffrey J. Crow. "The Social Order and Violent Disorder: An
Analysis of North Carolina in the Revolution and the Civil War." *Journal of
Southern History* 52, no. 3 (August 1986): 373–402.

Faust, Drew Gilpin. "Altars of Sacrifice: Confederate Women and the Narratives
of War." *Journal of American History* 76, no. 4 (March 1990): 1200–28.

Inscoe, John C. "Coping in Confederate Appalachia: Portrait of a Mountain
Woman and Her Community at War." *North Carolina Historical Review* 69, no.
4 (October 1992): 388–413.

Vandiver, Frank E. "The Confederacy and the American Tradition." *Journal of
Southern History* 28, no. 3 (August 1962): 277–86.

Wynne, Lewis N., and Guy Porcher Harrison. " 'Plain Folk' Coping in the
Confederacy: The Garrett-Asbell Letters." *Georgia Historical Quarterly* 72, no.
1 (Spring 1988): 102–18.

Civil War Historiography

Cain, Marvin R. "A 'Face of Battle' Needed": An Assessment of Motives and
Men in Civil War Historiography." *Civil War History* 28, no. 1 (March 1982):
5–27.

Gallagher, Gary W. "Home Front and Battlefield: Some Recent Literature on
Virginia and the Confederacy." *Virginia Magazine of History and Biography* 98,
no. 2 (April 1990): 135–68.

Glatthaar, Joseph T. "The 'New' Civil War History: An Overview." *Pennsylvania
Magazine of History and Biography* 115, no. 3 (July 1991): 339–69.

Sutherland, Daniel E. "Getting the 'Real War' into the Books." *Virginia Magazine of History and Biography* 98, no. 2 (April 1990): 193–220.

Wiley, Bell Irvin. "Historians and the National Register." *American Archivist* 17, no. 4 (October 1954): 325–30.

BOOK REVIEWS

Castel, Albert. "The Civil War and the Quest for Originality." Review of J. Matthew Gallman, *The North Fights the Civil War: The Home Front*, Joseph T. Glatthaar, *Partners in Command: The Relationships between Leaders in the Civil War*, and James M. McPherson, *What They Fought For, 1861–1865. Reviews in American History* 22, no. 4 (December 1994): 596–601.

Gallagher, Gary W. "Building a Legend and Prolonging a War: Another Look at Two of Robert E. Lee's Victories." Review of John J. Hennessy, *Return to Bull Run: The Campaign and Battle of Second Manassas*, and Ernest B. Furgurson, *Chancellorsville, 1863: The Souls of the Brave. Reviews in American History* 21, no. 3 (September 1993): 424–29.

Hess, Earl J. Review of Emil Rosenblatt and Ruth Rosenblatt, eds., *Hard Marching Every Day: The Civil War Letters of Private Wilbur Fisk, 1861– 1865*, and Daniel E. Sutherland, ed., *Reminiscences of a Private: William E. Bevens of the First Arkansas Infantry, C. S. A. Georgia Historical Quarterly* 77, no. 1 (Spring 1993): 200–202.

Index

17, 25, 26, 54, 62, 85–86, 109, 117, 119, 126, 177, 184, 187, 192, 206, 221, 226, 243, 262, 274, 284; Fourth (Beauregard's), 117, 118, 177, 184, 202, 206, 212, 221, 227, 231, 262, 272, 273, 275, 284; Cavalry, 19–20, 24, 56–57, 78–79, 144, 177, 204, 272, 275

—divisions: Breckinridge's, 58, 62, 64; Butler's, 239; Early's (Gordon), 45, 56; Field's, 85, 119, 211; Grimes's, 237, 249; Hampton's, 58, 144; Hill's (Wilcox), 87; Hoke's, 123, 201–2, 210–11, 239; Bushrod R. Johnson's, 115, 136, 137; Edward Johnson's, 37, 56, 240; Kershaw's, 87, 108, 147, 154, 161, 228, 259; Fitzhugh Lee's, 144; W. H. F. Lee's, 185; Mahone's, 118, 137, 186, 255, 273, 282; Pegram's (Johnston), 257–58; Pickett's, 57–58, 85, 180, 226, 233, 238, 256, 260, 272, 298; Rodes's, 29, 33; Rosser's, 108; Wilcox's, 273

—strength, 10, 17, 79, 212, 213–14, 225–27, 239–40, 264, 275, 300–301, 319–20, 333 (n. 52), 404–5 (n. 144)

Army of Tennessee, 11, 83, 132, 228, 284, 311, 319; opinions of, 23–24, 133–34, 201, 202

Army of the James, 205; strength, 82

Army of the Potomac, 1, 9–10, 13, 15, 17, 23, 24, 28, 36, 52, 54, 65, 68, 77, 79, 85, 108, 110, 119, 122, 194, 199, 204, 206, 230, 318; strength, 81, 330 (n. 51), 333 (n. 52)

Army of the Shenandoah, 167; strength, 148

Army of the Valley, 89, 90–91, 94, 132, 140, 289, 299, 318–19; raid to Maryland and Washington, 94–99, 101–2; inspections, 100–101, 103–4, 163–65, 172, 176; criticism of, 104, 145–46, 158–61; rations, 107; stragglers, 156, 158; and plundering, 164–65; and exhaustion, 165, 176; breakup of, 177

—brigades: Battle's, 161, 170; Cox's, 164; Evans's (Atkinson), 150, 158; Grimes's, 104, 150, 161; Johnston's, 150; Kershaw's (Conner), 162; Lewis's, 94;

Lomax's, 101; Patton's, 153; Pegram's (Hoffman), 164; Simms's, 170; Terry's, 103; York's, 103, 150

—cavalry: 94, 143–45, 154

—corps: Breckinridge's, 94

—divisions: Breckinridge's, 79, 91; Breckinridge's (Wharton), 154; Gordon's, 94, 96, 97, 100–101, 103, 146, 147, 148, 149, 150, 155, 164, 168, 169, 174; Grimes's, 172, 176; Kershaw's, 162, 168, 169, 170, 177; Fitzhugh Lee's, 156; Lee's (Rosser), 165; Lomax's, 177; Pegram's, 155, 168, 169; Ramseur's, 100, 146, 147, 148, 149, 155, 163–64, 168, 169; Ramseur's (Pegram), 154; Rodes's, 146, 147, 148, 149, 152; Rodes's (Ramseur), 154, 175; Rosser's, 177; Wharton's, 146, 147, 148, 153, 155, 168, 169, 177

—strength, 79, 107–8, 147–48, 161–63, 164, 177

"Artisavis," 264–65

Atkinson, Col. Edmund N., 158

Atlanta Campaign, 102–3, 133–34, 200–201

Augusta, Ga., 304

Aycock, Sgt. William H., 95, 101

Bailey, Pvt. Henry M.: photograph, 27

Bailey, Pvt. William T.: photograph, 27

Baldwin, Lt. Col. Briscoe G., 74–75

Baltimore, Md., 96, 109, 132

Bardolph, Richard, 311

Barksdale, Capt. C. D., 195

Barksdale, Ethelbert, 251

Barnes, Pvt. Edward C., 233

Barnes, Capt. Ruffin, 90, 107

Barton, Lt. E. Harleston, 121

Barton, Michael, 292

Bass, Pvt. Sidney, 320

Battle, Brig. Gen. Cullen A., 150, 161, 170

Battle, Pvt. Walter R., 30, 34, 107, 230

Baughman, Corp. Charles C., 205

Bearden, Pvt. William P., 47

Beauregard, Gen. P. G. T., 60–61, 86, 109, 122, 187, 211–12; correspondence with Confederate authorities, 57, 81, 84; faith

28–51, 52–54, 56–61, 63–79, 85–89, 288, 293. *See also individual battles*
Owen, Capt. Henry T., 213
Owen, Col. Thomas H., 252

Page, Thomas Nelson, 297
Paris, Chaplain John, 282–83
Park, Robert E.: as lieutenant, 95, 142–43; as captain, 151
Parker, Pvt. Alexander, 114
Parks, Commissary Sgt. David C., 131
Parsley, Lt. Col. William M., 10
Parsons, Simeon, 321
Patton, Col. George S., 153
Patton, Sgt. Jacob, 3
Peace: hopes for and rumors of, 199–200, 240–42
Pearsall, Pvt. George W., 21, 29, 47
Peebles Farm, Battle of, 206, 209
Pegram, Maj. James W., 268
Pegram, Brig. Gen. John, 154, 243
Pegram, Lt. Col. William J., xvi, 131–32, 179, 202, 209–10, 268, 269, 417–18 (n. 112)
Pendleton, Brig. Gen. William N., 74–75
Perry, Capt. Heman H., 197
Petersburg, Siege of, 86–89, 108, 109–29, 131–40, 179–97, 199–245, 247–65, 267–74, 298, 302; hopes for, 102–3; stalemate, 112, 117–19, 180–81, 197, 199, 264–65; Confederate accounts of, 112–17, 118–19, 121–29, 131–32, 134–40, 177–78, 179–84, 185–87, 188–91, 192–97, 199, 201–5, 207–10, 212–15, 219–43, 243–45, 247–65, 267–74, 288–89, 291; daily casualties, 113–14, 115–17; exhaustion and disease, 122–24; perceptions of, 315–19; historians on, 316–18. *See also individual battles*
Petersburg, Va., 79, 81, 83–85, 102, 105, 141, 144, 147, 161, 163, 177
Peyton, Lt. Col. H. E., 224–25, 226
Phillips, Pvt. Peter, 189
Phillips, Sgt. William H., 73, 228, 264, 268, 309
Pickett, Maj. Gen. George E., 82, 272
Platt, Rev. William H., 126

Poague, Lt. Col. William T., 45, 207–8, 247
Point Lookout, Md., 309
Pollard, Edward A., 319
Poor: soldiers' donations to, 6, 73–74, 232–33
Pope, Maj. Gen. John, 24
Poplar Spring Church, Battle of. *See* Squirrel Level Road and Poplar Spring Church, Battles of
Port Republic, Va., 158, 162
Port Walthall Junction, Battle of, 82, 123
Potomac River, 94, 95, 99, 132, 146, 199
Proffit, Pvt. Alfred N., 220, 222–23; photograph, 222

Ramseur, Maj. Gen. Stephen D., 99, 101–2, 104, 147, 149–50, 153–54, 161, 163, 166, 169–70, 175
Ramsey, Capt. N. A., 67
Ransom, Maj. Gen. Robert, 144
Rapidan River, 10, 17
Rations, 7, 72–74, 124–25, 181, 224–25, 229–33, 236–37, 257–60, 277–78, 302, 308, 346 (n. 24)
Ray, Pvt. James, 214–15
Read, Capt. Stephen P., 220
Reams Station, Battle of, 191–94, 196, 202, 204
Reams Station, Va., 191, 192
Redding, Capt. William R., Jr., 5–6
Redwood, Lt. R. G., 231
Reenlistments, 3–4
Religion, 4–6, 125–27, 193–94, 259–60
Reynolds, Pvt. James A., 24, 121–22
Reynolds, Pvt. Powell B., 9, 56
Rice's Depot, Va., 276, 277
Richmond, Va., 6, 8, 24, 41, 52, 53, 54, 57, 59, 60, 72, 75, 76–77, 78, 81, 82, 85, 90, 101, 108, 134, 184, 189, 201, 202, 229–30, 231, 241, 250, 253, 268, 273–74, 283, 316, 317–18, 319
Richmond and Danville Railroad, 274, 275
Ring, Capt. George P., 20, 37, 46, 102, 151, 154
Robertson, James I., Jr., 406 (n. 5)
Rodes, Maj. Gen. Robert E., 29, 104, 106, 153, 161, 175